Professional Review Guide for the RHIA and RHIT Examinations
2013 Edition

Professional Review Guide for the RHIA and RHIT Examinations 2013 Edition

Patricia J. Schnering, RHIA, CCS
Debora J. Butts, EdD, RHIA
Debra W. Cook, MAEd, RHIA
Lauralyn Kavanaugh-Burke,DrPH, RHIA,CHES
Marjorie H. McNeill, PhD, RHIA, CCS, FAHIMA
Toni Cade, MBA, RHIA, CCS, FAHIMA
Lisa Delhomme, MHA, RHIA
Lon'Tejuana S. Cooper, PhD, RHIA, CPM
Barbara W. Mosley, PhD, RHIA
Nanette B. Sayles, EdD, RHIA, CCS, CHPS, CPHIMS, FAHIMA
Kathy C. Trawick, EdD, RHIA
Charlotte McCuen, MS,RHIA
Anita Hazelwood, MLS, RHIA, FAHIMA
Carol A. Venable, MPH, RHIA, FAHIMA
Mary Teslow, MLIS, RHIA
Sheila Carlon, PhD, RHIA, FAHIMA
Leslie Moore, RHIT, CCS

DELMAR
CENGAGE Learning·

Australia • Brazil • Japan • Korea • Mexico • Singapore • Spain • United Kingdom • United States

Professional Review Guide for the RHIA and RHIT Examinations, 2013 Edition
Patricia J. Schnering, RHIA, CCS; et al

Vice President, Careers & Computing:
Dave Garza

Healthcare Publisher: Steve Helba

Associate Acquisitions Editor:
Jadin Kavanaugh

Director, Development-Career and
Computing: Marah Bellegarde

Product Development Manager:
Juliet Steiner

Product Manager: Amy Wetsel

Editorial Assistant: Courtney Cozzy

Brand Manager: Wendy Mapstone

Market Development Manager:
Nancy Bradshaw

Senior Production Director:
Wendy Troeger

Production Manager: Andrew Crouth

Senior Content Project Manager:
Kenneth McGrath

Senior Art Director: Jack Pendleton

Media Editor: Bill Overrocker

Cover image(s): iStock.com

The 2013 versions of CPT, ICD-9-CM, ICD-10-CM, and ICD-10-PCS were used in preparation of this product.

CPT copyright 2012 American Medical Association. All rights reserved. CPT is a registered trademark of the American Medical Association. Applicable FARS/DFARS Restrictions Apply to Government Use. Fee schedules, relative value units, conversion factors and/or related components are not assigned by the AMA, are not part of CPT, and the AMA is not recommending their use. The AMA does not directly or indirectly practice medicine or dispense medical services. The AMA assumes no liability for data contained or not contained herein.

For product information and technology assistance, contact us at
**Cengage Learning Customer & Sales Support,
1-800-354-9706**
For permission to use material from this text or product, submit all requests online at **www.cengage.com/permissions**
Further permissions questions can be emailed to
permissionrequest@cengage.com

Library of Congress Control Number: 2012954472

Book Only ISBN-13: 978-1-133-60832-5
Package ISBN-13: 978-1-133-60830-1

Delmar
5 Maxwell Drive
Clifton Park, NY 12065-2919
USA

Cengage Learning is a leading provider of customized learning solutions with office locations around the globe, including Singapore, the United Kingdom, Australia, Mexico, Brazil, and Japan. Locate your local office at: **international.cengage.com/region**

Cengage Learning products are represented in Canada by Nelson Education, Ltd.

To learn more about Delmar, visit **www.cengage.com/delmar**

Purchase any of our products at your local college store or at our preferred online store **www.cengagebrain.com**

Notice to the Reader
Publisher does not warrant or guarantee any of the products described herein or perform any independent analysis in connection with any of the product information contained herein. Publisher does not assume, and expressly disclaims, any obligation to obtain and include information other than that provided to it by the manufacturer. The reader is expressly warned to consider and adopt all safety precautions that might be indicated by the activities described herein and to avoid all potential hazards. By following the instructions contained herein, the reader willingly assumes all risks in connection with such instructions. The publisher makes no representations or warranties of any kind, including but not limited to, the warranties of fitness for particular purpose or merchantability, nor are any such representations implied with respect to the material set forth herein, and the publisher takes no responsibility with respect to such material. The publisher shall not be liable for any special, consequential, or exemplary damages resulting, in whole or part, from the reader's use of, or reliance upon, this material.

Printed in United States of America
1 2 3 4 5 6 7 17 16 15 14 13

ABOUT THE AUTHORS

Patricia J. Schnering, RHIA, CCS

Patricia J. Schnering founded PRG Publishing, Inc. and Professional Review Guides, Inc. Mrs. Schnering is a 1995 graduate of the Health Information Management program at St. Petersburg College in St. Petersburg, Florida. In 1998, she was certified as a CCS and in 1999 she received her RHIA certification. Her education includes a Baccalaureate degree from the University of South Florida in Tampa, Florida, with a major in Business Administration. Her HIM experience includes working as Health Information Services supervisor, as an HIM consultant, and as an adjunct HIM instructor at St. Petersburg College. Pat received the Florida Health Information Management Association (FHIMA) Literary Award in 2000 and 2005.

Debora J. Butts, EdD, RHIA

Debora J. Butts is a 1979 graduate of the Health Information Management (formerly Medical Record Administration) program of Clark Atlanta University in Atlanta, Georgia. Ms. Butts received her Master's degree in Management from Webster University in St. Louis, Missouri, in 1983. Her HIM experience includes:

- Twelve years as HIM Program Director and Assistant Professor in the Baccalaureate RHIA program at Texas Southern University, College of Pharmacy and Health Sciences in Houston, Texas.
- Three years as Evening Supervisor for Medical Records at Sierra Medical Center in El Paso, Texas.
- Two years as Coding Analyst at Grady Memorial Hospital in Atlanta, Georgia.
- Numerous consultant and other positions in Health Information Management.
- Director of Health Information Management Department at North Harris College in Houston, Texas.
- Currently, she is the Document Specialist at Triumph Health care in Houston, Texas.

Debra W. Cook, MAEd, RHIA

Debra W. Cook is a graduate of the Medical Record Administration and the Adult Education programs at East Carolina University in Greenville, North Carolina. Her HIM experience includes five years in acute health care practice in a variety of positions, such as management, utilization management, coding, and consulting. She also has over 24 years' experience in HIM education at Alderson-Broaddus College and Marshall University in West Virginia, and Catawba Valley Community College in Hickory, North Carolina. Currently, she is the Department Head of Health Information Technology at CVCC and Director of the Workforce Development Program for Electronic Record Specialists. In addition to this, she serves on the Panel of Accreditation Reviewers for the Commission of Health Informatics and Information Management Education.

Nanette B. Sayles, EdD, RHIA, CCS, CHPS, CPHIMS, FAHIMA

Nanette Sayles is a 1985 graduate of the University of Alabama at Birmingham Medical Record Administration (now the Health Information Management) program. She earned her Master's of Science in Health Information Management (1995) and her Master's in Public Administration (1990) from the University of Alabama at Birmingham. She earned her doctorate in Adult Education from the University of Georgia (2003). She is currently Associate Professor for the Health Information Management program at East Central College in Union, Missouri. She has a wide range of health information management experience in hospitals, consulting, system development/implementation, and education. She also received the 2005 American Health Information Management Association Triumph Educator Award.

Anita Hazelwood, MLS, RHIA, FAHIMA

Anita Hazelwood is an Associate Professor in the Health Information Management Department at the University of Louisiana at Lafayette, located in Lafayette, Louisiana. She has a Bachelor's degree in Medical Record Science and a Master's degree in Library Science, and has been a credentialed Registered Health Information Administrator (RHIA) for 28 years.

Some of the courses she teaches include coding and classification systems such as ICD-9-CM and CPT coding; reimbursement methodologies such as DRGs and RBRVS; fraud and abuse; principles of health information management and alternative delivery systems. She is also the Clinical Experience Coordinator.

Anita has actively consulted in hospitals, nursing homes, clinics, facilities for the mentally retarded, and in other educational institutions. She has conducted numerous ICD-9-CM and CPT coding workshops throughout the state for hospitals and physicians' offices.

On a professional level, Anita has been a member of the American Health Information Management Association (AHIMA) for several years. She is also a member of the Society for Clinical Coding (SCC) and served on the SCC board as Secretary in 1998. Anita has been the Internet Task Force Chair for several years. She is a member of the AHIMA's Assembly on Education (AOE) and has served as Membership Chair, a member of the Nominating Committee, and on the Board of Directors.

Anita is a member of the Louisiana Health Information Management Association and was selected as its 1997 Distinguished Member.

Mary Spivey Teslow, MLIS, RHIA

Mary Spivey Teslow is a 1981 graduate of the University of Illinois at Chicago program in Health Information Management (formerly Medical Record Administration) and has been a credentialed RHIA for over 29 years. She received her first Bachelor's degree from Governors State University in Women's Studies in 1976 and her Master's degree in Library and Information Science from the University of South Florida in 1994. In 1998, Ms. Teslow was awarded an Endowed Teaching Chair in the Health Sciences. Her HIM experience includes:

- Twenty years as an HIM educator. She is currently Program Director in HIM at Western Carolina University in North Carolina.
- Fifteen years at Broward Community College in Ft. Lauderdale, Florida, where she developed and directed the Health Information Technology program.
- Seven years in HIM practice, including various management positions in acute care in both an academic medical center and a community hospital as well as managed care.
- Ongoing consulting and publication projects, including creation of the PRG Quick Notes series with Patricia Schnering, and editing and authoring several titles.

Lisa M. Delhomme, MPA, RHIA

Lisa M. Delhomme is an Instructor in the Health Information Management Department at the University of Louisiana at Lafayette located in Lafayette, Louisiana. She has a Bachelor's degree in Health Information Management and a Master's degree in Health Services Administration. She teaches several courses, including CPT coding, legal aspects for health care, and computers in health care organizations. Prior to teaching, she held a management position at a physician practice and ambulatory surgery center. Mrs. Delhomme has been an active member of the American Health Information Management Association for 11 years. In addition, she has been involved with committees and projects for the Louisiana Health Information Management Association and Louisiana Medical Group Management Association.

Toni Cade, MBA, RHIA, CCS, FAHIMA

Toni Cade is a tenured Associate Professor in the Health Information Management Department at the University of Louisiana at Lafayette. She teaches several courses including health care reimbursement methodologies (MS-DRGs, APCs, RUGs, etc.), hospital statistics, case management, performance improvement, medical terminology, and health care risk management. Mrs. Cade is also the Management Internship Site Coordinator, coordinating affiliation sites throughout the United States.

Mrs. Cade has 33 years of experience with previous positions, including Data Analyst for the QIO, Utilization Review Supervisor, and Coding Supervisor in a large acute care hospital.

She is listed in *Marquis' Who's Who in Medicine and Health Care* and serves on the Editorial Advisory Board of For the Record. She has reviewed and authored publications on topics including medical terminology, billing, reimbursement, and health care statistics.

As an independent consultant, Mrs. Cade has extensive experience conducting seminars in coding and reimbursement. She also consults at acute care hospitals and works as an expert health care data analyst and expert witness with attorneys involved in medical malpractice cases.

Mrs. Cade has served the American Health Information Management Association (AHIMA) in various positions, including Delegate, Nominating Committee member, and Fellowship Review Committee member. She was also nominated for AHIMA's Champion Award and Educator's Award.

In her state association (Louisiana Health Information Management Association), she was awarded the Distinguished Member Award and the Outstanding Volunteer Award. At the university, she received the Excellence in Teaching Award and holds the Louisiana Health Systems / BoRSF Professorship in Health Care Administration.

Charlotte McCuen, MS, RHIA

Charlotte McCuen has 30 years of experience in health information management. She currently is an independent contractor as editor and coauthor of HIM textbooks. She served as Associate Professor and Clinical Coordinator for 14 years in the Health Information Management baccalaureate and associate degree programs at Macon State College in Macon, Georgia. She also served 15 years as HIM Director of an acute care hospital and a state psychiatric / forensic acute care hospital. She has consulted for long-term care facilities, a behavioral health hospital, physician offices, and renal dialysis centers. She received her Master's degree from Mercer University in Health Care Policy and Administration and a Baccalaureate degree from the Medical College of Georgia in Medical Record Administration. She volunteers professional services to both AHIMA and Georgia Health Information Management Association (GHIMA), most recently serving on the AHIMA program committee and acting as President of GHIMA (2011–2012). She was the recipient of the Mentor Award for GHIMA in 2004.

Lon'Tejuana S. Cooper, MSHA, RHIA, CPM

Lon'Tejuana S. Cooper is a 1998 graduate of the Health Informatics and Information Management (formerly Health Information Management) program at Florida A&M University in Tallahassee, Florida. She completed the Certified Public Manager's program at Florida State University in 2002 and received her Master's of Science degree in Healthcare Administration in 2004 at Florida A&M University. Mrs. Cooper has completed 45 hours of course work toward her doctoral degree in Educational Leadership and Human Services. She has more than 8 years of experience in managing PHI in electronic format. Mrs. Cooper has developed policies and procedures on implementing HIPAA requirements, developed training modules for staff training, and designed HIPAA assessment tools. For the past 6 years, Mrs. Cooper has served as a faculty member in the Division of Health Informatics and Information Management at Florida A&M University.

Barbara W. Mosley, PhD, RHIA

Barbara W. Mosley is a 1976 graduate of the Health Information Management (formerly Medical Record Administration) program at the University of Tennessee Center for the Health Sciences in Memphis, Tennessee. She received her Master's degree in Public Administration with a concentration in Health Services Administration from the University of Memphis (formerly Memphis State University) in 1980. She earned her doctorate degree in Adult Education in 1990 from Florida State University. In 1996, Dr. Mosley was chosen Teacher of the Year at Florida A&M University. In 1998, she was chosen as the Advanced Teacher of the Year at Florida A&M University. Her experience in health information management includes:

- Twenty-six years as Health Information Management educator. Currently, she is a Professor in the Health Information Management Program and the Associate Dean for the School of Allied Health Sciences at Florida A&M University in Tallahassee, Florida.
- Nineteen years of consulting experience at several long-term care facilities in Tallahassee, Florida, and surrounding cities.
- Formerly, Assistant Director of Medical Record Department at the City of Memphis Hospital and the VA Medical Center in Birmingham, Alabama, and Director of Medical Records at the Southeast Memphis Mental Health Center.

Carol A. Venable, MPH, RHIA, FAHIMA

Carol A. Venable is a Professor and Department Head of Health Information Management at the University of Louisiana at Lafayette (ULL). She has a Bachelor's degree in Medical Record Science, a Master's degree in Public Health and Tropical Medicine, and has been a credentialed Registered Health Information Administrator (RHIA) for over 30 years. Prior to teaching at ULL, Ms. Venable held the position of Director of Medical Records at Lafayette General Medical Center and has actively consulted in hospitals, nursing homes, clinics, home health agencies, educational institutions, physicians' offices, and facilities for the mentally retarded. She has written numerous articles and coedited several coding publications. She has coauthored the books ICD-9-CM Diagnostic Coding and Reimbursement for Physician Services and ICD-10 Preview. She was coauthor of a chapter in the book, Health Information: Management of a Strategic Resource, 2nd edition. She has been a member of the Louisiana Health Information Management Association and has served as President, President-elect, Treasurer, Delegate, and a member of the Board of Directors, as well as serving on various committees and projects. Carol has also been active in the American Health Information Management Association. She has served on the Item Writing Committee, Benchmarking the Best Practices in HIM Education Project, Council on Education, and the Council on Certification's Roles and Functions Committee. She also serves as a member of the Panel of Accreditation Surveyors. In addition, Carol was awarded the Legacy Award by the American Health Information Management Association. She was elected to serve on the Assembly on Education's (AOE) Board of Directors and has served as chair of the Membership and Nomination Committees of the AOE. She also serves on the Editorial Review Board for Educational Perspectives in Health Information Management, the journal of the Assembly on Education of the American Health Information Management Association.

Sheila A. Carlon, PhD, RHIA, FAHIMA

Dr. Carlon has a PhD in Organizational Development and Systems, a Master's degree in Health Services Administration, and Bachelor's degrees in Broadcast Journalism and Health Care Management. She is a Fellow of AHIMA and received the Educator of the Year Award in 2006 and Cypress College's Distinguished Alumni Award in 2008. Dr. Carlon has been a Program Director and Degree Chair in Regis University's College for Health Professions for the past 8 years, where she administers and teaches in four-degree programs. She also has extensive hospital and physician office management experience and has been a Health Care Consultant for Deloitte, Touche International. She is a frequent meeting facilitator and speaker both locally and nationally on such topics as technology, HIPAA, the Global EHR, E- HIM, leadership and management theory and development, HIM advocacy, education trends, and organizational assessment. Dr. Carlon volunteers as an Ombudsman for the Aging Services Division of the Denver Regional Council of Governments. She serves as a Board Member of the Golden Gate Fire Department in Golden, Colorado. She is a volunteer for the Ronald McDonald House, Project Homeless, Quarters for Kids, and Project Mercy in Yetebon, Ethiopia. She is currently helping to launch the field of HIM into the country of Ethiopia.

Marjorie H. McNeill, PhD, RHIA, CCS, FAHIMA

Marjorie H. McNeill is a graduate of the Health Information Management (formerly Medical Record Administration) program at the Medical College of Georgia in Augusta. She received her MS degree in Health Education at Florida State University and her PhD in Educational Leadership at Florida A&M University. Her experience in health information management includes:

- Twenty-seven years as an HIM educator
- Director of the Division of Health Informatics and Information Management at the School of Allied Health Sciences, Florida A&M University in Tallahassee, Florida
- Former Director of the Health Information Management program at Armstrong State College in Savannah, Georgia
- Nine years of management and consulting experience in various health care facility practice settings (mental retardation, ambulatory surgery, and nursing home) including acute care hospital experience as Associate Director of Medical Records at St. Joseph's Hospital in Savannah, Georgia

Marjorie was the recipient of the 2008 Florida Health Information Management Association Distinguished Services Award and the 2010 Florida Health Information Management Association Literary Award.

Kathy C. Trawick, EdD, RHIA

Dr. Kathy Trawick is the chairman and associate professor of the Health Information Management Department at the University of Arkansas for Medical Sciences in Little Rock, Arkansas. She is a 1985 graduate of the University of Alabama at Birmingham, Health Information Management (formerly Medical Record Administration) program. Dr. Trawick has expertise in Higher Education and in the Allied Health Sciences. Her basic research interests with keywords under the ERIC database include higher educational administration effectiveness, institutional effectiveness, and student satisfaction. Dr. Trawick has been a practitioner for 10 years in acute care facilities, as well as an HIM educator and program chairman since 1999. Topics of instruction include health care statistics, legal issues, HIM systems and the CPR, health administration, quality improvement, and cancer registry principles. She has coauthored a text (for AHIMA) on computer systems in HIT and has been a contributing author of texts on medical terminology and medical law and ethics. She has published articles in the *AHIMA Journal* and *Advance* magazine and written for Educational Perspectives in Health Information Management and the Mid-South Educational Research Association Proceedings. She is also a consultant to various types of health care facilities in Arkansas. In addition to holding offices at the state level in HIM and Cancer Registry associations, she currently serves on the CAHIIM Panel of Reviewers for HIT/HIA program accreditation.

Lauralyn Kavanaugh-Burke, DrPH, RHIA, CHES, HITPRO-IM

After receiving a BS degree in Medical Record Administration with a minor in biology from York College of Pennsylvania, Dr. Burke worked in several hospitals in Virginia and Maryland in various management positions, including DRG Analyst, Assistant Director, and Director of the Medical Record / Health Information departments. During this time, her interest in pathophysiology intensified after working with several physicians in their research endeavors. She started teaching at an associate's degree Health Information Technology (HIT) program at Fairmont State College in West Virginia where she was able to strengthen her anatomy and pathophysiology skills, not only instructing HIT students, but also working with the medical laboratory and veterinary technology programs there. This position gave her the chance to complete her MS degree in Community Health Education from West Virginia University, which perfectly blended health information management and education. She achieved her Certified Health Education Specialist (CHES) credential shortly afterward. She then moved back to Pennsylvania and returned to the hospital arena as a DRG and coding consultant. Dr. Burke had the opportunity to teach at her alma mater and lay the foundation for an associate's degree program in HIT at a local community college.

Subsequent to relocating to Florida, she became a faculty member at Florida A&M University's BS degree program in Health Informatics & Information Management Division. She continued her pursuit of more training in pathophysiology, and soon after received her Doctor of Public Health (DrPH) with a concentration in epidemiology from Florida A&M University. Dr. Burke's main areas of interest are in disaster preparedness for hospitals, and bioterrorism and infectious diseases. She recently achieved certification as a Health Information Technology Implementation Manager (HITPRO-IM) after completing her HITECH training through Santa Fe College.

ACKNOWLEDGMENTS

First and foremost, I wish to express my gratitude to the contributing authors who created and revised the various chapters. They are wonderful people and have graciously provided whatever is needed at the right time while the work is in process. Each of the authors is a seasoned professional and an excellent educator. I can only say that they inspire me to work harder to produce a better product for each edition. With their contributions and assistance, we have been able to provide a broad overview of content from both the RHIA and RHIT programs. I am honored to call them my friends and associates.

I have enjoyed working with the staff at Delmar Cengage Learning. They have been quite accommodating and have taught me a lot about the process of publishing. Thank you, Rhonda, Jadin, Amy, Lauren and the rest of the wonderful staff at Delmar Cengage Learning.

There have been very special people in my life who always knew I could do it when I was not sure I could. My late husband, Bob, always continued to keep me grounded while I would spin off in space working on the book. My mother, Emma Miller, has been my role model for perseverance leading to success. She embodied grace, courage, strength, and endurance. I will always be grateful for having had them in my life.

My thanks would not be complete without acknowledging all the HIM/HIT educators and students who support our efforts by using PRG products. I have been so fortunate in meeting such wonderful people in the HIM profession.

My reward is knowing that the materials you study here may assist you in preparing for the challenge of your examination. Thank you for the letters and words of encouragement.

Whichever credential you seek, I wish you the very best now and throughout your career.

Until we meet...

Patricia J. Schnering, RHIA, CCS

PJSPRG@AOL.COM

TABLE OF CONTENTS

INTRODUCTION ....**xv**
Patricia J. Schnering, RHIA, CCS

I. EXAMINATION STUDY STRATEGIES AND RESOURCES **1**
Patricia J. Schnering, RHIA, CCS

II. TEST-TAKING SKILLS **9**
Patricia J. Schnering, RHIA, CCS
Debora J. Butts, EdD, RHIA

III. HEALTH DATA CONTENT AND STANDARDS **21**
Debra W. Cook, MAEd, RHIA

IV. INFORMATION RETENTION AND ACCESS **55**
Marjorie H. McNeill, PhD, RHIA, CCS, FAHIMA

V. CLASSIFICATION SYSTEMS AND SECONDARY DATA SOURCES **89**
Lisa M. Delhomme, MHA, RHIA

VI. MEDICAL BILLING AND REIMBURSEMENT SYSTEMS **125**
Toni Cade, MBA, RHIA, CCS, FAHIMA

VII. MEDICAL SCIENCE **157**
Lauralyn Kavanaugh-Burke, DrPH, RHIA, CHES, HITPRO-IM

VIII. ICD-9-CM CODING **187**
Leslie Moore, RHIT, CCS

IX. CPT CODING...**243**
Lisa M. Delhomme, MHA, RHIA

X. INFORMATICS AND INFORMATION SYSTEMS **295**
Nanette B. Sayles, EdD, RHIA, CCS, CHPS, CPHIMS, FAHIMA

XI. HEALTH INFORMATION PRIVACY AND SECURITY **321**
Nanette B. Sayles, EdD, RHIA, CCS, CHPS, CPHIMS, FAHIMA

XII. HEALTH LAW **353**
Barbara W. Mosley, PhD, RHIA
Lon'Tejuana S. Cooper, MSHA, RHIA, CPM

XIII. HEALTH STATISTICS AND RESEARCH **383**
Kathy C. Trawick, EdD, RHIA

XIV. QUALITY AND PERFORMANCE IMPROVEMENT **441**
Charlotte McCuen, MS, RHIA

XV. ORGANIZATION AND MANAGEMENT **477**
Anita Hazelwood, MLS, RHIA, FAHIMA
Carol A. Venable, MHP, RHIA, FAHIMA

XVI. HUMAN RESOURCES **507**
Mary Spivey Teslow, MLIS, RHIA

XVII. MOCK EXAMINATION **539**
Debra W. Cook, MAEd, RHIA
Sheila Carlon, PhD, RHIA, FAHIMA

Evaluation Form **607**

Introduction

Patricia J. Schnering, RHIA, CCS

Introduction

Although we have no way of knowing what exactly will be on the examination, the authors tried to cover as many HIM concepts as possible. We have carefully selected questions that are generic enough to cover the broad topic categories. Researching the questions as you study should expand your knowledge such that, when you encounter similar questions, you can arrive at the correct answer. We believe this review material will jog your memory and serve to help you build on information you have already gained through your education.

With the collaboration of Health Information Administration and Technology educators, many questions have been updated and new questions added to enhance topic categories in this edition of the book. The more advanced questions for RHIA candidates are at the end of the chapters, where appropriate.

Professional Review Guide for the RHIA and RHIT Examinations by Content Areas

This review guide is arranged by content sections much as you studied in your classes. See Table I-1 for content areas and the number of questions in each content area. The number of questions does not indicate the importance of any one subject; it is merely an accounting of the questions in each section of this book.

Table I-1 Professional Review Guide for the RHIA and RHIT Examinations, 2013 Edition Content Areas and Number of Questions

Professional Review Guide for the RHIA and RHIT Examinations, 2013 Edition Content Areas and Number of Questions	
Health Information Content Topic	Number of Questions
Health Data Contents and Standards	98
Information Access and Retention	125
Classification Systems and Secondary Data Sources	110
Medical Billing and Reimbursement	114
Medical Science	138
ICD-9-CM Coding	210
CPT-4 Coding	217
Informatics and Information Systems	101
Health Information Privacy and Security	98
Health Law	100
Health Statistics and Research	106
Quality and Performance Improvement	107
Organization and Management	106
Human Resources	100
Mock Examination	180
Total Questions	1900

Examination Content and Insights

The test uses competency categories known as domains, subdomains, and tasks that have been shown to be essential entry-level competencies for HIM practice.

Before you begin your review for the examinations, we suggest that you obtain the latest RHIA/RHIT Examination Candidate Handbook. The handbook can be downloaded from AHIMA's Web site at www.ahima.org. Visit the Certification and Credentials section of the AHIMA Web site for the latest certification information.

The entry-level tasks are grouped into six domains for the RHIA and seven domains for the RHIT examination, as shown in Table I-2.

Table I-2 Entry-Level Domains for RHIA and RHIT (Effective October 2011)

Entry-Level Domains for RHIA and RHIT	
RHIA	RHIT
1. Health Data Management	1. Data Analysis and Management
2. Health Statistics and Research Support	2. Coding
3. Information Technology and Systems	3. Compliance
4. Organization and Management	4. Information Technology
5. Privacy, Security, and Confidentiality	5. Quality
6. Legal and Regulatory Standards	6. Legal
	7. Revenue Cycle

These domains are divided further into subdomains that modify the domains. Weights for each domain and subdomain are assigned by the number of questions in the domain or subdomain. Thus, each weight correlates to the degree of emphasis, or importance, given to each domain statement as it relates to the HIM practice.

The examinations are based on the competencies. The competencies are aligned with knowledge statements. On the following pages, you will find additional information on the competencies and their corresponding knowledge statements listed for the RHIA and RHIT examinations.

Look at the differences in the level of knowledge needed for the RHIA and RHIT examinations. It may help you understand what is expected in each examination by competency. You can expect a higher level of knowledge in statistics, research, management, and information systems for the RHIA, whereas the RHIT will be focused more on Domain 1 and Domain 2 in data analysis and coding.

COMPETENCIES FOR THE RHIA EXAMINATION

The RHIA examination has 180 questions (160 questions scored and 20 that are not scored for the exam). The 160 scored questions are the basis for scoring your examination. The 20 unscored questions on the RHIA examination are to be used in obtaining statistical information to help in the construction of questions for future examinations. These 20 questions will not be identified in the exam, nor will they count toward the examination pass/fail score. Table I-3 presents the domains and equivalent weights for the RHIA examination. Review the current RHIA and RHIT Examination Candidate Handbook from AHIMA.

Table I-3 Domains and Equivalent Weights for the RHIA Certification Examination

Domains and Equivalent Weights for the RHIA Certification Examination			
Domain	Domain Name	Questions	Weight
1	Health Data Management	32	20%
2	Health Statistics and Research Support	17	11%
3	Information Technology and Systems	32	20%
4	Organization and Management	48	30%
5	Privacy, Security, and Confidentiality	21	13%
6	Legal and Regulatory Standards	10	6%
Total		160	100%

COMPETENCIES FOR THE RHIT EXAMINATION

The RHIT examination has 150 questions (130 questions scored and 20 that are not scored for the exam). The 130 scored questions are the basis for scoring the examination. The 20 unscored questions on the RHIT examination are to be used in obtaining statistical information to help in the construction of questions for future examinations. These 20 questions will not be identified in the exam, nor will they count toward the examination pass/fail score. Table I-4 presents the domains and equivalent weights for the RHIT examination. Review the current RHIA and RHIT Examination Candidate Handbook from AHIMA to verify the competencies.

Table I-4 Domains and Equivalent Weights for the RHIT Certification Examination

Domains and Equivalent Weights for the RHIT Certification Examination			
Domain	Domain Name	Questions	Weights
1	Data Analysis and Management	26	20%
2	Coding	23	18%
3	Compliance	21	16%
4	Information Technology	16	12%
5	Quality	16	12%
6	Legal	14	11%
7	Revenue Cycle	14	11%
Total		130	100%

In creating the review guide, we wanted to cover the competencies for both the RHIA and the RHIT. The questions in the chapters of this review guide relate to the competencies according to the breakdown of content for both the RHIA and RHIT exams.

Table I-5 provides a crosswalk between the RHIA competencies for and the number of questions in each competency by chapter.

Table I-6 provides a crosswalk of RHIT Competencies by number of questions in each Chapter.

Table I-7 shows the pass rates for the RHIA and RHIT examinations given in 2009, 2010, and 2011.

Table I-5 Crosswalk of RHIA Competencies by Chapter

Crosswalk of RHIA Competencies by Chapter							
Chapter Name	Competency Domain						
	1	2	3	4	5	6	Total
Health Data Content and Standards	40	3	18	3	0	34	98
Information Retention and Access	57	3	31	15	17	16	139
Classification Systems and Secondary Data Sources	105	0	5	0	0	0	110
Medical Billing and Reimbursement Systems	114	0	0	0	0	0	114
Medical Science	138	0	0	0	0	0	138
ICD-9-CM Coding	210	0	0	0	0	0	210
CPT Coding	217	0	0	0	0	0	217
Informatics and Information Systems	0	0	101	0	0	0	101
Health Information Privacy and Security	0	0	0	0	98	0	98
Health Statistics and Research	0	106	0	0	0	0	106
*Health Law	0	0	0	0	50	50	100
Quality and Performance Improvement	0	107	0	0	0	0	107
Organization and Management	0	0	0	106	0	0	106
Human Resources	0	0	0	100	0	0	100
Mock Examination	48	40	23	36	14	19	180
Total RHIA Questions	929	259	182	254	164	120	1900

*Competencies for the Health Law questions fit in both domains 5 and 6.

Table I-6 RHIT Competencies by Chapter

Crosswalk of RHIT Competencies by Chapter								
Chapter Name	Competency Domain							
	1	2	3	4	5	6	7	Total
Health Data Content and Standards	44	5	30	16	1	0	0	98
Information Retention and Access	79	1	15	18	5	6	0	125
Classification Systems and Secondary Data Sources	42	68	0	0	0	0	0	110
Medical Billing and Reimbursement Systems	0	0	0	0	0	0	114	114
Medical Science	138	0	0	0	0	0	0	138
ICD-9-CM Coding	0	210	0	0	0	0	0	210
CPT Coding	0	217	0	0	0	0	0	217
Informatics and Information Systems	0	0	0	55	0	0	0	55
Health Information Privacy and Security	0	0	0	0	0	98	0	98
Health Statistics and Research	42	7	0	0	30	0	0	79
Health Law	0	0	0	0	0	100	0	100
Quality and Performance Improvement	0	0	0	0	107	0	0	107
Organization and Management	24	0	0	0	0	0	0	24
Human Resources	28	2	0	0	3	18	0	51
Mock Examination	37	32	10	16	31	17	8	150
Total RHIT Questions	434	541	57	106	177	238	122	1679

Table I-7 Passing Rates for the First-Time Test Taker for 2009, 2010, and 2011

Passing Rates for the First-Time Test Taker (2009–2011)			
*Pass Rates for First-Time Test Takers	2011	2010	2009
Registered Health Information Administrator (RHIA)	70.9%	77.0%	70.6%
Registered Health Information Technician (RHIT)	71.3%	76.4%	82.7%
*Exam pass rates are based on the calendar year. Exam pass rates for 2012 will be posted by March 31, 2013.			

Source: AHIMA (AHIMA.org).

KNOWLEDGE STATEMENTS For The RHIA And RHIT

In addition to the competencies, AHIMA and the COC have identified the knowledge statements that emerged from the Roles and Function Study for the RHIA and RHIT. Mastery of these knowledge statements is necessary to successfully perform the competencies.

Table I-8 lists the knowledge statements by domain for the baccalaureate degree program (RHIA).

Table I-9 lists the knowledge statements by domain for the associate degree program (RHIT).

Table I-8 Knowledge Statements for RHIA Domains

Domain 1 Health Data Management
1. Manage health data elements and/or data sets
2. Develop and maintain organizational policies, procedures, and guidelines for management of health information
3. Ensure accuracy and integrity of health data and health record documentation
4. Manage and/or validate coding accuracy and compliance
5. Manage the use of clinical data required in reimbursement systems and prospective payment systems (PPS) in healthcare delivery
6. Code diagnosis and procedures according to established guidelines
7. Present data for organizational use (e.g., summarize, synthesize, and condense information) Health information media (paper, electronic/computer-based; e-health-personal, web-based)
Domain 2 Healthcare Statistics, Biomedical Research, and Quality Management
1. Identify and/or respond to the information needs of internal and external healthcare customers
2. Filter and/or interpret information for the end customer
3. Analyze and present information for organizational management (e.g., quality, utilization, risk)
4. Use data mining techniques to query and report from databases
Domain 3 Information Technology and Research Support
1. Implement and manage use of technology applications
2. Develop data dictionary and data models for database design
3. Manage and maintain databases (e.g., data migration, updates)
4. Apply data and functional standards to achieve interoperability of healthcare information systems
5. Apply data/record storage principles and techniques associated with the medium (e.g., paper-based, hybrid, electronic)
6. Evaluate and recommend clinical, administrative, and specialty service applications (e.g., financial systems, electronic record, clinical coding)
7. Manage master person index (e.g., patient record integration, customer–client relationship management)
Domain 4 Organization and Management
1. Develop and support strategic and operational plans for facility-wide health information management
2. Monitor industry trends and organizational needs to anticipate changes
3. Perform human resource management activities (e.g., recruiting staff, creating job descriptions, resolving personnel issues)
4. Conduct training and educational activities (e.g., HIM systems, coding, medical and institutional terminology, documentation and regulatory requirements)
5. Establish and monitor productivity standards for the HIM function
6. Optimize reimbursement through management of the revenue cycle (e.g., chargemaster maintenance)
7. Develop, motivate, and support work teams and/or individuals (e.g., coaching, mentoring)
8. Prepare and manage budgets
9. Analyze and report on budget variances
10. Determine resource needs by performing analyses (e.g., cost-benefit, business planning)
11. Evaluate and manage contracts (e.g., vendor, contract personnel, maintenance)
12. Organize and facilitate meetings
13. Advocate for department, organization, and/or profession
14. Manage projects
15. Prepare for accreditation and licensing processes (e.g., Joint Commission, Medicare, state regulators)

Table I-8 Knowledge Statements for RHIA Domains (continued)

Domain 5 Privacy, Security, and Confidentiality
1. Design and implement security measures to safeguard Protected Health Information (PHI)
2. Manage access, disclosure, and use of Protected Health Information (PHI) to ensure confidentiality
3. Investigate and resolve healthcare privacy and security issues/problems
4. Develop and maintain healthcare privacy and security training programs

Domain 6 Legal and Regulatory Standards
1. Administer organizational compliance with healthcare information laws, regulations, and standards (e.g., audit, report, and/or inform; legal health record)
2. Prepare for accreditation and licensing processes (e.g., Joint Commission, Medicare, state regulators)

Table I-9 Knowledge Statements for RHIT Domains

Domain 1 Data Analysis and Management
1. Abstract information found in health records (i.e., coding, research, physician deficiencies, etc.)
2. Analyze data (i.e., productivity reports, quality measures, health record documentation, case-mix index)
3. Maintain filing and retrieval systems for health records
4. Identify anomalies in data
5. Resolve risks and/or anomalies of data findings
6. Maintain the master patient index (i.e., enterprise systems merge/unmerge medical record numbers, etc.)
7. Eliminate duplicate documentation
8. Organize data into a useable format
9. Review trends in data
10. Gather/compile data from multiple sources
11. Generate reports or spreadsheets (i.e., customize, create, etc.)
12. Present data findings (i.e., study results, delinquencies, conclusion/summaries, gap analysis, graphical)
13. Implement workload distribution
14. Design workload distribution
15. Participate in the data management plan (i.e., determine data elements, assemble components, set time frame)
16. Input and/or submit data to registries
17. Summarize findings from data research/analysis
18. Follow data archive and backup policies
19. Develop data management plan
20. Calculate healthcare statistics (i.e., occupancy rates, length of stay, delinquency rates, etc.)
21. Determine validation process for data mapping
22. Maintain data dictionaries

Domain 2 Coding
1. Apply all official current coding guidelines
2. Assign diagnostic and procedure codes based on health record documentation
3. Insure physician documentation supports coding
4. Validate code assignment
5. Abstract data from health record
6. Sequence codes
7. Query physician when additional clinical documentation is needed
8. Review and resolve coding edits (i.e. correct coding initiative, outpatient code editor, National Coverage Determination, Local Coverage Determination, etc.)
9. Review the accuracy of abstracted data
10. Assign POA (present on admission) indicators
11. Provide educational updates to coders
12. Validate grouper assignment (i.e. MS-DRG, APC, etc.)
13. Identify HAC (hospital acquired condition)
14. Develop and manage a query process
15. Create standards for coding productivity and quality
16. Develop educational guidelines for provider documentation
17. Perform concurrent audits

Table I-9 Knowledge Statements for RHIT Domains (continued)

Domain 3 Compliance

1. Ensure patient record documentation meets state and federal regulations
2. Ensure compliance with privacy and security guidelines (HIPAA, state, hospital, etc.)
3. Control access to health information
4. Monitor documentation for completeness
5. Develop a coding compliance plan (i.e., current coding guidelines)
6. Manage release of information
7. Perform continual updates to policies and procedures
8. Implement internal and external audit guidelines
9. Evaluate medical necessity (CDMP – clinical documentation management program)
10. Collaborate with staff to prepare the organization for accreditation, licensing, and/or certification surveys
11. Evaluate medical necessity (Outpatient services)
12. Evaluate medical necessity (Data management)
13. Responding to fraud and abuse
14. Evaluate medical necessity (ISSI utilization review)
15. Develop forms (i.e., chart review, documentation, EMR, etc.)
16. Evaluate medical necessity (Case management)
17. Analyze access audit trails
18. Ensure valid healthcare provider credentials

Domain 4 Information Technology

1. Train users on software
2. Maintain database
3. Set up secure access
4. Evaluate the functionality of applications
5. Create user accounts
6. Troubleshoot HIM software or support systems
7. Create database
8. Perform end user audits
9. Participate in vendor selection
10. Perform end user needs analysis
11. Design data archive and backup policies
12. Perform system maintenance of software and systems
13. Create data dictionaries

Domain 5 Quality

1. Audit health records for content, completeness, accuracy, and timeliness
2. Apply standards, guidelines, and/or regulations to health records
3. Implement corrective actions as determined by audit findings (internal and external)
4. Design efficient workflow processes
5. Comply with national patient safety goals
6. Analyze standards, guidelines, and/or regulations to build criteria for audits
7. Apply process improvement techniques
8. Provide consultation to internal and external users of health information on HIM subject matter
9. Develop reports on audit findings
10. Perform data collection for quality reporting (core measures, PQRI, medical necessity, etc.)
11. Use trended data to participate in performance improvement plans/initiatives
12. Develop a tool for collecting statistically valid data
13. Conduct clinical pertinence reviews
14. Monitor physician credentials to practice in the facility

Table I-9 Knowledge Statements for RHIT Domains (continued)
Domain 6 Legal
1. Ensure confidentiality of the health records (paper and electronic)
2. Adhere to disclosure standards and regulations (HIPAA privacy, HITECH Act, breach notifications, etc.) at both state and federal levels
3. Demonstrate and promote legal and ethical standards of practice
4. Maintain integrity of legal health record according to organizational bylaws, rules, and regulations
5. Follow state mandated and/or organizational record retention and destruction policies
6. Serve as the custodian of the health records (paper or electronic)
7. Respond to Release of Information (ROI) requests from internal and external requestors
8. Work with risk management department to provide requested documentation
9. Identify potential health record related risk management issues through auditing
10. Respond to and process patient amendment requests to the health record
11. Facilitate basic education regarding the use of consents, healthcare Power of Attorney, Advanced Directives, DNRs, etc.
12. Represent the facility in court related matters as it applies to the health record (subpoenas, depositions, court orders, warrants)
Domain 7 Revenue Cycle
1. Communicate with providers to discuss documentation deficiencies (i.e., queries)
2. Participate in clinical documentation improvement programs to ensure proper documentation of health records
3. Collaborate with other departments on monitoring accounts receivable (i.e., unbilled, uncoded)
4. Provide ongoing education to healthcare providers (i.e. regulatory changes, new guidelines, payment standards, best practices, etc.)
5. Identify fraud and abuse
6. Assist with appeal letters in response to claim denials
7. Monitor claim denials/over-payments to identify potential revenue impact
8. Prioritize the work according to accounts receivable, patient type, etc.
9. Distribute the work according to accounts receivable, patient type, etc.
10. Maintain the chargemaster
11. Ensure physicians are credentialed with different payers for reimbursement

ADDITIONAL INSIGHTS ABOUT PAST EXAMINATIONS

1. **Computerized exam.** The test is taken electronically in an approved testing center. You will be able to return to previously answered questions to check your answers before you close the exam file on the computer. Visit AHIMA's Web site for examples of the screens you will be using.

2. **Statistical formulas** needed to complete the questions on health statistics will be available if needed in some form so that you can see it on the screen, thus eliminating the need to memorize all the formulas. You will be expected to know basic formulas like those for average, mean, and median. However, it is critical that you know how to apply the formulas accurately. We recommend that you spend time working through as many statistical problems as possible.

3. **Math throughout.** Be aware that mathematical calculations may also be required in other types of questions (for instance, calculating FTE requirements, budget questions, etc.), so basic math skills are a must! Become proficient in making mathematical calculations on the computer by practicing on the calculator provided in the accessories folder on your computer. If math is not a strong area for you, seek out assistance and practice, practice, practice. On the examination, you will need to use the calculator function on the computer.

4. **Informatics and information systems questions are interspersed throughout the other topics.** From the workplace setting you experienced during your professional practice experiences, you know that computers are involved in almost every aspect of HIM functions, e.g., coding, record tracking, incomplete charts, release of information, etc. Therefore, it stands to reason that questions related to information systems could show up in many other categories.

5. **Legal questions are at the national level.** In reference to questions in the category of health care legal aspects, keep in mind that this is a national examination. Therefore, any state-specific laws would not be applicable. Concentrate on federal legislation, statutes, and legal issues that would be appropriate nationally in all 50 states. You can count on federal questions that relate to the HIPAA standards for privacy and security.

6. **Questions on the examinations are scrambled** and change topics from question to question. Therefore, you may have a legal question, followed by a management question, followed by a coding question, followed by a quality assurance question, etc. Be prepared to shift gears quickly throughout the exam.

7. **Quality and performance improvement focus.** Because the implementation of QA/PI is at the forefront of the health care industry, give special attention to Quality Assessment and Performance Improvement issues. Become familiar with the various QA/PI tools. Several resources for this subject are listed at the end of the Quality Assessment and Performance Improvement chapter of this book.

8. **Be sure to spend some time reviewing organization and management** functions and techniques, especially those preparing for the RHIA examination.

9. **You will not need to bring your ICD-9-CM or CPT-4 coding books to the test.** The questions are in a narrative form and any necessary codes and/or code narratives will be supplied on the computer screen for you to choose from. Study the Official ICD-9-CM Guidelines for Coding and Reporting. Review reimbursement methodologies and compliance issues as they have become more and more important in the health care arena.

10. **Application and analysis emphasis.** The questions on both the RHIA and RHIT examinations have been increasingly skewed toward application and analysis rather than recall level of question difficulty. Questions on the examination may combine several concepts into one question, increasing the level of difficulty of the question. Effective October 2011, the test specifications have been updated for the RHIT exam. The cognitive levels for this exam are as follows: 40% Recall/Understanding, 35% Application, and 25% Analysis and Higher Thinking. (Source: AHIMA.org.)

THE DAY BEFORE AND THE MORNING OF THE EXAM

1. Avoid studying the night before the exam. Last-minute studying tends to increase your anxiety level. However, you may want to spend a little time reviewing content you must memorize.

2. Organize in advance all the materials you need to take with you to the exam. Review the Candidate Handbook carefully and be sure to have all the items required, especially the admission card and appropriate proof of identity.

3. Get a good night's sleep and have a healthy meal before the exam.

4. Allow yourself plenty of time so that you arrive at the test site early. If necessary, spend the night before the examination in a hotel or motel near the exam test site.

5. Dress comfortably and plan for possible variations in room temperature. Dressing in layers may prove helpful.

TAKING THE EXAMINATION

You have stuck to your study schedule and have conditioned yourself to be in the best physical and mental shape possible. Now comes the moment of truth: the examination pops up on the screen before your eyes. Every paratrooper knows that, in addition to having a parachute, one must know how to open it. You have mastered the major topics; you have the parachute. Now you need to utilize good test-taking techniques to apply the knowledge you have gained; open the parachute!

1. Prior to starting the exam, you will be given a chance to practice taking an examination on the computer. Ten minutes will be allotted for this practice test; however, you may quit the practice test and begin the actual exam when you are comfortable with the computerized testing process.

2. Read all directions and questions carefully. Try to avoid reading too much into the questions. Be sensible and practical in your interpretation. Read ALL of the possible answers, because the first one that looks good may not be the best one.

3. Scan the computer screen quickly for the general format of the questions. Like the marathon runner, pace yourself for the distance. A good rule of thumb is 1 to 1.5 minutes per question. You may wish to keep the timer displayed on the computer to check your schedule throughout the exam. For example, at question 31, about one-half hour will have elapsed, etc.

4. Some people answer all questions that they are certain of first, and then go back through the exam a second time to answer any questions they were uncertain about. Others prefer not to skip questions but make their best choice on encountering each question and go on. Both can be good approaches; choose the one that works best for you. You can "mark" questions that you have left unanswered and/or those questions you may want to review. Before you sign off of the exam or run out of time, you have the ability to go back to those questions for a final review.

5. Answer all the questions. There are no penalties for guessing, but putting no answer is definitely a wrong answer.

6. Use deductive reasoning and the process of elimination to arrive at the most correct answer. Some questions will have more than one correct answer. You will be asked to select the "best" possible answer based on the information presented.

7. If the question is written in a scenario format, first identify the question being asked and then review the entire question for the information needed to determine the correct answer.

8. Use all the time available to recheck your answers. However, avoid changing your answers unless you are absolutely certain it is necessary. Second-guessing yourself often results in a wrong answer.

AFTER THE EXAM

Our advice is to reclaim your life and focus on your career. One good way to start is to plan a special reward for yourself at some point immediately following or shortly after the exam. Schedule a family vacation or a relaxing weekend get-away. Just find some way of being good to yourself. You certainly deserve it! You have worked hard, so relish your success.

WebTutor™ Online Course Cartridges Now Available

WebTutor™ online course management cartridges are available to accompany this text. WebTutor™ is available on WebCT and Blackboard, and other platforms upon request. WebTutor is an online course management and delivery system designed to accompany a specific textbook. WebTutors designed for the Professional Review Guide self-study examination titles contain the following items:

- Learning objectives
- Class notes
- Multiple choice quizzes (taken directly from the books)
- Discussion questions
- Web links

Contact your Delmar Cengage Learning sales representative or go to www.webtutor.cengage.com for more information.

I. Examination Study Strategies and Resources

Patricia J. Schnering, RHIA, CCS

FORMAT OF THE EXAMINATION

The questions developed for the examinations are based on specifications currently referred to as domains and subdomains. A complete copy of these entry-level specifications will be provided in the RHIA/RHIT Candidate Handbook provided by AHIMA.

The general format of the exams is primarily designed to engage your problem-solving and critical-thinking skills. These types of questions require that you translate what you have learned and apply it to a situation. To get a preview, you can access sample questions on AHIMA's Web site: www.ahima.org.

EXAMINATION STRATEGIES

Preparing for a major exam is similar to preparing for a marathon athletic event. The time allotted for the RHIA examination is 4 hours. The time allotted for the RHIT examination is 3½ hours. One suggestion is to use your study process to slowly build up your concentration time until you can focus your energy for the appropriate time. This is like the runner who begins jogging for 30 minutes and builds up to 1 hour, then 1½ hours, and so on, and gradually increases the endurance time to meet the demands of the race. Try this strategy; it could work for you!

Everyone has his or her own particular study style. Some people prefer to study alone and others work best in a group. Regardless of your preference, we strongly recommend that you take advantage of group study at least some of the time. Studying with others can prove very helpful when working through your weakest areas. Each member of the study team will bring strengths and weaknesses to the table, and all can benefit from the collaboration. So, even if you are a solitary learner, you may occasionally want to work with a group for those topics you find more challenging.

Theoretically, material known thoroughly after one's learning will fade predictably with time. After one day, the average person retains only 80% of what was learned; ultimately he or she will remember about 30% of it. That is why you are now relearning information you acquired over a period of years. Your aim is to achieve maximum recall through effective review.

Make your study process systematic. To facilitate this effort, we recommend that you design a 10-week study program. You should plan on spending an average of 10 to 12 hours per week studying. The idea is to study smart, not to bulldoze through tons of material in a haphazard way.

DEVELOPING YOUR STUDY HABITS

First, you must get organized. You have to be deliberate about making sure that you develop and stick to a regular study routine. Find a place where you can study, either at home or at the library.

How you schedule your study time during the week is an individual decision. However, we recommend that you avoid all-nighters and other unreasonably long study sessions. The last thing you want to do is burn yourself out by working too long and too hard at one time. Try to do a little bit at a time and maintain a steady pace that is manageable for you.

Develop your individual study program. Write the topics and subjects in a list. Outline the chapters in your HIM text. Pause at each chapter outline and recall basic points. Do you draw a blank, recall them more or less, or do you feel comfortable with your recall? Pinpoint your weakest subjects. By using this approach, you can see where you stand.

Weigh the importance of each subject. How were the topics emphasized in textbooks, in your class notes, and on previous exams (review the examination content information in the introduction of this book)? Try to pick out concepts that would make good exam questions.

Avoid trying to make a head-on attack by giving equal time and attention to all topics. Use the outlines to identify your weakest topics. Determine which topics will require a significant amount of study time and which will only require a brief review. Make a list of the topics in the order that you plan to study them.

Your list will give you a clear mental picture of what you need to do and will keep you on track. There are three additional advantages to a list:

1. It builds your morale as you steadily cross off the items that you have completed, and you can monitor your progress.

2. Glancing back at the list from time to time serves to reassure you that you are on target.

3. You can readily see that you are applying your time and effort where they are most needed.

Keep the list conspicuously in view. Carefully plan your pre-exam study time and stick to your plan. Go to the exam like a trained and disciplined runner going to a marathon event!

A SUMMARY OF TIPS FOR ORGANIZING YOUR TIME AND MATERIALS

1. **Assess your strengths and weaknesses.** Review the major topic categories and the AHIMA competency listing to help in determining where your areas of strength are and what areas are in need of improvement.

2. **Set up a realistic study schedule.** Refer to the sample schedule provided in this book and customize it to meet your needs.

3. **Focus on your weaknesses.** Spend more time and energy studying your areas of weakness, especially if these categories had a significant percentage of questions associated with them on the AHIMA competency list. Remember, every question counts toward that passing score!

4. **Organize and review all of the following items:**
   a. Course syllabi and outlines
   b. Class notes
   c. Tests and examinations
   d. Textbooks
   e. AHIMA test information and materials

5. **Take tests.** One of the best ways to study for a test is to take tests. Practice answering questions and working problems as much as possible. Work with your watch in front of you. Time yourself so that you become accustomed to taking only 1 to 1½ minutes per question. Practice using the calculator on your computer to make mathematical calculations. When you take the practice tests contained on the CD included in this book, you can practice by choosing the section and then picking the competency you want to focus on.

6. **Read the AHIMA Candidate Handbook for the Certification Examinations.** If anything in the Candidate Handbook is unclear, seek assistance from your program director or call AHIMA. You are held accountable for the important information, deadlines, and instructions addressed in this material.

SAMPLE STUDY SCHEDULE

Week 1   Health Data Contents and Standards, and Information Retention and Access

Week 2   Legal and Ethical Aspects, and Health Information Privacy and Security

Week 3   Informatics and Information Systems

Week 4   Organization and Management and Human Resources

Week 5   Classification Systems and Secondary Data Sources

Week 6   Billing and Reimbursement and Medical Science

Week 7   CPT Coding

Week 8   ICD-9-CM Coding

Week 9   Quality and Performance Improvement

Week 10   Health Statistics and Research

STUDY RESOURCES

There are three basic sources of information: books, people, and your educational program or college. If your studies become stagnant, do not sit and grind yourself down. If your text is not making the subject clear for you, don't spend time trying to memorize something you do not understand. The main issue is to understand the material so you can use the knowledge in a practical way. Search for additional information that will help make the subject clear to you.

Books and other written resources may use another style of presentation that you are more receptive to. A different textbook may be all you need to gain better insight into the subject. It can offer a fresh point of view, provide relief from boredom, and encourage critical thinking in the process of comparing the texts.

Periodical literature in the health field provides well-written articles that may open up the subject to you and turn study into an adventure in learning. AHIMA publishes authoritative and insightful information on every aspect of HIM. Sometimes an article can help put the text material into practical perspective and pull it together so that you gain a deeper understanding. With the rapidly changing health care world, HIM journals and magazines have the most current information and are frequently used as references for test questions.

Take advantage of the college library by using reserved materials set aside for your study purposes.

Professional contacts in your HIM community can also be helpful in your study effort. Most people in our field are eager to share their knowledge and are flattered by appeals for information.

Collaborating with classmates may reveal fresh viewpoints, stimulate thought by disagreement, or at least let you see that you are not alone in your quest. Organize study groups and set aside specific times to work together. This interaction can be truly beneficial in keeping you motivated and on task.

Classes, workshops, and seminars present opportunities to learn and review the subject matter in a new light. Take advantage of any examination review sessions available in your area. Talking to graduates who have recently taken the exam can also be of great assistance.

Don't overlook the power of AHIMA's Web site. In this dynamic, changing environment, the most up-to-date materials may not be available in a book. The AHIMA resources online are extensive and quite easy to access at www.ahima.org. In addition, the Communities of Practice (CoPs) are a phenomenal source of contact with HIM professionals and other students on a myriad of subjects.

In summary, some of the study resources available to you include the following:

1. HIM textbooks and Class text books: There is a large variety of textbooks for HIM and coding available on the market. Both Delmar Cengage Learning (www.cengage.com) and AHIMA (www.ahima.org) have a variety of HIM products. For example, see the partial listing of books available through Delmar Cengage Learning.

2. Review books written for the RHIA and RHIT examinations.

3. Mock exam questions on the CD-ROM is included in the back of this book for practice taking computerized tests.

4. Class notes as well as the class tests and exams.

5. Examination review sessions.

6. On-the-job experience (be cautious because the exam tests theory and not each particular practice and the test uses national laws, rules, and regulations—not state and facility practice).

7. Study groups or partners.

8. Visit various Internet sites such as www.ahima.org and www.cms.gov for the latest information on the health care industry.

AHIMA has developed a series of HIM and coding resources.
> To place an order, call (800) 335-5535.
> Visit the AHIMA Web site at http://www.ahima.org for additional resources and information about the coding certification examinations.

Ingenix has an array of coding, reimbursement, and compliance products. Ingenix is now OPUMInsight, part of Optum—a leading health services business.
> Contact them at 1-800-INGENIX.
> Visit their Web site at http//www.shopingenix.com.

Delmar Cengage Learning has a multitude of HIM products. In addition, they have partnered with Ingenix so that you can order your Ingenix resources through Delmar Cengage Learning.

For additional information on these Health Information resources, visit Delmar Cengage Learning at http//www.cengage.com.

The following is a partial listing of Cengage products for Health Information:

3-2-1 Code It! (3rd Edition)
> Green, Michelle A.

A Guide to Health Insurance Billing
> (Includes Ingenix Trial Printed Access Card and Premium Web Site Printed Access Card)
> Moisio, Marie A.

Basic Allied Health Statistics and Analysis
> Koch, G.

Case Studies for Health Information Management
> McCuen, Charlotte; Sayles, Nanette; and Schnering, Patricia

Coding Basics: Medical Billing and Reimbursement Fundamentals
> Richards, Cynthia

Coding Basics: Understanding Medical Collections
> Rimmer, Michelle

Coding for Medical Necessity in the Physician Office
> Kelly-Farwell, Deborah and Favreau, Cecile

Coding Surgical Procedures: Beyond the Basics
> Smith, Gail I.

Cengage products for Health Information (continued)

Coding Workbook for the Physician's Office
  Covell, Alice

Comparative Health Information Management
  Peden, Ann

Essentials of Health Information Management Principles and Practices (2nd Edition)
  Green, M. A. and Bowie, M. J.

Essentials of Healthcare Compliance
  Safian, Shelly

Ethics Case Studies for Health Information Management
  Grebner, Leah

Guide to Coding Compliance
  Becker, Joanne M.

Health Services Research Methods
  Shi, L.

HIPAA for Medical Office Personnel
  Krager, Dan and Krager, Carole

ICD-10: A Comprehensive Guide: Education, Planning and Implementation
  Dawlish, Carline

ICD-10-CM Diagnostic Coding System: Education, Planning and Implementation
  Dagleish, Carline

ICD-10-PCS Coding System: Education, Planning and Implementation
  Dagleish, Carline

Legal and Ethical Aspects of Health Information Management
  McWay, Dana C.

Medical Terminology for Insurance and Coding
  Moisio, Marie A.

Today's Health Information Management: An Integrated Approach
  McWay, D. C.

Understanding Health Insurance: A Guide to Billing and Reimbursement
  Green, Michelle A. and Rowell, Jo Anne

Understanding Hospital Billing and Coding: A Worktext
  Diamond, Marsha S.

Understanding ICD-9-CM: A Worktest
  Bowie, Mary Jo and Schaffer, Regina M.

Understanding ICD-9-CM Coding
  Bowie, Mary Jo and Schaffer, Regina M.

Understanding ICD-10-CM and ICD-10-PCS: A Worktext
  Bowie, Mary Jo and Schaffer, Regina M.

Understanding Medical Coding: A Comprehensive Guide
  Johnson, S. L. and McHugh, C. S.

Understanding Hospital Billing and Coding
  Diamond, M. S.

Understanding Procedural Coding: A Worktext
  Bowie, Mary Jo and Schaffer, Regina M.

Using the Electronic Health Record in the Healthcare Provider Practice
  Eichenwald Maki, Shirley and Petterson, Bonnie

II. Test-Taking Skills

Patricia J. Schnering, RHIA, CCS

Debora J. Butts, EdD, RHIA

This section of the review book is designed to provide students with techniques that will help maximize their chances for success on the RHIA and RHIT national certification examinations. Five major areas are explored in this section:

1. Becoming "test wise"
2. The "truth" about test taking
3. Characteristics of successful test takers
4. Multiple-choice test question construction
5. Practical advice for exam preparation

Health Information Administration/Technology (HIA/HIT) students may view the test-taking experience as one that causes great anxiety and concern. Test-taking does not have to be a negative experience. Students can equip themselves with an array of techniques and practical strategies to master the test-taking situation. After all, the ultimate goal of taking the exam is to pass it and move forward with one's career aspirations.

BECOMING "TEST WISE"

This section will assist the student in becoming "test wise." Becoming test wise involves a set of skills that is acquired through practice and instruction. Being test wise does not mean that one will always achieve a very high score on the exam. What it does mean is that one will learn to overcome such factors as test anxiety, which often prevent students from passing examinations. The ultimate key to being test wise is knowledge of the subject matter that will be covered on the certification examination. No amount of tips or techniques can replace adequate preparation. A colleague I know in academia often states, "Adequate preparation prevents poor performance." If one does not have thorough knowledge of the subject, no amount of test-taking knowledge or skills will improve test performance. Now, let's turn our discussion to the first topic—the "truth" about test taking.

THE "TRUTH" ABOUT TEST TAKING

It is important to be realistic about what a test really is and what it is not. The exam is not a measure of your intelligence. It is not directly a measure of your knowledge of the course material. It is not a complete picture of what you know. It is certainly not a measure of your worth as a human being. Most importantly, failing to pass the certification examination does not imply that you are in the wrong profession. Many lawyers and certified public accountants require several attempts to obtain their credentials.

Now let's look at what a test is really all about. What does it measure? A test may measure your performance on a given day. It tells you how much you know about the questions you were asked, which represent a small sampling of the material you actually covered while studying to become a health information management professional. To some degree, a test measures your skills as a test taker, such as your ability to apply reasoning and logic, as well as your critical-thinking and problem-solving skills. The test also measures your ability to recall "correct answers."

It is important as you prepare for the certification examination that you maintain a realistic perspective. The certification examination is a professionally designed test that has been developed by educators and practitioners in health information management. It will measure your ability to answer questions in the major domains.

Knowing what is expected of you in order to pass the examination and improving your test-taking skills will provide you with valuable tools to apply in your study process. If you keep the examination in the proper perspective and prepare well, you will obtain the credentials that you so rightly deserve.

Learning how to take tests will usually help you overcome inappropriate test-taking habits and allow you to demonstrate what you know to the fullest degree in the testing situation. Here are 10 truths that you should know before attempting the certification examination.

10 TRUTHS

TRUTH 1: Test-taking skills can be learned.
Good test-taking skills make the most of what you know. That's just what this chapter is focused on.

TRUTH 2: Test-taking skills make a difference.
Two people can get scores that differ greatly on the test because one person has better test-taking skills.

TRUTH 3: Good preparation reduces anxiety.
Reducing anxiety by proper preparation improves test performance.

TRUTH 4: Attitude does make a difference.
A significant percentage of success on the test will depend on your attitude toward test-taking and your general attitude about yourself. Students should strive to feel good about the test-taking experience, knowing that they have done everything possible to prepare in advance for the examination.

TRUTH 5: Always answer the easy questions first.
Avoid attempting to answer the most difficult questions first, because they will interfere with your positive attitude and confidence. Agonizing over difficult questions will result in loss of time and points.

TRUTH 6: Failure to plan to pass the exam ensures planning to fail the exam.
This might sound a bit harsh and bitter to swallow, but it is indeed the truth. Do not let poor planning and a lack of preparation hinder you from peak performance on the examination. As the saying goes, "Plan your work and work your plan."

TRUTH 7: Usually your first hunch is your best.
Changing answers after you have selected what you believe or know to be the correct answer is not recommended. Usually, your first hunch is your best, unless of course you discover or uncover information in the examination that disqualifies or nullifies your first choice.

TRUTH 8: Educated guessing is better than guessing randomly.
It is appropriate to guess after you have narrowed down the four options to two possible answers.

TRUTH 9: The only thing that stands between you and passing the exam is …
You guessed it: "YOU." If passing the exam is your number one goal at this point in your life, then your priorities should reflect this goal. Priority number one should be to find the time to plan to be successful on the exam.

TRUTH 10: No amount of "tips and tricks" replaces content knowledge.
As mentioned previously, strong content knowledge is essential. The suggestions in this chapter are meant to make the most of what you know, not to take the place of content preparation.

CHARACTERISTICS OF SUCCESSFUL TEST TAKERS

Have you ever wondered why it seems that some people pass the exam and others do not? What are the characteristics of successful test takers? If one looks at successful people in general, you will probably find that they demonstrate these traits and habits in different aspects of their personal and professional lives. Here are some of the characteristics of successful test takers in general.

1. **Good time management.** Time is looked upon by the successful test taker as something not to be feared, but rather a medium that must be mastered and controlled in order to complete the exam with confidence. Completion of the exam with confidence means that one will be able to manage his or her time effectively and have sufficient time to attempt to answer every question without heavily depending on guessing, whether educated guessing or guessing randomly. Ultimately, if your time is not managed well, the minutes will pass whether you have completed the exam or not. Remember to avoid spending excessive time on any one question.

2. **Read questions carefully.** Read the question twice, if necessary, to fully understand the directions or to fully comprehend what exactly is being asked. In lengthy scenario questions, it may be helpful to read the question portion of the statement first. Also, have a good understanding of key terms or phrases often used in health information management, such as "confidentiality" or "skilled nursing facility." Remember, there is no substitute for knowing the facts.

3. **Take the question at face value.** In other words, avoid reading something into the question that was not intended or explicitly stated. For example, consider the following question:

   In progressive counseling, the first step in disciplining for a first offense is
   A. termination.
   B. suspension.
   C. oral reprimand.
   D. written warning.

   The student who reads into the question may decide that in order to answer this question, he or she must know more about the specific offense. However, such details are not necessary. This question assumes that the offense is one that would not require immediate termination for the first offense. Therefore, in the process of applying progressive disciplinary action, an oral reprimand (answer C) is the correct answer.

4. **Read and consider all four options carefully.** One approach in answering multiple-choice questions is to read the answers first. In using this method, you will evaluate each answer separately and equally. Look for an answer that not only seems right on its own, but completes the question statement smoothly. Statistically, the least likely correct answer on a multiple-choice question is the first option.

   If you have narrowed the options down to two that seem correct, then you must study the options and compare them with each other to see what makes them different. Using deductive reasoning and the process of elimination, you should be able to arrive at the best answer.

5. **Approach questions systematically.** Break down each question into manageable parts and proceed systematically. Consider the following question:

> For a 2-week period, the HIM department had 1,200 worked hours and 1,280 total (or paid) hours on its payroll. During this same 2 weeks, there were 375 discharges. The department's standard is 3.3 worked hours per discharge. The number of worked hours per discharge for this 2-week period was
> A. 3.0.
> B. 3.2.
> C. 3.4.
> D. 3.8.

Following the above principle of breaking down the question into component parts, what would you do to make this question more manageable? There are often several ways to arrive at the same answer. Some students may answer, "I would first pull out the number of discharges," or some may answer, "I would pull out the total hours worked." Whatever works for you to manage answering the question correctly is the right approach for you. The calculation for this question is 1,200 hours worked divided by 375 discharges equals 3.2 (answer B).

6. **Read carefully.** Reading directions thoroughly and identifying key words and phrases in the question are essential to test-taking success. For example, consider the following question:

> The health information manager exercises staff authority in the hospital when he or she
> A. abstracts a medical record.
> B. advises on a file system for the radiology department.
> C. teaches a file clerk a new procedure.
> D. writes a procedure for the correct filing of records.

The stem states "exercises staff authority." If the student did not read the question carefully, he or she may have missed these key terms, which are critical to selecting the correct answer, which is B.

7. **Avoid applying preset solutions.** The successful test taker does not try to remember solutions to similar problems; rather, he or she solves each new problem independently.

WHEN AND HOW TO GUESS

There will be questions on the exam that will be totally unfamiliar to you. Choosing the correct answer may lie in the concept of "informed guessing." In applying this technique, the test taker eliminates the absurd options and guesses on the basis of familiarity.

It is helpful to relate possible answers to the question being asked. Read all the options before selecting the correct one. Usually, you can narrow the possible answers down to two by asking yourself:

* What is the question really asking?
* What is the main idea or point of this question?
* What answer would make the most sense?
* How can I rephrase or break down the question?

Sometimes the test taker can gain information about the correct answers from cues and information from other questions. Remember, however, this is when you are in the "informed guessing" mode. There will be information in a question that is irrelevant, and it is important for you to get to the heart of the question. Don't get too preoccupied with the content or meaning of a scenario before you know what the question is asking. Use logic and common sense whenever possible.

MULTIPLE-CHOICE TEST QUESTION CONSTRUCTION

The entire multiple-choice question is called an item. Each item consists of two main parts:

* **Stem:** The first part is known as the stem. The purpose of the stem is to present a problem in a clear and concise manner. The stem should contain all the details necessary to answer the question. The stem of an item can be a complete sentence that asks a question. It can also be presented as an incomplete sentence that becomes a complete sentence when it is combined with one of the options in the item.

* **Answer options:** The second part of the item is comprised of the options or possible answers. One of the options will answer the question posed in the stem correctly. The remaining options are called *distracters*. They are referred to as distracters because they are designed to distract you from the correct answer. Consider the following sample item.

	ITEM	
Stem	In quantitative research, the formulation of the hypothesis is an activity usually associated with	
Distracter	A.	data collection.
Correct	B.	identification of the problem.
Distracter	C.	analysis.
Distracter	D.	assembling the results.

COGNITIVE LEVELS

In addition to the stem and distracters, the item may also be measuring different cognitive levels. These levels are used to identify the candidates' knowledge of subject matter at different levels needed to perform on the job (see Table 2–1). An example of each of the three levels is shown after the table.

Table 2–1 Cognitive Levels

Cognitive Levels		
Cognitive Level	**Purpose**	**Performance Required**
Recall (RE)	Primarily, to measure memory.	Identify terms, specific facts, methods, procedures, basic concepts, basic theories, principles, and processes.
Application (AP)	To measure simple interpretation of limited data.	Apply concepts and principles to new situations, recognize relationships among data, apply laws and theories to practical situations, calculate solutions to mathematical problems, interpret charts and translate graphic data, classify items, interpret information.
Analysis (AN)	To measure the application of knowledge to solving a specific problem and the assembly of various elements into a meaningful whole.	Select an appropriate solution for responsive action; revise policy, procedure, or plan; evaluate a solution, case scenario, report, or plan; compare solutions, plans, ideas, or aspects of a problem; evaluate information or a situation; perform multiple calculations to arrive at one answer.

© Cengage Learning 2014

Recall: This question is at the "recall level." The student needs to be able to recall pertinent facts.

The medical record is the property of the
  A. patient.
  B. medical facility.
  C. health information management department.
  D. attending physician.

The answer is, of course, B. This question relied on your memory of this fact.

Application: Now let's look at the second highest cognitive level, an application level question, which tests the student's ability to apply information.

The medical record is the property of the medical facility and can be removed in which of the following situations?
- A. The patient is suing the hospital and wants the original record mailed to the attorney representing his case.
- B. The attending physician wants to take the patient's original record to a professional conference for presentation.
- C. The court issues a subpoena and needs the original record in court within 24 hours.
- D. The attending physician is being sued and he wants to take the original patient record to court with him.

The correct answer in this case is C. The only instance when the original record should be removed from the hospital is in the case of the issuance of a subpoena *duces tecum*. This question requires the student to apply information about when a record can be removed from the health care facility. The application level goes beyond the student recalling the rule about who has legal ownership of the record.

Analysis (problem solving): The third and highest cognitive level utilized by test developers is the analysis level. At this level the student will demonstrate the ability to analyze familiar information in new and different situations. This is often referred to as a problem-solving or critical-thinking question.

The information below is from a transcription service in your department.

Total average lines transcribed/month:	270,000
Standard per person:	1,200 lines in one day
21 workdays in a month	15% adjustment factor

The number of transcriptionists needed by this facility is
- A. 10.7.
- B. 11.7.
- C. 12.3.
- D. 16.0.

The correct answer for this question is C.

The mathematical calculation to achieve the answer is
270,000 x 0.15 adjustment factor = 40,500
270,000 + 40,500 = 310,500 potential lines of transcription per month
1,200 lines x 21 days = 25,200 lines one employee can produce in one month
310,500/25,200 = 12.3 transcriptionists

After reviewing the cognitive levels, it is clear that for both the RHIA and RHIT examinations the student must be prepared to answer questions from the lowest cognitive level (recall) to the highest cognitive level (analysis). Testing at all three levels will help ensure that students can apply their newly acquired knowledge and skills on the job.

As always, refer to the current copy of the AHIMA Candidate Handbook for a complete listing of the domains, subdomains, and task competencies.

PRACTICAL ADVICE FOR EXAM PREPARATION

As you become more proficient at applying effective test-taking techniques, you will truly understand the phrase that "knowledge is power." This is exactly what this information hopes to do, and that is to provide you with the knowledge and skills to empower you to achieve your ultimate goal—certification.

Research demonstrates that the test taker who approaches a test with physical, mental, and emotional authority is in a better position to master the testing situation and the outcome. Remember, failing to plan means planning to fail. Here are some recommendations for you to incorporate as part of your "success plan."

Recommendation 1: Follow your regular routine.
Follow your regular nightly routine the evening before and morning of the exam. Abruptly changing your schedule and habits for this testing event could throw your system off balance and negatively affect your performance.

Recommendation 2: Arrive early for the examination.
It is always better to have 15 to 30 minutes of extra time prior to the start of a major examination. By arriving early on test day, you will be able to visit the restroom, survey the situation, and collect your thoughts. Decide where you want to sit in the test area, if the seats are not assigned. By collecting your thoughts prior to the start of the exam, you can improve your mental attitude by knowing you are truly prepared for this time, this situation, and this test-taking process. Remember, you want to be in control of the test anxiety that is normal, despite all of your preparation. If you are unfamiliar with the test site, it is usually a good practice to travel to the test site in advance of the exam date. Becoming familiar with the test site will prevent you from getting lost on the exam day.

Recommendation 3: Maintain a positive mental attitude.
Perhaps you are sometimes plagued by a negative inner voice that says something like: "Well look at you… trying to pass the certification examination. Why don't you stop kidding yourself? You know you are not as smart as your classmates. They will probably all pass and you will probably fail!" Almost all of us have critical voices inside our heads. Sometimes the voice may tell us that we don't measure up to others in the class. At other times it tries to blame our performance on the test, the teacher, or some other convenient scapegoat. You can learn to replace your negative inner dialogue with positive self-talk.

Start by programming your inner voice to remind you of how long and hard you have prepared for this examination. Remind yourself that you deserve to pass because of the time and energy you have spent in school preparing for this examination. Repeat positive affirmation statements to yourself, such as "I am a wonderful, worthy person who is capable of achieving my goal of becoming an RHIA/RHIT."

Recommendation 4: Answer the questions you know first.
It is a good idea to begin the test by answering questions that build your confidence. Getting off to a good start allows you to establish a positive momentum, which will assist you when you encounter more difficult questions. Because time is critical, answering the easier questions first will assure you of getting credit for what you know.

Recommendation 5: Check your answers before exiting the computerized exam.
Make sure you have answered every question. Be careful about changing your answers. You may need to revisit any items in which you have made an educated guess or items you discovered answers to as you progressed through the questions. Submit your test knowing that you did your very best.

CONCLUSION

As you study for the exam, take a moment now and then to review the test-taking skills addressed in this section. Using these techniques will help you develop the characteristics of a successful test taker. Working through questions will help you become more and more comfortable with multiple-choice testing.

Knowing how questions are constructed and what to look for should greatly improve your correct answer ratio. A sense of the scheme of the test structure and cognitive levels will become second nature with practice.

During your exam preparation, you will find that you actually enjoy taking multiple-choice examinations as a study aid. Be sure to obtain any mock computerized test exams available on your CD-ROM or online to gain experience taking the test on the computer.

This comfort zone will free you to apply your knowledge and skills effectively during the examination process. The real bonus is that you will be more focused on demonstrating your knowledge through the medium of testing than on the exam process itself.

III. Health Data Content and Standards

Debra W. Cook, MAEd, RHIA

1. In preparation for an EHR, you are conducting a total facility inventory of all forms currently used. You must name each form for bar coding and indexing into a document management system. The unnamed document in front of you includes a microscopic description of tissue excised during surgery. The document type you are most likely to give to this form is
    A. recovery room record.
    C. operative report.
    B. pathology report.
    D. discharge summary.

REFERENCE: Abdelhak, p 114
                Green and Bowie, p 167
                Johns, p 77
                Odom-Wesley, p 171
                LaTour and Eichenwald-Maki, p 200

2. Patient data collection requirements vary according to health care setting. A data element you would expect to be collected in the MDS, but NOT in the UHDDS would be
    A. personal identification.
    C. procedures and dates.
    B. cognitive patterns.
    D. principal diagnosis.

REFERENCE: Abdelhak, pp 137–138, 141
                Johns, pp 99, 203
                LaTour and Eichenwald-Maki, p 168
                Davis and LaCour, pp 148–149

3. In the past, Joint Commission standards have focused on promoting the use of a facility-approved abbreviation list to be used by hospital care providers. With the advent of the Commission's national patient safety goals, the focus has shifted to the
    A. prohibited use of any abbreviations.
    B. flagrant use of specialty-specific abbreviations.
    C. use of prohibited or "dangerous" abbreviations.
    D. use of abbreviations in the final diagnosis.

REFERENCE: Abdelhak, p 117
                LaTour and Eichenwald-Maki, p 539
                Odom, pp 111, 230

4. Engaging patients and their families in health care decisions is one of the core objectives for
    A. achieving meaningful use of EHRs.
    B. the Joint Commission's National Patient Safety goals.
    C. HIPAA 5010 regulations.
    D. establishing flexible clinical pathways.

REFERENCE: HealthIT.hhs.gov

5. A risk manager needs to locate a full report of a patient's fall from his bed, including witness reports and probable reasons for the fall. She would most likely find this information in the
   A. doctors' progress notes.
   C. incident report.
   B. integrated progress notes.
   D. nurses' notes.

REFERENCE: Abdelhak, pp 460–461, 544–545
Green and Bowie, p 88
Johns, p 653
LaTour and Eichenwald-Maki, p 302
Davis and LaCour, pp 299–301
Odom-Wesley, p 54
McWay, p 110

6. For continuity of care, ambulatory care providers are more likely than providers of acute care services to rely on the documentation found in the
   A. interdisciplinary patient care plan.
   C. transfer record.
   B. discharge summary.
   D. problem list.

REFERENCE: Abdelhak, p 136
Green and Bowie, p 91
Johns, p 95
Davis and LaCour, pp 71, 73
Odom-Wesley, pp 326–327
LaTour and Eichenwald-Maki, p 202

7. Joint Commission does not approve of auto authentication of entries in a health record. The primary objection to this practice is that
   A. it is too easy to delegate use of computer passwords.
   B. evidence cannot be provided that the physician actually reviewed and approved each report.
   C. electronic signatures are not acceptable in every state.
   D. tampering too often occurs with this method of authentication.

REFERENCE: Green and Bowie, p 78
LaTour and Eichenwald-Maki, p 213

8. As part of a quality improvement study, you have been asked to provide information on the menstrual history, number of pregnancies, and number of living children on each OB patient from a stack of old obstetrical records. The best place in the record to locate this information is the
   A. prenatal record.
   C. postpartum record.
   B. labor and delivery record.
   D. discharge summary.

REFERENCE: Abdelhak, pp 114–115
Green and Bowie, p 182
Odom-Wesley, pp 180–186

9. As a concurrent record reviewer for an acute care facility, you have asked Dr. Crossman to provide an updated history and physical for one of her recent admissions. Dr. Crossman pages through the medical record to a copy of an H&P performed in her office a week before admission. You tell Dr. Crossman
   A. a new H&P is required for every inpatient admission.
   B. that you apologize for not noticing the H&P she provided.
   C. the H&P copy is acceptable as long as she documents any interval changes.
   D. Joint Commission standards do not allow copies of any kind in the original record.

REFERENCE: Abdelhak, p 109
               Green and Bowie, p 145
               LaTour and Eichenwald-Maki, p 196
               Odom-Wesley, p 367

10. You have been asked to identify every reportable case of cancer from the previous year. A key resource will be the facility's
    A. disease index.   C. physicians' index.
    B. number control index.   D. patient index.

REFERENCE: Abdelhak, pp 486–487
               Johns, p 487
               LaTour and Eichenwald-Maki, p 332
               McWay, p 116

11. Joint Commission requires the attending physician to countersign health record documentation that is entered by
    A. interns or medical students.   C. consulting physicians.
    B. business associates.   D. physician partners.

REFERENCE: Green and Bowie, p, 78
               Davis and LaCour, pp 97, 118–119

12. The minimum length of time for retaining original medical records is primarily governed by
    A. Joint Commission.   C. state law.
    B. medical staff.   D. readmission rates.

REFERENCE: Abdelhak, pp 196–197
               Green and Bowie, p 93
               Johns, p 423
               LaTour and Eichenwald-Maki, p 282
               Odom-Wesley, pp 67–69
               Davis and LaCour, p 212

13. The use of personal signature stamps for authentication of entries in a paper-based record requires special measures to guard against delegated use of the stamp. In a completely computerized patient record system, similar measures might be utilized to govern the use of
    A. fingerprint signatures.   C. expert systems.
    B. voice recognition systems.   D. electronic signatures.

REFERENCE: Abdelhak, pp 117–118, 191
               Green and Bowie, pp 78–79
               LaTour and Eichenwald-Maki, p 213

14. Discharge summary documentation must include
    A. a detailed history of the patient.
    B. a note from social services or discharge planning.
    C. significant findings during hospitalization.
    D. correct codes for significant procedures.

REFERENCE: Abdelhak, pp 111, 113
              Green and Bowie, p 144
              Johns, p 78
              Odom-Wesley, pp 200–205
              Davis and LaCour, p 98
              LaTour and Eichenwald-Maki, pp 200–201

15. The performance of qualitative analysis is an important tool in ensuring data quality. These reviews evaluate
    A. quality of care through the use of preestablished criteria.
    B. adverse effects and contraindications of drugs utilized during hospitalization.
    C. potentially compensable events.
    D. the overall quality of documentation.

REFERENCE: Abdelhak, pp 130–131
              LaTour and Eichenwald-Maki, p 214
              Odom-Wesley, pp 251–256
              Davis and LaCour, pp 294–298

16. Ultimate responsibility for the quality and completion of entries in patient health records belongs to the
    A. chief of staff.   C. HIM director.
    B. attending physician.   D. risk manager.

REFERENCE: LaTour and Eichenwald-Maki, p 214

17. The federally mandated resident assessment instrument used in long-term care facilities consists of three basic components, including the new care area assessment, utilization guidelines, and the
    A. UHDDS.   C. OASIS.
    B. MDS.   D. DEEDS.

REFERENCE: Peden, p 357

18. The foundation for communicating all patient care goals in long-term care settings is the
    A. legal assessment.   C. interdisciplinary plan of care.
    B. medical history.   D. Uniform Hospital Discharge Data Set.

REFERENCE: Abdelhak, p 109
              Johns, p 98
              Odom-Wesley, p 371
              LaTour and Eichenwald-Maki, p 203

19. As the Director of a Health Information Technology Program, your community college has been selected to participate in the workforce development of electronic health record specialists as outlined by ARRA and HITECH. In order to keep abreast of changes in this program, you will need to regularly access the Web site of this governmental agency.
    A. ONC
    B. CMS
    C. OSHA
    D. CDC

REFERENCE: Johns, p 221

20. As part of Joint Commission's National Patient Safety Goal initiative, acute care hospitals are now required to use a preoperative verification process to confirm the patient's true identity, and to confirm that necessary documents such as x-rays or medical records are available. They must also develop and use a process for
    A. including the primary caregiver in surgery consults.
    B. including the surgeon in the preanesthesia assessment.
    C. marking the surgical site.
    D. apprising the patient of all complications that might occur.

REFERENCE: Abdelhak, p 459
LaTour and Eichenwald-Maki, p 530

21. In preparing your facility for initial accreditation by the Joint Commission, you are trying to improve the process of ongoing record review. All health record reviews are presently performed by a team of HIM department personnel. The committee meets quarterly and reports to a Quality Management Committee. In reviewing Joint Commission standards, your first recommended change is to
    A. have more frequent committee meetings.
    B. have the committee report to the Executive Committee.
    C. have a physician perform all the reviews.
    D. provide for record reviews to be performed by an interdisciplinary team of care providers.

REFERENCE: Abdelhak, pp 126–130
Davis and LaCour, pp 296–298
LaTour and Eichenwald-Maki, p 545
Odom-Wesley, p 253

22. According to the Joint Commission's National Patient Safety Goals, which of the following abbreviations would most likely be prohibited?
    A. 0.4 mg Lasix
    B. 4 mg Lasix
    C. 40 mg Lasix
    D. .4 mg Lasix

REFERENCE: Odom, pp 230–231

23. A qualitative review of a health record reveals that the history and physical for a patient admitted on June 26 was performed on June 30 and transcribed on July 1. Which of the following statements regarding the history and physical is true in this situation? Completion and charting of the H&P indicates
    A. noncompliance with Joint Commission standards.
    B. compliance with Joint Commission standards.
    C. compliance with Medicare regulations.
    D. compliance with Joint Commission standards for nonsurgical patients.

REFERENCE: Abdelhak, p 109
               Odom-Wesley, p 367
               LaTour and Eichenwald-Maki, p 196

24. Using the SOAP method of recording progress notes, which entry would most likely include a differential diagnosis?
    A. assessment
    B. plan
    C. subjective
    D. objective

REFERENCE: Abdelhak, pp 118–119
               Odom, pp 215, 217
               Green, pp 91, 343
               Johns, p 114
               LaTour and Eichenwald-Maki, p 204

25. You have been asked by a peer review committee to print a list of the medical record numbers of all patients who had CABGs performed in the past year at your acute care hospital. Which secondary data source could be used to quickly gather this information?
    A. disease index   C. master patient index
    B. physician index   D. operation index

REFERENCE: Johns, pp 451–452
               LaTour and Eichenwald-Maki, p 331

26. The best example of point-of-care service and documentation is
    A. using an automated tracking system to locate a record.
    B. using occurrence screens to identify adverse events.
    C. doctors using voice recognition systems to dictate radiology reports.
    D. nurses using bedside terminals to record vital signs.

REFERENCE: Abdelhak, p 38
               LaTour and Eichenwald-Maki, p 239

27. Many of the principles of forms design apply to both paper-based and computer-based systems. For example, the physical layout of the form and/or screen should be organized to match the way the information is requested. Facilities that are scanning and imaging paper records as part of a computer-based system must give careful consideration to
    A. placement of hospital logo.   C. use of box design.
    B. signature line for authentication. D. bar code placement.

REFERENCE: Abdelhak, pp 274–275
               LaTour and Eichenwald-Maki, p 216

28. Which of the following is a form or view that is typically seen in the health record of a long-term care patient but is rarely seen in records of acute care patients?
    A. pharmacy consultation
    B. medical consultation
    C. physical exam
    D. emergency record

REFERENCE: Abdelhak, p 141

29. The health record states that the patient is a female, but the registration record has the patient listed as male. Which of the following characteristics of data quality has been compromised in this case?
    A. data comprehensiveness
    B. data granularity
    C. data precision
    D. data accuracy

REFERENCE: Green, pp 247–248
               Abdelhak, pp 133–134
               LaTour and Eichenwald-Maki, pp 134, 342–343

30. The first patient with cancer seen in your facility on January 1, 2012, was diagnosed with colon cancer with no known history of previous malignancies. The accession number assigned to this patient is
    A. 12-0000/00.
    B. 12-0000/01.
    C. 12-0001/00.
    D. 12-0001/01.

REFERENCE: Johns, p 487
               LaTour and Eichenwald-Maki, p 332

31. Setting up a drop down menu to make sure that the registration clerk collects "gender" as "male, female, or unknown" is an example of ensuring data
    A. reliability.
    B. timeliness.
    C. precision.
    D. validity.

REFERENCE: Green and Bowie, p 258
               LaTour and Eichenwald-Maki, pp 134, 342–343
               Abdelhak, pp 133–134

32. In determining your acute care facility's degree of compliance with prospective payment requirements for Medicare, the best resource to reference for recent certification standards is the
    A. CARF manual.
    B. hospital bylaws.
    C. Joint Commission accreditation manual.
    D. Federal Register.

REFERENCE: Abdelhak, p 441
               Green and Bowie, p 29
               LaTour and Eichenwald-Maki, p 391
               Odom-Wesley, p 288

33. In an acute care hospital, a complete history and physical may not be required for a new admission when
    A. the patient is readmitted for a similar problem within 1 year.
    B. the patient's stay is less than 24 hours.
    C. the patient has an uneventful course in the hospital.
    D. a legible copy of a recent H&P performed in the attending physician's office is available.

REFERENCE: Abdelhak, p 109
               Green and Bowie, p 145
               LaTour and Eichenwald-Maki, p 196
               Odom-Wesley, p 367

34. You are developing a complete data dictionary for your facility. Which of the following resources will be most helpful in providing standard definitions for data commonly collected in acute care hospitals?
    A. Minimum Data Set
    B. Uniform Hospital Discharge Data Set
    C. Conditions of Participation
    D. Federal Register

REFERENCE: Abdelhak, pp 102–105, 134–136
               Green and Bowie, p 124
               Johns, p 202
               LaTour and Eichenwald-Maki, pp 131–133, 165
               Odom-Wesley, pp 84–85, 92–94, 310
               Davis and LaCour, pp 240–242

35. Gerda Smith has presented to the ER in a coma with injuries sustained in a motor vehicle accident. According to her sister, Gerda has had a recent medical history taken at the public health department. The physician on call is grateful that she can access this patient information using the area's
    A. EDMS system.   B. CPOE.
    C. expert system.   D. RHIO.

REFERENCE: Green and Bowie, p 112
               Johns, pp 150–151

36. When developing a data collection system, the most effective approach first considers
    A. the end user's needs.   C. hardware requirements.
    B. applicable accreditation standards. D. facility preference.

REFERENCE: Odom-Wesley, p 230

37. A key data item you would expect to find recorded on an ER record but would probably NOT see in an acute care record is the
    A. physical findings.   C. time and means of arrival.
    B. lab and diagnostic test results.   D. instructions for follow-up care.

REFERENCE: Abdelhak, pp 138–139
               Peden, p 37
               Johns, p 93
               LaTour and Eichenwald-Maki, p 202
               Odom-Wesley, p 171
               Davis and LaCour, p 165

38. A data item to include on a qualitative review checklist of infant and children inpatient health records that need not be included on adult records would be
    A. chief complaint.
    B. condition on discharge.
    C. time and means of arrival.
    D. growth and development record.

REFERENCE: Johns, p 97
               Peden, p 83

39. The authors of all entries in a health care record should be
    A. identified by a PIN.
    B. identified by biometrics.
    C. approved by the HIM Director.
    D. clearly identified.

REFERENCE: Green and Bowie, p 78
               Johns, p 107
               LaTour and Eichenwald-Maki, p 301
               Odom-Wesley, pp 113, 115

40. In creating a new form or computer view, the designer should be most driven by
    A. QIO standards.
    B. medical staff bylaws.
    C. needs of the users.
    D. flow of data on the page or screen.

REFERENCE: Abdelhak, p 120
               Green and Bowie, p 201
               Johns, p 414
               LaTour and Eichenwald-Maki, p 216
               Odom-Wesley, p 230
               Davis and LaCour, pp 75–78

41. Under which of the following conditions can an original paper-based patient health record be physically removed from the hospital?
    A. when the patient is brought to the hospital emergency department following a motor vehicle accident and, after assessment, is transferred with his health record to a trauma designated emergency department at another hospital
    B. when the director of health records is acting in response to a subpoena *duces tecum* and takes the health record to court
    C. when the patient is discharged by the physician and at the time of discharge is transported to a long-term care facility with his health record
    D. when the record is taken to a physician's private office for a follow-up patient visit postdischarge

REFERENCE: Abdelhak, pp 531–534
               Johns, p 804

42. According to the following table, the most serious record delinquency problem occurred in which of the following months?

Record Delinquency for Second Quarter	April	May	June
Percentage incomplete records	70%	88%	79%
Percentage delinquent records	51%	43%	61%
Percentage delinquent due to missing H&P	3%	1.4%	0.5%

    A. April
    B. May
    C. June
    D. cannot determine from these data

REFERENCE: Abdelhak, pp 128–129
               Green and Bowie, pp 99, 145

43. Using the SOAP style of documenting progress notes, choose the "subjective" statement from the following.
    A. sciatica unimproved with hot pack therapy
    B. patient moving about very cautiously, appears to be in pain
    C. adjust pain medication; begin physical therapy tomorrow
    D. patient states low back pain is as severe as it was on admission

REFERENCE: Abdelhak, pp 118–119
               Green and Bowie, p 91
               LaTour and Eichenwald-Maki, p 91
               Odom-Wesley, pp 217, 331–332
               Davis and LaCour, pp 96–97

44. In 1987, OBRA helped shift the focus in long-term care to patient outcomes. As a result, core assessment data elements are collected on each SNF resident as defined in the
    A. UHDDS.   C. Uniform Clinical Data Set.
    B. MDS.   D. Uniform Ambulatory Core Data.

REFERENCE: Abdelhak, pp 141–143
               Green and Bowie, p 253
               Johns, p 98
               LaTour and Eichenwald-Maki, p 166
               Peden, pp 357–360
               Odom-Wesley, pp 365, 368–378
               Davis and LaCour, p 175

45. As the Chair of a Forms Review Committee, you need to track the field name of a particular data field and the security levels applicable to that field. Your best source for this information would be the
    A. facility's data dictionary.   C. glossary of health care terms.
    B. MDS.   D. UHDDS.

REFERENCE: Abdelhak, pp 502–503
               Johns, p 906
               LaTour and Eichenwald-Maki, p 131

46. You notice on the admission H&P that Mr. McKahan, a Medicare patient, was admitted for disc surgery, but the progress notes indicate that due to some heart irregularities, he may not be a good surgical risk. Because of your knowledge of COP regulations, you expect that a(n) _____ will be added to his health record.
    A. interval summary   C. advance directive
    B. consultation report   D. interdisciplinary care plan

REFERENCE: Abdelhak, pp 111–112
               Green and Bowie, p 148
               Davis and LaCour, p 91
               Odom-Wesley, pp 117–118
               LaTour and Eichenwald-Maki, p 198

47. An example of objective entry in the health record supplied by a health care practitioner is the
    A. past medical history.
    B. physical assessment.
    C. chief complaint.
    D. review of systems.

REFERENCE: Abdelhak, pp 118–119
               Green and Bowie, p 148
               Johns, p 62
               LaTour and Eichenwald-Maki, pp 195–196, 204
               Odom-Wesley, pp 217, 331–332
               Davis and LaCour, pp 96–97

48. You have been appointed as Chair of the Health Record Committee at a new hospital. Your committee has been asked to recommend time-limited documentation standards for inclusion in the medical staff bylaws, rules, and regulations. The committee documentation standards must meet the standards of both the Joint Commission and the Medicare Conditions of Participation. The standards for the history and physical exam documentation are discussed first. You advise them that the time period for completion of this report should be set at
    A. 12 hours after admission.
    B. 24 hours after admission.
    C. 12 hours after admission or prior to surgery.
    D. 24 hours after admission or prior to surgery.

REFERENCE: Abdelhak, p 109
               Green and Bowie, p 145
               LaTour and Eichenwald-Maki, p 196
               Odom-Wesley, p 108
               Davis and LaCour, p 94

49. Based on the following documentation in an acute care record, where would you expect this excerpt to appear?

    "With the patient in the supine position, the right side of the neck was appropriately prepped with betadine solution and draped. I was able to pass the central line, which was taped to skin and used for administration of drugs during resuscitation."

    A. physician progress notes
    B. operative record
    C. nursing progress notes
    D. physical examination

REFERENCE: Johns, p 73
               Abdelhak, pp 113–114
               Davis and LaCour, p 100
               Odom-Wesley, p 164

50. A surgeon on the Health Record Committee voices a concern that, although he has been told that the operative report is to be dictated immediately after surgery, he has often had to deal with the problem of transcription backlog, which prevented the report from getting on the health record in a timely manner. Your advice to this doctor is that when a known backlog exists, he should
    A. provide the dictated tape to his staff.
    B. request a "stat" report.
    C. write a detailed operative note in the record.
    D. request that administration hire more transcriptionists.

REFERENCE: Abdelhak, pp 113–114
               Green and Bowie, pp 162–165
               LaTour and Eichenwald-Maki, p 200

51. Joint Commission standards require that a complete history and physical be documented on the health records of operative patients. Does this report carry a time requirement?
    A. Yes, within 8 hours postsurgery   C. Yes, prior to surgery
    B. No, as long as it is done ASAP   D. Yes, within 24 hours postsurgery

REFERENCE: Abdelhak, p 109
               Green and Bowie, p 145
               LaTour and Eichenwald-Maki, p 196
               Odom-Wesley, p 108
               Davis and LaCour, p 94

52. The old practices of flagging records for deficiencies and requiring retrospective documentation add little or no value to patient care. You try to convince the entire health care team to consistently enter data into the patient's record at the time and location of service instead of waiting for retrospective analysis to alert them to complete the record. You are proposing
    A. quantitative record review.   C. concurrent record analysis.
    B. clinical pertinence review.   D. point-of-care documentation.

REFERENCE: Abdelhak, p 38
               LaTour and Eichenwald-Maki, p 212

53. An example of a primary data source for health care statistics is the
    A. disease index.   C. MPI.
    B. accession register.   D. hospital census.

REFERENCE: Abdelhak, pp 480–481
               Horton, p 4
               Koch, p 65
               Davis and LaCour, p 240
               LaTour and Eichenwald-Maki, p 330
               Odom-Wesley, p 83

54. In the computerization of forms, good screen view design, along with the options of alerts and alarms, makes it easier to ensure that all essential data items have been captured. One essential item to be captured on the physical exam is the
    A. general appearance as assessed by the physician.
    B. chief complaint.
    C. family history as related by the patient.
    D. subjective review of systems.

REFERENCE: Abdelhak, p 109
              Green and Bowie, p 149
              Johns, p 65
              LaTour and Eichenwald-Maki, p 197
              Odom-Wesley, p 230
              Davis and LaCour, pp 75–78

55. During a retrospective review of Rose Hunter's inpatient health record, the health information clerk notes that on day 4 of hospitalization there was one missed dose of insulin. What type of review is this clerk performing?
    A. utilization review   C. legal review
    B. quantitative review   D. qualitative review

REFERENCE: Abdelhak, pp 130–131
              Green and Bowie, p 99
              LaTour and Eichenwald-Maki, p 214

56. Which of the following is least likely to be identified by a deficiency analysis technician?
    A. missing discharge summary
    B. need for physician authentication of two verbal orders
    C. discrepancy between post-op diagnosis by the surgeon and pathology diagnosis by the pathologist
    D. x-ray report charted on the wrong record

REFERENCE: Abdelhak, pp 130–131
              Green and Bowie, p 99
              Johns, p 410

57. The Conditions of Participation requires that the medical staff bylaws, rules, and regulations address the status of consultants. Which of the following reports would normally be considered a consultation?
    A. tissue examination done by the pathologist
    B. impressions of a cardiologist asked to determine whether patient is a good surgical risk
    C. interpretation of a radiologic study
    D. technical interpretation of electrocardiogram

REFERENCE: Abdelhak, pp 111–112
              Green and Bowie, p 148
              Davis and LaCour, p 91
              Odom-Wesley, p 117–118
              LaTour and Eichenwald-Maki, p 198

58. The health care providers at your hospital do a very thorough job of periodic open record review to ensure the completeness of record documentation. A qualitative review of surgical records would likely include checking for documentation regarding
    A. the presence or absence of such items as preoperative and postoperative diagnosis, description of findings, and specimens removed.
    B. whether a postoperative infection occurred and how it was treated.
    C. the quality of follow-up care.
    D. whether the severity of illness and/or intensity of service warranted acute level care.

REFERENCE: Abdelhak, pp 113–114
               Green and Bowie, p 99
               LaTour and Eichenwald-Maki, p 200
               Davis and LaCour, pp 296–298
               Odom-Wesley, pp 251–256

59. In your facility it has become critical that information regarding patients who are transferred to the oncology unit be sent to an outpatient scheduling system to facilitate outpatient appointments. This information can be obtained most efficiently from
    A. generic screens used by record abstractors.
    B. disease index.
    C. R-ADT system.
    D. indicator monitoring program.

REFERENCE: Abdelhak, pp 162–163
               Johns, p 947

60. In your facility, the health care providers from every discipline document progress notes sequentially on the same form. Your facility is utilizing
    A. integrated progress notes.   C. source-oriented records.
    B. interdisciplinary treatment plans.   D. SOAP notes.

REFERENCE: Abdelhak, pp 118–119
               Green and Bowie, p 153
               LaTour and Eichenwald-Maki, pp 204–205
               Odom-Wesley, pp 217–221

61. Which of the following services is LEAST likely to be provided by a facility accredited by CARF?
    A. chronic pain management   C. brain injury management
    B. palliative care   D. vocational evaluation

REFERENCE: Abdelhak, pp 26–29
               Green and Bowie, p 30
               Johns, p 101

62. Which method of identification of authorship or authentication of entries would be inappropriate to use in a patient's health record?
    A. written signature of the provider of care
    B. identifiable initials of a nurse writing a nursing note
    C. a unique identification code entered by the person making the report
    D. delegated use of computer key by radiology secretary

REFERENCE: Abdelhak, pp 117–118
               Green and Bowie, pp 78–79
               LaTour and Eichenwald-Maki, p 213

63. Though you work in an integrated delivery network, not all systems in your network communicate with one another. As you meet with your partner organizations, you begin to sell them on the concept of an important development intended to support the exchange of health information across the continuum within a geographical community. You are promoting that your organization join a
   A. data warehouse.
   B. regional health information organization.
   C. continuum of care.
   D. data retrieval portal group.

REFERENCE: Abdelhak, pp 86–90
                LaTour and Eichenwald-Maki, p 51
                McWay, p 181
                Davis and LaCour, p 263
                Odom-Wesley, p 15

64. As a trauma registrar working in an emergency department, you want to begin comparing your trauma care services to other hospital-based emergency departments. To ensure that your facility is collecting the same data as other facilities, you review elements from which data set?
   A. DEEDS   C. MDS
   B. UHDDS   D. ORYX

REFERENCE: Green and Bowie, p 253
                LaTour and Eichenwald-Maki, p 169

65. As a new HIM manager of an acute care facility, you have been asked to update the facility's policy for a physician's verbal orders in accordance with Joint Commission standards and state law. Your first area of concern is the qualifications of those individuals in your facility who have been authorized to record verbal orders. For this information, you will consult the
   A. Consolidated Manual for Hospitals.
   B. Federal Register.
   C. Policy and Procedure Manual.
   D. Hospital Bylaws, Rules, and Regulations.

REFERENCE   Green and Bowie, p 154
               Johns, p 107
               LaTour and Eichenwald-Maki, p 197
               Davis and LaCour, p 96
               Odom-Wesley, pp 111, 113, 290–291, 339

66. Reviewing a medical record to ensure that all diagnoses are justified by documentation throughout the chart is an example of
   A. peer review.   C. qualitative review.
   B. quantitative review.   D. legal analysis.

REFERENCE: Abdelhak, pp 130–131
                Green and Bowie, p 99
                LaTour and Eichenwald-Maki, p 214
                McWay, p 104
                Odom-Wesley, pp 251–252
                Davis and LaCour, p 298

67. Accreditation by Joint Commission is a voluntary activity for a facility and it is
    A. considered unnecessary by most health care facilities.
    B. required for state licensure in all states.
    C. conducted in each facility annually.
    D. required for reimbursement of certain patient groups.

REFERENCE: Abdelhak, pp 113–114
                     Odom-Wesley, p 299
                     LaTour and Eichenwald-Maki, p 280
                     Davis and LaCour, p 24

68. Which of the following indices might be protected from unauthorized access through the use of unique identifier codes assigned to members of the medical staff?
    A. disease index
    B. procedure index
    C. master patient index
    D. physician index

REFERENCE: Green and Bowie, p 240
                     Johns, p 453
                     LaTour and Eichenwald-Maki, p 331

69. Which of the four distinct components of the problem-oriented record serves to help index documentation throughout the record?
    A. database
    B. problem list
    C. initial plan
    D. progress notes

REFERENCE: Abdelhak, pp 118–119
                     Green and Bowie, p 91
                     Johns, p 114
                     Odom-Wesley, pp 215–216
                     Davis and LaCour, pp 71–74

70. As supervisor of the cancer registry, you report the registry's annual caseload to administration. The most efficient way to retrieve this information would be to use
    A. patient abstracts.
    B. patient index.
    C. accession register.
    D. follow-up files.

REFERENCE: Johns, p 487
                     LaTour and Eichenwald-Maki, p 332

71. As the Compliance Officer for an acute care facility, you are interested in researching recent legislation designed to provide significant funding for health information technology for your next committee meeting. You begin by googling
    A. EMTALA.
    B. Health Care Quality Improvement Act.
    C. HIPAA.
    D. ARRA.

REFERENCE: Johns, p 820

72. Select the appropriate situation for which a final progress note may legitimately be substituted for a discharge summary in an inpatient medical record.
    A. Patient admitted with COPD 1/4/2011 and discharged 1/7/2011
    B. Baby Boy Hiltz, born 1/5/2011, maintained normal status, discharged 1/7/2011
    C. Baby Boy Hiltz's mother admitted 1/5/2011, C-section delivery, and discharged 1/7/2011
    D. Baby Boy Doe admitted 1/3/2011, died 1/4/2011

REFERENCE: Abdelhak, p 113
               Green and Bowie, p 142
               LaTour and Eichenwald-Maki, p 201
               Odom-Wesley, pp 180, 201

73. Based on the following documentation in an acute care record, where would you expect this excerpt to appear?

    "Initially the patient was admitted to the medical unit to evaluate the x-ray findings and the rub. He was started on Levaquin 500 mg initially and then 250 mg daily. The patient was hydrated with IV fluids and remained afebrile. Serial cardiac enzymes were done. The rub, chest pain, and shortness of breath resolved. EKGs remained unchanged. Patient will be discharged and followed as an outpatient."

    A. discharge summary
    B. physical exam
    C. admission note
    D. clinical laboratory report

REFERENCE: Johns, p 78
               Abdelhak, p 113
               Davis and LaCour, p 100
               Odom-Wesley, p 164

74. The information security officer is revising the policies at your rehabilitation facility for handling all patient clinical information. The best resource for checking out specific voluntary accreditation standards and guidelines is the
    A. Conditions of Participation for Rehabilitation Facilities.
    B. Medical Staff Bylaws, Rules, and Regulations.
    C. Joint Commission manual.
    D. CARF manual.

REFERENCE: Johns, p 103
               LaTour and Eichenwald-Maki, p 36
               Odom-Wesley, pp 191–196
               Davis and LaCour, pp 25–26, 286

75. Stage I of meaningful use focuses on data capture and sharing. Which of the following is included in the menu set of objectives for eligible hospitals in this stage?
    A. Use CPOE for medication orders
    B. Smoking cessation counseling for MI patients
    C. Appropriate use of HL-7 standards
    D. Establish critical pathways for complex, high-dollar cases

REFERENCE: HealthIT.hhs.gov

76. Which of the following is a secondary data source that would be used to quickly gather the health records of all juvenile patients treated for diabetes within the past 6 months?
    A. disease index
    B. patient register
    C. pediatric census sheet
    D. procedure index

REFERENCE: Green and Bowie, pp 240–243
               Johns, p 451
               LaTour and Eichenwald-Maki, p 331

77. As the Coding Supervisor, your job description includes working with agents who have been charged with detecting and correcting overpayments made to your hospital in the Medicare Fee for Service program. You will need to develop a professional relationship with
    A. the OIG.
    B. MEDPAR representatives.
    C. QIO physicians.
    D. recovery audit contractors.

REFERENCE: Green and Bowie, pp 325–326
               Johns, pp 364–365

78. Using a template to collect data for key reports may help to prompt caregivers to document all required data elements in the patient record. This practice contributes to data
    A. timeliness.
    B. accuracy.
    C. comprehensiveness.
    D. security.

REFERENCE: Abdelhak, pp 133–134
               Green and Bowie, p 258

79. In preparation for an upcoming site visit by Joint Commission, you discover that the number of delinquent records for the preceding month exceeded 50% of discharged patients. Even more alarming was the pattern you noticed in the type of delinquencies. Which of the following represents the most serious pattern of delinquencies? Fifteen percent of delinquent records show
    A. missing signatures on progress notes.
    B. missing discharge summaries.
    C. absence of SOAP format in progress notes.
    D. missing operative reports.

REFERENCE: Abdelhak, p 128
               Green and Bowie, pp 162–165
               LaTour and Eichenwald-Maki, p 215

80. A primary focus of screen format design in a health record computer application should be to ensure that
    A. programmers develop standard screen formats for all hospitals.
    B. the user is capturing essential data elements.
    C. paper forms are easily converted to computer forms.
    D. data fields can be randomly accessed.

REFERENCE: Abdelhak, pp 119–120, 124
               Johns, p 439
               LaTour and Eichenwald-Maki, p 216
               Odom-Wesley, p 230
               Davis and LaCour, pp 75–78

81. A quality improvement team is focusing on the unacceptable number of unsigned doctors' orders in your facility. The most effective method for increasing the timeliness of signatures on orders and positively impacting the patient care process would be
    A. performing a retrospective review where all orders can be flagged at one time.
    B. holding a printed order sheet on the medical care unit at least 24 hours postdischarge to give the physician time to sign.
    C. developing an open-record review process.
    D. devising a signature sheet for the attending physician to sign prospectively that will apply to all orders given during the current episode of his patient's care.

REFERENCE: LaTour and Eichenwald-Maki, pp 214–215

82. Before making recommendations to the Executive Committee regarding new physicians who have applied for active membership, the Credentials Committee must query the
    A. peer review organization.
    B. National Practitioner Data Bank.
    C. risk manager.
    D. Health Plan Employer Data and Information Set.

REFERENCE: Abdelhak, pp 471–472
               Green and Bowie, pp 251, 255
               LaTour and Eichenwald-Maki, p 17

83. A qualitative analysis of OB records reveals a pattern of inconsistent data entries when comparing documentation of the same data elements captured on both the prenatal form and labor and delivery form. The characteristic of data quality that is being compromised in this case is data
    A. reliability.   C. legibility.
    B. accessibility.   D. completeness.

REFERENCE: Green and Bowie, p 258
               LaTour and Eichenwald-Maki, p 120

84. Medicare rules state that the use of verbal orders should be infrequent and used only when the orders cannot be written or given electronically. In addition, verbal orders must be
    A. written within 24 hours of the patient's admission.
    B. accepted by charge nurses only.
    C. co-signed by the attending physician within 4 hours of giving the order.
    D. recorded by persons authorized by hospital regulations and procedures.

REFERENCES: Green and Bowie, p 154
               LaTour and Eichenwald-Maki, p 197
               Davis and LaCour, p 96
               Odom-Wesley, pp 111, 113, 290–291, 339

85. The lack of a discharge order may indicate that the patient left against medical advice. If this situation occurs, you would expect to see the circumstances of the leave
    A. documented in an incident report and filed in the patient's health record.
    B. reported as a potentially compensable event.
    C. reported to the Executive Committee.
    D. documented in both the progress notes and the discharge summary.

REFERENCE: LaTour and Eichenwald-Maki, p 202
               Odom-Wesley, p 446

86. Your committee is charged with developing procedures for the Health Information Services staff of a new home health agency. You recommend that the staff routinely check to verify that a summary on each patient is provided to the attending physician so that he or she can review, update, and recertify the patient as appropriate. The time frame for requiring this summary is at least every
    A. week.
    B. month.
    C. 60 days.
    D. 90 days.

REFERENCE: Abdelhak, p 143
                Peden, p 441
                Odom-Wesley, pp 401–402

87. You want to review one document in your facility that will spell out the documentation requirements for patient records, designate the time frame for completion by the active medical staff, and indicate the penalties for failure to comply with these record standards. Your best resource will be
    A. medical staff bylaws.
    B. quality management plan.
    C. Joint Commission accreditation manual.
    D. medical staff rules and regulations.

REFERENCE: Green and Bowie, p 16
                LaTour and Eichenwald-Maki, p 191
                Odom-Wesley, p 367

88. A quarterly review reveals the following data for Springfield Hospital:

Springfield Hospital Quarterly Statistics	
Average monthly discharges	1,820
Average monthly operative procedures	458
Number of incomplete records	1,002
Number of delinquent records	590

What is the percentage of incomplete records during this quarter?
    A. 55%
    B. 54%
    C. 33%
    D. 32%

REFERENCE: Horton, p 19
                Koch, p 48

89. Referring to the data in the previous question, determine the delinquent record rate for Springfield Hospital.
    A. 55%
    B. 32%
    C. 33%
    D. 54%

REFERENCE: Green and Bowie, p 84
                Horton, p 19
                Koch, p 48

90. Still referring to the information in the table in question 88 and the delinquent record rate shown in the answer for question 89, would the facility be out of compliance with Joint Commission standards?
   A. Yes
   B. No

REFERENCE: Abdelhak, p 128
              Green and Bowie, p 84
              Horton, p 19

91. In an acute care facility, the responsibility for educating physicians and other health care providers regarding proper documentation policies belongs to the
   A. information security manager.   C. health information manager.
   B. clinical data specialist.   D. risk manager.

REFERENCE: Green and Bowie, p 98
              LaTour and Eichenwald-Maki, p 227
              Odom-Wesley, pp 246–248

92. For inpatients, the first data item collected of a clinical nature is usually
   A. principal diagnosis.   C. admitting diagnosis.
   B. expected payer.   D. review of systems.

REFERENCE: Green and Bowie, p 140
              Davis and LaCour, pp 90, 122–123

93. Documentation found in acute care health records should include core measure quality indicators required for compliance with Medicare's Health Care Quality Improvement Program (HCQIP). A typical indicator for patients with pneumonia is
   A. beta blocker at discharge.
   B. blood culture before first antibiotic received.
   C. early administration of aspirin.
   D. discharged on antithrombotic.

REFERENCE: CMS, p 3

94. One record documentation requirement shared by BOTH acute care and emergency departments is
   A. patient's condition on discharge.   C. advance directive.
   B. time and means of arrival.   D. problem list.

REFERENCE: Abdelhak, pp 109, 133

95. In addition to diagnostic and therapeutic orders from the attending physician, you would expect every completed inpatient health record to contain
   A. standing orders.   C. stop orders.
   B. telephone orders.   D. discharge order.

REFERENCE: Abdelhak, p 108
              Green and Bowie, p 154
              LaTour and Eichenwald-Maki, p 198
              Odom-Wesley, p 115

96. As the Chair of the Forms Committee at your hospital, you are helping to design a template for house staff members to use while collecting information for the history and physical. When asked to explain how "review of systems" differs from "physical exam," you explain that the review of systems is used to document
    A. objective symptoms observed by the physician.
    B. past and current activities, such as smoking and drinking habits.
    C. a chronological description of patient's present condition from time of onset to present.
    D. subjective symptoms that the patient may have forgotten to mention or that may have seemed unimportant.

REFERENCE: Green and Bowie, p 147
              Odom-Wesley, p 331
              Davis and LaCour, p 95

97. Skilled nursing facilities may choose to submit MDS data using RAVEN software, or software purchased commercially through a vendor, provided that the software meets
    A. Joint Commission standards.
    B. NHIN standards.
    C. HL-7 standards.
    D. CMS standards.

REFERENCE: Peden, p 374
              Green and Bowie, p 253

98. Based on the following documentation in an acute care record, where would you expect this excerpt to appear?

    "The patient is alert and in no acute distress. Initial vital signs: T 98, P 102 and regular, R 20 and BP 120/69…"

    A. physical exam
    B. past medical history
    C. social history
    D. chief complaint

REFERENCE: Abdelhak, p 107
              LaTour and Eichenwald-Maki, pp 195–197
              Odom-Wesley, pp 108–109
              Davis and LaCour, pp 94–96

Answer Key for Health Data Content and Standards

    ANSWER   EXPLANATION

1. B (C and D) Although a gross description of tissue removed may be mentioned on the operative note or discharge summary, only the pathology report will contain a microscopic description.
2. B Answers A, C, and D represent items collected on Medicare inpatients according to UHDDS requirements. Only B represents a data item collected more typically in long-term care settings and required in the MDS.
3. C The Joint Commission requires hospitals to prohibit abbreviations that have caused confusion or problems in their handwritten form, such as "U" for unit, which can be mistaken for "O" or the number "4." Spelling out the unit is preferred.
4. A There are several core objectives for achieving meaningful use. Engaging patients and their families is one of these objectives.
5. C Factual summaries investigating unexpected facility events should not be treated as part of the patient's health information and therefore would not be recorded in the health record.
6. D (A, B, and C) Patient care plans, pharmacy consultations, and transfer summaries are likely to be found on the records of long-term care patients.
7. B Auto authentication is a policy adopted by some facilities that allow physicians to state in advance that transcribed reports should automatically be considered approved and signed (or authenticated) when the physician fails to make corrections within a preestablished time frame (e.g., "Consider it signed if I do not make changes within 7 days."). Another version of this practice is when physicians authorize the HIM department to send weekly lists of unsigned documents. The physician then signs the list in lieu of signing each individual report. Neither practice ensures that the physician has reviewed and approved each report individually.
8. A The antepartum record should include a comprehensive history and physical exam on each OB patient visit with particular attention to menstrual and reproductive history.
9. C Joint Commission and COP allow a legible copy of a recent H&P done in a doctor's office in lieu of an admission H&P as long as interval changes are documented in the record upon admission. In addition, when the patient is readmitted within 30 days for the same or a related problem, an interval history and physical exam may be completed if the original H&P is readily available.
10. A The major sources of case findings for cancer registry programs are the pathology department, the disease index, and the logs of patients treated in radiology and other outpatient departments. B. The number index identifies new health record numbers and the patients to whom they were assigned. C. The physicians' index identifies all patients treated by each doctor. D. The patient index links each patient treated in a facility with the health number under which the clinical information can be located.
11. A Those who make entries in the medical record are given that privilege by the medical staff. Only house staff members who are under the supervision of active staff members require countersignatures once the privilege has been granted.
12. C The statute of limitations for each state is information that is crucial in determining record retention schedules.
13. D Authentication by signature stamps requires a written agreement with the facility not to delegate the use of the stamps. Similarly, in a computer-based system, it is important to ensure that personal identification codes used to authenticate entries are used only by the persons to whom they are assigned. A. Fingerprint signatures are individualized automatically.

Answer Key for Health Data Content and Standards

  ANSWER   EXPLANATION

14. C A. Some reference to the patient's history may be found in the discharge summary but not a detailed history. B. The attending physician records the discharge summary. D. Codes are usually recorded on a different form in the record.

15. D A and B deal with issues directly linked to quality of care reviews. C deals with risk management. Only D points to a review aimed at evaluating the quality of documentation in the health record.

16. B Although the nursing staff, hospital administration, and the health information management professional play a role in ensuring an accurate and complete record, the major responsibility lies with the attending physician.

17. B The Minimum Data Set is a basic component of the long-term care RAI. A. UHDDS used in acute care; C. OASIS used in home health; D. DEEDS used in emergency departments.

18. C Unlike the acute care hospital, where most health care practitioners document separately, the patient care plan is the foundation around which patient care is organized in long-term care facilities because it contains the unique perspective of each discipline involved.

19. A B. Utilization review committees deal with the issues of the medical necessity of admissions and efficient utilization of facility resources. C. Risk management committees consider methods for reducing injury and financial loss. D. Joint conference committees act as a liaison between the governing body and the medical staff.

20. C The Joint Commission requires hospitals to mark the correct surgical site and to involve the patient in the marking process to help eliminate wrong site surgeries.

21. D Joint Commission suggests that HIM department, nursing, medical staff, administrative personnel, and other services participate in the record reviews.

22. D Among those abbreviations considered confusing or likely to be misinterpreted are those containing a leading decimal.

23. A Joint Commission specifies that H&Ps must be completed within 24 hours.

24. A The assessment statement combines the objective and subjective into a diagnostic conclusion, sometimes in the form of a differential diagnosis, such as "peritonitis vs. appendicitis."

25. D A. The disease index is a listing in diagnostic code number order. B. The physician index is a listing of cases in order by physician name or number. C. The MPI cross-references the patient name and medical record number.

26. D A, B, and C all refer to a computer application of managing health information, but only answer D deals with the clinical application of data entry into the patient's record at the time and location of service.

27. D Most facilities use bar-coded patient identification to ensure proper indexing into the imaging system.

28. A Pharmacy consults are required for elderly patients who typically take multiple medications. These consults review for potential drug interactions and/or discrepancies in medications given and those ordered.

29. D Data accuracy/validity denotes that data are correct values and are valid. A. Data comprehensiveness denotes that all data items are included. B. Data granularity denotes that the attributes and values of data should be defined at the correct level of detail. C. Data precision denotes that data values should be just large enough to support the application of process.

Answer Key for Health Data Content and Standards

ANSWER EXPLANATION

30. C In accession number 12–0001/00, "12" represents the year that the patient first entered the database; "0001" indicates that this was the first case entered that year; "00" indicates that this patient has only one known neoplasm.

31. C Validity refers to the accuracy of data, while reliability refers to consistency of data. Timeliness refers to data being available within a time frame helpful to the user, and precision refers to data values that are just large enough to support the application of the process.

32. D CMS publishes both proposed and final rules for the Conditions of Participation for hospitals in the daily Federal Register.

33. D A. An interval H&P can be used when a patient is readmitted for the same or related problem within 30 days. B and C. No matter how long the patient stays or how minor the condition, an H&P is required.

34 B A. The MDS is designed for use in long-term care facilities. C. The COP is the set of regulations that health care institutions must follow to receive Medicare reimbursement. D. The *Federal Register* is a daily government newspaper for publishing proposed and final rules of federal agencies.

35. D With the increasing number of health care entities implementing EHR systems, the networking of electronic information between facilities has become a reality in some areas due to the establishment of regional health information organizations. A. EDMS = electronic data management system. B. CPOE = computerized provider order entry system

36. A The needs of the end user are always the primary concern when designing systems.

37. C Answers A, B, and D are required items in BOTH acute and ER records.

38. D Answers A and B are items that should be documented on any inpatient record. Answer C reflects a data item you would expect to find on ER records only.

39. B All health record signatures should be identified by a minimum of name and discipline, e.g., "J. Smith, P.T." Other types of authentication other than signature (such as written initials or computer entry) must be uniquely identifiable.

40. C The needs of the user are the primary concern in forms design.

41. B A and C. In these situations a transfer summary or pertinent copies from the inpatient health record may accompany the patient, but the original record stays on the premises.

42. A A recommendation for improvement from Joint Commission is indicated if the number of delinquent records is greater than 50% or if the percentage of records with delinquent records due to missing H&Ps exceeds 2% of the average monthly discharges. In the month of April, both of these delinquency problems are reflected. The percentage of incomplete records is not relevant.

43. D A represents the assessment statement, B the objective, and C the plan.

44. B OBRA mandates comprehensive functional assessments of long-term care residents using the Minimum Data Set for Long-Term Care.

45. A Answers B and D are types of data sets for collecting data in long-term (MDS) and acute care (UHDDS) facilities. A data dictionary should include security levels for each field as well as definitions for all entities.

46. B COP requires a consultation report on patients who are not a good surgical risk as well as those with obscure diagnoses, patients whose physicians have doubts as to the best therapeutic measure to be taken, and patients for whom there is a question of criminal activity.

Answer Key for Health Data Content and Standards

    ANSWER   EXPLANATION

47. B The medical history, including a review of systems and chief complaint, is information supplied by the patient. A physical assessment adds objective data to the subjective data provided by the patient in the history.

48. D This meets both Joint Commission and COP standards.

49. B This entry is typical of a surgical procedure.

50. C Joint Commission requires that a detailed OP note be written in the health record when expeditious transcription of the dictated report is impossible to maintain continuity of care.

51. C Joint Commission standards require the surgeon to document the history and physical examination prior to surgery.

52. D AHIMA's Position Statement supports that point-of-care documentation raises documentation standards and improves patient care. It is defined as data entry that occurs at the point and location of service.

53. D Answers A, B, and C are examples of secondary data sources.

54. A The medical history (including chief complaint, history of present illness, past medical history, personal history, family history, and a review of systems) is provided by the patient or the most knowledgeable available source. The physical examination adds objective data to the subjective data provided by the patient. This exam begins with the physician's objective assessment of the patient's general condition.

55. D Quantitative analysis involves checking for the presence or absence of necessary reports and/or signatures, while qualitative analysis may involve checking documentation consistency, such as comparing a patient's pharmacy drug profile with the medication administration record.

56. C A, B, and D all represent common checks performed by a quantitative analysis clerk: missing reports, signatures, or patient identification. Answer C represents a more in-depth review dealing with the quality of the data documented.

57. B A, C, and D represent routine interpretations that are not normally considered to be consultations.

58. A B represents an appropriate job for the infection control officer. Answer C represents the clinical care evaluation process, rather than the review of quality documentation. Answer D is a function of the utilization review program.

59. C For tracking in-house patients who have been transferred to a specialty unit, the best source of information is the registration-admission, discharge, and transfer system.

60. A Progress notes may be integrated or they may be separated, with nurses, physicians, and other health care providers writing on designated forms for each discipline.

61. B The Commission on Accreditation of Rehabilitation Facilities is an independent accrediting agency for rehabilitation facilities. Palliative care (answer B) is most likely to be provided at a hospice.

62. D Written signatures, identifiable initials, unique computer codes, and rubber stamp signatures may all be allowed as legitimate means of authenticating an entry. However, the use of codes and stamped signatures MUST be confined to the owners and they are never to be used by anyone else.

63. B Regional health information organizations are intended to support health information exchange within a geographic region.

Answer Key for Health Data Content and Standards

ANSWER   EXPLANATION

64. A   A. Data Elements for Emergency Departments—recommended data set for hospital-based emergency departments; B. Uniform Hospital Data Set—required data set for acute care hospitals; C. Minimum Data Set—required data set for long-term care facilities; D. ORYX—an initiative of Joint Commission whereby five core measures are implemented to improve safety and quality of health care.

65. D   Although Joint Commission, CMS, and state laws may include standards for verbal orders, the specific information regarding which employees have been given authority to transcribe verbal orders in your facility should be located in your hospital's bylaws, rules, and regulations.

66. C   A. Peer review typically involves quality of care issues rather than quality of documentation issues. D. Legal analysis ensures that the record entries would be acceptable in a court of law.

67. D   A. Advantages of accreditation are numerous and include financial and legal incentives. B. State licensure is required for accreditation but not the reverse. C. Joint Commission conducts unannounced on-site surveys approximately every 3 years.

68. D   Because information contained in the physicians' index is considered confidential, identification codes are often used rather than the physicians' names.

69. B   In a POMR, the database contains the history and physical; the problem list includes titles, numbers, and dates of problems and serves as a table of contents of the record; the initial plan describes diagnostic, therapeutic, and patient education plans; and the progress notes document the progress of the patient throughout the episode of care, summarized in a discharge summary or transfer note at the end of the stay.

70. C   The accession register is a permanent log of all the cases entered into the database. Each number assigned is preceded by the accession year, making it easy to assess annual workloads.

71. D   The American Recovery and Reinvestment Act was signed into law in 2009, and included significant funding for health information technology.

72. B   A final progress note may substitute for a discharge summary in the following cases: patients who are hospitalized less than 48 hours with problems of a minor nature, normal newborns, and uncomplicated obstetrical deliveries. Answer A does not qualify because of the nature of the problem and the length of stay. Answer C describes a complicated delivery, and answer D cites a severely ill patient rather than one with a minor problem.

73. A   The excerpt clearly indicates an overall summary of the patient's course in the hospital, which is a common element of the discharge summary.

74. D   The manual published by the Commission on Accreditation of Rehabilitation Facilities will have the most specific and comprehensive standards for a rehabilitation facility.

75. A   See all objectives for Stage I of meaningful use on the HealthIT.hhs.gov website.

76. A   The disease index is compiled as a result of abstracting patient code numbers into a computer database, allowing a variety of reports to be generated.

Answer Key for Health Data Content and Standards

ANSWER   EXPLANATION

77. D   The RAC program is mandated to find and correct improper Medicare payments paid to health care providers participating in the Medicare reimbursement program. (A) OIG (Office of Inspector General); (B) MEDPAR (Medicare Provider Analysis and Review); (C) QIO (Quality Improvement Organization)

78. C   Data comprehensiveness refers specifically to the presence of all required data elements.

79. D   Answers A and B. Both signature omissions and discharge summary reports can be captured after discharge, but history and physicals should be on the chart within 24 hours of the patient's admission. Answer C. The SOAP format is not a requirement of Joint Commission. Answer D. Institutions are given a Type I recommendation when 2% of delinquent records are due to missing history and physicals or operative reports.

80. B   Both paper-based and computer-based records share similar forms and view design considerations. Among these are the selection and sequencing of essential data items.

81. C   A and B. Signing orders after discharge does not affect the patient's care process. D. Although this process would speed up the signature process, it is not a legally sound method of obtaining signatures on orders.

82. B   With the passage of the Health Care Quality Improvement Act of 1986, the NPDB was established. Hospitals are required to query the data bank before granting clinical privileges to physicians.

83. A   Data reliability implies that data are consistent no matter how many times the same data are collected and entered into the system. Accessibility implies that data are available to authorized people when and where needed. Legibility implies data that are readable. Completeness implies that all required data are present in the information system.

84. D   Only persons designated by hospital policies and procedures and state and federal law are to accept verbal orders.

85. D   A. Incident reports are written accounts of unusual events that have an adverse effect on a patient, employee, or facility visitor and should never be filed with the patient's record. B. PCEs are occurrences that could result in financial liability at some future time. A patient leaving AMA does not in itself suggest a PCE. C. It is not typical to report AMAs to the Executive Committee. D. Documenting the event is crucial in protecting the legal interests of the health care team and facility.

86. C   This 60-day time frame is often referred to as the patient's certification period. Recertification can continue every 62 days until the patient is discharged from home health services.

87. D   Although the medical staff bylaws reflect general principles and policies of the medical staff, the rules and regulations outline the details for implementing these principles, including the process and time frames for completing records, and the penalties for failure to comply.

88. A   Using the basic rate formula, calculate as follows:
Incomplete records × 100 divided by average monthly discharges, or
$$\frac{1,002 \times 100}{1820} = 55.1\%$$

89. B   Using the basic rate formula, calculate as follows:
Delinquent records × 100 divided by average monthly discharges, or
$$\frac{590 \times 100}{1820} = 32.4\%$$

Answer Key for Health Data Content and Standards

ANSWER   EXPLANATION

90. B   Using the basic rate formula, the delinquent record rate is 32%. Even though the delinquent record rate is 32%, this does not exceed the Joint Commission requirement to keep this statistic below 50%.

91. C   Although all of the positions listed have an interest in proper documentation in an acute care facility, the health information manager is in the best position to keep abreast of documentation standards and advocate change where poor documentation patterns exist.

92. C   Clinical data include all health care information collected during a patient's episode of care. During the registration or intake process, the admitting diagnosis, provided by the attending physician, is entered on the face sheet. If the patient is admitted through the ED, the chief complaint listed on the ED record is usually the first clinical data collected. A. The principal diagnosis is often not known until after diagnostic tests are conducted. B. Demographic data are not clinical in nature. D. The review of systems is collected during the history and physical, which is typically done after admission to the hospital.

93 B   Answers A and C represent quality indicators for patients with acute myocardial infarction; answer D represents a quality indicator for stroke patients.

94. A   B. Time and means of arrival is required on ED records only. C. Evidence of known advance directive is required on inpatient records only. D. Problem list is required on ambulatory records by the third visit.

95. D   Although many patient health records may feasibly contain all of the orders listed, only the discharge order is required to document the formal release of a patient from the facility. Absence of a discharge order would indicate that the patient left against medical advice and this event should be thoroughly documented as well.

96. D   Answer A refers to the Physical Exam. Answer B refers to the Social History. Answer C refers to the History of Present Illness.

97. D   MDS data are reported directly to the Centers for Medicare and Medicaid Services and must conform to agency standards.

98. A   Answers B, C, and D represent components of the medical history as supplied by the patient, while the physical exam is an entry obtained through objective observation and measurement made by the provider.

REFERENCES

Abdelhak, M., Grostick, S., Hanken, M.A., (2012). *Health information: Management of a strategic resource* (4th ed.). Philadelphia: W. B. Saunders, an imprint of Elsevier.

CMS. Fiscal Year 2009 Quality Measure Reporting for 2010 Payment Update https://www.cms.gov/HospitalQualityInits/downloads/HospitalRHQDAPU200808.pdf

Davis and LaCour. (2007). *Health information technology* (2nd ed.). Maryland, MO: Elsevier (Saunders).

Green, M. A., & Bowie, J. (2011). *Essentials of health information management: Principles and practices.* Clifton Park, NY: Delmar Cengage Learning.

Horton, L. (2011) *Calculating and reporting healthcare statistics* (4th ed.) Chicago: American Health Information Management Association (AHIMA).

Johns, M. L. (2011). *Health information management technology: An applied approach* (3rd ed.). Chicago: American Health Information Management Association (AHIMA).

Koch, G. (2008). *Basic allied health statistics and analysis* (3rd ed.). Clifton Park, NY: Delmar Cengage Learning.

LaTour, K., & Eichenwald-Maki, S. (2010). *Health information management: Concepts, principles and practice* (3rd ed.). Chicago: American Health Information Management Association (AHIMA).

McWay, D. C. (2008). *Today's health information management, an integrated approach.* Clifton Park, NY: Delmar Cengage Learning.

Odom-Wesley, B., Brown, D., & Meyers, C. (2009). *Documentation for medical records.* Chicago: American Health Information Management Association (AHIMA).

Peden, A. H. (2012). *Comparative health information management* (3rd ed.). Clifton Park, NY: Delmar Cengage Learning.

| | RHIA AND RHIT COMPETENCIES BY QUESTION FOR HEALTH DATA | | | | | | | | | | | | | |
| Question | RHIA Domain Competencies | | | | | | | RHIT Domain Competencies | | | | | | |
	1	2	3	4	5	6		1	2	3	4	5	6	7
1			X							X				
2	X							X						
3						X						X		
4			X							X				
5	X											X		
6	X							X						
7						X					X			
8	X							X						
9						X				X				
10	X							X						
11						X				X				
12						X							X	
13			X								X			
14	X							X						
15	X							X						
16						X						X		
17	X							X						
18	X							X						
19				X							X			
20						X						X		
21						X						X		
22						X						X		
23						X		X						
24	X							X						
25		X						X						
26			X					X						
27			X							X				
28	X							X						
29	X							X						
30	X							X						
31	X										X			
32						X				X				
33						X		X						
34	X							X						
35				X							X			
36			X					X						
37	X							X						
38	X							X						
39						X		X						
40				X							X			
41						X							X	
42						X		X						
43	X							X						
44	X									X				
45			X					X						
46						X				X				
47	X							X						
48						X				X				
49	X							X						
50						X		X						
51						X				X				
52			X					X						
53		X						X						

Question	RHIA Domain Competencies							RHIT Domain Competencies						
	1	2	3	4	5	6		1	2	3	4	5	6	7
54			X					X						
55	X							X						
56	X							X						
57						X		X						
58	X									X				
59			X								X			
60	X							X						
61						X		X						
62						X				X				
63			X								X			
64	X									X				
65						X				X				
66	X							X						
67						X				X				
68			X									X		
69	X							X						
70			X					X						
71			X								X			
72						X		X						
73	X							X						
74						X							X	
75			X							X				
76			X					X						
77			X						X					
78	X							X						
79						X				X				
80			X								X			
81		X						X						
82						X					X			
83			X					X						
84						X					X			
85	X							X						
86						X		X						
87	X							X						
88						X		X						
89						X		X						
90						X		X						
91				X					X					
92	X							X						
93						X				X				
94	X							X						
95	X							X						
96	X									X				
97						X				X				
98	X							X						

Table title: RHIA AND RHIT COMPETENCIES BY QUESTION FOR HEALTH RECORDS

IV. Information Retention and Access

Marjorie H. McNeill, PhD, RHIA, CCS, FAHIMA

1. Which one of the following actions would not be included in the professional obligations of the health information practioner that lead to responsible handling of patient health information?
   A. Educate consumers about their rights and responsibilities regarding the use of their personal health information.
   B. Extend privacy and security principles into all aspects of the data use, access, and control program adopted in the organization.
   C. Honor the patient-centric direction of the national agenda.
   D. Take a compromising position toward optimal interpretation of nonspecific regulations and laws.

REFERENCE: LaTour and Eichenwald-Maki, pp 310–313

2. If there is more than one patient with the identical last name, first name, and middle initial, the master patient index entries are then arranged according to the
   A. date of birth.   C. social security number.
   B. date of admission.   D. mother's maiden name.

REFERENCE: Johns, p 392
               Odom, pp 41–42, 93

3. Which one of the following is NOT a step in developing a record retention schedule?
   A. conducting an inventory of the facility's records
   B. determining the format and location of storage
   C. assigning all records the same retention period
   D. destroying records that are no longer needed

REFERENCE: Green and Bowie, pp 93–94
               LaTour and Eichenwald-Maki, pp 221–225
               Johns, pp 404–405
               McWay, pp 112–113
               Odom, pp 67–69
               Abdelhak, pp 196–197, 529

4. What type of filing system is being used if records are filed in the following order: 12-23-75, 12-34-29, 12-35-71, 13-42-14, and 14-32-79?
   A. terminal digit   C. social security number
   B. straight numeric   D. middle digit

REFERENCE: Green and Bowie, pp 212–214
               Johns, p 393
               LaTour and Eichenwald-Maki, p 218

5. If there are 150,000 records and the HIM Department receives 3,545 requests for records within a given period of time, what is the request rate?
   A. 2.4%   C. 4.6%
   B. 3.5%   D. 5.1%

REFERENCE: LaTour and Eichenwald-Maki, p 220
               McWay, pp 193–197

6. Which of the following would not be an advantage of a centralized filing system?
   A. There is less transportation time and effort when a facility operates from several sites.
   B. There is less duplication of effort to create, maintain, and store records.
   C. Record control and security are easier to maintain.
   D. There is decreased cost in space and equipment.

REFERENCE: Green and Bowie, pp 214–215
              McWay, pp 111–113

7. In a terminal digit filing system, what would be the record number immediately in front of record number 01-06-26?
   A. 00-06-26   C. 03-06-26
   B. 02-06-26   D. 99-99-25

REFERENCE: Abdelhak, p 225
              Green and Bowie, pp 212–214
              LaTour and Eichenwald-Maki, pp 218–219
              Johns, p 393

8. The HIM Department at General Hospital has been experiencing an average 30-minute delay in the retrieval of records requested by the Emergency Department. Which one of the following corrective actions would be most effective in reducing the delay in retrieval of requested records?
   A. Offer a prize to the employee who locates the requested records first.
   B. Review and possibly reengineer the retrieval process to decrease retrieval time.
   C. Allow the requesters to retrieve the record themselves.
   D. Increase file area staff to include one additional file clerk devoted to pulling records for the emergency room.

REFERENCE: McWay, pp 261–262
              LaTour and Eichenwald-Maki, p 220

9. Which one of the following is NOT an advantage of a computerized master patient index?
   A. It allows access to data alphabetically, phonetically, or by date of birth, social security number, medical record, or billing number.
   B. It solves most space and retrieval problems.
   C. It provides other departments with immediate access to the information maintained in the master patient index.
   D. Duplication of patient registration can never occur.

REFERENCE: Green and Bowie, pp 237–239
              Johns, p 484
              McWay, pp 115–116
              LaTour and Eichenwald-Maki, pp 226–227

10. Color coding of record folders is used to assist in the control of
    A. record tracking.   C. record completion.
    B. loose reports.   D. misfiles.

REFERENCE: Green and Bowie, pp 220–221
              LaTour and Eichenwald-Maki, p 221

11. Which of the following would NOT be considered secondary data?
    A. disease index   C. x-ray
    B. implant registry   D. incident report

REFERENCE: Green and Bowie, p 88
                      McWay, p 115
                      LaTour and Eichenwald-Maki, pp 330–331

12. Under the Patient Self-Determination Act of 1990, advance directives
    A. are required to be included in the health record.
    B. are not required to be included in the health record.
    C. require a doctor's approval.
    D. must be prepared by an attorney.

REFERENCE: Abdelhak, pp 13, 108
                      Green and Bowie, p 129
                      Johns, pp 89–90
                      McWay, pp 65, 85
                      LaTour and Eichenwald-Maki, pp 194–195

13. A new Health Information Department has purchased 200 units of 6-shelf files and plans to implement a terminal digit filing system. How many shelves should be allocated to each primary number?
    A. 6   C. 10
    B. 8   D. 12

REFERENCE: LaTour and Eichenwald-Maki, pp 220–221

14. A 200-bed acute care hospital currently has 15 years of records in hard copy and filing space is limited. What action should be taken?
    A. Return inactive records to each individual patient.
    B. Destroy records of all deceased patients.
    C. Destroy inactive records that exceed the statute of limitations.
    D. Maintain the records indefinitely in hard copy.

REFERENCE: Abdelhak, pp 196–197
                      Green and Bowie, pp 93–94
                      LaTour and Eichenwald-Maki, pp 221–222
                      McWay, pp 110–113

15. Which filing system would provide the most convenient method for the record retrieval of 200 patients consecutively admitted to the hospital?
    A. terminal digit   C. straight numeric
    B. unit   D. serial unit

REFERENCE: Green and Bowie, p 212
                      Johns, p 393
                      McWay, p 11
                      LaTour and Eichenwald-Maki, pp 218–219

16. What is the chief criterion for determining record inactivity?
    A. Medicare's definition of inactivity
    B. amount of space available for storage of newer records
    C. efficiency of microfilming
    D. preference of the medical staff

REFERENCE: Green and Bowie, pp 93–94
              LaTour and Eichenwald-Maki, p 220

17. Out of 2,543 records requested from the HIM Department, 2,375 were located. What is the filing accuracy rate?
    A. 6.61%   C. 89.01%
    B. 75.33%   D. 93.39%

REFERENCE: McWay, pp 193–194
              LaTour and Eichenwald-Maki, p 220

18. Which set of records filed consecutively on a shelf displays terminal digit filing order?
    A. 00-79-99, 00-79-01, 99-78-99   C. 99-05-26, 01-06-26, 49-04-02
    B. 57-78-00, 57-78-01, 56-78-99   D. 55-55-55, 33-33-33, 44-44-44

REFERENCE: Green and Bowie, pp 212–214
              LaTour and Eichenwald-Maki, pp 218–219
              Johns, p 393

19. In the master patient index, which is filed by last name, Jill Thomas-Jones would be
    A. J-I-L-L-T-H-O-M-A-S-J-O-N-E-S
    C. T-H-O-M-A-S-J-O-N-E-S, J-I-L-L
    B. T-H-O-M-A-S, J-I-L-L-J-O-N-E-S
    D. J-O-N-E-S, J-I-L-L-T-H-O-M-A-S

REFERENCE: Green and Bowie, p 210
              Johns, p 392
              McWay, p 111

20. According to terminal digit filing, what would be the number of the record immediately after record number 99-99-30?
    A. 99-98-30   C. 01-00-31
    B. 00-00-31   D. 99-99-31

REFERENCE: Green and Bowie, pp 212–214
              LaTour and Eichenwald-Maki, pp 218–219
              Johns, p 393

21. Medicare's Conditions of Participation for Hospitals requires that patient health records be retained for at least _____ years unless a longer period is required by state or local laws.
    A. 3   C. 7
    B. 5   D. 10

REFERENCE: Green and Bowie, p 93
              LaTour and Eichenwald-Maki, p 222

22. Your state regulations require records to be kept for a statute of limitations period of 7 years. Federal law requires records to be retained for 5 years. The minimum retention period for health records in your facility should be
   A. 5 years.   C. 10 years.
   B. 7 years.   D. either 5 or 7 years, as determined by the facility.

REFERENCE: Abdelhak, p 526
                LaTour and Eichenwald-Maki, pp 221–222
                Johns, p 405
                McWay, pp 112–113

23. Which of the following technologies works best with automated record-tracking systems to speed the data entry process?
   A. discharge lists   C. compressible filing units
   B. bar codes   D. computerized chart-out slips

REFERENCE: Abdelhak, p 280
                Green and Bowie, p 226
                LaTour and Eichenwald-Maki, p 55
                Johns, p 403

24. A HIM Department, currently using 2,540 linear filing inches to store records, plans to purchase new open-shelf filing units. Each of the shelves in a new 6-shelf unit measures 36 linear filing inches. It is estimated that an additional 400 filing inches should be planned for to allow for 5-year expansion needs. How many new file shelving units should be purchased?
   A. 11   C. 13
   B. 12   D. 14

REFERENCE: Green and Bowie, p 219
                LaTour and Eichenwald-Maki, p 221
                Johns, pp 397–399
                McWay, pp 110–112

25. Microfilmed records are considered
   A. inadmissible evidence.
   B. never admissible as hearsay evidence.
   C. acceptable as courtroom evidence.
   D. not admissible as secondary evidence.

REFERENCE: Johns, p 401

26. A research request has been received by the HIM Department from the Quality Improvement Committee. The Committee plans to review the records of all patients who were admitted with CHF in the month of January 2013. Which of the following indices would be the best source in locating the needed records?
   A. master patient index   C. disease index
   B. physicians' index   D. operation index

REFERENCE: Green and Bowie, p 240
                Johns, pp 451–452, 485
                LaTour and Eichenwald-Maki, p 331
                McWay, pp 116–117

27. When using stationary open-shelf files, _____ inches are recommended for aisles between file units.
    A. 24   C. 60
    B. 36   D. 72

REFERENCE: LaTour and Eichenwald-Maki, pp 220–221

28. In a manual record-tracking system, no record should be removed from the file without being replaced by a(n)
    A. 8½ × 11-inch charge-out slip.   C. paddle.
    B. empty file folder.   D. outguide.

REFERENCE: Green and Bowie, p 226
                 Johns, p 402

29. Which of the following should not be included in documentation of record destruction?
    A. statement that records were destroyed in the normal course of business
    B. method of destruction
    C. signature of the individuals supervising and witnessing the destruction
    D. dates not covered in destruction

REFERENCE: AHIMA Practice Brief "Destruction of Patient Health Information"
                 Green and Bowie, pp 96–97
                 LaTour and Eichenwald-Maki, p 222
                 McWay, pp 112–113
                 Johns, pp 405–408
                 Odom, pp 69–70

30. If the HIM Department has purchased 100 units of 8-shelf files and plans to use the terminal digit filing system, how many shelves should be allocated to each primary number?
    A. 8   C. 12
    B. 10   D. 100

REFERENCE: McWay, pp 112–113
                 LaTour and Eichenwald-Maki, pp 220–221

31. In the event of water damage to a large volume of records, what action should be taken immediately to assist in disaster recovery?
    A. Turn on the heat to help retard mold or mildew from forming.
    B. Turn off the air conditioning to reduce temperature and humidity.
    C. Turn off the fans to prevent circulation of air.
    D. Freeze the records to prevent mold or mildew from forming.

REFERENCE: LaTour and Eichenwald-Maki, p 220

32. Which of the following lists is in correct alphabetical order?
    A. Ferlazzo, Joshua; Ferlazzo, Joshua P.; Ferlazzo, Joshua Philip; Ferlazzo, J.
    B. Ferlazzo, J.; Ferlazzo, Joshua; Ferlazzo, Joshua P.; Ferlazzo, Joshua Philip
    C. Ferlazzo, Joshua; Ferlazzo, Joshua P.; Ferlazzo, J.; Ferlazzo, Joshua Philip
    D. Ferlazzo, Joshua A.; Ferlazzo, B.; Ferlazzo, Joshua; Ferlazzo, Joshua Phillip

REFERENCE: Green and Bowie, p 210
                 Johns, p 392
                 McWay, pp 111–112

33. Mary Schnering was admitted to Community Hospital on 1/3/12 and assigned a record number of 54-47-53. The patient was later admitted on 2/14/12 and assigned the number 54-88-42. Both records were eventually filed under 54-88-42. What type of numbering/filing system is being used at Community Hospital?
   A. serial-unit
   B. serial
   C. unit
   D. terminal digit

REFERENCE: Green and Bowie, p 209
                 Johns, p 388
                 LaTour and Eichenwald-Maki, p 218
                 McWay, p 111

34. North Port Health Center is moving to a new facility in 2014. The CEO is projecting a conversion to paperless health records by then. This new facility will not include space for the filing of paper health records. Which of the following items would not be considered when planning this conversion?
   A. changing role of department functions and work flow
   B. challenges of maintaining records that are partially paper and partially electronic
   C. whether to scan older paper records
   D. relationship with the microfilm vendor

REFERENCE: LaTour and Eichenwald-Maki, pp 256–262
                 McWay, pp 113–115

35. What microform should the HIM practitioner select if the records must be unitized and color-coded for filing purposes?
   A. roll microfilm
   B. cartridge
   C. jacket microfilm
   D. cassette

REFERENCE: LaTour and Eichenwald-Maki, p 223
                 Johns, p 400

36. In retrieval of optical image files, cache memory
   A. decreases access time for all users on the system.
   B. increases exchange time on the jukebox.
   C. is resident on the jukebox.
   D. is a way of defragmenting a WORM platter.

REFERENCE: Sayles and Trawick, p 15

37. At Community Hospital the average admission will create a file that will take up 0.25 inch of file space. Each new ER record requires 0.125 inch of file space. Approximately 25,000 new patients are admitted per year and 15,000 ER patients are treated per year. The shelving cost is $1.05 per filing inch. How much money should be allocated for storage space in next year's budget?
   A. $8,531.25
   B. $8,125.00
   C. $853.25
   D. $1,875.00

REFERENCE: LaTour and Eichenwald, p 221
                 Johns, pp 397–399
                 McWay, pp 111–112

38. On his 5/23/12 admission to Metropolitan Hospital, David Robinson was assigned the medical record number 07-23-38. The previous record number assigned to Mr. Robinson during a 4/1/12 admission was 07-10-47. In a serial numbering/filing system, how would these records be filed?
    A. Both records are combined under 07-10-47.
    B. Both records are combined under 07-23-38.
    C. Each admission is filed under its own number.
    D. Previous records are brought forward and filed under the latest number issued.

REFERENCE: Green and Bowie, pp 206–207
               LaTour and Eichenwald-Maki, p 218
               Johns, p 387
               McWay, p 111

39. The same patient was admitted on three different occasions and assigned a new medical record number each time. In order to correct this situation in a unit numbering system, which medical record number should be used given the following information?
                    Admitted 5/04/12   Patty Miller   23-33-56
                    Admitted 6/05/12   P. J. Miller   25-56-88
                    Admitted 9/27/12   Patricia Miller   27-12-12
    A. Void the first and last numbers and file all admissions under 25-56-88.
    B. Delete all previous numbers and assign a completely new number.
    C. Void the first two numbers and file all admissions under 27-12-12.
    D. Void the last two numbers and file all admissions under 23-33-56.

REFERENCE: Green and Bowie, pp 207–208
               LaTour and Eichenwald-Maki, p 218
               Johns, pp 387–388
               McWay, p 111

40. The health care providers in a large teaching hospital require access to health records 24 hours a day, 7 days a week. To secure the area and continue to maintain accessibility, the Director of the HIM Department should
    A. staff the department with personnel 24 hours a day.
    B. be on call every evening and weekends for emergency requests.
    C. train security guards to retrieve records after the department closes.
    D. arrange for records to be retrieved at 7:00 AM every morning.

REFERENCE: Green and Bowie, pp 28–29

41. As a prerequisite to phasing in a new imaging system, what process would facilitate automatic indexing?
    A. redesigning forms to include bar codes
    B. removing portions of the patient record that will not be scanned
    C. converting all microfilm to optical disk format
    D. scanning only emergency room records initially

REFERENCE: LaTour and Eichenwald-Maki, p 216

42. Which of the following is NOT a safety hazard in the file area of the HIM Department?
    A. tightly packed open-shelf files
    B. heavy objects placed in top file drawers
    C. stepladders that are fully open and locked in place
    D. plastic wastebasket for trash

REFERENCE: Abdelhak, p 650

43. A HIM Department wants to buy new open-shelf filing units for its file expansion. Each of the shelves in a new 6-shelf unit measures 33 linear filing inches. There will be an estimated 1,000 records to file. The average record is 1-inch thick. How many filing units should be purchased?
   A. 2
   B. 4
   C. 6
   D. 8

REFERENCE: Green and Bowie, p 219
                LaTour and Eichenwald-Maki, p 221
                Johns, pp 397–399
                McWay, pp 111–112

44. Which of the following microform types is the least expensive to prepare and results in the greatest storage density?
   A. microfilm jackets
   B. roll microfilm
   C. microfiche
   D. ultrafiche

REFERENCE: Green and Bowie, p 95
                LaTour and Eichenwald-Maki, p 223

45. Brian Hills was discharged from the hospital after a 3-day hospitalization and instructed to return to the outpatient department for follow-up care. On his first visit as an outpatient, a new record was created and he was assigned a new record number. Following completion of the outpatient appointment, his outpatient record is filed permanently in the outpatient department. What is the filing system used in this situation?
   A. decentralized
   B. unit record
   C. centralized
   D. terminal digit

REFERENCE: Green and Bowie, pp 215–216
                McWay, p 111

46. The master patient index must, at a minimum, include sufficient information to
   A. summarize the patient's medical history.
   B. list all physicians who have ever treated the patient.
   C. uniquely identify the patient.
   D. justify the patient's hospital bill.

REFERENCE: Abdelhak, p 126
                Green and Bowie, p 237
                LaTour and Eichenwald-Maki, pp 226–227
                Johns, p 382
                McWay, pp 115–116
                Odom, p 78
                Eichenwald-Maki and Petterson, pp 65–68

47. Dr. Gray has applied for medical staff privileges at your hospital. What database would you research to determine if he has been denied medical staff privileges at another hospital?
   A. National Practitioner Data Bank
   B. Healthcare Integrity and Protection Data Bank
   C. MEDPAR file
   D. State Administrative Data Bank

REFERENCE: Abdelhak, p 472
                Green and Bowie, pp 251, 255
                LaTour and Eichenwald-Maki, p 338
                Johns, pp 498–499

48. Which type of patient information system does the Joint Commission suggest that hospitals use?
    A. unit record
    B. computer-based patient record
    C. protocol for requesting information, whereby the request is provided to the practitioner in a timely manner
    D. any one of the above

REFERENCE: Joint Commission

49. A health information manager develops a formal plan or record retention schedule for the automatic transfer of records to inactive storage and potential destruction based on all but which one of the following factors?
    A. statute of limitations   C. readmission rate
    B. volume of research   D. file area staffing

REFERENCE: Green and Bowie, pp 93–94
               LaTour and Eichenwald-Maki, pp 221–225, 282
               McWay, pp 112–114

50. Which of the following is NOT a benefit of the electronic document management system in the HIM Department?
    A. online availability of information
    B. multiuser simultaneous access
    C. decreased use of computer technology
    D. system security and confidentiality

REFERENCE: Green and Bowie, p 109
               McWay, p 104

51. Which one of the following is an advantage of straight numeric filing over terminal digit filing?
    A. All sections of the file expand uniformly.
    B. The training period is short.
    C. Work can be evenly distributed, causing accountability for accuracy in each of the 100 sections.
    D. Inactive records can be purged evenly.

REFERENCE: Green and Bowie, pp 212–214
               LaTour and Eichenwald-Maki, pp 218–219
               Johns, p 393

52. Which one of the following is NOT an electronic document management system component?
    A. the scanner   C. the jukebox
    B. the file server   D. the reader-printer

REFERENCE: Sayles and Trawick, pp 161–163

53. Which of the following items should the Health Information Manager be primarily concerned with when purchasing file guides?
    A. cost and color   C. cost and visibility
    B. durability and visibility   D. color and durability

REFERENCE: Johns, p 399

54. Palm Beach Healthcare Center has been in operation for 13 years. It has 6,000 admissions per year. The facility has expanded and will allow for 200 more admissions per year from now on. There are 2,500 linear feet of filing space available and half is being used. The facility expects a 30% readmission rate. If a unit numbering/filing system is used, how many file folders will be needed for the next year?
   A. 1,800   C. 4,340
   B. 1,860   D. 6,200

REFERENCE: LaTour and Eichenwald-Maki, p 218
                  McWay, pp 111–112

55. As Director of the HIM Department you have become aware of instances of unauthorized access to the record file area. After considering several options to limit or restrict access to the area, you decide to
   A. install a computerized access panel.
   B. hire a security guard to monitor entrance to the file area.
   C. convert from a terminal digit filing system to serial unit filing.
   D. utilize a sign-in and sign-out log for admittance to the file area.

REFERENCE: Abdelhak, p 543

56. What technical security controls do electronic health record systems employ that are different from paper-based health record systems?
   A. audit trails
   B. data encryption protocols
   C. user-based access controls
   D. all of the above

REFERENCE: Eichenwald-Maki and Petterson, p 38

57. The Chief of the Medical Staff requests a report on the number of coronary artery bypass grafts performed by a particular physician in April of the previous year. Where would the health information manager look for this information?
   A. patient register   C. operation index
   B. disease index   D. birth defects register

REFERENCE: Green and Bowie, p 240
                  LaTour and Eichenwald-Maki, p 331
                  Johns, pp 451–452
                  McWay, pp 115–116
                  Odom, p 79

58. A major consideration in a hospital or facility closure is to
   A. notify all patients to pick up their original records by the date of closure.
   B. seek approval for destruction of all records with a last date of treatment over 3 years ago.
   C. ensure that authorized parties have access to the information as provided by law.
   D. arrange for donating the records to an HIA/HIT education program for student use.

REFERENCE: Green and Bowie, pp 97–98
                  LaTour and Eichenwald-Maki, p 222
                  McWay, p 113

59. The American College of Surgeons mandates a successful follow-up rate for all cancer cases of at
    least _____ to meet approval requirements as a cancer program.
    A. 70%   C. 90%
    B. 80%   D. 100%

REFERENCE: LaTour and Eichenwald-Maki, pp 232–233
                  American College of Surgeons' Cancer Program Manual

60. In negotiating a contract with a commercial storage company for storage of inactive records, what
    would be the most important issue to clarify in writing?
    A. who completes the list of what records are to be stored
    B. what are the billing terms
    C. who will purge inactive files for transfer
    D. confidentiality policies and liability concerns

REFERENCE: Green and Bowie, pp 94–95
                  LaTour and Eichenwald-Maki, p 225

61. Which one of the following master patient index core data elements is optional, not
    recommended, by AHIMA?
    A. internal patient identification   C. marital status
    B. discharge date   D. ethnicity

REFERENCE: AHIMA Practice Brief "Master Patient (Person) Index (MPI)—Recommended Core
                  Data Elements"
                  Odom, pp 80–81

62. Unless state or federal laws require longer time periods, AHIMA recommends that patient health
    information for minors be retained for at least how long?
    A. age of majority plus statute of limitation
    B. 10 years after the most recent encounter
    C. 10 years after the age of majority
    D. permanently

REFERENCE: AHIMA Practice Brief "Retention of Health Information"
                  Green and Bowie, p 94
                  Johns, p 406
                  McWay, pp 112–113
                  LaTour and Eichenwald-Maki, pp 221–225

63. A health care facility has made a decision to destroy computerized data. AHIMA recommends
    which one of the following as the preferred method of destruction for computerized data?
    A. overwriting data with a series of characters
    B. disk reformatting
    C. magnetic degaussing
    D. overwriting the backup tapes

REFERENCE: AHIMA Practice Brief "Retention and Destruction of Health Information"
                  McWay, p 113
                  Odom, p 69

64. Which of the following statements would be found in the laboratory report section of the health record?
    A. BUN reported as 20 mg
    B. Morphine sulfate gr. 1/4 q.4h. for pain
    C. IV sodium Pentothal 1% started at 9:05 AM
    D. TPR recorded q.h. for 12 hours

REFERENCE: Abdelhak, p 115
                    Green and Bowie, p 170
                    LaTour and Eichenwald-Maki, p 199
                    Odom, p 141

65. Which of the following is a disadvantage of terminal digit filing as compared to straight numeric filing?
    A. File personnel are crowded in the highest numbers.
    B. Inactive records are pulled from one common area.
    C. The training period is slightly longer.
    D. Files expand at the end of the number series, requiring back shifting.

REFERENCE: Green and Bowie, pp 212–214

66. The main advantage of phonetic filing is
    A. typographical errors are eliminated.
    B. spelling accuracy is encouraged.
    C. emphasis is placed on a foreign language.
    D. names that sound alike are filed together.

REFERENCE: Green and Bowie, p 199

67. Technologies that can make data capture easier include all but which one of the following?
    A. digital dictation
    B. direct data capture from a medical device attached to the HIM department employee
    C. handheld wireless devices
    D. speech recognition

REFERENCE: LaTour and Eichenwald-Maki, pp 245–247

68. If the file clerks are having trouble locating the terminal digit sections quickly, the filing supervisor could add more
    A. outguides.   C. requisitions.
    B. file guides.   D. file maintenance staff.

REFERENCE: Green and Bowie, p 224

69. The HIM Department receives a request for a certified copy of a birth certificate on a patient born in the hospital 30 years ago. The Department should
    A. issue a copy of the birth certificate from the patient's record.
    B. direct the request to the state's office of vital records.
    C. direct the request to the attending physician.
    D. issue a copy of the newborn's record.

REFERENCE: Abdelhak, p 108
                    Green and Bowie, pp 134–135

70. A surgeon requests the name of a patient he admitted on January 11, 2013. Which of the following would be used to retrieve this information?
   A. master patient index
   B. number index
   C. admission register
   D. operation index

REFERENCE: Green and Bowie, p 244
               LaTour and Eichenwald-Maki, p 331McWay, p 117

71. Which of the following is NOT a consideration in file folder size and design?
   A. reinforced top and side panels
   B. scoring on folder bottoms
   C. vendor location
   D. weight of folder

REFERENCE: Green and Bowie, pp 219–220
               Johns, p 399

72. Where in the health record would the following statement be located?

   "Microscopic Diagnosis: Liver (needle biopsy), metastatic adenocarcinoma"?
   A. operative report
   B. pathology report
   C. anesthesia report
   D. radiology report

REFERENCE: Abdelhak, p 114
               Green and Bowie, pp 165–168
               LaTour and Eichenwald-Maki, p 200
               Johns, pp 77–78
               Odom, p 171

73. The HIM Department is located in a hospital that provides health record access 24 hours a day, 7 days a week. To secure the file area and continue to maintain accessibility, the department director should
   A. be on call during the evening hours.
   B. staff the file area with file clerks on all three shifts.
   C. instruct medical staff in record retrieval.
   D. instruct nurse supervisors in record retrieval.

REFERENCE: Green and Bowie, pp 28–29

74. A file area has limited space, medium file activity, and two file clerks. The HIM department would benefit from choosing which type of storage equipment?
   A. compressible filing units
   B. lateral filing cabinets
   C. open shelf files
   D. motorized revolving units

REFERENCE: Johns, pp 395–397
               LaTour and Eichenwald-Maki, pp 220–221

75. When evaluating a microfilm service bureau, all but which of the following are important factors to rate?
   A. cost
   B. emergency returns
   C. storage after filming
   D. cache memory

REFERENCE: LaTour and Eichenwald-Maki, p 223

76. AHIMA recommends converting all but which one of the following minimum data elements when merging or overwriting demographic information for duplicate and overlap master patient index entries?
    A. encounter type
    B. alias/previous name
    C. attending physician
    D. facility identification

REFERENCE: AHIMA Practice Brief "Merging Master Patient (Person) Indexes"

77. Which of the following steps would NOT be taken when bringing all patient health information together in a complete record, regardless of the media output form?
    A. Look at the past composition of records in the facility.
    B. Determine storage requirements for information currently not filed in the medical record.
    C. Decide if all patient health information is being collected and managed uniformly.
    D. Evaluate what patient data, if any, are not incorporated in the medical record.

REFERENCE: AHIMA Practice Brief "Managing Multimedia Medical Records: A Health Information Manager's Role"
               McWay, p 110

78. When operating under the Health Insurance Portability and Accountability Act of 1996 (HIPAA), what is a basic tenet in information security for health care professionals to follow?
    A. Security training is provided to all levels of staff.
    B. Patients are not educated about their right to confidentiality of health information.
    C. The information system encourages mass copying, printing, and downloading of patient records.
    D. When paper-based records are no longer needed, they are bundled and sent to a recycling center.

REFERENCE: AHIMA Practice Brief "Information Security: A Checklist for Health care Professionals"
               McWay, pp 322–323

79. When designing a computer view for information capture, all of the following should be considered except for which one?
    A. external standards such as those developed by HL7 and NCVHS
    B. standardized vocabularies
    C. size of the document
    D. forms committee membership

REFERENCE: AHIMA Practice Brief "Developing Information Capture Tools"
               McWay, pp 109–112

80. When health care facilities close or medical practices dissolve, procedures for disposition of patient records should take into consideration all of the following EXCEPT for
    A. state laws and licensing standards.
    B. Communities of Practice requirements.
    C. needs and wishes of patients.
    D. Medicare requirements.

REFERENCE: AHIMA Practice Brief "Protecting Patient Information After a Facility Closure"
               Green and Bowie, pp 97–98
               McWay, pp 113–114

81. Case finding methods for patients with diabetes include a review of all but which one of the following?
    A. health plans
    B. CPT diagnostic codes
    C. billing data
    D. medication lists

REFERENCE: LaTour and Eichenwald-Maki, p 335
               Johns, p 492

82. To protect health information from catastrophes such as fire, flooding, bomb threats, and theft, Joint Commission-accredited facilities are required to maintain a _____ plan.
    A. budget
    B. disaster
    C. case management
    D. patient care

REFERENCE: AHIMA Practice Brief, "Disaster Planning for Health Information (Updated)"
               McWay, p 112

83. Which of the following is NOT an alternative storage method for paper-based records?
    A. microfilm
    B. optical imaging
    C. computer
    D. outguide

REFERENCE: Green and Bowie, pp 94–96
               LaTour and Eichenwald-Maki, pp 223–225
               Johns, p 395

84. Which of the following issues would be of LEAST concern when storing health records in off-site storage?
    A. operating hours of the storage facility
    B. safety and confidentiality procedures
    C. filing order of the records
    D. procedure for request of a record in an emergency

REFERENCE: Green and Bowie, pp 94–95
               LaTour and Eichenwald-Maki, p 225
               Johns, p 401

85. The HIM Department maintains 500,000 records and responds to 5,000 requests for records in a given period of time. What is the record usage rate?
    A. 0.01%
    B. 1%
    C. 5%
    D. 10%

REFERENCE: LaTour and Eichenwald-Maki, p 220
               McWay, pp 193–194

86. Which one of the following is NOT a data retrieval technology?
    A. Color
    B. Sound
    C. Point and click fields
    D. Icons

REFERENCE: LaTour and Eichenwald-Maki, p 245

87. When engaging the services of a microfilm vendor, all but which one of the following factors should be included in the contract?
    A. Cost
    B. Provision for destruction of original records
    C. Type of reader or printer needed to view the microfilm
    D. Confidentiality of information being filmed

REFERENCE: LaTour and Eichenwald-Maki, pp 222–225

88. What would be the most cost-effective and prudent course of action for the storage or disposition of 250,000 records at a large teaching and research hospital?
    A. Storing the records off-site at a cost of $25,000 per year
    B. Microfilming all 250,000 records for the cost of $195,000
    C. Purging all death records and storing them off-site
    D. Destroying all records older than the time frame required by the statute of limitations

REFERENCE: Abdelhak, pp 196–197
               McWay, p 112
               LaTour and Eichenwald-Maki, pp 220–225

89. The total number of records filed during the month is 2,500 and, upon completion of a filing accuracy study, 90 records were not found. What is the accuracy rate for filing?
    A. 1%   C. 28%
    B. 4%   D. 96%

REFERENCE: Johns, pp 417–418
               McWay, pp 192–194
               LaTour and Eichenwald-Maki, p 220

90. A quality control measure that should be established for the filing, storage, and retrieval of health records includes criteria for the
    A. accuracy of analyzing records.   C. filing of loose materials.
    B. number of incomplete records.   D. tracking of release of information requests.

REFERENCE: Johns, pp 417–418
               LaTour and Eichenwald-Maki, p 220

91. According to AHIMA's recommended retention standards, which one of the following types of health information does NOT need to be retained permanently?
    A. Physician index   C. Register of surgical procedures
    B. Register of births   D. Register of deaths

REFERENCE: AHIMA Practice Brief "Retention of Health Information"
               McWay, p 112

92. For a health care facility to meet its document destruction needs, the certificate of destruction should include all but which one of the following elements?
    A. Unique and serialized transaction number
    B. Location of destruction
    C. Patient notification
    D. Acceptance of fiduciary responsibility

REFERENCE: LaTour and Eichenwald-Maki, pp 222, 225
               Johns, pp 405–408
               McWay, p 112
               Odom, pp 69–70

93. The steps in developing a record retention program include all but which one of the following?
    A. Determining the format and location of storage
    B. Notifying the courts of the destruction
    C. Assigning each record a retention period
    D. Destroying records that are no longer needed

REFERENCE: LaTour and Eichenwald-Maki, p 223
                McWay, pp 112–114
                Odom, pp 67–68

94. A health care facility has received a request to participate in a statewide study on cleft lip and cleft palate. This study would include data from the past year and subsequent years. Given that each of the data sources cited below contains the necessary information, the initial data would be most easily collected from the
    A. newborn records.   C. maternal records.
    B. state bureau of vital statistics.   D. birth defects registry.

REFERENCE: LaTour and Eichenwald-Maki, p 334
                Abdelhak, pp 492–494
                Johns, pp 490–491

95. An example of a primary data source is the
    A. physician index.   C. cancer registry.
    B. health record.   D. hospital statistical report.

REFERENCE: LaTour and Eichenwald-Maki, p 330
                Abdelhak, p 481
                Johns, p 481
                McWay, p 115

96. Which one of the following is NOT considered a challenge in the adoption of an electronic health record system?
    A. executive commitment and support
    B. physician willingness to adopt
    C. contribution to the quality of patient care
    D. individual state legal and regulatory issues

REFERENCE: LaTour and Eichenwald-Maki, pp 256–260

97. Fetal monitoring strips are part of the _____ record and should be maintained_____.
    A. newborn's; 10 years past the age of majority
    B. mother's; according to the length of time required for a minor's records
    C. newborn's; according to the time period specified in the state's statute of limitations
    D. mother's; 10 years

REFERENCE: LaTour and Eichenwald-Maki, p 222

98. Which one of the following would NOT be a strategy when purchasing an electronic health record system?
    A. Identify stakeholders from different organizational levels and engage them appropriately.
    B. Identify return on investment or cost-benefit analysis.
    C. Identify system requirements.
    D. Broaden the vendor field and select several vendors of choice.

REFERENCE: AHIMA Practice Brief "Purchasing Strategies for EHR Systems"

99. Which one of the following describes the electronic health record's impact on the record retrieval function?
    A. This function will be eliminated except for historical files maintained in paper or on microform.
    B. There will be more online management through computer-generated reports using logic rules.
    C. This function will remain the same as the paper record function.
    D. There will be increased record pulling as records are scanned or online documents become available.

REFERENCE: AHIMA Practice Brief "The EHR's Impact on HIM Functions"

100. What data cannot be retrieved from the MEDPAR?
    A. ICD-9-CM diagnosis and procedure codes
    B. Charges broken down by specific types of services
    C. Non-Medicare patient data
    D. Data on the provider

REFERENCE: LaTour and Eichenwald-Maki, p 338

101. As the filing and retrieval supervisor, you are evaluating storage devices for a new health information management system. Which one of the following would you NOT consider as an option for storing health information?
    A. light pen   C. microfilm
    B. optical disc   D. magnetic disk

REFERENCE: Johns, pp 399–401
              Sayles and Trawick, pp 12, 20, 165

102. General Hospital utilizes various related files that include clinical and financial data to generate reports such as MS-DRG case mix reports. What application would be MOST effective for this activity?
    A. desktop publishing
    B. word processing
    C. database management system
    D. command interpreter

REFERENCE: Abdelhak, p 268
              LaTour and Eichenwald-Maki, p 125

103. The Director of Health Information Management has been asked by the Board of Trustees to justify support for the use of handheld devices by the medical staff for point-of-service input. Which one of the following reasons would NOT be included in the Director's response?
    A. decreased clinical documentation errors
    B. increased work efficiency
    C. faster access to health data
    D. elimination of the need for expensive desktop computers

REFERENCE: Abdelhak, p 279
              LaTour and Eichenwald-Maki, p 247

104. The Assistant Director of Record Processing is evaluating software packages for a chart tracking system in the HIM Department. What is the BEST method to verify that the software will work as marketed?
    A. Visit corporate headquarters of the vendor.
    B. Perform a vendor reference check.
    C. Read consumer reports before buying.
    D. Test the software prior to purchase.

REFERENCE: Abdelhak, pp 343–345
                LaTour and Eichenwald-Maki, p 264

105. Concern for health data loss and misuse within the HIM department requires that the health information practitioner evaluate
    A. security controls and access privileges of staff.
    B. policies and procedures developed to safeguard privacy and security.
    C. use of a back-up system.
    D. all of the above.

REFERENCE: LaTour and Eichenwald-Maki, pp 134, 250–251

106. Lewis-Beck Medical Center has been collecting data on patient satisfaction for six months. It is ready to start retrieving data from the database so that it can be used to improve clinical services. Which tool should be used?
    A. HTML   C. XML
    B. SQL   D. data dictionary

REFERENCE: LaTour and Eichenwald-Maki, p 127

107. The Assistant Director of HIM is evaluating software that would use electronic logging of the location of incomplete and delinquent records as they move through the completion process. What departmental function is this most useful for?
    A. release of information   C. chart tracking
    B. coding   D. transcription

REFERENCE: LaTour and Eichenwald-Maki, p 215
                Green and Bowie, pp 224–226

108. The hospital administrator is making a strategic decision by querying various institutional databases for information. What type of system is the hospital administrator using?
    A. electronic health record system
    B. results reporting system
    C. financial information system
    D. executive information system

REFERENCE: Sayles and Trawick, p 213
                LaTour and Eichenwald-Maki, p 614

109. University Hospital has the messaging technology to securely route an alert for a patient's possible drug interaction or abnormal lab result to the appropriate physician's pager number. Which one of the following is the medical staff using?
   A. Intranet
   B. Extranet
   C. Internet
   D. Clinical information system

REFERENCE: LaTour and Eichenwald-Maki, p 60
                      Sayles and Trawick, p 226

110. The HIM practitioner's duty to retain health information by archiving and storage of health data includes
   A. strategies that consider accessibility, natural disasters, and innovations in storage technology.
   B. strategies ensuring that inactive records are as secure as active records.
   C. a retention plan for multiple volumes of records.
   D. all of the above.

REFERENCE: Abdelhak, pp 196–197

111. As Chief Privacy Officer, you are evaluating software programs that will support the hospital's policy on security controls for computer terminals. One of the required items you include in the RFP to vendors is
   A. time-out feature.
   B. encryption.
   C. voice recognition.
   D. unique identifier for log-on.

REFERENCE: LaTour and Eichenwald-Maki, pp 250–251

112. Health Informatics, Inc. is a vendor with a large collection of clinical information systems and hospital information systems that are designed to share data without human or technical intervention. This is a(an)
   A. interfaced system.
   B. integrated system.
   C. OLAP.
   D. standard.

REFERENCE: LaTour and Eichenwald-Maki, pp 243, 246
                      Sayles and Trawick, pp 110–111

113. The function of a(an) _____ is limited to data retrieval.
   A. electronic health record
   B. executive information system
   C. database management system
   D. clinical data repository

REFERENCE: Abdelhak, pp 186–187
                      LaTour and Eichenwald-Maki, p 242
                      Odom, p 225
                      Trawick and Sayles, pp 72, 100

114. The Director of the HIM Department is explaining incentives to physicians for entering their clinical documentation in the electronic health record. Which one of the following would be the key advantage in using this type of data entry?
    A. Enhanced databases will provide information for improved clinical care.
    B. Training will be offered by the hospital.
    C. Those physicians not in compliance will be denied admitting privileges.
    D. Multiple users will not have access to the same information simultaneously.

REFERENCE: LaTour and Eichenwald-Maki, p 239
                   Odom, p 224

115. University Hospital, a 900 bed tertiary health care organization, is undergoing an information systems development. The system that would best meet its needs is the _____.
    A. application service provider model
    B. clinical workstation
    C. IBM Medical Information Systems Program
    D. legacy system

REFERENCE: Abdelhak, p 291
                   LaTour and Eichenwald-Maki, pp 64–65, 149, 258
                   Sayles and Trawick, p 108

116. A 16-year-old female delivers a stillborn infant in Mercy Hospital. The clinical documentation on the stillborn infant would
    A. be filed in a health record created for the infant.
    B. be filed in the mother's record.
    C. be retained in a separate file in the administrative offices.
    D. not be retained in hospital records.

REFERENCE: Odom, p 180

117. Which one of the following is a major management challenge in the storage and retention of electronic health record systems?
    A. Following state and federal laws and accreditation requirements when developing retention and destruction policies.
    B. Keeping technology updated in order to retrieve data.
    C. Ensuring that health information can be retrieved in a timely manner.
    D. All of the above are challenges.

REFERENCE: Abdelhak, pp 196–197

118. When implementing the electronic health record, what is the technical security standard that requires unique user identification, emergency access procedures, automatic log-off, and encryption and decryption of data?
    A. audit control
    B. person or entity authentication
    C. transmission security
    D. access control

REFERENCE: LaTour and Eichenwald-Maki, pp 254–255

119.Which of the following is NOT a factor to consider when developing a record retention program?
   A. legal requirements as determined by statute of limitations
   B. record usage in the facility determined by health care provider activity
   C. reimbursement guidelines
   D. cost of space to maintain hard copy records

REFERENCE: LaTour and Eichenwald-Maki, pp 222–223
                Green and Bowie, p 94

120. Of 750 records filed during the week, 75 were not located. What is the filing error rate?
   A. 10%
   B. 90%
   C. 0.1%
   D. 0.9%

REFERENCE: McWay, pp 193–194
                LaTour and Eichenwald-Maki, p 220

121.Which one of the following is NOT an example of document capture in the electronic document management system?
   A. scanning
   B. bar codes
   C. microfilming
   D   forms recognition

REFERENCE: Sayles and Trawick, p 153

122.Which of the following statements is FALSE when addressing characteristics of the legal health record in an electronic document management system?
   A. The storage media used and the format of the scanned documents must protect data from loss and damage.
   B. The storage format must be efficient, manageable, and in compliance with laws and regulations.
   C. The backup and disaster recovery process is certified to ensure that all data can be recovered.
   D. Direct electronic interfaces from ancillary department systems to the document imaging system will not eliminate the need to scan documents and integrate the data from these ancillary systems.

REFERENCE: Sayles and Trawick, p 154

123.Which of the following is NOT a data retrieval tool?
   A. light pen
   B. SQL
   C. color, animation, sound, icons
   D. screen design

REFERENCE: Sayles and Trawick, pp 176–178

124.Messenger, pneumatic tube, dumbwaiter, and conveyor belt are all examples of
   A. record security systems.
   B. mechanical circulation systems.
   C. loose filing.
   D. filing controls.

REFERENCE: Green and Bowie, pp 228–229

125. Which item is collected and maintained in the transplant registry?
    A. vaccine manufacturer
    B. histocompatibility information
    C. cytogenetic results
    D. stage at the time of diagnosis

REFERENCE: LaTour and Eichenwald-Maki, p 336
                Abdelhak, pp 495–496

Answer Key for Information Retention and Access

NOTE: *Explanations are provided for those questions that require mathematical calculations and questions that are not clearly explained in the references that are cited.*

ANSWER   EXPLANATION

1. D
2. A
3. C
4. B
5. A $(3,545 \times 100)$ divided by $15,000 = 2.36\% = 2.4\%$
6. A
7. A
8. B
9. D
10. D
11. C
12. B
13. D   200 units $\times$ 6 shelves per unit = 1,200 shelves total
            1,200 shelves divided by 100 primary numbers (00–99) = 12 shelves per primary number
14. C
15. C
16. B
17. D   (2,375 records retrieved from proper locations $\times$ 100) divided by 2,543 records requested = 93.39% filing accuracy
18. B
19. C
20. B
21. B
22. B
23. B
24. D   2,540 + 400 = 2,940 inches needed
            $36 \times 6 = 216$ inches per unit
            2,940 (inches needed) divided by 216 (inches per unit) = 13.61 shelves
            You must buy 14 units because you cannot purchase a 0.14 filing shelf.
25. C
26. C
27. B
28. D
29. D
30. A   8 shelves per unit $\times$ 100 units = 800 total shelves
            800 shelves divided by 100 primary digits (00–99) = 8 shelves per primary digit
31. D
32. B
33. A
34. D
35. C
36. A

Answer Key for Information Retention and Access

	ANSWER	EXPLANATION
37.	A	25,000 inpatients × 0.25 inch/record = 6,250 inches
		15,000 ER patients × 0.125 inch/record = 1,875 inches
		6,250 inches + 1,875 inches = 8,125 total inches of filing space/year
		8,125 total inches × $1.05/filing inch = $8,531.25 budget allocation for storage space
38.	C	
39.	D	
40.	A	
41.	A	
42.	C	
43.	C	33 inches per shelf × 6 shelves per unit = 198 linear filing inches per unit
		1,000 records × 1 inch per record = 1,000 inches of records to be filed
		1,000 (inches of records needed) divided by 198 inches per unit = 5.05 filing units
		In order to provide for the total expansion, 6 filing units need to be purchased.
44.	B	
45.	A	
46.	C	
47.	A	
48.	D	
49.	D	
50.	C	
51.	B	
52.	D	
53.	B	
54.	C	6,000 admissions (year currently)
		+ 200 additional admissions/year
		6,200 total admissions next year
		6,200 total admissions
		× 30% readmission rate
		1,860 readmissions next year
		6,200 total admissions
		−1,860 readmissions
		4,340 new file folders needed for next year
55.	A	
56.	D	
57.	C	
58.	C	
59.	C	
60.	D	
61.	C	
62.	A	
63.	D	
64.	A	
65.	C	

Answer Key for Information Retention and Access

	ANSWER	EXPLANATION
66.	D	
67.	B	
68.	B	
69.	B	
70.	C	
71.	C	
72.	B	
73.	B	In a hospital where records are routinely requested 24 hours a day, it would be beneficial to have 24-hour staffing. If it were a small facility with few requests in the evenings, it could be more appropriate to have a nurse supervisor assigned responsibility for record retrieval.
74.	A	
75	D	
76	C	
77.	A	The current, not the past, composition of records is studied.
78.	A	
79.	D	
80.	B	
81.	B	
82.	B	
83.	D	
84.	C	
85.	B	$(5{,}000 \times 100)$ divided by $500{,}000 = 1\%$
86.	C	
87.	C	
88.	B	
89.	D	$2{,}500 - 90 = 2{,}410$ $(2{,}410 \times 100)$ divided by $2{,}500 = 96.4\%$ filing accuracy
90.	C	
91.	A	
92.	C	
93.	B	
94.	D	
95.	B	
96.	C	
97.	B	
98.	D	
99.	A	
100.	C	
101.	A	
102.	C	
103.	D	
104.	D	
105	D	
106.	B	
107.	C	

Answer Key for Information Retention and Access

ANSWER   EXPLANATION

108. D
109. D
110. D
111. A
112. A
113. D
114. A
115. A
116. B
117. D
118. D
119. C
120. A
121. C
122. D
123. A
124. B
125. B

REFERENCES

Abdelhak, M., Grostick, S., and Hanken, M. (2012). *Health information: Management of a strategic resource* (4th ed.). St. Louis: Saunders Elsevier.

AHIMA Practice Briefs. All are published by the American Health Information Management Association, Chicago.

AHIMA Practice Brief: "Managing Multimedia Medical Records: A Health Information Manager's Role"

AHIMA Practice Brief: "Information Security: A Checklist for Health care Professionals"

AHIMA Practice Brief: "Developing Information Capture Tools"

AHIMA Practice Brief: "Protecting Patient Information After a Facility Closure Updated"

AHIMA Practice Brief: "Disaster Planning for Health Information (Updated)"

AHIMA Practice Brief: "Master Patient (Person) Index (MPI) – Recommended Core Data Elements"

AHIMA Practice Brief: "Retention of Health Information (Updated)"

AHIMA Practice Brief: "Retention and Destruction of Health Information (Updated)"

AHIMA Practice Brief: "Merging Master Patient (Person) Indexes"

AHIMA Practice Brief: "Purchasing Strategies for EHR Systems"

AHIMA Practice Brief: "EHR's Impact on HIM Functions"

American College of Surgeons. (2011). *Cancer program standards 2012: Ensuring patient-centered care.* Chicago: American College of Surgeons Commission on Cancer.

Eichenwald-Maki, S., & Petterson, B. (2008). *Using the electronic health record in the health care provider practice.* Clifton Park, NY: Thomson Delmar Learning.

Green, M. A., & Bowie, M. J. (2011). *Essentials of health information management: Principles and practices.* Clifton Park, NY: Delmar Cengage Learning.

Johns, M. L. (2011). *Health information management technology: An applied approach* (3rd ed.). Chicago: American Health Information Management Association.

Joint Commission. (2012) *Comprehensive accreditation manual for hospitals: The official handbook.* Oakbrook Terrace, IL: Author.

LaTour, K., & Eichenwald-Maki, S. (2010). *Health information management: Concepts, principles and practice* (3rd ed.). Chicago: American Health Information Management Association.

McWay, D. C. (2008). *Today's health information management: An integrated approach.* Clifton Park, NY: Delmar Cengage Learning.

Odom-Wesley, B., & Brown, D. (2009). *Documentation for medical records.* Chicago: American Health Information Management Association.

Sayles, N., & Trawick, K. (2010). *Introduction to computer systems for health information technology.* Chicago: American Health Information Management Association.

RHIA AND RHIT COMPETENCIES BY QUESTION FOR INFORMATION RETENTION AND ACCESS

Question	RHIA Domain Competencies						RHIT Domain Competencies						
	1	2	3	4	5	6	1	2	3	4	5	6	7
1					X						X		
2	X						X						
3	X										X		
4	X						X						
5	X						X						
6	X						X						
7	X						X						
8	X						X						
9			X							X			
10	X						X						
11	X						X						
12				X								X	
13	X						X						
14	X						X						
15	X						X						
16	X						X						
17	X						X						
18	X						X						
19	X						X						
20	X						X						
21						X			X				
22						X			X				
23			X							X			
24				X								X	
25						X	X						
26		X					X						
27	X						X						
28	X								X				
29						X	X						
30	X						X						
31	X						X						
32	X						X						
33	X						X						
34				X			X						
35	X						X						
36			X							X			
37	X						X						
38	X						X						
39	X						X						
40				X			X						
41			X				X						
42				X			X						
43	X						X						
44	X						X						
45	X						X						
46			X				X						
47						X				X			
48						X				X			
49						X						X	
50			X								X		
51	X						X						
52			X								X		
53	X						X						

Question	RHIA Domain Competencies							RHIT Domain Competencies						
	1	2	3	4	5	6		1	2	3	4	5	6	7
54				X				X						
55				X				X						
56				X				X						
57		X						X						
58						X							X	
59	X									X				
60				X				X						
61	X									X				
62						X				X				
63			X										X	
64	X							X						
65	X							X						
66	X							X						
67			X								X			
68	X							X						
69						X		X						
70	X							X						
71	X							X						
72	X							X						
73				X				X						
74				X				X						
75				X				X						
76			X					X						
77						X				X				
78						X				X				
79			X								X			
80						X				X				
81	X							X						
82						X				X				
83	X							X						
84	X							X						
85	X							X						
86			X					X						
87	X							X						
88				X				X						
89	X							X						
90	X							X						
91	X									X				
92						X				X				
93	X									X				
94		X						X						
95	X							X						
96			X								X			
97	X							X						
98			X								X			
99			X					X						
100			X						X					
101	X							X						
102						X		X						
103			X								X			

RHIA AND RHIT COMPETENCIES BY QUESTION FOR INFORMATION RETENTION AND ACCESS													
Question	RHIA Domain Competencies							RHIT Domain Competencies						
	1	2	3	4	5	6		1	2	3	4	5	6	7
104			X								X			
105				X				X						
106			X					X						
107			X					X						
108			X								X			
109			X								X			
110				X				X						
111						X					X			
112			X								X			
113			X								X			
114			X								X			
115			X								X			
116	X							X						
117			X					X						
118			X							X				
119	X									X				
120	X							X						
121			X								X			
122						X							X	
123			X									X		
124			X					X						
125	X							X						

V. Classification Systems and Secondary Data Sources

Lisa M. Delhomme, MHA, RHIA

1. Which of the following is a valid ICD-9-CM principal diagnosis code?
   A. V27.2   outcome of delivery, twins, both live born
   B. V30.00   single live born, born in hospital
   C. E867   accidental poisoning by gas distributed by pipeline
   D. M9010/0   fibroadenoma, NOS

REFERENCE: Frisch, pp 150–151
                Green, p 185
                Johnson and Linker, pp 17, 52, 63–64
                Brown, pp 270–272, 314, 379–381, 407–408

2. A physician performed an outpatient surgical procedure on the eye orbit of a patient with Medicare. Upon searching the CPT codes and consulting with the physician, the coder is unable to find a code for the procedure. The coder should assign
   A. an unlisted Evaluation and Management code from the E/M section.
   B. an unlisted procedure code located in the eye and ocular adnexa section.
   C. a HCPCS Level Two (alphanumeric) code.
   D. an ophthalmologic treatment service code.

REFERENCE: AMA (2013), p 55
                Green, pp 487–488
                Frisch, p 254
                Smith, p 23

3. A system of preferred terminology for naming disease processes is known as a
   A. set of categories.   C. medical nomenclature.
   B. classification system.   D. diagnosis listing.

REFERENCE: Green, p 11
                Green and Bowie, p 304
                McWay, pp 125–128
                Abdelhak, p 224
                Johns, p 236
                LaTour and Eichenwald-Maki, pp 192, 348

4. Which of the following is NOT included as a part of the minimum data maintained in the MPI?
   A. principal diagnosis   C. full name (last, first, and middle)
   B. patient medical record number   D. date of birth

REFERENCE: McWay, pp 115–116
                Green and Bowie, pp 237–239
                Abdelhak, p 107
                Johns, p 382
                LaTour and Eichenwald-Maki, pp 226, 331

5. The Health Information Department receives research requests from various committees in the hospital. The Medicine Committee wishes to review all patients having a diagnosis of anterolateral myocardial infarction within the past 6 months. Which of the following would be the best source to identify the necessary charts?
   A. operation index
   B. consultation index
   C. disease index
   D. physician's index

REFERENCE: Green and Bowie, pp 240–243
McWay, pp 116–117
Johns, pp 451–452
LaTour and Eichenwald-Maki, p 331

6. One of the major functions of the cancer registry is to ensure that patients receive regular and continued observation and management. How long should patient follow-up be continued?
   A. until remission occurs
   B. 10 years
   C. for the life of the patient
   D. 1 year

REFERENCE: McWay, p 117
Abdelhak, p 485
Johns, pp 487–488
LaTour and Eichenwald-Maki, pp 332–333

7. In reviewing the medical record of a patient admitted for a left herniorrhaphy, the coder discovers an extremely low potassium level on the laboratory report. In examining the physician's orders, the coder notices that intravenous potassium was ordered. The physician has not listed any indication of an abnormal potassium level or any related condition on the discharge summary. The best course of action for the coder to take is to
   A. confer with the physician and ask him or her to list the condition as a final diagnosis if he or she considers the abnormal potassium level to be clinically significant.
   B. code the record as is.
   C. code the condition as abnormal blood chemistry.
   D. code the abnormal potassium level as a complication following surgery.

REFERENCE: Bowie and Shaffer (2012), p 69
Green, p 239
Johnson and Linker, pp 5–36
Brown, p 33

8. DSM-IV-TR is used most frequently in what type of health care setting?
   A. behavioral health centers
   B. ambulatory surgery centers
   C. home health agencies
   D. nursing homes

REFERENCE: Green, p 832
McWay, p 134
LaTour and Eichenwald-Maki, pp 353–354
Johns, pp 262–263

9. A coder notes that a patient is taking prescription Pilocarpine. The final diagnoses on the discharge summary are congestive heart failure and diabetes mellitus. The coder should query the physician about adding a diagnosis of

A. arthritis.   C. bronchitis.
B. glaucoma.   D. laryngitis.

REFERENCE: Green, p 16
               Nobles, p 689

10. The patient is diagnosed with congestive heart failure. A drug of choice is

A. ibuprofen.   C. haloperidol.
B. oxytocin.   D. digoxin.

REFERENCE: Nobles, p 329

11. ICD-10-CM utilizes a placeholder character. This is used as a 5th character placeholder at certain 6 character codes to allow for future expansion. The placeholder character is

A. "Z."   B. "O."
C. "1."   D. "x."

REFERENCE: Bowie and Schaffer (2), p 29

12. The local safety council requests statistics on the number of head injuries occurring as a result of skateboarding accidents during the last year. To retrieve this data, you will need to have the correct

A. CPT code.
B. Standard Nomenclature of Injuries codes.
C. E-codes and ICD-9-CM codes.
D. HCPCS Level II codes.

REFERENCE: Bowie and Shaffer (2012), pp 358–362
               Frisch, pp 150–151
               Green, pp 188–189
               Johnson and Linker, pp 16, 66–69
               McWay, p 130
               Brown, pp 405–407
               Schraffenberger (2012), pp 400–401

13. A patient was admitted with severe abdominal pain, elevated temperature, and nausea. The physical examination indicated possible cholecystitis. Acute and chronic pancreatitis secondary to alcoholism was recorded on the face sheet as the final diagnosis. The principal diagnosis is

A. alcoholism.   C. cholecystitis.
B. abdominal pain.   D. acute pancreatitis.

REFERENCE: AHA, Coding Clinic, 2nd quarter, 1990, p 4
               Brown, pp 57–58
               Green, p 120
               Johnson and Linker, p 79

14. In general, all three key components (history, physical examination, and medical decision making) for the E/M codes in CPT should be met or exceeded when
    A. the patient is established.
    B. a new patient is seen in the office.
    C. the patient is given subsequent care in the hospital.
    D. the patient is seen for a follow-up inpatient consultation.

REFERENCE: AMA (2013), p 10
               Bowie and Shaffer (2011), pp 39–53
               Green, pp 405–406
               Johnson and Linker, p 144

15. A direction to "code first underlying disease" should be considered
    A. only when coding inpatient records.
    B. a mandatory instruction.
    C. mandatory dependent on the code selection.
    D. a suggestion only.

REFERENCE: Bowie and Shaffer (2012), pp 47–48
               Frisch, p 130
               Green, pp 93–95
               Brown, pp 18–19
               Schraffenberger (2012), p 23
               Hazelwood and Venable, p 22

16. Which classification system was developed to standardize terminology and codes for use in clinical laboratories?
    A. Systematized Nomenclature of Human and Veterinary Medicine International (SNOMED)
    B. Systematized Nomenclature of Pathology (SNOP)
    C. Read Codes
    D. Logical Observation Identifiers, Names and Codes (LOINC)

REFERENCE: McWay, p 127
               Abdelhak, pp 237–239
               LaTour and Eichenwald-Maki, pp 357–358

17. Which classification system is used to classify neoplasms according to site, morphology, and behavior?
    A. International Classification of Diseases for Oncology (ICD-O)
    B. Systematized Nomenclature of Human and Veterinary Medicine International (SNOMED)
    C. Diagnostic and Statistical Manual of Mental Disorders (DSM)
    D. Current Procedural Terminology (CPT)

REFERENCE: Green, pp 48–49
               McWay, p 135
               Abdelhak, p 252
               LaTour and Eichenwald-Maki, p 351

18. According to the UHDDS, a procedure that is surgical in nature, carries a procedural or anesthetic risk, or requires special training is defined as a
    A. principal procedure.   C. operating room procedure.
    B. significant procedure.   D. therapeutic procedure.

REFERENCE: Brown, p 65
               Green, p 241
               Johnson and McHugh, pp 573–574
               Schraffenberger (2012), p 65

19. The "cooperating party" responsible for maintaining the ICD-9-CM disease classification is the
    A. Centers for Medicare and Medicaid Services (CMS).
    B. National Center for Health Statistics (NCHS).
    C. American Hospital Association (AHA).
    D. American Health Information Management Association (AHIMA).

REFERENCE: Green, p 69
               Johns, pp 238–239
               Johnson and Linker, p 6
               LaTour and Eichenwald-Maki, p 349

20. An encoder that prompts the coder to answer a series of questions and choices based on the documentation in the medical record is called a(n)
    A. logic-based encoder.   C. grouper.
    B. automated codebook.   D. automatic code assignment.

REFERENCE: LaTour and Eichenwald-Maki, p 400
               McWay, p 132

21. Which of the following classification systems was designed with electronic systems in mind and is currently being used for problem lists, ICU unit monitoring, patient care assessments, data collection, medical research studies, clinical trials, disease surveillance, and image d?
    A. SNOMED CT
    B. SNDO
    C. ICDPC-2
    D. GEM

REFERENCE: Abdelhak, pp 235–237
               LaTour and Eichenwald-Maki, pp 356–357
               McWay, p 127

22. The Unified Medical Language System (UMLS) is a project sponsored by the
    A. National Library of Medicine.   C. World Health Organization.
    B. CMS.   D. Office of Inspector General.

REFERENCE: Johns, pp 276–277
               LaTour and Eichenwald-Maki, p 364
               McWay, p 127

23. A patient is admitted with shortness of breath and hemoptysis. A chest x-ray revealed patchy infiltrates in the left lung and possible pneumonia. On the third day of hospitalization a bronchoscopy with biopsy was done which revealed a small cell carcinoma of the left upper lobe of the lung. A metastatic lesion in the brain was detected. The principal diagnosis is the
    A.   metastatic brain carcinoma.
    B.   small cell lung carcinoma.
    C.   hemoptysis.
    D.   pneumonia.

REFERENCE: Bowie and Shaffer (2012), pp 66, 116
               Brown, pp 27–28
               Frisch, pp 132–133
               Green, pp 137–139
               Johnson and Linker, pp 63–64
               Schraffenberger (2012), pp 67–69

24. Jane Moore was admitted to the ambulatory care unit of the hospital for a planned cholecystectomy for cholelithiasis. Shortly before surgery, Jane developed tachycardia, and the surgery was canceled. After a thorough workup for the tachycardia, Jane was discharged. This outpatient admission should be coded in the following sequence:
    A.   V code for canceled surgery, tachycardia, cholelithiasis
    B.   tachycardia, V code for canceled surgery, cholelithiasis
    C.   cholelithiasis, V code for canceled surgery
    D.   cholelithiasis, tachycardia, V code for canceled surgery

REFERENCE: Bowie and Shaffer (2012), pp 67, 375
               Brown, pp 72–73
               Green, p 246
               Schraffenberger (2012), pp 46–47

25. A 75-year-old female was admitted for repair of a hiatal hernia that was performed on the first day of admission. While recovering, the patient fell out of her bed and sustained a fractured femur, which was surgically reduced. Further complications included severe angina for which a cardiac catheterization and PTCA were performed. The principal procedure is
    A.   femur reduction.
    B.   herniorrhaphy.
    C.   catheterization.
    D.   PTCA.

REFERENCE: Brown, pp 65–66
               Green, p 241
               Johnson and Linker, p 17
               Schraffenberger (2012), p 65

26. Code 402, Hypertensive Heart Disease, would appropriately be used in which of the following situations?
    A. left heart failure with benign hypertension
    B. congestive heart failure; hypertension
    C. hypertensive cardiovascular disease with congestive heart failure
    D. cardiomegaly with hypertension

REFERENCE: Bowie and Schaffer (2012), pp 194–195
               Brown, pp 347–348
               Frisch, pp 146–147
               Green, pp 157–160
               Hazelwood and Venable, pp 165–167
               Johnson and Linker, pp 289–290
               Schraffenberger (2012), pp 181–185

27. A patient is admitted to the hospital 6 weeks post myocardial infarction with severe chest pains. Which is the correct code?
    A. 414.8   chronic MI
    B. 410.1x   acute MI
    C. 412   old MI
    D. 413.0   angina

REFERENCE: Bowie and Schaffer (2012), pp 197–199
               Brown, pp 333–334
               Hazelwood and Venable, pp 167–169
               Johnson and Linker, pp 42–43
               Schraffenberger (2012), pp 156–159

28. Susan Dawn is status post mastectomy (6 weeks) due to carcinoma of the breast. She is admitted to the outpatient clinic for chemotherapy. What is the correct sequencing of the codes?
    A. V58.11 chemotherapy; 174.9 malignant neoplasm of breast
    B. V58.11 chemotherapy; V10.3 personal history of neoplasm of the breast
    C. V67.00 follow-up exam after surgery; V58.11 chemotherapy
    D. V10.3 personal history of neoplasm of the breast; V58.11 chemotherapy

REFERENCE: Bowie and Schaffer (2012), pp 115, 120
               Brown, pp 391–394
               Frisch, p 153
               Green, p 143
               Hazelwood and Venable, pp 102–103
               Johnson and Linker, pp 63–64
               Schraffenberger (2012), pp 97–98

29. Which of the following is coded as an adverse effect in ICD-9-CM?
    A. mental retardation due to intracranial abscess
    B. rejection of transplanted kidney
    C. tinnitus due to allergic reaction after administration of eardrops
    D. nonfunctioning pacemaker due to defective soldering

REFERENCE: Bowie and Schaffer (2012), pp 334–336, 627–629
               Brown, pp 443–444
               Frisch, pp 149–150
               Green, pp 189–192
               Hazelwood and Venable, pp 294–299
               Johnson and Linker, pp 73–74
               Schraffenberger (2012), pp 376–381

30. A service provided by a physician whose opinion or advice regarding evaluation and/or management of a specific problem is requested by another physician is referred to as
    A. a referral.   C. risk factor intervention.
    B. a consultation.   D. concurrent care.

REFERENCE: AMA (2013), p 18
               Bowie and Shaffer (2013), pp 61–63
               Frisch, p 77
               Green, pp 412–414
               Johnson and Linker, pp 153–154, 644
               Smith, p 213

31. A patient with leukemia is admitted for chemotherapy 5 weeks after experiencing an acute myocardial infarction. How will the MI be coded?
    A. acute MI with 5th digit 1—initial episode of care
    B. acute MI with 5th digit 2—subsequent episode of care
    C. history of MI
    D. chronic MI

REFERENCE: Bowie and Schaffer (2012), pp 197–199
               Brown, pp 333–334
               Hazelwood and Venable, pp 167–169
               Johnson and Linker, pp 42–43
               Schraffenberger (2012), pp 186–189

32. In ICD-9-CM, when an exploratory laparotomy is performed followed by a therapeutic procedure, the coder lists
    A. therapeutic procedure first, exploratory laparotomy second.
    B. exploratory laparotomy, therapeutic procedure, closure of wound.
    C. therapeutic procedure only.
    D. exploratory laparotomy first, therapeutic procedure second.

REFERENCE: Bowie and Schaffer (2012), p 374
               Brown, p 68
               Green, p 254
               Schraffenberger (2012), pp 43–44

33. The most widely discussed and debated unique patient identifier is the
   A. patient's date of birth.
   B. patient's first and last names.
   C. patient's social security number.
   D. Unique Physician Identification Number (UPIN).

REFERENCE: LaTour and Eichenwald-Maki, pp 179–180

34. The Central Office on ICD-9-CM, which publishes *Coding Clinic*, is maintained by the
   A. National Center for Health Statistics.
   B. Centers for Medicare and Medicaid Services.
   C. American Hospital Association.
   D. American Health Information Management Association.

REFERENCE: Johnson and Linker, pp 16–17
               Schraffenberger and Kuehn, p 15

35. A nomenclature of codes and medical terms that provides standard terminology for reporting physicians' services for third-party reimbursement is
   A. Current Medical Information and Terminology (CMIT).
   B. Current Procedural Terminology (CPT).
   C. Systematized Nomenclature of Pathology (SNOP).
   D. Diagnostic and Statistical Manual of Mental Disorders (DSM).

REFERENCE: Bowie and Schaffer (2013) pp 2, 8
               Frisch, p 5
               Green, p 9
               Johnson and Linker, p 110
               Schraffenberger and Kuehn, p 10

36. A cancer program is surveyed for approval by the
   A. American Cancer Society.
   B. Commission on Cancer of the American College of Surgeons.
   C. State Department of Health.
   D. Joint Commission on Accreditation of Healthcare Organizations.

REFERENCE: Abdelhak, p 483
               Johns, p 488
               LaTour and Eichenwald-Maki, p 333

37. The nursing staff would most likely use which of the following to facilitate aggregation of data for comparison at local, regional, national, and international levels?
   A. READ codes   C. SPECIALIST Lexicon
   B. ABC codes   D. LOINC

REFERENCE: Green and Bowie, p 309
               McWay, p 135

38. The Level II (national) codes of the HCPCS coding system are maintained by the
    A. American Medical Association.
    B. CPT Editorial Panel.
    C. local fiscal intermediary.
    D. Centers for Medicare and Medicaid Services.

REFERENCE: Bowie and Schaffer (2013), p 8
                Green and Bowie, p 24
                Johnson and Linker, pp 110–111

39. A patient is admitted with alcohol withdrawal suffering from delirium tremens. The patient is a chronic alcoholic and cocaine addict. Which of the following is the principal diagnosis?
    A. alcoholic withdrawal   C. cocaine dependence
    B. chronic alcoholism   D. delirium tremens

REFERENCE: Bowie and Schaffer (2012), pp 159–160
                Brown, pp 143–144
                Frisch, p 132
                Schraffenberger (2012), p 148

40. A patient is admitted with pneumonia. Cultures are requested to determine the infecting organism. Which of the following, if present, would alert the coder to ask the physician whether or not this should be coded as gram-negative pneumonia?
    A. pseudomonas   C. staphylococcus
    B. clostridium   D. listeria

REFERENCE: Brown, p 112
                Green, pp 14–16

41. The Level I (CPT) codes of the HCPCS coding system are maintained by the
    A. American Medical Association.
    B. American Hospital Association.
    C. local fiscal intermediary.
    D. Centers for Medicare and Medicaid Services.

REFERENCE: Bowie and Schaffer (2013), pp 2, 8
                Frisch, p 5
                Green, p 9
                Green and Bowie, pp 24, 307–308
                Johnson and Linker, pp 110–111
                McWay, pp 127–130

42. A physician excises a 3.1 cm malignant lesion of the scalp that requires full-thickness graft from the thigh to the scalp. In CPT, which of the following procedures should be coded?
    A. full-thickness skin graft to scalp only
    B. excision of lesion; full-thickness skin graft to scalp
    C. excision of lesion; full-thickness skin graft to scalp; excision of skin from thigh
    D. code 15004 for surgical preparation of recipient site; full-thickness skin graft to scalp

REFERENCE: AMA, CPT Assistant, vol. 7, no. 9, Sept. 1997, pp 1–3
                Green, pp 493–495, 501–503
                Johnson and Linker, pp 222, 227–229
                Smith, pp 59–60, 71–74

43. A patient is seen by a surgeon who determines that an emergency procedure is necessary. Identify the modifier that may be reported to indicate that the decision to do surgery was made on this office visit.
    A. −25   B. −55   C. −57   D. −58

REFERENCE: AMA (2013), pp 595–600
                Bowie and Schaffer (2013), pp 16–25
                Frisch, pp 18–19
                Green, p 365
                Smith, p 201

44. A patient develops difficulty during surgery and the physician discontinues the procedure. Identify the modifier that may be reported by the physician to indicate that the procedure was discontinued.
    A. −52   B. −53   C. −73   D. −74

REFERENCE: AMA (2013), pp 595–600
                Bowie and Schaffer (2013), pp 6–25
                Frisch, p 18
                Green, p 365
                Johnson and Linker, p 456
                Smith, p 44

45. A barrier to widespread use of automated code assignment is
    A. inadequate technology.   C. resistance by physicians.
    B. poor quality of documentation. D. resistance by HIM professionals.

REFERENCE: LaTour and Eichenwald-Maki, pp 400–401
                McWay, p 136

46. In assigning E/M codes, three key components are used. These are
    A. history, examination, counseling.
    B. history, examination, time.
    C. history, nature of presenting problem, time.
    D. history, examination, medical decision making.

REFERENCE: AMA (2013), p 9
                Bowie and Schaffer (2011), pp 39–40
                Frisch, p 12
                Green, p 391
                Johnson and Linker, p 131
                Smith, pp 194–195

47. Mrs. Jones had an appendectomy on November 1. She was taken back to surgery on November 2 for evacuation of a hematoma of the wound site. Identify the modifier that may be reported for the November 2 visit.
    A. −58   B. −76   C. −78   D. −79

REFERENCE: AMA (2013), pp 595–600
                Bowie and Schaffer (2011), pp 22–23
                Frisch, pp 22, 240
                Green, p 368
                Johnson and Linker, p 461
                Smith, p 46

48. The primary goal of a hospital-based cancer registry is to
    A. improve patient care.
    B. allocate hospital resources appropriately.
    C. determine the need for professional and public education programs.
    D. monitor cancer incidence.

REFERENCE: Abdelhak, p 486
               McWay, p 117

49. A pregnant patient was admitted to the hospital with uncontrolled diabetes mellitus. She has type 1 diabetes and was brought under control and subsequently discharged. The following code was assigned:

> 648.03 Other current condition in the mother classifiable elsewhere but complicating pregnancy, childbirth of the puerperium, diabetes mellitus

    Which of the following describes why the coding is in error?
    A. The incorrect fifth digit was used.
    B. The condition should have been coded as gestational diabetes because she is pregnant.
    C. An additional code describing the diabetes mellitus should be used.
    D. Only the code for the diabetes mellitus should have been used.

REFERENCE: Bowie and Schaffer (2012), pp 256–257
               Brown, pp 276–277
               Frisch, p 130
               Green, pp 173–174
               Johnson and Linker, pp 47–50, 343
               Schraffenberger (2012), p 275

50. A secondary data source that houses and aggregates extensive data about patients with a certain diagnosis is a
    A. disease index.   C. disease registry.
    B. master patient index.   D. admissions register.

REFERENCE: Green and Bowie, pp 240–243
               LaTour and Eichenwald-Maki, pp 331–332
               McWay, pp 116–117

51. After reviewing the following excerpt from CPT, code 27646 would be interpreted as

27645	Radical resection of tumor; tibia
27646	fibula
27647	talus or calcaneus

    A. 27646   radical resection of tumor; tibia and fibula.
    B. 27646   radical resection of tumor; fibula.
    C. 27646   radical resection of tumor; fibula or tibia.
    D. 27646   radical resection of tumor; fibula, talus or calcaneus.

REFERENCE: Bowie and Schaffer (2013), pp 4–5
               Green, p 350
               Smith, pp 18–19

52. A patient was admitted to the hospital with hemiplegia and aphasia. The hemiplegia and aphasia were resolved before discharge and the patient was diagnosed with cerebral thrombosis. What is the correct coding and sequencing?
    A. hemiplegia; aphasia
    B. cerebral thrombosis
    C. cerebral thrombosis; hemiplegia; aphasia
    D. hemiplegia; cerebral thrombosis; aphasia

REFERENCE: Hazelwood and Venable, p 175

53. A 36-year-old woman was admitted to the hospital for an obstetrical delivery of her third child. During the admission, a sterilization procedure was performed for contraceptive purposes. The V25.2 code for sterilization would be
    A. assigned as a principal diagnosis.
    B. assigned as a secondary diagnosis.
    C. not assigned because this was the patient's third child.
    D. not assigned because it is the same admission as the delivery.

REFERENCE: Brown, pp 283–284
               Schraffenberger (2012), pp 440–441

54. According to ICD-9-CM, which one of the following is NOT a mechanical complication of an internal implant?
    A. erosion of skin by pacemaker electrodes
    B. inflammation of urethra due to indwelling catheter
    C. leakage of breast prosthesis
    D. IUD embedded in uterine wall

REFERENCE: Brown, pp 458–460
               Hazelwood and Venable, pp 315–316
               Johnson and Linker, pp 76–77
               Schraffenberger (2012), pp 386–387

55. A population-based cancer registry that is designed to determine rates and trends in a defined population is a(n)
    A. incidence-only population-based registry.
    B. cancer control population-based registry.
    C. research-oriented population-based registry.
    D. patient care population-based registry.

REFERENCE: Abdelhak, p 487
               Johns, p 486
               LaTour and Eichenwald-Maki, p 332

56. Given the diagnosis "carcinoma of axillary lymph nodes and lungs, metastatic from breast," what is the primary cancer site(s)?
    A. axillary lymph nodes
    B. lungs
    C. breast
    D. A and B

REFERENCE: Bowie and Schaffer (2012), pp 111–114
            Brown, p 375
            Frisch, pp 142–144
            Green, pp 137–139
            Hazelwood and Venable, p 109
            Johnson and Linker, p 63
            Schraffenberger (2012), p 106

57. When is it appropriate to use category V10, history of malignant neoplasm?
    A. Primary malignancy recurred at the original site and adjunct chemotherapy is directed at the site.
    B. Primary malignancy has been eradicated and no adjunct treatment is being given at this time.
    C. Primary malignancy has been eradicated and the patient is admitted for adjunct chemotherapy to the primary site.
    D. Primary malignancy is eradicated; adjunct treatment is refused by the patient even though there is some remaining malignancy.

REFERENCE: Bowie and Schaffer (2012), pp 114–117, 346
            Frisch, pp 142–144
            Green, p 140
            Johnson and Linker, p 63
            Schraffenberger (2012), pp 97–98, 436–438

58. According to CPT, in which of the following cases would an established E/M code be used?
    A. A home visit with a 45-year-old male with a long history of drug abuse and alcoholism. The man is seen at the request of Adult Protective Services for an assessment of his mental capabilities.
    B. John and his family have just moved to town. John has asthma and requires medication to control the problem. He has an appointment with Dr. You and will bring his records from his previous physician.
    C. Tom is seen by Dr. X for a sore throat. Dr. X is on call for Tom's regular physician, Dr. Y. The last time that Tom saw Dr. Y was a couple of years ago.
    D. A 78-year-old female with weight loss and progressive agitation over the past 2 months is seen by her primary care physician for drug therapy. She has not seen her primary care physician in 4 years.

REFERENCE: AMA (2013), pp 4–5
            AMA, CPT Assistant, vol. 8, no. 10, Oct. 1998
            Bowie and Schaffer (2013), pp 37–38
            Frisch, pp 49–50
            Green, pp 388–389
            Smith, p 193

59. In order to use the inpatient CPT consultation codes, the consulting physician must
    A. order diagnostic tests.
    B. document his findings in the patient's medical record.
    C. communicate orally his opinion to the attending physician.
    D. use the term "referral" in his report.

REFERENCE: AMA (2013), pp 61–63
              Bowie and Schaffer (2011), pp 59–61
              Frisch, pp 77–78
              Green, pp 412–413
              Smith, p 213

60. The attending physician requests a consultation from a cardiologist. The cardiologist takes a detailed history, performs a detailed examination, and utilizes moderate medical decision making. The cardiologist orders diagnostic tests and prescribes medication. He documents his findings in the patient's medical record and communicates in writing with the attending physician. The following day the consultant visits the patient to evaluate the patient's response to the medication, to review results from the diagnostic tests, and to discuss treatment options. What codes should the consultant report for the two visits?
    A. an initial inpatient consult and a follow-up consult
    B. an initial inpatient consult for both visits
    C. an initial inpatient consult and a subsequent hospital visit
    D. an initial inpatient consult and initial hospital care

REFERENCE: AMA (2013), pp 18–19
              Bowie and Schaffer (2013), pp 61–63
              Frisch, pp 82–86
              Green, pp 414–415
              Smith, p 213

61. According to the American Medical Association, medical decision making is measured by all of the following except the
    A. number of diagnoses or management options.
    B. amount and complexity of data reviewed.
    C. risk of complications.
    D. specialty of the treating physician.

REFERENCE: AMA (2013), p 10
              Bowie and Schaffer (2013), pp 52–54
              Frisch, p 322
              Green, p 391
              Johnson and Linker, pp 139–140
              Smith, pp 202–205

62. CPT provides Level I modifiers to explain all of the following situations EXCEPT
    A. when a service or procedure is partially reduced or eliminated at the physician's discretion.
    B. when one surgeon provides only postoperative services.
    C. when a patient sees a surgeon for follow-up care after surgery.
    D. when the same laboratory test is repeated multiple times on the same day.

REFERENCE: AMA (2013), pp 565–600
                Bowie and Schaffer (2013), pp 16–25
                Frisch, pp 13–23
                Green, pp 364–371
                Johnson and Linker, pp 449–464

63. The best place to ascertain the size of an excised lesion for accurate CPT coding is the
    A. discharge summary.   C. operative report.
    B. pathology report.   D. anesthesia record.

REFERENCE: Green, pp 493–496
                Johnson and Linker, pp 220–221
                Smith, pp 59–60

64. Which of the following is expected to enable hospitals to collect more specific information for use in patient care, benchmarking, quality assessment, research, public health reporting, strategic planning, and reimbursement?
    A. LOINC
    B. ICD-10-CM
    C. NDC
    D. NANDA

REFERENCE: Abdelhak, p 249
                Johnson and Linker, pp 82–89

65. Case definition is important for all types of registries. Age will certainly be an important criterion for accessing a case in a(n) _____ registry.
    A. implant   C. HIV/AIDS
    B. trauma   D. birth defects

REFERENCE: LaTour and Eichenwald-Maki, p 334

66. To gather statistics for surgical services provided on an outpatient basis, which of the following codes are needed?
    A. ICD-9-CM codes
    B. evaluation and management codes
    C. HCPCS Level II Codes
    D. CPT codes

REFERENCE: Green and Bowie, pp 240–243
                McWay, p 116
                Schraffenberger and Kuehn, p 10

67. The Cancer Committee at your hospital requests a list of all patients entered into your cancer registry in the last year. This information would be obtained by checking the
   A. disease index.
   B. tickler file.
   C. accession register.
   D. suspense file.

REFERENCE: Johns, p 487
                        LaTour and Eichenwald-Maki, p 332

68. The reference date for a cancer registry is
   A. January 1 of the year in which the registry was established.
   B. the date when data collection began.
   C. the date that the Cancer Committee is established.
   D. the date that the cancer program applies for approval by the American College of Surgeons.

REFERENCE: Abdelhak, p 486

69. The abstract completed on the patients in your hospital contains the following items: patient demographics; prehospital interventions; vital signs on admission; procedures and treatment prior to hospitalization; transport modality; and injury severity score. The hospital uses these data for its
   A. AIDS registry.
   B. diabetes registry.
   C. implant registry.
   D. trauma registry.

REFERENCE: Abdelhak, p 496
                        Johns, pp 489–490
                        LaTour and Eichenwald-Maki, pp 333–334

70. In relation to birth defects registries, active surveillance systems
   A. use trained staff to identify cases in all hospitals, clinics, and other facilities through review of patient records, indexes, vital records, and hospital logs.
   B. are commonly used in all 50 states.
   C. miss 10% to 30% of all cases.
   D. rely on reports submitted by hospitals, clinics, or other sources.

REFERENCE: Abdelhak, p 492

71. In regard to quality of coding, the degree to which the same results (same codes) are obtained by different coders or on multiple attempts by the same coder refers to
   A. reliability.
   B. validity.
   C. completeness.
   D. timeliness.

REFERENCE: LaTour and Eichenwald-Maki, p 399

72. The Healthcare Cost and Utilization Project (HCUP) consists of a set of databases that include data on inpatients whose care is paid for by third-party payers. HCUP is an initiative of the
   A. Agency for Healthcare Research and Quality.
   B. Centers for Medicare and Medicaid Services.
   C. National Library of Medicine.
   D. World Health Organization.

REFERENCE: LaTour and Eichenwald-Maki, p 341
                        McWay, p 145

73. The coding supervisor notices that the coders are routinely failing to code all possible diagnoses and procedures for a patient encounter. This indicates to the supervisor that there is a problem with

    A. reliability.   C. completeness.
    B. validity.   D. timeliness.

REFERENCE: LaTour and Eichenwald-Maki, p 399

74. When coding free skin grafts, which of the following is NOT an essential item of data needed for accurate coding?

    A. recipient site   C. size of defect
    B. donor site   D. type of repair

REFERENCE: Bowie and Schaffer (2013), p 110
               Green, pp 501–503
               Johnson and McHugh, pp 123–130
               Smith, pp 70–74

75. In CPT, Category III codes include codes

    A. to describe emerging technologies.
    B. to measure performance.
    C. for use by nonphysician practitioners.
    D. for supplies, drugs, and durable medical equipment.

REFERENCE: AMA (2013), p 597
               Bowie and Schaffer (2013), p 8
               Green, p 349
               Johnson and Linker, pp 120, 130
               Smith, p 3

76. The information collected for your registry includes patient demographic information, diagnosis codes, functional status, and histocompatibility information. This type of registry is a

    A. birth defects registry.   C. transplant registry.
    B. diabetes registry.   D. trauma registry.

REFERENCE: LaTour and Eichenwald-Maki, p 336

77. In the ICD-9-CM classification system, shooting pain in the right eye due to the presence of an intact, correctly positioned permanent contact lens would be coded as a(n)

    A. current injury.
    B. late effect.
    C. mechanical complication of an internal prosthetic device.
    D. abnormal reaction of the body to the presence of an internal prosthetic device.

REFERENCE: Brown, pp 458–460
               Hazelwood and Venable, pp 315–316
               Schraffenberger (2012), pp 386–388

78. In the ICD-9-CM classification system, severe shock due to third-degree burns sustained in an industrial accident would be coded as a(n)
    A. current injury.
    B. late effect.
    C. mechanical complication of an internal prosthetic device.
    D. abnormal reaction of the body to the presence of an internal prosthetic device.

REFERENCE: Bowie and Schaffer (2012), pp 331–334
                     Brown, pp 434–436
                     Frisch, p 137
                     Johnson and Linker, pp 76–78

79. In the ICD-9-CM classification system, a nonfunctioning pacemaker due to the disintegration of the electrodes (leads) would be coded as a(n)
    A. current injury.
    B. late effect.
    C. mechanical complication of an internal prosthetic device.
    D. abnormal reaction of the body to the presence of an internal prosthetic device.

REFERENCE: Brown, pp 458–460
                     Hazelwood and Venable, pp 315–316
                     Johnson and Linker, p 76
                     Schraffenberger (2012), pp 386–388

80. In the ICD-9-CM classification system, an esophageal stricture due to a burn received in a house fire several years ago would be coded as a(n)
    A. current injury.
    B. late effect.
    C. mechanical complication of an internal prosthetic device.
    D. abnormal reaction of the body to the presence of an internal prosthetic device.

REFERENCE: Bowie and Schaffer (2012), pp 63–65
                     Brown, p 425
                     Hazelwood and Venable, pp 284–286
                     Schraffenberger (2012), p 364

81. Dizziness and blurred vision following ingestion of prescribed Allegra and a glass of wine at dinner would be reported as a(n)
    A. poisoning.
    B. adverse reaction to a drug.
    C. late effect of a poisoning.
    D. late effect of an adverse reaction.

REFERENCE: Bowie and Schaffer (2012), pp 334–336, 627–629
                     Brown, pp 443–444
                     Frisch, pp 149–150
                     Green, pp189–192
                     Hazelwood and Venable, pp 294–299
                     Johnson and Linker, pp 73–75
                     Schraffenberger (2012), pp 382–384

82. Tachycardia after taking a correct dosage of prescribed Lortab would be reported as a(n)
    A. poisoning.
    B. adverse reaction to a drug.
    C. late effect of a poisoning.
    D. late effect of an adverse reaction.

REFERENCE: Bowie and Schaffer (2012), pp 334–336, 627–629
                Brown, pp 443–444
                Frisch, pp 149–150
                Green, pp 189–192
                Hazelwood and Venable, pp 294–299
                Johnson and Linker, pp 73–75
                Schraffenberger (2012), pp 376–381

83. Blindness due to an allergic reaction to ampicillin administered 6 years ago would be reported as a(n)
    A. poisoning.   C. late effect of a poisoning.
    B. adverse reaction to a drug.   D. late effect of an adverse reaction.

REFERENCE: Bowie and Schaffer (2012), pp 334–336, 627–629
                Brown, p 451
                Frisch, pp 134–135
                Green, p 196
                Hazelwood and Venable, p 295
                Johnson and Linker, pp 75–77
                Schraffenberger (2012), p 378

84. The patient underwent bypass surgery for life-threatening coronary artery disease. With the aid of extracorporeal circulation, the right internal mammary artery was taken down to the left anterior descending artery and saphenous vein grafts were brought from the aorta to the diagonal, the right coronary artery, and the posterior descending artery. What is the correct ICD-9-CM coding for this procedure?
    A. single internal mammary artery bypass; aortocoronary artery bypass of three vessels
    B. aortocoronary bypass of three coronary arteries
    C. aortocoronary bypass of four coronary arteries
    D. single internal mammary artery bypass; aortocoronary bypass of three vessels, extracorporeal circulation

REFERENCE: Brown, pp 360–362
                Schraffenberger (2012), pp 203–204

85. Patient Jamey Smith has been seen at Oceanside Hospital three times prior to this current encounter. Unfortunately, because of clerical errors, Jamey's information was entered into the MPI incorrectly on the three previous admissions and consequently has three different medical record numbers. The unit numbering system is used at Oceanside Hospital. Jamey's previous entries into the MPI are as follows:

09/03/09	Jamey Smith	MR# 10361
03/10/10	Jamey Smith Doe	MR# 33998
07/23/11	Jamie Smith Doe	MR# 36723

The next available number to be assigned at Oceanside Hospital is 41369. Duplicate entries in the MPI should be scrubbed and all of Jamey's medical records should be filed under medical record number

   A. 10361.
   B. 33998.
   C. 36723.
   D. 41369.

REFERENCE: Green and Bowie, pp 237–240
                      McWay, p 111

86. The method of calculating errors in a coding audit that allows for benchmarking with other hospitals, and permits the reviewer to track errors by case type, is the
   A. record-over-record method.
   B. benchmarking method.
   C. code method.
   D. focused review method.

REFERENCE: Schraffenberger and Kuehn, p 319

87. The most common type of registry located in hospitals of all sizes and in every region of the country is the
   A. trauma registry.
   B. cancer registry.
   C. AIDS registry.
   D. birth defects registry.

REFERENCE: Green and Bowie, p 248
                      McWay, p 117

88. A radiologist is asked to review a patient's CT scan that was taken at another facility. The modifier - 26 attached to the code indicates that the physician is billing for what component of the procedure?
   A. professional
   B. technical
   C. global
   D. confirmatory

REFERENCE: Bowie and Schaffer (2013), pp 17–18
                      Frisch, pp 14, 16
                      Green, pp 370, 702
                      Johnson and Linker, pp 453–454

89. When coding neoplasms, topography means
   A. cell structure and form.
   B. site.
   C. variation from normal tissue.
   D. extent of the spread of the disease.

REFERENCE: Abdelhak, p 488

90. According to CPT, antepartum care includes all of the following EXCEPT
    A. initial and subsequent history.
    C. monthly visits up to 36 weeks.
    B. physical examination.
    D. routine chemical urinalysis.

REFERENCE: Bowie and Schaffer (2013), pp 293–295
                Green, p 656
                Johnson and Linker, pp 346–347
                Smith, p 143

91. The Cancer Committee at Wharton General Hospital wants to compare long-term survival rates for pancreatic cancer by evaluating medical versus surgical treatment of the cancer. The best source of these data is the
    A. disease index.
    C. master patient index.
    B. operation index.
    D. cancer registry abstracts.

REFERENCE: Abdelhak, pp 487–488
                LaTour and Eichenwald-Maki, pp 332–333
                McWay, p 117

92. A list or collection of clinical words or phrases with their meanings is a
    A. data dictionary.
    C. medical nomenclature.
    B. language.
    D. clinical vocabulary.

REFERENCE: McWay, pp 125–128

93. The main difference between concurrent and retrospective coding is
    A. when the coding is done.
    B. what classification system is used.
    C. the credentials of the coder.
    D. the involvement of the physician.

REFERENCE: Schraffenberger and Kuehn, p 30

94. A patient was discharged from the acute care hospital with a final diagnosis of bronchial asthma. As the coder reviews the record, she notes that the patient was described as having prolonged and intractable wheezing, airway obstruction that was not relieved by bronchodilators, and the lab values showed decreased respiratory function. The coder queried the physician to determine whether the code for _____ is appropriate to be added to the final diagnoses.
    A. acute and chronic bronchitis
    B. chronic obstructive pulmonary disease
    C. respiratory failure
    D. status asthmaticus

REFERENCE: Bowie and Schaffer (2012), p 215
                Brown, pp 187–188
                Frisch, p 139
                Green, p 164
                Hazelwood and Venable, pp 190–191
                Schraffenberger (2012), pp 222–223

95. A patient is undergoing hemodialysis for end-stage renal disease in the outpatient department of an acute care hospital. The patient develops what is believed to be severe heartburn but is sent to observation for several hours, at which time the patient is admitted to inpatient care for further workup. The cardiologist diagnoses the patient's problem as unstable angina. What is the principal diagnosis for the acute hospital stay?
    A. complications of hemodialysis
    B. heartburn
    C. unstable angina
    D. renal disease

REFERENCE: Bowie and Schaffer (2012), p 66
                Green, pp 233–234
                Johnson and Linker, p 17
                Schraffenberger (2012), pp 189–190

96. A patient is seen in the emergency room of an acute care hospital with tachycardia and hypotension. The patient had received an injection of tetanus toxoid (correct dosage) earlier at his primary care physician's office. Which of the following is the appropriate sequencing for this encounter?
    A. hypotension; tachycardia; accidental poisoning E code (tetanus toxoid)
    B. unspecified adverse reaction to tetanus toxoid; undetermined cause E code (tetanus toxoid)
    C. hypotension; tachycardia; therapeutic use E code (tetanus toxoid)
    D. poisoning code (tetanus toxoid); hypotension; tachycardia; accidental poisoning E code (tetanus toxoid)

REFERENCE: Bowie and Schaffer (2012), pp 334–336, 627–629
                Brown, pp 443–446
                Frisch, pp 149–150
                Green, pp 189–192
                Hazelwood and Venable, pp 294–299
                Johnson and Linker, pp 73–78
                Schraffenberger (2012), pp 376–381

97. A rare malignant tumor often associated with AIDS is
    A. Kaposi's sarcoma.
    B. glioblastoma multiforme.
    C. pheochromocytoma.
    D. melanoma.

REFERENCE: Schraffenberger (2012), pp 83–84

98. A PEG procedure would most likely be done to facilitate
    A. breathing.
    B. eating.
    C. urination.
    D. none of the above.

REFERENCE: Johnson and Linker, p 89
                Schraffenberger (2012), p 241

99. What ICD-9-CM coding scheme is used to show that a therapeutic abortion resulted in a live fetus?
    A. spontaneous abortion; V30 code to show a newborn birth
    B. Code 644.21, early onset of delivery; V27 code (outcome of delivery)
    C. abortion by type; V27 code (outcome of delivery)
    D. therapeutic abortion

REFERENCE: Bowie and Schaffer (2012), p 256
               Brown, p 297
               Green, p 176
               Hazelwood and Venable, p 233
               Johnson and Linker, p 343
               Schraffenberger (2012), p 267

100. Prolonged pregnancy is a pregnancy that has advanced beyond _____ completed weeks of gestation.
    A. 39   C. 41
    B. 40   D. 42

REFERENCE: Hazelwood and Venable, pp 233–234
               Schraffenberger (2012), p 269

101. CMS published a final rule indicating a compliance date to implement ICD-10-CM and ICD-10-PCS. The use of these two code sets will be effective on
    A. January 1, 2014.   C. January 1, 2014.
    B. October 1, 2013.   D. October 1, 2012.

REFERENCE: DeVault, Barta, and Endicott, p 3
               Bowie and Schaffer (2), p 3

102. Mappings between ICD-9-CM and ICD-10-CM were developed and released by the National Center for Health Statistics (NCHS) to facilitate the transition from one code set to another. They are called
    A. GEMS (General Equivalency Mappings).
    B. Medical Mappings.
    C. Code Maps.
    D. ICD Code Maps.

REFERENCE: DeVault, Barta, and Endicott, p 6

103. The code structure for ICD-10-CM differs from the code structure of ICD-9-CM. An ICD-10-CM code consists of
    A. five alphanumeric characters.   C. three to seven characters.
    B. 10 characters.   D. seven digits.

REFERENCE: Bowie and Schaffer (2), p 47
               DeVault, Barta, and Endicott, pp 7–8

104. The first character for all of the codes assigned in ICD-10-CM is
    A. an alphabet.   C. an alphabet or a number.
    B. a number.   D. a digit.

REFERENCE: DeVault, Barta, and Endicott, p 7

105. ICD-10-PCS will be implemented in the United States to code
   A. hospital inpatient procedures.
   B. physician office procedures.
   C. hospital inpatient diagnoses.
   D. hospital outpatient diagnoses.

REFERENCE: Barta, DeVault, and Endicott, p 2

106. ICD-10-PCS codes have a unique structure. An example of a valid code in the ICD-10-PCS system is
   A. L03.311.
   B. 013.2.
   C. B2151.
   D. 2W3FX1Z.

REFERENCE: Barta, DeVault, and Endicott, pp 6–10
                  Schraffenberger (2012), p 51

107. ICD-10-PCS utilizes the third character in the Medical and Surgical section to identify the "root operation." The name of the root operation that describes "cutting out or off, without replacing a portion of a body part" is
   A. destruction.
   B. extirpation.
   C. excision.
   D. removal.

REFERENCE: Barta, DeVault, and Endicott, p 101
                  Schraffenberger (2012), p 55

108. In ICD-10-PCS, to code "removal of a thumbnail," the root operation would be
   A. removal.
   B. extraction.
   C. fragmentation.
   D. extirpation.

REFERENCE: Barta, DeVault, and Endicott, p 109
                  Schraffenberger (2012), p 55
                  DeVault, Barta, and Endicott, p 24

109. In ICD-10-CM, the final character of the code indicates laterality. An unspecified side code is also provided should the site not be identified in the medical record. If no bilateral code is provided and the condition is bilateral, the ICD-10-CM Official Coding Guidelines direct the coder to
   A.   assign the unspecified side code.
   B.   assign separate codes for both the left and right side.
   C.   not assign a code.
   D.   query the physician.

REFERENCE: Bowie and Schaffer (2), pp 35, 50
                  DeVault, Barta, and Endicott, p 24

110. An example of a valid code in ICD-10-CM is
   A. 576.212D.
   B. Z2358.J.
   C. 329.6677.
   D. BJRT23x.

REFERENCE: Bowie and Schaffer (2), p 19
                  DeVault, Barta, and Endicott, p 24

Answer Key for Classification Systems and Secondary Data Sources

NOTE: Explanations are provided for those questions that require mathematical calculations and questions that are not clearly explained in the references that are cited.

ANSWER   EXPLANATION

1.   B   M codes and E codes are never principal diagnosis codes and, in fact, are optional for coding. V codes to describe the outcome of delivery are always secondary codes on the mother's chart.

2.   B

3.   C

4.   A

5.   C

6.   C

7.   A   A coder should never assign a code on the basis of laboratory results alone. If findings are clearly outside the normal range and the physician has ordered additional testing or treatment, it is appropriate to consult with the physician as to whether a diagnosis should be added or whether the abnormal finding should be listed.

8.   A

9.   B   Pilocarpine is used to treat open-angle and angle-closure glaucoma to reduce intraocular pressure.

10.   D   Digoxin is used for maintenance therapy in congestive heart failure, atrial fibrillation, atrial flutter, and paroxysmal atrial tachycardia. Ibuprofen is an anti-inflammatory drug. Oxytocin is used to initiate or improve uterine contractions at term, and haloperidol is used to manage psychotic disorders.

11.   D

12.   C   HCPCS codes (Levels I and II) would only give the code for any procedures that were performed and would not identify the diagnosis code or cause of the accident. The correct name of the nomenclature for athletic injuries is the Standard Nomenclature of Athletic Injuries and is used to identify sports injuries. It has not been revised since 1976.

13.   D

14.   B   All three key components (history, physical examination, and medical decision making) are required for new patients and initial visits. At least two of the three key components are required for established patients, and subsequent visits.

15.   B

16.   D

17.   A

18.   B

19.   B

20.   A

21.   A

22.   A

23.   B

Answer Key for Classification Systems and Secondary Data Sources

ANSWER   EXPLANATION

24. D There are V codes that indicate various reasons for canceled surgery. Review codes V64.0x, V64.1, V64.2, and V64.3. As usual, the principal diagnosis is always the reason for admission, in this case, the cholelithiasis. The contraindication (the tachycardia) should also be coded.

25. B The principal procedure is defined as the procedure performed for definitive treatment (rather than for diagnostic purposes) or one that was necessary to take care of the complication. If two or more procedures meet this definition, the one most related to the principal diagnosis is designated as the principal procedure.

26. C In order to use category 402 there must be a cause and effect relationship shown between the hypertension and the heart condition. "With" does not show this relationship, nor does the fact that both conditions are listed on the same chart. The term "hypertensive" indicates a cause and effect relationship.

27. B An acute MI is considered to be anything under 8 weeks' duration from the time of initial onset. A chronic MI is considered anything over 8 weeks with symptoms. An old MI is considered anything over 8 weeks with NO symptoms.

28. A The patient is admitted for chemotherapy (V58.11) and, because the breast cancer is still actively being treated, it is still coded as current.

29. C Mental retardation is a late effect, rejection of the kidney is a complication, and a nonfunctioning pacemaker is a mechanical complication.

30. B
31. B
32. C
33. C
34. C
35. B
36. B
37. B
38. D
39. D
40. A
41. A
42. B
43. C
44. B
45. B
46. D
47. C
48. A
49. C
50. C

Answer Key for Classification Systems and Secondary Data Sources

	ANSWER	EXPLANATION
51.	B	
52.	C	Codes for hemiplegia and aphasia are assigned in addition to the code for cerebral thrombosis even if they are no longer present at discharge.
53.	B	
54.	B	
55.	A	
56.	C	
57.	B	
58.	C	
59.	B	
60.	C	The first visit would be an inpatient consult. Because the physician continued to treat the patient and participate in his care, all subsequent visits are considered as subsequent hospital care and are no longer consults.
61.	D	
62.	C	Modifier -52 can be used if a physician elects to partially reduce or eliminate a service or procedure. Modifier -55 is used by a physician who only provides postoperative services. Modifier -91 is used when a laboratory test is repeated multiple times on the same day. CPT code 99024 is used to report a follow-up visit after surgery.
63.	C	
64.	B	
65.	D	
66	D	
67.	C	
68.	B	
69.	D	
70.	A	
71.	A	
72.	A	
73.	C	
74.	B	
75.	A	
76.	C	
77.	D	
78.	A	
79.	C	
80.	B	
81.	A	
82.	B	
83.	D	

Answer Key for Classification Systems and Secondary Data Sources

ANSWER   EXPLANATION

84.   D   The procedure described includes one internal mammary artery, which is not considered an aortocoronary bypass. There were three aortocoronary bypasses: aorta to diagonal, aorta to right coronary artery, and aorta to the posterior descending artery. The description states that extracorporeal circulation was used.

85.   A

86.   A

87.   B

88.   A   With CPT radiology codes, there are three components that have to be considered. These are the professional, technical, and global components. The professional component describes the services of a physician who supervises the taking of an x-ray film and the interpretation with report of the results. The technical component describes the services of the person who uses the equipment, the film, and other supplies. The global component describes the combination of both professional and technical components. If the billing radiologist's services include only the supervision and interpretation component, the radiologist bills the procedure code and adds the modifier -26 to indicate that he or she did only the professional component of the procedure.

89.   B

90.   C

91.   D

92.   D

93.   A

94.   D

95.   C

96.   C

97.   A

98.   B

99.   B

100. D

101. B

102. A

103. C

104. A

105. A

106. D

107. C

108. B   The root operation "removal" is incorrect because by definition, a removal in ICD-10-PCS is defined as "taking out or off a device from a body part."

109. B

110. A   ICD-10-CM codes begin with an alphabet. There is a decimal after the third character. Codes can consist of three to seven characters.

REFERENCES

Abdelhak, M., Grostick, S., Hanken, M.A., & Jacobs, E. (Eds.). (2012). *Health information: Management of a strategic resource* (4th ed.). St. Louis, MO: Saunders Elsevier.

American Hospital Association (AHA). *Coding clinic.* Chicago: AHA, Coding Clinic, 2nd quarter, 1990, p 4.

American Medical Association (AMA). *CPT assistant.* Chicago: AMA, CPT Assistant, vol. 7, no. 9, Sept. 1997, pp 1–3.

American Medical Association (AMA). (2012). *Physicians' current procedural terminology (CPT) 2013, Professional Edition.* Chicago: AMA, CPT Assistant, vol. 8, no. 10, Oct. 1998.

Bowie, M. J., & Schaffer, R. (2013). *Understanding procedural coding: A worktext* (3rd ed.). Clifton Park, NY: Delmar Cengage Learning.

Bowie, M. J., & Schaffer, R. (2012). *Understanding ICD-9-CM: A worktext.* Clifton Park, NY: Delmar Cengage Learning.

Bowie, M. J., & Schaffer, R. (2012). *Understanding ICD-10-CM and ICD-10-PCS: A worktext.* Clifton Park, NY: Delmar Cengage Learning.

Brown, F. (2011). *ICD-9-CM coding handbook 2012 with answers.* Chicago: American Hospital Association (AHA).

Frisch, B. (2007). *Correct coding for Medicare, compliance, and reimbursement.* Clifton Park, NY: Delmar Cengage Learning.

Green, M. (2012). *3-2-1 Code it* (3rd ed.). Clifton Park, NY: Delmar Cengage Learning.

Green, M. A., & Bowie, M. J. (2011). *Essentials of health information management: Principles and practices* (2nd ed.). Clifton Park, NY: Delmar Cengage Learning.

Hazelwood, A.C., & Venable, C. A. (2012). *ICD-9-CM and ICD-10-CM diagnostic coding and reimbursement for physician services.* Chicago: American Health Information Management Association (AHIMA).

ICD-9-CM. (2013). *Code book professional edition.* Salt Lake City, UT: INGINEX.

Johns, M. (2011). *Health information management technology: An applied approach* (3rd ed.). Chicago: American Health Information Management Association (AHIMA).

Johnson, S. L., & Linker, C. S. (2013). Understanding medical coding: A comprehensive guide (3rd ed.). Clifton Park, NY: Delmar Cengage Learning.

LaTour, K., & Eichenwald-Maki, S. (2010). *Health information management: Concepts, principles and practice* (3rd ed.). Chicago: American Health Information Management Association (AHIMA).

McWay, D. C. (2008). *Today's health information management: An integrated approach.* Clifton Park, NY: Delmar Cengage Learning.

Nobles, S. (2002). *Delmar's drug reference for health care professionals.* Clifton Park, NY: Delmar Cengage Learning.

REFERENCES (continued)

Schraffenberger, L. A. (2012). *Basic ICD-10-CM/PCS and ICD-9-CM coding*. Chicago: American Health Information Management Association (AHIMA).

Schraffenberger, L. A., & Kuehn, L. (2011). *Effective management of coding services* (4th ed.). Chicago: American Health Information Management Association (AHIMA).

Smith, G. (2012). *Basic current procedural terminology and HCPCS coding 2012*. Chicago: American Health Information Management Association (AHIMA).

RHIA AND RHIT COMPETENCIES BY QUESTION FOR
CLASSIFICATION SYSTEMS AND SECONDARY DATA SOURCES

Question	RHIA Domain Competencies							RHIT Domain Competencies						
	1	2	3	4	5	6		1	2	3	4	5	6	7
1	X								X					
2	X								X					
3	X							X						
4			X					X						
5	X							X						
6	X							X						
7	X								X					
8	X							X						
9	X								X					
10	X							X						
11	X							X						
12	X							X						
13	X								X					
14	X							X						
15	X								X					
16	X							X						
17	X							X						
18	X								X					
19	X							X						
20			X						X					
21			X					X						
22	X							X						
23	X								X					
24	X								X					
25	X								X					
26	X								X					
27	X								X					
28	X								X					
29	X								X					
30	X							X						
31	X								X					
32	X								X					
33	X							X						
34	X							X						
35	X							X						
36	X							X						
37	X							X						
38	X							X						
39	X								X					
40	X								X					
41	X							X						
42	X								X					
43	X								X					
44	X								X					
45			X						X					
46	X								X					
47	X								X					
48	X							X						
49	X								X					
50	X							X						
51	X								X					
52	X								X					
53	X								X					

Question	RHIA Domain Competencies							RHIT Domain Competencies						
	1	2	3	4	5	6		1	2	3	4	5	6	7
54	X								X					
55	X							X						
56	X								X					
57	X								X					
58	X								X					
59	X								X					
60	X								X					
61	X								X					
62	X								X					
63	X								X					
64			X					X						
65	X							X						
66	X							X						
67	X							X						
68	X							X						
69	X							X						
70	X							X						
71	X								X					
72	X							X						
73	X								X					
74	X								X					
75	X								X					
76	X							X						
77	X								X					
78	X								X					
79	X								X					
80	X								X					
81	X								X					
82	X								X					
83	X								X					
84	X								X					
85	X							X						
86	X							X						
87	X							X						
88	X								X					
89	X							X						
90	X								X					
91	X							X						
92	X							X						
93	X								X					
94	X								X					
95	X								X					
96	X								X					
97	X								X					
98	X								X					
99	X								X					
100	X								X					
101	X							X						
102	X								X					
103									X					

Question	RHIA Domain Competencies							RHIT Domain Competencies						
	1	2	3	4	5	6		1	2	3	4	5	6	7
104	X								X					
105	X							X						
106	X								X					
107	X								X					
108	X								X					
109	X								X					
110	X								X					

RHIA AND RHIT COMPETENCIES BY QUESTION FOR CLASSIFICATION SYSTEMS AND SECONDARY DATA SOURCES

VI. Medical Billing and Reimbursement Systems

Toni Cade, MBA, RHIA, CCS, FAHIMA

1. The case-mix management system that utilizes information from the Minimum Data Set (MDS) in long-term care settings is called
    A. Medicare Severity Diagnosis Related Groups (MS-DRGs).
    B. Resource Based Relative Value System (RBRVS).
    C. Resource Utilization Groups (RUGs).
    D. Ambulatory Patient Classifications (APCs).

REFERENCE: Green and Rowell, p 27
                  Green, p 829

2. The prospective payment system used to reimburse home health agencies for patients with Medicare utilizes data from
    A. MDS (Minimum Data Set).
    B. OASIS (Outcome and Assessment Information Set).
    C. UHDDS (Uniform Hospital Discharge Data Set).
    D. UACDS (Uniform Ambulatory Core Data Set).

REFERENCE: Green, p 829
                  Green and Rowell, pp 27, 367
                  Schraffenberger and Kuehn, p 140

3. _____ indicates that the claim is suspended in the billing system awaiting late charges, diagnoses/procedure codes that are soft coded by the coders, and/or insurance verification.
    A. Bill hold   C. Bill drop
    B. Accounts receivables   D. Concurrent review

REFERENCE: Schraffenberger and Kuehn, p 231

4. All of the following items are "packaged" under the Medicare outpatient prospective payment system, EXCEPT for
    A. recovery room.   C. anesthesia.
    B. medical supplies.   D. medical visits.

REFERENCE: Johns, p 330
                 LaTour and Eichenwald-Maki, p 393

5. Under the RBRVS, each HCPCS/CPT code contains three components, each having assigned relative value units. These three components are
    A. geographic index, wage index, and cost of living index.
    B. fee-for-service, per diem payment, and capitation.
    C. conversion factor, CMS weight, and hospital-specific rate.
    D. physician work, practice expense, and malpractice insurance expense.

REFERENCE: Green, p 833

6. The prospective payment system used to reimburse hospitals for Medicare hospital outpatients is called
   A. APGs.
   B. RBRVS.
   C. APCs.
   D. MS-DRGs.

REFERENCE: Green and Rowell, p 28
                      Green, p 830
                      Kuehn, p 65
                      Schraffenberger and Kuehn, p 196

7. A patient was seen by Dr. Zachary. The charge for the office visit was $125. The Medicare beneficiary had already met his deductible. The Medicare fee schedule amount is $100. Dr. Zachary does not accept assignment. The office manager will apply a practice termed as "balance billing," which means that the patient is
   A. financially liable for the Medicare fee schedule amount.
   B. financially liable for charges in excess of the Medicare fee schedule, up to a limit.
   C. not financially liable for any amount.
   D. financially liable for only the deductible.

REFERENCE: Green and Rowell, pp 64–65
                      Johns, p 326
                      LaTour and Eichenwald-Maki, p 405

8. The prospective payment system based on resource utilization groups (RUGs) is used for reimbursement to _____ for patients with Medicare.
   A. freestanding ambulatory surgery centers
   B. hospital-based outpatients
   C. intermediate care facilities
   D. skilled nursing facilities

REFERENCE: Green and Rowell, p 27
                      Schraffenberger and Kuehn, p 212

9. The _____ is a statement sent to the provider to explain payments made by third-party payers.
   A. remittance advice
   B. advance beneficiary notice
   C. attestation statement
   D. acknowledgment notice

REFERENCE: Green, p 853
                      Green and Rowell, pp 8, 87, 79
                      Kuehn, p 11

10. How many major diagnostic categories are there in the MS-DRG system?
   A. 100
   B. 2,000
   C. 80
   D. 25

REFERENCE: Scott, p 37
                      Kuehn, pp 54–55

11. The computer-to-computer transfer of data between providers and third-party payers in a data format agreed upon by both parties is called
    A. HIPPA (Health Insurance Portability and Accountability Act).
    B. electronic data interchange (EDI).
    C. health information exchange (HIE).
    D. health data exchange (HDE).

REFERENCE: Green and Rowell, p 76

12. A computer software program that assigns appropriate MS-DRGs according to the information provided for each episode of care is called a(n)
    A. encoder.   C. grouper.
    B. case-mix analyzer.   D. scrubber.

REFERENCE: Casto and Layman, p 128
               Kuehn, p 21
               Scott, p 32

13. The standard claim form used by hospitals to request reimbursement for inpatient and outpatient procedures performed or services provided is called the
    A. UB-04.   C. CMS-1491.
    B. CMS-1500.   D. CMS-1600.

REFERENCE: Green and Rowell, pp 391–392
               Scott, p 76
               Kuehn, pp 17–18

14. Under ASCs, when multiple procedures are performed during the same surgical session, a payment reduction is applied. The procedure in the highest level group is reimbursed at _____ and all remaining procedures are reimbursed at _____.
    A. 50%, 25%   C. 100%, 25%
    B. 100%, 50%   D. 100%, 75%

REFERENCE: Casto and Layman, p 192

15. The _____ refers to a statement sent to the patient to show how much the provider billed, how much Medicare reimbursed the provider, and what the patient must pay the provider.
    A. Medicare summary notice   C. advance beneficiary notice
    B. remittance advice   D. coordination of benefits

REFERENCE: Green and Rowell, pp 380–382
               Johns, pp 343–344
               LaTour and Eichenwald-Maki, pp 401–403

16. Currently, which prospective payment system is used to determine the payment to the physician for outpatient surgery performed on a Medicare patient?
    A. MS-DRGs   C. RBRVS
    B. APGs   D. ASCs

REFERENCE: Schraffenberger and Kuehn, p 210
               Green, p 833

17. Which of the following best describes the situation of a provider who agrees to accept assignment for Medicare Part B services?
    A. The provider is reimbursed at 15% above the allowed charge.
    B. The provider is paid according to the Medicare Physician Fee Schedule (MPFS) plus 10%.
    C. The provider cannot bill the patients for the balance between the MPFS amount and the total charges.
    D. The provider is a nonparticipating provider.

REFERENCE: Green and Rowell, pp 64–65

18. When the MS-DRG payment received by the hospital is lower than the actual charges for providing the inpatient services for a patient with Medicare, then the hospital
    A. makes a profit.
    B. can bill the patient for the difference.
    C. absorbs the loss.
    D. can bill Medicare for the difference.

REFERENCE: LaTour and Eichenwald-Maki, p 390

19. Under ASCs, bilateral procedures are reimbursed at _____ of the payment rate for their group.
    A. 50%   C. 200%
    B. 100%   D. 150%

REFERENCE: Casto and Layman, p 192

Use the following table to answer questions 20 through 23.

Plantation Hospital's TOP 10 MS-DRGs

MS-DRG	Description	Number of Patients	CMS Relative Weight
470	Major joint replacement or reattachment of lower extremity w/o MCC	2,750	1.9871
392	Esophagitis, gastroent & misc. digestive disorders w/o MCC	2,200	0.7121
194	Simple pneumonia & pleurisy w CC	1,150	1.0235
247	Perc cardiovasc proc 2 drug-eluting stent w/o MCC	900	2.1255
293	Heart failure & shock w/o CC/MCC	850	0.8765
313	Chest pain	650	0.5489
292	Heart failure & shock w CC	550	1.0134
690	Kidney & urinary tract infections w/o MCC	400	0.8000
192	Chronic obstructive pulmonary disease w/o CC/MCC	300	0.8145
871	Septicemia w/o MV 96+ hours w MCC	250	1.7484

20. The case-mix index (CMI) for the top 10 MS-DRGs above is
    A. 1.164.   C. 0.782.
    B. 1.278.   D. 1.097.

REFERENCE: Casto and Layman, p 119
               Johns, p 324
               Kuehn, pp 53–54

21. Which individual MS-DRGs has the highest reimbursement?
   A. 247
   B. 470
   C. 871
   D. 293
REFERENCE: Casto and Layman, p 119
                Johns, p 324

22. Based on this patient volume, during this time period, the MS-DRG that brings in the highest "total" reimbursement to the hospital is
   A. 470.
   B. 247.
   C. 392.
   D. 871.
REFERENCE: Casto and Layman, p 119
                Johns, p 324

23. Based on this patient volume, the MS-DRG that brings in the highest total profit to the hospital is
   A. 470.
   B. 247.
   C. 392.
   D. It cannot be determined from this information.
REFERENCE: Casto and Layman, p 119
                Johns, p 324

24. The Health Insurance Portability and Accountability Act (HIPAA) requires the retention of health insurance claims and accounting records for a minimum of ____ years, unless state law specifies a longer period.
   A. six
   B. five
   C. seven
   D. ten
REFERENCE: Green and Rowell, p 114

25. ____ is an act that represents a crime against payers or other health care programs (e.g., Medicare), or attempts or conspiracies to commit those crimes.
   A. Fraud
   B. Whistle-blowing
   C. Abuse
   D. Assault
REFERENCE: Green and Bowie, p 323

26. These are assigned to every HCPCS/CPT code under the Medicare hospital outpatient prospective payment system to identify how the service or procedure described by the code would be paid.
   A. geographic practice cost indices
   B. major diagnostic categories
   C. minimum data set
   D. payment status indicator
REFERENCE: Casto and Layman, pp 175–176, 178, 183, 186
                Green and Rowell, pp 373–374

27. The term used to indicate that the service or procedure is reasonable and necessary for the diagnosis or treatment of illness or injury consistent with generally accepted standards of care is
   A. appropriateness.
   B. evidence-based medicine.
   C. benchmarking.
   D. medical necessity.
REFERENCE: Green and Rowell, pp 4, 146

28. This law prohibits a physician from referring Medicare patients to clinical laboratory services where the doctor or a member of their family has a financial interest.
    A. the False Claims Act
    B. the Civil Monetary Penalties Act
    C. the Federal Antikickback Statute
    D. the Stark I Law

REFERENCE: Green and Bowie, p 325
            Johns, pp 322–324

29. ____ are errors in medical care that are clearly identifiable, preventable, and serious in their consequences for patients.
    A. Sentinel events
    B. Adverse preventable events
    C. Never events
    D. Potential compensable events

REFERENCE: Green and Bowie, p 326

30. When a provider, in order to increase their reimbursement, reports codes to a payer that are not supported by documentation in the medical record, this is called
    A. fraud.
    B. abuse.
    C. unbundling.
    D. hypercoding.

REFERENCE: Green and Bowie, p 323

31. What prospective payment system reimburses the provider according to prospectively determined rates for a 60-day episode of care?
    A. home health resource groups
    B. inpatient rehabilitation facility
    C. long-term care Medicare severity diagnosis-related groups
    D. the skilled nursing facility prospective payment system

REFERENCE: Green and Bowie, p 313

32. If the Medicare nonPAR approved payment amount is $128.00 for a proctoscopy, what is the total Medicare approved payment amount for a doctor who does not accept assignment, applying the limiting charge for this procedure?
    A. $140.80   C. $192.00
    B. $143.00   D. $147.20

REFERENCE: Green and Rowell, pp 64–65

33. Under the inpatient prospective payment system (IPPS), there is a 3-day payment window (formerly referred to as the 72-hour rule). This rule requires that outpatient preadmission services that are provided by a hospital up to three calendar days prior to a patient's inpatient admission be covered by the IPPS MS-DRG payment for
   A. diagnostic services.
   B. therapeutic (or nondiagnostic) services whereby the inpatient principal diagnosis code (ICD-9-CM) exactly matches the code used for preadmission services.
   C. therapeutic (or nondiagnostic) services whereby the inpatient principal diagnosis code (ICD-9-CM) does not match the code used for preadmission services.
   D. both A and B.

REFERENCE: Green, p 826
                  Green and Rowell, pp 371–372
                  Green and Bowie, p 313

34. A new initiative by the government to eliminate fraud and abuse and recover overpayments involves the use of _____. Charts are audited to identify Medicare overpayments and underpayments. These entities are paid based on a percentage of money they identify and collect on behalf of the government.
   A. Clinical Data Abstraction Centers (CDAC)
   B. Quality Improvement Organizations (QIO)
   C. Medicare Code Editors (MCE)
   D. Recovery Audit Contractors (RAC)

REFERENCE: Scott, p 119
                  Green, p 818
                  Kuehn, pp 23, 96

35. A discharge in which the patient was discharged from the inpatient rehabilitation facility and returned within three calendar days (prior to midnight on the third day) is called a(n)
   A. interrupted stay.
   B. transfer.
   C. per diem.
   D. qualified discharge.

REFERENCE: Casto and Layman, p 226
                  Scott, pp 68–69

36. In a global payment methodology, which is sometimes applied to radiological and similar types of procedures that involve professional and technical components, all of the following are part of the "technical" components EXCEPT
   A. radiological equipment.
   B. physician services.
   C. radiological supplies.
   D. support services.

REFERENCE: Johns, p 318
                  LaTour and Eichenwald-Maki, p 387
                  Green and Rowell, p 320

37. Changes in case-mix index (CMI) may be attributed to all of the following factors EXCEPT
   A. changes in medical staff composition.
   B. changes in coding rules.
   C. changes in services offered.
   D. changes in coding productivity.

REFERENCE: Schraffenberger and Kuehn, pp 484–485

38. This prospective payment system replaced the Medicare physician payment system of "customary, prevailing, and reasonable (CPR)" charges whereby physicians were reimbursed according to their historical record of the charge for the provision of each service.
    A. Medicare Physician Fee Schedule (MPFS)
    B. Medicare Severity-Diagnosis Related Groups (MS-DRGs)
    C. Global payment
    D. Capitation

REFERENCE: Green, p 833
               Green and Rowell, pp 379–380
               Kuehn, pp 77–78

39. CMS-identified "Hospital-Acquired Conditions" mean that when a particular diagnosis is not "present on admission," CMS determines it to be
    A. medically necessary.
    B. reasonably preventable.
    C. a valid comorbidity.
    D. the principal diagnosis.

REFERENCE: Kuehn, pp 59–61
               LaTour and Eichenwald-Maki, p 391

40. This process involves the gathering of charge documents from all departments within the facility that have provided services to patients. The purpose is to make certain that all charges are coded and entered into the billing system.
    A. precertification
    B. insurance verification
    C. charge capturing
    D. revenue cycle

REFERENCE: Diamond, p 9

41. The Correct Coding Initiative (CCI) edits contain a listing of codes under two columns titled "comprehensive codes" and "component codes." According to the CCI edits, when a provider bills Medicare for a procedure that appears in both columns for the same beneficiary on the same date of service
    A. code only the component code.
    B. do not code either one.
    C. code only the comprehensive code.
    D. code both the comprehensive code and the component code.

REFERENCE: Green, pp 372–375
               Green and Rowell, pp 24, 111, 125

42. The following type of hospital is considered excluded when it applies for and receives a waiver from CMS. This means that the hospital does not participate in the inpatient prospective payment system (IPPS)
    A. rehabilitation hospital
    B. long-term care hospital
    C. psychiatric hospital
    D. cancer hospital

REFERENCE: Green, p 825

43. These are financial protections to ensure that certain types of facilities (e.g., children's hospitals) recoup all of their losses due to the differences in their APC payments and the pre-APC payments.
   A. limiting charge
   B. indemnity insurance
   C. hold harmless
   D. pass through

REFERENCE: Casto and Layman, p 174

44. LCDs and NCDs are review policies that describe the circumstances of coverage for various types of medical treatment. They advise physicians which services Medicare considers reasonable and necessary and may indicate the need for an advance beneficiary notice. They are developed by the Centers for Medicare and Medicaid Services (CMS) and Medicare Administrative Contractors. LCD and NCD are acronyms that stand for
   A. local covered determinations and noncovered determinations.
   B. local coverage determinations and national coverage determinations.
   C. list of covered decisions and noncovered decisions.
   D. local contractor's decisions and national contractor's decisions.

REFERENCE: Green, p 744
              Green and Rowell, pp 418–419
              Scott, p 23

Use the following table to answer questions 45 through 50.

EXAMPLE OF A CHARGE DESCRIPTION MASTER (CDM) FILE LAYOUT

Charge Code	Item Description	General Ledger Key	HCPCS Code		Charges	Revenue Code	Activity Date
			Medicare	Medicaid			
49683105	CT scan; head; w/out contrast	3	70450	70450	500.00	0351	1/1/2013
49683106	CT scan; head; with contrast	3	70460	70460	675.00	0351	1/1/2013

45. This information is printed on the UB-04 claim form to represent the cost center (e.g., lab, radiology, cardiology, respiratory, etc.) for the department in which the item is provided. It is used for Medicare billing.
   A. HCPCS
   B. revenue code
   C. charge code
   D. general ledger key

REFERENCE: Green, p 839
              Green and Rowell, pp 386–387
              Schraffenberger and Kuehn, pp 225–226

46. This information is used because it provides a uniform system of identifying procedures, services, or supplies. Multiple columns can be available for various financial classes.
   A. HCPCS code
   B. revenue code
   C. general ledger key
   D. charge code

REFERENCE: Green, p 839
              Green and Rowell, pp 386–387
              Schraffenberger and Kuehn, pp 226–227

47. This information provides a narrative name of the services provided. This information should be presented in a clear and concise manner. When possible, the narratives from the HCPCS/CPT book should be utilized.
    A. general ledger key
    B. HCPCS
    C. item description/service description
    D. revenue code

REFERENCE: Green, p 839
             Green and Rowell, pp 386–387
             Schraffenberger and Kuehn, p 225

48. This information is the numerical identification of the service or supply. Each item has a unique number with a prefix that indicates the department number (the number assigned to a specific ancillary department) and an item number (the number assigned by the accounting department or the business office) for a specific procedure or service represented on the chargemaster.
    A. charge code/service code
    B. HCPCS code
    C. revenue code
    D. general ledger key

REFERENCE: Green, p 839
             Green and Rowell, pp 386–387
             Schraffenberger and Kuehn, p 225

49. This information is used to assign each item to a particular section of the general ledger in a particular facility's accounting section. Reports can be generated from this information to include statistics related to volume in terms of numbers, dollars, and payer types.
    A. general ledger key
    B. charge code
    C. revenue code
    D. HCPCS code

REFERENCE: Schraffenberger and Kuehn, p 225

50. Under APCs, the patient is responsible for paying the coinsurance amount based upon ____ of the national median charge for the services rendered.
    A. 50%
    B. 15%
    C. 20%
    D. 80%

REFERENCE: Green and Bowie, p 314

51. ____ is a program that pays for medical assistance to individuals and families with low incomes and limited financial resources.
    A. Medigap
    B. Medicare Part A
    C. Medicaid
    D. Medicare Part B

REFERENCE: Johns, p 305

52. The DNFB report includes all patients who have been discharged from the facility but for whom, for one reason or another, the billing process is not complete.
    A. diagnosis not finally balanced
    B. days not fiscally balanced
    C. dollars not fully billed
    D. discharged not final billed

REFERENCE: Schraffenberger and Kuehn, p 461

53. The limiting charge is a percentage limit on fees specified by legislation that the nonparticipating physician may bill Medicare beneficiaries above the nonPAR fee schedule amount. The limiting charge is
A. 10%.
B. 15%.
C. 20%.
D. 50%.

REFERENCE: Green and Rowell, pp 380–383

Use the following case scenario to answer questions 54 through 58.

A patient with Medicare is seen in the physician's office.
The total charge for this office visit is $250.00.
The patient has previously paid his deductible under Medicare Part B.
The PAR Medicare fee schedule amount for this service is $200.00.
The nonPAR Medicare fee schedule amount for this service is $190.00.

54. The patient is financially liable for the coinsurance amount, which is
A. 80%.
B. 100%.
C. 20%.
D. 15%.

REFERENCE: Green and Rowell, pp 380–383

55. If this physician is a participating physician who accepts assignment for this claim, the total amount the physician will receive is
A. $200.00.
B. $250.00.
C. $218.50.
D. $190.00.

REFERENCE: Green and Rowell, pp 380–383

56. If this physician is a nonparticipating physician who does NOT accept assignment for this claim, the total amount the physician will receive is
A. $250.00.
B. $200.00.
C. $218.50.
D. $190.00.

REFERENCE: Green and Rowell, pp 380–383

57. If this physician is a participating physician who accepts assignment for this claim, the total amount of the patient's financial liability (out-of-pocket expense) is
A. $200.00.
B. $40.00.
C. $160.00.
D. $30.00.

REFERENCE: Green and Rowell, pp 380–383

58. If this physician is a nonparticipating physician who does NOT accept assignment for this claim, the total amount of the patient's financial liability (out-of-pocket expense) is
A. $66.50.
B. $38.00.
C. $190.00.
D. $152.00.

REFERENCE: Green and Rowell, pp 380–383

59. A fiscal year is a yearly accounting period. It is the 12-month period on which a budget is planned. The federal fiscal year is
A. October 1st through September 30 of the next year.
B. January 1st through December 31.
C. July 1st through the June 30 of the next year.
D. April 1st through March 31 of the next year.

REFERENCE: Casto and Layman, p 299

60. There are times when documentation is incomplete or insufficient to support the diagnoses found in the chart. The most common way of communicating with the physician for answers is by
    A. e-mailing physicians.
    B. using physician query forms.
    C. calling the physician's office.
    D. leaving notes in the chart.

REFERENCE: Green, p 16
                      Scott, pp 189–199

61. Under APCs, payment status indicator "X" means
    A. ancillary services.
    B. clinic or emergency department visit (medical visits).
    C. significant procedure, multiple procedure reduction applies.
    D. significant procedure, not discounted when multiple.

REFERENCE: Casto and Layman, p 176
                      Diamond, p 337
                      LaTour and Eichenwald-Maki, p 393

62. Under APCs, payment status indicator "V" means
    A. ancillary services.
    B. clinic or emergency department visit (medical visits).
    C. inpatient procedure.
    D. significant procedure, not discounted when multiple.

REFERENCE: Casto and Layman, p 176
                      Diamond, p 337
                      LaTour and Eichenwald-Maki, p 393

63. Under APCs, payment status indicator "S" means
    A. ancillary services.
    B. clinic or emergency department visit (medical visits).
    C. significant procedure, multiple procedure reduction applies.
    D. significant procedure, multiple procedure reduction does not apply.

REFERENCE: Casto and Layman, p 176
                      Diamond, p 337
                      Green and Rowell, pp 373–374
                      LaTour and Eichenwald-Maki, p 393

64. Under APCs, payment status indicator "T" means
    A. ancillary services.
    B. clinic or emergency department visit (medical visits).
    C. significant procedure, multiple procedure reduction applies.
    D. significant procedure, not discounted when multiple.

REFERENCE: Casto and Layman, p 176
                      Diamond, p 337
                      Green, p 831
                      Green and Rowell, pp 373–374
                      LaTour and Eichenwald-Maki, p 393

65. Under APCs, payment status indicator "C" means
    A. ancillary services.
    B. inpatient procedures/services.
    C. significant procedure, multiple procedure reduction applies.
    D. significant procedure, not discounted when multiple.

REFERENCE: Casto and Layman, p 176
         Diamond, p 337
         LaTour and Eichenwald-Maki, p 393

66. This is a 10-digit, intelligence-free, numeric identifier designed to replace all previous provider legacy numbers. This number identifies the physician universally to all payers. This number is issued to all HIPAA-covered entities. It is mandatory on the CMS-1500 and UB-04 claim forms.
    A. National Practitioner Databank (NPD)
    B. Universal Physician Number (UPN)
    C. Master Patient Index (MPI)
    D. National Provider Identifier (NPI)

REFERENCE: Green and Rowell, pp 29, 126

67. In the managed care industry, there are specific reimbursement concepts, such as "capitation." All of the following statements are true in regard to the concept of "capitation," EXCEPT
    A. each service is paid based on the actual charges.
    B. the volume of services and their expense do not affect reimbursement.
    C. capitation means paying a fixed amount per member per month.
    D. capitation involves a group of physicians or an individual physician.

REFERENCE: Casto and Layman, p 102
         Green and Rowell, p 45

68. When billing for the admitting physician for a patient who is admitted to the hospital as an inpatient, one must use a CPT Evaluation and Management code based on the level of care provided.

These are the codes to be selected from for initial hospital care.

99221 Initial hospital care, per day, for the evaluation and management of a patient, which requires these three key components:
- a detailed or comprehensive history
- a detailed or comprehensive examination and
- medical decision making that is straightforward or of low complexity

99222 Initial hospital care, per day, for the evaluation and management of a patient, which requires these three key components:
- a comprehensive history
- a comprehensive examination and
- medical decision making of moderate complexity

99223 Initial hospital care, per day, for the evaluation and management of a patient, which requires these three key components:
- a comprehensive history
- a comprehensive examination and
- medical decision making of high complexity

The following statement is true.
    A. This code can be used only once per hospitalization.
    B. This code can be used by the admitting physician or consulting physician.
    C. This code can be used for patients admitted to observation status.
    D. This code can be used by the hospital to bill for facility services.

REFERENCE: Green and Rowell, pp 290–304

69. This document is published by the Office of Inspector General (OIG) every year. It details the OIG's focus for Medicare fraud and abuse for that year. It gives health care providers an indication of general and specific areas that are targeted for review. It can be found on the Internet on CMS' Web site.
    A. the OIG's Evaluation and Management Documentation Guidelines
    B. the OIG's Model Compliance Plan
    C. the Federal Register
    D. the OIG's Workplan

REFERENCE: Johns, p 360

70. Accounts Receivable (A/R) refers to
    A. cases that have not yet been paid.
    B. the amount the hospital was paid.
    C. cases that have been paid.
    D. denials that have been returned to the hospital.

REFERENCE: Schraffenberger and Kuehn, p 458

71. The following coding system(s) is/are utilized in the MS-DRG prospective payment methodology for assignment and proper reimbursement.
    A. HCPCS/CPT codes
    B. ICD-9-CM codes
    C. both HCPCS/CPT codes and ICD-9-CM codes
    D. none of the above

REFERENCE: Green, p 828
               Green and Rowell, p 371
               Johns, p 323
               Kuehn, p 9

72. The following coding system(s) is/are utilized in the Inpatient Psychiatric Facilities (IPFs) prospective payment methodology for assignment and proper reimbursement.
    A. HCPCS/CPT codes
    B. ICD-9-CM codes
    C. both HCPCS/CPT codes and ICD-9-CM codes
    D. none of the above

REFERENCE: Green, p 832
               Johns, p 339

73. An Advance Beneficiary Notice (ABN) is a document signed by the
    A. utilization review coordinator indicating that the patient stay is not medically necessary.
    B. physician advisor indicating that the patient's stay is denied.
    C. patient indicating whether he/she wants to receive services that Medicare probably will not pay for.
    D. provider indicating that Medicare will not pay for certain services.

REFERENCE: Green, p 334
               LaTour and Eichenwald-Maki, pp 405–406

74. CMS identified Hospital-Acquired Conditions (HACs). Some of these HACs include foreign objects retained after surgery, blood incompatibility, and catheter-associated urinary tract infection. The importance of the HAC payment provision is that the hospital
    A. will receive additional payment for these conditions when they are not present on admission.
    B. will not receive additional payment for these conditions when they are not present on admission.
    C. will receive additional payment for these conditions whether they are present on admission or not.
    D. will not receive additional payment for these conditions when they are present on admission.

REFERENCE: LaTour and Eichenwald-Maki, pp 390–391

75. Under Medicare Part B, all of the following statements are true and are applicable to nonparticipating physician providers, EXCEPT
    A. providers must file all Medicare claims.
    B. nonparticipating providers have a higher fee schedule than that for participating providers.
    C. fees are restricted to charging no more than the "limiting charge" on nonassigned claims.
    D. collections are restricted to only the deductible and coinsurance due at the time of service on an assigned claim.

REFERENCE: Green and Rowell, pp 380–383

76. Under Medicare, a beneficiary has lifetime reserve days. All of the following statements are true, EXCEPT
    A. the patient has a total of 60 lifetime reserve days.
    B. lifetime reserve days are usually reserved for use during the patient's final (terminal) hospital stay.
    C. lifetime reserve days are paid under Medicare Part B.
    D. lifetime reserve days are not renewable, meaning once a patient uses all of their lifetime reserve days, the patient is responsible for the total charges.

REFERENCE: Green and Rowell, pp 528–529

77. The term used to describe a diagram depicting grouper logic in assigning MS-DRGs is
    A. interrelationship diagram.   C. decision tree.
    B. case-mix index.   D. grouper hierarchy.

REFERENCE: Casto and Layman, p 124
              Schraffenberger and Kuehn, pp 198–200

78. Once all data are posted to a patient's account, the claim can be reviewed for accuracy and completeness. Many facilities have internal auditing systems. The auditing systems run each claim through a set of edits specifically designed for the various third-party payers. The auditing system identifies data that have failed edits and flags the claim for correction. These "internal" auditing systems are called
    A. scrubbers.   C. groupers.
    B. pricers.   D. encoders.

REFERENCE: Casto and Layman, p 252

79. To compute the reimbursement to a particular hospital for a particular MS-DRG, multiply the hospital's base payment rate by the
    A. conversion factor.
    B. case-mix index.
    C. geographic practice cost index.
    D. relative weight for the MS-DRG.

REFERENCE: Casto and Layman, p 128
               Green and Rowell, p 367

80. Under the APC methodology, discounted payments occur when
    A. there are two or more (multiple) procedures that are assigned to status indicator "T."
    B. there are two or more (multiple) procedures that are assigned to status indicator "S."
    C. modifier-73 is used to indicate a procedure is terminated after the patient is prepared but before anesthesia is started.
    D. both A and C.

REFERENCE: Green and Rowell, pp 373–374
               Schraffenberger and Kuehn, pp 207–209

81. This prospective payment system is for _____ and utilizes a Patient Assessment Instrument (PAI) to classify patients into case-mix groups (CMGs).
    A. skilled nursing facilities
    B. inpatient rehabilitation facilities
    C. home health agencies
    D. long-term acute care hospitals

REFERENCE: Green and Rowell, p 377
               Schraffenberger and Kuehn, p 213

82. Home Health Agencies (HHAs) utilize a data entry software system developed by the Centers for Medicare and Medicaid Services (CMS). This software is available to HHAs at no cost through the CMS Web site or on a CD-ROM.
    A. PACE (Patient Assessment and Comprehensive Evaluation)
    B. HAVEN (Home Assessment Validation and Entry)
    C. HHASS (Home Health Agency Software System)
    D. PEPP (Payment Error Prevention Program)

REFERENCE: Green and Rowell, p 367
               Johns, p 334
               LaTour and Eichenwald-Maki, p 395

83. This information is published by the Medicare Administrative Contractors (MACs) to describe when and under what circumstances Medicare will cover a service. The ICD-9-CM and CPT/HCPCS codes are listed in the memoranda.
    A. LCD (Local Coverage Determinations)
    B. SI/IS (Severity of Ilness/Intensity of Service Criteria)
    C. OSHA (Occupational Safety and Health Administration)
    D. PEPP (Payment Error Prevention Program)

REFERENCE: Green and Rowell, p 417
               Schraffenberger and Kuehn, p 461

84. The term "hard coding" refers to
    A. HCPCS/CPT codes that are coded by the coders.
    B. HPCS/CPT codes that appear in the hospital's chargemaster and will be included automatically on the patient's bill.
    C. ICD-9-CM codes that are coded by the coders.
    D. ICD-9-CM codes that appear in the hospital's chargemaster and that are automatically included on the patient's bill.

REFERENCE: Schraffenberger and Kuehn, pp 228–229

85. This is the amount collected by the facility for the services it bills.
    A. costs
    B. charges
    C. reimbursement
    D. contractual allowance

REFERENCE: Schraffenberger and Kuehn, pp 433–434

86. Assume the patient has already met his or her deductible and that the physician is a Medicare participating (PAR) provider. The physician's standard fee for the services provided is $120.00. Medicare's PAR fee is $60.00. How much reimbursement will the physician receive from Medicare?
    A. $120.00   C. $ 48.00
    B. $ 60.00   D. $ 96.00

REFERENCE: Green and Rowell, pp 380–383

87. This accounting method attributes a dollar figure to every input required to provide a service.
    A. cost accounting   C. reimbursement
    B. charge accounting   D. contractual allowance

REFERENCE: Schraffenberger and Kuehn, p 433

88. This is the amount the facility actually bills for the services it provides.
    A. costs   C. reimbursement
    B. charges   D. contractual allowance

REFERENCE: Schraffenberger and Kuehn, p 433

89. This is the difference between what is charged and what is paid.
    A. costs   C. reimbursement
    B. charges   D. contractual allowance

REFERENCE: Schraffenberger and Kuehn, p 433

90. When appropriate, under the outpatient PPS, a hospital can use this CPT code in place of, but not in addition to, a code for a medical visit or emergency department service.
    A. CPT Code 99291 (critical care)
    B. CPT Code 99358 (prolonged evaluation and management service)
    C. CPT Code 35001 (direct repair of aneurysm)
    D. CPT Code 50300 (donor nephrectomy)

REFERENCE: Kirchoff, p 42

91. To monitor timely claims processing in a hospital, a summary report of "patient receivables" is generated frequently. Aged receivables can negatively affect a facility's cash flow; therefore, to maintain the facility's fiscal integrity, the HIM manager must routinely analyze this report. Though this report has no standard title, it is often called the
    A. remittance advice.
    B. periodic interim payments.
    C. DNFB (discharged, no final bill).
    D. chargemaster.

REFERENCE: LaTour and Eichenwald-Maki, p 794

92. Assume the patient has already met his or her deductible and that the physician is a nonparticipating Medicare provider but does accept assignment. The standard fee for the services provided is $120.00. Medicare's PAR fee is $60.00 and Medicare's nonPAR fee is $57.00. How much reimbursement will the physician receive from Medicare?
    A. $120.00   C. $57.00
    B. $60.00   D. $45.60

REFERENCE: Green and Rowell, pp 58, 306, 308, 423–424, 459–462

93. CMS assigns one _____ to each APC and each _____ code.
    A. payment status indicator, HCPCS
    B. CPT code, HCPCS
    C. MS-DRG, CPT
    D. payment status indicator, ICD-9-CM

REFERENCE: Kirchoff, p 11

94. All of the following statements are true of MS-DRGs, EXCEPT
    A. a patient claim may have multiple MS-DRGs.
    B. the MS-DRG payment received by the hospital may be lower than the actual cost of providing the services.
    C. special circumstances can result in an outlier payment to the hospital.
    D. there are several types of hospitals that are excluded from the Medicare inpatient PPS.

REFERENCE: Green and Rowell, pp 367–370
                Johns, pp 321–324
                LaTour and Eichenwald-Maki, pp 387–390

95. This program, formerly called CHAMPUS (Civilian Health and Medical Program—Uniformed Services), is a health care program for active members of the military and other qualified family members.
    A. TRICARE
    B. CHAMPVA
    C. Indian Health Service
    D. workers' compensation

REFERENCE: Green and Rowell, p 602
               Johns, p 736

96. Under Medicare Part B, Medicare participating (PAR) providers
    A. will be able to collect his or her total charges.
    B. agree to charge no more than 15% (limiting charge) over the allowed charge from the nonPAR fee schedule.
    C. accept, as payment in full, the allowed charge from the PAR fee schedule.
    D. agree to charge no more than 10% (limiting charge) over the allowed charge from the nonPAR fee schedule.

REFERENCE: Green and Rowell, pp 380–383

97. Regarding hospital emergency department and hospital outpatient evaluation and management CPT code assignment, which statement is true?
    A. Each facility is accountable for developing and implementing its own methodology.
    B. The level of service codes reported by the facility must match those reported by the physician.
    C. Each facility must use the same methodology used by physician coders based on the history, examination, and medical decision-making components.
    D. Each facility must use acuity sheets with acuity levels and assign points for each service performed.

REFERENCE: Diamond, pp 285–287

98. CMS adjusts the Medicare Severity DRGs and the reimbursement rates every
    A. calendar year beginning January 1.
    B. quarter.
    C. month.
    D. fiscal year beginning October 1.

REFERENCE: Johns, p 323

99. In calculating the fee for a physician's reimbursement, the three relative value units are each multiplied by the
    A. geographic practice cost indices.
    B. national conversion factor.
    C. usual and customary fees for the service.
    D. cost of living index for the particular region.

REFERENCE: Green, p 833
               Green and Rowell, pp 379–380

100. If a participating provider's usual fee for a service is $700.00 and Medicare's allowed amount is $450.00, what amount is written off by the physician?
    A. none of it is written off
    B. $250.00
    C. $340.00
    D. $391.00

REFERENCE: Green and Rowell, pp 380–383

101. Health plans that use _____ reimbursement methods issue lump-sum payments to providers to compensate them for all the health care services delivered to a patient for a specific illness and/or over a specific period of time.
     A. episode-of-care (EOC)   C. fee-for-service
     B. capitation   D. bundled

REFERENCE: Johns, p 317

102. _____ offers voluntary, supplemental medical insurance to help pay for physician's services, outpatient hospital services, medical services, and medical-surgical supplies not covered by the hospitalization plan.
     A. Medicare Part A
     B. Medicare Part B
     C. Medicare Part C
     D. Medicare Part D

REFERENCE: Kirchoff, p 296

103. Commercial insurance plans usually reimburse health care providers under some type of _____ payment system, whereas the federal Medicare program uses some type of _____ payment system.
     A. prospective, retrospective   C. retrospective, prospective
     B. retrospective, concurrent   D. prospective, concurrent

REFERENCE: Green and Rowell, pp 360–361
               Johns, p 315

104. The difference between a rejected claim and a denied claim is that
     A. a rejected claim is sent back to the provider, errors may be corrected and the claim resubmitted.
     B. a denied claim is sent back to the provider, errors may be corrected and the claim resubmitted.
     C. a rejected claim may be appealed, but a denied claim may not be appealed.
     D. if a procedure or service is unauthorized, the claim will be rejected, not denied.

REFERENCE: Green and Rowell, pp 87–88

105. Some services are performed by a nonphysician practitioner (such as a Physician Assistant). These services are an integral yet incidental component of a physician's treatment. A physician must have personally performed an initial visit and must remain actively involved in the continuing care. Medicare requires direct supervision for these services to be billed. This is called
     A. "Technical component" billing.
     B. "Assignment" billing.
     C. "Incident to" billing.
     D. "Assistant" billing.

REFERENCE: Green and Rowell, p 385

106. The term used to describe the information-gathering fields on the UB-04 billing form is
     A. form locator.
     B. data field.
     C. field box.
     D. data locator.

REFERENCE: Diamond, p 100

107. The following services are excluded under the Hospital Outpatient Prospective Payment System (OPPS) Ambulatory Payment Classification (APC) methodology.
    A. surgical procedures
    B. clinical lab services
    C. clinic/emergency visits
    D. radiology/radiation therapy

REFERENCE: Diamond, p 333

108. A HIPPS (Health Insurance Prospective Payment System) code is a five-character alphanumeric code. A HIPPS code is used by
    A. ambulatory surgery centers (ASC).
    B. home health agencies (HHA).
    C. inpatient rehabilitation facilities (IRF).
    D. B and C.

REFERENCE: Casto and Layman, pp 226, 239–241
              Green and Rowell, p 367

109. The Centers for Medicare and Medicaid Services (CMS) will make an adjustment to the MS-DRG payment for certain conditions that were not present on hospital admission but were acquired during the hospital stay. Therefore, hospitals are required to report an indicator for each diagnosis. This indicator is referred to as
    A. a sentinel event.
    B. a payment status indicator.
    C. a hospital acquired condition.
    D. present on admission.

REFERENCE: Casto and Layman, pp 283–284
              Kuehn, pp 59–61

110. A patient is admitted for a diagnostic workup for cachexia. The final diagnosis is malignant neoplasm of lung with metastasis. The present on admission (POA) indicator is
    A. Y = Present at the time of inpatient admission.
    B. N = Not present at the time of inpatient admission.
    C. U = Documentation is insufficient to determine if condition was present at the time of admission.
    D. W = Provider is unable to clinically determine if condition was present at the time of admission.

REFERENCE: Casto and Layman, p 283
              Kuehn, pp 59–61
              Green, p 828
              LaTour and Eichenwald-Maki, p 391

111. A patient undergoes outpatient surgery. During the recovery period, the patient develops atrial fibrillation and is subsequently admitted to the hospital as an inpatient. The present on admission (POA) indicator is
    A. Y = Present at the time of inpatient admission.
    B. N = Not present at the time of inpatient admission.
    C. U = Documentation is insufficient to determine if condition was present at the time of admission.
    D. W = Provider is unable to clinically determine if condition was present at the time of admission.

REFERENCE: Casto and Layman, p 283
                Green, p 828
                Kuehn, pp 59–61
                LaTour and Eichenwald-Maki, p 391

112. A patient is admitted to the hospital for a coronary artery bypass surgery. Postoperatively, he develops a pulmonary embolism. The present on admission (POA) indicator is
    A. Y = Present at the time of inpatient admission.
    B. N = Not present at the time of inpatient admission.
    C. U = Documentation is insufficient to determine if condition was present at the time of admission.
    D. W = Provider is unable to clinically determine if condition was present at the time of admission.

REFERENCE: Casto and Layman, p 283
                Green, p 828
                Kuehn, pp 59–61
                LaTour and Eichenwald-Maki, p 391

113. The nursing initial assessment upon admission documents the presence of a decubitus ulcer. There is no mention of the decubitus ulcer in the physician documentation until several days after admission. The present on admission (POA) indicator is
    A. Y = Present at the time of inpatient admission.
    B. N = Not present at the time of inpatient admission.
    C. U = Documentation is insufficient to determine if condition was present at the time of admission.
    D. W = Provider is unable to clinically determine if condition was present at the time of admission.

REFERENCE: Casto and Layman, p 283
                Green, p 828
                Kuehn, pp 59–61
                LaTour and Eichenwald-Maki, p 391

114. The present on admission (POA) indicator is required to be assigned to the _____ diagnosis(es) for _____ claims on _____ admissions.
    A. principal and secondary, Medicare, inpatient
    B. principal, all, inpatient
    C. principal and secondary, all, inpatient and outpatient
    D. principal, Medicare, inpatient and outpatient

REFERENCE: Casto and Layman, p 283
             Green, p 828
             Kuehn, pp 59–61
             LaTour and Eichenwald-Maki, p 391

Answer Key for Medical Billing and Reimbursement Systems

	ANSWER	EXPLANATION
1.	C	
2.	B	
3.	A	
4.	D	
5.	D	
6.	C	
7.	B	
8.	D	
9.	A	
10.	D	
11.	B	
12.	C	
13.	A	The UB-04 is used by hospitals. The CMS-1500 is used by physicians and other noninstitutional providers and suppliers. The CMS-1491 is used by ambulance services.
14.	B	
15.	A	
16.	C	
17.	C	Since the provider accepts assignment, he will accept the Medicare Physician Fee Schedule (MPFS) payment as payment in full.
18.	C	
19.	D	
20.	B	12781.730/10,000 = 1.278

MS-DRG	Description	Number of Patients	CMS Relative Weight	Total CMS Relative Weight
470	Major joint replacement or reattachment of lower extremity w/o MCC	2,750	1.9871	5464.525
392	Esophagitis, gastroent & misc. digestive disorders w/o MCC	2,200	0.7121	1566.620
194	Simple pneumonia & pleurisy w CC	1,150	1.0235	1177.025
247	Perc cardiovasc proc 2 drug-eluting stent w/o MCC	900	2.1255	1912.950
293	Heart failure & shock w/o CC/MCC	850	0.8765	745.025
313	Chest pain	650	0.5489	356.785
292	Heart failure & shock w CC	550	1.0134	557.350
690	Kidney & urinary tract infections w/o MCC	400	0.8000	320.000
192	Chronic obstructive pulmonary disease w/o CC/MCC	300	0.8145	244.350
871	Septicemia w/o MV 96+ hours w MCC	250	1.7484	437.100
	Total	10,000		12781.730
	Case-Mix Index Total CMS Relative Weights (12781.730) divided by (10,000) patients			1.278

Answer Key for Medical Billing and Reimbursement Systems

ANSWER   EXPLANATION

21.   A (See table on answer key under question 20.)
22.   A (See table on answer key under question 20.)
23.   D Total profit cannot be determined from this information alone. A comparison of the total charges on the bills and the PPS amount (reimbursement amount) that the hospital would receive for each MS-DRG could identify the total profit.
24.   A
25.   A
26.   D
27.   D
28.   D
29.   C
30.   B
31.   A
32.   D The limiting charge is 15% above Medicare's approved payment amount for doctors who do NOT accept assignment ($128.00 × 1.15 = $147.20).
33.   D
34.   D
35.   A
36.   B
37.   D Coding productivity will not directly affect CMI. Inaccuracy or poor coding quality can affect CMI.
38.   A The Medicare Physician Fee Schedule (MPFS) reimburses providers according to predetermined rates assigned to services.
39.   B
40.   C
41.   C
42.   D Cancer hospitals can apply for and receive waivers from the Centers for Medicare and Medicaid Services (CMS) and are therefore excluded from the inpatient prospective payment system (MS-DRGs). Rehabilitation hospitals are reimbursed under the Inpatient Rehabilitation Prospective Payment System (IRF PPS). Long-term care hospitals are reimbursed under the Long-Term Care Hospital Prospective Payment System (LTCH PPS). Skilled nursing facilities are reimbursed under the Skilled Nursing Facility Prospective Payment System (SNF PPS).
43.   C
44.   B
45.   B
46.   A
47.   C
48.   A
49.   A
50.   C
51.   C
52.   D
53.   B
54.   C

Answer Key for Medical Billing and Reimbursement Systems

ANSWER   EXPLANATION

55.   A   If a physician is a participating physician who accepts assignment, he will receive the lesser of "the total charges" or "the PAR Medicare fee schedule amount." In this case, the Medicare fee schedule amount is less; therefore, the total received by the physician is $200.00.

56.   C   If a physician is a nonparticipating physician who does not accept assignment, he can collect a maximum of 15% (the limiting charge) over the nonPAR Medicare fee schedule amount. In this case, the nonPAR Medicare fee schedule amount is $190.00 and 15% over this amount is $28.50; therefore, the total that he can collect is $218.50.

57.   B   The PAR Medicare fee schedule amount is $200.00. The patient has already met the deductible. Of the $200.00, the patient is responsible for 20% ($40.00). Medicare will pay 80% ($160.00). Therefore, the total financial liability for the patient is $40.00.

58.   A   If a physician is a nonparticipating physician who does not accept assignment, he may collect a maximum of 15% (the limiting charge) over the nonPAR Medicare fee schedule amount.

$190.00 = nonPAR Medicare schedule amount

$190.00 \times 0.20 = \underline{\$38.00}$ = patient liable for 20% coinsurance

$190.00 \times 0.80 = \underline{\$152.00}$ = Medicare pays 80%

$190.00 \times 0.15 = \underline{\$28.50}$ = 15% (limiting charge) over nonPAR Medicare fee schedule amount

Physician can balance bill and collect from the patient the difference between the nonPAR Medicare fee schedule amount and the total charge amount. Therefore, the patient's financial liability is $38.00 + 28.50 = $66.50.

59.   A

60.   B

61.   A   Under the APC system, there exists a list of status indicators (also called service indicators, payment status indicators, or payment indicators). This indicator is provided for every HCPCS/CPT code and identifies how the service or procedure would be paid (if covered) by Medicare for hospital outpatient visits.

62.   B   Under the APC system, there exists a list of status indicators (also called service indicators, payment status indicators, or payment indicators). This indicator is provided for every HCPCS/CPT code and identifies how the service or procedure would be paid (if covered) by Medicare for hospital outpatient visits.

63.   D   Under the APC system, there exists a list of status indicators (also called service indicators, payment status indicators, or payment indicators). This indicator is provided for every HCPCS/CPT code and identifies how the service or procedure would be paid (if covered) by Medicare for hospital outpatient visits. Payment Status Indicator (PSI) "S" means that if a patient has more than one CPT code with this PSI, none of the procedures will be discounted or reduced. They will all be paid at 100%.

64.   C   Under the APC system, there exists a list of status indicators (also called service indicators, payment status indicators, or payment indicators). This indicator is provided for every HCPCS/CPT code and identifies how the service or procedure would be paid (if covered) by Medicare for hospital outpatient visits. Payment Status Indicator (PSI) "T" means that if a patient has more than one CPT code with this PSI, the procedure with the highest weight will be paid at 100% and all others will be reduced or discounted and paid at 50%.

Answer Key for Medical Billing and Reimbursement Systems

ANSWER   EXPLANATION

65. B Under the APC system, there exists a list of status indicators (also called service indicators, payment status indicators, or payment indicators). This indicator is provided for every HCPCS/CPT code and identifies how the service or procedure would be paid (if covered) by Medicare for hospital outpatient visits.

66. D
67. A
68. A
69. D
70. A
71. B
72. B
73. C

74. B When these conditions are present on admission, the hospital may receive additional payment.

75. B Under Medicare Part B, Congress has mandated special incentives to increase the number of health care providers signing PAR (participating) agreements with Medicare. One of those incentives includes a 5% higher fee schedule for PAR providers than for nonPAR (nonparticipating) providers.

76. C Lifetime reserve days are applicable for hospital inpatient stays that are payable under Medicare Part A.

77. C
78. A

79. D Each hospital's prospective payment system (PPS) rate is a dollar amount based on that hospital's costs of operating as determined by several blended factors. This blended rate is multiplied by the MS-DRG's (relative) weight to calculate that hospital's reimbursement for a given MS-DRG. The (relative) weight is a number assigned to each MS-DRG published in the Federal Register, and it is used as a multiplier to determine reimbursement.

80. D Discounts are applied to those multiple procedures identified by CPT codes with status indicator "T" and also those CPT codes assigned with the modifier-73.

81. B
82. B
83. A Local Coverage Determinations (LCDs) were formerly called local medical review policies (LMRPs).

84. B
85. C
86. C The physician receives 80% of the MPFS amount ($48.00) from Medicare. (The remaining 20% ($12.00) is paid by the patient to the physician. The total amount paid is $60.00.)

87. A
88. B
89. D
90. A When a patient meets the definition of critical care, the hospital must use CPT Code 99291 to bill for outpatient encounters in which critical care services are furnished. This code is used instead of another E&M code.

Answer Key for Medical Billing and Reimbursement Systems

ANSWER   EXPLANATION

91.   C

92.   D   Since the physician is a nonparticipating physician, he will receive the nonPAR fee.
          The Medicare nonPAR fee is $57.00.
          Medicare will pay 80% of the nonPAR fee ($57.00 x 0.80 = $45.60).
          The patient will pay 20% of the nonPAR fee ($57.00 x 0.20 = $11.40).
          Since the physician is accepting assignment on this claim, he cannot charge the patient any
          more than the 20% co-payment. This question asked what Medicare would pay, which is
          $45.60.

93.   A

94.   A   Only one MS-DRG is assigned per inpatient hospitalization.

95.   A

96.   C

97.   A

98.   D

99.   A   After the three relative value units are each multiplied by the geographic practice cost
          indices, then this total is multiplied by the national conversion factor.

100. B   The participating physician agrees to accept Medicare's fee as payment in full; therefore,
          the physician would collect $450.00. The remainder ($700.00 – $450.00 = $250.00) is written
          off.

101. A

102. B

103. C

104. A

105. C

106. A

107. B

108. D   Inpatient Rehabilitation Facilities (IRF) reports the HIPPS (Health Insurance Prospective
          Payment System) code on the claim. The HIPPS code is a five-digit CMG (Case Mix
          Group). Therefore, the HIPPS code for a patient with tier 1 comorbidity and a CMG of 0109
          is B0109. Home Health Agencies (HHA) report the HIPPS code on the claim. The HIPPS
          code is a five-character alphanumeric code. The first character is the letter "H." The second,
          third, and fourth characters represent the HHRG (Home Health Resource Group). The fifth
          character represents what elements are computed or derived. Therefore, the HIPPS code
          for the HHRG C0F0S0 would be HAEJ1.

109. D

110. A   The malignant neoplasm was clearly present on admission, although it was not diagnosed
          until after the admission occurred.

111. A   The atrial fibrillation developed prior to a written order for inpatient admission; therefore,
          it was present at the time of inpatient admission.

112. B   The pulmonary embolism is an acute condition that was not present on admission because
          it developed after the patient was admitted and after the patient had surgery.

113. C   Query the physician as to whether the decubitus ulcer was present on admission or
          developed after admission.

114. A

REFERENCES

Casto, A. B., & Layman, E. (2011). *Principles of healthcare reimbursement* (3rd ed.). Chicago: American Health Information Management Association (AHIMA).

CMS Web site: http://www.cms.hhs.gov/home/Medicare.asp (This Web site provides links to pages containing official informational materials on all of the Medicare Fee-For-Service Payment Systems.)

Diamond, M. S. (2012) *Understanding hospital coding and billing: A worktext* (2nd ed.).Clifton Park, NY: Delmar Cengage Learning.

Green, M. A. (2012). *3-2-1-Code It!* (3rd ed.). Clifton Park, NY: Delmar Cengage Learning.

Green, M. A., & Rowell, J. C. (2011). *Understanding health insurance: A guide to billing and reimbursement* (10th ed.). Clifton Park, NY: Delmar Cengage Learning.

Green, M. A., & Bowie, M. J. (2011). *Essentials of health information management: Principles and practices* (2nd ed.). Clifton Park, NY: Delmar Cengage Learning.

Johns, M. L. (2011). *Health information management technology: An applied approach* (3rd ed.). Chicago: American Health Information Management Association (AHIMA).

Kirchoff, S. (2009). *Coding and reimbursement for hospital outpatient services.* Chicago: American Health Information Management Association (AHIMA).

Kuehn, L. (2010). *A practical approach to analyzing healthcare data.* Chicago: American Health Information Management Association (AHIMA).

LaTour, K., & Eichenwald-Maki, S. (2010). *Health information management: Concepts, principles, and practice* (3rd ed.). Chicago: American Health Information Management Association (AHIMA).

Rimmer, M. (2008). *Medical billing 101.* Clifton Park, NY: Delmar Cengage Learning.

Schraffenberger, L. A., & Kuehn, L. (2011). *Effective management of coding services* (4th ed.). Chicago: American Health Information Management Association (AHIMA).

Scott, K. (2011). *Coding and reimbursement for hospital inpatient services* (3rd ed.). Chicago: American Health Information Management Association (AHIMA).

Medical Billing and Reimbursement Systems Competencies

Question	RHIA Domain	RHIT Domain
1–114	1	7

VII. Medical Science

Lauralyn Kavanaugh-Burke, DrPH, RHIA, CHES, HITPRO-IM

1. The etiology of aplastic anemia is
   A. acute blood loss.
   B. bone marrow failure.
   C. chronic blood loss.
   D. inadequate iron intake.

REFERENCE: Jones, pp 331, 337, 340
               Moisio, p 213
               Neighbors & Tannehill-Jones, p 117
               Scott & Fong, p 250

2. The most common etiology of dementia in the United States is
   A. autism.
   B. Alzheimer's disease.
   C. alcohol abuse.
   D. anxiety disorder.

REFERENCE: Jones, p 1084
               Neighbors & Tannehill-Jones, p 273

3. Dr. Zambrano ordered a CEA test for Mr. Logan, a 67-year-old African-American male patient. Dr. Zambrano may be considering a diagnosis of
   A. cancer.
   B. carpal tunnel syndrome.
   C. cardiomyopathy.
   D. congestive heart failure.

REFERENCE: NLM (4)

4. The prevention of illness through vaccination occurs due to the formation of
   A. helper B cells.
   B. immunosurveillance.
   C. mast cells.
   D. memory cells.

REFERENCE: Jones, pp 350–351
               Scott & Fong, p 338

5. A bee stung little Bobby. He experiences itching, erythema, and respiratory distress caused by laryngeal edema and vascular collapse. In the emergency department where he is treated with an epinephrine injection, Bobby is diagnosed with
   A. allergic rhinitis.
   B. allergic sinusitis.
   C. anaphylactic shock.
   D. asthma.

REFERENCE: Jones, pp 965, 974
               Neighbors & Tannehill-Jones, p 69

6. Genital warts are caused by
   A. HAV.
   B. HIV.
   C. HPV.
   D. VZV.

REFERENCE: Jones, p 716
               Moisio, p 436
               Scott & Fong, p 468

7. A patient's history includes the following documentation:
   - Small ulcers (chancres) appeared on the genitalia and resolved after four to six weeks
   - Elevated temperature, skin rash, and enlarged lymph nodes

   Which procedure will be used to initially diagnose the patient?
   A. bone marrow test   C. serology test
   B. chest x-ray   D. thyroid scan

   REFERENCE: Jones, p 328
                  Moisio, p 437
                  Neighbors & Tannehill-Jones, p 329

8. Which of the following cells produce histamine in a type I hypersensitivity reaction?
   A. lymphocyte   C. mast cells
   B. macrophages   D. neutrophils

   REFERENCE: Jones, p 106
                  Neighbors & Tannehill-Jones, p 47
                  Rizzo, p 104

9. Which one of the following cells produces antibodies?
   A. A cells   C. helper T cells
   B. cytotoxic T cells   D. plasma cells

   REFERENCE: Neighbors & Tannehill-Jones, p 64
                  Rizzo, pp 349, 350, 352
                  Scott & Fong, p 338

10. Which of the following conditions is NOT a predisposing risk associated with essential hypertension?
    A. age   C. low dietary sodium intake
    B. cigarette smoking   D. obesity

    REFERENCE: Jones, p 404
                  Neighbors & Tannehill-Jones, p 134
                  Scott & Fong, pp 300–301

11. A patient, who is HIV positive, has raised lesions, red or purple in color appearing on the skin, in the mouth, or anywhere on the body. What is the stage of his disease process in today's medical terminology?
    A. ARC   C. AZT
    B. AIDS   D. HIV positive

    REFERENCE: Jones, pp 714–715
                  Neighbors & Tannehill-Jones, p 78

12. Each of the following conditions fall under the category of COPD EXCEPT
    A. chronic bronchitis.   C. pneumonia.
    B. emphysema.   D. smoking.

    REFERENCE: Moisio, pp 238, 240
                  Neighbors & Tannehill-Jones, pp 160–161
                  Rizzo, p 407
                  Scott & Fong, p 368

13. Which of the following is a lethal arrhythmia?
    A. atrial fibrillation
    B. atrial tachycardia
    C. bradycardia
    D. ventricular fibrillation

REFERENCE: Jones, p 411
                Neighbors & Tannehill-Jones, p 144

14. The drug commonly used to treat bipolar mood swings is
    A. Lanoxin.
    B. Lasix.
    C. lithium carbonate.
    D. lorazepam.

REFERENCE: Neighbors & Tannehill-Jones, p 417
                Woodrow, pp 358, 360

15. The leading cause of blindness in the United States is a vision-related pathology caused by diabetes. It is called
    A. retinal detachment.
    B. retinoblastoma.
    C. retinopathy.
    D. rhabdomyosarcoma.

REFERENCE: Jones, pp 569, 606–607, 1075–1077
                Moisio, p 403
                Neighbors & Tannehill-Jones, pp 254–255, 289, 294–295, 300
                Scott & Fong, pp 195, 231–232

16. Penicillin is effective in the treatment of all the following diseases EXCEPT
    A. influenza.
    B. Lyme disease.
    C. strep throat.
    D. syphilis.

REFERENCE: Jones, pp 452, 070
                Neighbors & Tannehill-Jones, pp 89–90, 190, 345, 325
                Rizzo, p 459

17. Impetigo can be
    A. spread through autoinoculation.
    B. caused by *Streptococcus pyogenes.*
    C. caused by *Staphylococcus aureus.*
    D. either A or B.

REFERENCE: Jones, pp 121, 855
                Neighbors & Tannehill-Jones, pp 344, 393
                Scott & Fong, pp 78–79

18. Diagnostic testing for meningitis usually involves
    A. blood cultures.
    B. cerebrospinal fluid analysis.
    C. stool C&S.
    D. testing urine.

REFERENCE: Jones, p 292
                Neighbors & Tannehill-Jones, p 266

19. Which disease is a malignancy of the lymphatic system?
    A. cystic fibrosis
    B. Hodgkin's disease
    C. neutropenia
    D. Von Willebrand's disease

REFERENCE: Jones, p 355
                Moisio, p 216
                Neighbors & Tannehill-Jones, pp 114, 119,121, 380
                Rizzo, p 354
                Scott & Fong, p 312

20. Which of the following is a hereditary disease of the cerebral cortex that includes progressive muscle spasticity and mental impairment leading to dementia?
    A. Huntington chorea
    B. Lou Gehrig's disease
    C. Bell's palsy
    D. Guillain--Barré syndrome

REFERENCE: Jones, pp 277–278
                        Moisio, p 294
                        Neighbors & Tannehill-Jones, p 280
                        Scott & Fong, p 481

21. Which of the following autoimmune diseases affects tissues of the nervous system?
    A. Goodpasture's syndrome
    B. Hashimoto's disease
    C. myasthenia gravis
    D. rheumatoid arthritis

REFERENCE: Jones, pp 281–282, 356
                        Neighbors & Tannehill-Jones, pp 72, 107
                        Scott & Fong, p 139

22. Pain is a symptom of which of the following conditions?
    A. first-degree burn (superficial)
    B. second-degree burn (partial thickness)
    C. third-degree burn (full thickness)
    D. both A and B

REFERENCE: Jones, pp 116–117
                        Neighbors & Tannehill-Jones, p 356
                        Scott & Fong, pp 81–82

23. A 75-year-old patient has a sore tongue with tingling and numbness of the hands and feet. She has headaches and is fatigued. Following diagnostic workup, the doctor orders monthly injections of vitamin B_{12}. This patient most likely has which of the following conditions?
    A. aplastic anemia
    B. autoimmune hemolytic anemia
    C. pernicious anemia
    D. sickle cell anemia

REFERENCE: Jones, p 332
                        Moisio, p 213
                        Neighbors & Tannehill-Jones, p 116
                        Scott & Fong, p 250

24. Which one of the following is NOT a pathophysiological factor in anemia?
    A. excessive RBC breakdown
    B. lack of RBC maturation
    C. loss of bone marrow function
    D. loss of spleen function

REFERENCE: Jones, pp 331–333, 338–341
                        Neighbors & Tannehill-Jones, p 116
                        Rizzo, p 308
                        Scott & Fong, pp 250–251

25. Many bacterial diseases are transmitted directly from person to person. Which of the diseases listed below is a bacterial disease that is transmitted by way of a tick vector?
   A. Legionnaires' disease
   B. Lyme disease
   C. tetanus
   D. tuberculosis

REFERENCE: Jones, pp 228–229
               Moisio, p 434
               Neighbors & Tannehill-Jones, p 345
               Scott & Fong, p 335

26. Necrosis extending down to the underlying fascia is characteristic of a decubitus ulcer in stage
   A. one.
   B. two.
   C. three.
   D. four.

REFERENCE: Scott & Fong, p 83

27. Scabies, a highly contagious condition that produces intense pruritus and rash, is caused by
   A. pediculous capitis.
   B. itch mites.
   C. candidiasis.
   D. ringworm.

REFERENCE: Jones, pp 124–125
               Moisio, p 108
               Neighbors & Tannehill-Jones, p 347

28. A physician prescribes a diuretic for his patient. He could be treating any of the following disorders EXCEPT
   A. congestive heart failure.
   B. mitral stenosis.
   C. pneumonia.
   D. pulmonary edema.

REFERENCE: Neighbors & Tannehill-Jones, p 162
               Scott & Fong, pp 274, 366

29. All of the following are examples of direct transmission of a disease EXCEPT
   A. contaminated foods.
   B. coughing or sneezing.
   C. droplet spread.
   D. physical contact.

REFERENCE: Neighbors & Tannehill-Jones, pp 5–6
               Scott & Fong, pp 332–336

30. _____ is the most common type of skin cancer and _____ is the most deadly type of skin cancer.
   A. Malignant melanoma, basal cell carcinoma
   B. Basal cell carcinoma, malignant melanoma
   C. Oat cell carcinoma, squamous cell carcinoma
   D. Squamous cell carcinoma, oat cell carcinoma

REFERENCE: Jones, pp 117, 122–123, 934–935, 939–940
               Neighbors & Tannehill-Jones, p 351
               Rizzo, p 132
               Scott & Fong, p 81
               Sormunen, pp 114, 115

31. John Palmer was in a car accident and sustained severe chest trauma resulting in a tension pneumothorax. Manifestations of this disorder include all of the following EXCEPT

    A. severe chest pain.   C. shock.

    B. dyspnea.   D. clubbing.

REFERENCE: Jones, p 454

                   Neighbors & Tannehill-Jones, p 166

32. Cancer derived from epithelial tissue is classified as a(n)

    A. adenoma.   C. lipoma.

    B. carcinoma.   D. sarcoma.

REFERENCE: Jones, p 931

                   Neighbors & Tannehill-Jones, p 26

                   Rizzo, p 90

                   Sormunen, p 302

33. Sex-linked genetic diseases

    A. are transmitted during sexual activity.

    B. involve a defect on a chromosome.

    C. occur equally between males and females.

    D. occur only in males.

REFERENCE: Neighbors & Tannehill-Jones, p 14

                   Rizzo, p 457

                   Scott & Fong, pp 480–485

34. A stapedectomy is a common treatment for

    A. atherosclerosis.   C. otosclerosis.

    B. multiple sclerosis.   D. scoliosis.

REFERENCE: Jones, p 630

                   Moisio, pp 412–413

                   Neighbors & Tannehill-Jones, p 298

                   Scott & Fong, p 201

35. In systemic circulation, which of the following vessels carries oxygenated blood?

    A. right vena cava

    B. renal arteries

    C. pulmonary arteries

    D. left ventricle

REFERENCE: Jones, pp 380–382

                   Moisio, pp 176–178

                   Neighbors & Tannehill-Jones, p 128

                   Rizzo, pp 322, 335

                   Scott & Fong, pp 286–287, 295

                   Sormunen, p 206

36. Which of the following sequences correctly depicts the flow of blood through the heart to the lungs in order for gas exchange to occur?
    A. right atrium, right ventricle, lungs, pulmonary artery
    B. right atrium, right ventricle, pulmonary artery, lungs
    C. right ventricle, right atrium, lungs, pulmonary artery
    D. right ventricle, right atrium, pulmonary artery, lungs

REFERENCE: Jones, pp 380–382
               Moisio, pp 176–177
               Neighbors & Tannehill-Jones, p 128
               Rizzo, pp 322, 325
               Scott & Fong, pp 286–288, 295
               Sormunen, p 206

37. Diastole occurs when
    A. cardiac insufficiency is present.   C. the ventricles contract.
    B. the atria contracts.   D. the ventricles fill.

REFERENCE: Jones, pp 384, 387
               Neighbors & Tannehill-Jones, p 130
               Rizzo, p 333
               Scott & Fong, p 295
               Sormunen, p 207

38. The most fatal type of lung cancer is
    A. adenocarcinoma.   C. small cell cancer.
    B. large cell cancer.   D. squamous cell cancer.

REFERENCE: Scott & Fong, p 368–369

39. Gas exchange in the lungs takes place at the
    A. alveoli.   C. bronchioles.
    B. bronchi.   D. trachea.

REFERENCE: Neighbors & Tannehill-Jones, p 154
               Rizzo, pp 402–404
               Scott & Fong, p 358
               Sormunen, p 345

40. O_2 is carried in the blood
    A. bound to hemoglobin.   C. plasma.
    B. in the form of carbonic acid.   D. serum.

REFERENCE: Moisio, p 208
               Neighbors & Tannehill-Jones, p 112
               Rizzo, pp 408, 413
               Sormunen, p 247

41. Which of the following anatomical parts is involved in both the respiratory and digestive systems?
    A. larynx
    B. nasal cavity
    C. pharynx
    D. trachea

REFERENCE: Moisio, p 233
               Rizzo, p 371
               Scott & Fong, pp 355–356
               Sormunen, p 344

42. A disease of the inner ear with fluid disruption in the semicircular canal that causes vertigo is
    A. labyrinthitis.
    B. mastoiditis.
    C. Meniere's disease.
    D. both A and C.

REFERENCE: Moisio, pp 411–412
               Neighbors & Tannehill-Jones, pp 300–301
               Scott & Fong, p 201

43. Softening of the bone in children is termed _____.
    A. Raynaud's disease
    B. Reye's syndrome
    C. Rickets
    D. Rubella

REFERENCE: Neighbors & Tannehill-Jones, p 92
               Rizzo, p 147
               Scott & Fong, p 112

44. A pathological diagnosis of transitional cell carcinoma is made. The examined tissue was removed from the
    A. bladder.
    B. esophagus.
    C. oral cavity.
    D. pleura.

REFERENCE: Neighbors & Tannehill-Jones, p 235
               Rizzo, pp 102–103

45. Most carbon dioxide is carried in the
    A. blood as CO_2 gas.
    B. blood bound to hemoglobin.
    C. blood plasma in the form of carbonic acid.
    D. red blood cells.

REFERENCE: Rizzo, pp 408, 413
               Scott & Fong, p 243
               Sormunen, p 247

46. The key diagnostic finding for typical pneumonia is
    A. abnormal chemical electrolytes.
    B. elevated WBC.
    C. lung consolidation on CXR.
    D. positive sputum culture.

REFERENCE: Neighbors & Tannehill-Jones, p 162

47. The presence of fluid in the alveoli of the lungs is characteristic of
    A. COPD.
    B. Crohn's disease.
    C. pneumonia.
    D. tuberculosis.

REFERENCE: Neighbors & Tannehill-Jones, p 163
               Rizzo, p 407

48. Full-blown AIDS sets in as
    A. CD4 receptors increase.
    B. helper T-cell concentration decreases.
    C. HIV virus concentration decreases.
    D. immunity to HIV increases.

REFERENCE: Scott & Fong, pp 321–324
               Sormunen, p 271

49. Which of the following BEST describes tuberculosis?
    A. a chronic, systemic disease whose initial infection is in the lungs
    B. an acute bacterial infection of the lung
    C. an ordinary lung infection
    D. a viral infection of the lungs

REFERENCE: Neighbors & Tannehill-Jones, pp 49, 392–393
               Scott & Fong, p 366
               Sormunen, p 272

50. A treatment for sensorineural hearing loss is
    A. cochlear implants.   C. removal of impacted cerumen.
    B. myringotomy.   D. stapedectomy.

REFERENCE: Jones, p 628
               Scott & Fong, p 202

51. Mary Mulholland has diabetes. Her physician has told her about some factors that put her more at risk for infections. Which of the following factors would probably NOT be applicable?
    A. hypoxia   C. increased blood supply
    B. increased glucose in body fluids   D. both A and C

REFERENCE: Neighbors & Tannehill-Jones, pp 253–257

52. Most of the digestion of food and absorption of nutrients occur in the
    A. ascending colon.   C. small intestine.
    B. esophagus.   D. stomach.

REFERENCE: Neighbors & Tannehill-Jones, p 185
               Rizzo, pp 377–378
               Scott & Fong, pp 385–386
               Sormunen, p 374

53. The Phalen's wrist flexor test is a noninvasive method for diagnosing
    A. carpal tunnel syndrome.   C. severe acute respiratory syndrome.
    B. Down syndrome.   D. Tourette's syndrome.

REFERENCE: NINDS

54. A chronic inflammatory bowel disease where affected segments of the bowel may be separated by normal bowel tissue is characteristic of
    A. appendicitis.   C. diverticulitis.
    B. Crohn's disease.   D. Graves' disease.

REFERENCE: Moisio, p 270
               Neighbors & Tannehill-Jones, pp 193, 198
               Rizzo, p 381
               Sormunen, p 392

55. The patient's pathology report revealed the presence of Reed-Sternberg cells. This is indicative of
    A. Hodgkin's disease.
    B. leukemia.
    C. non-Hodgkin's lymphoma.
    D. sarcoma.

REFERENCE: Neighbors & Tannehill-Jones, p 119

56. The most common rickettsial disease in the United States is
    A. hantavirus.
    B. Lyme disease.
    C. Rocky Mountain spotted fever.
    D. syphilis.

REFERENCE: Moisio, pp 434–435
Neighbors & Tannehill-Jones, p 57
Scott & Fung, pp 331–332

57. Early detection programs apply screening guidelines to detect cancers at an early stage, which provides the likelihood of increased survival and decreased morbidity. Which of the following would NOT be a diagnostic or screening test for colorectal cancer?
    A. double contrast barium enema
    B. sigmoidoscopy
    C. fecal occult blood test
    D. upper GI x-ray

REFERENCE: American Cancer Society
Neighbors & Tannehill-Jones, p 200
Scott & Fong, p 399

58. Prevention programs identify risk factors and use strategies to modify attitudes and behaviors to reduce the chance of developing cancers. Which of the following would NOT be an identified risk factor for colorectal cancer?
    A. alcohol use
    B. physical inactivity
    C. high-fiber diet
    D. obesity

REFERENCE: American Cancer Society

59. In general, excessive RBC breakdown could result in
    A. Crohn's disease.
    B. elevated BUN.
    C. high bilirubin levels.
    D. peptic ulcers.

REFERENCE: Labtestsonline (1)
Neighbors & Tannehill-Jones, p 209
NLM (1)

60. The most common bloodborne infection in the United States is
    A. *Helicobacter pylori.*
    B. hepatitis A.
    C. hepatitis C.
    D. hemophilia.

REFERENCE: Scott & Fong, p 397

61. The first stage of alcoholic liver disease is
    A. alcoholic hepatitis.
    B. cirrhosis.
    C. fatty liver.
    D. jaundice.

REFERENCE: Neighbors & Tannehill-Jones, p 211

62. Portal hypertension can contribute to all of the following EXCEPT
    A. ascites.
    B. dilation of blood vessels lining the intestinal tract.
    C. esophageal varices.
    D. kidney failure.

REFERENCE: Mayo Clinic (1)
                    Neighbors & Tannehill-Jones, pp 211–214

63. Which of the following is a liver function test?
    A. AST (SGOT)   C. ECG
    B. BUN   D. TSH

REFERENCE: Neighbors & Tannehill-Jones, pp 211–214
                    Sormunen, p 389

64. Which of the following is a risk factor involved in the etiology of gallstones?
    A. being overweight   C. low-fat diets
    B. being an adolescent   D. presence of peptic ulcer

REFERENCE: Rizzo, p 215

65. A serum potassium level of 2.8 would indicate
    A. Addison disease.   C. diabetic ketoacidosis.
    B. anemia.   D. hypokalemia.

REFERENCE: Mayo Clinic (2)
                    NLM (3)

66. A procedure performed with an instrument that freezes and destroys abnormal tissues (including seborrheic keratoses, basal cell carcinomas, and squamous cell carcinomas) is
    A. cryosurgery.   C. phacoemulsification.
    B. electrodesiccation.   D. photocautery.

REFERENCE: Moisio, p 110
                    Rizzo, pp 81, 469

67. Which of the organs listed below has endocrine and exocrine functions?
    A. kidney   C. lung
    B. liver   D. pancreas

REFERENCE: Moisio, p 266
                    Neighbors & Tannehill-Jones, p 252
                    Rizzo, pp 282–283, 274
                    Scott & Fong, p 386

68. Which of the following is an effect of insulin?
    A. decreases glycogen concentration in liver
    B. increases blood glucose
    C. increases the breakdown of fats
    D. increases glucose metabolism

REFERENCE: Moisio, pp 301–302, 304
                    Neighbors & Tannehill-Jones, pp 244, 252–256
                    Rizzo, pp 274–276, 282, 284–285
                    Scott & Fong, pp 225–226, 233, 504
                    Sormunen, p 554

69. The causative organism for severe acute respiratory syndrome (SARS) is a
    A. bacterium.
    B. coronavirus.
    C. fungus.
    D. retrovirus.

    REFERENCE: Moisio, p 241
                  Neighbors & Tannehill-Jones, p 165
                  Scott & Fong, p 366

70. Before leaving the hospital, all newborns are screened for an autosomal recessive genetic disorder of defective enzymatic conversion in protein metabolism. With early detection and a protein-restricted diet, brain damage is prevented. This disease is
    A. cystic fibrosis.
    B. hereditary hemochromatosis.
    C. phenylketonuria.
    D. Tay--Sachs disease.

    REFERENCE: Neighbors & Tannehill-Jones, p 378
                  Scott & Fong, p 481

71. Diabetic microvascular disease occurs
    A. as a direct result of elevated serum glucose.
    B. as a result of elevated fat in blood.
    C. due to damage to nerve cells.
    D. only in patients with type 1 diabetes.

    REFERENCE: Neighbors & Tannehill-Jones, pp 254–255
                  Rizzo, pp 284–285
                  Scott & Fong, pp 231–232

72. Older age, obesity, and family history of diabetes are all characteristics of
    A. type 1 diabetes.
    B. type 2 diabetes.
    C. juvenile diabetes.
    D. IDDM.

    REFERENCE: Rizzo, pp 284–285
                  Scott & Fong, p 232

73. An elevated serum amylase would be characteristic of
    A. acute pancreatitis.
    B. gallbladder disease.
    C. postrenal failure.
    D. prerenal failure.

    REFERENCE: Neighbors & Tannehill-Jones, p 219

74. Clinical manifestations of this disease include polydipsia, polyuria, polyphagia, weight loss, and hyperglycemia. Which of the following tests would be ordered to confirm the disease?
    A. fasting blood sugar
    B. glucagon
    C. glucose tolerance test
    D. postprandial blood sugar

    REFERENCE: Neighbors & Tannehill-Jones, pp 253–254
                  Rizzo, pp 84–85
                  Scott & Fong, pp 231, 235

75. Common kidney stone treatments that allow small particles to be flushed out of the body through the urinary system include all of the following EXCEPT
    A. extracorporeal shock wave lithotripsy.
    B. fluid hydration.
    C. ureteroscopy and stone basketing.
    D. using medication to dissolve the stone(s).

    REFERENCE: Neighbors & Tannehill-Jones, p 229

76. When a decubitus ulcer has progressed to a stage in which osteomyelitis is present, the ulcer has extended to the
    A. bone.
    B. fascia.
    C. muscle.
    D. subcutaneous tissue.

REFERENCE: Neighbors & Tannehill-Jones, pp 92–93
              Scott & Fong, pp 83–84

77. The 68-year-old female patient has no visible bleeding, but remains anemic. Her physician is concerned about possible gastrointestinal bleeding. Which of the following tests might be ordered?
    A. DEXA scan
    B. guaiac smear test
    C. Pap smear test
    D. prostatic-specific antigen test

REFERENCE: Estridge & Reynolds, pp 680–681
              Sormunen, p 388

78. When a physician orders a liver panel, which of the following tests are NOT included?
    A. albumin
    B. alkaline phosphatase
    C. bilirubin
    D. creatinine

REFERENCE: Estridge & Reynolds, pp 608–609

79. Maria Giovanni is in the hospital recovering from colon resection surgery. Based on her symptoms, her doctors are concerned about the possibility that she has developed a pulmonary embolism. Which of the following procedures will provide the definitive diagnosis?
    A. chest x-ray
    B. lung scan
    C. pulmonary angiography
    D. none of the above

REFERENCE: Neighbors & Tannehill-Jones, p 168
              Scott & Fong, p 369

80. A condition that involves the fifth cranial nerve, also known as "tic douloureux," causes intense pain in the eye and forehead; lower lip, the section of the cheek closest to the ear and the outer segment of the tongue; or the upper lip, nose, and cheek.
    A. Bell's palsy
    B. thrush
    C. trigeminal neuralgia
    D. Tourette's disorder

REFERENCE: Jones, pp 283, 288
              Moisio, p 396
              Scott & Fong, p 182

81. Which of the following is a congenital condition that is the most severe neural tube defect?
    A. meningocele
    B. myelomeningocele
    C. severe combined immunodeficiency
    D. spina bifida occulta

REFERENCE: Neighbors & Tannehill-Jones, p 374

82. Which of the following tubes conveys sperm from the seminal vesicle to the urethra?
    A. ejaculatory duct
    B. epididymis
    C. oviduct
    D. vas deferens

REFERENCE: Moisio, p 332
              Neighbors & Tannehill-Jones, p 481
              Rizzo, p 444

83. The most common type of vaginitis is
    A. yeast.
    B. protozoan.
    C. viral.
    D. both A and B.

REFERENCE: Neighbors & Tannehill-Jones, p 315

84. The childhood viral disease that unvaccinated pregnant women should be prevented from because it may be passed to the fetus, causing congenital anomalies such as mental retardation, blindness, and deafness, is
    A. rickets.
    B. rubeola.
    C. rubella.
    D. tetanus.

REFERENCE: Moisio, p 435
               Neighbors & Tannehill-Jones, p 389

85. In _____ anemia, the red blood cells become shaped like elongated crescents in the presence of low oxygen concentration.
    A. aplastic
    B. folic acid
    C. sickle cell
    D. vitamin B_{12}

REFERENCE: Jones, p 333
               Moisio, p 213
               Rizzo, p 308
               Scott & Fong, pp 250–251

86. _____ is usually the first symptom of benign prostate hyperplasia.
    A. Abdominal pain
    B. Burning pain during urination
    C. Difficulty in urinating
    D. Pelvic pain

REFERENCE: Neighbors & Tannehill-Jones, pp 322–324
               Rizzo, p 444
               Scott & Fong, pp 467–468

87. The hypothalamus, thalamus, and pituitary gland are all parts of the
    A. brainstem.
    B. cerebellum.
    C. exocrine system.
    D. limbic system.

REFERENCE: Rizzo, pp 157–158

88. Which of the following BEST summarizes the current treatment of cervical cancer?
    A. A new three-shot vaccination series protects against the types of HPV that cause most cervical cancer cases.
    B. All stages have extremely high cure rates.
    C. Early detection and treatment of cervical cancer does not improve patient survival rates.
    D. Over 99% of cases are linked to long-term HPV infections.

REFERENCE: CDC (1)

89. Children at higher risk for sudden infant death syndrome (SIDS) include those
    A. with sleep apnea.
    B. with respiratory problems.
    C. who are premature infants.
    D. all of the above.

REFERENCE: Jones, pp 455, 867–868
               Neighbors & Tannehill-Jones, p 395
               Scott & Fong, p 369

90. Increasing peristalsis of intestines, increasing salivation, and slowing heart rate are examples of
    A. automatic nervous system responses.
    B. higher brain function.
    C. parasympathetic nervous system responses.
    D. sympathetic nervous system responses.

REFERENCE: Jones, p 263
                Rizzo, pp 227, 251
                Scott & Fong, pp 177–179
                Sormunen, p 585

91. Photophobia or visual aura preceding a severe headache is characteristic of
    A. malnutrition.   C. migraines.
    B. mastitis.   D. myasthenia gravis.

REFERENCE: Jones, pp 275–276
                Neighbors & Tannehill-Jones, p 271
                Scott & Fong, p 163

92. Which of the following is characteristic of Graves' disease?
    A. is an autoimmune disease.   C. usually cannot be treated.
    B. most commonly affects males.   D. usually affects the elderly.

REFERENCE: Jones, p 560
                Neighbors & Tannehill-Jones, p 248
                Rizzo, pp 280, 285
                Scott & Fong, p 228

93. A "pill-rolling" tremor of the hand is a characteristic symptom of
    A. epilepsy.   C. myasthenia gravis.
    B. Guillain--Barré syndrome.   D. Parkinson disease.

REFERENCE: Jones, pp 282–283, 1066–1067
                Neighbors & Tannehill-Jones, p 281
                Scott & Fong, pp 162–164

94. Rheumatoid arthritis typically affects the
    A. intervertebral disks.
    B. hips and shoulders.
    C. knees and small joints of the hands and feet.
    D. large, weight-bearing joints.

REFERENCE: Jones, p 230
                Moisio, p 149
                Neighbors & Tannehill-Jones, pp 71–72, 94–95
                Rizzo, p 183
                Scott & Fong, pp 110–111

95. Henry experienced sudden sharp chest pain that he described as heavy and crushing. His pain and past medical history caused Dr. James to suspect that Henry was having an acute myocardial infarction (AMI). Which of the following tests is a more specific marker for an AMI?
    A. AST   C. LDH1
    B. CK-MB   D. Troponin I

REFERENCE: Labtestsonline (2)

96. A radiological test for bone mineral density (BMD) is a useful diagnostic tool for diagnosing
    A. osteoarthritis.
    B. osteomyelitis.
    C. osteoporosis.
    D. rheumatoid arthritis.

REFERENCE: Jones, p 184
               Neighbors & Tannehill-Jones, pp 90–92
               Scott & Fong, p 113

97. A 72-year-old white male patient is on Coumadin therapy. Which of the following tests is commonly ordered to monitor the patient's Coumadin levels?
    A. bleeding time
    B. blood smear
    C. partial thromboplastin time
    D. prothrombin time

REFERENCE: Jones, p 339
               Labtestsonline (3)
               Moisio, p 219
               Neighbors & Tannehill-Jones, p 235
               NLM (2)

98. A toxic goiter has what distinguishing characteristic?
    A. iodine deficiency
    B. parathyroid involvement
    C. presence of muscle spasm
    D. thyroid hyperfunction

REFERENCE: Moisio, p 304
               Neighbors & Tannehill-Jones, pp 247–248
               Rizzo, p 280
               Sormunen, p 567

99. How can Graves' disease be treated?
    A. antithyroid drugs
    B. radioactive iodine therapy
    C. surgery
    D. all of the above

REFERENCE: Jones, pp 560–561
               Neighbors & Tannehill-Jones, pp 247–248
               Rizzo, p 285
               Sormunen, p 567

100. Fractures occur in patients with osteoporosis due to
    A. falling from loss of balance.
    B. fibrous joint adhesions tearing apart small bones.
    C. loss of bone mass.
    D. tendency to fall from lack of joint mobility.

REFERENCE: Jones, pp 174–175
               Moisio, p 149
               Neighbors & Tannehill-Jones, pp 90–92
               Scott & Fong, p 113

101. United States health care providers are concerned about a possible pandemic of avian flu because
    A. there is no vaccine currently available.
    B. it is caused by a group of viruses that mutate very easily.
    C. the causative virus is being spread around the world by migratory birds.
    D. of all of the above.

REFERENCE: CDC (2)

102. A sweat test was done on a patient with the following symptoms: frequent respiratory infections, chronic cough, and foul-smelling bloody stools. Which of the following diseases is probably suspected?
    A. cystic breast disease
    B. cystic fibrosis
    C. cystic lung disease
    D. cystic pancreas

REFERENCE: Neighbors & Tannehill-Jones, p 380

103. Margaret Vargas needs to have her mitral valve replaced. Her surgeon will discuss which of the following issues with her before the surgery?
    A. A mechanical valve will require that she take a "blood thinner" for the rest of her life.
    B. A biological valve (usually porcine) will last 10 to 15 years.
    C. A mechanical valve increases the risk of blood clots that can cause stroke.
    D. All of the above.

REFERENCE: NHLBI

104. Cervical cerclage is a procedure used to help prevent
    A. breathing restrictions.
    B. miscarriage.
    C. torsion.
    D. torticollis.

REFERENCE: Jones, pp 802, 817

105. Sam Spade has been severely injured in an MVA because he was not wearing a seat belt. The organ in his body, situated at the upper left of his abdominal cavity, under the ribs, that is part of his lymphatic system has been ruptured and he is bleeding internally. Sam needs a surgical procedure known as
    A. sequestrectomy.
    B. sialoadenectomy.
    C. sigmoidoscopy.
    D. splenectomy.

REFERENCE: Jones, p 345
                 Moisio, p 219
                 Rizzo, p 346
                 Sormunen, pp 275, 399

106. Henrietta Dawson presents with a chief complaint of pain and weakness in her arms and neck. After an H&P and review of diagnostic tests that include a myelogram, her doctor diagnoses a herniated nucleus pulposus at the _____ level of her spine.
    A. cervical
    B. lumbar
    C. sacral
    D. thoracic

REFERENCE: Jones, pp 160, 228, 277
                 Moisio, p 147
                 Neighbors & Tannehill-Jones, p 103
                 Rizzo, pp 157, 170
                 Scott & Fong, pp 99, 112
                 Sormunen, pp 158, 161

107. Ingrid Anderson presents with a skin infection that began as a raised, itchy bump, resembling an insect bite. Within 1 to 2 days, it developed into a vesicle. Now it is a painless ulcer, about 2 cm in diameter, with a black necrotic area in the center. During the history, her doctor learns that she has recently returned from an overseas vacation and becomes concerned that she may have become infected with anthrax. He will prescribe an
    A. antibiotic.
    B. antineoplastic.
    C. antiparasitic.
    D. antiviral.

REFERENCE: Scott & Fong, pp 342, 366–367

108. Etiologies of dementia include
    A. brain tumors.
    B. ischemia.
    C. trauma.
    D. all of the above.

REFERENCE: Neighbors & Tannehill-Jones, p 414
               Rizzo, pp 937, 946
               Scott & Fong, p 164
               Sormunen, p 597

109. Carpal tunnel syndrome is caused by entrapment of the
    A. medial nerve.
    B. radial nerve.
    C. tibial nerve.
    D. ulnar nerve.

REFERENCE: Jones, p 270
               Moisio, p 142
               Neighbors & Tannehill-Jones, p 104
               NINDS
               Rizzo, p 182
               Sormunen, p 158

110. The organism transmitted by a mosquito bite that causes malaria is a
    A. bacteria.
    B. prion.
    C. protozoa.
    D. virus.

REFERENCE: Moisio, p 432
               Neighbors & Tannehill-Jones, pp 54–55, 57
               Rizzo, p 309
               Scott & Fong, p 309

111. Contributing factors of mental disorders include
    A. heredity.
    B. stress.
    C. trauma.
    D. all of the above.

REFERENCE: Jones, pp 1008, 1010
               Neighbors & Tannehill-Jones, p 408

112. A 13-year-old patient is brought to her pediatrician with a 2-week history of fatigue, an occasional low-grade fever, and malaise. The pediatrician indicates it is a possible infection but needs to know what type of infection. She orders a hematology laboratory test to determine the relative number and percentage of each type of leukocytes. This test is referred to as a(n)
    A. hematocrit.
    B. CBC.
    C. WBC diff.
    D. hemoglobin determination.

REFERENCES: Estridge & Reynolds, p 198
               Merck, p 1080

113. A 62-year-old female presents to her family doctor complaining of fatigue; constantly feeling cold, especially in her hands and feet; weakness; and pallor. O_2 must be transported to the cells and exchanged with CO_2, which is then transported back to the lungs to be expelled. A hematology laboratory test that evaluates the oxygen-carrying capacity of blood is referred to as a(n)

A. hematocrit
B. CBC.
C. WBC diff.
D. hemoglobin determination.

REFERENCES: Estridge & Reynolds, pp 206–207
                     Merck, p 926

114. An African-American couple are undergoing genetic counseling to determine the likelihood of producing children with a recessively genetic blood condition. The genetic tests reveal that the father carries the trait to produce abnormal hemoglobin, HbS, which causes crystallization in RBCs and deforms their shape when O_2 is low. This condition causes painful crises and multiple infarcts and is termed

A. hemophilia.
B. thalassemia.
C. sickle cell anemia.
D. iron-deficiency anemia.

REFERENCES: Estridge & Reynolds, pp 328–330
                     Labtestsonline (4)

115. A 37-year-old female goes to her family physician complaining of dysuria, urgency, fever, and malaise. A UA is performed and upon gross examination is found to be turbid and has an unusual odor. Microscopic examination reveals a rod-shaped microorganism. A 24-hour culture produces a colony count greater than 100,000/mL of *Escherichia coli*. This would indicate a diagnosis of

A. UTI.
B. FUO.
C. PID.
D. KUB.

REFERENCES: Estridge & Reynolds, pp 751–753
                     Labtestsonline (5)

116. A 57-year-old male patient is having his annual physical. Due to a family history of coronary artery disease and his sedentary lifestyle, his doctor orders a total blood cholesterol panel. What is the optimal level of total cholesterol in the blood for adults?

A. < 200 mg/dL
B. 200–239 mg/dL
C. 300–339 mg/dL
D. >500 mg/dL

REFERENCES: Estridge & Reynolds, pp 662–667
                     Labtestsonline (6)

117. A pharyngeal culture is taken from a 13-year-old male patient presenting to the ER with fever, painful cervical lymph nodes, purulent tonsillar exudate, and difficulty swallowing. Blood agar culture plate shows complete hemolysis around *Streptococcus pyogenes* bacterial colonies. The patient is given a prescription for erythromycin. The diagnosis in this case is

A. group A beta-hemolytic streptococcal throat infection.
B. methicillin-resistant *Staphylococcus aureus* skin infection.
C. tuberculosis with drug-resistant *Mycobacterium tuberculosis*-positive sputum.
D. meningitis due to *Neisseria meningitidis*-positive cerebrospinal fluid.

REFERENCES: Estridge & Reynolds, pp 739–742
                     Labtestsonline (7)
                     Merck, p 1232

118. An 81-year-old male with arteriosclerosis and a long-standing history of taking Coumadin presents to his physician's office for his bi-weekly prothrombin time (PT) test. The PT test is one of the most common hemostasis tests used as a presurgery screening and monitoring Coumadin (warfarin) therapy. This test evaluates
    A. coagulation of the blood.
    B. iron-binding capacity of RBCs.
    C. oxygen-carrying capacity of RBCs.
    D. type and cross-match of blood.

REFERENCES: Estridge & Reynolds, p 394
                        Labtestsonline (8)

119. A 28-year-old female presents to her general practitioner with morning nausea and vomiting, weight gain, and two missed menstrual cycles. The physician orders a pregnancy test. What chemical in the urine does this lab test detect?
    A. alpha-fetoprotein   C. carcinoembryonic antigen
    B. creatine phophokinase   D. human chorionic gonadotropin

REFERENCES: Estridge & Reynolds, pp 471–472
                        Labtestsonline (9).

120. A 19-year-old college student, who lives on campus in a dormitory, is brought to the ER by his roommates complaining of a severe headache, nuchal rigidity, fever, and photophobia. The ER physician performs an LP and orders a CSF analysis with a bacterial culture and sensitivity. The young man is admitted to the ICU with a provisional diagnosis of
    A. group A beta-hemolytic streptococcal throat infection.
    B. methicillin-resistant *Staphylococcus aureus* skin infection.
    C. tuberculosis with drug-resistant *Mycobacterium tuberculosis*-positive sputum.
    D. meningitis due to *Neisseria meningitidis*-positive cerebrospinal fluid.

REFERENCES: Labtestsonline (10)
                        Merck, p 1735

121. Microbiological lab culture and sensitivity tests were performed on the skin scrapings of a groin lesion on a 27-year-old male patient who presented to a local health department clinic. The results confirm infection with *Treponema pallidum*. He was given a prescription for penicillin and told to return for a follow-up visit in within 2 weeks. His diagnosis is
    A. syphilis.   C. herpes.
    B. HIV.   D. HPV.

REFERENCES: Labtestsonline (11)
                        Merck, p 1476

122. The HPV vaccine, Gardasil, is recommended for all children/young adults between the ages of 9 and 26 years. It is a quadrivalent vaccine. What is the definition of quadrivalent?
    A. It must be administered every 4 years to be effective.
    B. It is administered in a series of four shots over a 6-month period.
    C. It prevents infection from the four most prevalent types of HPV that cause cervical cancer.
    D. It reduces the risk of infection by four times.

REFERENCES: CDC (3)
                       FDA
                       Labtestsonline (12)
                       Merck, p 1471

123. *Mycobacterium tuberculosis* is the organism that causes tuberculosis (TB), typically a respiratory disorder. It is currently experiencing a resurgence in the United States and many other countries. What is the average time frame all patients with new, previously untreated TB must have daily antibiotic therapy?
    A. 4–7 days   C. 6–9 weeks
    B. 6–9 months   D. 4–7 years

REFERENCES: CDC (4)
                       Labtestsonline (13)
                       Merck, p 1310

124. A 63-year-old patient with terminal pancreatic cancer has started palliative chemotherapy. Palliative means
    A. alleviating or eliminating distressing symptoms of the disease.
    B. increasing the immune response to fight infections.
    C. quick destruction of cancerous cells.
    D. the combining of several medications to cure the cancer.

REFERENCES: ACS (3)
                       Merck, p 1076
                       Woodrow, pp 221–222

125. Why are there "black box warnings" on antidepressant medications regarding children and adolescents?
    A. Antidepressants increase the risk of suicidal thinking and behavior in some children and adolescents.
    B. Dosage requirements must be significantly higher in children and adolescents compared to adults.
    C. There is no established medical need for treatment of depression in children and adolescents.
    D. Antidepressants interfere with physiological growth patterns in children and adolescents.

REFERENCES: Merck, p 3057
                       Woodrow, p 354

126. The positive belief in a drug and its ability to cure a patient's illness, even if this drug is an inactive or inert substance, typically positively influences a patient's perception of their outcome. This effect is termed
    A. synergistic effect.
    B. potentiation effect.
    C. placebo effect.
    D. antagonistic effect.

REFERENCES: Merck, p 3169
               Woodrow, pp 34–36

127. A common cardiac glycoside medication that increases the force of the cardiac contraction without increasing the oxygen consumption, thereby increasing the cardiac output is typically given to patients with heart failure. However, a very narrow therapeutic window between effectiveness and toxicity and the patient must be monitored closely. This common cardiac medication is
    A. COX-2 inhibitor.
    B. nitroglycerin.
    C. digoxin.
    D. acetylsalicylic acid.

REFERENCES: Merck, p 2131
               Woodrow, pp 461–462

128. The interaction of two drugs working together to where each simultaneously helps the other achieve an effect that neither could produce alone is termed
    A. placebo effect.
    B. synergistic effect.
    C. potentiation effect.
    D. antagonistic effect.

REFERENCES: Woodrow, p 35

129. The opposing interaction of two drugs in which one decreases or cancels out the effects of the other is termed
    A. placebo effect.
    B. potentiation effect.
    C. synergistic effect.
    D. antagonistic effect.

REFERENCES: Woodrow, p 35

130. One of the most common causes of peptic ulcer disease is the consumption of aspirin and NSAIDs. Another common cause is the infection of *Helicobacter pylori,* and the usual treatment for this condition is with the use of
    A. antivirals.
    B. antibiotics.
    C. antifungals.
    D. antiemetics.

REFERENCES: Merck, p 134
               Woodrow, p 254

131. A common contraceptive that is implanted in the uterus induces slight endometrial inflammation, which attracts neutrophils to the uterus. These neutrophils are toxic to sperm and prevent the fertilization of the ovum. This contraception is termed
    A. oral contraceptives.
    B. progestin injections.
    C. spermicides.
    D. IUD.

REFERENCES: Merck, p 2589
               Woodrow, p 447

132. There has been a significant increase in the number of cases and deaths from pertussis. Health care professionals attribute this disease trend to which of the following?
    A. A decrease in the number of people immunized with TDaP
    B. An increase in the virulence of the bacteria
    C. Drug-resistant strains of the bacteria
    D. All of the above

REFERENCES: CDC (5)

133. Which of the following is a severe, chronic, two-phased, bacterial respiratory infection that has become increasingly difficult to treat because many antibiotics are no longer effective against it?
    A. SARS
    B. MDR-TB
    C. MRSA
    D. H1N1

REFERENCES: CDC (6)

134. A new strain of influenza, H1N1, is a highly virulent strain that spread all over the world. This type of epidemiological disease pattern is referred to as a(n)
    A. cluster.
    B. outbreak.
    C. epidemic.
    D. pandemic.

REFERENCES: CDC (7)

135. Mary Smith, a 48-year-old patient, is receiving an IV mixture of four different medications to treat stage 2 invasive ductal breast carcinoma. Each of the medications acts upon a different aspect of the cancer cells. This mixture is typically termed a(n)
    A. amalgamation.
    B. cocktail.
    C. blend.
    D. mash-up.

REFERENCES: CDC (8)

136. Some immunizations, such as tetanus, require a second application, to strengthen or "remind" the immune system in response to antigens. The subsequent injections are termed
    A. alerting shots.
    B. warning shots.
    C. booster shots.
    D. unnecessary shots.

REFERENCES: CDC (9)

137. What common vitamin should be taken by pregnant women to substantially reduce the occurrence of neural tube defects, such as spina bifida, in a developing fetus?
    A. Folic acid
    B. Calcium

REFERENCES: CDC (10)

138. Why must influenza immunizations be developed and administered on an annual basis?
    A. The virus mutates significantly each year.
    B. People develop resistance to the vaccine.
    C. The immunization is only strong enough for one year.
    D. The pharmaceutical companies produce the lowest dosage possible.

REFERENCES: CDC (11)

Answer Key for Medical Science

1.	B	49.	A	97.	D
2.	B	50.	A	98.	D
3.	A	51.	C	99.	D
4.	D	52.	C	100.	C
5.	C	53.	A	101.	D
6.	C	54.	B	102.	B
7.	C	55.	A	103.	D
8.	C	56.	C	104.	B
9.	D	57.	D	105.	D
10.	C	58.	C	106.	A
11.	B	59.	C	107.	A
12.	C	60.	C	108.	D
13.	D	61.	C	109.	A
14.	C	62.	D	110.	C
15.	C	63.	A	111.	D
16.	A	64.	A	112.	C
17.	D	65.	C	113.	D
18.	B	66.	A	114.	C
19.	B	67.	D	115.	A
20.	A	68.	D	116.	A
21.	C	69.	B	117.	A
22.	D	70.	C	118.	A
23.	C	71.	A	119.	D
24.	D	72.	B	120.	D
25.	B	73.	A	121.	A
26.	C	74.	C	122.	C
27.	B	75.	C	123.	B
28.	C	76.	A	124.	A
29.	A	77.	B	125.	A
30.	B	78.	D	126.	C
31.	D	79.	C	127.	C
32.	B	80.	C	128.	B
33.	B	81.	B	129.	D
34.	C	82.	A	130.	B
35.	D	83.	D	131.	D
36.	B	84.	C	132.	A
37.	D	85.	C	133.	B
38.	C	86.	C	134.	D
39.	A	87.	D	135.	B
40.	A	88.	A	136.	C
41.	C	89.	D	137.	B
42.	D	90.	C	138.	A
43.	C	91.	C		
44.	A	92.	A		
45.	D	93.	D		
46.	C	94.	C		
47.	C	95.	D		
48.	B	96.	C		

REFERENCES

American Cancer Society (ACS). http://www.cancer.org

ACS (1)

http://www.cancer.org/acs/groups/cid/documents/webcontent/003096-pdf.pdf

http://www.cancer.org/Cancer/ColonandRectumCancer/DetailedGuide/colorectal-cancer-detection

ACS (3)

http://www.cancer.org/Cancer/CancerofUnknownPrimary/DetailedGuide/cancer-unknown-primary-treating-palliative-care

Centers for Disease Control and Prevention (CDC). http://www.cdc.gov/index.htm

CDC (1)

http://www.cdc.gov/std/Hpv/STDFact-HPV-vaccine-young-women.htm#why

CDC (2)

http://www.cdc.gov/flu/avian/gen-info/pdf/avian_facts.pdf

CDC (3)

http://www.cdc.gov/Features/HPVvaccine/

CDC (4)

http://www.cdc.gov/tb/topic/treatment/default.htm

CDC (5)

http://www.cdc.gov/pertussis/outbreaks-faqs.html

CDC (6)

http://www.cdc.gov/tb/topic/treatment/default.htm

CDC (7)

http://www.cdc.gov/flu/spotlights/pandemic-global-estimates.htm

CDC (8)

http://www.cdc.gov/cancer/breast/basic_info/

CDC (9)

http://www.cdc.gov/vaccines/vac-gen/default.htm

CDC (10)

http://www.cdc.gov/NCBDDD/folicacid/about.html

CDC (11)

http://www.cdc.gov/vaccines/vac-gen/default.htm

Estridge, B. H., & Reynolds, A. P. (2012). *Basic clinical laboratory techniques* (6th ed.). Clifton Park, NY: Delmar Cengage Learning.

Food and Drug Administration (FDA). http://www.fda.gov/default.htm

http://www.fda.gov/BiologicsBloodVaccines/Vaccines/ApprovedProducts/ucm094042.htm

Jones, B. D. (2011). *Comprehensive medical terminology* (4th ed.). Clifton Park, NY: Delmar Cengage Learning.

Labtestsonline. http://www.labtestsonline.org

Labtestsonline (1).

http://www.labtestsonline.org/understanding/analytes/bilirubin/glance.html

Labtestsonline (2).

http://www.labtestsonline.org/understanding/analytes/troponin/related.html

Labtestsonline (3).

http://www.labtestsonline.org/understanding/analytes/pt/test.html

Labtestsonline (4).

http://labtestsonline.org/understanding/conditions/sickle

Labtestsonline (5).
  http://labtestsonline.org/understanding/analytes/urinalysis/tab/test
Labtestsonline (6).
  http://labtestsonline.org/understanding/analytes/cholesterol/tab/test
Labtestsonline (7)
  http://labtestsonline.org/understanding/analytes/strep/tab/sample
Labtestsonline (8)
  http://labtestsonline.org/understanding/analytes/pt/tab/sample
Labtestsonline (9)
  http://labtestsonline.org/understanding/wellness/pregnancy/first-hcg
Labtestsonline (10)
  http://labtestsonline.org/understanding/conditions/meningitis?start=3
Labtestsonline (11)
  http://labtestsonline.org/understanding/analytes/syphilis/tab/glance
Labtestsonline (12)
  http://www.cdc.gov/vaccines/vpd-vac/hpv/default.htm
Labtestsonline (13)
  http://labtestsonline.org/understanding/conditions/tuberculosis/?start=4

Mayo Clinic. http://www.mayoclinic.com
  Mayo Clinic (1).
    http://www.mayoclinic.com/print/esophageal-varices/DS00820/
  Mayo Clinic (2)
    http://www.mayoclinic.com/health/diabetic-ketoacidosis/DS00674

The Merck manual of diagnosis and therapy (19th ed.). (2011). Rahway, NJ: Merck.

Moisio, M. A. (2010). *Medical terminology for insurance and coding.* Clifton Park, NY: Delmar Cengage Learning.

National Library of Medicine. http://www.nlm.nih.gov/medlineplus/
  NLM (1).

    http://www.nhlbi.nih.gov/health/dci/Diseases/ha/ha_diagnosis.html
    http://www.nlm.nih.gov/medlineplus/ency/article/003479.htm

  NLM (2).
    http://www.nlm.nih.gov/medlineplus/ency/article/003652.htm

  NLM (3)
    http://www.nlm.nih.gov/medlineplus/ency/article/003498.htm

  NLM (4)
    http://www.nlm.nih.gov/medlineplus/ency/article/003574.htm

NHLBI—National Heart Lung and Blood Institute. http://www.nhlbi.nih.gov
  http://www.nhlbi.nih.gov/health/dci/Diseases/hvd/hvd_treatments.html

NINDS—National Institute of Neurological Disorders and Stroke.
  http://www.ninds.nih.gov/disorders/carpal_tunnel/detail_carpal_tunnel.htm

Scott, A. S., & Fong, P.E. (2009). *Body structures and functions* (11th ed.). Clifton Park, NY: Delmar Cengage Learning.

Sormunen, C. (2010). *Terminology for allied health professionals* (6th ed.). Clifton Park, NY: Delmar Cengage Learning.

Woodrow, R. (2011). *Essentials of pharmacology for health occupations* (6th ed.). Clifton Park, NY: Delmar Cengage Learning.

Medical Sciences Competencies

Question	RHIA Domain	RHIT Domain
1–138	1	1

VIII. ICD-9-CM Coding

Leslie Moore, RHIT, CCS

Infectious and Parasitic Diseases

1. A patient is admitted with a left ankle fracture. The patient also has AIDS with Kaposi's sarcoma of the skin. He had a closed reduction with internal fixation of the ankle fracture.
    A. 042, 176.0, 824.8, 79.16
    B. 824.8, 176.0, V08, 79.16
    C. 176.1, 824.8, V08, 79.16
    D. 824.8, 042, 176.0, 79.16

REFERENCE: Brown, pp 115–116, 413–408, 416–417
              Schraffenberger, pp 82–84
              Ingenix, pp 617–618

2. A patient was admitted with septicemia due to methicillin-resistant *Staphylococcus aureus*. The patient also was admitted with septic shock and decubitus ulcer of the sacrum. She had a central line inserted and infusion of drotrecogin alfa.
    A. 038.19, 785.59, 707.02, 38.91
    B. 038.12, 707.03, 995.92, 785.52, 707.20, 38.93, 00.11
    C. 707.00, 038.11, 785.59, 38.93, 00.11
    D. 038.11, 785.59, 995.92, 38.93

REFERENCE: Bowie and Shaffer, pp 92–93
              Brown, pp 109–113, 241–242
              Schraffenberger, pp 80–82
              Ingenix, pp 47, 348

3. A patient was diagnosed with nephropathy due to tuberculosis (confirmed histologically) of the kidney. He had a right nephrectomy performed.
    A. 016.05, 583.81, 55.51
    B. 583.81, 016.06, 55.52
    C. 016.02, 583.81, 55.51
    D. 016.02, 583.81, 55.52

REFERENCE: Brown, pp 108–109, 220–222
              Schraffenberger, p 78
              Ingenix, pp 466–467

4. A patient is admitted with fever and severe headache. The diagnostic workup revealed viral meningitis. She also has asthma with acute exacerbation and hypertension, both of which are treated.
    A. 047.9, 780.60, 784.0, 493.90, 401.9
    B. 047.8, 493.92, 401.1
    C. 047.9, 493.92, 401.9
    D. 780.60, 784.0, 047.9, 493.90, 401.9

REFERENCE: Brown, pp 107, 161–162, 186–187, 347–349
              Schraffenberger, pp 78, 181–182, 184–186

5. Nurse Jones suffers a needlestick and presents for HIV testing. She sees her physician for the test results and counseling.
    A. V72.60, 795.71
    B. 795.71, V65.8
    C. V08, V72.60, V65.44
    D. V73.89, V65.44, V01.79

REFERENCE: Brown, pp 115–116
              Schraffenberger, p 84

6. A patient presents with right arm paralysis due to poliomyelitis that the patient suffered from as a child.
   A. 045.11, 342.81
   B. 138, 344.41
   C. 344.40, 138
   D. 138, 344.41

REFERENCE: Brown, pp 108–109

Neoplasms

7. A patient is admitted for chemotherapy for treatment of breast cancer with liver metastasis. She had a mastectomy 4 months ago. Chemotherapy is given today.
   A. 197.7, V10.3, 99.25
   B. 174.9, 197.7, 99.25
   C. V58.11, V10.3, 197.7, 99.25
   D. V58.11, 174.9, V45.71, 197.7, 99.25

REFERENCE: Bowie and Schaffer, pp 119–120
               Brown, pp 380–381, 383–385, 391–395
               Schraffenberger, pp 94–98
               Ingenix, pp 807–808

8. A patient with a history of malignant neoplasm of the lung is admitted with seizures. The workup revealed metastasis of the lung cancer to the brain.
   A. 780.39, V10.11, 198.3
   B. 162.9, V10.11, 198.3, 780.39
   C. 198.3, 780.39, V10.11
   D. 198.3, 780.39, 162.9

REFERENCE: Bowie and Schaffer, p 116
               Brown, pp 380–381, 383–385
               Schraffenberger, pp 107–109

9. A patient is admitted to the hospital for treatment of dehydration following chemotherapy as treatment for ovarian cancer.
   A. 276.51, 183.0
   B. 183.0, 276.51, 99.25
   C. 276.50, 183.0, 99.25
   D. 183.0, 276.51

REFERENCE: Bowie and Schaffer, p 118
               Brown, pp 391–395

10. A patient has malignant melanoma of the skin of the back. She undergoes a radical excision of the melanoma with full-thickness skin graft.
    A. 173.59, 86.4, 86.63
    B. 172.5, 86.4, 86.63
    C. 173.59, 86.3, 86.63
    D. 172.5, 86.3, 86.63

REFERENCE: Brown, p 377
               Schraffenberger, p 94
               Ingenix, p 718

11. A patient is admitted with abdominal pain. The needle biopsy of the liver reveals secondary malignancy of the liver. The patient has an exploratory laparotomy to determine the primary site. The primary site is unknown at the time of discharge.
    A. 197.7, 199.1, 54.11, 50.12
    B. 197.7, 789.00, 54.11, 50.11
    C. 197.7, 199.1, 54.11, 50.11
    D. 197.7, 199.1, 789.00, 54.11, 50.12

REFERENCE: Brown, pp 383–385
               Ingenix, pp 431, 452

12. A patient with a history of cancer of the colon and status postcolostomy is admitted for closure of the colostomy. The patient is also being treated for chronic obstructive pulmonary disease and diastolic heart failure. He has a takedown of the colostomy.
    A. 153.2, 496, 428.30, 46.52
    B. V55.3, 496, V10.05, 428.30, 46.52
    C. V55.3, 496, V10.05, 428.0, 46.52, 45.79
    D. V10.05, 492.8, 428.30, 46.52

REFERENCE: Brown, pp 187, 339–340, 391
              Schraffenberger, pp 436, 447–448
              Ingenix, pp 409–410, 414

Endocrine, Nutritional, and Metabolic Diseases and Immunity Disorders

13. A female, 68 years old, was admitted with type 2 diabetes mellitus with a diabetic ulcer of the left heel. The patient was taken to the operating room for excisional debridement of the ulcer.
    A. 250.80, 707.14, 86.22   C. 250.81, 707.13, 86.22
    B. 707.14, 250.80, 86.22   D. 250.82, 707.14, 86.28

REFERENCE: Brown, pp 119–126, 242–243
              Schraffenberger, pp 122–124, 294
              Ingenix, pp 715–716

14. A 67-year-old man is admitted with acute dehydration secondary to nausea and vomiting that is due to acute gastroenteritis. He is treated for dehydration. An esophagogastroduodenoscopy is performed.
    A. 558.9, 787.01, 276.51, 45.13   C. 276.51, 787.01, 558.9, 45.13
    B. 558.9, 787.01, 276.51, 45.16   D. 276.51, 558.9, 45.13

REFERENCE: Schraffenberger, pp 126, 236
              Ingenix, pp 404–405

15. A patient was found at home in a hypoglycemic coma. This patient had never been diagnosed as being diabetic.
    A. 250.30   C. 251.1
    B. 251.0   D. 251.2

REFERENCE: Brown, p 128

16. A patient is admitted with aplastic anemia secondary to chemotherapy administered for multiple myeloma.
    A. 284.89, 203.00, E933.1   C. 284.9, 203.00, E933.1
    B. 203.00, 284.81, E933.1   D. 203.01, 284.89, E933.1

REFERENCE: Bowie and Schaffer, p 145
              Brown, pp 153–154, 445–446

17. A male patient is admitted with gastrointestinal hemorrhage resulting in acute blood-loss anemia. A colonoscopy and esophagogastroduodenoscopy fail to reveal the source of the bleed.
    A. 285.9, 578.1, 45.13, 45.23   C. 578.9, 285.1, 45.13, 45.23
    B. 578.1, 285.1, 45.13, 45.23   D. 578.9, 280.0, 45.13, 45.23

REFERENCE: Brown, pp 152–153, 199–200
              Ingenix, pp 404–407

18. A patient is admitted with severe malnutrition. The physician performs a percutaneous endoscopic gastrostomy.
    A. 263.9, 43.11   C. 261, 43.19
    B. 261, 43.11   D. 263.8, 43.11

REFERENCE: Brown, p 129
                 Ingenix, pp 392–393

Diseases of the Blood and Blood-Forming Organs

19. A patient is admitted with thrombocytopenia and purpura. A splenectomy is performed.
    A. 287.49, 41.5   C. 287.9, 41.42
    B. 287.8, 41.5   D. 287.30, 41.5

REFERENCE: Schraffenberger, p 136
                 Ingenix, pp 379–380

20. A patient is admitted with sickle cell anemia with crisis.
    A. 282.61   C. 282.63
    B. 282.62   D. 282.69

REFERENCE: Brown, p 154
                 Schraffenberger, p 134

21. A patient is admitted with sickle cell pain crisis.
    A. 282.62   C. 282.5
    B. 282.60   D. 282.42

REFERENCE: Bowie and Schaffer, p 145
                 Brown, p 154
                 Schraffenberger, p, 134

22. A patient is admitted with Cooley's anemia.
    A. 282.41   C. 282.49
    B. 282.0   D. 282.44

REFERENCE: Brown, p 151
                 Schraffenberger, p 134

23. A patient is admitted with anemia due to end-stage renal disease. The patient is treated for anemia.
    A. 285.8   C. 285.22, 585.6
    B. 285.21, 585.6   D. 285.9

REFERENCE: Brown, p 151
                 Schraffenberger, p 135

24. A patient is admitted with pernicious anemia.
    A. 280.9   C. 281.1
    B. 280.8   D. 281.0

REFERENCE: Brown, p 151
                 Schraffenberger, pp 133–134

Mental Disorders

25. A patient is admitted with mild mental retardation due to an old viral encephalitis.
    A. 319, 049.8
    B. 317, 326
    C. 317, 047.8
    D. 317, 139.0

REFERENCE: Brown, p 108

26. A patient is admitted with anxiety with depression.
    A. 300.11, 311
    B. 300.4
    C. 309.28
    D. 300.00, 311

REFERENCE: Brown, p 139

27. A patient is admitted with delirium tremens with alcohol dependence.
    A. 291.0, 303.90
    B. 303.91, 291.0
    C. 291.3, 303.90
    D. 291.0, 303.00

REFERENCE: Brown, pp 141–142
               Schraffenberger, pp 143, 146–149

28. A patient is admitted with latent schizophrenia, chronic with acute exacerbation.
    A. 295.52
    B. 295.55
    C. 295.54
    D. 295.53

REFERENCE: Bowie and Schaffer, pp 157–158
               Brown, p 137

29. A patient with chronic paranoia due to continuous cocaine dependence is admitted. Drug rehabilitation is provided.
    A. 301.0, 305.61, 94.63
    B. 297.1, 304.21, 94.64
    C. 297.1, 305.61, 94.64
    D. 297.1, 304.21, 94.63

REFERENCE: Brown, p 143
               Schraffenberger, pp 143, 146–149
               Ingenix, pp 784-786

30. A patient is diagnosed with psychogenic paroxysmal tachycardia.
    A. 427.2, 316
    B. 306.2, 427.1
    C. 427.1, 306.2
    D. 316, 427.2

REFERENCE: Brown, p 139

Diseases of the Nervous System and Sense Organs

31. A 5-year-old female is admitted to ambulatory surgery with chronic otitis media. She has bilateral myringotomy with insertion of tubes.
    A. 381.20, 20.01
    B. 381.3, 20.01
    C. 382.9, 20.01, 20.01
    D. 381.89, 20.01

REFERENCE: Schraffenberger, p 165
               Ingenix, pp 208–209

32. A patient is a type 2 diabetic with a diabetic cataract. He has phacoemulsification of the cataract with synchronous insertion of the lens.
    A. 250.51, 366.42, 13.59, 13.71
    B. 250.50, 366.41, 13.41, 13.71
    C. 250.52, 366.41, 13.41, 13.71
    D. 366.41, 250.50, 13.41, 13.71

REFERENCE: Brown, pp 125, 172
               Schraffenberger, pp 122–124, 164
               Ingenix, pp 171–174

33. A patient has epilepsy and paraplegia as residuals of a head injury he suffered 5 years ago.
    A. 345.90, 344.1, 907.0
    B. 345.91, 344.1, 907.0
    C. 959.01, 345.90, 344.1
    D. 345.81, 344.2, 907.0

REFERENCE: Brown, pp 164–165
               Schraffenberger, pp 161–162

34. A patient is diagnosed with Alzheimer's disease with dementia.
    A. 331.0, 294.8
    B. 294.8
    C. 331.0, 294.10
    D. 331.0

REFERENCE: Brown, p 136

35. A patient is admitted with meningitis sarcoidosis.
    A. 321.2, 136.1
    B. 135, 321.4
    C. 136.1, 321.2
    D. 321.4, 135

REFERENCE: Brown, p 162

36. A patient with carpal tunnel syndrome is admitted for arthroscopic release of the carpal tunnel.
    A. 354.0, 04.43
    B. 354.1, 80.23
    C. 354.1, 04.43, 80.23
    D. 354.0, 04.43, 80.23

REFERENCE: Brown, p 167
               Ingenix, pp 110–111, 623

Diseases of the Circulatory System

37. A patient is admitted with acute cerebral infarction with left hemiparesis. The hemiparesis resolved by discharge.
    A. 342.90
    B. 434.91
    C. 436, 342.90
    D. 434.91, 342.90

REFERENCE: Brown, pp 343–344

38. A patient is admitted with multiple problems. He has hypertensive kidney disease, congestive heart failure, and acute systolic heart failure.
    A. 593.9, 401.9, 482.0, 428.21
    B. 404.11, 428.0, 428.21
    C. 403.90, 428.0, 428.21
    D. 404.91

REFERENCE: Brown, pp 348–349
               Schraffenberger, pp 182, 192–193

39. A patient is admitted with acute inferior wall myocardial infarction with unstable angina. He also has coronary artery disease and atrial fibrillation.
    A. 410.41, 411.1, 414.01, 427.31   C. 410.40, 414.00, 427.31
    B. 410.41, 414.00, 411.1, 427.31   D. 410.41, 414.00, 427.31

REFERENCE: Bowie and Schaffer, pp 197–199
                Brown, pp 333–339
                Schraffenberger, pp 186–191, 194

40. A patient with a diagnosis of aortic valve stenosis and mitral valve regurgitation is admitted for aortic valve replacement. The patient is also under treatment for congestive heart failure. He undergoes the placement of aortic valve prosthesis with cardiopulmonary bypass.
    A. 396.2, 398.91, 35.22, 39.61   C. 396.2, 428.0, 35.22, 39.61
    B. 424.1, 424.0, 428.0, 35.22   D. 424.1, 424.0, 428.0, 35.21, 39.61

REFERENCE: Brown, pp 329–332
                Schraffenberger, p 179
                Ingenix, pp 303–304, 357–358

41. A patient with atherosclerotic peripheral vascular disease of the lower leg with claudication is admitted for angioplasty of the lower leg artery.
    A. 440.20, 39.50   C. 444.22, 38.08
    B. 440.21, 39.50   D. 443.9, 39.50

REFERENCE: Brown, pp 351–352
                Ingenix, pp 340–342, 355

Diseases of the Respiratory System

42. A patient presents to the outpatient department for a chest x-ray. The physician's order lists the following reasons for the chest x-ray: fever and cough, rule out pneumonia. The radiologist reports that the chest x-ray is positive for pneumonia.
    A. 486   C. 780.61, 786.2
    B. 486, 780.61, 786.2, V72.5   D. V72.5, 780.60, 786.2

REFERENCE: Brown, pp 179–184
                Schraffenberger, p 219

43. A patient has aspiration pneumonia with pneumonia due to *Staphylococcus aureus*. The patient also has emphysema.
    A. 507.0, 482.9, 496   C. 507.0, 491.21
    B. 507.0, 482.41, 496   D. 507.0, 482.41, 492.8

REFERENCE: Brown, pp 179–183
                Schraffenberger, pp 218–219

44. A patient is admitted with acute respiratory failure due to congestive heart failure. The patient is placed on the ventilator for 3 days following insertion of the endotracheal tube.
    A. 518.81, 428.0, 96.71, 96.04   C. 428.0, 518.81, 96.71, 96.04
    B. 518.81, 428.0, 96.72, 96.04   D. 428.0, 518.83, 96.72, 96.04

REFERENCE: Brown, pp 157–159, 189–191, 339–340
                Schraffenberger, pp 192–194, 223–226
                Ingenix, pp 793, 798

45. A child has hypertrophic tonsillitis and is admitted for bilateral tonsillectomy and adenoidectomy.
   A. 463, 28.3, 28.3
   B. 474.00, 28.3
   C. 474.02, 28.3, 28.3
   D. 463, 28.3

REFERENCE: Schraffenberger, p 218
             Ingenix, p 257

46. A patient is admitted with chronic obstructive pulmonary disease with an exacerbation of acute bronchitis.
   A. 491.22
   B. 496, 466.0
   C. 466.0, 496
   D. 491.22, 466.0

REFERENCE: Brown, pp 186–187
             Schraffenberger, p 218

47. A patient is admitted with extrinsic asthma with status asthmaticus.
   A. 493.11
   B. 493.90
   C. 493.01
   D. 493.81

REFERENCE: Brown, pp 186–188
             Schraffenberger, pp 222-223

48. A patient is experiencing exacerbation of myasthenia gravis resulting in acute respiratory failure. The patient required mechanical ventilation for 10 hours, following endotracheal intubation.
   A. 358.00, 518.81, 96.71, 96.04
   B. 518.81, 358.01, 96.71, 96.04
   C. 358.00, 581.89, 96.71, 96.05
   D. 518.82, 358.00, 96.72, 96.04

REFERENCE: Brown, pp 189–191, 194–195
             Schraffenberger, pp 223-226
             Ingenix, pp 793–794, 798

Diseases of the Digestive System

49. A patient is admitted to the hospital for repair of a ventral hernia. The surgery is canceled after the chest x-ray revealed lower lobe pneumonia. The patient is placed on antibiotics to treat the pneumonia.
   A. 553.20, 486, V64.1
   B. 486, 553.20, V64.3
   C. 486, 553.20
   D. 553.20, 486

REFERENCE: Brown, pp 72–73, 181–182, 208–210
             Schraffenberger, pp 45–46, 220, 235

50. A patient is admitted with gastric ulcer with hemorrhage resulting in acute blood-loss anemia. An esophagogastroduodenoscopy is performed.
   A. 531.20, 285.1, 45.13
   B. 285.1, 531.20, 45.13
   C. 531.40, 280.0, 45.14
   D. 531.40, 285.1, 45.13

REFERENCE: Bowie and Schaffer, pp 218–219
             Brown, pp 116–117, 203
             Schraffenberger, pp 135, 234
             Ingenix, pp 404–405

51. A patient has diverticulitis of the large bowel with abscess. The physician performs a right hemicolectomy with colostomy.

    A. 562.10, 45.74, 46.03
          C. 562.11, 569.5, 45.73, 46.10

    B. 562.11, 45.73, 46.10
             D. 562.11, 569.5, 45.74, 46.11

REFERENCE: Brown, p 205
                       Ingenix, pp 109, 411

52. A patient is admitted with acute and chronic cholecystitis with cholelithiasis. A laparoscopic cholecystectomy was attempted, and then it was converted to an open procedure.

    A. 574.00, 574.10, V64.41, 51.22
      C. 574.00, 51.22, 51.23

    B. 574.00, 574.10, 51.22, 51.23
       D. 574.00, V64.41, 51.22

REFERENCE: Brown, pp 206–207
                       Schraffenberger, p 224
                       Ingenix, p 437

53. A patient is admitted with bleeding esophageal varices with alcoholic liver cirrhosis and portal hypertension. The patient is alcohol dependent. An esophagogastroduodenoscopy is performed for control of the hemorrhage.

    A. 456.20, 571.2, 303.90, 42.33
      C. 572.3, 571.2, 303.90, 456.20, 42.33

    B. 571.2, 456.20, 303.90, 280.0, 42.33
    D. 303.90, 456.20, 303.90, 42.33

REFERENCE: Brown, pp 141–145, 203
                       Ingenix, pp 385–386

54. A patient is admitted for workup for melena. The laboratory results reveal chronic blood-loss anemia. The colonoscopy with biopsy reveals Crohn's disease of the descending colon.

    A. 578.1, 555.1, 45.25, 45.43
        C. 555.1, 578.1, 45.25

    B. 555.1, 45.25
                    D. 555.1, 578.1, 45.25, 45.23

REFERENCE: Brown, p 151
                       Schraffenberger, p 236
                       Ingenix, pp 405–408

Diseases of the Genitourinary System

55. A patient is admitted with acute urinary tract infection due to *E. coli*.

    A. 599.0, 041.49
              C. 041.49, 599.0

    B. 599.0
                  D. 590.2, 041.49

REFERENCE: Brown, p 112
                       Schraffenberger, pp 250–251

56. A patient presents with complaints of gross hematuria. The diagnosis is benign prostatic hypertrophy and the patient undergoes a transurethral prostatectomy.

    A. 600.01, 60.21
           C. 600.00, 599.71, 60.29

    B. 600.00, 60.29
           D. 600.00, 599.71, 60.21

REFERENCE: Brown, pp 225–226
                       Ingenix, p 507

57. A male patient presents to the ED with acute renal failure. He is also being treated for hypertension.
   A. 410.00, 586
   B. 401.9, 584.9
   C. 585.9, 401.1
   D. 584.9, 401.9

REFERENCE: Brown, pp 219–221

58. A patient is admitted with hemorrhagic cystitis. A cystoscopy with biopsy of the bladder is performed.
   A. 595.9, 57.33
   B. 595.9, 041.49, 57.32
   C. 595.82, 57.33
   D. 596.7, 57.33

REFERENCE: Brown, p 217
              Schraffenberger, p 251
              Ingenix, p 484

59. A patient is admitted with chronic kidney disease due to hypertension and type 1 diabetes mellitus.
   A. 250.41, 403.90, 585.9
   B. 250.40, 403.10, 585.1
   C. 403.90, 250.41, 585.9, V58.67
   D. 403.10, 250.41, 585.2

REFERENCE: Brown, p 220

60. A patient has end-stage kidney disease, which resulted from malignant hypertension.
   A. 403.01, 585.6
   B. 585.9, 401.0
   C. 403.00
   D. 401.0, 585.9

REFERENCE: Brown, pp 219–220
              Schraffenberger, pp 182, 250

Complications of Pregnancy, Childbirth, and the Puerperium

61. A woman has a vaginal delivery of a full-term liveborn infant. She undergoes an episiotomy with repair and post delivery elective tubal ligation.
   A. 650, V25.2, V27.0, 73.6, 66.32
   B. 648.91, V27.0, 73.6, 66.32
   C. 650, V27.0, 66.32
   D. 650, V27.0

REFERENCE: Bowie and Schaffer, p 260
              Brown, pp 269–271, 282–283
              Schraffenberger, pp 272–274
              Ingenix, pp 540–541, 585–586

62. A woman has an incomplete spontaneous abortion complicated by excessive hemorrhage. The physician performs a dilation and curettage.
   A. 634.12, 69.09
   B. 634.12, 285.1, 69.09
   C. 634.11, 69.02
   D. 634.91, 69.02

REFERENCE: Brown, pp 293–295
              Schraffenberger, pp 264–265
              Ingenix, p 562

63. A patient has obstructed labor due to breech presentation. A single liveborn infant was delivered via cesarean section.
    A. 660.81, 74.1
    B. 660.01, 652.21, V27.0, 74.99
    C. 660.01, V27.0, 74.1
    D. 660.81, 652.21, 74.99

REFERENCE: Brown, pp 269–271, 283
               Ingenix, pp 587–588

64. A woman was admitted for delivery of a single newborn at 43 weeks gestation. It was a manually assisted delivery.
    A. 650, V27.0, 73.59
    B. 645.20, V27.0, 73.59
    C. 644.21, V27.0, 73.59
    D. 645.21, V27.0, 73.59

REFERENCE: Brown, pp 280–283
               Schraffenberger, pp 274–275
               Ingenix, p 585

65. A female who is 26 weeks pregnant is treated for a fractured distal radius and ulna. A closed reduction of the fracture is performed.
    A. 813.44, 79.02
    B. 648.93, 813.44, 79.02
    C. 813.44, V22.2, 79.02
    D. V22.2, 813.44, 79.02

REFERENCE: Brown, pp 269–270
               Schraffenberger, pp 275–277, 353
               Ingenix, p 617

66. A patient is diagnosed with a tubal pregnancy. She undergoes a unilateral salpingectomy for removal of the tubal pregnancy.
    A. 633.20, 66.63
    B. 633.11, 66.62
    C. 633.00, 66.61
    D. 633.10, 66.62

REFERENCE: Brown, pp 298–299
               Schraffenberger, pp 270–273
               Ingenix, p 542

Diseases of the Skin and Subcutaneous Tissue

67. A patient is admitted with an abscess with cellulitis of the abdominal wall. The culture is positive for *Staphylococcus aureus*.
    A. 682.8, 041.11
    B. 682.2, 041.11
    C. 682.2, 707.8
    D. 682.2

REFERENCE: Brown, p 292
               Schraffenberger, p 244

68. A patient had a cholecystectomy 6 days ago and is now coming back with evidence of staphylococcal cellulitis at the site of operative incision.
    A. 958.3, 682.2, 041.19
    B. 998.51, 682.8, 041.11
    C. 958.3, 682.8, 041.11
    D. 998.59, 682.2, 041.10

REFERENCE: Brown, pp 242–243

69. A patient has chronic ulcers of the calf and the back. Both ulcers are excisionally debrided and the ulcer on the back has a split-thickness skin graft.
    A. 707.12, 707.8, 86.22, 86.22, 86.69
    B. 707.12, 707.8, 86.22
    C. 707.8, 86.22, 86.69
    D. 707.8, 86.22, 86.22, 86.69

REFERENCE: Brown, pp 242–244
              Schraffenberger, pp 294, 296–297
              Ingenix, pp 717, 719

70. A patient presents with dermatitis due to prescription topical antibiotic cream used as directed by physician.
    A. 692.4
    B. 692.3, E930.9
    C. 692.3
    D. 692.3, E930.1

REFERENCE: Brown, pp 239–240
              Schraffenberger, p 292

71. A patient developed a boil on the left side of the face. An incision and drainage was performed.
    A. 680.0, 86.04
    B. 680.0, 86.09
    C. 680.8, 86.11
    D. 680.0, 86.04, 86.11

REFERENCE: Brown, p 239
              Ingenix, p 712–715

72. A patient has an abscessed pilonidal cyst. An excision of the cyst was performed.
    A. 685.1, 86.04
    B. 686.09, 86.04
    C. 685.0, 86.21
    D. 686.01, 86.22

REFERENCE: Brown, p 239
              Ingenix, pp 712–713, 715

Diseases of the Musculoskeletal System and Connective Tissue

73. A patient has a pathological fracture of the femur due to metastatic bone cancer. He has a history of lung cancer.
    A. 198.5, 733.14, V10.11
    B. 733.14, 198.5, V10.11
    C. 733.19, 198.5, V10.11
    D. 821.00, 162.9

REFERENCE: Brown, p 255
              Schraffenberger, pp 108, 305–306

74. A 69-year-old man has a herniated lumbar intervertebral disc with paresthesia. A lumbar laminectomy with diskectomy is performed.
    A. 722.11, 80.51, 03.09
    B. 839.20, 80.51
    C. 722.10, 80.59, 03.09
    D. 722.10, 80.51

REFERENCE: Brown, pp 251–252
              Schraffenberger, pp 304–305
              Ingenix, pp 99–100, 624–626

75. A patient developed pyogenic arthritis of the hip due to Group A *Streptococcus*. An arthrocentesis was done.
    A. 716.95, 041.01, 81.91   C. 711.05, 041.01, 81.91
    B. 715.95, 041.01, 81.92   D. 711.05, 81.91

REFERENCE: Brown, p 253
                Schraffenberger, pp 79–80, 304–305
                Ingenix, p 655

76. A patient is admitted with a bunion of the left foot and a hammertoe of the right foot. Keller procedure and hammer toe repair were performed.
    A. 727.1, 735.4, 77.59, 77.56   C. 727.2, 735.4, 77.52, 77.58
    B. 727.1, 735.8, 77.52, 77.59   D. 727.1, 735.3, 77.56, 77.59

REFERENCE: Schraffenberger, pp 304–305
                Ingenix, pp 608–610

77. A patient developed a malunion of the humeral fracture. The original injury occurred 1 year ago. Open reduction with internal fixation was performed.
    A. 812.20, 79.39   C. 733.81, 905.2, 79.31
    B. 733.82, 905.2, 79.31   D. 733.94, 905.2, 79.32

REFERENCE: Schraffenberger, p 306
                Ingenix, pp 618–619

78. A patient has recurrent internal derangement of the left knee. A diagnostic arthroscopy of the knee is performed.
    A. 715.96, 80.26   C. 836.2, 80.26
    B. 718.36, 80.26   D. 718.36, 80.6

REFERENCE: Brown, p 254
                Ingenix, pp 623, 626

Congenital Anomalies

79. A liveborn infant is born in hospital with a cleft palate and cleft lip.
    A. 749.00, 749.10   C. V30.00, 749.20
    B. 749.20   D. V30.00, 749.00, 749.10

REFERENCE: Bowie and Schaffer, pp 290–291
                Brown, pp 307, 314
                Schraffenberger, pp 320, 442–443

80. A newborn is born in the hospital with tetralogy of Fallot.
    A. 745.8   C. 745.2
    B. V30.01, 746.09   D. V30.00, 745.2

REFERENCE: Brown, pp 307, 314

81. A newborn infant is transferred to Manasota Hospital for treatment of an esophageal atresia. What is the code for Manasota Hospital?
    A. V30.00   C. V30.00, 750.3
    B. 750.3   D. 750.3, V30.00

REFERENCE: Brown, p 307

82. A patient presents with cervical spina bifida with hydrocephalus.
    A. 741.02
    B. 741.93
    C. 741.01
    D. 741.91

REFERENCE: Brown, p 307
Schraffenberger, pp 316–317

83. An infant is seen with clubfoot, which is corrected by the Evans operation.
    A. 754.70, 83.84
    B. 754.71, 83.84
    C. 736.71, 83.84
    D. 736.79, 83.84

REFERENCE: Brown, p 307
Schraffenberger, p 322
Ingenix, p 667

84. A full-term infant born in hospital is diagnosed with polycystic kidneys.
    A. 753.12
    B. V30.00, 753.12
    C. V30.00
    D. 753.12, V30.00

REFERENCE: Brown, pp 307, 314
Schraffenberger, pp 317, 321, 442–443

Certain Conditions Originating in the Perinatal Period

85. A full-term newborn is born in hospital to a mother who is addicted to cocaine; however, the infant tested negative.
    A. V30.00, 760.75
    B. 779.5 V29.8
    C. V30.00, 779.5
    D. V30.00, V29.8

REFERENCE: Brown, pp 314, 318–319
Schraffenberger, pp 317, 442–443

86. A preterm infant is born via cesarean section and has severe birth asphyxia.
    A. V30.01, 765.10, 768.5
    B. 765.10, 768.5, V30.01
    C. 768.5, 765.10
    D. 768.5

REFERENCE: Brown, pp 315–316

87. A preterm infant born in the hospital has neonatal jaundice. Phototherapy is done to treat the jaundice.
    A. V30.00, 774.2, 99.83
    B. 774.2, 99.83
    C. V30.00, 99.83
    D. V30.00, 774.2

REFERENCE: Brown, p 314
Ingenix, p 811

88. A 1-week-old infant is admitted to the hospital with a diagnosis of urinary tract infection contracted prior to birth. The urine culture is positive for *E. coli.*
    A. V30.00, 599.0
    B. 599.0, 041.49
    C. V30.00, 599.0, 041.49
    D. 771.82, 041.49

REFERENCE: Brown, pp 107, 319

89. An infant has hypoglycemia with a mother with diabetes.
    A. 251.2
    B. 775.1
    C. 775.0
    D. 251.1

REFERENCE: Brown, p 313, 320–321

90. A full-term infant is born in the hospital. The birth is complicated by cord compression, which affected the newborn.
   A. V30.00, 762.5
   B. V30.00
   C. 762.5
   D. 762.6, V30.00

REFERENCE: Bowie and Schaffer, pp 300–301
               Brown, pp 314, 319
               Schraffenberger, pp 317, 442–443

Symptoms, Signs, and Ill-Defined Conditions

91. A patient is admitted with abdominal pain. The discharge diagnosis is listed as abdominal pain due to gastroenteritis or diverticulosis.
   A. 789.00
   B. 562.10, 558.9
   C. 789.00, 558.9, 562.10
   D. 558.9, 562.10, 789.00

REFERENCE: Bowie and Schaffer, pp 317–318
               Brown, pp 97–99
               Schraffenberger, pp 236, 338–340

92. A patient has a lung mass. A diagnostic bronchoscopy is performed.
   A. 518.89, 33.23
   B. 786.6, 33.23
   C. 793.19, 33.27
   D. 786.6, 33.27

REFERENCE: Brown, pp 97–99
               Ingenix, pp 278–280

93. A woman has a Pap smear that detected cervical high-risk human papillomavirus (HPV). The DNA test was positive.
   A. 795.05
   B. 795.09
   C. 795.04
   D. 795.02

REFERENCE: Brown, pp 97–99

94. A patient presents to the emergency department with ascites. A paracentesis was done.
   A. 789.30, 54.91
   B. 789.51, 54.91
   C. 789.59, 54.91
   D. 782.3, 54.91

REFERENCE: Brown, pp 97–99
               Ingenix, p 456

95. A patient is admitted with fever due to bacteremia.
   A. 780.61, 790.7
   B. 038.9
   C. 780.61
   D. 790.7, 780.61

REFERENCE: Brown, pp 97–99

96. A patient has urinary retention requiring the insertion of a Foley catheter.
   A. 788.21, 57.94
   B. 788.20, 57.93
   C. 788.20, 57.94
   D. 788.29, 57.93

REFERENCE: Brown, pp 97–99
               Ingenix, p 489

Injury and Poisoning

97. A patient has a fracture of the medial malleolus due to a fall down some steps. The fracture was treated with a closed reduction procedure.
    A. 824.1, E880.9, 79.05
    B. 824.0, E880.9, 79.06
    C. 824.0, 79.09
    D. 824.1, E880.1, 79.05

REFERENCE: Bowie and Schaffer, pp 325–328
               Brown, pp 413–414, 416
               Schraffenberger, pp 354–355
               Ingenix, p 617

98. A patient experienced a closed head injury. He was a passenger in a motor vehicle involved in a head-on collision with another motor vehicle.
    A. 959.01, E812.1
    B. 959.09, E812.2
    C. 959.01, E813.1
    D. 959.09, E813.1

REFERENCE: Brown, pp 405–408
               Schraffenberger, pp 367–368

99. A man appears with a gunshot wound to the abdomen. There is a moderate laceration of the liver. The patient stated that he was assaulted with a pistol.
    A. 864.00, E965.1
    B. 864.10, E965.0
    C. 864.13, E965.1
    D. 864.13, E965.0

REFERENCE: Brown, pp 405–408
               Schraffenberger, pp 359–360

100. A patient was admitted with third-degree burns to his upper back, which involved 20% of his body surface. There was an explosion and fire at his home.

    A. 942.25, 948.22, E890.2
    B. 942.44, 948.21, E895
    C. 942.34, 948.22, E890.3
    D. 942.24, 949.3, E897

REFERENCE: Brown, pp 433–436
               Schraffenberger, pp 363–364

101. A woman experienced third-degree burns to her thigh and second-degree burns to her foot. She stated that the burns were from hot liquid.
    A. 945.36, 945.22, E924.0
    B. 945.22, 945.36, E924.0
    C. 945.22, E924.0
    D. 945.29, 945.39, E924.0

REFERENCE: Brown, pp 433–436
               Schraffenberger, pp 363–364

102. A patient presents with a laceration of left wrist with injury to the radial nerve as a result of an accident, with embedded glass. The wrist laceration was repaired with sutures.
    A. 881.02, 86.59
    B. 881.12, E920.8, 86.59
    C. 955.3, E920.8, 86.59
    D. 881.12, 955.3, E920.8, 86.59

REFERENCE: Brown, pp 405–408, 421
               Schraffenberger, p 352
               Ingenix, pp 717–718

103. A 76-year-old female is admitted with tachycardia due to theophylline toxicity.
    A. 785.0, E942.1   C. 785.0, E944.1
    B. 995.20, E942.1   D. 995.20, E944.1

REFERENCE: Brown, pp 443–446
                      Schraffenberger, pp 338–339

104. A patient suffered dizziness as a result of taking prescribed phenobarbital. The patient took his medication with beer.
    A. 780.4, 980.0, E860.0
    B. 967.0, 980.0, 780.4, E851, E860.0
    C. 967.0, 708.4, E851
    D. 780.4, E851, E860.0

REFERENCE: Brown, pp 443–446
                      Schraffenberger, pp 382–383

105. A patient is experiencing pain in the hip due to a displaced hip prosthesis. The patient is admitted and undergoes a revision of the hip prosthesis.
    A. 996.49, 81.53   C. 719.45, 81.53
    B. 996.77, 81.53   D. 996.49, 719.45, 81.53

REFERENCE: Schraffenberger, pp 386–388
                      Ingenix, p 645

106. A patient has postoperative hemorrhage, resulting in acute blood-loss anemia.
    A. 997.72, 285.1   C. 998.11, 285.1
    B. 999.1, 285.1   D. 998.11

REFERENCE: Brown, pp 152, 462
                      Schraffenberger, p 389

V-Codes

107. A patient is admitted for colostomy takedown. The takedown procedure is performed.
    A. V44.3, 46.52   C. 997.49, 46.52
    B. 569.60, 46.52   D. V55.3, 46.52

REFERENCE: Brown, pp 83–85
                      Schraffenberger, pp 447–448
                      Ingenix, p 414

108. The patient is being admitted for a preoperative EKG on an outpatient basis. He is scheduled to have an elective cholecystectomy tomorrow for chronic cholecystitis and cholelithiasis. The EKG reveals atrial flutter.
    A. 574.10   C. V72.81, 574.10, 427.32
    B. V72.81, 51.23   D. 427.32

REFERENCE: Brown, p 88
                      Schraffenberger, pp 457–459

109. The patient presents for a screening examination for lung cancer.
    A. V72.82   C. V72.5
    B. 162.9   D. V76.0

REFERENCE: Brown, p 89
                      Schraffenberger, p 459

110. A patient is admitted for observation for a head injury following a fall. The patient also suffered a minor laceration to the forehead. Head injury was ruled out.
   A. V71.4, 873.42, E888.9
   B. 873.42, E888.9
   C. 959.01, 873.42, E888.9
   D. V71.4, E888.9

REFERENCE: Brown, pp 86–87
               Schraffenberger, pp 260–361, 457

When the question has the ICD-9-CM codes and their respective narrative description, you should practice answering the question without using your coding book.

111. An elderly man was admitted through the emergency department for severe urinary retention. Upon study, it was determined that his hypertension was uncontrolled (215/108). Prior medical records show admission 8 weeks ago for the same problem. As per conditions on previous admission, his BPH is complicated by acute cystitis. He is noncompliant with medications. Medication for the hypertension was immediately started and his hypertension was quickly brought under control. Urinary retention was relieved by placement of a Foley catheter. Transurethral resection of the prostate was done.

401.0	Essential hypertension, malignant
401.9	Essential hypertension, unspecified benign or malignant
595.0	Acute cystitis
595.9	Cystitis, unspecified
600.00	Hypertrophy (benign) of prostate without urinary obstruction and other lower urinary tract symptoms (LUTS)
600.01	Hypertrophy (benign) of prostate with urinary obstruction and other lower urinary tract symptoms (LUTS)
600.3	Cyst of prostate
788.20	Retention of urine, unspecified
V15.81	Personal history of noncompliance with medical treatment
57.92	Dilation of bladder neck
57.94	Insertion of indwelling urinary catheter
60.29	Other transurethral prostatectomy
60.61	Local excision of lesion of prostate

   A. 600.01, 595.0, 788.20, 401.9, V15.81, 57.94, 60.29
   B. 600.3, 595.0, 401.0, V15.81, 57.92, 60.61
   C. 600.00, 595.9, 788.20, 401.9, V15.81, 57.94, 60.61
   D. 600.3, 595.0, 788.20, 401.0, V15.81, 57.94, 60.61

REFERENCE: Brown, pp 83–84, 97–98, 347-348
               Schraffenberger, pp 180–181, 251–252, 338–339

112. A 32-year-old female known to be HIV positive was admitted with lesions of the anterior trunk. Excisional biopsies of the skin lesions were positive for Kaposi's sarcoma. Further examination revealed thrush.

042	Human Immunodeficiency Virus (HIV) Disease
112.0	Candidiasis of mouth
176.0	Kaposi's sarcoma of skin
528.9	Other and unspecified diseases of the oral soft tissues
686.00	Pyoderma, unspecified
795.71	Nonspecific serological evidence of Human Immunodeficiency Virus (HIV)
86.11	Closed biopsy of skin and subcutaneous tissue
86.22	Excisional debridement of wound, infection, or burn

A. 042, 686.00, 112.0, 86.22   C. 795.71, 176.0, 528.9, 86.11
B. 042, 176.0, 112.0, 86.11   D. 795.71, 686.00, 528.9, 86.22

REFERENCE: Brown, pp 115–117
               Schraffenberger, pp 82–84

113. A female patient was admitted with uncontrolled type 2 diabetes. She also had an abscessed diabetic ulcer of the foot that was treated with incision and drainage. The culture and sensitivity of the abscess shows growth of methicillin-resistant *Staphylococcus aureus*. The patient was started on the appropriate antibiotic. The patient is on oral as well as injectional insulin for control of her diabetes.

041.11	Bacterial infection in conditions classified elsewhere and of unspecified site, methicillin-susceptible *staphylococcus aureus* (MSSA)
041.12	Methicillin-resistant *staphylococcus aureus* (MSRA)
041.19	Bacterial infection in conditions classified elsewhere and of unspecified site, other staphylococcus
250.82	Diabetes mellitus with other specified manifestations, type 2 or unspecified type, uncontrolled
250.83	Diabetes mellitus with other specified manifestations, type 1 (juvenile type), uncontrolled
682.7	Other cellulitis and abscess of foot, except toes
682.8	Other cellulitis and abscess of other specified sites
707.00	Chronic ulcer of skin, pressure ulcer, unspecified site
707.15	Ulcer of lower limbs, except pressure ulcer, of other part of foot (toes)
707.8	Chronic ulcer of other specified sites
V09.0	Infection with microorganisms resistant to penicillins
86.01	Aspiration of skin and subcutaneous tissue
86.04	Other incision with drainage of skin and subcutaneous tissue

A. 250.83, 682.8, V09.0, 86.04
B. 682.7, 682.8, 707.15, 041.19, 86.01
C. 682.8, 041.19, 250.82, 707.00, 86.04,
D. 250.82, 682.7, 707.15, 041.12, V09.0, 86.04

REFERENCE: Brown, pp 112, 121–126, 239–242
               Schraffenberger, pp 79–80, 112–124, 292–294
               Ingenix, p 712

114. A patient was admitted to a nursing home with acute respiratory failure due to congestive heart failure. Chest x-ray also showed pulmonary edema. Patient was intubated and placed on mechanical ventilation and expired the day after admission.

428.0	Congestive heart failure, unspecified
428.1	Left heart failure
428.20	Systolic heart failure, unspecified as to acute, chronic, or acute on chronic
518.4	Acute edema of lung, unspecified
518.81	Acute respiratory failure
518.84	Acute and chronic respiratory failure
96.71	Continuous invasive mechanical ventilation for less than 96 consecutive hours
96.04	Insertion of endotracheal tube

A. 428.1, 518.84, 518.4, 96.71, 96.04
B. 428.20, 428.0, 518.81, 518.4, 96.71, 96.04
C. 518.81, 428.0, 96.71, 96.04
D. 428.0, 518.4, 96.04, 96.71

REFERENCE: Brown, pp 189–192, 194–195
              Schraffenberger, pp 192–194, 224–226
              Ingenix, pp 793, 798

115. The patient has hypertensive heart disease and nephrosclerosis with end-stage renal disease. The patient had placement of arteriovenous fistula in his left wrist to prepare for the hemodialysis. Dialysis was also performed on this admission.

404.92	Hypertensive heart and chronic kidney disease, unspecified as malignant or benign, without heart failure and with chronic kidney disease Stage V or end-stage renal disease
404.93	Hypertensive heart and chronic kidney disease unspecified as malignant or benign, with heart failure and chronic kidney disease Stage V or end-stage renal disease
585.6	End-stage renal disease
585.9	Chronic kidney disease, unspecified
V56.0	Encounter for extracorporeal dialysis
39.27	Arteriovenostomy for renal dialysis
38.95	Venous catheterization for renal dialysis
39.95	Hemodialysis
54.98	Peritoneal dialysis

A. 404.93, 585.9, 54.98, 39.27   C. 404.93, 585.6, 39.95, 39.27
B. 404.92, 585.6, 39.95, 39.27   D. 404.92, 585.9, 38.95, 39.27

REFERENCE: Brown, pp 221–222
              Ingenix, pp 348–349, 352, 365

116. The patient has had abnormal heavy uterine bleeding and abdominal pain. There was bright red blood in the vagina and the right adnexa was enlarged. The woman was admitted. During surgery, a laparoscopy revealed a right follicular ovarian cyst. A laparoscopic ovarian cystectomy was performed. Following surgery, she was transfused two units of packed red blood cells for acute blood-loss anemia.

    280.0   Iron-deficiency anemia secondary to blood loss (chronic)
    285.1   Acute posthemorrhagic anemia
    620.0   Follicular cyst of ovary
    65.25   Other laparoscopic local excision or destruction of ovary
    65.39   Other unilateral oophorectomy

    A. 620.0, 285.1, 65.25   C. 620.0, 285.1, 65.39
    B. 620.0, 280.0, 65.39   D. 620.0, 280.0, 65.25

REFERENCE: Brown, p 153
                 Schraffenberger, pp 135, 253
                 Ingenix, pp 530–531

117. Jane Doe is 6 weeks post mastectomy for carcinoma of the breast. She is admitted for chemotherapy. What is the correct sequencing of the codes?
    A. V58.11 (chemotherapy), 174.9 (malignant neoplasm of the breast), V45.71 (acquired absence of breast)
    B. V58.11 (chemotherapy), V10.3 (personal history of malignant neoplasm of breast), V45.71 (acquired absence of breast)
    C. V67.00 (follow-up exam after surgery), V58.11 (chemotherapy)
    D. V10.3 (personal history of malignant neoplasm of breast)

REFERENCE: Brown, pp 391–396
                 Schraffenberger, pp 445–446, 449–450

118. The patient was admitted due to increasingly severe pain in his right arm, shoulder, and neck for the past 6 weeks. MRI tests showed herniation of the C5-C6 disc. Patient underwent cervical laminotomy and diskectomy for C5-C6 disc. The patient is currently being treated for COPD and CAD with a history of a PTCA.

    414.00   Coronary atherosclerosis of unspecified type of vessel, native or graft
    414.01   Coronary atherosclerosis of native coronary artery
    492.8   Other emphysema
    496   Chronic airway obstruction, not elsewhere classified
    722.0   Displacement of cervical intervertebral disc without myelopathy
    722.11   Displacement of thoracic intervertebral disc without myelopathy
    V45.82   Percutaneous transluminal coronary angioplasty status
    80.51   Excision of intervertebral disc
    03.09   Other exploration and decompression of spinal canal

    A. 722.0, 492.8, 414.01, V45.82, 80.51
    B. 722.11, 496, 414.01, V45.82, 03.09, 80.51
    C. 722.11, 492.8, 414.00, 03.09, 80.51
    D. 722.0, 496, 414.01, V45.82, 80.51

REFERENCE: Brown, pp 186, 251–252, 337, 355
                 Schraffenberger, pp 190–193, 224, 304, 445–446
                 Ingenix, pp 99–100, 624–625

119. A 75-year-old man is admitted with acute cerebral embolism with infarction. He had hemiplegia and dysphagia. Physical therapy was given for the hemiplegia. The hemiplegia was resolved at the time of discharge.

    342.90   Hemiplegia, unspecified, affecting unspecified side
    434.11   Cerebral embolism with cerebral infarction
    787.20   Dysphagia, unspecified
    V57.1   Other physical therapy

    A.   434.11, 342.90, V57.1   C.   434.11, 342.90
    B.   434.11, 342.90, 787.20   D.   434.11, 342.90, 787.20, V57.1

REFERENCE: Brown, pp 343–345

Infectious and Parasitic Diseases

120. Patient is admitted to St. Mary's Hospital with hyperthermia, tachycardia, hypoxemia, and altered mental status. Urinalysis is positive for *E. coli* and blood cultures are negative. Patient is immediately started on broad-spectrum IV antibiotics. Physician documents urosepsis as the final diagnosis. The coder should
    A.   report 599.0 (UTI) and 041.4 (*E. coli*).
    B.   report 038.42 (septicemia due to *E. coli*) and 995.91 (SIRS-sepsis).
    C.   report 038.42 (septicemia due to *E. coli*), 599.0 (UTI) and 995.91 (SIRS-sepsis).
    D.   confer with physician for reporting 038.9 (unspecified septicemia) based on the clinical findings with 041.4 (*E. coli*) and 995.91 (SIRS-sepsis).

REFERENCE: Brown, pp 109–110
                      Schraffenberger, pp 80–82

121. Six-year-old Alex attended a birthday party where hot dogs and potato salad were served for lunch. Several hours after returning home, Alex began vomiting and having severe diarrhea. Alex was admitted to the hospital for treatment of his vomiting and diarrhea and was diagnosed with salmonella food poisoning. Alex was given IV fluids for dehydration. Alex also has asthma, so he was given respiratory treatments while in the hospital.

    003.9   Salmonella infection, unspecified
    005.9   Food poisoning, unspecified
    276.51   Dehydration
    493.90   Asthma, unspecified, unspecified as to with status asthmaticus or with acute exacerbation
    787.03   Vomiting alone
    787.91   Diarrhea

    A.   003.9, 276.51, 493.90   C.   005.9, 276.51, 493.90
    B.   005.9, 003.9, 276.51, 493.90   D.   005.9, 003.9, 267.51, 787.03, 787.91, 493.90

REFERENCE: Schraffenberger, pp 78–79, 126, 222–224

122. A patient is admitted to the hospital with listlessness, fever, and persistent cough. Workup reveals HIV infection with HIV-related pneumonia. The patient is treated for pneumonia.

    042   Human Immunodeficiency Virus (HIV) disease
    486   Pneumonia, organism unspecified
    795.71   Nonspecific serologic evidence of Human Immunodeficiency Virus (HIV)
    V08   Asymptomatic Human Immunodeficiency Virus (HIV) infection status

    A. 486, 042   C. 486, 795.71
    B. 042, 486   D. 486, V08

REFERENCE: Brown, p 115
               Schraffenberger, pp 82–85, 220

123. David was experiencing chronic fatigue and was experiencing flulike symptoms. Blood testing indicated that he had hepatitis C. A percutaneous liver biopsy was performed to determine the stage of the disease.

    070.41   Acute viral hepatitis C with hepatic coma
    070.51   Acute viral hepatitis C without mention of hepatic coma
    487.1   Influenza with other respiratory manifestations
    780.79   Other malaise and fatigue
    50.11   Closed (percutaneous) (needle) biopsy of liver
    50.12   Open biopsy of liver

    A. 070.51, 487.1, 780.79, 50.12   C. 070.51, 487.1, 50.11
    B. 070.41, 50.11   D. 070.51, 50.11

REFERENCE: Brown, pp 70–71, 107
               Schraffenberger, p 79
               Ingenix, p 491

124. A 40-year-old female suddenly develops a painful rash. A visit to her physician reveals she has shingles. She is experiencing a great amount of anxiety and stress, so her physician prescribes medication for the shingles and for the anxiety that occurred as a reaction to the stress.

    053.8   Herpes zoster with unspecified complication
    053.9   Herpes zoster without mention of complication
    300.00   Anxiety state, unspecified
    308.0   Predominant disturbance of emotions
    308.3   Other acute reactions to stress

    A. 053.9, 308.0   C. 053.8, 300.00
    B. 053.9, 308.3, 300.00   D. 053.8, 308.0

REFERENCE: Brown, pp 107, 139–140
               Schraffenberger, pp 79, 143

Neoplasms

125. James is admitted to the hospital for severe anemia that is a result of the chemotherapy treatments he is receiving for metastatic prostate cancer to bone. James receives blood transfusions and is discharged home.

185	Malignant neoplasm of prostate
198.5	Secondary malignant neoplasm, bone and bone marrow
285.22	Anemia in neoplastic disease
E933.1	Adverse effect of antineoplastic and immunosuppressive drugs

A. 185, 198.5, 285.22, E933.1   C. 285.22, E933.1
B. E933.1, 285.22   D. 285.22, 185, 198.5, E933.1

REFERENCE: Brown, pp 151, 153, 383–385
Schraffenberger, pp 103–111, 135

126. Mary had resection of the large bowel for carcinoma of the colon. She is admitted for further staging of her cancer and receives radiation therapy during this admission.

153.9	Malignant neoplasm of colon, unspecified
V10.05	Personal history of malignant neoplasm of large intestine
V58.0	Encounter for radiotherapy
V67.09	Follow-up examination following other surgery
92.29	Other radiotherapeutic procedure

A. 153.9, 92.29   C. V67.09, V58.0
B. V58.0, V10.05   D. V10.05, V58.0

REFERENCE: Brown, pp 382–383, 391–392

127. Jackie has developed a lesion on her right shoulder. A biopsy was obtained and was positive for malignant melanoma. She is now admitted for radical excision of the melanoma lesion and full-thickness skin graft.

172.6	Malignant melanoma of skin, upper limb, including shoulder
173.69	Malignant neoplasm of skin of upper limb, including shoulder
86.3	Other local excision or destruction of lesion or tissue of skin and subcutaneous tissue
86.4	Radical excision of skin lesion
86.63	Full-thickness skin graft to other sites

A. 172.6, 86.4, 86.63   C. 173.69, 86.3, 86.63
B. 173.69, 86.4, 86.63   D. 172.6, 86.3, 86.63

REFERENCE: Brown, pp 243, 377–379
Schraffenberger, p 103
Ingenix, pp 716–718

128. Richard is admitted for chemotherapy for leukemia. Chemotherapy is administered. Given this information,
    A. the leukemia code and a procedure code for the chemotherapy will be assigned.
    B. an admission for chemotherapy code and a chemotherapy procedure code will be assigned.
    C. an admission for chemotherapy code, a leukemia code, and a procedure code for the chemotherapy should be assigned and the principal diagnosis will be the admission for chemotherapy V code.
    D. an admission for chemotherapy code, a leukemia code, and a procedure code for the chemotherapy should be assigned and the principal diagnosis will be the leukemia code.

REFERENCE: Brown, pp 382–385
              Schraffenberger, p 111

129. Sophia has been diagnosed with metastatic carcinoma of lung, primary site breast. Simple mastectomy performed 2 years ago. What is the principal diagnosis?
    A. metastatic carcinoma of the lung
    B. carcinoma of breast
    C. history of carcinoma of breast
    D. status post mastectomy

REFERENCE: Brown, pp 382–385
              Schraffenberger, pp 108–109

130. Given the following diagnosis: "Carcinoma of axillary lymph nodes and lungs, metastatic from breast." What is the primary cancer site(s)?
    A. axillary lymph nodes   C. breast
    B. lungs   D. both A and B

REFERENCE: Brown, pp 382–385
              Schraffenberger, pp 107–109

131. When is it appropriate to use category V10, history of malignant neoplasm?
    A. Primary malignancy recurred at the original site and adjunct chemotherapy is directed at the site.
    B. Primary malignancy has been eradicated and no adjunct treatment is being given at this time.
    C. Primary malignancy is eradicated and the patient is admitted for adjunct chemotherapy to primary site.
    D. Primary malignancy is eradicated; adjunct treatment is refused by the patient even though there is some remaining malignancy.

REFERENCE: Brown, pp 89–90
              Schraffenberger, pp 102–104

Endocrine, Nutritional, and Metabolic Diseases and Immunity Disorders

132. Ralph is a 96-year-old nursing home resident who is admitted for malnutrition. He has suffered a previous stroke that has left him with dysphagia. He is treated for malnutrition with hyperalimentation. He was also found to have hypokalemia that was treated with IV potassium replacement. On the day prior to discharge, Ralph underwent a PEG tube insertion.

263.9	Unspecified protein-calorie malnutrition
276.8	Hypopotassemia (Hypokalemia)
438.82	Dysphagia, late effect of cerebrovascular disease
787.20	Dysphagia, unspecified
43.11	Percutaneous endoscopic gastrostomy (PEG) insertion

A. 438.82, 263.9, 787.20, 43.11   C. 263.9, 276.8, 438.82, 43.11
B. 787.20, 276.8, 43.11   D. 263.9, 787.20, 276.8, 43.11

REFERENCE: Brown, pp 129, 343–344
                         Schraffenberger, pp 122, 126, 198
                         Ingenix, pp 391–392

133. Jessica has been diagnosed with hyperthyroidism due to toxic multinodular goiter with crisis. She also has hypertension and has a history of sick sinus syndrome with pacemaker insertion. Jessica has a partial thyroidectomy on this admission.

240.9	Goiter, unspecified
241.1	Nontoxic multinodular goiter
242.21	Toxic multinodular goiter with mention of thyrotoxic crisis or storm
401.0	Essential hypertension, malignant
401.9	Essential hypertension, unspecified benign or malignant
427.81	Sinoatrial node dysfunction
V45.01	Other postprocedural states, cardiac pacemaker
06.39	Other partial thyroidectomy
06.4	Complete thyroidectomy

A. 240.9, 401.0, 427.81, 06.4
B. 242.21, 401.9, 427.81, V45.01, 06.39
C. 240.9, 242.21, 401.9. V45.01, 06.4
D. 242.21, 401.9. V45.01, 06.39

REFERENCE: Brown, p 347
                         Schraffenberger, pp 121–122, 180–182, 445–446
                         Ingenix, p 120

134. Laura is 7 years old and has acute bronchitis and cystic fibrosis. She is admitted to ambulatory surgery for bronchoscopy.

    277.00   Cystic fibrosis without mention of meconium ileus
    277.01   Cystic fibrosis with meconium ileus
    466.0   Acute bronchitis
    33.23   Other bronchoscopy
    33.24   Closed (endoscopic) biopsy of bronchus
    96.56   Other lavage of bronchus and trachea

  A. 466.0, 277.00, 33.23   C. 277.00, 96.56, 33.23
  B. 466.0, 277.01, 33.24   D. 277.00, 33.23, 33.24, 96.56

REFERENCE: Brown, p 129
                    Schraffenberger, pp 113, 181
                    Ingenix, pp 378–379, 797

135. Estelle has had nausea and vomiting and is unable to eat. She develops dehydration and is subsequently admitted for rehydration with intravenous fluids.

    276.51   Dehydration
    787.01   Nausea with vomiting
    787.02   Nausea alone
    787.03   Vomiting alone

  A. 276.51, 787.01   C. 276.51, 787.02
  B. 276.51   D. 276.51, 787.02, 787.03

REFERENCE: Schraffenberger, p 112

136. A patient is admitted for treatment of peripheral vascular disease, renal failure, and diabetes mellitus. The coder would
  A. assign codes for PVD, renal failure, and diabetes.
  B. assign codes for diabetes with peripheral vascular and renal manifestations.
  C. query physician for causal relationship between the PVD, renal failure, and diabetes.
  D. assign codes of diabetes with PVD and a code for renal failure.

REFERENCE: Brown, pp 123–126

137. Lucy is admitted because of diabetic coma. She has type 2 diabetes with nephritic syndrome and gangrene of her toes, all due to her diabetes.

> 250.30   Diabetes mellitus with other coma, type 2 or unspecified type, not stated as uncontrolled
>
> 250.31   Diabetes mellitus with other coma, type 1 (juvenile type), not stated as uncontrolled
>
> 250.40   Diabetes mellitus with renal manifestations, type 2 or unspecified type, not stated as uncontrolled
>
> 250.41   Diabetes mellitus with renal manifestations, type 1 (juvenile type), not stated as uncontrolled
>
> 250.70   Diabetes mellitus with peripheral circulatory disorders, type 2 or unspecified type, not stated as uncontrolled
>
> 581.81   Nephrotic syndrome in diseases classified elsewhere (manifestation)
>
> 785.4   Gangrene

A. 250.30, 250.40, 581.81, 250.70, 785.4
B. 250.31, 581.81, 785.4
C. 250.30, 250.40, 581.81
D. 250.30, 250.41, 785.4

REFERENCE: Brown, pp 121–126
              Schraffenberger, pp 122–124, 250

138. George has type 2 diabetes and is admitted in a coma with blood glucose of 876. He is diagnosed with diabetic ketoacidosis. George also has a diabetic cataract.

> 250.10   Diabetes mellitus with ketoacidosis, type 2 or unspecified type, not stated as uncontrolled
>
> 250.11   Diabetes mellitus with ketoacidosis, type 1 (juvenile type), not stated as uncontrolled
>
> 250.30   Diabetes mellitus with other coma, type 2 or unspecified type, not stated as uncontrolled
>
> 250.31   Diabetes mellitus with other coma, type 1 (juvenile type), not stated as uncontrolled
>
> 250.32   Diabetes mellitus with other coma, type 2 or unspecified type, uncontrolled
>
> 250.50   Diabetes mellitus with ophthalmic manifestations, type 2 or unspecified type, not stated as uncontrolled
>
> 250.51   Diabetes mellitus with ophthalmic manifestations, type 1 (juvenile type), not stated as uncontrolled
>
> 250.52   Diabetes mellitus with ophthalmic manifestations, type 2 or unspecified type, uncontrolled
>
> 366.41   Diabetic cataract (manifestation)
>
> 366.9   Unspecified cataract

A. 250.11, 250.31, 366.9   C. 250.32, 250.52, 366.41
B. 250.10, 250.30, 250.50, 366.9   D. 250.31, 250.51, 366.41

REFERENCE: Brown, pp 121–126
              Schraffenberger, pp 122–124, 164

139. Spencer has hypercholesterolemia and is treated with medication.

    272.0   Pure hypercholesterolemia
    272.1   Pure hyperglyceridemia
    272.3   Hyperchylomicronemia
    272.8   Other disorders of lipoid metabolism

    A.   272.0   C.   272.3
    B.   272.1   D.   272.8

REFERENCE: Schraffenberger, p 121

140. Edward is diagnosed with syndrome of inappropriate antidiuretic hormone with resultant electrolyte imbalance.

    253.6   Other disorders of neurophyophysis (syndrome of inappropriate secretion of antidiuretic hormone—ADH)
    272.9   Unspecified disorder of lipoid metabolism
    276.50   Volume depletion, unspecified
    276.8   Hypopotassemia (hypokalemia)
    276.9   Electrolyte and fluid disorders, not elsewhere classified

    A.   276.50   C.   253.6, 276.9
    B.   276.9, 272.9   D.   253.6. 276.8

REFERENCE: Schraffenberger, pp 121–126

Diseases of the Blood and Blood-Forming Organs

141. Ruth is admitted for an axillary lymph node biopsy to determine the cause of her chronic lymphadenitis. She is on medication for gout and atrial fibrillation.

    274.9   Gout, unspecified
    289.1   Chronic lymphadenitis
    289.2   Nonspecific mesenteric lymphadenitis
    427.31   Atrial fibrillation
    40.11   Biopsy of lymphatic structure
    40.23   Excision of axillary lymph node
    40.51   Radical excision of axillary lymph nodes

    A.   289.1, 274.9, 427.31, 40.11   C.   289.1, 427.31, 40.23
    B.   274.9, 289.2, 427.31, 40.11   D.   289.1, 427.31, 274.9, 40.51

REFERENCE: Brown, pp 70–71
                      Schraffenberger, pp 126, 137–138, 194
                      Ingenix, pp 368–369, 371

142. Elizabeth has a history of von Willebrand's disease and frequently requires transfusions for chronic blood-loss anemia associated with her condition. She presents to the outpatient department for routine blood transfusion.

280.0	Iron-deficiency anemia secondary to blood loss (chronic)
280.1	Iron-deficiency anemia secondary to inadequate dietary iron intake
285.1	Acute posthemorrhagic anemia
286.4	Von Willebrand's disease
286.7	Acquired coagulation factor deficiency

A. 285.1, 286.4   C. 286.4, 280.1
B. 286.7, 286.4   D. 280.0, 286.4

REFERENCE: Brown, pp 151–153
                           Schraffenberger, pp 132–136

143. Steven, a 7-year-old, is seen in the emergency department with severe joint pain. Following workup, it is discovered that he is having a severe crisis due to sickle cell anemia.

282.61	Sickle cell disease (Hb-SS disease without crisis)
282.62	Sickle cell disease (Hb-SS disease with crisis)
282.63	Sickle cell/Hb-C disease without crisis
282.69	Other sickle cell disease with crisis

A. 282.61   C. 282.63
B. 282.62   D. 282.69

REFERENCE: Bowie and Schaffer, p 145
                           Brown, p 154
                           Schraffenberger, p 132

144. Angela has just undergone orthopedic surgery. Documentation indicates that she lost 700 cc of blood during surgery. Her hemoglobin and hematocrit are monitored following surgery. Subsequently, she is transfused. The physician documents anemia as a secondary diagnosis. The coder would

A. query the physician to clarify the type of anemia as acute blood loss.
B. assign a code for unspecified anemia.
C. assign a code for acute blood-loss anemia.
D. not assign a code for anemia.

REFERENCE: Brown, p 152

145. Liza has been diagnosed with anemia. She is being admitted for a bone marrow aspiration to determine the specific type of anemia. The pathology report indicates that she has iron-deficiency anemia.

280.0   Iron-deficiency anemia secondary to blood loss (chronic)
280.8   Other specified iron-deficiency anemias
280.9   Iron-deficiency anemia, unspecified
41.31   Biopsy of bone marrow
41.38   Other diagnostic procedures on bone marrow
41.91   Aspiration of bone marrow from donor for transplant

A. 280.0, 41.38   C. 280.9, 41.91
B. 280.9, 41.31   D. 280.8, 41.38

REFERENCE: Bowie and Schaffer, pp 144–145
              Brown, p 151
              Ingenix, pp 377–378, 380

146. Peggy has thymic dysplasia with immunodeficiency.

254.0   Persistent hyperplasia of thymus
254.8   Other specified diseases of thymus gland
254.9   Unspecified disease of thymus gland
279.2   Combined immunity deficiency (thymic aplasia or dysplasia with immunodeficiency)
279.3   Unspecified immunity deficiency

A. 279.3, 254.8   C. 279.2
B. 254.0   D. 279.2, 254.9

REFERENCE: Brown, p 130

147. Aaron has suffered a hypoglycemic reaction due to alcohol intoxication. Hypoglycemia is treated.

250.80   Diabetes mellitus with other specified manifestations, type 2 or unspecified type, not stated as uncontrolled
251.2   Hypoglycemia, unspecified
303.90   Other and unspecified alcohol dependence, unspecified
305.00   Alcohol abuse, unspecified
995.29   Unspecified adverse effect of other drug, medicinal, and biological substance

A. 251.2, 305.00   C. 995.29, 303.90
B. 251.2, 303.90   D. 250.80, 305.00

REFERENCE: Brown, pp 128, 141–142

Mental Disorders

148. Joe is being admitted for treatment of chronic alcoholism. As a result of Joe's drinking he also has chronic alcoholic gastritis for which he receives medication. Joe is scheduled to spend 30 days in the inpatient rehab unit of Sunshine Hospital.

    303.01   Acute alcoholic intoxication, continuous
    303.90   Other and unspecified alcohol dependence, unspecified
    303.91   Other and unspecified alcohol dependence, continuous
    535.00   Acute gastritis without mention of hemorrhage
    535.30   Alcoholic gastritis without mention of hemorrhage
    535.31   Alcoholic gastritis with hemorrhage
    94.61   Alcohol rehabilitation
    94.62   Alcohol detoxification
    94.63   Alcohol rehabilitation and detoxification

    A. 303.01, 535.00, 94.63   C. 303.90, 535.30, 94.61
    B. 303.91, 535.00, 94.63   D. 303.01, 303.90, 535.30, 94.63

    REFERENCE: Brown, pp 141–142, 201
                  Schraffenberger, pp 234–235
                  Ingenix, pp 786–787

149. Sheila has paranoid alcoholic psychosis with chronic alcoholism, continuous. She is admitted for treatment of her psychosis.

    291.5   Alcohol-induced psychotic disorder with delusions
    303.91   Other and unspecified alcohol dependence, continuous
    V57.89   Other specified rehabilitation procedure

    A. 291.5, 303.91   C. V57.89, 303.91
    B. 303.91, 291.5   D. 291.5, 303.91, V57.89

    REFERENCE: Brown, pp 135, 141–142
                  Schraffenberger, pp 143, 148

150. Sybil has been admitted to Shady Acres Psychiatric facility for treatment of schizophrenia. Sybil is also manic depressive and has been noncompliant with her medications.

    295.40   Schizophreniform disorder, unspecified
    295.41   Schizophreniform disorder, subchronic
    295.90   Unspecified schizophrenia, unspecified
    296.7   Bipolar I disorder, most recent episode (or current) unspecified
    296.80   Bipolar disorder, unspecified
    296.89   Other bipolar disorders (manic-depressive psychosis, mixed type)
    V15.81   Personal history, presenting hazards to health (noncompliance with medical treatment)

    A. V15.81, 296.89, 295.40   C. 296.7, 295.90
    B. 296.89, 295.41, V15.81   D. 295.90, 296.80, V15.81

    REFERENCE: Brown, p 137

151. Allen is addicted to Vicodin. He has stopped taking the drug and is now having withdrawal symptoms. Allen has chronic back pain for which he has been prescribed the medication. He is admitted for treatment of his withdrawal symptoms.

292.0	Drug withdrawal
292.11	Drug-induced psychotic disorder with delusions
292.2	Pathological drug intoxication
304.00	Drug dependence, opioid type dependence, unspecified
304.91	Unspecified drug dependence, continuous
724.5	Backache, unspecified

A. 292.2, 724.5

B. 292.11, 292.2, 304.91

C. 292.0, 304.00, 724.5

D. 292.11, 304.91, 724.5

REFERENCE: Brown, pp 141–142
              Schraffenberger, pp 143, 147–148

152. Acute epileptic twilight state with delirium.

293.0	Delirium due to conditions classified elsewhere (epileptic twilight state)
293.1	Subacute delirium
294.0	Amnestic disorder in conditions classified elsewhere
345.00	Generalized nonconvulsive epilepsy without mention of intractable epilepsy
780.02	Transient alteration of awareness

A. 293.0

B. 780.02

C. 293.1

D. 294.0, 345.00

REFERENCE: Brown, pp 164–165

153. Sally has been diagnosed with panic attacks and is prescribed Xanax. She has been taking the medication as prescribed by her physician for 3 days and is now having hallucinations. Her physician advises her to stop taking the medication and her symptoms abate. Her doctor determines that the hallucinations were due to the Xanax.

292.12	Drug-induced psychotic disorder with hallucinations
300.01	Panic disorder without agoraphobia
E939.4	Benzodiazepine-based tranquilizers

A. 292.12, E939.4, 300.01

B. 292.12

C. E939.4, 292.12

D. 300.01, 292.12

REFERENCE: Brown, pp 443–446
              Schraffenberger, p 143

154. Lou has profound mental retardation due to mongolism.

    317   Mild intellectual abilities
    318.0   Moderate intellectual abilities
    318.2   Profound intellectual abilities
    758.0   Down's syndrome
    759.0   Congenital anomaly of spleen

    A. 318.2, 758.0   C. 758.0, 318.2
    B. 318.0, 759.0   D. 317, 758.0

REFERENCE: Schraffenberger, pp 130, 283–284

Diseases of the Nervous System and Sense Organs

155. Mark has a long history of epilepsy. He is brought to the emergency department and is admitted with intractable epileptic seizures. Mark's epilepsy is the result of a head injury he suffered several years ago.

    345.11   Generalized convulsive epilepsy with intractable epilepsy
    345.10   Generalized convulsive epilepsy, without mention of intractable epilepsy
    345.3   Grand mal status
    345.91   Epilepsy, unspecified, with intractable epilepsy
    780.39   Other convulsions
    907.0   Late effect of intracranial injury without mention of skull fracture

    A. 780.39, 907.0   C. 345.3
    B. 345.91, 907.0   D. 345.10, 780.39

REFERENCE: Brown, pp 59–60, 164–165
                      Schraffenberger, pp 161–162

156. Jeff was in a car accident when he was 25 years old and suffered a spinal cord injury. As a result, he is a paraplegic and has neurogenic bladder. Jeff also has chronic ulcers of the buttocks. He is being seen for evaluation of his paraplegia.

    344.1   Paraplegia
    344.60   Cauda equina syndrome without mention of neurogenic bladder
    596.53   Paralysis of bladder
    596.54   Neurogenic bladder, not otherwise specified
    707.00   Chronic pressure ulcer of skin, unspecified site
    707.8   Chronic ulcer of other specified sites
    907.2   Late effect of spinal cord injury

    A. 344.1, 907.2, 596.54, 707.8   C. 344.1, 596.53, 907.2
    B. 344.60, 596.53, 707.00, 907.2   D. 344.1, 596.54, 707.8

REFERENCE: Brown, pp 60, 425

157. Josephine has developed senile cataracts in both eyes. She is admitted for right extracapsular cataract extraction with synchronous lens insertion.

    366.10   Senile cataract, unspecified
    366.9   Unspecified cataract
    13.59   Other extracapsular extraction of lens
    13.71   Insertion of intraocular lens prosthesis at time of cataract extraction, one stage

    A. 366.9, 13.71   C. 366.9, 13.59, 13.71
    B. 366.10, 13.59, 13.71   D. 366.10, 13.59

REFERENCE: Brown, p 172
                     Schraffenberger, p 164
                     Ingenix, pp 172–174

158. A patient presents with diabetic macular or retinal edema.

    250.50   Diabetes mellitus with ophthalmic manifestations, type 2 or unspecified type, not stated as uncontrolled
    250.51   Diabetes mellitus with ophthalmic manifestations, type 1 (juvenile type), not stated as uncontrolled
    362.01   Background diabetic retinopathy (manifestation)
    362.02   Proliferative diabetic retinopathy (manifestation)
    362.07   Diabetic macular edema

    A. 250.51, 362.07, 360.02   C. 250.50, 362.07, 362.01
    B. 362.07, 250.51, 362.02   D. 362.02, 362.07, 250.50

REFERENCE: Schraffenberger, pp 122–124, 163–164

159. A patient presents with bilateral sensorineural conductive hearing loss.

    389.20   Mixed hearing loss, unspecified
    389.21   Mixed hearing loss, unilateral
    389.22   Mixed hearing loss, bilateral
    389.9   Unspecified hearing loss

    A. 389.22   C. 389.9
    B. 389.21   D. 389.20

REFERENCE: Schraffenberger, p 165

Diseases of the Circulatory System

160. Madeline is diagnosed with bilateral carotid stenosis. She is being admitted for a bilateral endarterectomy. Madeline is also treated for Parkinson's disease and glaucoma.

    332.0   Paralysis agitans (Parkinson's disease)
    365.9   Unspecified glaucoma
    433.30   Occlusion and stenosis of precerebral arteries, multiple and bilateral, without mention of cerebral infarction
    38.12   Endarterectomy, other vessels of head and neck

    A. 433.30, 38.12   C. 433.30, 332.0, 365.9, 38.12
    B. 433.30, 38.12, 38.12   D. 433.30, 332.0, 365.9, 38.12, 38.12

REFERENCE: Brown, pp 172–173, 343–344
                     Schraffenberger, p 159, 164, 197
                     Ingenix, pp 341–342

161. Jonathan is admitted with bleeding prolapsed internal hemorrhoids and chronic constipation. The physician performed a rubber band ligation of the internal hemorrhoids.

455.1	Internal thrombosed hemorrhoids
455.2	Internal hemorrhoids with other complication
564.09	Other constipation
49.44	Destruction of hemorrhoids by cryotherapy
49.45	Ligation of hemorrhoids
49.46	Excision of hemorrhoids

A. 455.1, 564.09, 49.44
B. 455.1, 49.45
C. 455.2, 564.09 49.45
D. 455.1, 455.2, 49.45

REFERENCE: Schraffenberger, p 234
Ingenix, p 428

162. Frank has been diagnosed with sick sinus syndrome and is being admitted for dual chamber pacemaker and leads insertion. Frank also has type 2 diabetes on oral medication as well as insulin regimen. Surgery is carried out without complication.

250.00	Diabetes mellitus without mention of complication, type 2 or unspecified type, not stated as uncontrolled
250.01	Diabetes mellitus without mention of complication, type 1 (juvenile type), not stated as uncontrolled
427.81	Sinoatrial node dysfunction
V58.67	Long-term (current) use of insulin
37.70	Initial insertion of lead (electrode), not otherwise specified
37.71	Initial insertion of transvenous lead (electrode) into ventricle
37.72	Initial insertion of transvenous leads (electrode) into atrium and ventricle
37.82	Initial insertion of single-chamber device, rate responsive
37.83	Initial insertion of dual chamber device

A. 427.81, 250.00, V58.67, 37.72, 37.83
B. 427.81, 250.01, 37.71, 37.83
C. 427.81, 37.70, 37.83
D. 427.81, 250.00, 250.01, 37.72, 37.83

REFERENCE: Brown, pp 121–122, 358
Ingenix, pp 335–338

163. A patient is treated for congestive heart failure with pleural effusion. A therapeutic thoracentesis is performed.

428.0	Congestive heart failure, unspecified
511.9	Unspecified pleural effusion
34.04	Insertion of intercostal catheter for drainage
34.91	Thoracentesis

A. 511.9, 34.91
B. 428.0, 34.04
C. 428.0, 511.9
D. 428.0, 511.9, 34.91

REFERENCE: Brown, pp 189, 339–340
Schraffenberger, pp 192–193
Ingenix, pp 287–288, 296

164. A patient presents to the emergency department complaining of a severe headache. Workup revealed a ruptured berry aneurysm.

430   Subarachnoid hemorrhage
437.3   Cerebral aneurysm, nonruptured
784.0   Headache

A. 430
B. 784.0
C. 784.0, 430
D. 437.3

REFERENCE: Brown, pp 343–344

Diseases of the Respiratory System

165. Joseph has had cough, fever, and painful respirations for 2 days. He also has congestive heart failure and COPD. Joseph presents to the emergency department with severe shortness of breath, using accessory muscles to assist with breathing. Upon examination, Joseph is diagnosed with acute respiratory failure, congestive heart failure, pneumonia, and exacerbation of COPD. Joseph is intubated and placed on mechanical ventilation. He is weaned from the ventilator on the third day of admission. Two days later, he again goes into respiratory failure, requiring reintubation and placement on the ventilator. Fortunately, he is able to breathe on his own the following day, so was extubated.

428.0   Congestive heart failure, unspecified
486   Pneumonia, organism unspecified
491.21   Obstructive chronic bronchitis with (acute) exacerbation
496   Chronic airway obstruction, not elsewhere classified
518.81   Acute respiratory failure
96.04   Insertion of endotracheal tube
96.71   Continuous invasive mechanical ventilation for less than 96 consecutive hours
96.72   Continuous invasive mechanical ventilation for 96 consecutive hours or more

A. 428.0, 486, 496, 518.81, 96.04, 96.71
B. 518.81, 428.0, 491.21, 96.04, 96.71
C. 486, 428.0, 518.81, 491.21, 96.04, 96.72
D. 518.81, 486, 428.0, 491.21, 96.04, 96.71, 96.04, 96.71

REFERENCE: Bowie and Schaffer, p 216
Brown, pp 189–191, 194–195, 339–340
Schraffenberger, pp 192–193, 219, 223–224
Ingenix, pp 793, 798

166. Ronald is admitted for stenosis of his tracheostomy. He is a quadriplegic, C1-C4 secondary to spinal cord injury suffered in a diving accident. He has chronic respiratory failure and is maintained on mechanical ventilation. He undergoes revision of his tracheostomy.

344.00	Quadriplegia, unspecified
344.01	Quadriplegia, C1-C4, complete
518.83	Chronic respiratory failure
519.02	Mechanical complication of tracheostomy
519.09	Other tracheostomy complications
907.2	Late effect of spinal cord injury
V46.11	Dependence on respirator status (ventilator)
31.74	Revision of tracheostomy
31.79	Other repair and plastic operations on trachea
96.71	Continuous invasive mechanical ventilation for less than 96 consecutive hours
96.72	Continuous invasive mechanical ventilation for 96 consecutive hours or more

   A.   518.83, 519.09, 907.2, 31.74
   B.   344.01, 518.83, 519.02, 31.79, V46.11
   C.   519.02, 344.01, 518.83, 907.2, V46.11, 31.74, 96.72
   D.   519.02, 518.83, 907.2, 31.74

REFERENCE: Brown, pp 189–191, 194–195
              Schraffenberger, pp 161, 224–226, 446
              Ingenix, pp 270, 798–799

167. Jennifer presents to the emergency department with severe chest pain and shortness of breath. Chest x-ray revealed a secondary spontaneous pneumothorax. Jennifer also has acute bronchitis. The emergency department physician inserts a chest tube and Jennifer is admitted.

466.0	Acute bronchitis
491.20	Obstructive chronic bronchitis without exacerbation
491.21	Obstructive chronic bronchitis with (acute) exacerbation
512.0	Spontaneous tension pneumothorax
512.1	Iatrogenic pneumothorax
512.81	Primary spontaneous pneumothorax
512.82	Secondary spontaneous pneumothorax
34.01	Incision of chest wall
34.04	Insertion of intercostal catheter for drainage

   A.   466.0, 512.82, 34.04   C.   466.0, 491.21, 512.1, 34.04
   B.   512.0, 491.21, 34.01   D.   491.20, 466.0, 512.82, 34.01

REFERENCE: Schraffenberger, pp 217–218
              Ingenix, pp 287–288

168. Dale is admitted with emphysematous nodules. He undergoes, without complication, a wedge resection of the right upper lobe. Dale developed atelectasis postoperatively that required monitoring with portable chest x-rays and extended his length of stay.

492.8	Other emphysema
518.0	Pulmonary collapse (atelectasis)
518.89	Other diseases of lung, not elsewhere classified
997.39	Respiratory complications
32.29	Other local excision or destruction of lesions or tissue of lung
32.30	Thoracoscopic segmental resection of lung

A. 518.89, 997.39, 32.30   C. 492.8, 997.39, 518.0, 32.29
B. 997.39, 518.0, 518.89, 32.29   D. 518.89, 518.0, 32.29

REFERENCE: Brown, pp 188–189
                 Schraffenberger, pp 223, 387–390
                 Ingenix, pp 274–275

169. Agnes is admitted with cough, fever, and dysphagia. Chest x-ray shows infiltrates in both lower lobes. Sputum culture is positive for *Staphylococcus aureus*. Swallow study indicates that Agnes aspirates. Physician documents aspiration pneumonia and *Staphylococcus aureus* pneumonia. As a coder, you would assign codes for the following conditions in this proper sequence.
A. *Staphylococcus aureus* pneumonia, dysphagia
B. *Staphylococcus aureus* pneumonia, aspiration pneumonia
C. Aspiration pneumonia, dysphagia
D. Aspiration pneumonia, *Staphylococcus aureus* pneumonia, dysphagia

REFERENCE: Bowie and Schaffer, p 212
                 Brown, pp 181–183
                 Schraffenberger, p 219

170. This patient has pneumonia. She also has acute exacerbation of COPD.

486	Pneumonia, organism unspecified
491.20	Obstructive chronic bronchitis, without exacerbation
491.21	Obstructive chronic bronchitis, with (acute) exacerbation

A. 491.21   C. 491.20, 486
B. 486, 491.21   D. 486

REFERENCE: Brown, pp 181–182, 186
                 Schraffenberger, p 219

171. Matthew has acute and chronic maxillary sinusitis. He had a maxillary sinusectomy performed.

461.0	Acute maxillary sinusitis
461.2	Acute ethmoidal sinusitis
473.0	Chronic maxillary sinusitis
22.62	Excision of lesion of maxillary sinus with other approach

A. 461.0, 22.62   C. 461.0, 473.0, 22.62
B. 473.0, 22.62   D. 461.2, 22.62

REFERENCE: Schraffenberger, p 217
                 Ingenix, p 234

Diseases of the Digestive System

172. Grace has been having abdominal pain for several weeks and has been vomiting blood for 2 days. Her physician performs an esophagogastroduodenoscopy and biopsies a lesion in the duodenum. The pathology report indicates Grace has acute and chronic gastritis.

> 532.00   Acute duodenal ulcer with hemorrhage without mention of obstruction
> 535.01   Acute gastritis with hemorrhage
> 535.11   Chronic (atrophic) gastritis with hemorrhage
> 789.00   Abdominal pain, unspecified site
> 45.13   Esophagogastroduodenoscopy (EGD)
> 45.16   Esophagogastroduodenoscopy with closed biopsy

   A.   532.00, 789.00, 45.13   C.   535.01, 535.11, 789.00. 45.13
   B.   535.01, 789.00, 45.16   D.   535.01, 535.11, 45.16

REFERENCE: Brown, p 201
                     Ingenix, pp 404–405

173. Mary presents to the emergency department with complaints of chest pain. Myocardial infarction is ruled out; however, gastrointestinal studies indicate Mary is suffering from gastroesophageal reflux disease (GERD). Mary is given medication to relieve her symptoms and instructed to follow up with her physician.

> 410.91   Acute myocardial infarction, unspecified site, initial episode of care
> 530.81   Gastroesophageal reflux (GERD)
> 786.50   Chest pain, unspecified

   A.   530.81   C.   530.81, 410.91
   B.   786.50   D.   410.91, 786.50

REFERENCE: Brown, p 203

174. Crystal has been vomiting for 24 hours with complaint of right lower quadrant pain. Examination is suspicious for acute appendicitis. Crystal is taken to surgery and laparoscopic appendectomy is carried out. Pathological diagnosis is consistent with acute appendicitis. Crystal developed postoperative paralytic ileus.

> 540.0   Acute appendicitis with generalized peritonitis
> 540.9   Acute appendicitis without mention of peritonitis
> 560.1   Paralytic ileus
> 997.49   Digestive system complications
> 47.01   Laparoscopic appendectomy
> 47.09   Other appendectomy
> 47.11   Laparoscopic incidental appendectomy

   A.   540.0, 997.49, 47.11   C.   540.9, 997.49, 560.1, 47.01
   B.   540.0, 997.49, 47.09   D.   997.49, 560.1, 540.9, 47.09

REFERENCE: Brown, pp 210–211
                     Ingenix, pp 417–418

175. A patient presents with intestinal obstruction due to adhesions. He also has peripheral vascular disease and chronic urinary tract infections; both conditions were treated with oral medication.

    443.9   Peripheral vascular disease, unspecified
    560.81   Intestinal or peritoneal adhesions with obstruction (postoperative) (post infection)
    560.89   Other specified intestinal obstruction
    560.9   Unspecified intestinal obstruction
    599.0   Urinary tract infection, site not specified

    A.   560.81, 443.9, 599.0   C.   560.9, 443.9, 599.0
    B.   560.9   D.   560.89, 443.9, 599.0

REFERENCE: Brown, pp 208, 217

176. This patient has chronic diarrhea associated with Crohn's disease. She also has protein-calorie malnutrition. She is admitted for bowel resection of the diseased colon.

    263.9   Unspecified protein-calorie malnutrition
    555.1   Regional enteritis, large intestine (Crohn's disease)
    556.9   Ulcerative colitis, unspecified
    787.91   Diarrhea
    45.79   Other and unspecified partial excision of large intestine
    45.94   Large-to-large intestinal anastomosis

    A.   556.9, 263.9, 45.79, 45.94   C.   555.1, 787.91, 263.9, 45.79
    B.   555.1, 263.9, 45.79   D.   556.9, 263.9, 45.79, 45.94

REFERENCE: Schraffenberger, p 236
                    Ingenix, pp 409–410

177. A patient is admitted with hepatic coma with ascites due to Laennec's cirrhosis.

    571.2   Alcoholic cirrhosis of liver (Laennec's cirrhosis)
    572.2   Hepatic encephalopathy (hepatic coma)
    789.59   Other ascites

    A.   572.2, 571.2, 789.59   C.   789.59, 572.2
    B.   571.2, 789.59   D.   789.59, 572.2, 571.2

REFERENCE: Schraffenberger, p 234

Diseases of the Genitourinary System

178. Chantel is admitted with infertility secondary to pelvic peritoneal adhesions. She had a laparoscopic lysis of adhesions performed.

    614.6   Pelvic peritoneal adhesions, female (postoperative) (post infection)
    628.2   Infertility, female, of tubal origin
    54.21   Laparoscopy
    65.81   Laparoscopic lysis of adhesions of ovary and fallopian tube

    A.   628.2, 614.6, 65.81   C.   614.6, 65.81, 54.21
    B.   628.2, 54.21, 65.81   D.   614.6, 54.21

REFERENCE: Brown, p 208
                    Ingenix, pp 453, 535–536

179. Betsy has chronic pelvic inflammatory disease with dysmenorrhea. She undergoes a diagnostic laparoscopy.

614.4	Chronic or unspecified parametritis and pelvic cellulitis
625.3	Dysmenorrhea
54.21	Laparoscopy
54.4	Excision or destruction of peritoneal tissue

A. 625.3, 54.21
B. 614.4, 54.4
C. 625.3, 614.4, 54.21
D. 614.4, 625.3, 54.21

REFERENCE: Schraffenberger, p 253
                 Ingenix, pp 453–454

180. David has chronic interstitial cystitis. The physician performs a cystoscopy with biopsy.

595.1	Chronic interstitial cystitis
595.2	Other chronic cystitis
599.0	Urinary tract infection, site not specified
57.32	Other cystoscopy
57.33	Closed (transurethral) biopsy of bladder

A. 599.0, 57.32
B. 595.1, 57.33
C. 595.2, 57.32, 57.33
D. 595.1, 599.0, 57.32

REFERENCE: Brown, p 217

181. Cynthia has fibrocystic disease of the breast and undergoes a needle biopsy of the breast.

610.1	Diffuse cystic mastopathy (fibrocystic disease of breast)
610.2	Fibroadenosis of breast
610.3	Fibrosclerosis of breast
610.9	Benign mammary dysplasia, unspecified
85.11	Closed (percutaneous) (needle) biopsy of breast
85.12	Open biopsy of breast

A. 610.1, 85.11
B. 610.3, 85.12
C. 610.2, 85.11
D. 610.9, 85.12

REFERENCE: Brown, p 229
                 Ingenix, pp 702–703

Complications of Pregnancy, Childbirth, and the Puerperium

182. Tammy has an intrauterine pregnancy and delivers a set of twins at 33 weeks. She had premature rupture of membranes. The spontaneous delivery of the premature twins was via a vertex presentation, and both infants were born alive.

644.20	Early onset of delivery, unspecified episode of care
644.21	Early onset of delivery, delivered, with or without mention of antepartum condition
651.01	Twin pregnancy, delivered, with or without mention of antepartum condition
658.11	Premature rupture of membranes, delivered, with or without mention of antepartum condition
659.11	Failed medical or unspecified induction, delivered, with or without mention of antepartum condition
V27.2	Outcome of delivery, twins, both live born
73.59	Other manually assisted delivery

A. 644.21, 658.11, 651.01, V27.2, 73.59
B. 644.20, 659.11, V27.2
C. 644.20, 658.11, 651.02, 73.59
D. 658.11, 651.01, V27.2, 73.59

REFERENCE: Brown, pp 269–275
Schraffenberger, pp 223, 230, 235–236
Ingenix, p 585

183. A pregnant patient was admitted to the hospital with uncontrolled diabetes mellitus. She has type 1 diabetes and was brought under control. The following code was assigned:

648.03	Other current conditions in the mother classifiable elsewhere but complicating pregnancy, childbirth or the puerperium, diabetes mellitus, antepartum condition, or complication

Which of the following describe why the coding is in error?
A. The incorrect fifth digit was used.
B. The condition should have been coded as gestational diabetes because she is pregnant.
C. An additional code describing the diabetes mellitus should be used.
D. Only the code for the diabetes mellitus should be used.

REFERENCE: Brown, pp 126–127, 276–277
Schraffenberger, pp 108–110

Disease of the Skin and Subcutaneous Tissue

184. Max is 80% bald. He is admitted for a hair transplant, which he undergoes without complication. Max is also treated for congestive heart failure and hypertension for which he is on medication.

401.9	Essential hypertension, unspecified benign or malignant
402.91	Hypertensive heart disease unspecified as to malignant or benign, with heart failure
428.0	Congestive heart failure, unspecified
704.00	Alopecia, unspecified
704.8	Other specified diseases of hair and hair follicles
86.64	Hair transplant

A. 704.00, 402.91, 86.64
B. 704.8, 401.9, 428.0, 86.64
C. 704.00, 401.9, 428.0, 86.64
D. 704.8, 402.91, 86.64

REFERENCE: Brown, pp 278, 339–340
Schraffenberger, pp 180–181, 192–194, 291
Ingenix, p 712

185. Melissa is status post mastectomy due to breast cancer. There has been no recurrence of the disease. She is admitted for insertion of unilateral breast implant.

174.9	Malignant neoplasm of breast (female), unspecified
V10.3	Personal history of malignant neoplasm of breast
V45.71	Acquired absence of breast and nipple
V51.0	Encounter for breast reconstruction following mastectomy
V58.42	Aftercare following surgery for neoplasm
85.53	Unilateral breast implant
85.54	Bilateral breast implant

A. V51.0, V10.3, 85.54
B. V58.42, V51.0, V45.71, V10.3, 85.53
C. V45.71, 174.9, 85.53
D. V51.0, V45.71, V10.3, 85.53

REFERENCE: Brown, pp 83–84, 89–90
Ingenix, p 707

186. Roscoe is 57 years old and has been diagnosed with gynecomastia. Roscoe also is on medication for temporal arteritis. Roscoe is admitted and bilateral mammectomy is performed. Roscoe's intravenous catheter infiltrates and he develops cellulitis at the IV site in the arm. This condition requires additional treatment.

446.5	Giant cell arteritis
611.1	Hypertrophy of breast
682.3	Other cellulitis and abscess upper arm and forearm
999.39	Infection following other infusion, injection, transfusion, or vaccination
85.34	Other unilateral subcutaneous mammectomy
85.36	Other bilateral subcutaneous mammectomy

A. 611.1, 85.36, 85.36
B. 611.1, 999.39, 446.5, 85.36
C. 611.1, 999.39, 682.3, 446.5, 85.36
D. 611.1, 682.3, 446.5, 85.34

REFERENCE: Brown, pp 462–464
Schraffenberger, pp 252, 292, 389–390
Ingenix, p 705

187. Brandon has an infected ingrown toenail that his physician removes.

    681.11   Onychia and paronychia of toe
    703.0   Ingrowing nail
    77.89   Other partial ostectomy, other site
    86.23   Removal of nail, nail bed, or nail fold
    86.27   Debridement of nail, nail bed, or nail fold

    A. 703.0, 86.23   C. 681.11, 86.27
    B. 681.11, 86.23   D. 703.0, 86.23, 77.89

REFERENCE: Schraffenberger, p 291
                Ingenix, pp 715–716

Disease of the Musculoskeletal System and Connective Tissue

188. Julia is an 80-year-old female with osteoporosis. She presents to the emergency department complaining of severe back pain. X-rays revealed pathological compression fractures of several vertebrae.

    721.90   Spondylosis of unspecified site without mention of myelopathy
    733.00   Osteoporosis, unspecified
    733.13   Pathological fracture of vertebrae
    805.8   Fracture of vertebral column without mention of spinal cord injury, unspecified, closed

    A. 733.13, 733.00   C. 721.90, 733.13
    B. 805.8, 733.00   D. 733.00, 733.13

REFERENCE: Brown, pp 255–256, 415
                Schraffenberger, pp 305–306

189 Scott has a deformity of his left ring finger, due to an old tendon injury. He is admitted and undergoes a transfer of the flexor tendon from the distal phalanx to the middle phalanx.

    727.82   Calcium deposits in tendon and bursa
    736.20   Unspecified deformity of finger (acquired)
    834.02   Closed dislocation of finger, interphalangeal (joint), hand
    905.8   Late effect of tendon injury
    82.55   Other change in hand muscle or tendon length
    82.56   Other hand tendon transfer or transportation

    A. 727.82, 82.56   C. 834.02, 82.55
    B. 736.20, 905.8, 82.56   D. 727.82, 82.55

REFERENCE: Schraffenberger, p 305
                Ingenix, p 664

190. Sara has Dupuytren's contracture of the right middle finger. She has an incision and division of the palmar fascia.

   728.6   Contracture of palmar fascia (Dupuytren's contracture)
   728.71   Plantar fascial fibromatosis
   728.86   Necrotizing fasciaitis
   82.12   Fasciotomy of hand
   82.19   Other division of soft tissue of hand

   A. 728.6, 82.12   C. 728.6, 82.19
   B. 728.71, 82.19   D. 728.86, 82.12

REFERENCE: Schraffenberger, pp 304–305
                Ingenix, pp 659–660

191. Cheryl has had chronic worsening pain of her left knee from rheumatoid arthritis. She has decided to undergo a total knee replacement as recommended by her physician. The surgery goes well; however, she develops a urinary tract infection that requires an additional day of stay in the hospital.

   599.0   Urinary tract infection, site not specified
   714.0   Rheumatoid arthritis
   714.31   Polyarticular juvenile rheumatoid arthritis, acute
   715.96   Osteoarthrosis, unspecified whether generalized or localized, low leg
   81.53   Revision of hip replacement, not otherwise specified
   81.54   Total knee replacement

   A. 715.96, 599.0, 81.54   C. 714.31, 81.53
   B. 714.0, 599.0, 81.54   D. 714.31, 81.54

REFERENCE: Brown, pp 218, 251–252, 256–257
                Schraffenberger, pp 250–251, 303
                Ingenix, pp 645–650

Injury and Poisoning

192. A patient who is HIV positive and currently asymptomatic is admitted with a compound fracture of the tibia. The patient was treated previously for Pneumocystis carinii pneumonia. Given the following codes, which is the correct coding and sequencing?

   042   Human Immunodeficiency Virus (HIV) disease
   136.3   Pneumocystosis (pneumonia due to *Pneumocystis carinii*)
   V08   Asymptomatic HIV infection status
   823.80   Fracture of tibia alone, unspecified part, closed
   823.90   Fracture of tibia alone, unspecified part, open

   A. 823.90, V08   C. 823.80, V08, 136.3
   B. 823.90, 042   D. 823.80, 042

REFERENCE: Brown, pp 115–116
                Schraffenberger, pp 80–81, 291

193. The diagnosis reads "first-, second-, and third-degree burns of the right arm." You would code:
   A. the first degree only.   C. the third degree only.
   B. the second degree only.   D. each degree of burn separately.

REFERENCE: Brown, pp 433–434
                Schraffenberger, pp 363–364

V Codes

194. A patient is admitted for elective cholecystectomy to treat chronic cholecystitis with cholelithiasis. Prior to administration of general anesthesia, the patient suffers cerebral thrombosis. The surgery is subsequently canceled. Code and sequence appropriately the codes.

434.00   Cerebral thrombosis, without mention of cerebral infarction
574.10   Calculus of gallbladder with other cholecystitis without mention of obstruction
V64.1   Surgical or other procedure not carried out because of contraindication
997.02   Iatrogenic cerebrovascular infarction or hemorrhage
51.22   Cholecystectomy

A. 997.02, 574.10, 51.22
B. 574.10, 434.00, V64.1
C. 997.02, 434.00, V64.1
D. 434.00, V64.1

REFERENCE: Brown, pp 72–73
Schraffenberger, pp 45–47, 197, 237
Ingenix, p 437

And Just a Few More Coding Questions for Practice

195. A physician lists the final diagnosis as diarrhea and constipation due to either irritable bowel syndrome or diverticulitis. The following codes are assigned:

562.10   Diverticulosis of colon without mention of hemorrhage
562.11   Diverticulitis of colon without mention of hemorrhage
564.00   Constipation, unspecified
564.1   Irritable bowel syndrome
787.91   Diarrhea

A. 564.1, 562.11
B. 562.10, 564.1
C. 564.00, 787.91, 564.1, 562.11
D. 564.1, 562.10, 564.00, 787.91

REFERENCE: Brown, pp 28–29
Schraffenberger, pp 234, 338–339

196. When an open biopsy is followed by a more extensive definitive procedure the coder reports
A. the open biopsy.
B. the extensive definitive procedure and the open biopsy.
C. no procedures.
D. the extensive definitive procedure.

REFERENCE: Brown, pp 70–71

197. In ICD-9-CM, when an exploratory laparotomy is performed followed by a therapeutic procedure, the coder reports
A. therapeutic procedure first, exploratory laparotomy second.
B. exploratory laparotomy, therapeutic procedure, closure of wound.
C. exploratory laparotomy first, therapeutic procedure second.
D. therapeutic procedure only.

REFERENCE: Brown, p 68

198. Codes from category 655, known or suspected fetal abnormality affecting the mother, should
    A. be assigned if the fetal conditions are documented.
    B. be assigned at the discretion of the physician.
    C. be assigned when they affect the management of the mother.
    D. never be assigned.

REFERENCE: Brown, p 276

199. There are a limited number of late effect codes in ICD-9-CM. When coding a residual condition where there is no applicable late effect code, one should code
    A. the residual condition followed by its cause.
    B. the cause followed by the residual condition.
    C. only the residual condition.
    D. only the cause of the residual condition.

REFERENCE: Brown, pp 59–60

200. A patient is admitted for a total hip replacement because of rheumatoid arthritis. Following admission, but prior to surgery, the patient develops congestive heart failure, which necessitates transfer to ICU. The hip replacement is canceled and the patient is treated for the heart failure. What is the principal diagnosis?
    A. congestive heart failure   C. hip replacement
    B. rheumatoid arthritis   D. canceled surgical procedure

REFERENCE: Brown, pp 72–73

201. According to the UHDDS guidelines, the principal procedure is performed for _____ rather than for _____.
    A. diagnostic or exploratory purposes; definitive treatment
    B. exploratory purposes; complications
    C. definitive treatment; diagnostic or exploratory purposes
    D. complications; definitive treatment

REFERENCE: Schraffenberger, p 65

202. A patient with diabetes is admitted to the hospital with acute gastrointestinal hemorrhage due to ulcer disease. In this case, the diabetes would be
    A. the principal diagnosis.
    B. a comorbid condition.
    C. a complication.
    D. irrelevant and not coded.

REFERENCE: Brown, pp 27–28
               Schraffenberger, p 65

203. Which of the following are considered late effects regardless of time?
    A. congenital defect
    B. nonunion, malunion, scarring
    C. fracture, burn
    D. poisoning

REFERENCE: Brown, p 425

204. When a patient is admitted in respiratory failure due to a chronic nonrespiratory condition
    A. the respiratory failure is the principal diagnosis.
    B. the chronic nonrespiratory problem is the principal diagnosis.
    C. only the respiratory failure is coded.
    D. only the chronic nonrespiratory condition is coded.

REFERENCE: Brown, pp 189–191
               Schraffenberger, pp 188–190

205. When Robert was discharged, his physician listed his diagnoses as congestive heart failure with acute pulmonary edema. You will code
    A. the CHF only.
    B. the edema only.
    C. both the CHF and the edema; sequence the CHF first.
    D. both the CHF and the edema; sequence the edema first.

REFERENCE: Brown, pp 27, 31

206. A patient was admitted with severe abdominal pain, elevated temperature, and nausea. The physical examination indicated possible cholecystitis. Acute and chronic pancreatitis secondary to alcoholism was recorded on the face sheet as the final diagnosis. The principal diagnosis is
    A. alcoholism.   C. cholecystitis.
    B. abdominal pain.   D. acute pancreatitis.

REFERENCE: Brown, pp 27, 30

207. A patient was admitted to the hospital with hemiplegia and aphasia. The hemiplegia and aphasia were resolved before discharge and the patient was diagnosed with cerebral thrombosis. What is the correct coding and sequencing?
    A. Hemiplegia; aphasia
    B. Cerebral thrombosis
    C. Cerebral thrombosis; hemiplegia; aphasia
    D. Hemiplegia; cerebral thrombosis; aphasia

REFERENCE: Brown, pp 27–28, 342–344

Use this information to answer questions 208–210:

Present on admission (POA) guidelines were established to identify and report diagnoses that are present at the time of a patient's admission. The reporting options for each ICD-9-CM code are
   A. Y = Yes
   B. N = No
   C. U = Unknown
   D. W = clinically undetermined
   E. Unreported/Not Used (Exempt from POA) reporting

208. The physician explicitly documents that a condition is not present at the time of admission.
   A. Y = Yes
   B. N = No
   C. U = Unknown
   D. W = clinically undetermined
   E. Unreported/Not Used (Exempt from POA) reporting

REFERENCE: Brown, pp 541–544

209. The physician documents that the patient has diabetes that was diagnosed prior to admission.
   A. Y = Yes
   B. N = No
   C. U = Unknown
   D. W = clinically undetermined
   E. Unreported/Not Used (Exempt from POA) reporting

REFERENCE: Brown, pp 541–544

210. The medical record documentation is unclear as to whether the condition was present on admission.
   A. Y = Yes
   B. N = No
   C. U = Unknown
   D. W = clinically undetermined
   E. Unreported/Not Used (Exempt from POA) reporting

REFERENCE: Brown, pp 541–544

Answer Key for ICD-9-CM Coding

1.	D	40.	A	
2.	B	41.	B	
3.	A	42.	A	
4.	C	43.	D	
5.	D	44.	A	
6.	C	45.	B	
7.	D	46.	A	
8.	C	47.	C	
9.	A	48.	B	
10.	B	49.	A	
11.	C	50.	D	
12.	B	51.	C	
13.	A	52.	A	
14.	D	53.	C	
15.	B	54.	B	The physician should be asked if the blood loss should be added as a discharge diagnosis.
16.	A			
17.	C			
18.	B	55.	A	
19.	D	56.	C	
20.	B	57.	D	
21.	A	Pain is a symptom that is integral to the sickle cell crisis and therefore is not coded.	58.	A
		59.	C	
		60.	A	
22.	D	61.	A	
23.	B	62.	C	
24.	D	63.	B	
25.	D	64.	D	
26.	B	65.	B	
27.	A	66.	D	
28.	C	67.	B	
29.	B	68.	D	
30.	D	69.	A	
31.	C	70.	B	
32.	B	71.	A	
33.	A	72.	C	
34.	C	73.	B	
35.	B	74.	D	
36.	D	75.	C	
37.	D	Effective October 1, 2010 the *Official ICD-9-CM Coding Guidelines* state, "Additional codes should be assigned for any neurologic deficits associated with the acute CVA, regardless of whether or not the neurologic deficit resolves prior to discharge."	76.	D
		77.	C	
		78.	B	
		79.	C	
		80.	D	
		81.	B	Newborn V-code is not assigned by the receiving facility when a newborn is transferred.
38.	C	82.	C	
39.	D	83.	A	

Answer Key for ICD-9-CM Coding

84. B

85. D

86. A

87. A

88. D

89. C

90. A

91. C

92. B

93. A

94. C

95. D

96. C

97. B

98. A

99. D

100. C

101. A

102. D

103. C

104. B

105. A

106. C

107. D

108. C

109. D

110. A

111. A

112. B

113. D

114. C

115. B

116. A

117. A

118. D

119. D Effective October 1, 2010, the *Official ICD-9-CM Coding Guidelines* state, "Additional codes should be assigned for any neurologic deficits associated with the acute CVA, regardless of whether or not the neurologic deficit resolves prior to discharge."

120. D

121. A

122. B

123. D Fatigue and flulike symptoms/signs of hepatitis would not be coded.

124. A

125. D

126. A

127. A

128. C

129. A

130. C

131. B

132. C

133. D SSS would not be reported as a current condition because the pacemaker would have taken care of this condition.

134. A

135. B

136. C The coder cannot assume a causal relationship between the diabetes and conditions that are usually related to the diabetes unless a physician confirms this relationship.

137. A

138. C Diabetic ketoacidosis by definition is uncontrolled.

139. A

140. C

141. A

142. D

143. B

144. A

145. B

146. C

147. A

148. C The term "continuous" refers to daily intake of large amounts of alcohol, or regular heavy drinking on weekends or days off. The coder should not assume to use the fifth digit "1" unless documented as continuous.

149. A

150. D

151. C

152. A

153. A

154. A

Answer Key for ICD-9-CM Coding

155. B

156. A

157. B

158. C

159. A

160. D

161. C

162. A

163. D

164. A

165. D   COPD (496) is a general term. It will present as chronic obstructive bronchitis.

166. C

167. A

168. C   The atelectasis is coded because it required monitoring and extended his length of stay

169. D

170. B

171. C   The alphabetic index is misleading and directs the coder to use one code for acute and chronic sinusitis. The Tabular List, however, directs the coder to use two separate codes.

172. D

173. A

174. C   The note under category 997 instructs the coder to "use additional code to identify complication."

175. A

176. B

177. A

178. A

179. D

180. B

181. A

182. A

183. C

184. C

185. B

186. C

187. A

188. A

189. B

190. A

191. B

192. B   A "compound" fracture is considered an "open" fracture.

193. C   Code the highest degree burn ONLY of the same site.

194. B

195. C

196. B

197. D

198. C

199. C

200. B

201. C

202. B

203. B

204. A

205. A

206. D

207. C   Effective October 1, 2010, the *Official ICD-9-CM Coding Guidelines* state, "Additional codes should be assigned for any neurologic deficits associated with the acute CVA, regardless of whether or not the neurologic deficit resolves prior to discharge."

208. B

209. A

210. C

REFERENCES

Bowie, M., & Schaffer, R. (2012). *Understanding ICD-9-CM coding: A worktext (3rd ed.).* Clifton Park, NY: Delmar Cengage Learning.

Brown, F. (2012). *ICD-9-CM Coding handbook with answers.* Chicago: American Hospital Association (AHA).

Ingenix. (2012). *ICD-9-CM Expert for hospitals* (Vols. 1, 2 and 3). St. Louis, MO: Author.

Ingenix. (2012). *ICD-9-CM Procedures Answers to your toughest ICD-9-CM coding questions.* St. Louis, MO: Author.

Schraffenberger, L. A. (2012). *Basic ICD-9-CM coding.* Chicago: American Health Information Management Association (AHIMA).

ICD-9-CM Chapter Competencies

Question	RHIA Domain	RHIT Domain
1–210	1	2

IX. CPT Coding

Lisa M. Delhomme, MHA, RHIA

Evaluation and Management

1. Patient is admitted to the hospital with acute abdominal pain. The attending medical physician requests a surgical consult. The consultant agrees to see the patient and conducts a comprehensive history and physical examination. The physician ordered lab work to rule out pancreatitis, along with an ultrasound of the gallbladder and abdominal x-ray. Due to the various diagnosis possibilities and the tests reviewed, a moderate medical decision was made.

    A. 99244
    B. 99222
    C. 99254
    D. 99204

    REFERENCE: AMA (6th ed.), p 66
                          Frisch, pp 82–85
                          Green, pp 412–414
                          Johnson and Linker, pp 153–154
                          Smith, p 213

2. An established patient returns to the physician's office for follow-up on his hypertension and diabetes. The physician takes the blood pressure and references the patient's last three glucose tests. The patient is still running above normal glucose levels, so the physician decides to adjust the patient's insulin. An expanded history was taken and a physical examination was performed.

    A. 99213
    B. 99232
    C. 99202
    D. 99214

    REFERENCE: AMA (6th ed.), p 54
                          Frisch, pp 53–55
                          Green, pp 405–407
                          Johnson and Linker, p 149
                          Smith, pp 211–212

3. Patient arrives in the emergency room via a medical helicopter. The patient has sustained multiple life-threatening injuries due to a multiple car accident. The patient goes into cardiac arrest 10 minutes after arrival. An hour and 30 minutes of critical care time is spent trying to stabilize the patient.

    A. 99285; 99288; 99291
    B. 99291; 99292
    C. 99291; 99292; 99285
    D. 99282

    REFERENCE: AMA (6th ed.), pp 70–71
                          Frisch, pp 27–29
                          Green, pp 416–418
                          Johnson and Linker, pp 155–157
                          Smith, p 214

4. The physician provided services to a new patient who was in a rest home for an ulcerative sore on the hip. A problem-focused history and physical examination were performed and a straightforward medical decision was made.

    A. 99304
    B. 99325
    C. 99324
    D. 99334

    REFERENCE: AMA (6th ed.), pp 76–77
                          Green, p 420
                          Johnson and Linker, pp 158–159
                          Smith, p 215

5. A doctor provides critical care services in the emergency department for a patient in respiratory failure. He initiates ventilator management and spends an hour and 10 minutes providing critical care for this patient.
   A. 99281, 99291, 99292, 94002
   B. 99291, 99292, 94002
   C. 99291, 94002
   D. 99291

REFERENCE: AMA (6th ed.), pp 68–71
                     Green, pp 416–418
                     Johnson and Linker, pp 155–157
                     Smith, pp 215

6. Services were provided to a patient in the emergency room after the patient twisted her ankle stepping down from a curb. The emergency room physician ordered x-rays of the ankle, which came back negative for a fracture. A problem-focused history and physical examination were performed and ankle strapping was applied. A prescription for pain was given to the patient. Code the emergency room visit only.
   A. 99201   C. 99281
   B. 99282   D. 99211

REFERENCE: AMA (6th ed.), p 66–68
                     Frisch, pp 71–72
                     Green, pp 415–416
                     Johnson and Linker, pp 155–157
                     Smith, pp 213–214

7. An established patient was seen in her primary physician's office. The patient fell at home and came to the physician's office for an examination. Due to a possible concussion, the patient was sent to the hospital to be admitted as an observation patient. A detailed history and physical examination were performed and the medical decision was low complexity. The patient stayed overnight and was discharged the next afternoon.
   A. 99214; 99234   C. 99218
   B. 99214; 99218; 99217   D. 99218; 99217

REFERENCE: AMA, 2013
                     AMA (6th ed.), pp 54–56
                     Frisch, p 69–71
                     Green, pp 407–409
                     Johnson and Linker, p 155
                     Smith, p 212

8. An out-of-town patient presents to a walk-in clinic to have a prescription refilled for a nonsteroidal anti-inflammatory drug. The physician performs a problem-focused history and physical examination with a straightforward decision.

   A. 99211   C. 99212
   B. 99201   D. 99202

   REFERENCE: AMA (6th ed.), p 52–53
                 Frisch, pp 49–51
                 Green, pp 405–406
                 Johnson and Linker, p 149
                 Smith, p 211

9. An office consultation is performed for a postmenopausal woman who is complaining of spotting in the past 6 months with right lower quadrant tenderness. A detailed history and physical examination were performed with a low-complexity medical decision.

   A. 99242   C. 99253
   B. 99243   D. 99254

   REFERENCE: AMA (6th ed.), pp 64–65
                 Frisch, pp 77–81
                 Green, pp 412–414
                 Johnson and Linker, pp 153–154
                 Smith, p 213

Anesthesia

10. Code anesthesia for upper abdominal ventral hernia repair.

    A. 00832   C. 00752
    B. 00750   D. 00830

    REFERENCE: AMA (6th ed.), pp 99–101
                 Green, pp 460–461
                 Johnson and Linker, p 175
                 Smith, pp 245–248

11. Code anesthesia for total hip replacement.

    A. 01210   C. 01230
    B. 01402   D. 01214

    REFERENCE: AMA (6th ed.), pp 99–101
                 Green, p 462
                 Smith, pp 245–248

12. Code anesthesia for vaginal hysterectomy.

    A. 00846   C. 00840
    B. 00944   D. 01963

    REFERENCE: AMA (6th ed.), pp 99–101
                 Green, pp 461–462
                 Smith, pp 245–248

13. Code anesthesia for placement of vascular shunt in forearm.
    A. 01844
    B. 01850
    C. 00532
    D. 01840

REFERENCE: AMA (6th ed.), pp 99–101
              Green, p 463
              Smith, pp 245–248

14. Code anesthesia for decortication of left lung.
    A. 01638
    B. 00542
    C. 00546
    D. 00500

REFERENCE: AMA (6th ed.), pp 99–101
              Green, pp 459–460
              Smith, pp 245–248

15. Code anesthesia for total shoulder replacement.
    A. 01760
    B. 01630
    C. 01402
    D. 01638

REFERENCE: AMA (6th ed.), pp 99–101
              Green, pp 458–459
              Smith, pp 245–248

16. Code anesthesia for cesarean section.
    A. 00840
    B. 01961
    C. 00940
    D. 01960

REFERENCE: AMA (6th ed.), pp 99–101
              Green, pp 464–465
              Smith, pp 245–248

17. Code anesthesia for procedures on bony pelvis.
    A. 00400
    B. 01170
    C. 01120
    D. 01190

REFERENCE: AMA (6th ed.), pp 99–101
              Green, pp 462
              Smith, pp 245–248

18. Code anesthesia for corneal transplant.
    A. 00144
    B. 00140
    C. 00147
    D. 00190

REFERENCE: AMA (6th ed.), pp 99–101
              Green, pp 457–458
              Smith, pp 245–248

Surgery—Integumentary System

19. Patient presents to the hospital for skin grafts due to previous third-degree burns. The burn eschar of the back was removed. Once the eschar was removed, the defect size measured 10 cm x 10 cm. A skin graft from a donor bank was placed onto the defect and sewn into place as a temporary wound closure.
   A. 15002, 15130
   B. 15002, 15271, 15272, 15272, 15272
   C. 15002, 15200
   D. 15002, 15273

REFERENCE: AMA, 2013

20. Patient presents to the operating room for excision of a 4.5 cm malignant melanoma of the left forearm. A 6 cm x 6 cm rotation flap was created for closure.
   A. 14021
   B. 11606; 14020
   C. 14301
   D. 11606; 15100

REFERENCE: AMA, 2013
             AMA (6th ed.), pp 132–133
             Green, p 501
             Smith, pp 70–71
             Smith (2), pp 26–27

21. Female patient has a percutaneous needle biopsy of the left breast lesion in the lower outer quadrant. Following the biopsy frozen section results, the physician followed this with an excisional removal of the same lesion.
   A. 19100; 19125
   B. 19100; 19120-LT
   C. 19120-LT
   D. 19100; 19120; 19120

REFERENCE: AMA (6th ed.), pp 142–143
             Green, pp 509–511
             Smith, p 77
             Smith (2), p 30

22. Patient presents to the emergency room with lacerations of right lower leg that involved the fascia. Lacerations measured 5 cm and 2.7 cm.
   A. 11406; 11403
   B. 12034
   C. 12032; 12031
   D. 12032

REFERENCE: AMA (6th ed.), p 131
             Smith, pp 64–66
             Smith (2), p 21

23. Ten sq cm epidermal autograft to the face from the back.
   A. 15110
   B. 15115
   C. 15110, 15115
   D. 15120

REFERENCE: AMA, 2013
             AMA (6th ed.), p 134
             Smith (2), p 27

24. Nonhuman graft for temporary wound closure. Patient has a 5 cm defect on the scalp.
    A. 15275, 15276
    B. 15271
    C. 15275
    D. 15271, 15272

REFERENCE: AMA, 2013

25. Patient is admitted for a blepharoplasty of the left lower eyelid and a repair for a tarsal strip of the left upper lid.
    A. 67917-E1; 15822-E2
    B. 67917-E1; 15820-E2
    C. 67917-E1
    D. 67917-E1; 15823-E2

REFERENCE: AMA (6th ed.), p 300
             CPT Assistant, January 2005, p 46
             Smith (2), p 165

26. Patient presents to the emergency room with lacerations sustained in an automobile accident. Repairs of the 3.3 cm skin laceration of the left leg that involved the fascia, 2.5 cm and 3 cm lacerations of the left arm involving the fascia, and 2.7 cm of the left foot, which required simple sutures, were performed. Sterile dressings were applied.
    A. 12032; 12032-59; 12031-59; 12002-59
    B. 12002, 12002-59
    C. 12034, 12002-59
    D. 13150; 12032-59, 12032-59, 12001-59

REFERENCE: AMA (6th ed.), pp 131–132
             Green, pp 498–500
             Smith, pp 64–66
             Smith (2), p 24

27. Patient presents to the operating room for excision of three lesions. The 1.5 cm and 2 cm lesions of the back were excised with one excision. The 0.5 cm lesion of the hand was excised. The pathology report identified both back lesions as squamous cell carcinoma. The hand lesion was identified as seborrheic keratosis.
    A. 11604; 11420
    B. 11402; 11420; 11403
    C. 11403; 11642; 11462
    D. 11602; 11402

REFERENCE: AMA (6th ed.), pp 124–129
             CPT Assistant, November 2002, pp 5–6, 8
             Green, pp 493–496
             Smith, pp 59–60
             Smith (2), pp 21–22

28. Patient presents to the radiology department where a fine-needle aspiration of the breast is performed utilizing computed tomography.
    A. 19120; 77012
    B. 19102
    C. 19125
    D. 10022, 77012

REFERENCE: AMA (6th ed.), p 380
             CPT Assistant, November 2002, pp 2–3
             Green, p 509
             Smith (2), p 29

29. Patient presents to the operating room where a 3.2 cm malignant lesion of the shoulder was excised and repaired with simple sutures. A 2 cm benign lesion of the cheek was excised and was repaired with a rotation skin graft.
    A. 11604, 11442; 14040; 12001
    B. 14040, 11604
    C. 15002, 15120
    D. 17264, 17000; 12001

REFERENCE: AMA (6th ed.), pp 126, 128, 132–133
              CPT Assistant, July 1999, pp 3–4
              CPT Assistant, August 2002, p 5
              CPT Assistant, November 2002, pp 5–8
              Green, pp 493–496, 501
              Smith, pp 59–61, 64–66, 71
              Smith (2), pp 26–27

30. Patient was admitted to the hospital for removal of excessive tissue due to massive weight loss. Liposuction of the abdomen and bilateral thighs was performed.
    A. 15830
    B. 15830; 15833; 15833
    C. 15877; 15879-50
    D. 15839

REFERENCE: AMA, 2013

Surgery—Musculoskeletal

31. Patient presents to the hospital with ulcer of the right foot. Patient is taken to the operating room where a revision of the right metatarsal head is performed.
    A. 28104-RT
    B. 28111-RT
    C. 28288-RT
    D. 28899-RT

REFERENCE: AMA, 2013

32. Patient presents to the emergency room following a fall. X-rays were ordered for the lower leg and results showed a fracture of the proximal left tibia. The emergency room physician performed a closed manipulation of the fracture with skeletal traction.
    A. 27532-LT
    B. 27536-LT
    C. 27530-LT
    D. 27524-LT

REFERENCE: Green, pp 520–523
              Smith, pp 82–83
              Smith (2), pp 42–44

33. Trauma patient was rushed to the operating room with multiple injuries. Open reduction with internal fixation of intertrochanteric femoral fracture; open reduction of the tibial and fibula shaft with internal fixation was performed.
    A. 27245; 27759
    B. 20690
    C. 27248; 27756
    D. 27244; 27758

REFERENCE: Green, pp 520–523
              Smith, pp 82–83
              Smith (2), pp 42–44

34. Open I&D of a deep abscess of the cervical spine.
    A. 22010
    B. 22015
    C. 10060
    D. 10140

REFERENCE: AMA, 2013

35. Patient presents to the emergency room following an assault. Examination of the patient reveals blunt trauma to the face. Radiology reports that the patient suffers from a fracture to the frontal skull and a blow-out fracture of the orbital floor. Patient is admitted and taken to the operating room where a periorbital approach to the orbital fracture is employed and an implant is inserted.
   A. 21407; 21275
   B. 21387; 61330
   C. 21390
   D. 61340; 21401

REFERENCE: Smith, pp 82–83
             Smith (2), pp 42–44

36. Patient presents with a traumatic partial amputation of the second, third, and fourth fingers on the right hand. Patient was taken to the operating room where completion of the amputation of three fingers was performed with direct closure.
   A. 26910-F6; 26910-F7; 26910-F8
   B. 26843-RT
   C. 26951-F6; 26951-F7; 26951-F8
   D. 26550-RT

REFERENCE: AMA, 2013

37. Patient is brought to the emergency room following a shark attack. The paramedics have the patient's amputated foot. The patient is taken directly to the operating room to reattach the patient's foot.
   A. 28800
   B. 28200; 28208
   C. 28110
   D. 20838

REFERENCE: AMA, 2013

38. Patient presents to the hospital with a right index trigger finger. Release of the trigger finger was performed.
   A. 26060-F7
   B. 26055-F6
   C. 26170-F6
   D. 26110

REFERENCE: AMA, 2013

39. Patient had been diagnosed with a bunion. Patient was taken to the operating room where a simple resection of the base of the proximal phalanx along with the medial eminence was performed. Kirschner wire was placed to hold the joint in place.
   A. 28292
   B. 28290
   C. 28293
   D. 28294

REFERENCE: AMA, 2013
             AMA (6th ed.), pp 116–117, 166
             CPT Assistant, December 1995, pp 5–7
             Smith (2), pp 47–49

Surgery—Respiratory

40. Patient has a bronchoscopy with endobronchial biopsies of three sites.
   A. 31625; 31625; 31625
   B. 31625
   C. 31622; 31625
   D. 31622; 31625; 31625; 31625

REFERENCE: AMA (6th ed.), pp 176–179
             CPT Assistant, June 2004, p 11
             Green, pp 549–550
             Smith, pp 97–98
             Smith (2), p 61

41. Patient presents to the surgical unit and undergoes unilateral endoscopy, partial ethmoidectomy, and maxillary antrostomy.
    A. 31254; 31256-51   C. 31290; 31267-51
    B. 31201; 31225-51   D. 31233; 31231-51

REFERENCE: AMA (6th ed.), pp 174–175
              CPT Assistant, January 1997, pp 4–6
              Green, pp 549–550
              Smith, p 91
              Smith (2), p 59

42. Patient has been diagnosed with metastatic laryngeal carcinoma. Patient underwent subtotal supraglottic laryngectomy with radical neck dissection.
    A. 31540   C. 31365
    B. 31367   D. 31368

REFERENCE: Green, pp 547–548

43. Patient was involved in an accident and has been sent to the hospital. During transport the patient develops breathing problems and, upon arrival at the hospital, an emergency transtracheal tracheostomy was performed. Following various x-rays, the patient was diagnosed with traumatic pneumothorax and a thoracentesis with insertion of tube was performed.
    A. 31603; 31612   C. 31603; 32555
    B. 31610; 32555   D. 31603; 32555

REFERENCE: AMA, 2013

44. Patient with laryngeal cancer has a tracheoesophageal fistula created and has a voicebox inserted.
    A. 31611   C. 31395
    B. 31580   D. 31502

REFERENCE: AMA, 2013

45. Upper lobectomy of the right lung with repair of the bronchus.
    A. 32480   C. 32320
    B. 32486   D. 32480, 32501

REFERENCE: AMA (6th ed.), pp 180–181
              Green, pp 551–552
              Smith (2), pp 61–62

46. Patient with a deviated nasal septum that was repaired by septoplasty.
    A. 30400   C. 30520
    B. 30620   D. 30630

REFERENCE: AMA, 2013

47. Lye burn of the larynx repaired by laryngoplasty.
    A. 31588   C. 31360
    B. 16020   D. 31540

REFERENCE: AMA, 2013

48. Bronchoscopy with multiple transbronchial right upper and right lower lobe lung biopsy with fluoroscopic guidance.
    A. 31628-RT; 76000-RT
    B. 31717-RT; 31632-RT
    C. 32405-RT
    D. 31628-RT; 31632-RT

REFERENCE: AMA (6th ed.), pp 176–179
              CPT Assistant, March 1999, p 3
              Green, pp 549–550
              Smith, pp 97–98
              Smith (2), p 61

49. Patient has recurrent spontaneous pneumothorax which has resulted in a chemical pleurodesis by thoracoscopy.
    A. 32650
    B. 32310; 32601
    C. 32601
    D. 32960

REFERENCE: AMA, 2013
              AMA (6th ed.), pp 179–180

50. Laryngoscopic stripping of vocal cords for leukoplakia of the vocal cords.
    A. 31535
    B. 31540
    C. 31541
    D. 31570

REFERENCE: AMA (6th ed.), p 175
              Green, p 548
              Smith, p 95

Surgery—Cardiovascular System

51. Patient returns to the operating room following open-heart bypass for exploration of blood vessel to control postoperative bleeding in the chest.
    A. 35820
    B. 20101
    C. 35761
    D. 35905

REFERENCE: AMA, 2013

52. Patient undergoes construction of apical aortic conduit with an insertion of a single-ventricle ventricular assist device.
    A. 33400
    B. 33975
    C. 33977
    D. 33975; 33404

REFERENCE: CPT Assistant, January 2004, p 28

53. Patient presents to the operating room where a CABG x 3 is performed using the mammary artery and two sections of the saphenous vein.
    A. 33534; 33511
    B. 33534; 33518; 33511
    C. 33535
    D. 33533; 33518

REFERENCE: AMA (6th ed.), pp 195–198
              Green, pp 571–572
              Smith, p 104
              Smith (2), pp 74–75

54. Patient complains of recurrent syncope following carotid thromboendarterectomy. Patient returns 2 weeks after initial surgery and undergoes repeat carotid thromboendarterectomy.
   A. 33510
   B. 35301
   C. 35201
   D. 35301; 35390

REFERENCE: CPT Assistant, Winter 1993, p 3
             Smith (2), pp 78–79

55. Patient is admitted with alcohol cirrhosis and has a TIPS procedure performed.
   A. 35476; 36011; 36481
   B. 37183
   C. 37182
   D. 37140

REFERENCE: CPT Assistant, December 2003, pp 1–3

56. Eighty-year-old patient has carcinoma and presents to the operating room for placement of a tunneled implantable centrally inserted venous access port.
   A. 36558
   B. 36571
   C. 36561
   D. 36481

REFERENCE: CPT Assistant, February 1999, pp 1–5
             CPT Assistant, November 1999, pp 19–20
             Green, pp 385–387
             Smith (2), pp 79–80
             Smith, pp 106–109

57. Patient presents to the operating room and undergoes an endovascular repair of an infrarenal abdominal aortic aneurysm utilizing a unibody bifurcated prosthesis.
   A. 34800; 34813
   B. 34802
   C. 34804
   D. 35081

REFERENCE: AMA (6th ed.), p 200
             CPT Assistant, September 2002, p 4
             CPT Assistant, February 2003, pp 2–4, 16
             Green, pp 577–578
             Smith (2), pp 76–77

58. The physician punctures the left common femoral to examine the right common iliac.
   A. 36245
   B. 36246
   C. 36247
   D. 36140

REFERENCE: AMA, 2013
             AMA (6th ed.), pp 335–336

59. Patient has a history of PVD for many years and experiences chest pains. The patient underwent Doppler evaluation, which showed a common femoral DVT. Patient is now admitted for thromboendarterectomy.
   A. 35371
   B. 35372
   C. 37224
   D. 35256

REFERENCE: AMA, 2013
             Smith (2), pp 78–79

60. Patient undergoes percutaneous transluminal iliac artery balloon angioplasty.
    A. 37228   C. 37222
    B. 37220   D. 37224

REFERENCE: AMA, 2013
               Smith, pp 109–110

Surgery—Hemic and Lymphatic Systems, Mediastinum, and Diaphragm

61. Patient has breast carcinoma and is now undergoing sentinel node biopsy. Patient was injected for sentinel node identification and two deep axillary lymph nodes showed up intensely. These two lymph nodes were completely excised. Path report was positive for metastatic carcinoma.
    A. 38525; 38790   C. 38308; 38790
    B. 38589   D. 38525; 38792

REFERENCE: CPT Assistant, November 1998, pp 15–16
               CPT Assistant, July 1999, pp 6–12
               Green, p 593

62. Patient has a history of hiatal hernia for many years, which has progressively gotten worse. The decision to repair the hernia was made and the patient was sent to the operating room where the repair took place via the thorax and abdomen.
    A. 39545   C. 43332
    B. 43336   D. 39503

REFERENCE: AMA, 2012

63. Patient has a bone marrow aspiration of the iliac crest and of the tibia.
    A. 38220, 38220-59   C. 38230
    B. 38221   D. 38220

REFERENCE: AMA (6th ed.), p 374
               CPT Assistant, January 2004, p 26
               Green, pp 592–593

64. Trauma patient is rushed to the operating room with multiple injuries. The patient had his spleen removed due to massive rupture with repair of lacerated diaphragm.
    A. 38115; 39501   C. 38102; 39540
    B. 38120; 39599   D. 38100; 39501

REFERENCE: AMA, 2013

65. Laparoscopic retroperitoneal lymph node biopsy.
    A. 38570   C. 49323
    B. 38780   D. 38589

REFERENCE: AMA, 2013

66. Excision of mediastinal cyst.
    A. 11400   C. 17000
    B. 39200   D. 39400

REFERENCE: AMA, 2013

67. Patient diagnosed with cystic hygroma of the axilla, which was excised.
    A. 38555
    B. 11400
    C. 38550
    D. 38300

REFERENCE: AMA, 2013

68. Laparoscopy with multiple biopsies of retroperitoneal lymph nodes.
    A. 38570
    B. 38571
    C. 38570-22
    D. 38572

REFERENCE: AMA, 2013

69. Cannulation of the thoracic duct.
    A. 38794
    B. 36810
    C. 36260
    D. 38999

REFERENCE: AMA, 2013

70. Patient has been on the bone marrow transplant recipient list for 3 months. A perfect match was made and the patient came in and received peripheral stem cell transplant.
    A. 38242
    B. 38230
    C. 38241
    D. 38240

REFERENCE: Green, pp 592–593

Surgery—Digestive System

71. Laparoscopic gastric banding.
    A. 43842
    B. 43843
    C. 43770
    D. 43771

REFERENCE: AMA, 2013

72. Patient presents with a history of upper abdominal pain. Cholangiogram was negative and patient was sent to the hospital for ERCP. During the procedure the sphincter was incised and a stent was placed for drainage.
    A. 43260; 43262; 43264
    B. 43262; 43269
    C. 43267
    D. 43262; 43268

REFERENCE: CPT Assistant, Spring 1994, pp 5–7
              Smith (2), pp 92–93

73. Patient presents to the emergency room with right lower abdominal pains. Emergency room physician suspects possible appendicitis. Patient was taken to the operating room where a laparoscopic appendectomy was performed. Pathology report was negative for appendicitis.
    A. 44950
    B. 44950; 49320
    C. 44970
    D. 44901

REFERENCE: AMA, 2013
              AMA (6th ed.), p 214
              Smith (2), p 97

74. Morbidly obese patient comes in for vertical banding of the stomach.
    A. 43848
    B. 43659
    C. 43842
    D. 43999

REFERENCE: CPT Assistant, May 1998, pp 5–6

75. Patient underwent anoscopy followed by colonoscopy. The physician examined the colon to 60 cm.
    A. 46600; 45378
    B. 46600; 45378-59
    C. 45378
    D. 45999

REFERENCE: Green, pp 620–622
            Smith, pp 117–118
            Smith (2), p 93

76. Injection snoreplasty for treatment of palatal snoring.
    A. 42299
    B. 42145
    C. 42999
    D. 40899

REFERENCE: CPT Assistant, December 2004, p 19

77. Patient arrives to the hospital and has a Nissen fundoplasty done laparoscopically.
    A. 43410
    B. 43415
    C. 43502
    D. 43280

REFERENCE: AMA, 2013
            Smith (2), p 97

78. Young child presents with cleft lip and cleft palate. This is the first attempt of repair, which includes major revision of the cleft palate and unilateral cleft lip repair.
    A. 42200; 40701
    B. 42225; 40700
    C. 42220; 40720
    D. 42215; 40700

REFERENCE: AMA, 2013

79. Patient has a history of chronic alcohol abuse with portal hypertension. Patient has been vomiting blood for the past 3 days and presented to his physician's office. Patient was sent to the hospital for evaluation and an EGD was performed. Biopsy findings showed gastritis, esophagitis, and bleeding esophageal varices, which were injected with sclerosing solution.
    A. 43235; 43244; 43204
    B. 43239; 43244
    C. 43239; 43243
    D. 43239; 43243; 43204

REFERENCE: AMA (6th ed.), p 220
            Green, pp 611–614
            Smith, p 115
            Smith (2), p 92

Surgery—Urinary System

80. Patient is admitted for contact laser vaporization of the prostate. The physician performed a TURP and transurethral resection of the bladder neck at the same time.
    A. 52648
    B. 52648; 52450; 52500
    C. 52450; 53500
    D. 52648; 52450

REFERENCE: AMA (6th ed.), p 242
            CPT Assistant, July 2005, p 15
            Smith (2), p 122

81. Patient comes to the hospital with a history of right flank pain. Urine tests are negative. Radiology examination reveals that the patient has renal cysts. Patient is now admitted for laparoscopic ablation of the cysts.
   A. 50541
   B. 50390
   C. 50280
   D. 50920

REFERENCE: AMA (6th ed.), p 234
              CPT Assistant, November 1999, p 25
              CPT Assistant, May 2000, p 4
              CPT Assistant, October 2001, p 8
              CPT Assistant, January 2003, p 19

82. Patient has extensive bladder cancer. She underwent a complete cystectomy with bilateral pelvic lymphadenectomy and creation of ureteroileal conduit.
   A. 51575; 50820
   B. 50825; 51570; 38770
   C. 51595
   D. 51550; 38770

REFERENCE: AMA, 2013

83. Patient presents to the hospital with right ureteral calculus. Patient is taken to the operating room where a cystoscopy with ureteroscopy is performed to remove the calculus.
   A. 52353
   B. 52310
   C. 51065
   D. 52352

REFERENCE: Green, pp 632–633
              Smith, p 131
              Smith (2), pp 111–112

84. Female with 6 months of stress incontinence. Outpatient therapies are not working and the patient decides to have the problem fixed. Laparoscopic urethral suspension was completed.
   A. 51992
   B. 51990
   C. 51840
   D. 51845

REFERENCE: CPT Assistant, November 1999, p 26
              CPT Assistant, May 2000, p 4
              CPT Changes: An Insider's View, 2000

85. Patient has ovarian vein syndrome and has ureterolysis performed.
   A. 58679
   B. 58660
   C. 52351
   D. 50722

REFERENCE: AMA, 2013

86. Male patient has been diagnosed with benign prostatic hypertrophy and undergoes a transurethral destruction of the prostate by radiofrequency thermotherapy.
   A. 52648
   B. 53852
   C. 52601
   D. 53850

REFERENCE: AMA (6th ed.), p 242
              CPT Assistant, November 1997, p 20
              CPT Assistant, April 2001, p 4

87. Nephrectomy with resection of half of the ureter.
   A. 50220
   B. 50234
   C. 50230; 50650
   D. 50546

REFERENCE: AMA (6th ed.), p 234
             Green, pp 628–629

88. Male with urinary incontinence. Sling procedure was performed 6 months ago and now the patient has returned for a revision of the sling procedure.
   A. 53449
   B. 53442
   C. 53440
   D. 53431

REFERENCE: AMA, 2013

89. Excision of 2.5 cm bladder tumor with cystoscopy.
   A. 51550
   B. 51530
   C. 52235
   D. 51060

REFERENCE: AMA (6th ed.), pp 238–239
             Green, pp 632–633
             Smith, p 131

90. Closure of ureterocutaneous fistula.
   A. 50930
   B. 50920
   C. 57310
   D. 50520

REFERENCE: AMA, 2013

Surgery—Male Genital System

91. Removal of nephrostomy tube with fluoroscopic guidance.
   A. 50387
   B. 50389
   C. 99212
   D. 99213

REFERENCE: AMA, 2013
             AMA (6th ed.), pp 232–233, 240

92. Patient has been diagnosed with prostate cancer. Patient arrived in the operating room where a therapeutic orchiectomy is performed.
   A. 54560
   B. 54530
   C. 55899
   D. 54520

REFERENCE: CPT Assistant, October 2001, p 8
             Smith (2), p 122

93. Patient undergoes laparoscopic orchiopexy for intra-abdominal testes.
   A. 54650
   B. 54699
   C. 54692
   D. 55899

REFERENCE: CPT Assistant, November 1999, p 27
             CPT Assistant, May 2000, p 4
             CPT Assistant, October 2001, p 8
             Smith (2), p 122

94. Scrotal wall abscess drainage.
   A. 55100
   B. 55150
   C. 54700
   D. 55110

REFERENCE: AMA, 2013

95. Hydrocelectomy of spermatic cord.
   A. 55500
   B. 55000
   C. 55041
   D. 55520

REFERENCE: CPT Assistant, October 2001, p 8

96. Patient has been followed by his primary care physician for elevated PSA. Patient underwent prostate needle biopsy in the physician office 2 weeks ago and final pathology was positive for carcinoma. Patient is admitted for prostatectomy. Frozen section of the prostate and one lymph node is positive for prostate cancer with metastatic disease to the lymph node. Prostatectomy became a radical perineal with bilateral pelvic lymphadenectomy.
   A. 55845
   B. 55815
   C. 55815; 38562
   D. 38770

REFERENCE: Green, pp 644–648
             Smith (2), p 122

97. Male presented to operating room for sterilization by bilateral vasectomy.
   A. 55200
   B. 55400
   C. 55250
   D. 55450

REFERENCE: CPT Assistant, June 1998, p 10
             CPT Assistant, July 1998, p 10

98. Laser destruction of penile condylomas.
   A. 54057
   B. 17106
   C. 17270
   D. 54055

REFERENCE: AMA, 2013
             Smith, p 136

99. First-stage repair for hypospadias with skin flaps.
   A. 54300
   B. 54308; 14040
   C. 54322
   D. 54304

REFERENCE: AMA, 2013

100. Priapism operation with spongiosum shunt.
   A. 54450
   B. 54352
   C. 54430
   D. 55899

REFERENCE: AMA, 2013

Surgery—Female Genital System

101. Patient was admitted to the hospital with sharp pelvic pains. A pelvic ultrasound was ordered and the results showed a possible ovarian cyst. The patient was taken to the operating room where a laparoscopic destruction of two corpus luteum cysts was performed.
   A. 49321
   B. 58925
   C. 58561
   D. 58662

REFERENCE: AMA, 2013
Smith (2), p 534

102. Patient was admitted with a cystocele and rectocele. An anterior colporrhaphy was performed.
   A. 57250
   B. 57260
   C. 57240
   D. 57110

REFERENCE: AMA, 2013

103. Patient has a Bartholin's gland cyst that was marsupialized.
   A. 54640
   B. 10060
   C. 58999
   D. 56440

REFERENCE: AMA, 2013

104. Patient is at a fertility clinic and undergoes intrauterine embryo transplant.
   A. 58679
   B. 58322
   C. 58323
   D. 58974

REFERENCE: AMA, 2013

105. Patient has been diagnosed with carcinoma of the vagina and she has a radical vaginectomy with complete removal of the vaginal wall.
   A. 57107
   B. 57110
   C. 58150
   D. 57111

REFERENCE: AMA, 2013
Smith (2), p 133

106. Patient has been diagnosed with uterine fibroids and undergoes a total abdominal hysterectomy with bilateral salpingo-oophorectomy.
   A. 58200
   B. 58150
   C. 58262
   D. 58150; 58720

REFERENCE: AMA (6th ed.), p 246
Green, p 652
Johnson and Linker, p 380
Smith, pp 142–143
Smith (2), p 133

107. Hysteroscopy with D&C and polypectomy.
   A. 58563   C. 58120; 58100; 58555
   B. 58558   D. 58558; 58120

REFERENCE: AMA (6th ed.), p 250
               Green, p 652
               Smith, p 142
               Smith (2), p 132

108. Laparoscopic tubal ligation utilizing Endoloop.
   A. 58670   C. 58671
   B. 58615   D. 58611

REFERENCE: AMA (6th ed.), pp 250–251
               Green, p 654

109. Laser destruction extensive herpetic lesions of the vulva.
   A. 17106   C. 56515
   B. 17004   D. 56501

REFERENCE: AMA, 2013
               Smith (2), p 131

110. Patient undergoes hysteroscopy with excision uterine fibroids.
   A. 58545   C. 58561
   B. 58140   D. 58140; 49320

REFERENCE: AMA (6th ed.), pp 249–250
               Green, p 652
               Smith, p 142
               Smith (2), p 132

Surgery—Maternity Care and Delivery

111. Attempted vaginal delivery in a previous cesarean section patient, which resulted in a repeat cesarean section.
   A. 59409   C. 59620
   B. 59612   D. 59514

REFERENCE: AMA (6th ed.), pp 254–255
               Green, p 658
               Smith, p 143

112. Patient is admitted to the hospital following an ultrasound at 25 weeks, which revealed fetal pleural effusion. A fetal thoracentesis was performed.
   A. 59074   C. 32555
   B. 32554   D. 76815

REFERENCE: AMA (6th ed.), p 252
               CPT Assistant, May 2004, pp 3–4

113. Patient in late stages of labor arrives at the hospital. Her OB physician is not able to make the delivery and the house physician delivers the baby vaginally. Primary care physician resumes care after delivery. Code the delivery.
    A. 59409
    B. 59612
    C. 59620
    D. 59400

REFERENCE: AMA (6th ed.), pp 255–256
              Green, pp 656–657
              Smith, p 143

114. Patient is 24 weeks pregnant and arrives in the emergency room following an automobile accident. No fetal movement or heartbeat noted. Patient is taken to the OB ward where prostaglandin is given to induce abortion.
    A. 59200
    B. 59855
    C. 59821
    D. 59410

REFERENCE: Green, pp 658–659

115. Patient is 6 weeks pregnant and complains of left-sided abdominal pains. Patient is suspected of having an ectopic pregnancy. Patient has a laparoscopic salpingectomy with removal of the ectopic tubal pregnancy.
    A. 59120
    B. 59200
    C. 59121
    D. 59151

REFERENCE: AMA, 2013
              AMA (6th ed.), p 252

116. Cesarean delivery with antepartum and postpartum care.
    A. 59610
    B. 59514
    C. 59400
    D. 59510

REFERENCE: AMA (6th ed.), p 254
              Green, pp 655–658
              Smith, p 143

117. A pregnant patient has an incompetent cervix, which was repaired using a vaginal cerclage.
    A. 57700
    B. 57531
    C. 59320
    D. 59325

REFERENCE: AMA, 2013
              AMA (6th ed.), p 253

118. A D&C is performed for postpartum hemorrhage.
    A. 59160
    B. 58120
    C. 58558
    D. 58578

REFERENCE: AMA, 2013

119. Hysterotomy for hydatidifom mole and tubal ligation.
    A. 58285; 58600
    B. 58150; 58605
    C. 51900; 58605
    D. 59100; 58611

REFERENCE: AMA, 2013

120. D&C performed for patient with a diagnosis of incomplete abortion at 8 weeks.
A. 59812　　　　　　　　　　　　C. 58120
B. 59820　　　　　　　　　　　　D. 59160

REFERENCE:　　AMA (6th ed.), p 258
　　　　　　　　Green, pp 658–659

Surgery—Endocrine System

121. Patient comes in for a percutaneous needle biopsy of the thyroid gland.
A. 60000　　　　　　　　　　　　C. 60699
B. 60270　　　　　　　　　　　　D. 60100

REFERENCE:　　CPT Assistant, June 1997, p 5

122. Laparoscopic adrenalectomy, complete.
A. 60650　　　　　　　　　　　　C. 60659
B. 60650-50　　　　　　　　　　 D. 60540

REFERENCE:　　AMA, 2013

123. Left carotid artery excision for tumor of carotid body.
A. 60650　　　　　　　　　　　　C. 60605
B. 60600　　　　　　　　　　　　D. 60699

REFERENCE:　　AMA, 2013

124. Patient undergoes total thyroidectomy with parathyroid autotransplantation.
A. 60240; 60512　　　　　　　　　C. 60260; 60512
B. 60520; 60500　　　　　　　　　D. 60650; 60500

REFERENCE:　　Green, pp 659–660

125. Unilateral partial thyroidectomy.
A. 60252　　　　　　　　　　　　C. 60220
B. 60210　　　　　　　　　　　　D. 60520

REFERENCE:　　Green, pp 659–660

Surgery—Nervous System

126. Patient comes in through the emergency room with a wound that was caused by an electric saw. Patient is taken to the operating room where two ulna nerves are sutured.
A. 64837　　　　　　　　　　　　C. 64836; 64837
B. 64892; 69990　　　　　　　　　D. 64856; 64859

REFERENCE:　　AMA, 2013
　　　　　　　　Smith (2), p 153

127. Laminectomy and excision of intradural lumbar lesion.
A. 63272　　　　　　　　　　　　C. 63282
B. 63267　　　　　　　　　　　　D. 63252

REFERENCE:　　AMA, 2013
　　　　　　　　Smith (2) p 149

128. Patient comes in for steroid injection for lumbar herniated disk. Marcaine and Aristocort were injected into the L2-L3 space.
    A. 64520
    B. 64483
    C. 62311
    D. 64714

REFERENCE: AMA (6th ed.), p 279
              CPT Assistant, September 1997, p 10
              Smith, p 150
              Smith (2), p 148

129. Patient with Parkinson's disease is admitted for insertion of a brain neurostimulator pulse generator with one electrode array.
    A. 61885
    B. 61850; 61863
    C. 61888
    D. 61867; 61870

REFERENCE: AMA (6th ed.), pp 272–273
              CPT Assistant, April 2001, pp 8–9
              CPT Assistant, June 2000, pp 4, 12
              Smith (2), p 145

130. Patient has rhinorrhea, which requires repair of the CSF leak with craniotomy.
    A. 63707
    B. 63709
    C. 62100
    D. 62010

REFERENCE: AMA, 2013
              Smith (2), pp 143–144

131. Patient has metastatic brain lesions. Patient undergoes stereotactic radiosurgery gamma knife of two lesions.
    A. 61533
    B. 61500
    C. 61796; 61797
    D. 61796

REFERENCE: AMA, 2013
              AMA (6th ed.), pp 269–270

132. Patient has right sacroiliac joint dysfunction and requires a right S2-S3 paravertebral facet joint anesthetic nerve block with image guidance.
    A. 62311
    B. 64493
    C. 64490
    D. 64520

REFERENCE: AMA, 2013
              Smith (2), pp 152–153

133. Patient requires repair of a 6 cm meningocele.
    A. 63700
    B. 63709
    C. 63180
    D. 63702

REFERENCE: AMA, 2013
              Smith (2), pp 151–152

134. Patient comes in through the emergency room with a laceration of the posterior tibial nerve. Patient is taken to the operating room where the nerve requires transposition and suture.
   A. 64856
   B. 64831; 64832; 64876
   C. 64840; 64874
   D. 64834; 64859; 64872

REFERENCE: AMA, 2013
             Smith (2), p 153

Surgery—Eye and Ocular Adnexa

135. Patient returns to the physician's office complaining of obscured vision. Patient has had cataract surgery 6 months prior. Patient requires laser discission of secondary cataract.
   A. 66821
   B. 66940
   C. 67835
   D. 66830

REFERENCE: AMA (6th ed.), p 297
             Smith, pp 155–156
             Smith (2), pp 162–163

136. Patient undergoes enucleation of left eye and muscles were reattached to an implant.
   A. 65135-LT
   B. 65105-LT
   C. 65730-LT
   D. 65103-LT

REFERENCE: AMA, 2013
             Smith (2), p 161

137. Patient suffers from strabismus and requires surgery. Recession of the lateral rectus (horizontal) muscle with adjustable sutures was performed.
   A. 67340; 67500
   B. 67314; 67320
   C. 67332; 67334
   D. 67311; 67335

REFERENCE: AMA, 2013
             AMA (6th ed.), pp 300–301
             CPT Assistant, Summer 1993, p 20
             CPT Assistant, March 1997, p 5
             CPT Assistant, November 1998, p 1
             CPT Assistant, September 2002, p 10
             Smith, p 157
             Smith (2), p 165

138. Radial keratotomy.
   A. 92071
   B. 65855
   C. 65767
   D. 65771

REFERENCE: Green, p 676
             Smith (2), pp 162–163

139. Correction of trichiasis by incision of lid margin.
   A. 67840
   B. 67830
   C. 67835
   D. 67850

REFERENCE: AMA, 2013
             Smith (2), p 165

140. Patient undergoes ocular resurfacing construction utilizing stem cell allograft from a cadaver.
    A. 67320   C. 68371
    B. 66999   D. 65781

REFERENCE: CPT Assistant, May 2004, pp 9–11
                        Smith (2), pp 162–163

141. Aphakia penetrating corneal transplant.
    A. 65755   C. 65750
    B. 65730   D. 65765

REFERENCE: AMA, 2013
                        AMA (6th ed.), pp 296–297
                        Smith (2), pp 162–163

142. Lagophthalmos correction with implantation using gold weight.
    A. 67912   C. 67901
    B. 67911   D. 67121

REFERENCE: CPT Assistant, May 2004, p 12
                        Smith (2), p 165

143. Lacrimal fistula closure.
    A. 68760   C. 68700
    B. 68761   D. 68770

REFERENCE: AMA, 2013
                        AMA (6th ed.), pp 302–303
                        Smith (2), pp 165–166

Surgery—Auditory

144. Patient comes into the office for removal of impacted earwax.
    A. 69210   C. 69222
    B. 69200   D. 69000

REFERENCE: AMA (6th ed.), p 305
                        Green, p 681
                        Smith (2), p 120

145. Patient with a traumatic rupture of the eardrum. Repaired with tympanoplasty with incision of the mastoid. Repair of ossicular chain not required.
    A. 69641   C. 69642
    B. 69646   D. 69635

REFERENCE: AMA, 2013
                        AMA (6th ed.), p 307
                        Smith (2), p 173

146. Patient came in for excision of a middle ear lesion.
    A. 11440   C. 69552
    B. 69540   D. 69535

REFERENCE: AMA, 2013
                        Smith (2), p 173

147. Patient with chronic otitis media requiring eustachian tube catheterization.
   A. 69400
   B. 69424
   C. 69421
   D. 69405

REFERENCE: AMA, 2013
               AMA (6th ed.), pp 304–305
               Smith (2), p 173

148. Modified radical mastoidectomy.
   A. 69511
   B. 69505
   C. 69635
   D. 69641

REFERENCE: AMA, 2013
               Smith (2), p 173

149. Decompression internal auditory canal.
   A. 69979
   B. 69915
   C. 69970
   D. 69960

REFERENCE: AMA, 2013
               AMA (6th ed.), p 308
               Smith (2), pp 172–173

150. Myringoplasty.
   A. 69620
   B. 69635
   C. 69610
   D. 69420

REFERENCE: AMA (6th ed.), p 306
               CPT Assistant, March 2001, p 10

151. Insertion of cochlear device inner ear.
   A. 69711
   B. 69949
   C. 69930
   D. 69960; 69990

REFERENCE: AMA, 2013
               AMA (6th ed.), p 307
               Smith (2), p 173

152. Patient with Bell's palsy requiring a total facial nerve decompression.
   A. 64742
   B. 64771
   C. 69955
   D. 64864

REFERENCE: AMA, 2013
               Smith (2), p 173

153. Drainage of simple external ear abscess.
   A. 69000
   B. 69100
   C. 10060
   D. 69020

REFERENCE: AMA (6th ed.), p 304
               CPT Assistant, October 1997, p 11
               CPT Assistant, October 1999, p 10
               Smith (2), p 173

Radiology

154. Administration of initial oral radionuclide therapy for hyperthyroidism.
 A. 78015   C. 78099
 B. 77402   D. 79005

REFERENCE: Green, p 733

155. Patient comes into the outpatient department at the local hospital for an MRI of the cervical spine with contrast. Patient is status post automobile accident.
 A. 72156   C. 72149
 B. 72142   D. 72126

REFERENCE: AMA (6th ed.), p 328
        Smith, pp 173–174

156. Obstetric patient comes in for a pelvimetry with placental placement.
 A. 74710   C. 76805
 B. 76946   D. 76825

REFERENCE: AMA, 2013

157. Patient comes into his physician's office complaining of wrist pain. Physician gives the patient an injection and sends the patient to the hospital for an arthrography. Code the complete procedure.
 A. 73115   C. 73110
 B. 73100   D. 25246; 73115

REFERENCE: AMA, 2013
        AMA (6th ed.), p 329

158. Patient has carcinoma of the breast and undergoes proton beam delivery of radiation to the breast with a single port.
 A. 77523   C. 77520
 B. 77432   D. 77402

REFERENCE: AMA (6th ed.), p 349
        Green, pp 728–729
        Smith, pp 177–178

159. CT scan of the head with contrast.
 A. 70460   C. 70551
 B. 70542   D. 70470

REFERENCE: AMA (6th ed.), p 323
        Smith, pp 173–174

160. Patient undergoes x-ray of the foot with three views.
 A. 73620   C. 73630
 B. 73610   D. 27648; 73615

REFERENCE: Smith, pp 173–174

161. Unilateral mammogram with computer-aided detection with further physician review and interpretation.
    A. 77055, 77032   C. 77056-52, 77051
    B. 77055-22   D. 77055, 77051

REFERENCE: AMA, 2013
              AMA (6th ed.), pp 342–343
              Green, pp 720–721

162. Pregnant female comes in for a complete fetal and maternal evaluation via ultrasound.
    A. 76856   C. 76811
    B. 76805   D. 76810

REFERENCE: AMA (6th ed.), p 340
              Green, p 719

163. Ultrasonic guidance for the needle biopsy of the liver. Code the complete procedure.
    A. 47000; 76942   C. 47000; 76999
    B. 47000; 76937   D. 47000; 77002

REFERENCE: AMA (6th ed.), pp 332–333
              Green, p 719

Pathology and Laboratory

164. What code is used for a culture of embryos less than 4 days?
    A. 89251   C. 89268
    B. 89272   D. 89250

REFERENCE: AMA (6th ed.), p 389
              CPT Assistant, April 2004, p 2
              CPT Assistant, May 2004, p 16
              CPT Assistant, June 2004, p 9
              Green, pp 759–760

165. Basic metabolic panel (calcium, total) and total bilirubin.
    A. 80048; 82247   C. 80100
    B. 80053   D. 82239; 80400; 80051

REFERENCE: AMA (6th ed.), pp 361–362
              Green, pp 747–748
              Smith, p 186

166. Huhner test and semen analysis.
    A. 89325   C. 89310
    B. 89258   D. 89300

REFERENCE: CPT Assistant, November 1997, p 36
              CPT Assistant, July 1998, p 10
              CPT Assistant, October 1998, p 1
              CPT Assistant, April 2004, p 3

167. Chlamydia culture.
     A. 87110
     B. 87106
     C. 87118
     D. 87109; 87168

REFERENCE: Green, pp 754–755

168. Partial thromboplastin time utilizing whole blood.
     A. 85732
     B. 85730
     C. 85245
     D. 85246

REFERENCE: AMA (6th ed.), pp 373–374
               Smith, p 187

169. Pathologist bills for gross and microscopic examination of medial meniscus.
     A. 88300
     B. 88302; 88311
     C. 88325
     D. 88304

REFERENCE: AMA (6th ed.), pp 383–389
               Green, pp 757–759
               Smith, pp 187–188

170. Cytopathology of cervical Pap smear with automated thin-layer preparation utilizing computer screening and manual rescreening under physician supervision.
     A. 88175
     B. 88148
     C. 88160; 88141
     D. 88161

REFERENCE: AMA (6th ed.), pp 377–379
               Green, pp 755–756
               CPT Assistant, July 2003, p 9
               CPT Assistant, March 2004, p 4

171. Pathologist performs a postmortem examination including brain of an adult. Tissue is being sent to the lab for microscopic examination.
     A. 88309
     B. 88025
     C. 88099
     D. 88028

REFERENCE: Green, p 755
               Smith, pp 187–188

172. Clotting factor VII.
     A. 85220
     B. 85240
     C. 85362
     D. 85230

REFERENCE: Smith, p 187

Medicine Section

173. IV push of one antineoplastic drug.
     A. 96401
     B. 96409
     C. 96411
     D. 96413

REFERENCE: AMA (6th ed.), pp 465–466
               Green, pp 796–797
               Smith, p 238

174. One-half hour of IV chemotherapy by infusion followed by IV push of a different drug.
    A. 96413
    B. 96413; 96411
    C. 96413; 96409
    D. 96409; 96411

REFERENCE: AMA (6th ed.), pp 464–466
              Green, pp 796–797
              Smith, p 238

175. Caloric vestibular test using air.
    A. 92543; 92700
    B. 92543; 92543
    C. 92700
    D. 92543

REFERENCE: AMA (6th ed.), p 417
              CPT Assistant, November 2004, p 10

176. Patient presents to the emergency room with chest pains. The patient is admitted as a 23-hour observation. The cardiologist orders cardiac workup and the patient undergoes left heart catheterization via the left femoral artery with visualization of the coronary arteries and left ventriculography. The physician interprets the report. Code the heart catheterization.
    A. 93452; 93455
    B. 93452; 93458
    C. 93458
    D. 93459

REFERENCE: AMA, 2013

177. Patient with hematochromatosis had a therapeutic phlebotomy performed on an outpatient basis.
    A. 99195
    B. 36522
    C. 36514
    D. 99199

REFERENCE: AMA (6th ed.), p 360
              CPT Assistant, June 1996, p 10

178. A physician performs a PTCA with drug-eluting stent placement in the left anterior descending artery and angioplasty only in the right coronary artery.
    A. 92928-LD; 92929-RC
    B. 92928-LD; 92920-RC
    C. 92928-LD; 92920-RC
    D. 92920-RC; 92929-LD

REFERENCE: AMA (6th ed.), pp 419–423
              CPT Assistant, April 2005, p 14
              Smith, pp 230–231

179. Transesophageal echocardiography (TEE) with probe placement, image, and interpretation and report.
    A. 93307
    B. 93303; 93325
    C. 93312; 93313; 93314
    D. 93312

REFERENCE: AMA (6th ed.), pp 429–430
              CPT Assistant, December 1997, p 5
              CPT Assistant, January 2000, p 10

180. Which code listed below would be used to report an esophageal electrogram during an EPS?
    A. 93600
    B. 93615
    C. 93612
    D. 93616

REFERENCE: AMA (6th ed.), pp 437–440
              CPT Assistant, April 2004, p 9
              Smith, pp 233–234

181. Cardioversion of cardiac arrhythmia by external forces.
    A. 92961
    B. 92950
    C. 92960
    D. 92970

REFERENCE: AMA (6th ed.), p 418
              CPT Assistant, Summer 1993, p 13
              CPT Assistant, November 1999, p 49
              CPT Assistant, June 2000, p 5
              CPT Assistant, November 2000, p 9
              CPT Assistant, July 2001, p 11

182. Osteopathic manipulative treatment to three body regions.
    A. 98926
    B. 98941
    C. 97110
    D. 97012

REFERENCE: Green, p 799

183. Patient presents to the Respiratory Therapy Department and undergoes a pulmonary stress test. CO_2 production with O_2 uptake with recordings was also performed.
    A. 94450
    B. 94620
    C. 94002
    D. 94621

REFERENCE: CPT Assistant, November 1998, p 35
              CPT Assistant, January 1999, p 8
              CPT Assistant, August 2002, p 10

For the following questions, you will be utilizing the codes provided for the scenarios. You will need to code appropriate ICD-9-CM and CPT-4 codes.

184. Patient presents to the hospital for debridement of a diabetic ulcer of the left ankle. The patient has a history of recurrent ulcers. Medication taken by the patient includes Diabeta and the patient was covered in the hospital with insulin sliding scales. The decubitus ulcer was debrided down to the bone.

250.70	Diabetes with peripheral circulatory disorders, type 2, or unspecified
250.71	Diabetes with peripheral circulatory disorders, type 1
250.80	Diabetes with other specified manifestations, type 2, or unspecified
250.81	Diabetes with other specified manifestations, type 1
707.06	Decubitus ulcer, ankle
707.09	Decubitus ulcer other site
707.20	Pressure ulcer unspecified stage
707.24	Pressure ulcer stage IV, Pressure ulcer with necrosis of soft tissues through to underlying muscle, tendon, or bone
11043	Debridement, muscle and/or fascia (includes epidermis, dermis, and subcutaneous tissue, if performed); first 20 sq cm or less
11044	Debridement, bone (includes epidermis, dermis, subcutaneous tissue, muscle and/or fascia, if performed); first 20 sq cm or less

A. 250.81, 707.06, 707.20, 11044   C. 250.80, 707.06, 707.24, 11044
B. 250.71, 707.24, 11043   D. 250.81, 250.70, 707.09, 707.20, 11044

REFERENCE: AMA, 2013
                        Brown, pp 121–126

185. Patient presents to the emergency room following a fall from a tree. X-rays were ordered for the left upper arm, which showed a fracture of the humerus shaft. The emergency room physician performed a closed reduction of the fracture and placed the patient in a long arm spica cast. Code the diagnoses and procedures, excluding the x-ray.

812.21	Fracture humerus, shaft, closed
812.31	Fracture, humerus, shaft, open
E000.9	unspecified external cause status
E030	Unspecified activity
E884.9	Other fall from one level to another
24500	Closed treatment of humeral shaft fracture; without manipulation
24505	Closed treatment of humeral shaft fracture; with manipulation, with or without skeletal traction
24515	Open treatment of humeral shaft fracture with plate/screws, with or without cerclage
29065	Application, cast; shoulder to hand (long arm)
LT	Left side

A. 812.21, E884.9, E030, E000.9, 24505-LT
B. 812.21, 24515-LT
C. 812.21, E884.9, E030, E000.9, 24505-LT, 29065
D. 812.31, 24500-LT

REFERENCE: AMA (6th ed.), pp 169–170
Brown, pp 407–408
Green, pp 520–523
Smith, pp 82–83

186. Patient was admitted with hemoptysis and underwent a bronchoscopy with transbronchial lung biopsy. Following the bronchoscopy the patient was taken to the operating room where a left lower lobe lobectomy was performed without complications. Pathology reported large cell carcinoma of the left lower lobe.

162.5	Malignant neoplasm of the lower lobe of the lung
162.8	Malignant neoplasm of other parts of bronchus or lung
162.9	Malignant neoplasm of the bronchus and lung, unspecified
31625	Bronchoscopy with biopsy, with or without fluoroscopic guidance
31628	Bronchoscopy with transbronchial lung biopsy, with or without fluoroscopic guidance
32405	Biopsy, lung or mediastinum, percutaneous needle
32440	Removal of lung, total pneumonectomy
32480	Removal of lung, other than total pneumonectomy, single lobe (lobectomy)
32484	Removal of lung, other than total pneumonectomy, single segment (segmentectomy)

A. 162.9, 31625   C. 162.9, 32405, 32484
B. 162.5, 31628, 32480   D. 162.8, 32440

REFERENCE: AMA (6th ed.), pp 177–178, 180–181
CPT Assistant, June 2001, p 10
CPT Assistant, June 2002, p 10
CPT Assistant, September 2004, p 9
Green, pp 549–550
Smith, pp 97–98

187. Patient was admitted for right upper quadrant pain. Workup included various x-rays that showed cholelithiasis. Patient was taken to the operating room where a laparoscopic cholecystectomy was performed. During the procedure, the physician was unable to visualize through the ports and an open cholecystectomy was elected to be performed. Intraoperative cholangiogram was performed. Pathology report states acute and chronic cholecystitis with cholelithiasis.

574.00	Calculus of gallbladder with acute cholecystitis without obstruction
574.10	Calculus of gallbladder with other cholecystitis without obstruction
789.01	Abdominal pain of the right upper quadrant
V64.41	Laparoscopic procedure converted to open procedure
47605	Cholecystectomy with cholangiography
47563	Laparoscopy, surgical; cholecystectomy with cholangiography

A. 789.01, 574.10, 47563
B. 789.01, 574.00, 574.10, 47563, 47605
C. 574.00, 574.10, V64.41, 47605
D. 574.00, 47563, 47605

REFERENCE: AMA (6th ed.), p 225
Brown, p 206
Green, p 624
Hazelwood and Venable, p 208

188. Patient presents to the emergency room complaining of right forearm/elbow pain after racquetball last night. Patient states that he did not fall, but overworked his arm. Past medical history is negative and the physical examination reveals the patient is unable to supinate. A four-view x-ray of the right elbow is performed and is negative. The physician signs the patient out with right elbow sprain. Prescription of Motrin is given to the patient.

841.2	Sprain of radiohumeral joint
841.8	Sprain of other specified sites of the elbow and forearm
841.9	Sprain of unspecified site of the elbow and forearm
E000.8	External cause status
E008.2	Activities involving racquet and hand sports
E927.2	Excessive physical exertion from prolonged activity
E928.9	Unspecified accident
73040	X-ray of shoulder, arthrography radiological supervision and interpretation
73070	X-ray of elbow, two views
73080	X-ray of elbow, complete, minimum of three views
99281	E/M visit to emergency room—problem-focused history, problem-focused exam, straightforward medical decision.
99282	E/M visit to emergency room—expanded problem-focused history, expanded problem-focused exam, and medical decision of low complexity
-25	Significant, separately identifiable evaluation and management service by the same physician on the same day of the procedure or other service

A. 841.8, 73080
B. 841.9, E928.9, E000.8, E008.2, 99281, 73070
C. 841.2, 73080, 99282, 73040
D. 841.9, E927.2, E000.8, E008.2, 99281-25, 73080

REFERENCE: AMA, 2013
              AMA (6th ed.), pp 325–326
              Brown, pp 405–408
              Smith, pp 173, 213–214

189. A physician orders a lipid panel on a 54-year-old male with hypercholesterolemia, hypertension, and a family history of heart disease. The lab employee in his office performs and reports the total cholesterol and HDL cholesterol only.

272.0	Pure hypercholesterolemia
401.9	Essential hypertension, unspecified
402.90	Hypertensive heart disease, unspecified, without heart failure
V17.49	Family history of other cardiovascular disease
80061	Lipid panel; this panel must include the following: Cholesterol, serum, total (82465); Lipoprotein, direct measurement, high density cholesterol (HDL cholesterol) (83718); Triglycerides (84478)
82465	Cholesterol, serum or whole blood, total
83718	Lipoprotein, direct measurement; high density cholesterol (HDL cholesterol)
84478	Triglycerides
52	Reduced services

A. 272.0, 80061-52
B. 272.0, 401.9, V17.49, 80061-52
C. 272.0, 401.9, V17.49, 82465, 83718
D. 272.0, 402.90, 82465, 83718

REFERENCE: AMA (6th ed.), pp 360–361
                     Green, pp 747–748
                     Smith, pp 186–187

190. Chronic nontraumatic rotator cuff tear. Arthroscopic subacromial decompression with coracoacromial ligament release, and open rotator cuff repair.

726.10	Disorders of bursae and tendons in shoulder region, unspecified
727.61	Complete rupture of rotator cuff, nontraumatic
840.4	Sprains and strains of rotator cuff (capsule)
23410	Repair of ruptured musculotendinous cuff (e.g., rotator cuff); open, acute
23412	Repair of ruptured musculotendinous cuff (e.g. rotator cuff) open; chronic
29821	Arthroscopy, shoulder, surgical; synovectomy, complete
29823	Arthroscopy, shoulder, surgical; debridement, extensive
29826	Arthroscopy, shoulder, surgical; decompression of subacromial space with partial acromioplasty, with coracoacromial ligament release
29827	Arthroscopy, shoulder, surgical; with rotator cuff repair
-59	Distinct procedural service

A. 840.4, 726.10, 29823   C. 840.4, 29826, 29821
B. 727.61, 23412, 29826-59   D. 727.61, 23410

REFERENCE: AMA (6th ed.), p 498
                   Smith, p 86

191. The patient is on vacation and presents to a physician's office with a lacerated finger. The physician repairs the laceration and gives a prescription for pain control and has the patient follow up with his primary physician when he returns home. The physician fills out the superbill as a problem-focused history and physical examination with straightforward medical decision making. Also checked is a laceration repair for a 1.5 cm finger wound.

99201	New patient office visit with a problem-focused history, problem-focused examination and straightforward medical decision making
99212	Established patient office visit with a problem-focused history, problem-focused examination and straightforward medical decision making
12001	Simple repair of superficial wounds of scalp, neck, axillae, external genitalia, trunk and/or extremities (including hands and feet); 2.5 cm or less
13131	Repair, complex, forehead, cheeks, chin, mouth, neck, axillae, genitalia, hands and/or feet; 1.1 cm to 2.5 cm

A. 99212; 13131
B. 12001

C. 99212; 12001
D. 99201; 12001

REFERENCE: AMA (6th ed.), pp 53, 131
Green, pp 405–406, 499–500
Smith, p 193

192. A 69-year-old established female patient presents to the office with chronic obstructive lung disease, congestive heart failure, and hypertension. The physician conducts a comprehensive history and physical examination and makes a medical decision of moderate complexity. Physician admits the patient from the office to the hospital for acute exacerbation of CHF.

428.0	Congestive heart failure, unspecified
402.91	Hypertensive heart disease, with congestive heart failure
401.9	Essential hypertension, unspecified
401.1	Essential hypertension, benign
496	Chronic obstructive pulmonary disease
99212	Established office visit for problem-focused history and exam, straightforward medical decision making
99214	Established office visit for a detailed history and physical exam, moderate medical decision making
99222	Initial hospital care for comprehensive history and physical exam, moderate medical decision making
99223	Initial hospital care for comprehensive history and physical exam, high medical decision making

A. 402.91; 496; 99214
B. 428.0; 496; 401.1; 99223

C. 428.0; 496; 401.9; 99222
D. 402.91; 496; 401.1; 99212

REFERENCE: AMA (6th ed.), p 58
Brown, pp 347–349
Green, pp 405–406
Smith, p 213

193. Established 42-year-old patient comes into your office to obtain vaccines required for his trip to Sri Lanka. The nurse injects intramuscularly the following vaccines: hepatitis A and B vaccines, cholera vaccine, and yellow fever vaccine. As the coding specialist, what would you report on the CMS 1500 form?
A. office visit, hepatitis A and B vaccine, cholera vaccine and yellow fever vaccine
B. office visit, intramuscular injection; HCPCS Level II codes
C. office visit; administration of two or more single vaccines; vaccine products for hepatitis A and B, cholera, and yellow fever
D. administration of two or more single vaccines; vaccine products for hepatitis A and B, cholera, and yellow fever.

REFERENCE: AMA (6th ed.), pp 394–398
Green, pp 772–773
Smith, p 224

194. Patient presents to the operating room where the physician performed, using imaging guidance, a percutaneous breast biopsy utilizing a rotating biopsy device.

19000   Puncture aspiration of cyst of breast
19103   Biopsy of breast; percutaneous, automated vacuum assisted or rotating biopsy device, using imaging guidance
19120   Excision of cyst, fibroadenoma, or other benign or malignant tumor, aberrant breast tissue, duct lesion, nipple or areolar lesion (except 19300), open, male or female, one or more lesions
19125   Excision of breast lesion identified by preoperative placement of radiological marker, open; single lesion
+19295   Image guided placement, metallic localization clip, percutaneous, during breast biopsy (List separately in addition to code for primary procedure)

A. 19103
B. 19125; 19295
C. 19120
D. 19000

REFERENCE: AMA (6th ed.), p 142
CPT Assistant, January 2001, pp 10–11
Green, pp 509–511
Smith, p 77

195. Facelift utilizing the SMAS flap technique.

15788   Chemical peel, facial; epidermal
15825   Rhytidectomy; neck with platysmal tightening (platysmal flap, P-flap)
15828   Rhytidectomy; cheek, chin, and neck
15829   Rhytidectomy; superficial musculoaponeurotic system (SMAS) flap

A. 15825
B. 15788
C. 15829
D. 15828

REFERENCE: AMA, 2013
Green, p 505

196. Tracheostoma revision with flap rotation.

    31613   Tracheostoma revision; simple, without flap rotation
    31614   Tracheostoma revision; complex, with flap rotation
    31750   Tracheoplasty; cervical
    31830   Revision of tracheostomy scar

   A. 31830   C. 31614
   B. 31750   D. 31613

REFERENCE: AMA, 2013

197. Blood transfusion of three units of packed red blood cells.

    36430   Transfusion, blood or blood components
    36455   Exchange transfusion; blood, other than newborn
    36460   Transfusion, intrauterine, fetal

   A. 36430   C. 36460
   B. 36430; 36430; 36430   D. 36455

REFERENCE: AMA, 2013

198. Two-year-old patient returns to the hospital for cleft palate repair where a secondary lengthening procedure takes place.

    40720   Plastic repair of cleft lip/nasal deformity; secondary, by re-creation of defect and reclosure
    42145   Palatopharyngoplasty
    42220   Palatoplasty for cleft palate; secondary lengthening procedure
    42226   Lengthening of palate, and pharyngeal flap

   A. 40720   C. 42226
   B. 42220   D. 42145

REFERENCE: AMA, 2013

199. Tonsillectomy on a 14-year-old.

    42820   Tonsillectomy and adenoidectomy; under age 12
    42821   Tonsillectomy and adenoidectomy; age 12 or over
    42825   Tonsillectomy, primary or secondary; under age 12
    42826   Tonsillectomy, primary or secondary; age 12 or over

   A. 42820   C. 42825
   B. 42821   D. 42826

REFERENCE: Green, p 610

200. Laparoscopic repair of umbilical hernia.

    49580   Repair umbilical hernia, under age 5 years, reducible

    49585   Repair umbilical hernia, age 5 years or over, reducible

    49652   Laparoscopy, surgical, repair, ventral, umbilical, spigelian or epigastric hernia (includes mesh insertion when performed); reducible

    49654   Laparoscopy, surgical, repair, incisional hernia (includes mesh insertion when performed); reducible

    A. 49580   C. 49585

    B. 49654   D. 49652

REFERENCE: AMA, 2013

                AMA (6th ed.), p 230

201. Ureterolithotomy completed laparoscopically.

    50600   Ureterotomy with exploration or drainage (separate procedure)

    50945   Laparoscopy, surgical ureterolithotomy

    52325   Cystourethroscopy; with fragmentation of ureteral calculus

    52352   Cystourethroscopy, with urethroscopy and/or pyeloscopy; with removal or manipulation of calculus (ureteral catheterization is included)

    A. 52352   C. 50600

    B. 52325   D. 50945

REFERENCE: CPT Assistant, November 1999, p 26

                CPT Assistant, May 2000, p 4

                CPT Assistant, October 2001, p 8

202. Patient undergoes partial nephrectomy for carcinoma of the kidney.

    50220   Nephrectomy, including partial ureterectomy, any open approach including rib resection

    50234   Nephrectomy with total ureterectomy and bladder cuff; through same incision

    50240   Nephrectomy, partial

    50340   Recipient nephrectomy (separate procedure)

    A. 50234   C. 50340

    B. 50220   D. 50240

REFERENCE: AMA (6th ed.), p 234

                Green, pp 628–629

203. Patient presents to the operating room for fulguration of bladder tumors. The cystoscope was inserted and entered the urethra, which was normal. Bladder tumors measuring approximately 1.5 cm were removed.

50957	Ureteral endoscopy through established ureterostomy, with or without irrigation, instillation, or ureteropyelography, exclusive of radiologic service; with fulguration and/or incision, with or without biopsy
51530	Cystotomy; for excision of bladder tumor
52214	Cystourethroscopy, with fulguration of trigone, bladder neck, prostatic fossa, urethra, or periurethral glands
52234	Cystourethroscopy, with fulguration (including cryosurgery or laser surgery) and/or resection of small bladder tumor(s) (0.5 up to 2.0 cm)

A. 52234
B. 50957
C. 52214
D. 51530

REFERENCE: AMA (6th ed.), pp 237–239
Green, pp 632–633
Smith, p 131

204. Excision of Cowper's gland.

53220	Excision or fulguration of carcinoma of urethra
53250	Excision of bulbourethral gland (Cowper's gland)
53260	Excision or fulguration; urethral polyp(s), distal urethra
53450	Urethromeatoplasty, with mucosal advancement

A. 53250
B. 53450
C. 53260
D. 53220

REFERENCE: AMA, 2013

205. Placement of double-J stent.

52320	Cystourethroscopy (including ureteral catheterization); with removal of ureteral calculus
52330	Cystourethroscopy; with manipulation, without removal of ureteral calculus
52332	Cystourethroscopy with insertion of indwelling ureteral stent (e.g. Gibbons or double-J type)
52341	Cystourethroscopy, with treatment of ureteral stricture (e.g. balloon dilation, laser electrocautery, and incision)

A. 52341
B. 52320
C. 52330; 52332
D. 52332

REFERENCE: AMA (6th ed.), pp 237–239
Green, pp 632–633
Smith, p 131

206. Litholapaxy, 3 cm calculus.

    50590   Lithotripsy, extracorporeal shock wave
    52317   Litholapaxy, simple or small (less than 2.5 cm)
    52318   Litholapaxy, complicated or large (over 2.5 cm)
    52353   Cystourethroscopy, with ureteroscopy and/or pyeloscopy; with lithotripsy

    A. 52353   C. 52318
    B. 50590   D. 52317

REFERENCE: AMA, 2013

207. Patient presented to the operating room where an incision was made in the epigastric region for a repair of ureterovisceral fistula.

    50520   Closure of nephrocutaneous or pyelocutaneous fistula
    50525   Closure of nephrovisceral fistula, including visceral repair; abdominal approach
    50526   Closure of nephrovisceral fistula, including visceral repair; thoracic approach
    50930   Closure of ureterovisceral fistula (including visceral repair)

    A. 50526   C. 50520
    B. 50930   D. 50525

REFERENCE: AMA, 2013

208. Amniocentesis.

    57530   Trachelectomy, amputation of cervix (separate procedure)
    57550   Excision of cervical stump, vaginal approach
    59000   Amniocentesis, diagnostic
    59200   Insertion of cervical dilator (separate procedure)

    A. 59000   C. 57550
    B. 59200   D. 57530

REFERENCE: AMA, 2013
                   AMA (6th ed.), p 252

209. Patient is admitted to the hospital with facial droop and left-sided paralysis. CT scan of the brain shows subdural hematoma. Burr holes were performed to evacuate the hematoma.

432.1	Subdural hemorrhage
852.20	Subdural hemorrhage following injury without mention of open intra-cranial wound, unspecified state of unconsciousness
61150	Burr hole(s) or trephine; with drainage of brain abscess or cyst
61154	Burr hole(s) with evacuation and/or drainage of hematoma, extradural or subdural
61156	Burr hole(s); with aspiration of hematoma or cyst, intracerebral
61314	Craniectomy or craniotomy for evacuation of hematoma, infratentorial; extradural or subdural

A. 852.20; 61156
B. 432.1; 61314
C. 432.1; 61154
D. 852.20; 61150

REFERENCE: Brown, 412–413
Green, p 661

210. Spinal tap.

62268	Percutaneous aspiration, spinal cord cyst or syrinx
62270	Spinal puncture, lumbar diagnostic
62272	Spinal puncture, therapeutic, for drainage of cerebrospinal fluid (by needle or catheter)
64999	Unlisted procedure, nervous system

A. 62272
B. 64999
C. 62268
D. 62270

REFERENCE: AMA, 2013
AMA (6th ed.), p 276

211. Injection of anesthesia for nerve block of the brachial plexus.

64413	Injection, anesthetic agent; cervical plexus
64415	Injection, anesthetic agent; brachial plexus, single
64510	Injection, anesthetic agent; stellate ganglion (cervical sympathetic)
64530	Injection, anesthetic agent; celiac plexus, with or without radiologic monitoring

A. 64415
B. 64413
C. 64530
D. 64510

REFERENCE: AMA (6th ed.), p 285
Green, p 671

212. SPECT bone imaging.

77080	Dual energy x-ray absorptiometry (DXA), bone density study, one or more sites; axial skeleton (e.g. hips, pelvis, spine)
76977	Ultrasound bone density measurement and interpretation, peripheral site(s), any method
78300	Bone and/or joint imaging; limited area
78320	Bone and/or joint imaging; tomographic (SPECT)

A. 76977   C. 77080
B. 78320   D. 76977

REFERENCE: AMA, 2013
AMA (6th ed.), p 355
CPT Assistant, June 2003, p 11

213. Vitamin B$_{12}$.

82180	Ascorbic acid (vitamin C), blood
82607	Cyanocobalamin (vitamin B$_{12}$)
84590	Vitamin A
84591	Vitamin, not otherwise specified

A. 84590   C. 84591
B. 82180   D. 82607

REFERENCE: AMA (6th ed.), p 372
Green, p 751
Smith, p 187

214. Hepatitis C antibody.

86803	Hepatitis C antibody
86804	Hepatitis C antibody; confirmatory test (e.g., immunoblot)
87520	Infectious agent detection by nucleic acid (DNA or RNA); hepatitis C, direct probe technique
87522	Infectious agent detection by nucleic acid (DNA or RNA); hepatitis C, quantification

A. 86804   C. 87522
B. 86803   D. 87520

REFERENCE: AMA (6th ed.), p 376
Green, pp 753–754

215. Creatinine clearance.

82550	Creatine kinase (CK), (CPK); total
82565	Creatinine; blood
82575	Creatinine; clearance
82585	Cryofibrinogen

A. 82550
B. 82565

C. 82575
D. 82585

REFERENCE: Green, pp 709–710
               Smith, p 187

216. Comprehensive electrophysiologic evaluation (EPS) with induction of arrhythmia.

93618	Induction of arrhythmia by electrical pacing
93619	Comprehensive electrophysiologic evaluation with right atrial pacing and recording, right ventricular pacing and recording, His bundle recording, including insertion and repositioning of multiple electrode catheters, without induction or attempted induction of arrhythmia
93620	Comprehensive electrophysiologic evaluation including insertion and repositioning of multiple electrode catheters with induction or attempted induction of arrhythmia; with right atrial pacing and recording, right ventricular pacing and recording, His bundle recording
+93623	Programmed stimulation and pacing after intravenous drug infusion (list separately in addition to code for primary procedure)
93640	Electrophysiologic evaluation of single- or dual-chamber pacing cardioverter-defibrillator leads including defibrillation threshold evaluation (induction of arrhythmia, evaluation of sensing and pacing for arrhythmia termination) at time of initial implantation or replacement

A. 93618; 93620
B. 93620

C. 93640; 93623
D. 93619; 93620

REFERENCE: AMA (6th ed.), pp 438–439
               CPT Assistant, Summer 1994, p 12
               CPT Assistant, August 1997, p 9
               CPT Assistant, October 1997, p 10
               CPT Assistant, July 1998, p 10

217. Patient presents to the hospital for a two-view chest x-ray for a cough. The radiology report comes back negative. What would be the correct codes to report to the insurance company?

786.2	Cough
786.30	Hemoptysis
V72.5	Radiology examination, not elsewhere classified
71010	Radiologic examination, chest; single view, frontal
71020	Radiologic examination, chest, two views, frontal and lateral
71035	Radiologic examination, chest, special views

A. V72.5; 71020
B. 786.2; 71020

C. V72.5; 71035
D. 786.2; 786.30, 71010

REFERENCE: AMA, 2013
               Schraffenberger, pp 338–339

Answer Key for CPT-4 Coding

1.	C		43.	C	
2.	A		44.	A	
3.	B		45.	D	
4.	C		46.	C	
5.	D		47.	A	
6.	C		48.	D	
7.	D		49.	A	
8.	B		50.	B	
9.	B		51.	A	
10.	C		52.	B	
11.	D		53.	D	
12.	B		54.	B	
13.	A		55.	C	
14.	B		56.	C	
15.	D		57.	C	
16.	B		58.	A	
17.	C		59.	A	
18.	A		60.	B	
19.	D	The supply of skin substitutes graft(s) should be reported separately.	61.	D	
			62.	B	
			63.	A	
20.	C		64.	D	
21.	C		65.	A	
22.	B		66.	B	
23.	B		67.	C	
24.	C	The supply of skin substitutes graft(s) should be reported separately.	68.	A	
			69.	A	
			70.	D	
25.	B		71.	C	
26.	C		72.	D	Radiology codes would be used for the supervision and interpretation.
27.	A	See Principles of CPT Coding 6th edition, page 129. If two lesions are removed with one excision, only one excision code would be reported			
			73.	C	
			74.	C	
			75.	C	
28.	D		76.	A	
29.	B		77.	D	
30.	C		78.	D	
31.	D		79.	C	
32.	A		80.	A	
33.	D		81.	A	
34.	A	Codes 10060 and 10140 are used for I&Ds of superficial abscesses.	82.	C	
			83.	D	
35.	C		84.	B	
36.	C		85.	D	
37.	D		86.	B	
38.	B		87.	A	
39.	A		88.	B	
40.	B		89.	C	
41.	A		90.	B	
42.	D		91.	B	

Answer Key for CPT-4 Coding

92.	D	138.	D
93.	C	139.	B
94.	A	140.	D
95.	A	141.	C
96.	B	142.	A
97.	C	143.	D
98.	A	144.	A
99.	D	145.	D
100.	C	146.	B
101.	D	147.	D
102.	C	148.	B
103.	D	149.	D
104.	D	150.	A
105.	D	151.	C
106.	B	152.	C
107.	B	153.	A
108.	C	154.	D
109.	C	155.	B
110.	C	156.	A
111.	C	157.	D
112.	A	158.	C
113.	A	159.	A
114.	B	160.	C
115.	D	161.	D
116.	D	162.	C
117.	C	163.	A
118.	A	164.	D
119.	D	165.	A

119. D — When tubal ligation is performed at the same time as hysterotomy, use 58611 in addition to 59100

120.	A	166.	D
121.	D	167.	A
122.	A	168.	B
123.	C	169.	D
124.	A	170.	A
125.	B	171.	B
126.	C	172.	D
127.	A	173.	B
128.	C	174.	B
129.	A	175.	C
130.	C		
131.	C		
132.	B		
133.	D		
134.	C		
135.	A		
136.	B		
137.	D		

175. C — Code 92543 is for use when an irrigation substance is used.

176.	C
177.	A
178.	B
179.	D
180.	B
181.	C
182.	A

Answer Key for CPT-4 Coding

183. D
184. C
185. A   Casting is included in the surgical procedure.
186. B
187. C
188. D
189. C   In order to use the code for the panel, every test must have been performed.
190. B   Code both the arthroscopic procedure and the open procedure. Both need to be reported because there were two separate procedures. Modifier -59 must be added to code 29826 because it is a component of the comprehensive procedure 23412. That is allowed if an appropriate modifier is used per NCCI edits.
191. D
192. C   According to CPT guidelines, when a patient is admitted to the hospital on the same day as an office visit, the office visit is not billable. Code rules do not allow the use of 402.91 because the scenario given does not state that the patient has hypertensive heart disease.

193. D   According to the CPT coding guidelines for vaccines, only a separate identifiable Evaluation and Management code may be billed in addition to the vaccine. In this scenario, the patient was seen only for his vaccines. This guideline immediately eliminates all the other answers.
194. A
195. C
196. C
197. A   Report this code only once no matter how many units were given.
198. B
199. D
200. D
201. D
202. D
203. A
204. A
205. D
206. C
207. B
208. A
209. C   Codes starting with 852 are considered to be traumatic injuries. No injury was stated in the case, so 432.1, nontraumatic subdural hematoma, would be the appropriate code.
210. D
211. A
212. B
213. D
214. B
215. C
216. B
217. B

REFERENCES

American Medical Association (AMA). *CPT assistant.* Chicago: Author.

American Medical Association (AMA). (2010). *Principles of CPT coding* (6th ed.). Chicago: Author.

American Medical Association (AMA). (2012). *Physician's current procedural terminology (CPT) 2013, Professional Edition.* Chicago: Author.

Brown, F. (2011). *ICD-9-CM coding handbook 2012 with answers.* Chicago: American Hospital Association (AHA).

Frisch, B. (2007). *Correct coding for Medicare compliance and reimbursement.* Clifton Park, NY: Delmar Cengage Learning.

Green, M. (2012). *3-2-1 Code It!* (3rd ed.). Clifton Park, NY: Delmar Cengage Learning.

Hazelwood, A., & Venable, C. (2012). *ICD-9-CM and ICD-10-CM coding and reimbursement for physician services.* Chicago: American Health Information Management Association (AHIMA).

Johnson, S. L., & Linker, R. (2013). *Understanding medical coding: A comprehensive guide* (3rd ed.). Clifton Park, NY: Delmar Cengage Learning.

Schraffenberger, L. A. (2012). *Basic ICD-10-CM/PCS and ICD-9-CM coding.* Chicago: American Health Information Management Association (AHIMA).

Smith, G. (2012). *Basic current procedural terminology and HCPCS coding, 2011 edition.* Chicago: American Health Information Management Association (AHIMA).

Smith, G. (2) (2011). *Coding surgical procedures: Beyond the basics.* Clifton Park, NY. Delmar Cengage Learning.

CPT Competencies

Question	RHIA Domain	RHIT Domain
1–217	1	2

X. Informatics and Information Systems

Nanette B. Sayles, EdD, RHIA, CCS, CHPS, CPHIMS, FAHIMA

Special Note

The Information Technology and Systems domains are very different for the RHIA and RHIT Examinations. Questions with only an RHIA competency begin at question 56. We advise that RHIT students should also study these questions. It is always better to know more than less.

1. Which of the following is primary storage?
    A. RAM
    B. USB drive
    C. CD
    D. external hard drive

REFERENCE: Glandon, Smaltz, and Slovensky, p 138

2. Your release of information system has part of the computing on the workstation and part on the file server. What type of technology is being used?
    A. Internet
    B. client server
    C. LAN
    D. operating system

REFERENCE: Eichenwald-Maki and Petterson, pp 29–30, 288
               Johns, pp 912–913
               Marreel and McLellan, pp 8, 191

3. Dr. Smith is entering a medication order in a CPOE. A window pops up with the following message:

    Patient is on beta-blocker, which is a contraindication for this medication. Do you want to order this medication? Yes or No.

    This is an example of a(n)
    A. reminder.
    B. alert.
    C. allergy.
    D. structured entry.

REFERENCE: Eichenwald-Maki and Petterson, pp 128, 130, 131–133, 287
               Marreel and McLellan, p 16

4. Barbara is being seen at a physician's office that she has never been to before. This physician practice is independently owned and is not associated with a hospital or other physician practice. She did not have to request copies of her medical records, but the physician has everything that she needs. The physician must be part of a(n)
    A. integrated health network.
    B. corporation.
    C. regional health information organization.
    D. electronic health record.

REFERENCE: Eichenwald-Maki and Petterson, pp 5–7
               Johns, pp 149–152
               LaTour and Eichenwald-Maki, p 172
               Marreel and McLellan, pp 39, 181–182
               McWay, pp 39, 181–183

5. What types of software provide a front-end structure/interface that presents information in a familiar format leading to a natural style of interaction through the use of icons and a mouse?
   A. graphical user interface
   B. fiber optics
   C. assembly level language
   D. machine language

REFERENCE: Abdelhak, p 126
               Johns, p 900
               LaTour and Eichenwald-Maki, p 604
               Marreel and McLellan, p 196
               McWay, p 171

6. With data exchange standards, the ability to transfer data from one system to another system is called
   A. data sets.
   B. messaging standards.
   C. interfaces.
   D. interoperability.

REFERENCE: Eichenwald-Maki and Petterson, p 3
               Johns, p 1144
               LaTour and Eichenwald-Maki, p 356
               Marreel and McLellan, pp 75–76, 199

7. Which of the following would be a foreign key in the patient table?
   A. last name
   B. addres
   C. medical record number
   D. billing number

REFERENCE: LaTour and Eichenwald-Maki, p 130
               Sayles and Trawick, p 91

Cardiovascular Information

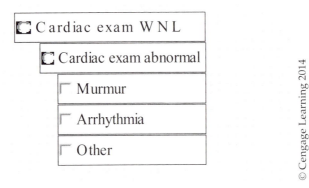

© Cengage Learning 2014

8. Review the simplistic screen above. This is an example of how _____ data can be entered.
   A. unstructured
   B. structured
   C. nomenclature
   D. template

REFERENCE: Amatayakul, p 248
               Eichenwald-Maki and Petterson, pp 35–37, 108

9. Why would the database administrator add a foreign key to one of the tables?
   A. the data element refers to ethnicity
   B. to indicate that it is a primary key in another table
   C. to ensure that each row is unique
   D. to separate two tables

REFERENCE: Johns, p 903
               LaTour and Eichenwald-Maki, p 130

10. The information systems manager is testing what the system can handle with regard to passing large amounts of data. This is called
   A. volume testing.   C. rigorous testing.
   B. acceptance testing.   D. final testing.

REFERENCE: Abdelhak, p 331

11. You need to identify some patterns in our database. What technology should you use?
   A. reminders   C. data mining
   B. alerts   D. clinical guidelines

REFERENCE: Amatayakul, p 30
               Green and Bowie, p 258
               LaTour and Eichenwald-Maki, p 242
               McWay, p 176

12. What controls the traffic on the Internet?
   A. the World Wide Web
   B. Internet protocol
   C. the ISDN
   D. domain names

REFERENCE: McWay, p 320

13. Which application design is used in a computer-assisted coding (CAC)?
   A. electronic data interchange   C. message standards
   B. intraoperability   D. natural language processing

REFERENCE: Eichenwald-Maki and Petterson, p 160
               Johns, pp 269–270, 469, 473
               LaTour and Eichenwald-Maki, p 400
               McWay, p 132

14. Mary is designing a computer screen that will be used to collect patient demographic information. What input design should be utilized for the state field?
    A. an icon
    B. a dialog box
    C. the drop-down menu
    D. free form text

REFERENCE: Abdelhak, p 126
               Eichenwald-Maki and Petterson, pp 33–35
               McWay, p 110

15. One of the coders is out on medical leave unexpectedly. At this facility, electronic workflow is used to distribute work. The supervisor needs the work normally sent to her to be distributed among the other coders. Which of the following statements is true?
    A. The supervisor will have to get a programmer to make the change.
    B. Each chart will have to be rerouted manually.
    C. The supervisor can change the established criteria.
    D. The vendor will have to be contacted to make the change.

REFERENCE: Sayles and Trawick, p 167

16. Which of the following tests determines how well new systems being implemented work with existing systems?
    A. volume test
    B. system test
    C. unit test
    D. integration test

REFERENCE: Abdelhak, p 331
               McWay, pp 318–319

17. You are working with a database that is created from multiple databases being stored in a single database. This is a(n)
    A. electronic health record.
    B. personal health record.
    C. clinical data repository.
    D. health information exchange.

REFERENCE: Green and Bowie, p 108
               Marreel and McLellan, p 175
               McWay, p 175

18. At an integrated delivery system, the hospital and clinic have separate networks. There are times when they need to share information across the network. This can be accomplished with a
    A. gateway.
    B. hub.
    C. router.
    D. bridge.

REFERENCE: Amatayakul, p 302
               Glandon, Smaltz, and Slovensky, p 154
               Marreel and McLellan, p 206

19. The data on the hard drive were erased by a corrupted file that had been attached to an e-mail message. Which software would be used to prevent this?
    A. productivity
    B. utility
    C. virus checker
    D. encryption

REFERENCE: Marreel and McLellan, pp 156–157
               McWay, p 321

20. In selecting a messaging standard for use in a picture archival communication system, the BEST choice would be
    A. Consolidated Health Informatics Initiatives.
    B. National Drug Code.
    C. HL7.
    D. DICOM.

REFERENCE: LaTour and Eichenwald-Maki, p 181

21. You have just inserted data contained in a spreadsheet into your word processed document. This is an example of a(n) _____ system.
    A. integrated   C. mapped
    B. interfaced   D. graphical user interface

REFERENCE: Glandon, Smaltz, and Slovensky, p 144
               Marreel and McLellan, pp 74–75
               McWay, p 171

22. Dr. Smith goes to Hollywood Hospital's Web site and logs in. He sees a list of patients currently in the hospital, test results, and more. Ms. Brown, a patient of Dr. Smith who is having surgery next week, logs onto the same Web site and only sees the date and time of her preoperative visit. This is an example of
    A. web portal.   C. application service provider.
    B. single sign-on technology. D. intranet.

REFERENCE: LaTour and Eichenwald-Maki, p 62
               McWay, p 321

23. Patient care can be improved through the use of technology. Which of the following is an example of how this happens?
    A. elimination of illegible orders   C. redundant testing
    B. scanning of medical record image   D. voice recognition

REFERENCE: Eichenwald-Maki and Petterson, pp 144–146
               McWay, p 328

24. In the RFP, you have asked for information regarding the amount of time that a vendor has been in business and the number of installations of the product under consideration. If you want to review this information, you would go to the _____ section.
    A. functional specifications
    B. organizational profile
    C. vendor information
    D. licensing and contractual details

REFERENCE: Abdelhak, p 340
               Amatayakul, p 385
               Marreel and McLellan, pp 109–110
               McWay, p 344
               Murphy, p 135

25. A facility wants to purchase a system that will use barcodes on all drug and biological products to help in ensuring patient safety. Which system should the facility purchase?
    A. BC-MAR
    B. EMAR
    C. CPOE
    D. EHR

REFERENCE: Amatayakul, p 27

26. One of the ways that an EHR is distinguished from a clinical data repository is that the EHR
    A. has clinical decision support capabilities.
    B. has data from multiple information systems.
    C. can have digital images.
    D. aggregates data.

REFERENCE: Green and Bowie, pp 114–116
                McWay, pp 175, 327

27. You have been asked to give an example of a clinical information system. Which one of the following would you cite?
    A. laboratory information system   C. billing system
    B. financial information system   D. Admission, Discharge, Transfer

REFERENCE: McWay, p 327

28. Which of the following systems would provide a snapshot of information about the patient's condition?
    A. EHR   C. personal health record
    B. continuity of care record   D. SMART card

REFERENCE: Sayles and Trawick, p 243

29. You are entering orders into an information system. This system prevented you from ordering a duplicate radiology test and prevented you from ordering a medication that the patient was allergic to. What system are you using?
    A. order entry/results reporting   C. clinical provider order entry
    B. electronic health record   D. decision support system

REFERENCE: Johns, p 949
                McWay, p 325

30. You are excited about the functionality of your firm's new EHR. Which of the following is an example of that functionality?
    A. its interactive voice recognition   C. the firewall
    B. its electronic communications   D. the modem

REFERENCE: McWay, p 328

31. You are developing a list of functions needed by users of a release of information system. You are also evaluating the current system to see what opportunities there are to improve the system. Which stage of the system developmental life cycle stages are you in?
    A. analysis
    B. implementation
    C. design
    D. obsolescence

REFERENCE: Johns, pp 883–884
              LaTour and Eichenwald-Maki, p 149
              Marreel and McLellan, pp 62–64, 317–319
              McWay, pp 317–319

32. Southside Community Hospital utilizes a wide area network to transport data across the Internet. This is done by using a private tunnel. This is a(n)
    A. WLAN.
    B. LAN.
    C. VPN.
    D. FDDI.

REFERENCE: Amatayakul, p 298
              Glandon, Smaltz, and Slovensky, p 147
              Marreel and McLellan, p 319
              McWay, p 319

33. In performing a "what if" query to determine if the facility should expand the emergency department, which of the following systems would be used?
    A. decision support system
    B. financial information system
    C. clinical decision support system
    D. knowledge based system

REFERENCE: Abdelhak, p 40
              Johns, p 880

34. What type of system would be purchased to provide information on the census, update the master patient index, and distribute demographic data?
    A. Admission, Discharge, Transfer
    B. executive information system
    C. clinical information system
    D. financial information system

REFERENCE: Abdelhak, p 179
              Green and Bowie, pp 237–240
              Marreel and McLellan, pp 8, 187

35. As HIM Department Director, you are on the implementation team for the new MPI. You have been assigned the responsibility of looking at every data element stored in the system and establishing criteria for the use of each. An example of what you are doing is shown below.

Name	Last name
Description	This field is for the patient's last name
Number of characters	30
Alphanumeric	Alpha
Acceptable characters	a–z
Responsible person	HIM Director
Used in reports	Admissions list, discharge list, transfer list, health record number list, UB-92, CMS-1500

You are responsible for the
A. data flow diagram.
B. decision tree.
C. data dictionary.
D. rules based algorithms.

REFERENCE: Amatayakul, p 270
              Eichenwald-Maki and Petterson, p 27
              Green and Bowie, pp 250, 253
              Johns, pp 169, 199–200, 907–907
              Marreel and McLellan, pp 79–81, 191
              McWay, p 170

36. A milestone is
    A. the distance between the users and the data center.
    B. a step in the path to the implementation of a system such as the EHR.
    C. a project plan.
    D. a module of an information system such as the EHR.

REFERENCE: Amatayakul, p 120

37. A common language used in data definition, and data manipulation is
    A. unified modeling language.
    B. metadata.
    C. HTML.
    D. SQL.

REFERENCE: LaTour and Eichenwald-Maki, p 127
              Marreel and McLellan, p 207
              McWay, p 171

38. What field monitors populations as a whole instead of patient specific data?
    A. informatics
    B. clinical informatics
    C. educational informatics
    D. public health informatics

REFERENCE: McWay, p 325

39. Differentiate between the physical and logical data models.
    A. The physical data model shows how the logical model will be created, and the logical data model shows the technology plan to be used.
    B. The logical data model shows what the system should do, and the physical data model shows how the logical data model will be created.
    C. The logical data model uses DFDs, and the physical data model uses entity relationship models.
    D. The physical data model uses DFDs, and the logical uses entity relationship model.

REFERENCE: LaTour and Eichenwald-Maki, p 128

40. The administrator has asked us to develop a patient satisfaction database internally. This database will be used to collect data that can be used to improve our services. He does not want this to be a long, drawn-out process. Which of the following could speed up this process?
    A. RFI   C. prototyping
    B. RFP   D. functional requirements

REFERENCE: LaTour and Eichenwald-Maki, pp 838–839

41. Cynthia wants to retrieve a list of patients from the new electronic document management system. She wants a list of patients admitted to the hospital by Dr. Smith. Which of the following would explain why she cannot generate this list?
    A. Improper scanning was done.
    B. The necessary indexing to retrieve this list was not done.
    C. The data are stored on optical disk so they are not readily available.
    D. The COLD technology has not downloaded the lab reports.

REFERENCE: Abdelhak, p 195
               Mahoney, p 28
               McWay, pp 115–117, 197

42. The medical staff wants a speech recognition system where the staff dictates and then the editing of the dictation is done by editors. What type of speech recognition is this?
    A. key-word spotting   C. back-end speech recognition
    B. hidden Markov model   D. front-end speech recognition

REFERENCE: Sayles and Trawick, p 284

43. The EHR system implementation team is using simulated patients and simulated patient information to add progress notes, nurses' notes, and so on, to the EHR prior to implementation. Which phase is the team involved in?
    A. conversion   C. analysis
    B. testing   D. site preparation

REFERENCE: Abdelhak, p 331
               Johns, p 890
               LaTour and Eichenwald-Maki, p 151
               McWay, pp 317–319

44. You are interested in performing some data analysis on patients with cardiac problems. You have downloaded the data that you need on the cardiology patients from the data warehouse into a smaller database that you can work with. You are using a
   A. data mart.   C. specialized data warehouse.
   B. clinical data repository.   D. executive information system.

REFERENCE: Abdelhak, p 293
                Amatayakul, p 274
                Johns, 958
                LaTour and Eichenwald-Maki, p 67
                McWay, p 176

45. The laboratory system was installed 3 years ago. It is running well and meeting the needs of the department. In which stage of the IS life cycle is the lab system?
   A. initiation   C. implementation
   B. development   D. operations (maintenance)

REFERENCE: Abdelhak, p 304
                Johns, pp 891-892
                LaTour and Eichenwald-Maki, p 151
                Marreel and McLellan, pp 62–64, 317–319
                McWay, pp 317–319

46. Drop boxes, radio buttons, and pick lists are used in
   A. structured data entry.   C. natural language processing.
   B. free text.   D. unstructured data entry.

REFERENCE: Amatayakul, p 321

47. The facility Hospital Information System team has been researching network topologies and has decided on one that combines the attributes of bus, ring, and star topologies. What topology has the team chosen?
   A. hybrid network   C. physical topology
   B. network protocol   D. TCP/IP

REFERENCE: Sayles and Trawick, p 28

48. The hospital utilizes the best of breed model for its information systems. The hospital is able to exchange data between the information systems from the various vendors seamlessly. This concept is
   A. interoperability.   C. transparency.
   B. networks.   D. EDI.

REFERENCE: Sayles and Trawick, p 265

49. The CEO needs to make a decision about the future of the health care facility. To make this decision, he utilizes an information system that queries a database containing data from a number of different information systems. What type of system is being used?
   A. EHR   C. financial information system
   B. results reporting   D. executive information system

REFERENCE: Abdelhak, p 277
                Johns, p 881, 957
                LaTour and Eichenwald-Maki, p 614

Requirement	Priority	System A	System B	System C	System A Weighted	System B Weighted	System C Weighted
Ad hoc reporting	2	1	3	2	2	6	4
Check-out chart	3	3	3	3	9	9	9
Mass check out of chart	3	3	3	3	9	9	9
Unlimited locations	1	2	2	1	2	2	1
Password security	2	2	3	2	4	6	4
User-friendly	3	3	2	3	9	6	9
Check-in chart	3	1	3	3	3	9	9
Total					38	47	45

System Evaluation: Chart Location System

50. The EHR system selection committee evaluated three systems on a scale of 1–3 with a score of 3 being the best. The priority is ranked on a scale of 1–3 with 3 being the highest. Based on the evaluation above, which of the following systems should be purchased?
    A. System A
    B. System B
    C. System C
    D. none of the above
    REFERENCE: Sayles and Trawick, pp 126–127

51. Upon final review of the RFP that is to be sent out to prospective vendors, you notice that there is content that should not be included in the operational requirement section of the document. Which of the following information should be deleted from this section?
    A. response time
    B. data architecture
    C. data conversion
    D. data analysis tools
    REFERENCE: Amatayakul, p 386
                  Marreel and McLellan, pp 90–100
                  McWay, pp 344–345

52. Dr. Smith needs something small and lightweight to use for dictating reports and entering data on the go. You suggest he use
    A. a laptop utilizing wireless technology.
    B. a VPN.
    C. voice recognition.
    D. a PDA.
    REFERENCE: Johns, pp 154, 166, 894–895
                  McWay, p 316

53. Maria has received a request to update a patient's insurance number. She accesses the _____and updates the system. What system is she using?
    A. executive information system
    B. clinical decision support system
    C. admission-discharge-transfer system
    D. laboratory information system

REFERENCE: Abdelhak, p 179
               Green and Bowie, pp 237–240
               Johns, pp 946–947
               Marreel and McLellan, pp 8, 187

54. The HIS department is involved in developing a plan that shows the fields that a database will contain, the operations that the database will exhibit, and the types of relationships. The team is developing the
    A. data model.   C. database manager.
    B. database design.   D. data dictionary.

REFERENCE: LaTour and Eichenwald-Maki, p 128
               McWay, p 171

55. To enter the results of a CBC into the computer system, you would use a(n)
    A. laboratory system.   C. pharmacy system.
    B. radiology system.   D. order entry/results reporting system.

REFERENCE: Green and Bowie, pp 156, 170-171
               Johns, p 948
               Marreel and McLellan, pp 14–15, 187

The following questions represent advanced competencies.

56. In developing your Information Systems Strategic Plan, which of the following should be the basis for the plan?
    A. business plan   C. consultant's recommendations
    B. previous IS strategic plan   D. previous IS budgets

REFERENCE: Johns, pp 875–876
               LaTour and Eichenwald-Maki, pp 116, 145–146
               McWay, pp 249–250

57. The vendor that you work for has decided to get into the EHR market. What standard should you suggest using in developing the functions performed by the EHR?
    A. DICOM   C. HL7 EHR functional model
    B. LOINC   D. IEEE 1073

REFERENCE: Abdelhak, p 70
               Johns, pp 138, 953

58. When negotiating an information system contract, which of the following would be an example of a performance warranty specified in the contract?
    A. remedies   C. insurances
    B. operational practices   D. uptime

REFERENCE: Amatayakul, p 420

59. Critique the following statement:

    The EHR utilizes existing source systems to supply data.

    A. This is true because the EHR uses many source systems to populate the data.
    B. This is false because the EHR is a stand-alone system.
    C. This is false because the EHR requires the latest and greatest system, thus eliminating legacy systems.
    D. This is true because the EHR obtains information SOLELY from the source documents.

REFERENCE: Amatayakul, p 417

60. You have been asked how to handle versioning of documents in the EDMS. Which of the following should be your response?
    A. Delete the first version and retain the second.
    B. Display the second version but identify that a previous version exists.
    C. Do not allow edits to the system.
    D. Display both versions side by side.

REFERENCE: Abdelhak, p 202

61. The physician will be called automatically when a lab result is at the panic level. This is an example of a
    A. data-driven rule.   C. clinical guideline.
    B. database.   D. reminder.

REFERENCE: Murphy, p 338

62. What type of databases utilize queries?
    A. transactional   C. relational
    B. hierarchical   D. object-oriented

REFERENCE: Amatayakul, p 266

63. Dr. Smith accesses the EHR in his office to see what patients are ready to be seen and what calls he needs to make. This functionality is called
    A. checkout   C. registration
    B. the in-basket function   D. the patient summary

REFERENCE: Amatayakul, p 515

64. Which one of the following is necessary during the strategic planning process for the EHR?
    A. gauging the user's readiness for the EHR
    B. writing the request for proposal to be used in selecting the EHR
    C. selecting the EHR to be used
    D. creating a newsletter to keep users informed of the status of EHR

REFERENCE: Amatayakul, p 77

65. The hospital is undergoing the development of an information system strategic plan. The part of the process where changes in the community, legislation, and other factors are monitored is called
    A. health information exchange.   C. environmental scanning.
    B. alerts.   D. critical path analysis.

REFERENCE: Glandon, Smaltz, and Slovensky, pp 124–125
                McWay, pp 249–250

66. Your transcription system utilizes disk mirroring. This is an example of a technology called
    A. RAID.   C. DASD.
    B. HL-7.   D. CPOE.

REFERENCE: Amatayakul, p 292

Patient
Last name
First name
Middle initial
Street address
City
State
Zip
Medical record number
Date of birth

67. You are developing an entity relationship diagram. In the entity of the patient shown above, which of the attributes is the primary key?
    A. last name
    B. combination of last and first names
    C. street address
    D. medical record number

REFERENCE: LaTour and Eichenwald-Maki, p 129
                McWay, pp 171–172

68. A preliminary step prior to issuing a formal RFP, which allows the facility to narrow down the field of potential vendors for procurement of a new hospital-wide computer system, would be to
    A. select the system to be purchased.
    B. create a Gantt chart to monitor project progress.
    C. issue a request for information (RFI) to potential vendors.
    D. initiate contract negotiations.

REFERENCE: Johns, p 889
               LaTour and Eichenwald-Maki, p 148
               Marreel and McLellan, pp 88–90
               McWay, p 344

69. Administration has asked the clinical provider order-entry task force to select the method of implementation that will reduce risk to the hospital. What method should they choose?
    A. Implement all modules across the entire organization.
    B. Implement one module in one unit while running the current system in parallel.
    C. Implement all modules across the entire organization while running the current system in parallel.
    D. Implement one module in one unit while shutting down the existing system.

REFERENCE: Johns, pp 888, 890

70. The EHR is expected to be operational 100% of the time. Which of the following assist in this level of availability?
    A. integrity   B. redundancy
    C. RAID   D. ECRM

REFERENCE: LaTour, p 250

71. You recently installed a new computer system and you just learned that the vendor does not have the right to use one portion of the system. Another company owns the rights to the information contained in this portion of the system. What clause in your contract would you review to see if you are protected from being sued by the other company?
    A. warranties   C. support
    B. indemnification   D. force majeure

REFERENCE: Abdelhak, p 347
               Marreel and McLellan, p 103
               McWay, p 344

72. Your facility has implemented the clinical systems needed to support the EHR. The knowledge-based and decision support systems will be installed next. Your team has a firm plan to indicate the direction you should take and the expected timeframe. This is called a
    A. cost-benefit analysis.   B. migration path.
    C. critical path.   D. value realization.

REFERENCE: Amatayakul, p 162

73. Which of the following is an example of two-factor authentication?
   A. user name and password
   B. token and smart card
   C. fingerprint and retinal scan
   D. password and token

REFERENCE: Abdelhak, p 287
                Johns, p 920
                LaTour and Eichenwald-Maki, pp 127–128
                McWay, p 170
                Sayles and Trawick, p 322

74. As Director of Health Information Services, you are negotiating a contract to purchase a new computerized dictation system that will be used across three satellite ambulatory clinics. What element is most critical in the contract negotiation to ensure use of the software in multiple environments?
   A. delivery terms
   B. scope and term of warranties
   C. price and payment terms
   D. license grant

REFERENCE: Abdelhak, p 347

75. The most secure model of signatures used in information systems is
   A. digital signature.
   B. electronic signature.
   C. digitized signature.
   D. there is no difference in the level of security between these models.

REFERENCE: McWay, pp 328–329

76. Which of the following situations would be an appropriate use of a DSS?
   A. determining the number of staff needed on the nursing unit
   B. establishing the productivity standard for the organization
   C. generating a report that aggregates data from multiple information system, including both clinical and financial data
   D. determining whether or not to purchase a new MRI machine so that there are two instead of just one

REFERENCE: LaTour and Eichenwald-Maki, pp 600–601

77. You need a report that includes only Medicare patients. What operation enables you to generate this report?
   A. filtering
   B. sorting
   C. grouping
   D. calculations

REFERENCE: Sayles and Trawick, p 174

78. Which of these functions is found in an ambulatory EHR but not in an acute care EHR?
   A. results review
   B. online documentation
   C. eMAR
   D. registration

REFERENCE: Amatayakul, p 511

79. Which of the following is a risky practice in the EHR?
   A. copy and paste
   B. data reuse
   C. free text
   D. graphical user interface

REFERENCE: Amatayakul, p 321

80. This small physician practice does not have the technical staff to manage the EHR. The physicians are looking for someone who can manage the software and hardware for them at a set monthly cost. Their technology support staff is limited, so you want to use a technology where the software and database is stored and maintained remotely. This is called
   A. the Internet
   B. cloud computing
   C. virtualization
   D. client-server architecture

REFERENCE: Amatayakul, p 297

81. The facility is implementing a new PACS. They know that the volume of data that will be passing over the Internet will significantly increase. As a result, they have updated their network. They want to determine if the updated network can handle the amount of data that is expected to be sent across the system. Which type of testing would they use?
   A. conversion
   B. functionality
   C. interface
   D. load or volume

REFERENCE: Abdelhak, p 331
               Amatayakul, p 419

© Cengage Learning 2014

82. Which of the following relationships does the diagram above demonstrate?
   A. one to one
   B. many to many
   C. one to many
   D. one and only one

REFERENCE: Abdelhak, p 316
               LaTour and Eichenwald-Maki, pp 130–131

83. There was an unexpected hardware failure for our EHR. It is expected to be up and operational in 3 hours. Until then, which of the following plans would you need to initiate?
   A. information system strategic plan
   B. implementation plan
   C. business continuity plan
   D. project planning

REFERENCE: Glandon, Smaltz and Slovensky, p 191
               McWay, pp 402–403

84. You have been asked to develop scenarios that will be used to design and program a new release of information system. These scenarios will include the processes to be used in detail. What are you designing?
    A. strategic plan
    B. functional requirements
    C. use cases
    D. request for proposal

REFERENCE: Abdelhak, p 319
              Sayles and Trawick, p 258

85. Mountaintop Hospital has decided to use the "best of breed" philosophy. Because of this, they need a(n) _____ to manage the sharing of data.
    A. DBMS
    B. RFP
    C. consultant
    D. interface engine

REFERENCE: Amatayakul, p 375
              Marreel and McLellan, p 198

86. The HIM supervisor is evaluating software that would utilize electronic logging and monitoring of requests for copies of patient information and develop an accounting of disclosure. What department function is this most useful for?
    A. release of information/disclosure management
    B. record completion
    C. record location/tracking
    D. transcription

REFERENCE: Green and Bowie, pp 296–298
              Johns, pp 443–446
              Sayles and Trawick, p 182

87. You have been asked to identify and display the existing record processing workflow with the paper record. After you finish this, you will redesign the process and display the new process. What tool should you use?
    A. policy and procedure
    B. data dictionary
    C. data flow diagram
    D data mapping

REFERENCE: Abdelhak, p 310
              Sayles and Trawick, p 97

88. Installation of a new electronic document management system is scheduled for the HIM department. The department director calls a meeting of the HIM supervisors to coordinate plans for training the HIM staff. What key factors must be taken into consideration as part of the training preparation process?
    A. the total storage capacity and price of the new system
    B. collecting the results of the RFP responses and vendor selection process used during the selection process
    C. presentation content and scheduling to accommodate all employee shifts
    D. scheduling training times and locations for all physicians and hospital personnel who will use the system

REFERENCE: Abdelhak, p 330
              LaTour and Eichenwald-Maki, p 754

89. The patient's blood pressure is automatically being recorded. This is an example of what type of clinical information system?
   A. patient monitoring system
   B. medical documentation
   C. nursing applications
   D. patient registration

REFERENCE: Green and Bowie, p 115

90. You have been asked to establish guidelines on screen design that will be used in all of your information system projects. Which of the following standards would be included in your guidelines?
   A. The screen should read right to left.
   B. Eliminate all hyperlinks.
   C. Provide instructions on how to complete the screen.
   D. Use red and green to flag key data.

REFERENCE: Abdelhak, p 121

91. You are entering the valid choices for each of the data elements, defining each data element and more. You must be managing the
   A. functional requirement.
   B. data dictionary.
   C. system analysis.
   D. data flow diagram.

REFERENCE: Abdelhak, p 121
               Johns, pp 169, 199–200, 904–907
               LaTour and Eichenwald-Maki, p 90
               McWay, p 170

92. Your department must send information electronically to the state health department every day. Currently this is taking a significant amount of time. What technology can be used to automatically send this information without human intervention?
   A. electronic data interchange
   B. LAN
   C. Internet
   D. network interface card

REFERENCE: Glandon, Smaltz, and Slovensky, p 159
               Johns, pp 144, 218–219, 348
               LaTour and Eichenwald-Maki, p 56
               Marreel and McLellan, pp 4, 55–60
               McWay, p 174

93. The CIO has given you a list of critical success factors developed for the EHR that your facility is developing. Which of the following would you expect to see on this list?
   A. implement e-prescribing
   B. get buy-in from the key players
   C. utilize thin clients
   D. utilize encryption

REFERENCE: LaTour and Eichenwald-Maki, pp 834–838

94. Which of the following is an example of a character?
    A. "abc"
    B. "123"
    C. "a"
    D. "123/abc"

REFERENCE: Green, p 113

95. You have had a problem with duplicate medical record numbers in your facility's MPI. Now you are joining a health information exchange, so you will need to clean up your database and prevent the duplicates from happening again. If you want to find near matches as well as identical matches in your MPI, you should implement a _____ algorithm.
    A. probabilistic
    B. deterministic
    C. fuzzy
    D. none of the above

REFERENCE: Gudea, p 51
               McWay, pp 115–116, 176

96. Juan has been asked to investigate e-health companies. Which of the following would NOT be included in his investigation?
    A. Health Data: a company that stores patient identifiable health information online.
    B. HealthInfo: a company that provides medical references to patients.
    C. Physician Services: a company that provides medical references to physicians.
    D. Café Services: a company that provides cafeteria services to the hospital.

REFERENCE: Fuller, p 50
               McWay, pp 325–326

97. If your network was graphed, it would show a hub in the middle with nodes surrounding it. What type of network is it and why would you choose it?
    A. Star, ease of adding computers
    B. Ring, operates over high distance
    C. Bus, ease of adding computers
    D. Ring, does not go down much

REFERENCE: Glandon, Smaltz, and Slovensky, p 158

98. Dr. Smith has a practice in Macon, Georgia. He is treating a patient who is physically located in Soperton, Georgia, which is about 70 miles away. What technology is required for Dr. Smith to treat the patient?
    A. EHR
    B. clinical data repository
    C. telehealth
    D. cloud computing

REFERENCE: LaTour and Eichenwald-Maki, p 608

99. The patient has been on medication X for several years. A physician ordered medication Y. The information system immediately sends the physician a message that says that medication Y is contraindicated due to medication X. What technology is being used?
   A. point-of-care system
   B. clinical decision support systems
   C. EHR
   D. order entry results reporting

REFERENCE: Abdelhak, p 182
                        Glandon, Smaltz, and Slovensky, p 222
                        Sayles and Trawick, p 249

100. The new computer hardware arrived and the technical staff was not able to install it because there was not enough space in the computer room. Which of the following implementation steps was not properly executed?
   A. system evaluation
   B. conversion
   C. site preparation
   D. user preparation

REFERENCE: Abdelhak, p 331
                        Johns, p 888

101. You are considering three vendors for your new encoder. Your facility wants to purchase the system from a stable company. After reviewing the vendor profile information below, which of the vendors would you eliminate from consideration?

Topic	Vendor A	Vendor B	Vendor C
Number of years in business	2	10	3
Number of installations	72	135	5
Number of installation staff	3	4	1
Age of product	2	6	3
Financial standing	Good	Excellent	Fair

   A. Vendor A
   B. Vendor B
   C. Vendor C
   D. You cannot eliminate any of the vendors.

REFERENCE: Johns, p 889
                        LaTour and Eichenwald-Maki, p 150
                        Marreel and McLellan, pp 101–106
                        McWay, pp 344–345

Answer Key for Informatics and Information Systems

1.	A		43.	B
2.	B		44.	A
3.	B		45.	D
4.	C		46.	A
5.	A		47.	A
6.	D		48.	A
7.	D		49.	D
8.	B		50.	B
9.	B		51.	C
10.	A		52.	D
11.	C		53.	C
12.	B		54.	A
13.	D		55.	A
14.	C		56.	A
15.	C		57.	C
16.	D		58.	D
17.	C		59.	A
18.	C		60.	B
19.	C		61.	A
20.	D		62.	C
21.	A		63.	B
22.	A		64.	A
23.	A		65.	C
24.	C		66.	A
25.	A		67.	D
26.	A		68.	C
27.	A		69.	B
28.	B		70.	B
29.	C		71.	A
30.	B		72.	B
31.	A		73.	D
32.	C		74.	D
33.	A		75.	A
34.	A		76.	D
35.	C		77.	A
36.	B		78.	D
37.	D		79.	A
38.	D		80.	B
39.	B		81.	D
40.	C		82.	A
41.	B		83.	C
42.	C		84.	C

Answer Key for Informatics and Information Systems

85. A Although the facility may benefit
        from the services of a consultant
        and they will need a DBMS to
        manage the database for the new
        systems, it is the interface engine
        that will be needed to manage
        communication between the various
        systems.
86. A
87. C
88. C
89. A

90. A
91. B
92. A
93. B
94. C
95. A
96. D
97. A
98. C
99. B
100. C
101. C

REFERENCES

Abdelhak, M., Grostick, S., Hanken, M. A., & Jacobs, E. (2012). *Health information: management of a strategic resource* (4th ed.). Philadelphia: W. B. Saunders.

Amatayakul, M. K. (2012). *Electronic health records: A practical guide for professionals and organizations* (5th ed.). Chicago: American Health Information Management Association.

Eichenwald-Maki, S., & Petterson, B. (2008). *Using the electronic health record.* Clifton Park, NY: Delmar Cengage Learning.

Fuller, S. (2000). To "E" or not to "E": HIM and the dawn of e-health. *Journal of AHIMA, 71*(4), 50–53. Chicago: American Health Information Management Association (AHIMA).

Glandon, G., Smaltz, D., & Slovensky, D. (2008). *Information systems for healthcare management.* Chicago: Health Administration Press.

Green, M. A., & Bowie, M. J. (2011). *Essentials of health information management* (2nd ed.). Clifton Park, NY: Delmar Cengage Learning.

Gudea, S. (2005). Deterministic, probabilistic, or fuzzy? A primer on the search algorithms that drive MPI quality. *Journal of AHIMA, 76*(8), 5–54. Chicago: American Health Information Management Association (AHIMA).

Johns, M. L. (2011). *Health information management technology: An applied approach* (3rd ed.). Chicago: American Health Information Management Association.

LaTour, K., & Eichenwald-Maki, S. (2010). *Health information management: Concepts, principles, and practice* (3rd ed.). Chicago: American Health Information Management Association (AHIMA).

Mahoney, M. E. (1997). Document imaging and workflow technology in health care today. *Journal of AHIMA, 68*(4), 28–36. Chicago: American Health Information Management Association (AHIMA).

Marreel, R., & McLellan, J. (1999). *Information management in health care.* Clifton Park, NY: Delmar Cengage Learning.

McWay, D. (2008). *Today's health information management: An integrated approach.* Chicago: Delmar Cengage Learning.

Murphy, G. F., Hanken, M. A., & Waters, K. (1999). *Electronic health records: Changing the vision.* Philadelphia: W. B. Saunders.

Sayles N. B., & Trawick, K. (2010). *Introduction to computer systems for health information technology.* Chicago: American Health Information Management Association.

Sheridan, C. (2001). Do you need an ASP ASAP? *Journal of AHIMA, 72*(8), 38–42. Chicago: American Health Information Management Association (AHIMA).

Informatics and Information Systems Chapter Domains

Question	RHIA Domain	RHIT Domain
1–101	3	
1–55		4

XI. Health Information Privacy and Security

Nanette B. Sayles, EdD, RHIA, CCS, CHPS, CPHIMS, FAHIMA

1. As Chief Privacy Officer for Premier Medical Center, you are responsible for which of the following?
   A. backing up data
   B. developing a plan for reporting privacy complaints
   C. writing policies on protecting hardware
   D. writing policies on encryption standards

REFERENCE: Brodnik, pp 186–187
             Green and Bowie, p 42
             Hjort (2001), p 64B
             Johns, pp 745, 856
             Krager and Krager, pp 11–12, 41
             McWay, pp 36, 57

2. Which of the following situations violate a patient's privacy?
   A. The hospital sends patients who are scheduled for deliveries information on free childbirth classes.
   B. The physician on the quality improvement committee reviews medical records for potential quality problems.
   C. The hospital provides patient names and addresses to a pharmaceutical company to be used in a mass mailing of free drug samples.
   D. The hospital uses aggregate data to determine whether or not to add a new operating room suite.

REFERENCE: Amatayakul (2001b), p 16B
             Brodnik, p 182
             Green and Bowie, p 294
             Johns, pp 855–856
             Krager and Krager, p 39

3. Margaret has signed an authorization to release information regarding her ER visit for a fractured finger to her attorney. Specifically, she says to release the ER history and physical, x-rays, and any procedure notes related to a finger fracture with laceration. Which of the following violates her privacy if released based on this authorization?
   A. release of face sheet used in ER as a history
   B. x-ray of chest
   C. x-ray of finger
   D. documentation of suturing of finger

REFERENCE: Brodnik, pp 176–177
             Hughes (2002b), p 56A
             Krager and Krager, pp 34, 41
             McWay, p 62

4. Mary processed a request for information and mailed it out last week. Today, the requestor, an attorney, called and said that all of the requested information was not provided. Mary pulls the documentation, including the authorization and what was sent. She believes that she sent everything that was required. She confirms this with her supervisor. The requestor still believes that some extra documentation is required. Given the above information, which of the following statements is true?
   A. Mary is not required to release the extra documentation because the facility has the right to interpret a request and apply the minimum standard rule.
   B. Mary is required to release the extra documentation because the requestor knows what is needed.
   C. Mary is required to release the extra documentation because, in the customer service program for the facility, the customer is always right.
   D. Mary is not required to release the additional information because her administrator agrees with her.

REFERENCE: Brodnik, pp 176–177
            Hughes (2002b), p 56A
            Johns, pp 777–779, 840
            Krager and Krager, pp 34–35, 41
            McWay, p 62

5. Mountain Hospital has discovered a security breach. Someone hacked into the system and viewed 50 medical records. According to ARRA, what is the responsibility of the covered entity?
   A. ARRA does not address this issue.
   B. All individuals must be notified within 30 days.
   C. All individuals must be notified within 60 days.
   D. ARRA requires oral notification.

REFERENCE: Johns, pp 853–855, 998–999, 1006–1007
            Rhodes (2009a), p 10
            U.S. DHHS 2

6. Physical safeguards include

    1. tools to monitor access
    2. tools to control access to computer systems
    3. fire protection
    4. tools preventing unauthorized access to data

   A. 1 and 2 only   C. 2 and 3 only
   B. 1 and 3 only   D. 2 and 4 only

REFERENCE: Green and Bowie, p 282
            Hartley and Jones, pp 168–170
            Johns, pp 1003, 1005
            Krager and Krager, pp 92–93
            McWay, pp 322–324

7. You are reviewing your privacy and security policies, procedures, training program, and so on, and comparing them to the HIPAA and ARRA regulations. You are conducting a
   A. policy assessment.
   B. risk assessment.
   C. compliance audit.
   D. risk management.

   REFERENCE: Brodnik, pp 292–294
                 Hjort (2001), p 64A
                 Krager and Krager, pp 86–87, 105
                 McWay, pp 252–253

8. A patient's medical record was breached. The written notification that goes out to the patient should contain only a message to call the hospital.
   A. True statement. This is too sensitive to address in a letter.
   B. False statement. The patient should receive a brief description of the breach, what the covered entity is doing about the breach, what the patient should do, and whom to contact.
   C. False statement, because the patient should be told to contact the Office of the Inspector General.
   D. False statement, because the patient should be told what happened and that the facility is sorry and hopes the patient will not have any problems as a result of the breach.

   REFERENCE: Johns, pp 854–855
                 Rhodes (2009a), p 11
                 U.S. DHHS 1

9. Kyle, the HIM Director, has received a request to amend a patient's medical record. The appropriate action for him to take is
   A. make the modification because you have received the request.
   B. file the request in the chart to document the disagreement with the information contained in the medical record.
   C. route the request to the physician who wrote the note in question to determine appropriateness of the amendment.
   D. return the notice to the patient because amendments are not allowed.

   REFERENCE: Brodnik, pp 179–180
                 Green and Bowie, pp 84–85
                 Johns, pp 831–833
                 Krager and Krager, pp 44–45
                 McWay, p 263
                 Thieleman, p 46

10. Dr. Brown has just approved the patient's request to amend the medical record. Dr. Brown has routed the request with his approval to the HIM Department. What should the HIM Department do?
    A. File the request where the erroneous information is located.
    B. File the request where the erroneous information is located and send a copy of the amendment to anyone who has a copy of the erroneous information.
    C. File in the front of the chart.
    D. File the request where the erroneous information is located and send a copy of the amendment to anyone who has a copy of the erroneous information plus anyone the patient requests.

REFERENCE: Brodnik, pp 179–180
                       Green and Bowie, pp 84–85
                       Johns, pp 284, 831–833
                       Thieleman, p 44

11. A patient has submitted an authorization to release information to a physician office for continued care. The release of information clerk wants to limit the information provided because of the minimum necessary rule. What should the supervisor tell the clerk?
    A. Good call.
    B. The patient is an exception to the minimum necessary rule, so process the request as written.
    C. The minimum necessary rule was eliminated with ARRA.
    D. The minimum necessary rule only applies to attorneys.

REFERENCE: McWay, p 62

12. Patricia is processing a request for medical records. The record contains an operative note and a discharge summary from another hospital. The records are going to another physician for patient care. What should Patricia do?
    A. Notify the requestor that redisclosure is illegal and so he must get the operative and discharge summary records from the original source hospital.
    B. Include the documents from the other hospital.
    C. Redisclose when necessary for patient care.
    D. Redisclose when allowed by law.

REFERENCE: Brodnik, p 176
                       Green and Bowie, pp 295–296
                       Hughes (2001b), p 72B
                       Johns, p 823
                       Krager and Krager, pp 127–128

13. You are writing a policy for the release of information area. This policy will include the requirements for a valid authorization. Which of the following would not be included?
    A. expiration
    B. request for an accounting of disclosure
    C. statement or right to revoke
    D. description of information to be disclosed

REFERENCE: Brodnik, p 169
               LaTour and Eichenwald-Maki, pp 571–572

14. Contingency planning includes which of the following processes?
    A. data quality   C. disaster planning
    B. systems analysis   D. hiring practices

REFERENCE: Brodnik, pp 227–231
               Green and Bowie, p 281
               Hartley and Jones, pp 158, 161
               Johns, pp 993–994
               Krager and Krager, pp 91–92
               McWay, pp 252–254

15. Which of the following disclosures would require patient authorization?
    A. law enforcement activities
    B. workers' compensation
    C. release to patient's attorney
    D. public health activities

REFERENCE: Brodnik, p 168
               Green and Bowie, pp 291–294
               Hartley and Jones, pp 103–198
               LaTour and Eichenwald-Maki, p 286

16. Your department was unable to provide a patient with a copy of his record within the 30-day limitation. What should you do?
    A. Call the patient and apologize.
    B. Call the patient and let him know that you will need a 30-day extension.
    C. Write the patient and tell him that you will need a 30-day extension.
    D. Both write and call the patient to tell him you need a 30-day extension.

REFERENCE: Green and Bowie, p 295

17. I have been asked if I want to be in the directory. The admission clerk explains that if I am in the directory
    A. my friends and family can find out my room number.
    B. my condition can be discussed with any caller in detail.
    C. my condition can be released to the news media.
    D. my condition can be released to hospital staff only.

REFERENCE: Brodnik, p 171
              Johns, pp 842–843
              Krager and Krager, pp 35–36, 40, 124–125
              Roach, p 172

18. Which of the following techniques would a facility employ for access control?

    1. automatic logoff
    2. authentication
    3. integrity controls
    4. unique user identification

    A. 1 and 4   C. 2 and 4 only
    B. 1 and 2 only   D. 3 and 4 only

REFERENCE: Brodnik, pp 212–214
              Green and Bowie, pp 282–283
              Hartley and Jones, pp 170–171
              Johns, pp 919–921
              Krager and Krager, pp 96–98
              McWay, pp 173, 323, 389

19. Which of the following statements is true about the Privacy Act of 1974?
    A. It applies to all organizations that maintain health care data in any form.
    B. It applies to all health care organizations.
    C. It applies to the federal government.
    D. It applies to federal government except for the Veterans Health Administration.

REFERENCE: Brodnik, p 157
              Green and Bowie, p 285
              LaTour and Eichenwald-Maki, p 281

20. Which of the following statements is true about a requested restriction?
    A. ARRA mandates that a CE must comply with a requested restriction.
    B. ARRA states that a CE does not have to agree to a requested restriction.
    C. ARRA mandates that a CE must comply with a requested restriction unless it meets one of the exceptions.
    D. ARRA does not address restrictions to PHI.

REFERENCE: Johns, p 835
              Rhodes (2009a), p 13

21. Facility access controls, workstation use, workstation security, and device/media controls are all part of
    A. physical safeguards.
    B. technical safeguards.
    C. administrative safeguards.
    D. organizational requirements.

REFERENCE: Green and Bowie, p 282
               Johns, pp 1003–1004

22. Encryption, access control, emergency access to records, and biometrics are examples of
    A. transmission security.
    B. technical security.
    C. a security incident.
    D. telecommunications.

REFERENCE: Brodnik, pp 201, 208
               Green and Bowie, pp 278, 283
               Johns, pp 1005–1007
               Krager and Krager, pp 96–100
               McWay, p 323
               Roach, pp 469–471

23. Intentional threats to security could include
    A. a natural disaster (flood).
    B. equipment failure (software failure).
    C. human error (data entry error).
    D. data theft (unauthorized downloading of files).

REFERENCE: Brodnik, p 225
               Johns, pp 996–998

24. Which of the following would be a business associate?
    A. release of information company
    B. bulk food service provider
    C. childbirth class instructor
    D. security force

REFERENCE: Brodnik, pp 158–159
               Johns, pp 822, 824–825
               Krager and Krager, p 42
               McWay, p 56

25. Which of the following statements demonstrates a violation of protected health information?
    A. "Can you help me find Mary Smith's record?"
    B. A member of the physician's office staff calls centralized scheduling and says, "Dr. Smith wants to perform a bunionectomy on Mary Jones next Tuesday."
    C. "Mary, at work yesterday I saw that Susan had a hysterectomy."
    D. Dr. Jones tells a nurse on the floor to give Ms. Brown Demerol for her pain.

REFERENCE: Johns, pp 701–702
               Krager and Krager, pp 19, 29–30
               McWay, pp 59–60
               Roach, p 45

26. Mark, a patient of Schnering Hospital, has asked for an electronic copy of his medical record to go to his physician. According to ARRA, what is the CE's obligation to Mark?
    A. None, as this is prohibited by HIPAA.
    B. None, as this is prohibited by ARRA.
    C. Mark has a right to an electronic copy, but it has to go to him, not a third party.
    D. Mark has a right to an electronic copy or to have it sent to someone else.

REFERENCE: Rhodes (2009a), p 16

27. Margot looked up PHI on her ex-sister-in-law. A routine audit discovered the violation. Which statement is true under ARRA?
    A. Margot cannot be prosecuted since she is not a covered entity.
    B. Margot cannot be prosecuted since she is not a covered entity or business associate.
    C. Margot cannot be prosecuted since she did not sell the PHI.
    D. Margot can be prosecuted.

REFERENCE: Rhodes (2009a), p 18

28. You are defining the designated record set for South Beach Healthcare Center. Which of the following would be included?
    A. quality reports
    B. psychotherapy notes
    C. discharge summary
    D. information compiled for use in civil hearing

REFERENCE: Amatayakul and Waymack, p 16A
               Brodnik, pp 124–125, 162
               Johns, p 822
               Krager and Krager, p 31
               LaTour and Eichenwald-Maki, p 300

29. You have been asked to provide examples of technical security measures. Which of the following would you include in your list of examples?
    A. locked doors   C. minimum necessary
    B. automatic logout   D. training

REFERENCE: Brodnik, pp 208–209
               Green and Bowie, p 283
               Johns, pp 105–107
               Krager and Krager, pp 90–100
               McWay, pp 322–323

30. Which security measure utilizes fingerprints or retina scans?
    A. audit trail
    B. biometrics
    C. authentication
    D. encryption

REFERENCE: Abdelhak, p 288
               Brodnik, pp 210–214
               Fuller, p 40
               Green and Bowie, p 283
               Johns, pp 1005–1006
               Krager and Krager, pp 96–97
               McWay, pp 222–223

31. Ms. Thomas was a patient at your facility. She has been told that there are some records that she cannot have access to. These records are most likely
    A. psychotherapy notes.
    B. alcohol and drug records.
    C. AIDS records.
    D. mental health assessment.

REFERENCE: Brodnik, pp 246–247
               Green and Bowie, pp 278, 294–295
               Hughes (2001a), p 90
               Johns, pp 826–827
               Krager and Krager, pp 38–39

32. Your organization is sending confidential patient information across the Internet using technology that will transform the original data into unintelligible code that can be re-created by authorized users. This technique is called
    A. a firewall.
    B. validity processing.
    C. a call-back process.
    D. data encryption.

REFERENCE: Abdelhak, p 289
               Brodnik, pp 217–218
               Green and Bowie, p 283
               Johns, pp 510, 1006–1007
               Krager and Krager, pp 99–100
               McWay, p 321

33. You are writing a policy on how to document the amendment process. What information should be required by the policy?
    A. none
    B. documentation of request and refusal
    C. documentation of request
    D. documentation of a request, a refusal, and a patient's right to write a statement of disagreement

REFERENCE: Amatayakul (2001b), p 16C
               Brodnik, pp 179–180
               Green and Bowie, pp 84–85
               Johns, pp 831–833
               Krager and Krager, pp 32–33
               McWay, pp 62, 85

34. Which of the following should the record destruction program include?
    A. the method of destruction
    B. the name of the supervisor of the person destroying the records
    C. citing the laws followed
    D. requirement of daily destruction

REFERENCE: Brodnik, pp 146–147
               Green and Bowie, pp 96–97
               Johns, pp 403, 405–408
               LaTour and Eichenwald-Maki, p 225
               McWay, pp 112–115

35. You are looking for potential problems and violations of the privacy rule. What is this security management process called?
    A. risk management
    B. risk assessment
    C. risk aversion
    D. business continuity planning

REFERENCE: Green, p 281

36. The administrator states that he should not have to participate in privacy and security training as he does not use PHI. How should you respond?
    A. "All employees are required to participate in the training, including top administration."
    B. "I will record that in my files."
    C. "Did you read the privacy rules?"
    D. "You are correct. There is no reason for you to participate in the training."

REFERENCE: Brodnik, pp 158–159
               Hartley and Jones, p 84
               Johns, p 857
               Krager and Krager, p 90
               McWay, pp 322–323

37. The surgeon comes out to speak to a patient's family. He tells them that the patient came through the surgery fine. The mass was benign and they could see the patient in an hour. He talks low so that the other people in the waiting room will not hear but someone walked by and heard. This is called a(n)
    A. privacy breach.   C. incidental disclosure.
    B. violation of policy. D. privacy incident.

REFERENCE: Brodnik, pp 174–175
               Johns, pp 847, 849
               Krager and Krager, pp 19, 36

38. The HIPAA security rule does not require specific technologies to be used but rather provides direction on the outcome. The term used to describe this philosophy is
   A. technology free.
   B. technology neutral.
   C. administrative rules.
   D. generic technology.

REFERENCE: Brodnik, p 197
               Krager and Krager, p 101
               Roach, p 460

39. A mechanism to ensure that PHI has not been altered or destroyed inappropriately has been established. This process is called
   A. entity authentication.
   B. audit controls.
   C. access control.
   D. integrity.

REFERENCE: Green, p 283

40. America LTD. has developed a PHR. According to ARRA, the health information that they store is
   A. not protected.
   B. protected.
   C. mandated to be de-identified.
   D. subject to security, but not privacy, requirements.

REFERENCE: Rhodes (2009a), p 2
               U.S. DHHS 6

41. The hospital has received a request for an amendment. How long does the facility have in order to accept or deny the request?
   A. 30 days   C. 14 days
   B. 60 days   D. 10 days

REFERENCE: Brodnik, pp 179–180
               Green and Bowie, pp 84–85
               Johns, pp 831–832
               Krager and Krager, pp 23–24, 44
               McWay, p 63
               Roach, p 233

42. You work for a 60-bed hospital in a rural community. You are conducting research on what you need to do to comply with HIPAA. You are afraid that you will have to implement all of the steps that your friend at a 900-bed teaching hospital is implementing at his facility. You continue reading and learn that you only have to implement what is prudent and reasonable for your facility. This is called
    A. scalable.
    B. risk assessment.
    C. technology neutral.
    D. access control.

REFERENCE: Brodnik, p 197
              Krager and Krager, p 87
              McWay, p 57

43. Barbara, a nurse, has been flagged for review because she logged in to the EHR in the evening when she usually works the day shift. Why should this conduct be reviewed?
    A. This is a privacy violation.
    B. This needs to be investigated before a decision is made because there may be a legitimate reason why she logged in at this time.
    C. This is not a violation since Barbara, as a nurse, has full access to data in the EHR.
    D. No action is required.

REFERENCE: Sayles and Trawick, p 324

44. Alisa has trouble remembering her password. She is trying to come up with a solution that will help her remember. Which one of the following would be the BEST practice?
    A. using the word "password" for her password
    B. using her daughter's name for her password
    C. writing the complex password on the last page of her calendar
    D. creating a password that utilizes a combination of letters and numbers

REFERENCE: Amatayakul and Walsh, p 16C
              Brodnik, pp 213–215
              Johns, p 920
              Krager and Krager, pp 88–89, 97
              McWay, p 321

45. Which statement is true about when a family member can be provided with PHI?
    A. The patient's mother can always receive PHI on their child.
    B. The family member lives out of town and cannot come to the facility to check on the patient.
    C. The family member is a health care professional.
    D. The family member is directly involved in the patient's care.

REFERENCE: Green & Bowie, p 273

The following questions represent advanced competencies.

46. Nicole is developing an agreement that will be used between the hospital and the health care clearing house. This agreement will require the two parties to protect the privacy of data exchanged. This is called
    A. a business associate agreement.   C. a trading partner agreement.
    B. a business contract.   D. none of the above.

REFERENCE: Amatayakul (2001a), p 16B
               Brodnik, pp 159–160, 246
               Johns, pp 824–825
               Krager and Krager, pp 42, 92, 100
               McWay, p 56

47. The computer system containing the electronic health record was located in a room that was flooded. As a result, the system is inoperable. Which of the following would be implemented?
    A. SWOT analysis
    B. information systems strategic planning
    C. request for proposal
    D. business continuity processes

REFERENCE: Brodnik, pp 52, 227–231
               Green and Bowie, pp 28–282
               Johns, pp 929–926
               Krager and Krager, pp 91–92
               McWay, pp 252–254

48. You have been given the responsibility of destroying the PHI contained in the system's old server before it is trashed. What destruction method do you recommend?
    A. crushing
    B. overwriting data
    C. degaussing
    D. incineration

REFERENCE: Sayles and Trawick, p 317

49. You are walking around the facility to identify any privacy and security issues. You walk onto the 6W nursing unit and from the desk where you are standing you are able to watch the nurse entering confidential patient information. How can you best improve the privacy of the patient's health information?
    A. Ask the nurse to type the data on another computer.
    B. Turn the computer screen so that the public cannot see it.
    C. Give the nurse additional training.
    D. None of the above.

REFERENCE: Amatayakul (2002a), p 16A-C
                Brodnik, p 217
                Krager and Krager, pp 86–87, 104–105
                McWay, p 252

50. In conducting an environmental risk assessment, which of the following would be considered in the assessment?
    A. placement of water pipes in the facility
    B. verifying that virus checking software is in place
    C. use of single sign-on technology
    D. authentication

REFERENCE: Brodnik, pp 206–207
                Dennis, p 18
                Johns, pp 989–992
                McWay, p 253

51. Which of the following documents is subject to the HIPAA security rule?
    A. document faxed to the facility
    B. copy of discharge summary
    C. paper medical record
    D. scanned operative report stored on CD

REFERENCE: Brodnik, p 196
                Krager and Krager, pp 6, 84–85
                McWay, p 57
                Roach, p 459

52. A hacker recently accessed our database. We are trying to determine how the hacker got through the firewall and exactly what was accessed. The process used to gather this evidence is called
    A. forensics.   C. security event.
    B. mitigation.   D. incident.

REFERENCE: Sayles and Trawick, p 310

53. As Chief Privacy Officer, you have been asked why you are conducting a risk assessment. Which reason would you give?
    A. to get rid of problem staff
    B. to change organizational culture
    C. to prevent breach of confidentiality
    D. none of the above

REFERENCE: Brodnik, p 187
               Dennis, p 36
               Johns, pp 989–990
               Krager and Krager, pp 86–87, 105
               McWay, pp 252–253

54. Which of the following situations would require authorization before disclosing PHI?
    A. releasing information to the Bureau of Disability Determination
    B. health oversight activity
    C. workers' compensation
    D. public health activities

REFERENCE: Green & Bowie, p 291

55. A covered entity
    A. is exempt from the HIPAA privacy and security rules.
    B. includes all health care providers.
    C. includes health care providers who perform specified actions electronically.
    D. must utilize business associates.

REFERENCE: Brodnik, p 164
               Johns, pp 823–824
               Krager and Krager, pp 10–11, 13
               McWay, p 56
               Roach, pp 141–142

56. Which of the following is an example of a security incident?
    A. Temporary employees were not given individual passwords.
    B. An employee took home a laptop with unsecured PHI.
    C. A handheld device was left unattended on the crash cart in the hall for 10 minutes.
    D. A hacker accessed PHI from off site.

REFERENCE: Sayles and Trawick, p 310

57. Protected health information includes
    A. only electronic individually identifiable health information.
    B. only paper individually identifiable health information.
    C. individually identifiable health information in any format stored by a health care provider.
    D. individually identifiable health information in any format stored by a health care provider or business associate.

REFERENCE: Brodnik, p 160
               Green and Bowie, pp 272–273
               Johns, pp 821–823
               Krager and Krager, pp 6–8, 28–29
               LaTour and Eichenwald-Maki, p 989
               McWay, p 57
               Roach, p 105

58. The HIM director received an e-mail from the technology support services department about her e-mail being full and asking for her password. The director contacted tech support and it was confirmed that their department did not send this e-mail. This is an example of what type of malware?
    A. phishing   C. denial of service
    B. spyware   D. virus

REFERENCE: Sayles and Trawick, p 326

59. You have been asked to create a presentation on intentional and unintentional threats. Which of the following should be included in the list of threats you cite?
    A. hard drive failures
    B. data deleted by accident
    C. data loss due to electrical failures
    D. a patient's Social Security number being used for credit card applications

REFERENCE: Sayles and Trawick, p 301

60. The housekeeping staff has access to the EHR. They can add notes, view, and print. This is an example of what?
    A. the termination process
    B. an information system activity review
    C. spoliation
    D. a workforce clearance procedure

REFERENCE: Green and Bowie, p 281

61. The information systems department was performing their routine destruction of data that they do every year. Unfortunately, they accidently deleted a record that is involved in a medical malpractice case. This unintentional destruction of evidence is called
    A. mitigation.
    B. spoliation.
    C. forensics.
    D. a security event.

REFERENCE: Sayles and Trawick, p 310

62. Mark is an HIM employee who utilizes six different information systems as part of his job. Each of these has a different password. In order to keep up with the password for each system, Mark has written them all on paper and taped it to the back of his wife's picture on his desk. What technology could be used to eliminate this problem for Mark and other employees in the same situation?
    A. role-based access   C. SSO
    B. user-based access   D. DAC

REFERENCE: Krager and Krager, pp 88–89, 97
               Miller and Gregory, p 40

63. Cindy, Tiffany, and LaShaundra are all nurses at Sandyshore Health Care. They all have access to the same functions in the information system. It is likely that this facility is using
    A. user-based access.   C. DAC.
    B. role-based access.   D. MAC.

REFERENCE: Brodnik, pp 211–212
               Krager and Krager, pp 88–89, 105
               Miller and Gregory, p 49

64. You will be choosing the type of encryption to be used for the new EHR. What are your choices?
    A. symmetric and conventional   C. symmetric and asymmetric
    B. asymmetric and public key   D. public key and integrity

REFERENCE: Stallings, p 651

65. You have been given some information that includes the patient's account number. Which statement is true?
    A. This is de-identified information because the patient's name and social security are not included in the data.
    B. This is not de-identified information, because it is possible to identify the patient.
    C. These data are individually identified data.
    D. These data are a limited data set.

REFERENCE: Brodnik, p 161

66. Which of the following is an example of a trigger that might be used to reduce auditing?
    A. A patient has not signed their notice of privacy practices.
    B. It is an example of the use of an audit trail.
    C. The use of an audit control.
    D. It is an example of the use of a trigger.

REFERENCE: Sayles and Trawick, p 323

67. Bob submitted his resignation from Coastal Hospital. His last day is today. He should no longer have access to the EHR and other systems as of 5:00 p.m. today. The removal of his privileges is known as
    A. terminating access.
    B. isolating access.
    C. password management.
    D. sanction policy.

REFERENCE: Green and Bowie, p 281

68. The company's policy states that audit logs, access reports, and security incident reports should be reviewed daily. This review is known as
    A. a data criticality analysis.
    B. a workforce clearinghouse.
    C. an information system activity review.
    D. a risk analysis.

REFERENCE: Green and Bowie, p 281

69. The term "de-identified" indicates
    A. the patient's name has been removed.
    B. the patient's name and medical record number have been removed.
    C. the patient's name, medical record number, and social security number have been removed.
    D. all of the HIPAA-specified patient identifiers have been removed.

REFERENCE: Abdelhak, p 538
               Brodnik, pp 160–161, 184–185
               Green and Rowell, p 20
               Johns, pp 826, 828
               Krager and Krager, pp 37–39
               LaTour and Eichenwald-Maki, pp 507, 963
               McWay, pp 60, 180, 233

70. An employee utilizes the patient's name and social security number to obtain a credit card. This is an example of
   A. identity theft.
   B. de-identified information.
   C. limited data set.
   D. security incident.

REFERENCE: Brodnik, pp 226–227
               Johns, pp 858–860
               Krager and Krager, pp 29–30, 44–45
               McWay, p 63

71. Your system just crashed. Fortunately, you have established a site that holds computer processors but not data. This site can be converted to meet our needs quickly. This is a
   A. hot site.   C. redundant site.
   B. cold site.   D. backup site.

REFERENCE: NIST, chap. 11, p 5

72. The purpose of the notice of privacy practices is to
   A. notify the patient of uses of PHI.
   B. notify the patient of audits.
   C. report incidents to the OIG.
   D. notify researchers of allowable data use.

REFERENCE: Brodnik, pp 165–166, 249
               Green and Bowie, pp 273–278
               Johns, pp 836–838
               Krager and Krager, p 43
               McWay, p 60

73. You have been asked to explain the purpose of the new security awareness program. Your response is to
   A. help staff realize the importance of security.
   B. remind users of procedures.
   C. lock down PHI.
   D. train staff on the security measures related to transmission security and physical security.

REFERENCE: Brodnik, p 215
               Johns, p 1003
               Green and Bowie, p 281
               Krager and Krager, p 90
               McWay, p 60
               NIST, chap. 13, p 10

74. Our Web site was attacked by malware that overloaded it. What type of malware was this?
   A. phishing   C. denial of service
   B. virus   D. spyware

REFERENCE: Sayles & Trawick, p 326

75. Mabel is a volunteer at a hospital. She works at the information desk. A visitor comes to the desk and says that he wants to know what room John Brown is in. What should Mabel do?
    A. Look the patient up and give the room number to the visitor.
    B. Look the patient up to see if John has agreed to be in the directory. If he has, then give the room number to the visitor.
    C. Look the patient up to see if the patient signed a notice of privacy practice. If so, then give the visitor the room number.
    D. Look the patient up in the system to determine if the patient has agreed to TPO usage and then give the room number to the visitor if he had.

REFERENCE: Brodnik, p 171
               Johns, pp 842–843
               LaTour and Eichenwald-Maki, p 285

76. Which of the following is a true statement about symmetric encryption?
    A. Symmetric encryption uses a private and public key.
    B. Symmetric encryption is also known as secure socket layer.
    C. Symmetric encryption assigns a public key to data.
    D. Symmetric encryption assigns a secret key to data.

REFERENCE: Brodnik, pp 206–207
               Roach, pp 466–468

77. The facility had a security breach. The breach was identified on October 10, 2012. The investigation was completed on October 15, 2012. What is the deadline that the notification must be completed?
    A. 60 days from October 10
    B. 60 days from October 15
    C. 30 days from October 10
    D. 30 days from October 15

REFERENCE: Johns, pp 854–855
               U.S. Department of Health and Human Services (n.d.)

78. Miles has asked you to explain the rights he has via HIPAA privacy standards. Which of the following is one of his HIPAA-given rights?
    A. He can review his bill.
    B. He can ask to be contacted at an alternative site.
    C. He can discuss financial arrangements with business office staff.
    D. He can ask a patient advocate to sit in on all appointments at the facility.

REFERENCE: Brodnik, pp 177–179
               Johns, p 835
               LaTour and Eichenwald, pp 283–284
               McWay, p 57
               U.S. Office of Civil Rights (n.d.), pp 1–2

79. The following is a sentence from the notice of privacy practices. What problem do you identify?

> The party of the first part vows to mitigate breaches should a security incident occur.

    A. None, because that is the responsibility of a covered entity.
    B. None, because that is the responsibility of a business associate.
    C. It is not the responsibility of a covered entity.
    D. It is not written in plain English.

REFERENCE: Brodnik, p 165
                   Krager and Krager, p 31
                   U.S. Department of Health and Human Services Office for Civil Rights

80. HIPAA workforce security requires
    A. a criminal background check.   C. that access to PHI be appropriate.
    B. a two-factor authentication.   D. the use of card keys.

REFERENCE: Brodnik, pp 211–212
                   Krager and Krager, pp 88–89
                   McWay, p 323
                   Roach, p 463

81. To prevent our network from going down, we have duplicated much of our hardware and cables. This duplication is called
    A. emergency mode plan.
    B. redundancy.
    C. contingency plan.
    D. business continuity planning.

REFERENCE: Sayles & Trawick, p 313

82. Richard has asked to view his medical record. The record is stored off-site. How long does the facility have to provide this record to him?
    A. 30 days   C. 14 days
    B. 60 days   D. 10 days

REFERENCE: Brodnik, p 178
                   Johns, p 710
                   U.S. Department of Health and Human Services Office for Civil Rights

83. A patient authorizes Park Hospital to send a copy of a discharge summary for the latest hospitalization to Flowers Hospital. The hospital uses the discharge summary in the patient's care and files it in the medical record. When Flowers Hospital receives a request for records, a copy of Park Hospital's discharge summary is sent. This is an example of
    A. a privacy violation.   C. satisfactory assurance.
    B. redisclosure.   D. inappropriate release.

REFERENCE: Abdelhak, p 540
                   Brodnik, p 126
                   Green and Bowie, pp 295–296
                   Johns, pp 842, 847, 849
                   Krager and Krager, pp 127–128
                   Servais, pp 345–349

84. You have to decide which type of firewall you want to use in your facility. Which of the following is one of your options?
    A. packet filter
    B. secure socket layer
    C. CCOW
    D. denial of service

REFERENCE: Abdelhak, p 289

85. A data use agreement is required when
    A. a complaint has been filed.
    B. a limited data set is used.
    C. a notice of disclosure is requested.
    D. information is provided to a business associate.

REFERENCE: Brodnik, pp 174–175
               McWay, p 180

86. What type of digital signature uses encryption?
    A. digitized signature
    B. electronic signature
    C. digital signature
    D. encryption is not a part of digital signatures

REFERENCE: Brodnik, pp 137–138
               LaTour and Eichenwald-Maki, p 256

87. The police came to the HIM Department today and asked that a patient's right to an accounting of disclosure be suspended for two months. What is the proper response to this request?
    A. "I'm sorry officer, but privacy regulations do not allow us to do this."
    B. "I'm sorry officer but we can only do this for one month."
    C. "Certainly officer. We will take care of that right now."
    D. "Certainly officer. We will be glad to do that as soon as we have the request in writing."

REFERENCE: Green and Bowie, p 296

88. Which of the following set(s) is an appropriate use of the emergency access procedure?
    A. A patient is crashing. The attending physician is not in the hospital, so a physician who is available helps the patient.
    B. One of the nurses is at lunch. The nurse covering for her needs patient information.
    C. The coder who usually codes the emergency room charts is out sick and the charts are left on a desk in the ER admitting area.
    D. A and B.

REFERENCE: Green and Bowie, pp 273, 275, 278
               Krager and Krager, pp 89, 105
               U.S. HHS OCR, 1 Brodnik, pp 176–177

89. Today is August 30, 2011. When can the training records for the HIPAA privacy training being conducted today be destroyed?
    A. August 30, 2017   C. August 30, 2019
    B. August 30, 2018   D. August 30, 2020

REFERENCE: Hjort (2002), p 60 A–G
                Krager and Krager, p 90

90. We have just identified that an employee looked up his own medical record. Which of the following actions should be taken?
    A. Notify his or her supervisor because this is a minor incident and therefore not subject to the incident response procedure.
    B. Follow the incident response procedure.
    C. Terminate the employee on the spot.
    D. Notify OCR.

REFERENCE: U.S. HHS, OCR, 2

91. Your facility just learned that one of its business associates is out of compliance with your contract and with the privacy rule. What should your response be according to ARRA?
    A. Educate the business associate and conduct an audit in 30 days.
    B. Educate the business associate. Request that the problem be corrected by the business associate within 60 days.
    C. Request that the problem be corrected by the business associate within 60 days.
    D. Request that the business associate correct the problem or stop doing business with the organization.

REFERENCE: Rhodes and Rode, p 39

92. You have been assigned the responsibility of performing an audit to confirm that all of the workforce's access is appropriate for their role in the organization. This process is called
    A. risk assessment.
    B. information system activity review.
    C. workforce clearance procedure.
    D. information access management.

REFERENCE: Sayles and Trawick, p 305

93. A data use agreement allows the organization receiving the data to
    A. use the non-PHI data any way they want.
    B. use PHI data any way they want.
    C. use data only within the bounds of the agreement.
    D. conduct business for the organization.

REFERENCE: Brodnik, pp 174–175
                U.S. Department of Health and Human Services Office for Civil Rights (2003), p 31

94. Which of the following is subject to the HIPAA security rule?
    A. x-ray films stored in radiology
    B. paper medical record
    C. faxed records
    D. clinical data repository

REFERENCE: Roach, p 459

95. You work for an organization that publishes a health information management journal and provides clearinghouse services. What must you do?
    A. Have the same security plan for the entire organization.
    B. Separate the e-PHI from the noncovered entity portion of the organization.
    C. Train the journal staff on HIPAA security awareness.
    D. Follow the same rules in all parts of the organization.

REFERENCE: Sayles and Trawick, p 306

96. Robert Burchfield was recently caught accessing his wife's medical record. The system automatically notified the staff of a potential breach due to the same last name for the user and the patient. This was an example of a
    A. trigger.
    B. biometrics.
    C. telephone callback procedures.
    D. transmission security.

REFERENCE: Sayles and Trawick, p 323

97. Your facility just learned that some PHI was posted to the Internet in error. The PHI was online for 2 days before the problem was found. Unfortunately, there were people who visited the Web page during this time. Four hundred patients were impacted. Which of the following applies?
    A. The media must be notified.
    B. Patients as well as Health and Human Services must be notified.
    C. Health and Human Services must be notified within 60 days.
    D. The media and Health and Human Services must be notified.

REFERENCE: U.S. Department of Health and Human Services (n.d.)

98. An organization that is a covered entity, that performs functions that are covered and noncovered by HIPAA, and that specifies the portion of the organization that will be subject to HIPAA is called a(n)
    A. hybrid entity.
    B. affiliated covered entity.
    C. organized health care arrangement.
    D. business associate.

REFERENCE: Brodnik, p 164
              Roach, p 149

Health Information Privacy and Security

ANSWER   EXPLANATION

1. B

2. C   The release of childbirth information is acceptable because it is related to the reason for admission. The mass mailing of samples violates giving out confidential information to outside agencies.

3. B   The chest x-ray has no bearing on the finger fracture.

4. A

5. C

6. C

7. B

8. B

9. C   The person who recorded the documentation in question should be the one who authorizes the change. While these references may not explicitly state this, it does state that the form should have a place for the provider's signature and comments.

10. D

11. B

12. B

13. B

14. C

15. C

16. C

17. A

18. A

19. C

20. C

21. A

22. B

23. D   Natural disasters, equipment failure, and human error are usually unintentional threats to security. Data theft is intentional.

24. A

25. C

26. D

27. A

28. C

29. B

30. B

31. A

32. D

33. D

34. A

35. B

36. A

37. C

38. B

39. D

40. B

41. A

42. A

43. B

44. D

45. D

46. A

47. D

48. C

49. B

50. A

51. D

52. A

53. C

54. D

55. C

56. D

57. D

58 A

59. D

60. D

61. B

62. C

63. B

64. C

65. B

66. D

Health Information Privacy and Security

ANSWER   EXPLANATION

67. A		83. B	
68. C		84. B	
69. D		85. B	
70. A		86. C	
71. B		87. D	
72. A		88. D	
73. A		89. B	
74. C		90. B	
75. B		91. D	
76. D		92. C	
77. A		93. C	
78. B		94. D	The security rule only applies to e-PHI.
79. D	The Notice of Privacy must be written in plain English so that it can be understood.	95. B	
80. C		96. A	
81. B		97. B	
82. B		98. A	

REFERENCES

Abdelhak, M., Grostick, S., Hanken, M. A., & Jacobs, E. (2012). *Health information: Management of a strategic resource* (4th ed.). Philadelphia: W. B. Saunders.

Amatayakul, M. (2001a). HIPAA on the job series: Five steps to reading the HIPAA rules. *Journal of AHIMA, 72*(8), 16A–C.

Amatayakul, M. (2001b). HIPAA on the job series: Managing individual rights requirements under HIPAA privacy. *Journal of AHIMA, 72*(6), 16A–D.

Amatayakul, M. (2002a). HIPAA on the job: A reasonable approach to physical security. *Journal of AHIMA, 73*(4), 16A–C.

Amatayakul, M. (2002b). United under HIPAA: A comparison of arrangements and agreements. *Journal of AHIMA, 73*(8), 24A–D.

Amatayakul, M. (2012). *Electronic health records a practical guide for professionals and organizations* (5th ed.). Chicago: American Health Information Management Association.

Amatayakul, M., & Walsh, T. (2001). Selecting strong passwords (HIPAA on the job series). *Journal of AHIMA, 72*, 40.9, 16A–D.

Amatayakul, M., & Waymack, P. (2002). What's your designated record set? *Journal of AHIMA, 73*(6), 16A–C.

Brodnik, M. S., McCain, M. C., Rinehart-Thompson, L. A., Reynolds, R. B.(2009). *Fundamentals of law for health informatics and information management.* Chicago: American Health Information Management Association.

Cassidy, B. S. (2000). HIPAA on the job: Understanding chain of trust and business partner agreements. *Journal of AHIMA, 71*(9), 16A–C.

Cassidy, B. S. (2001). HIPAA on the job: The next challenge: Employee training on privacy, security. *Journal of AHIMA, 72*(1), 16A–C.

Dennis, J. C. (2000). *Privacy and confidentiality of health information.* San Francisco: Jossey-Bass.

Dougherty, M. (2001). Practice brief: Accounting and tracking disclosure of protected health information. *Journal of AHIMA, 72*(10), 72E–H.

Fuller, S. (1999). Implementing HIPAA security standards—are you ready? *Journal of AHIMA, 70*(9), 38–44.

Green, M. A., & Bowie, M. J. (2011). *Essentials of health information management* (2nd ed.). Clifton Park, NY: Delmar Cengage Learning.

Hartley, C. P., & Jones, III, E. D. (2011). *HIPAA plain and simple: A compliance guide for health care professionals* (2nd ed). Chicago: American Medical Association.

Hjort, B. (2001). AHIMA practice brief: A HIPAA privacy checklist. *Journal of AHIMA, 72*(6), 64A–C.

REFERENCES (continued)

Hjort, B. (2002). Privacy and security training. *Journal of AHIMA, 73*(4), 60A–G.

Hjort, B. (2011). *Practice brief: Security audits.*
    Retrieved September 20, 2012, from http://ahima.org
    http://library.ahima.org/xpedio/groups/public/documents/ahima/bok1_048702.hcsp?dDocName=bok1_048702

Hjort, B. (2003). *Practice brief: Understanding the minimum necessary standard.*
    Retrieved September 20, 2012, from http://ahima.org
    http://library.ahima.org
    http://library.ahima.org/xpedio/groups/public/documents/ahima/bok1_018177.hcsp?dDocName=bok1_018177

Hughes, G. (2001a). Managing exceptions to HIPAA's patient access rule. *Journal of AHIMA, 72*(9), 90–92.

Hughes, G. (2001b). Practice briefs: Redisclosure of PHI. *Journal of AHIMA, 72*(8), 72A, 72B.

Hughes, G. (2002a). Practice briefs: Notice of information practices (updated). *Journal of AHIMA, 72*(5), 64I–M.

Hughes, G. (2002b). Practice brief: Understanding the minimum necessary standard. *Journal of AHIMA, 73*(1), 56A–B.

Hughes, G. (2002c). Simple steps to tracking disclosures. *Journal of AHIMA, 73*(7), 68–70.

Hughes, G. (2002d). Understanding the privacy rule's amendments. *Journal of AHIMA, 73*(10), 64–66.

Johns, M. L. (2011). *Health information technology: An applied approach* (3rd ed.). Chicago: American Health Information Management Association.

Krager, D., & Krager, C. (2008). *HIPAA for health care professionals.* Clifton Park, NY: Delmar Cengage Learning.

LaTour, K. M., & Eichenwald-Maki, S. (2010). *Health information management: Concepts, principles, and practice* (3rd ed.). Chicago: American Health Information Management Association.

McWay, D. (2008). *Today's health information management: An integrated approach.* Chicago: Thomson Delmar.

Miaoulis, W. M. (2010). Access, use, and disclosure: HITECH's impact on the HIPAA touchstones. *Journal of AHIMA, 81*(3), 38–39, 64.

Miller, L., & Gregory, P. (2002). *CISSP for dummies.* New York: Wiley.

National Institute of Standards and Technology (NIST). (2005). *Special Publication 800-12: An Introduction to Computer Security – The NIST Handbook.* Printed from http://csrc.nist.gov/publications/nistpubs/800-12/800-12-html/

Roach, M. (2001). HIPAA compliance questions for business partner agreements. *Journal of AHIMA, 72*(2), 45–51.

REFERENCES (continued)

Roach, W., Hoban, R., Broccolo, B., Roth, A., & Blanchard, T. (2006). *Medical records and the law*. Sudbury, MA: Jones and Bartlett.

Rhodes, H. (2009a). *Analysis of health care confidentiality, privacy, and security provisions of The American Recovery and Reinvestment Act of 2009, Public Law 111–5*. Retrieved from http://www.ahima.org/downloads/pdfs/advocacy/AnalysisofARRAPrivacy-fin-3-2009a.pdf

Rhodes, H. (2009b). Accounting of disclosures: ARRA's impact. *2009 AHIMA Convention Proceedings*.

Rhodes, H., & Rode, D. (2010). HIPAA, too: Many ARRA privacy provisions amend HIPAA, not create new regulations. *Journal of AHIMA, 81*(1), 38–39.

Sayles, N., & Trawick, K. (2010*). Introduction to computer systems for health information technology*. Chicago: AHIMA.

Servais, C., Olderman, N., & Trahan, K. (2008). *The legal health record*. Chicago: American Health Information Management Association.

Stallings, W. (2000). *Data and computer communication* (6th ed.). Upper Saddle River, NJ: Prentice-Hall.

Sullivan, T. (2002). Mind your business associate access: Six steps. *Journal of AHIMA, 73*(9), 92, 94, 96.

Thieleman, W. (2002). A patient friendly approach to the record amendment process. *Journal of AHIMA*, 73(5), 46–47.

U.S. Department of Health and Human Services. (n.d.). Breach notification rule. Retrieved from http://www.hhs.gov/ocr/privacy/hipaa/administrative/breachnotificationrule/index.html

U.S. DHHS 45 CFR Parts 164 and 164. Breach Notification for Unsecured Protected Health Information; Interim Final Rule. Retrieved from http://edocket.access.gpo.gov/2009/pdf/E9-20169.pdf

 U.S. DHHS 1, p. 42768/Section 164.404 (c) Implementation Specifications: Contents of Notification

 U.S. DHHS 2, p. 42768/Section 164.404(a)

 U.S. DHHS 3, p. 42767/Section 164.103 Definitions

 U.S. DHHS 4. p. 42743/Supplementary Information: 1. Background

 U.S. DHHS 5, p. 42760/Summary of Costs and Benefits, 1.a. Affected Entities

 U.S. DHHS 6, p. 42743/Supplementary Information: IV 1. Definitions-Section 164.402

 U.S. DHHS 7, p. 42757/Section V. Impact Statement and Other Required Analyses A Introduction

REFERENCES (continued)

U.S. Department of Health and Human Services Office for Civil Rights. *Standards for Privacy of Individually Identifiable Health Information Security Standards for the Protection of Electronic Protected Health Information General Administrative Requirements, Including Civil Money Penalties: Procedures for Investigations, Imposition of Penalties, and Hearings Regulation Text* 45 CFR Parts 160 and 164 (Unofficial version, as amended through February 16, 2006). Retrieved from http://www.hhs.gov/ocr/privacy/hipaa/administrative/privacyrule/adminsimpregtext.pdf
    U.S. HHS OCR, 1, Section 164.306(a) (1)
    U.S. HHS OCR, 2, Section 164.308(6) (i)

U.S. Office of Civil Rights. (n.d.). *For consumers.* Retrieved from http://www.hhs.gov/ocr/privacy/hipaa/understanding/consumers/index.html

Health Information Privacy and Security
Chapter Competencies

Question	RHIA Domain	RHIT Domain
1–98	5	6

XII. Health Law

Barbara W. Mosley, PhD, RHIA

Lon'Tejuana S. Cooper, MSHA, RHIA, CPM

CASE STUDY #1

Dr. Roberts, an orthopedic surgeon, and Nurse Parrish, head nurse on the orthopedic surgery unit, have had an acrimonious working relationship for years. While making rounds on the unit, Dr. Roberts discovered that the physical therapy evaluation he had ordered for one of his patients had not been performed and became outraged. Even though he did not have proof, Dr. Roberts placed the blame for the missed evaluation with Nurse Parrish. Dr. Roberts wrote in the patient's medical record that Nurse Parrish failed to properly order the physical therapy evaluation because she was incompetent and could not be trusted to carry out even the simplest order. After having read Dr. Roberts's note, Nurse Parrish countered by making a disparaging remark about Dr. Roberts to the medical personnel at the nurses' station. Nurse Parrish stated that Dr. Roberts was the one who was incompetent and was responsible for the needless suffering of countless patients over the years.

1. Referring to Case Study #1, the written statement by Dr. Roberts about Nurse Parrish's professional competence in the patient's medical record can constitute
    A. libel.   C. perjury.
    B. slander.   D. defamation.

REFERENCE: LaTour and Eichenwald-Maki, p 276
                McWay (2008), p 94
                Brodnik, pp 76–77
                McWay (2010), pp 80, 411
                Pozgar, pp 47–48, 580
                Roach, p 401

2. Referring to Case Study #1, the oral statement by Nurse Parrish about Dr. Roberts's professional practices at the nurses' station can constitute
    A. libel.   C. perjury.
    B. slander.   D. defamation.

REFERENCE: LaTour and Eichenwald-Maki, p 276
                McWay (2008), p 54
                Brodnik, pp 76–77
                McWay (2010), pp 80, 415
                Pozgar, p 600
                Roach, p 401

3. Referring to Case Study #1, what should Dr. Roberts be reminded of regarding his notation in the patient's chart about Nurse Parrish?
    A. It is against the law to mention names of persons who are not actively attending to his patient.
    B. His action violates the 1974 Privacy Act.
    C. The medical record must not be used as a battleground against another professional.
    D. He should erase his note about Nurse Parrish because it is malicious.

REFERENCE: Pozgar, pp 283, 297
                Brodnik, pp 6–8
                Roach, pp 291–292

4. Which type of law is constituted by rules and principles determined by legislative bodies?
    A. statutory law
    C. common law
    B. administrative law
    D. case law

REFERENCE: Green and Bowie, pp 265–267
                LaTour and Eichenwald-Maki, pp 273, 995
                McWay (2008), pp 46, 468
                Brodnik, pp 14–15
                McWay (2010), pp 8–10
                Pozgar, pp 16, 19, 582
                Roach, pp 6–7

5. Which of the following elements of negligence must be present in order to recover damages?
    A. duty of care; breach of duty of care; value attached to injury is greater than a certain value (ordinarily $1,000); provisions of the HIPAA Privacy Rule have been met
    B. duty of care; breach of the duty of care; suffered an injury; value attached to injury is greater than a certain value (ordinarily $1,000)
    C. duty of care; breach of duty of care; suffered an injury; defendant's conduct caused the plaintiff harm
    D. breach of duty of care; suffered an injury; value attached to injury is greater than a certain value (ordinarily $1,000); provision of HIPAA Privacy Rule have been met

REFERENCE: LaTour and Eichenwald-Maki, p 276
                Green and Bowie, p 267
                Brodnik, pp 70–71, 75–76, 79
                McWay (2008), p 55

6. When the physician failed to give the patient the lips of the famous actress as promised, the physician engaged in which of the following?
    A. slander
    C. libel
    B. a breach of contract
    D. invasion of privacy

REFERENCE: McWay (2008), p 54
                LaTour and Eichenwald-Maki, pp 278–279
                Pozgar, p 87
                McWay (2010), p 83

7. Laws that limit the period during which legal action may be brought against another party are known as
    A. case law.
    C. statutes of limitations.
    B. summons.
    D. common law.

REFERENCE: Green and Bowie, pp 94, 267
                McWay (2008), pp 112, 468
                McWay (2010), pp 84–85, 416
                Brodnik, pp 81–83
                Pozgar, pp 90, 130, 582
                Roach, pp 43–44
                LaTour and Eichenwald-Maki, pp 278, 995

8. The protection of a patient's health information is addressed in each of the following EXCEPT
   A. Health Insurance Portability and Accountability Act.
   B. Privacy Act.
   C. Drug Abuse and Treatment Act.
   D. U.S. Patriot Act.

REFERENCE: Green and Bowie, pp 284–285
               LaTour and Eichenwald-Maki, pp 280–282
               McWay (2010), pp 47, 285, 292
               Brodnik, pp 238–242, 247–248, 256, 263–264
               Pozgar, pp 26–27, 279–280
               Roach, pp 104–106

9. In a court of law, Attorney A, the attorney for Sun City Hospital, introduces the medical record from the hospital as evidence. However, Attorney B, the attorney for the defendant, objects on the grounds that the medical record is subject to the hearsay rule, which prohibits its admission as evidence. Attorney B's objection is overridden. Why?
   A. The medical record does not belong to the hospital; therefore, the hospital has no right to release the medical record as evidence.
   B. It would violate physician–patient privilege, even though the patient signed a proper release of information form.
   C. The doctrine of *res ipsa loquitur* prevails; therefore, reference to the medical record is moot.
   D. The medical record may be admitted as business records or as an explicit exception to hearsay rule.

REFERENCE: Green and Bowie, pp 270–271
               Brodnik, pp 57–58, 125, 127
               McWay (2010), pp 50–51, 409
               Pozgar, pp 120–122
               Roach, pp 383–384
               Servais, pp 4–5

10. Medical record information may be exempt from the Freedom of Information Act requirements if the request for information meets the test of being an unwarranted invasion of personal privacy. Which of the following is NOT one of the conditions of the test?
    A. The information must be contained in a personal, medical, or similar file.
    B. The information is generated from federally funded research conducted by a private health care organization.
    C. Disclosure of the information constitutes an invasion of personal privacy.
    D. The severity of the invasion must outweigh the public's interest in disclosure.

REFERENCE: LaTour and Eichenwald-Maki, p 281
               McWay (2010), p 177
               Brodnik, pp 154, 254
               Green and Bowie, p 284
               Roach, pp 123–127

11. The doctrine that the decisions of the court should stand as precedents for future guidance is
    A. res ipsa loquitur.
    B. respondeat superior.
    C. stare decisis.
    D. statute of limitations.

REFERENCE: Green and Bowie, p 257
                Brodnik, p 17
                McWay (2010), pp 12–13, 15, 18, 415
                Roach, pp 16–18
                Pozgar, pp18, 1582

12. The body of law founded on custom, natural justice and reason, and sanctioned by usage and judicial decision is known as
    A. common law.
    B. lien law.
    C. constitutional law.
    D. statutory law.

REFERENCE: Green and Bowie, pp 265–267
                LaTour and Eichenwald-Maki, pp 272, 959
                Brodnik, pp 17, 20
                McWay (2008), pp 46, 449
                McWay (2010), pp 12, 405
                Pozgar, pp 16–19, 578
                Roach, pp 10, 545

CASE STUDY #2

You are the Director of the Health Information Management Department for Bayshore Hospital. A former patient of the hospital, Barbara Masters, is suing the hospital for negligent care of an infected decubitus ulcer. You are asked by Barbara's attorney to provide sworn verbal testimony and/or written answers to questions.

13. Referring to Case Study #2, Barbara Masters is the _____ in this case.
    A. appellant
    B. appellee
    C. defendant
    D. plaintiff

REFERENCE: Green and Bowie, pp 265, 267
                LaTour and Eichenwald-Maki, p 274
                McWay (2008), pp 52, 463
                McWay (2010), pp 31, 413
                Brodnik, p 35
                Pozgar, pp 108, 531, 581

14. Referring to Case Study #2, Bayshore Hospital is the _____ in this case.
    A. appellant
    B. appellee
    C. defendant
    D. plaintiff

REFERENCE: Green and Bowie, pp 265, 337
                LaTour and Eichenwald-Maki, p 274
                McWay (2008), p 52
                McWay (2010), pp 31, 406
                Brodnik, p 35
                Pozgar, pp 108, 578

15. Referring to Case Study #2, the sworn verbal testimony you are asked to provide is called a(n)
  A. interrogatory.
  B. deposition.
  C. physical and mental examination.
  D. court order.

REFERENCE: Green and Bowie, pp 265, 337
              Brodnik, p 28
              McWay (2010), pp 34, 39, 57, 406
              Pozgar, p 578

16. Referring to Case Study #2, the written answers to questions you have been asked to provide are known as a(n)
  A. interrogatory.
  B. deposition.
  C. physical and mental examination.
  D. court order.

REFERENCE: Green and Bowie, pp 265, 342
              LaTour and Eichenwald-Maki, p 274
              McWay (2010), pp 34, 40, 57, 410
              Pozgar, p 580
              Brodnik, pp 29, 41
              Roach, p 375

17. Referring to Case Study #2, what phase of the lawsuit are you involved in?
  A. pretrial conference   C. discovery
  B. trial   D. appeal

REFERENCE: Pozgar, pp 110–111, 579
              Green and Bowie, pp 265, 338
              McWay (2008), pp 52–53
              McWay (2010), pp 34, 57, 263, 407
              Brodnik, p 35
              Roach, pp 374–375
              LaTour and Eichenwald-Maki, p 274

18. Which of the following claims of negligence fits into the category of *res ipsa loquitur*?
  A. incorrect administration of anesthesia
  B. failure to refer patient to a specialist
  C. leaving a foreign body inside a patient
  D. improper use of x-rays

REFERENCE: Green and Bowie, pp 267, 350
              McWay (2010), pp 75–76, 414
              Brodnik, pp 71–72
              Pozgar, pp 56, 115–117, 582
              LaTour and Eichenwald-Maki, p 278

19. The failure to obtain the written consent of the patient before performing a surgical procedure may constitute
    A. battery.   C. libel.
    B. contempt.   D. malpractice.

REFERENCE: Green and Bowie, p 333
               LaTour and Eichenwald-Maki, p 276
               McWay (2008), pp 54, 447
               McWay (2010), pp 80, 404
               Brodnik, pp 115–116
               Pozgar, pp 43–44, 577

20. The fee paid for reimbursement for expenses incurred from providing health information whether for subpoena or reproduction by health care providers is determined by the
    A. American Health Information Management Association.
    B. hospitals and lawyers.
    C. statute or court rules.
    D. plaintiff and defendant lawyers.

REFERENCE: Brodnik, pp 262–263
               McWay (2010), p 209

21. Who determines the retention period for health records?
    A. state and federal governments
    B. medical staff
    C. city and state governments
    D. commercial storage vendors

REFERENCE: Servais, pp 350–354
               Green and Bowie, p 93
               LaTour and Eichenwald-Maki, pp 221–223, 225, 282
               McWay (2008), pp 49, 112–113
               McWay (2010), pp 159–161, 163, 414
               Brodnik, pp 52, 140–146
               Pozgar, p 282
               Roach, pp 40–41

22. The extent to which the HIPAA privacy rule may regulate an individual's rights of access is not meant to preempt other existing federal laws and regulations. This means that if an individual's rights of access
    A. are less under another existing federal law, HIPAA must follow the directions of that law.
    B. are refused by a federal facility, HIPAA must also refuse the individual of the access.
    C. are greater under another applicable federal law, the individual should be afforded the greater access.
    D. are greater under another existing federal law, HIPAA can obstruct freedoms of the other federal law when using electronic health records.

REFERENCE: Servais, p 119
               Brodnik, pp 186, 271
               LaTour and Eichenwald-Maki, p 283

CASE STUDY #3

A 73-year-old male was admitted to the Sunset Nursing Facility with senility, cataracts, and S/P cerebrovascular accident with right-side hemiplegia. On his second day at the facility, the resident was discovered to have extensive thermal burns on his buttocks and legs by one of the facility's attendants.

23. Referring to Case Study #3, the resident's family brought legal action against the nursing facility for
    A. medical abandonment.
    B. vicarious liability.
    C. assault and battery.
    D. negligence.

REFERENCE: Green and Bowie, pp 267, 345
              LaTour and Eichenwald-Maki, pp 275–276, 982
              McWay (2008), pp 55, 461
              McWay (2010), pp 71–72, 412
              Brodnik, pp 69–71
              Pozgar, pp 32–40, 150–152, 581

24. Referring to Case Study #3, which of the following can the attorney of the resident's family also use as a basis for the lawsuit and why?
    A. The doctrine of *res ipsa loquitur* because it allows the plaintiff to shift the burden of proof to the defendant because direct evidence is available.
    B. The doctrine of charitable immunity because the nursing facility is a private institution and is shielded from liability for any torts committed on its property.
    C. The Good Samaritan Statutes because they protect the Director of Nursing, an employee of the nursing facility, who was not present when the injury occurred.
    D. The failure to warn theory because the doctor did not inform the resident's family that the resident was in danger at the nursing facility.

REFERENCE: Green and Bowie, pp 267, 350
              McWay (2008), pp 55, 466
              McWay (2010), pp 75–76, 414
              Brodnik, pp 71–72
              Pozgar, pp 56, 115–117, 582

25. In a negligence or malpractice case, all of the following elements must be present in order to shift the burden of proof onto the defendant EXCEPT the
    A. event would not normally have occurred in the absence of negligence.
    B. health care facility does not have a risk management program.
    C. defendant had exclusive control over the instrumentality that caused the injury.
    D. plaintiff did not contribute to the injury.

REFERENCE: McWay (2010), pp 71–75
              McWay (2008), p 55
              Brodnik, pp 70–71
              Pozgar, pp 33–41
              LaTour and Eichenwald-Maki, p 276

26. When a health care facility fails to investigate the qualifications of a physician hired to work as an independent contractor in the emergency room and is accused of negligence, the health care facility can be held liable under
    A. respondeat superior.
    B. corporate negligence.
    C. contributory negligence.
    D. general negligence.

REFERENCE: Brodnik, p 74
                Pozgar, pp 150–152
                McWay (2008), p 55
                McWay (2010), pp 77–78
                LaTour and Eichenwald-Maki, p 297

27. What source or document is considered the "supreme law of the land"?
    A. Bill of Rights
    B. Supreme Court decisions
    C. presidential power
    D. Constitution of the United States

REFERENCE: LaTour and Eichenwald-Maki, p 272
                McWay (2008), p 46
                Brodnik, pp 14–15
                Pozgar, p 19

28. Hospitals that destroy their own medical records must have a policy that
    A. ensures records are destroyed and confidentiality is protected.
    B. notifies the physicians when the records of their patients are destroyed.
    C. states that all records are destroyed annually.
    D. ensures that the type of equipment to be used for destruction of records is properly maintained.

REFERENCE: Green and Bowie, pp 96–97, 349
                LaTour and Eichenwald-Maki, p 222
                McWay (2008), pp 112–113, 115
                McWay (2010), pp 164–166
                Brodnik, p 147
                Roach, pp 49–50

29. A written authorization from the patient releasing copies of his or her medical records is required by all of the following EXCEPT
    A. the patient's attorney.
    B. a physician requesting copies from another physician.
    C. an insurance company.
    D. the hospital attorney for the facility where the patient is treated.

REFERENCE: Green and Bowie, p 291
                LaTour and Eichenwald-Maki, pp 286–289
                McWay (2008), p 6163
                McWay (2010), pp 207–208
                Brodnik, pp 163–164

30. Traditionally, the medical record is accepted as being the property of the
    A. patient's guardian. C. institution.
    B. court. D. patient.

REFERENCE: Green and Bowie, pp 72–73
                LaTour and Eichenwald-Maki, pp 282–283
                McWay (2008), p 61
                McWay (2010), pp 194–196
                Brodnik, pp 239–241
                Servais, p 54
                Pozgar, p 279

31. The ownership of the information contained in the physical medical/health record is considered to belong to the
    A. patient. C. physician.
    B. hospital. D. insurance company.

REFERENCE: Green and Bowie, pp 72–73
                LaTour and Eichenwald-Maki, pp 282–283
                McWay (2008), p 61
                McWay (2010), pp 194–196
                Brodnik, pp 239–241
                Servais, p 54
                Pozgar, p 279

32. When developing a record retention policy, the HIM professionals should consider all of the following EXCEPT
    A. current storage space.
    B. uses of and need for information.
    C. all applicable statutes and regulations.
    D. the thickness of the records.

REFERENCE: Green and Bowie, p 94
                LaTour and Eichenwald-Maki, pp 221–222, 282
                McWay (2008), pp 112–113, 466
                McWay (2010), pp 160–163
                Brodnik, pp 52, 146–147, 149
                Servais, pp 350–353
                Pozgar, pp 282–283

33. If the patient record is involved in litigation and the physician requests to make a change to that record, what should the HIM professional do?
    A. Refer request to legal counsel.
    B. Allow the change to occur.
    C. Notify the patient.
    D. Say the record is unavailable.

REFERENCE: Green and Bowie, pp 84–85
                Brodnik, pp 138–140
                Servais, pp 30–32
                McWay (2010), pp 157–158
                Pozgar, pp 287–288

34. One of the greatest threats to the confidentiality of health data is
    A. when medical information is reviewed as a part of quality assurance activities.
    B. disclosure of information for purposes not authorized in writing by the patient.
    C. lack of written authorization by the patient.
    D. when medical information is used for research or education.

REFERENCE: Green and Bowie, p 271
                LaTour and Eichenwald-Maki, pp 317–318
                Servais, pp 52–55
                McWay (2008), pp 61–62
                McWay (2010), pp 202–208

35. All of the following are areas in which electronically stored information, for example, the electronic health record, differs from paper-based information EXCEPT
    A. volume.
    B. metadata.
    C. variety of sources.
    D. confidentiality.

REFERENCE: McWay (2010), pp 34–35
                Brodnik, p 46
                McWay (2008), p 53

36. Spoliation is the term that refers to the wrongful destruction of evidence or the failure to preserve property, which addresses which of the following methods of discovery?
    A. interrogatories
    B. deposition
    C. e-discovery
    D. request for admissions

REFERENCE: McWay (2010), pp 34–35
                Brodnik, pp 50–51

37. What type of testimony is inappropriate for a health information manager serving as custodian of the record when he or she is called to be a witness in court?
    A. whether the record is in the practitioner's possession
    B. title and position held in the health care facility
    C. whether the medical record was made in the usual course of business
    D. interpretation of documentation in the record

REFERENCE: Brodnik, pp 29–31
                Servais, pp 4–5, 208

38. Internal disclosures of patient information for patient care purposes should not be granted
    A. to the facility's legal counsel.
    B. to the attending physician.
    C. on a need to know basis.
    D. to a family member who is a registered nurse at the facility.

REFERENCE: Green and Bowie, pp 271, 275
                McWay (2008), pp 59–60
                Servais, pp 7, 53–55

Case Study #4

William is a 16-year-old male who lives at home with his parents and works part-time as a dishwasher at one of the local restaurants. While emptying the dishwasher, William is severely scalded and rendered unconscious. He is taken to the emergency room of the local acute care hospital for emergency treatment.

39. Referring to Case Study #4, given the emergency of the situation, who should the health care provider seek consent from in order to provide treatment to William?
    A. the employer
    B. the parents
    C. the patient
    D. no consent is needed for emergency care

REFERENCE: Pozgar, pp 312, 314
                Roach, pp 89–91
                LaTour and Eichenwald-Maki, pp 287–288
                McWay (2010), pp 187–188
                Brodnik, pp 99–100

40. Referring to Case Study #4, in order to release information to his employer, the hospital must receive a
    A. consent signed by the patient.
    B. court order.
    C. consent signed by the doctor.
    D. consent signed by the patient's parent.

REFERENCE: LaTour and Eichenwald-Maki, pp 287–288
                McWay (2010), p 186
                Brodnik, pp 244–245, 255
                Pozgar, p 314

41. A valid authorization for the disclosure of health information should not be
    A. dated prior to discharge of the patient.
    B. in writing.
    C. addressed to the health care provider.
    D. signed by the patient.

REFERENCE: LaTour and Eichenwald-Maki, pp 255–256
                Brodnik, pp 259–260

42. Internal disclosures of patient information for patient care purposes should be granted
    A. to legal counsel.
    B. on a need to know basis.
    C. to any physician on staff.
    D. to a family member who is an employee.

REFERENCE: Green and Bowie, p 275
                LaTour and Eichenwald-Maki, p 288
                McWay (2010), pp 99, 102, 203–204
                McWay (2008), p 62
                Brodnik, pp 176–177

43. According to AHIMA's Position on Transmission of Health Information, the health information manager should engage in all of the following to ensure that information is properly sent via facsimile transmission EXCEPT
    A. to always follow up by sending the original record by mail.
    B. to preprogram into the machine the number of destination sites.
    C. encrypt the data if public channels are used for electronic transmittal.
    D. ask the sender to contact the recipient prior to and after transmission.

REFERENCE: Brodnik, p 261
               Roach, pp 492–495
               Servais, pp 263–264

44. All of the following need a proper authorization to access a patient's health information EXCEPT
    A. local and state law enforcement officers.
    B. IRS agents.
    C. medical examiners or coroners.
    D. FBI agents.

REFERENCE: Green and Bowie, p 289
               LaTour and Eichenwald-Maki, p 290

45. One best practice to follow in order to establish safeguards for the security and confidentiality of a patient's information when a person makes a request for his or her records in person is to
    A. ask the requester for identification and the request in writing.
    B. refuse the request.
    C. refer the requester to the facility's attorney.
    D. charge an exorbitant fee.

REFERENCE: Roach, pp 239–241
               Brodnik, pp 258–260

46. Which of the following acts was passed to stimulate the development of standards to facilitate electronic maintenance and transmission of health information?
    A. Health Insurance for the Aged
    B. Health Insurance Portability and Accountability Act
    C. Conditions of Participation
    D. Hospital Survey and Construction Act

REFERENCE: Green and Bowie, pp 10, 320
               LaTour and Eichenwald-Maki, p 281
               McWay (2008), p 360
               McWay (2010), p 161
               Brodnik, pp 155–156
               Pozgar, pp 27, 282

47. The premise that charitable institutions could be held blameless for their negligent acts is known as
    A. doctrine of respondeat superior.
    B. doctrine of res ipsa loquitur.
    C. doctrine of charitable immunity.
    D. negligence factor.

REFERENCE: Brodnik, pp 291–292
                      Pozgar, pp 151, 578
                      McWay (2010), pp 85, 405
                      Roach, pp 10–11

48. Under traditional rules of evidence, a medical/health record is considered _____ and is _____ into evidence.
    A. hearsay; admissible   C. reliable; admissible
    B. hearsay; inadmissible   D. reliable; inadmissible

REFERENCE: Green and Bowie, pp 270–271
                      LaTour and Eichenwald-Maki, p 292
                      McWay (2010), pp 50-51, 409
                      Brodnik, pp 56–58
                      Roach, pp 383–385

49. The hospital has a policy that states, "Original medical records may be removed from the Medical Record Department jurisdiction only by court order." Which situation would be a violation of the policy?
    A. A physician wishes to have the record sent to the physician lounge in the OR suite for final signatures.
    B. The Risk Manager requests the record for review by physicians at a quality assurance meeting.
    C. A lawyer has subpoenaed the record for deposition.
    D. The physician has been sued and wants to study the original record at home prior to his deposition.

REFERENCE: LaTour and Eichenwald-Maki, p 296
                      Green and Bowie, pp 270–271, 278

50. Who is legally responsible for obtaining the patient's informed consent for surgery?
    A. the admissions clerk
    B. the surgeon performing the surgery
    C. the nurse
    D. medical records personnel

REFERENCE: Green and Bowie, pp 129, 132
                      Brodnik, pp 116
                      McWay (2008), pp 64–65
                      McWay (2010), pp 188–189
                      Pozgar, pp 199–200
                      Roach, p 74

51. With regard to confidentiality, when HIM functions are outsourced (i.e., record copying, microfilming, or transcription), the HIM professional should confirm that the outside contractor's
    A. costs are not prohibitive, thus compromising confidentiality.
    B. hours of operation permit easy access by all health care providers.
    C. is contractually bound to handle confidential information appropriately by means of a signed business associate agreement.
    D. is located in an easy to find place.

REFERENCE: McWay (2010), pp 215–216
               LaTour and Eichenwald-Maki, p 254
               Brodnik, pp 158–159

52. A 21-year-old employee of National Services was treated in an acute care hospital for an illness unrelated to work. A representative from the personnel department of National Services calls to request information regarding the employee's diagnosis. What would be the appropriate course of action?
    A. Request that the personnel office send an authorization for release of information that is signed and dated by the patient.
    B. Require parental consent.
    C. Release the information because the employer is paying the patient's bill.
    D. Call the patient to obtain verbal permission.

REFERENCE: Green and Bowie, pp 291–292
               LaTour and Eichenwald-Maki, pp 286–287
               Brodnik, pp 244–245, 255

53. *Darling v. Charleston Community Memorial Hospital* is considered one of the benchmark cases in health care because it was with this case that the doctrine of _____ was eliminated for nonprofit hospitals.
    A. charitable immunity
    B. corporate negligence
    C. professional negligence
    D. contributory negligence

REFERENCE: Green and Bowie, p 267
               Brodnik, pp 291–292
               McWay (2010), p 77
               Pozgar, pp 150–152

54. All of the following are elements of a contract EXCEPT
    A. offer/communication.   C. price/consideration.
    B. duty.   D. acceptance.

REFERENCE: Pozgar, pp 87–88
               Brodnik, p 83

55. A valid authorization for release of information contains
    A. the name, agency, or institution to which the information is to be provided.
    B. the name of the hospital or provider who is releasing the medical information.
    C. the date and signature of the patient or the patient's authorized representative.
    D. all of the above.

REFERENCE: LaTour and Eichenwald-Maki, pp 286–287
               McWay (2010), pp 202–203
               Brodnik, pp 259–262

56. In which of the following circumstances would release of information without the patient's authorization be permissible?
    A. release to an attorney
    B. release to third-party payers
    C. release to state workers' compensation agencies
    D. release to insurance companies

REFERENCE: Green and Bowie, p 291
               LaTour and Eichenwald-Maki, pp 287–288
               Brodnik, pp 170–175, 281–282

57. Who decides whether all or portions of the medical record will be received in evidence in a court of law?
    A. presiding judge/court   C. clerk of the court
    B. subpoenaing attorney   D. defendant

REFERENCE: LaTour and Eichenwald-Maki, p 292
               Brodnik, p 44
               Servais, p 4

58. Which of the following health care systems have to comply with the requirements of the Freedom of Information Act?
    A. private hospitals   C. veterans' hospitals
    B. physicians' offices   D. single-day surgery clinics

REFERENCE: LaTour and Eichenwald-Maki, p 281
               Brodnik, p 157
               Roach, p 123

59. Which of the following measures should a health care facility incorporate into its institution-wide security plan to protect the confidentiality of the patient record?
    A. verification of employee identification
    B. locked access to data processing and record areas
    C. use of unique computer passwords, key cares, or biometric identification
    D. all of the above

REFERENCE: Green and Bowie, pp 282–283
               LaTour and Eichenwald-Maki, p 281
               Brodnik, pp 199–200
               Roach, pp 462–470
               Servais, pp 42–46

60. A signed consent for release of information dated December 1, 2010, is received with a request for the chart from the patient's admission of 12/5/2010. Indicate the appropriate response from the options below.
    A. Request another authorization that is dated closer but prior to the admission date.
    B. Request another authorization dated after the discharge date.
    C. Release the requested information.
    D. Call the patient for a verbal authorization.

REFERENCE: Brodnik, pp 168–171

61. Willful disregard of a subpoena is considered
    A. breach of contract.
    B. abuse of process.
    C. contributory negligence.
    D. contempt of court.

REFERENCE: McWay (2008), p 65
               Brodnik, p 30
               Pozgar, p 115
               Roach, p 322

62. HIM personnel charged with the responsibility of bringing a medical record to court would ordinarily do so in answer to a
    A. personal subpoena.
    B. deposition.
    C. subpoena duces tecum.
    D. judgment.

REFERENCE: Green and Bowie, p 289
               McWay (2008), p 65
               McWay (2010), pp 40–41, 54, 416
               Brodnik, p 31
               Pozgar, p 115
               Roach, p 317
               Servais, pp 36, 60, 63

63. HIPAA requires that certain covered entities provide every patient a Notice of Privacy Practices that sets forth all of the following EXCEPT
    A. covered entities provide every patient with its annual business report.
    B. how covered entities may use and disclose PHI.
    C. patient's rights regarding the covered entities' uses and disclosures.
    D. covered entities' obligations for protecting the patient's PHI.

REFERENCE: LaTour and Eichenwald-Maki, pp 283–284
               Green and Bowie, p, 273
               McWay (2008), pp 60, 107, 382, 389
               McWay (2010), pp 196–205
               Brodnik, pp 165–166
               Roach, pp 218–222

64. A record that has been requested by subpoena duces tecum is currently located at an off-site microfilm company. By contacting the microfilm provider, you learn that the microfilm is ready and the original copy of the record still exists. What legal requirement would compel you to produce the original record for the court?
    A. best evidence rule   C.   motion to quash
    B. hearsay rule   D.   subpoena instanter

REFERENCE: Roach, pp 487–488
               Brodnik, pp 56–57

65. Under which category of law would Marleana Harrison bring a cause of action against Dr. Billy Ray for disclosing information regarding her previous physical examination to his wife, Jana Ray, who is Ms. Harrison's hairstylist?
    A. administrative law
    B. criminal law
    C. private law
    D. procedural law

REFERENCE: McWay (2010), pp 45–46
Brodnik, p 14
Roach, p 2
Pozgar, pp 15–16
McWay (2008), pp 3–4

66. As a general rule, a person making a report in good faith and under statutory command (e.g., on child abuse, communicable diseases, births, deaths, etc.) is
    A. not protected from liability claims.
    B. subject to penalties imposed by federal law.
    C. subject to penalties imposed by state law.
    D. protected.

REFERENCE: Green and Bowie, p 288
Brodnik, pp 67–68
Pozgar, pp 323–324
Roach, pp 247–248

67. According to AHIMA and AHA guidelines, which of the following would be an acceptable authorization for release of information from the medical record of an adult, mentally competent patient hospitalized from 4/16/2011 to 5/10/2011? An authorization dated
    A. 7/10/2011 and presented 7/15/2011
    B. 5/09/2011 and presented 1/15/2012
    C. 3/10/2011 and presented 5/15/2011
    D. 2/15/2011 and presented 1/10/2012

REFERENCE: Green and Bowie, pp 122, 124–125
McWay (2008), p 62
McWay (2010), pp 96–98
Brodnik, pp 168–170

68. Which would be the better "best practice" for handling fax transmission of a physician's orders?
    A. Treat faxed orders like verbal orders and require authentication of the orders by appropriate medical staff within the required period.
    B. Faxed orders should be placed on the patient's chart immediately upon receipt after the head nurse signs the orders.
    C. Wait 24 hours before placing faxed orders on the patient's chart to ensure that the orders are legitimate.
    D. Faxed orders should never be accepted.

REFERENCE: Green and Bowie, p 81
Roach, p 494
Brodnik, pp 131, 386

69. The *Darling v. Charleston Community Memorial Hospital* case established the following doctrine for hospitals to observe and changed the way hospitals dealt with liability.
    A.   doctrine of respondeat superior
    B.   doctrine of continuing wrong
    C.   doctrine of res ipsa loquitur
    D.   doctrine of corporate negligence

REFERENCE: Green and Bowie, p 257
               Pozgar, p 150
               McWay (2010), pp 50–51
               Brodnik, pp 291–292

70. HIM professionals have a duty to maintain health information that complies with
    A.   state statutes.
    B.   federal statutes.
    C.   accreditation standards.
    D.   all of the above.

REFERENCE: Green and Bowie, p 273
               LaTour and Eichenwald-Maki, p 282
               McWay (2008), pp 60, 107
               McWay (2010), pp 147, 201
               Roach, pp 40–41
               Servais, pp 7–9
               Brodnik, p 128

71. In general, which of the following statements is correct?
    A.   When federal and state laws conflict, valid federal laws supersede state laws.
    B.   When federal and state laws conflict, valid state laws supersede federal laws.
    C.   When federal and state laws conflict, valid local laws supersede federal and state laws.
    D.   When federal and state laws conflict, valid corporate policies supersede federal and state laws.

REFERENCE: McWay (2008), p 58
               McWay (2010), p 201
               Brodnik, p 128

72. Which of the following statements is correct regarding HIPAA preemption analysis?
    A.   If the state law that recognizes a patient's right to health care information privacy is more stringent than the HIPAA federal rule, then the state law prevails.
    B.   State law regarding a patient's right to health care information privacy can never prevail over the HIPAA federal rule.
    C.   If a state law that recognizes a patient's right to health care information privacy is more stringent than the HIPAA federal rule, then the courts must decide which shall prevail.
    D.   Even if the state law that recognizes a patient's right to health care information privacy is more stringent than the HIPAA federal rule, the HIPAA federal rule will still prevail.

REFERENCE: Green and Bowie, p 283
               LaTour and Eichenwald-Maki, p 283
               McWay (2008), p 58
               McWay (2010), p 201
               Roach, pp 100–101
               Brodnik, pp 186, 271

73. The minimum record retention period for patients who are minors is
    A. age of majority.
    B. age of majority plus the statute of limitations.
    C. 5 years past treatment.
    D. 2 years past treatment.

REFERENCE: Green and Bowie, p 94
               LaTour and Eichenwald-Maki, p 225
               McWay (2008) pp 112–113
               Brodnik, pp 141–146
               Roach, pp 43–44
               Servais, p 350

74. In which type of facility does the Privacy Act of 1974 permit patients to request amendments to their medical record?
    A. private proprietary health care facility
    B. mental health and chemical dependency facility
    C. university-based teaching facility
    D. Department of Defense health care facility

REFERENCE: Green and Bowie, p 285
               Brodnik, p 157
               LaTour and Eichenwald-Maki, p 284
               Pozgar, pp 279–280

75. What advice should be given to a physician who has just informed you that she just discovered that a significant portion of a discharge summary she dictated last month was left out?
    A. Squeeze in the information omitted by writing in available spaces such as the top, bottom, and side margins.
    B. Dictate the portion omitted with the heading "Discharge Summary—Addendum" and make a reference to the addendum with a note that is dated and signed on the initial Discharge Summary (e.g., "9/1/11—See Addendum to Discharge Summary"—Signature).
    C. Redictate the discharge summary and replace the old one with the new one.
    D. Inform the physician that nothing can be done about the situation.

REFERENCE: Green and Bowie, pp 84–85
               Brodnik, pp 138–140
               Roach, p 70
               Servais, pp 30–32

76. While performing routine quantitative analysis of a record, a medical record employee finds an incident report in the record. The employee brings this to the attention of her supervisor. Which best practice should the supervisor follow to deal with this situation?
    A. Remove the incident report and send it to the patient.
    B. Tell the employee to leave the report in the record.
    C. Remove the incident report and have nursing personnel transfer all documentation from the report to the medical record.
    D. Refer this record to the Risk Manager for further review and removal of the incident report.

REFERENCE: Green and Bowie, p 88
                       LaTour and Eichenwald-Maki, pp 301–302
                       Brodnik, pp 295–297
                       McWay (2008), p 110
                       Pozgar, pp 329–330
                       Roach, p 393

77. Which of the following is considered confidential information if the patient is seeking treatment in a substance abuse facility?
    A. patient's name   C. patient's diagnosis
    B. patient's address   D. all of the above

REFERENCE: Green and Bowie, pp 284–285
                       Brodnik, pp 247–250

78. In electronic health records, authentication may be achieved by
    A. handwritten signature.   C. verbal statement.
    B. digital signature.   D. all the above.

REFERENCE: Green and Bowie, pp 26, 278
                       LaTour and Eichenwald-Maki, pp 79, 256
                       Brodnik, pp 133–135
                       McWay (2008), p 321
                       McWay (2010), p 286
                       Servais, pp 34–35, 269

79. It is common practice to forgo patient authorization for the release of information when the
    A. patient is an employee.
    B. patient is a physician.
    C. patient has a direct transfer from the hospital to a long-term care facility.
    D. patient is incompetent.

REFERENCE: LaTour and Eichenwald-Maki, pp 284, 287–288

80. Many states have recognized a minor's right to seek treatment without parental consent in all of the following situations EXCEPT a(n)
    A. minor seeking treatment for breast reduction.
    B. minor seeking treatment for a sexually transmitted disease.
    C. minor seeking treatment for alcohol and substance abuse.
    D. emancipated minor seeking treatment for breast enlargement.

REFERENCE: Pozgar, pp 313–314
                       Roach, pp 89–90
                       Brodnik, pp 113–115

81. When a health information professional (record custodian) brings the medical record to court in response to a subpoena duces tecum, it is his or her responsibility to
    A. confirm whether or not the record is complete, accurate, and made in the ordinary course of business.
    B. present the case favorably for the patient involved.
    C. leave the original record in the possession of the plaintiff's attorney.
    D. explain details of the medical treatment given to the patient.

REFERENCE: McWay (2010), p 52
               Servais, pp 36, 60, 63
               Brodnik, pp 30–31, 54–55

82. When substituting a photocopy of the original record in response to legal process, which of the following can be helpful in convincing the court to accept the photocopy as a true and exact copy of the original?
    A. certificate of authentication
    B. consent from the patient
    C. consent from the hospital administrator
    D. correspondence from the attending physician

REFERENCE: Servais, pp 6–7, 58–56
               Brodnik, pp 33–34, 54–55

83. Which of the following should be required to sign a confidentiality statement before having access to patients' medical information?
    A. nursing students   C.   HIM students
    B. medical students   D.   all of the above

REFERENCE: Green and Bowie, pp 43–48
               Pozgar, pp 290–292
               Brodnik, pp 158, 215, 442

84. All of the following have laws and regulations addressing medical records EXCEPT
    A. accrediting agencies.   C.   state laws.
    B. corporate law.   D.   federal laws.

REFERENCE: Green and Bowie, p 265
               Servais, pp 7–8
               Brodnik, pp 156–158

85. The proper method for correcting a documentation error in a medical record is for the author to
    A. draw an "X" through the incorrect documentation.
    B. draw a single line through the incorrect information, date and initial the change.
    C. white it out, date and initial the change.
    D. remove the form from the chart and add a revised form.

REFERENCE: Green and Bowie, pp 84–85
               LaTour and Eichenwald-Maki, p 193
               McWay (2010), p 157
               Roach, p 70
               Brodnik, pp 138–140
               Pozgar, p 297
               Servais, pp 30–32, 113–114

86. Dr. Vincent Orangeburg performed a cesarean on Mrs. Greentree, who later returned to the emergency room 5 days after the surgery with abdominal pain. An x-ray performed revealed that a sponge was left in the lower abdominal cavity from the cesarean. Which case law principle can be used in a lawsuit against Dr. Orangeburg?
    A. res gestae
    B. star decis
    C. res ipsa loquitur
    D. res judicata

REFERENCE: Green and Bowie, p 267
                McWay (2008), p 55
                McWay (2010), p 75
                Brodnik, pp 71–72
                Pozgar, pp 56, 115–117

87. To be admitted into court as evidence, medical records or health information are introduced as
    A. torts or contracts.
    B. privileged information.
    C. business records or exception to hearsay rule.
    D. product liability.

REFERENCE: Green and Bowie, pp 270–271
                LaTour and Eichenwald-Maki, p 292
                McWay (2010), p 51
                Roach, pp 383–386
                Brodnik, pp 44–45
                Servais, pp 4–5, 123–130

88. A health care organization's compliance plans should not only focus on regulatory compliance, but also have a
    A. strong personnel component that reduces the rapid turnover of nursing personnel.
    B. coding compliance program that prevents fraudulent coding and billing.
    C. component that increases the security of medical records.
    D. substantial program that increases the availability of clinical data.

REFERENCE: Green and Bowie, p 323
                LaTour and Eichenwald-Maki, p 412
                McWay (2008), pp 69, 133
                McWay (2010), p 318
                Brodnik, pp 316–318
                Pozgar, pp 332–333
                Servais, pp 224–228

89. A written consent from the patient is required from which of the following entities in order to learn a patient's HIV status?
    A. insurance companies
    B. emergency medical personnel
    C. spouse or needle partner
    D. health care workers

REFERENCE: Green and Bowie, p 292
               McWay (2008), p 90
               McWay (2010), pp 181–183
               Brodnik, pp 250–251
               Pozgar, pp 358–559
               Roach, pp 352–362

90. Dr. Sam Vineyard improperly performed a knee replacement surgery, which caused the patient to develop an infection that lead to the amputation of the leg and thigh. The best term to describe the action performed is
    A. misfeasance.
    B. malpractice.
    C. nonfeasance.
    D. malfeasance.

REFERENCE: LaTour and Eichenwald-Maki, p 275
               Brodnik, p 70
               Pozgar, p 33

91. The ideal consent for medical treatment obtained by the physician is
    A. expressed.   C. implied.
    B. informed.   D. verbal.

REFERENCE: Green and Bowie, pp 129, 132, 134
               McWay (2008), pp 64–65
               Brodnik, pp 96–99
               Roach, pp 78–81
               Pozgar, pp 302–303

92. Which of the following is an example of the breach of confidentiality?
    A. a nurse speaking with the physician in the patient's room
    B. staff members discussing patients in the elevator
    C. the admission clerk verifying over the phone that the patient is in-house
    D. the hospital operator paging code blue in room 3 north

REFERENCE: Pozgar, p 52
               LaTour and Eichenwald-Maki, p 277
               Brodnik, pp 78–79
               Roach, pp 406–408

93. Which of the following would be an inappropriate procedure for the custodian of the medical record to perform prior to taking a medical record from a health care facility to court?
    A. Number each page of the record in ink.
    B. Document in the file folder the total number of pages in the record.
    C. Remove any information that might prove detrimental to the hospital or physician.
    D. Prepare an itemized list of sheets contained in the medical record.

REFERENCE: LaTour and Eichenwald-Maki, p 292
               Pozgar, pp 284–287
               Brodnik, pp 33–34

94. Which of the following agencies is empowered to implement the law governing Medicare and Medicaid?
    A. Centers for Medicare and Medicaid Services (CMS) formerly known as Health Care Financing Administration (HCFA)
    B. Joint Commission
    C. Institutes of Health
    D. Department of Health and Human Services

REFERENCE: Green and Bowie, p 65
               LaTour and Eichenwald-Maki, p 372
               Brodnik, p 128
               McWay (2008), pp 50, 69
               McWay (2010), p 12
               Pozgar, pp 25–28

95. Consent forms may be challenged on all the following grounds EXCEPT
    A. wording was too technical.
    B. the treating physician obtained the patient's signature.
    C. it is written in a language that the patient could not understand.
    D. the signature was not voluntary.

REFERENCE: Green and Bowie, pp 129, 132, 134
               Roach, p 97
               Brodnik, pp 115–118

96. Mandatory reporting requirements for vital statistics generally
    A. do not require authorization by the patient.
    B. require authorization by the physician.
    C. require authorization by the payer.
    D. do not apply to health care facilities.

REFERENCE: Green and Bowie, p 277
               Brodnik, pp 172–175
               McWay (2008), pp 61–62
               Pozgar, p 330

97. The responsibility of obtaining an informed consent for a surgical or invasive procedure rests with the
    A. patient.
    B. nurse.
    C. physician.
    D. hospital.

REFERENCE: Green and Bowie, pp 129, 132, 134
              Brodnik, pp 115–118
              Pozgar, pp 302–303
              Roach, pp 91–94

98. Courts have released adoption records based on
    A. the request of the adoptee.
    B. the request of the biological parent(s).
    C. the Freedom of Information Act.
    D. a court order for good cause.

REFERENCE: Roach, p 301
              McWay (2010), p 218
              Brodnik, pp 152–153

99. The legislation that required all federally funded facilities to inform patients of their rights under state law to accept or refuse medical treatment is known as
    A. advance directives.
    B. living wills.
    C. Patient Self-Determination Act.
    D. durable power of attorney.

REFERENCE: Green and Bowie, p 129
              McWay (2008), p 65
              McWay (2010), pp 114, 142, 186–187
              Roach, p 97
              Brodnik, p 105
              Pozgar, pp 316–317, 424, 430

100. An improper disclosure of patient information to unauthorized individuals, agencies, or news media may be considered a(n)
    A. invasion of privacy.
    B. libel.
    C. slander.
    D. defamation.

REFERENCE: Pozgar, p 52
              Green and Bowie, p 271
              McWay (2008), p 54
              McWay (2010), p 81
              Roach, pp 406–407, 410

Answer Key for Health Law

1.	A	35.	B	69.	D
2.	B	36.	C	70.	D
3.	C	37.	D	71.	A
4.	A	38.	D	72.	A
5.	C	39.	D	73.	B
6.	B	40.	D	74.	D
7.	C	41.	A	75.	B
8.	D	42.	B	76.	D
9.	D	43.	A	77.	D
10.	B	44.	C	78.	B
11.	C	45.	A	79.	C
12.	A	46.	B	80.	A
13.	D	47.	C	81.	A
14.	C	48.	B	82.	A
15.	B	49.	D	83.	D
16.	A	50.	B	84.	B
17.	C	51.	C	85.	B
18.	C	52.	A	86.	C
19.	A	53.	A	87.	C
20.	C	54.	B	88.	B
21.	A	55.	D	89.	A
22.	C	56.	C	90.	A
23.	D	57.	A	91.	B
24.	A	58.	C	92.	B
25.	B	59.	D	93.	C
26.	B	60.	B	94.	A
27.	D	61.	D	95.	B
28.	A	62.	C	96.	A
29.	D	63.	A	97.	C
30.	C	64.	A	98.	D
31.	A	65.	C	99.	C
32.	D	66.	D	100.	A
33.	A	67.	A		
34.	B	68.	A		

REFERENCES

Brodnik, M. S., McCain, M. C., Rinehart-Thompson, L. A., Reynolds, R. B. et al. (2009). *Fundamentals of law for health informatics and information management.* Chicago: American Health Information Management Association.

Green, M. A., & Bowie, M. J. (2011). *Essentials of health information management: Principles and practices.* Clifton Park, NY: Delmar Cengage Learning.

LaTour, K., & Eichenwald-Maki, S. (2010). *Health information management: Concepts, principles, and practice* (3rd ed.). Chicago: American Health Information Management Association (AHIMA).

McWay, D. C. (2008). *Today's health information management: An integrated approach.* Clifton Park, NY: Delmar Cengage Learning.

McWay, D. C. (2010). *Legal and ethical aspects of health information management* (3rd ed.). Clifton Park, NY: Delmar Cengage Learning.

Pozgar, G. D. (2012). *Legal aspects of health care administration* (11th ed.). Sudbury, MA: Jones & Bartlett.

Roach, W. H. (2006). *Medical records and the law* (4th ed.). Sudbury, MA: Jones & Bartlett.

Servais, C. E. (2008). *The legal health record.* Chicago: American Health Information Management Association (AHIMA).

Health Law Competency Domains

Question	RHIA Domain	RHIT Domain
1–100	5–6	
1–100		6

XIII. Health Statistics and Research

Kathy C. Trawick, EdD, RHIA

As noted in the main Introduction section, you will be able to access some statistical formulas on the computer to use during the exam. You may not find them in any set location—be prepared to look around for them a little. Of course, there are some formulas, (for example: mean, median, and average) you will be responsible for knowing. When preparing for the exam, practice using the calculator located in the program accessories bar on your computer and the formulas that are provided in this text.

Although some questions are included from the Commonly Computed Rates and Percentages for Hospital Inpatients, you will often be asked to interpret everyday data and/or solve questions that have more to do with common sense and good math skills than with memorized formulas. To help you distinguish among the types of questions you might expect, and to make sure you realistically evaluate your skills in this area, this chapter has been divided into four sections:
1. Statistical basics
2. Commonly computed rates
3. Data display and interpretation
4. Research and financial statistics

According to the breakdown of content for both the RHIA and RHIT exams, the health statistics questions have been included in Domain II. This section not only covers statistics and research, but also may include data collection, interpretation, and presentation as well as knowledge of registries, specialized databases, and the Institutional Review Board (IRB). You should also be prepared to analyze and interpret statistical charts and graphs. Some questions will refer to a graphical representation of data when asking for the answer. Refer to the specific details of these items in the domain and subdomain competencies found in the Certification Guide.

You will want to work with statistical formulas from this chapter, from your formal courses, and from previous textbooks until you get your speed up. Sometimes the length of time it takes in calculating formulas and mathematical computations can make or break you on the entire examination as far as your testing time. Thus, increasing your speed by practicing formulas can really help you at exam time.

Most answers in this section should be rounded to the first decimal point. On the national examination, let the answers provided in the test be your guide, or follow the examination instructions in order to round correctly.

Do not let the word problems throw you off. Some of these are quite long; look for the pertinent data.

Do not panic—approach word problems just as you did in your formal classes. You will have the formulas provided for you as appropriately required on the exam. For problems that you may not have a formula for, try the memory device of—"what did happen divided by what could have happened." Here, the "what did happen" is always the numerator (top number) and the "what could have happened" is always the denominator (bottom number).

We recommend that you review the textbooks listed at the end of this chapter as you study for this section of your exam.

Health Statistics Definitions and Formulas

There are a number of important things to think about when you tackle census and occupancy statistics. First, remember that when it comes to occupancy, beds and bassinets are counted separately. This means newborn discharges are separated from the discharges of adults and children. Next, remember not to be fooled by beds set up temporarily to meet unusual admission needs; all occupancy statistics should be calculated based on approved, permanent beds only. The common rates used for census and occupancy statistics are as follows:

Census Statistics

Daily Inpatient Census	Total number of patients treated during a 24-hour period
Inpatient Service Day	Services received by one inpatient in one 24-hour period
Total Inpatient	Sum of all inpatient service days for each of the days in the period
Service Days	
FORMULA: Average Daily Census	$$\frac{\text{Total inpatient service days for a period (excluding newborns)}}{\text{Total number of days in the period}}$$

Length of Stay

Length of Stay (LOS)	Number of calendar days from admission to discharge
Total Length of Stay	Sum of the days' stay of any group of inpatients discharged during a specific period
FORMULA: Average LOS	$$\frac{\text{Total length of stay (discharge days)}}{\text{Total number of discharges}}$$

Bed Count

Inpatient Bed Count	Number of available hospital beds, both occupied and vacant, on any given day
Inpatient Bed Count Day	Counts the presence of one inpatient bed (occupied or vacant) that is set up and staffed for use in one 24-hour period
Total Inpatient Bed Count Day	Sum of inpatient bed count days for each of the days in a period

Percentage of Occupancy

FORMULA:	$$\frac{\text{Total number of inpatient service days for a period} \times 100}{\text{Total inpatient bed count days} \times \text{number of days in the period}}$$

Bed Turnover Rate

Direct Formula: $\dfrac{\text{Total number of discharges for a period}}{\text{Average bed count for the same period}}$

Indirect Formula: $\dfrac{\text{Percentage of occupancy} \times \text{Days in the period} \times 100}{\text{Average length of stay}}$

NOTE: The indirect formula must be used in cases where the bed count changes during the period in question.

Death (Mortality) Rates

Anesthesia Death Rate	$\dfrac{\text{Total number of deaths caused by an anesthetic agent} \times 100}{\text{Total number of anesthetics administered}}$
Fetal Death Rate (Stillbirth Rate)	$\dfrac{\text{Total number of intermediate and late fetal deaths} \times 100}{\text{Total number of births (plus intermediate and late fetal deaths)}}$
Gross Hospital Death Rate	$\dfrac{\text{Total number of inpatient deaths (including newborns)} \times 100}{\text{Total number of discharges (including deaths and newborns)}}$
Net Hospital Death Rate	$\dfrac{\text{Number of inpatient deaths (including NB) minus deaths} < 48 \text{ hours of admission} \times 100}{\text{Total discharges (including deaths and NB. minus deaths} <48 \text{ hours)}}$
Maternal Death Rate	$\dfrac{\text{Total number of maternal deaths for a period} \times 100}{\text{Total number of obstetrical discharges}}$
Neonatal Death Rate (Infant Mortality Rate)	$\dfrac{\text{Total number of newborn (NB. deaths for a period} \times 100)}{\text{Total number of newborn (NB. Discharges)}}$
Postoperative Death Rate	$\dfrac{\text{Number of deaths within 10 days of surgery} \times 100}{\text{Total number of patients operated on}}$

Autopsy Rates

Newborn (NB) Autopsy Rate	$\dfrac{\text{Number of autopsies on NB deaths} \times 100}{\text{Total number of NB deaths}}$
Fetal Autopsy Rate	$\dfrac{\text{Number of autopsies on intermediate and late fetal deaths} \times 100}{\text{Total number of intermediate and late fetal deaths}}$
Gross Autopsy Rate	$\dfrac{\text{Total inpatient autopsies for a period} \times 100}{\text{Total inpatient deaths for the period}}$
Net Autopsy Rate	$\dfrac{\text{Total inpatient autopsies for a period} \times 100}{\text{Total inpatient deaths minus unautopsied coroner's or medical examiner's cases for the period}}$
Hospital Autopsy Rate (Adjusted)	$\dfrac{\text{Total hospital autopsies} \times 100}{\text{Number of deaths of hospital patients whose bodies are available for hospital autopsy}}$

The hospital patients whose bodies after death are available for hospital autopsy include inpatients, unless the bodies are removed from the hospital by legal authorities. However, in any such case, if the hospital pathologist or delegated physician of the medical staff performs an autopsy while acting as an agent for the coroner, the autopsy is included in the numerator and the death in the denominator.

In addition, other hospital patients (including hospital home care patients, outpatients, and previous hospital patients who have died elsewhere) whose bodies have been made available for the performance of hospital autopsy, the autopsy is included in the numerator and the death in the denominator.

Infection (Morbidity) Rates

Total Hospital (Morbidity) Infection Rate	$\dfrac{\text{Total number of hospital infections} \times 100}{\text{Total number of discharges}}$
Nosocomial Infection Rate	$\dfrac{\text{Number of hospital acquired infections} \times 100}{\text{Total number of discharges (including deaths)}}$
Community-Acquired Infection Rate	$\dfrac{\text{Number of community-acquired infections} \times 100}{\text{Total number of discharges}}$
Postoperative Infection Rate	$\dfrac{\text{Number of postoperative infections for a period (within 10 days postoperatively)} \times 100}{\text{Total number of operations performed}}$

Other Rates

Cesarean Section Rate	$\dfrac{\text{Total number of cesarean sections performed in a period} \times 100}{\text{Total number of deliveries in the period}}$
Consultation Rate	$\dfrac{\text{Total number of consultations for a period} \times 100}{\text{Total number of discharges for the period}}$
Delinquent Medical Record Rate	$\dfrac{\text{Total number of delinquent records} \times 100}{\text{Average number of discharges during a completion period}}$
Incomplete Medical Record Rate	$\dfrac{\text{Total number of incomplete records} \times 100}{\text{Total number of discharges during the completion period}}$
Percentage of Medicare Patients	$\dfrac{\text{Total number of Medicare discharges} \times 100}{\text{Total number of adult and children discharges}}$
Percentage of Medicare Discharge Days	$\dfrac{\text{Total number of Medicare discharge days} \times 100}{\text{Total number of discharge days for adults and children}}$
Readmission Rate	$\dfrac{\text{Number of readmissions for a period} \times 100}{\text{Number of total admissions (including readmissions)}}$

Generic Formulas Percentage Rates	$\dfrac{\text{Total number of times events actually happened} \times 100}{\text{Total number of times events could have happened}}$
Mean	Add all the available values and divide the sum by the total number of values involved. Example: Average length of stay or average daily inpatient census.
Median	The midpoint of an ordered series of numbers arranged in numerical order from highest to lowest or vice versa.
Mode	The most frequently recurring value in a set of numbers is the mode.

Section I—Math and Statistical Basics

The basics include mathematical and statistical terminology as well as the measures of central tendency and variations around those measures. It is unlikely that you will get instructions for calculating the measures of central tendency, so they are supplied along with the statistical formulas at the beginning of this chapter.

1. Sandy Beach Hospital reports 1,652 discharges for September. The infection control report documents 21 nosocomial infections and 27 community-acquired infections for the same month. What is the community-acquired infection rate?
   A. 1.3
   B. 1.4
   C. 1.6
   D. 2.9

   REFERENCE: Koch, p 179
   Johns, pp 564–565

2. Physicians at South Seas Clinic are expected to see six patients per hour on average. The physicians with the highest productivity each week are exempted from on-call responsibilities for the weekend. Which physician will get the weekend off this week?

SOUTH SEAS CLINIC PHYSICIAN PRODUCTIVITY Week 1 January 2013		
PHYSICIAN NAME	NUMBER OF HOURS WORKED	NUMBER OF PATIENTS SEEN
Robinson	32	185
Beasley	30	161
Hiltz	35	200
Wolf	26	157

   A. Robinson
   B. Beasley
   C. Hiltz
   D. Wolf

   REFERENCE: Koch, pp 56–57
   Abdelhak, pp 368–369
   McWay, p 192
   Horton, pp 147–148
   LaTour and Eichenwald-Maki, p 690

3. If there are 150,000 medical records and the Health Information Department receives 3,545 requests for records in a week, what percentage of the records are requested weekly?
   A. 2.4%
   B. 3.5%
   C. 4.6%
   D. 5.1%

   REFERENCE: Horton, pp 14, 19–20
   Koch, p 49
   McWay, p 192
   Abdelhak, pp 368–369
   Johns, pp 526–527
   LaTour and Eichenwald-Maki, pp 424–425

4. You are conducting a study on the pain associated with a specific illness. For the purpose of your study, you classify pain level as follows:

CODE	PAIN LEVEL (as described by the patient)
01	None
02	Little or Minimal
03	Moderate
04	Heavy
05	Severe

These data are best described as
   A. discrete.
   B. continuous.
   C. nominal.
   D. ordinal.

REFERENCE: McWay, pp 199–201
             Abdelhak, pp 380–385
             Horton, pp 196–199
             Koch, pp 12–13

5. You are choosing restaurants where you might eat while you are in Chicago at the AHIMA Leadership Conference. You have collected the following information about four possible lunch restaurants that are all located within easy walking distance of the meeting site. The data are displayed below.

RESTAURANT NAME	MEAN LUNCH COST	STANDARD DEVIATION
Bon Appetite	$8.00	0.75
Mario's	$7.50	1
Au Courant	$9.00	1.25
The Windy City Grill	$7.50	1.5

You want to stay within the reimbursement rate allowed by your Component State Association, so it is important to you that you have at least a 95% chance of eating a lunch that costs no more than $10.00. Therefore, when lunchtime comes, you head to
   A. Bon Appetite or Mario's.
   B. Mario's or Au Courant.
   C. Au Courant or The Windy City Grill.
   D. The Windy City Grill or Bon Appetite.

REFERENCE: McWay, pp 194–195
             Koch, pp 246–247
             Horton, pp 184–186

6. Organizations collect statistics to increase their knowledge of a specified population. The knowledge does not come automatically—it is developed in the following sequence:
   A. data → facts → information → knowledge.
   B. data → information → facts → knowledge.
   C. facts → data → information → knowledge.
   D. facts → information → data → knowledge.

REFERENCE: Horton, pp 2–3
             Johns, p 28

Questions 7 and 8 are based on the study and data below.

The coding supervisor at Bayside Hospital regularly has the coders recode records from the previous week in an effort to improve and monitor coding consistency. The supervisor has collected the data displayed below on four coders.

Coder	Records Under Review	Same Code on Self-Coding Review	Same Code on Peer Coding Review
Coder A	28	22	20
Coder B	18	16	16
Coder C	45	42	43
Coder D	17	15	16

7. The data in the column on the far right were collected when the coders traded records for recoding. This is a common practice used to check
   A. interrater reliability.
   B. intrarater reliability.
   C. interrater validity.
   D. intrarater validity.

REFERENCE: McWay, p 231
               Abdelhak, pp 410–412
               Johns, p 509
               Shi, p 299

8. The coder with the highest overall accuracy rating will get the day after Thanksgiving off. Which coder will get to spend the day after Thanksgiving off rather than coding?
   A. Coder A
   B. Coder B
   C. Coder C
   D. Coder D

REFERENCE: Abdelhak pp 368–369
               Johns, pp 523–527
               Koch, p 48
               Horton, pp 14, 19–20

9. Which of the following interactions fits the definition of a patient encounter?

   Phyllis saw Dr. Holland during a scheduled office visit. Dr. Holland prescribed a new medication.

   Jean called Dr. Holland with a question about her medication. Dr. Holland returned the telephone call and answered Jean's question.

   Howard was seen by Dr. Holland in the hospital emergency department after having a reaction to his medication.

   The pharmacy received telephone approval from Dr. Horton for a refill on Jackson's prescription.

   A. Phyllis, Jean, Howard, and Jackson
   B. Jackson, Howard, and Jean
   C. Jean, Phyllis, and Howard
   D. Phyllis and Howard

REFERENCE: Horton, pp 4, 148
               LaTour and Eichenwald-Maki, p 438
               Abdelhak, p 138

10. A small portion of the form you are using for a research study is reproduced below.

| Male | 1 |
| Female | 2 |

This is an example of

A. ordinal data.
B. ranked data.
C. nominal data.
D. discrete data.

REFERENCE: McWay, pp 199–201
Abdelhak, pp 380–385
Horton, pp 196–199
Koch, pp 12–13
LaTour and Eichenwald-Maki, pp 423–424

11. You have made a list of the advantages and disadvantages of a measure of central tendency.

ADVANTAGES	DISADVANTAGES
Easy to obtain and interpret	May not be descriptive of the distribution
Not sensitive to extreme observations in the frequency distribution	May not be unique
Easy to communicate and explain to others	Does not provide information about the entire distribution

The measure of central tendency you are describing is the

A. mean.
B. median.
C. range.
D. mode.

REFERENCE: McWay, p 194
Horton, pp 175–181
Koch, pp 234–237
Abdelhak, pp 385–387
Johns, pp 529–532
LaTour and Eichenwald-Maki, pp 454–458

The following data were collected in your physician office practice from one morning's visits. Use the data for questions 12, 13, and 14.

Office Visit ID Number	Minutes with the Physician	Physician
508-123	5	Robinson
508-124	9	Robinson
508-125	8	Beasley
508-126	12	Wolf
508-127	6	Beasley
508-128	7	Beasley
508-129	5	Wolf
508-130	10	Baumstark
508-131	7	Baumstark
508-132	9	Robinson
508-133	11	Wolf

12. The median number of minutes with the physician (considering all physicians) is
   A. 7 minutes.
   B. 8 minutes.
   C. 8.4 minutes.
   D. 9 minutes.

REFERENCE: McWay, p 194
            Abdelhak, pp 385–387
            Koch, pp 234–237
            Johns, pp 529–533
            Horton, pp 175–181
            Shaw, p 56

13. The mean number of minutes with the physician (considering all physicians) is
   A. 7 minutes.
   B. 8 minutes.
   C. 8.4 minutes.
   D. 9 minutes.

REFERENCE: McWay, p 194
            Abdelhak, pp 385–387
            Koch, pp 234–237
            Johns, pp 529–532
            Horton, pp 175–181
            Shaw, pp 53–54

14. Which physician spent the longest average time with patients on that day?
   A. Beasley
   B. Wolf
   C. Baumstark
   D. Robinson

REFERENCE: Abdelhak, pp 385–387
            Koch, pp 234–237
            Johns, pp 529–532
            Shaw, pp 53–54

Use this portion of yesterday's discharges printout below to answer questions 15 and 16.

Discharge List					
Patient #	Admit Date	Service	Physician ID	Room #	LOS
12-32-21	1/02/13	MED	212	44-A	13
12-32-22	1/02/13	SURG	218	32	13
12-32-85	1/14/13	PEDS	214	23-B	1
11-99-94	1/12/13	MED	212	46-A	3
10-93-23	1/10/13	MED	212	45	5
12-35-94	1/11/13	SURG	218	33	4
10-85-14	1/01/13	PEDS	214	23-A	14

15. Without even performing any complex calculations, you can get a quick, simple measure of dispersion in the LOS for yesterday's discharges by computing the
    A. range of the data set.
    B. mean of the data set.
    C. variance of the data set.
    D. coefficient of variation of the data set.

REFERENCE: Koch, pp 234–243
                Abdelhak, pp 385–389
                Johns, pp 529–533
                Horton, pp 175–182

16. Looking more closely at the LOS for these patients, when you calculate the standard deviation on the data, you would expect
    A. a large standard deviation because the dispersion is large.
    B. a small standard deviation because the dispersion is small.
    C. a large standard deviation because the dispersion is small.
    D. a small standard deviation because the dispersion is large.

REFERENCE: Koch, pp 246–247
                McWay, pp 194–195
                Abdelhak, pp 387–389
                Johns, p 1171
                Horton, pp 183–186
                Shaw, pp 54–56

17. Englewood Health Center collected the following data on patients discharged on January 1, 2013. Which measure of central tendency would be most affected by Mallory's extremely long LOS?

Patient Name	Length of Stay
Ben	1
Josh	2
Emma	3
Bryan	4
Mallory	29
Taylor	2
Matthew	3
Aiden	2
Trevor	4
Tyler	2

A. variance
B. median
C. mean
D. mode

REFERENCE: McWay, p 194
              Horton, pp 175–181
              Koch, pp 234–243
              Johns, pp 531–533
              LaTour and Eichenwald-Maki, p 455–457
              Abdelhak, pp 385–387
              Shaw, pp 53–56

CASE NUMBER	BRIEF DESCRIPTION
101-43-26	A 32-year-old female was admitted through the ED following an automobile accident. She spontaneously delivered a 720 g fetus that showed no sign of life.
101-44-23	A 22-year-old female was admitted in labor. Following an uneventful course, she delivered a 7 lb 4 oz term male. The child developed sudden and unexpected respiratory distress. All attempts at resuscitation failed; the baby was pronounced dead less than 2 hours after delivery.
101-48-69	A 19-year-old female spontaneously delivered a 475 g fetus following a fall down the stairs at home.
101-56-29	A 28-year-old female was admitted for a late-term therapeutic abortion. The procedure was completed without complication; product of conception weighed 728 g.

18. The OB/GYN Department reported the information in the table shown above to the Quality Management/Statistics Committee. When the committee considers these adverse outcomes from the OB/GYN Department, which of the cases will be included in the numerator of the facility's fetal death rate?
    A. 101-43-26
    B. 101-43-26 and 101-44-23
    C. 101-43-26 and 101-48-69
    D. 101-43-26 and 101-56-29

REFERENCE: Horton, pp 88–89
              Koch, pp 147–148
              LaTour and Eichenwald-Maki, pp 431–432
              Johns, pp 557–559
              Abdelhak, pp 368–372

19. Which of the cases listed in the table above will have an impact on the facility's gross death rate?
    A. 101-43-26
    B. 101-44-23
    C. 101-48-69
    D. 101-56-29

REFERENCE: Horton, pp 72–74
               Koch, p 120
               LaTour and Eichenwald-Maki, pp 430–432
               Johns, pp 556–559
               Abdelhak, pp 368–373

20. Patients in the pediatrics ward were studied to determine their favorite color. The survey results are listed below. The results of the favorite color study are reported in a

REPORTED FAVORITE COLOR OF PEDIATRIC PATIENTS AZURE TIDES HOSPITAL JANUARY 18, 2013	
FAVORITE COLOR	NUMBER OF RESPONDENTS
RED	12
GREEN	14
BLUE	22
YELLOW	18
ORANGE	16

    A. frequency polygon.
    B. line graph.
    C. frequency distribution.
    D. systematic fashion.

REFERENCE: Shi, pp 359–360
               McWay, p 203
               Koch, pp 260–284
               Horton, pp 202–212
               Johns, pp 540–546
               Abdelhak, pp 382–385

21. All of the following items mean the same thing, EXCEPT
    A. inpatient service day.
    B. daily inpatient census.
    C. daily census.
    D. inpatient census.

REFERENCE: Koch, pp 64–67
               McWay, pp 198–199
               Abdelhak, pp 378–379
               Horton, pp 24–27
               LaTour and Eichenwald-Maki, pp 426–427

22. Pasadena Bay Hospital reports an average LOS in February of 3.7 days with a standard deviation of 20. This tells us that
    A. most patients had an LOS of 3–4 days.
    B. there was a small variation in the LOS.
    C. patients at Pasadena Bay stay longer than average.
    D. there was a large variation in the LOS.

REFERENCE: McWay, p 198
               Abdelhak, pp 385–388
               Koch, pp 246–247
               Johns, p 1171
               LaTour and Eichenwald-Maki, p 457
               Horton, pp 184–186
               Shaw, pp 54–56

23. Jason collected data on the length of stay (LOS) for 10 patients and then determined the median LOS as follows:

1	
2	
4	
3	
1	← median
3	
2	
4	
2	
8	

What is wrong with Jason's determination of the median?
    A. There is nothing wrong with Jason's determination of the median.
    B. Jason forgot to put the numbers in sequential order before determining the median.
    C. It is not possible to determine the median on such a small number of data points.
    D. It is not possible to determine the median on an even number of data points.

REFERENCE: McWay, p 194
               Koch, pp 234–237
               Horton, pp 175–181
               Johns, pp 529–532
               Abdelhak, pp 383–389
               Shaw, p 54

Section II—Commonly Computed Rates and Percentages for Hospital Inpatients

24. All Women's Hospital reports the following statistics:

Single births	
Vaginal	40
C-section	0
Twin births	
Twins—vaginal	12 (6 sets)
Twins—C-section	8 (4 sets)
Other multiple births	0
Intermediate fetal deaths	
Vaginal	5
C-section	0
Late fetal deaths	
Vaginal	2
C-section	0

How many deliveries occurred?
A. 50   C. 60
B. 57   D. 67

REFERENCE: Horton, pp 124–125
                       Koch, p 140

25. The inpatient census at midnight is 67. Two patients were admitted in the morning; one died 2 hours later; the second patient was transferred to another facility that same afternoon. The inpatient service days for that day will be
A. 65.   C. 68.
B. 67.   D. 69.

REFERENCE: Abdelhak, pp 378–380
                       Horton, pp 27–32
                       Koch, pp 68–69
                       Johns, p 548
                       LaTour and Eichenwald-Maki, p 427

26. Bayside Hospital has 275 adult beds, 30 pediatric beds, and 40 bassinets. In a nonleap year, inpatient service days were 75,860 for adults, 7,100 for pediatrics, and 11,800 for newborns. What was the average daily census for the year?
A. 227   C. 207
B. 208   D. 259

REFERENCE: Abdelhak, pp 378–380
                       Horton, pp 38–42
                       Koch, pp 75–77
                       Johns, pp 548–549
                       LaTour and Eichenwald-Maki, pp 427–430

27. In order to derive the total inpatient service days for any given day, you would need to
    A. subtract intra-hospital transfers from the inpatient census.
    B. add same-day admits and discharges to the inpatient census.
    C. add intra-hospital transfers to the inpatient census.
    D. subtract same day admits and discharges from the inpatient census.

REFERENCE: McWay, p 198
              Abdelhak, pp 378–380
              Horton, pp 27–32
              Koch, pp 68–69
              Johns, p 548
              LaTour and Eichenwald-Maki, p 427

28. Mr. McDonaldson was admitted to your hospital at 10:45 PM on January 1. He died at 4:22 AM on January 3. How many inpatient service days did Mr. McDonaldson receive?
    A. 1
    B. 2
    C. 3
    D. 4

REFERENCE: McWay, p 198
              Abdelhak, pp 382–384
              Horton, pp 27–32
              Koch, pp 68–69
              Johns, p 548
              LaTour and Eichenwald-Maki, p 427

29. A patient admitted to the hospital on January 24 and discharged on February 9 has a length of stay of
    A. 16 days.
    B. 15 days.
    C. 17 days.
    D. 14 days.

REFERENCE: McWay, p 198
              Abdelhak, pp 378–380
              Horton, pp 58–61
              Koch, pp 102–106
              Johns, pp 553–556

Use the data in the table below to answer the next two questions.

Royal Palm Hospital has 500 beds and 55 bassinets. In February of a nonleap year, it reported the following statistics:

Inpatient service days:	
Adult and pediatric	12,345
Newborn	553
Discharges:	
Adult and pediatric	1,351
Newborn	77
Discharge days:	
Adult and pediatric	9,457
Newborn	231

30. What was the percentage of occupancy for adults and pediatrics in February?
    A. 84.8%   C. 79.6%
    B. 88.2%   D. 80.5%

REFERENCE: McWay, p 199
                          Abdelhak, pp 378–380
                          Koch, pp 86–90
                          Johns, pp 550–552
                          Horton, pp 46–48
                          LaTour and Eichenwald-Maki, p 428

31. What was the average length of stay at Royal Palm Hospital in February?
    A. 6.8 days   C. 9 days
    B. 7 days   D. 9.1 days

REFERENCE: McWay, p 198
                          Abdelhak, pp 378–380
                          Koch, pp 106–110
                          Johns, pp 553–555
                          Horton, pp 63–65
                          LaTour and Eichenwald-Maki, pp 429–430

32. You are responsible for calculating and reporting average length of stay (ALOS) for your hospital each month. This month, there were 92 discharges, and the total discharge days equal 875. One of the patients discharged this month had a total of 428 discharge days, so the ALOS is distorted by this unusually long stay. In this situation, you should report an ALOS of
    A. 9.51 days— no further information is necessary.
    B. 9.61 days and make a note that the one patient with an unusually long LOS was subtracted prior to making the calculation.
    C. 4.86 days and make a note that one unusually long LOS was subtracted prior to making the calculation.
    D. 4.91 days and make a note that the data on one patient with an unusually long LOS were subtracted prior to making the calculation.

REFERENCE: McWay, p 198
               Horton, pp 63–65
               Johns, pp 553–555
               Abdelhak, pp 378–380
               Koch, pp 106–110
               Shaw, pp 46–48

33. A hospital reported the following statistics during a nonleap year. Calculate the percentage of occupancy for the entire year.

Time Period	Bed Count	Inpatient Service Days
January 1–May 31	200	28,690
June 1–October 15	250	27,400
October 16–December 31	275	19,250

    A. 85.2%   C. 90.0%
    B. 88%   D. 91.2%

REFERENCE: McWay, p 199
               Abdelhak, pp 378–380
               Koch, pp 86–90
               Johns, pp 550–552
               Horton, pp 46–48
               LaTour and Eichenwald-Maki, p 428

34. Lake City Health Center has 200 beds and 20 bassinets. In a nonleap year, Styles Hospital admitted 16,437 adults and children; 16,570 adults and children were discharged. There were 1,764 live births and 1,798 newborns discharged. The bed turnover rate for the year was
    A. 82.2.   C. 82.9.
    B. 82.7.   D. 93.5.

REFERENCE: Koch, pp 185–187
               Abdelhak, pp 378–380
               Horton, pp 52–53
               LaTour and Eichenwald-Maki, p 429

35. Sea Crest Hospital has 200 beds and 20 bassinets. There was a sudden spurt in the birth rate in the town in November. The hospital set up five additional bassinets for the entire month. Total bed count days for Sea Crest Hospital in a nonleap year would be
    A. 73,000.
    B. 80,300.
    C. 80,450.
    D. 80,455.

REFERENCE: Koch, pp 84–85
              Horton, p 45
              Abdelhak, pp 378–380
              Johns, p 551
              LaTour and Eichenwald-Maki, p 428

36. Use the statistics provided in the table to compute the fetal death rate at All Women's Hospital for March.

All Women's Hospital March Statistics	
Live births	225
Intermediate and late fetal deaths	5
Early fetal deaths	4
Newborn discharges	235

    A. 4.0%
    B. 1.78%
    C. 2.2%
    D. 1.77%

REFERENCE: Abdelhak, pp 372–373
              Koch, pp 147–149
              Johns, pp 557–558
              Horton, pp 88–89
              LaTour and Eichenwald-Maki, pp 431–432

The following obstetrical statistics were collected for the month of October. Use the data in the table below to answer the next two questions.

DELIVERED		TOTAL	DELIVERED BY C-SECTION
Live			
	Single infant	50	15
	Twins	3 sets	1 set
Dead			
	Early fetal	1	0
	Late fetal	1	1

37. The number of births in the facility in October is
    A. 53.
    B. 55.
    C. 56.
    D. 58.

REFERENCE: Koch, pp 209–210
              Johns, p 571
              Horton, pp 124–125

38. The number of deliveries in the facility in October is
    A. 53.   C. 56.
    B. 55.   D. 58.

REFERENCE: Koch, p 140
                  Johns, p 571
                  Horton, pp 124–125

39. Ocean View Healthcare Center recorded six fetal deaths during the last year; details are listed
    below.

Fetal Death Information		
ID	WEIGHT	GESTATIONAL AGE
A	526 g	22 weeks
B	405 g	18 weeks
C	817 g	26 weeks
D	1,023 g	30 weeks
E	629 g	24 weeks
F	1,113 g	29 weeks

   How should these deaths be counted in the hospital death rates?
    A. All the deaths except B will be included in the gross death rate.
    B. Deaths D and F will be included in the gross death rate.
    C. Deaths C, D, and F will be included in the gross death rate.
    D. None of these deaths will be included in the gross death rate.

REFERENCE: Abdelhak, p 372
                  Koch, p 120
                  LaTour and Eichenwald-Maki, p 431
                  Johns, p 556
                  Horton, pp 72–74

40. William Rumple was pronounced dead on arrival (DOA). The hospital pathologist performed an
    autopsy on Mr. Rumple's body. This statistical event would be counted in the
    A. net death rate.   C. net autopsy rate.
    B. gross death rate.   D. hospital autopsy rate.

REFERENCE: Horton, pp 72–76, 95–105
                  Koch, pp 119–121, 162–170
                  Johns, pp 556–564
                  LaTour and Eichenwald-Maki, pp 430–434
                  Abdelhak, pp 375–376

Tampa Bay Health Center discharged 6,069 adults/children and 545 newborns last year. A total of 1,648 adults/children and 1,279 newborns were seen in the emergency department. Information on the deaths at Happy Valley last year is listed below. Use the data to answer the next two questions.

INPATIENT DEATHS		
Adult/child	245 < 48 hr	105 > 48 hr
Newborn	8 < 48 hr	3 > 48 hr

OUTPATIENT (ED) DEATHS		
Adult/child	2	
Newborn	0	

FETAL DEATHS		
Early	1	
Intermediate	3	
Late	2	

41. What was the gross (hospital) death rate at Tampa Bay Health Center last year?
    A. 3.8%
    B. 5.4%
    C. 5.5%
    D. 5.6%

REFERENCE: Koch, p 120
               Horton, pp 72–74
               Johns, p 556
               LaTour and Eichenwald-Maki, p 431
               Abdelhak, pp 369–371

42. What was the net death rate at Tampa Bay Health Center last year?
    A. 1.6%
    B. 1.7%
    C. 1.8%
    D. 1.9%

REFERENCE: Abdelhak, pp 369–371
               Koch, pp 120–121
               LaTour and Eichenwald-Maki, p 431
               Johns, p 557
               Horton, pp 75–76

43. During the month of September, Superior Health Care Center had 1,382 inpatient discharges, including 48 deaths. There were 38 deaths over 48 hours. Statistics also show 4 fetal deaths, 3 DOAs, and 4 inpatient coroner's cases. Which of the following calculations is correct to figure the net death rate?
    A. $(48 \times 100)/(1,382 - 10)$
    B. $(48-10 \times 100)/(1,382 - 10)$
    C. $(1,382 \times 100)/(48 - 10)$
    D. $(1,382 - 10) \times 100/(48 - 10)$

REFERENCE: Abdelhak, pp 369–373
               Horton, pp 75–76
               Koch, pp 120–121
               Johns, p 557
               LaTour and Eichenwald-Maki, p 431

44. The best form/graph for demonstrating trends over time would be
    A. frequency polygon.
    B. line graph.
    C. pie chart.
    D. histogram.

REFERENCE: McWay, p 201
               Horton, p 212
               Koch, pp 273–274
               Shaw, pp 49–51, 57–63

45. Joseph Woodley has been on a third floor nursing unit since October 2011 and was finally discharged to a nursing home in December 2012. When the average length of stay is calculated for the year 2012, this very long length of stay will
    A. have little impact on the average length of stay.
    B. result in a special cause variation in the average length of stay.
    C. result in a small variation in the average length of stay.
    D. result in a common cause variation in the average length of stay.

REFERENCE: Koch, pp 106–110
               Johns, pp 553–555
               Horton, pp 62–64
               Abdelhak, pp 385–388
               Shaw, pp 44–46

46. Still thinking about Mr. Woodley and his long stay, if you were to graph the ALOS for the facility for 2012, which of the following graphs would you expect to see?

A.

C.

B.

D.

REFERENCE: Horton, pp 187–189
               Koch, pp 238–240
               LaTour and Eichenwald-Maki, pp 457–458
               Abdelhak, pp 387–389
               Shaw, pp 44–46

47. The New Beginnings Maternity Center recorded the following statistics in December:

FETAL DEATHS:	
EARLY	240
INTERMEDIATE	40
LATE	32
BIRTHS	980
DELIVERIES	994
NEWBORN DISCHARGES	1,008

What was the fetal death rate at New Beginnings Maternity Center in December?
A. 6.8%
B. 7.3%
C. 7.4%
D. 31.8%

REFERENCE: Johns, pp 557–558
Horton, pp 88–89
LaTour and Eichenwald-Maki, pp 431–432
Abdelhak, pp 369–372
Koch, pp 147–149

48. The statistics reported for a 300-bed hospital for 1 year were 20,932 discharges with 136,651 discharge days and 3,699 consultations performed. What was the consultation rate for the year?
A. 16.5%
B. 17.0%
C. 17.7%
D. 18.0%

REFERENCE: Horton, pp 126–127
Koch, pp 182–183
Johns, p 556

Section III—Data Display

You have already practiced reading tables in many of the preceding questions. Data display—the selection, interpretation, and construction of data—is an important part of HIM practice. Therefore, a number of data display questions should be expected. Examples of these kinds of questions follow.

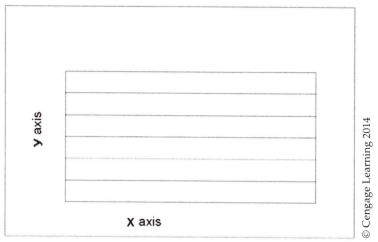

© Cengage Learning 2014

49. Look at the graph grid displayed above. If you want to follow accepted principles for graph construction, you will follow the three-quarter-high rule. That means the
   A. height of the graph should be three-fourths the length of the graph.
   B. length of the graph should be three-fourths the height of the graph.
   C. height of the graph should display three-fourths of the data in the graph.
   D. length of the graph should display three-fourths of the data in the graph.

REFERENCE: Johns, p 535
               Horton, p 207
               LaTour and Eichenwald-Maki, pp 445–446

50. You are preparing data from a series of weight loss studies for display. The data collected during the study are as follows:

POUNDS LOST	NUMBER IN GROUP A WITH THIS WEIGHT LOSS	NUMBER IN GROUP B WITH THIS WEIGHT LOSS
7.5–9.4	1	2
9.5–11.4	3	2
11.5–13.4	6	5
13.5–15.4	5	4
15.5–17.4	8	7
17.5–19.4	2	3

If you want to allow the reader to compare the results of Group A with those of Group B on one graphic display, your best choice would be to construct a

A. bar chart.
B. line graph.
C. histogram.
D. frequency polygon.

REFERENCE: McWay, p 203
Horton, pp 207–212
Koch, pp 264–284
Johns, pp 537–545
LaTour and Eichenwald-Maki, pp 445–449
Abdelhak, pp 382–385
Shaw, pp 48–51, 57–63

51. A distribution is said to be positively skewed when the mean is

A. bimodal.
B. multimodal.
C. shifted to the left.
D. shifted to the right.

REFERENCE: Koch, pp 238–240
Horton, pp 187–189
LaTour and Eichenwald-Maki, pp 457–458
Shaw, pp 56–58

52. You want to graph the number of patients admitted to three different medical staff services on each day of the last month. Because you have a large number of observations (one for each day of the month) and you want to be able to compare the observations for each of the three services on one data display, your best choice is a

A. table.
B. bar chart.
C. line graph.
D. histogram.

REFERENCE: McWay, pp 201–203
Johns, pp 537-545
Horton, pp 207–212
LaTour and Eichenwald-Maki, pp 445–449
Koch, pp 264–284
Shaw, pp 48–51, 57–63

53. You have just constructed the chart displayed below.

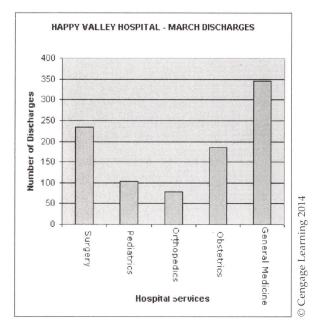

The names of the hospital services are hard to read. The best way to deal with this problem would be to
A. construct a line graph instead of a bar chart.
B. use a column chart instead of a bar chart.
C. plot your primary variable along the x axis.
D. divide the data into two charts.

REFERENCE: Koch, pp 264–273
                Horton, pp 206–209
                Johns, p 537
                LaTour and Eichenwald-Maki, pp 446–448

54. The display below is a

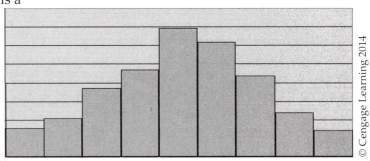

A. bar chart, which is commonly used to display continuous data.
B. bar chart, which is commonly used to display discrete data.
C. histogram, which is commonly used to display continuous data.
D. histogram, which is commonly used to display discrete data.

REFERENCE: McWay, p 203
                Horton, pp 207–212
                Koch, pp 264–283
                Johns, pp 537–543
                LaTour and Eichenwald-Maki, pp 446–448
                Shaw, pp 48–51, 57–63

55. The data display below is a

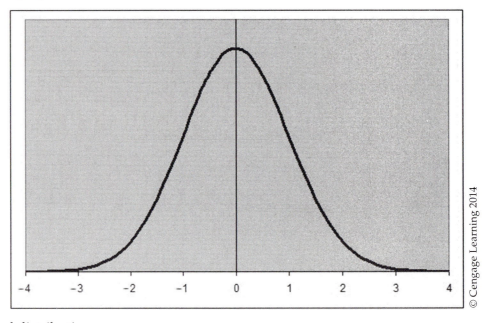

A. normal distribution or curve.
B. positive skewed curve.
C. negative skewed curve.
D. heterogeneous curve.

REFERENCE: McWay, p 208
                Koch, pp 238–240
                Shi, p 359
                Horton, pp 187–189
                Shaw, pp 56–58

56. What conclusion can you make from the pie graph below?

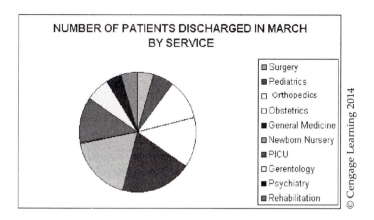

A. A pie graph should not be used, because there are too many categories for effective display.
B. A pie graph should not be used, because the data are representational instead of quantitative.
C. A pie graph should not be used, because the data are qualitative instead of quantitative.
D. A pie graph is a good choice and is often used to display this kind of data.

REFERENCE: McWay, pp 201, 203
              Horton, pp 210–211
              Koch, pp 273–274
              Abdelhak, pp 382–383
              Johns, pp 537–538
              LaTour and Eichenwald-Maki, pp 446–448
              Shaw, pp 48–51, 57–63

57. You are trying to improve communications with your staff by posting graphs of significant statistics on the employee bulletin board. You recently calculated the percentage of time employees spend on each of six major tasks. Because you would like the employees to appreciate each task as a percentage of their whole day, you will post these figures using a
A. line graph.   C. scatter diagram.
B. bar graph.   D. pie graph.

REFERENCE: McWay, pp 201, 203
              Abdelhak, pp 382–385
              Horton, pp 207–216
              Koch, pp 264–274
              Johns, pp 537–541
              LaTour and Eichenwald-Maki, pp 446–449
              Shaw, pp 48–51, 57–63

58. The graph below can best be described as

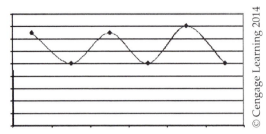

© Cengage Learning 2014

A. sequential.
B. multimodal.
C. substitutional.
D. erratic.

REFERENCE: Koch, pp 241–243
               Horton, pp 187–189

59. Looking at the data represented in the scatter diagram below, you would conclude that there is

Variable A

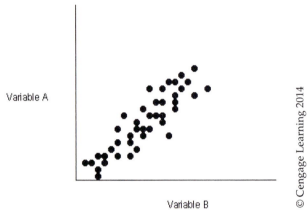

Variable B

© Cengage Learning 2014

A. no correlation between Variable A and Variable B.
B. a positive correlation between Variable A and Variable B.
C. a negative correlation between Variable A and Variable B.
D. a cause and effect relationship between Variable A and Variable B.

REFERENCE: McWay, pp 203–204
               LaTour and Eichenwald-Maki, pp 449, 451–452
               Horton, pp 216–219
               Johns, p 632

60. The data displayed in the histogram below could best be described as

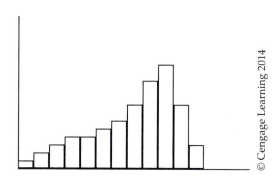

© Cengage Learning 2014

    A. negatively skewed.
    B. positively skewed.
    C. evenly distributed.
    D. normally distributed.

REFERENCE: Horton, pp 187–189
                  Koch, pp 238–240
                  Johns, p 634
                  LaTour and Eichenwald-Maki, pp 457–458
                  Shaw, pp 56–58

61. You want to construct a data display for a frequency distribution. You will use a
    A. frequency polygon or histogram.
    B. frequency polygon or bar chart.
    C. line graph or histogram.
    D. line graph or bar chart.

REFERENCE: McWay, p 203
                  Horton, pp 207–212
                  Abdelhak, pp 382–385
                  LaTour and Eichenwald-Maki, pp 446–449
                  Johns, pp 537–545
                  Shaw, pp 48–51, 57–63

62. Look at the graph below. It is an example of a

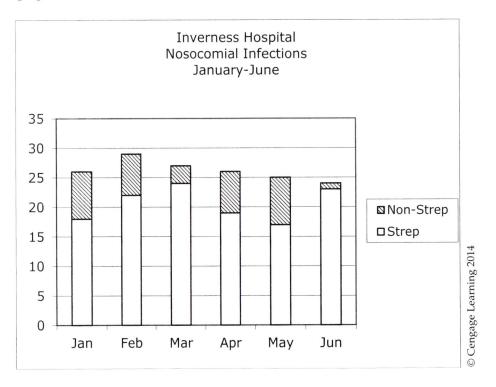

A. stacked bar chart; it is well constructed.
B. histogram; it is well constructed.
C. comparison bar chart; it is not well constructed.
D. frequency polygon; it is not well constructed.

REFERENCE: McWay, p 201
              Koch, pp 264–285
              Abdelhak, pp 382–385
              Johns, pp 537–545

Use the historical graph below to answer questions 63 and 64.

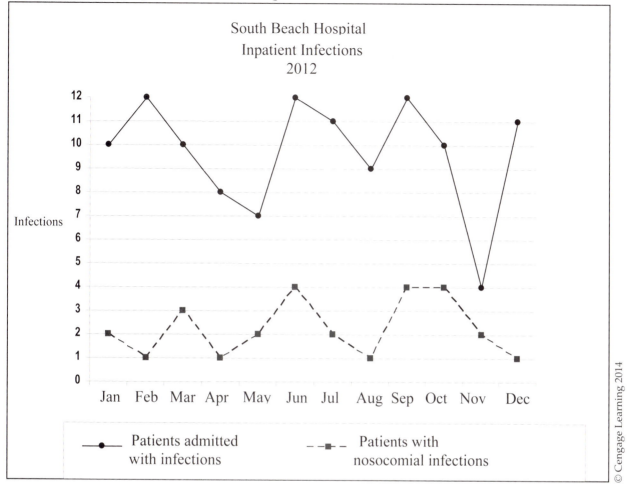

South Beach Hospital
Inpatient Infections
2012

63. The total number of infections at South Beach Hospital during the first quarter (January–March) 2012 was
   A. 6.
   B. 12.
   C. 22.
   D. 38.

REFERENCE: McWay, pp 203, 205
               Abdelhak, pp 382–385
               Koch, pp 274–278
               Johns, pp 540–543
               Horton, pp 212–214
               LaTour and Eichenwald-Maki, pp 448–451

64. Look again at the graph you used for the last question. From this graph, you can assume that more people
   A. were admitted to the facility with infections than without infections.
   B. were admitted to the facility with infections than is typical for U.S. hospitals.
   C. were admitted to the facility with infections than acquired infections in the hospital.
   D. acquired infections in the hospital than were admitted with infections.

REFERENCE: McWay, pp 203, 205
               Abdelhak, pp 382–385
               Koch, pp 274–278
               Horton, pp 212–214

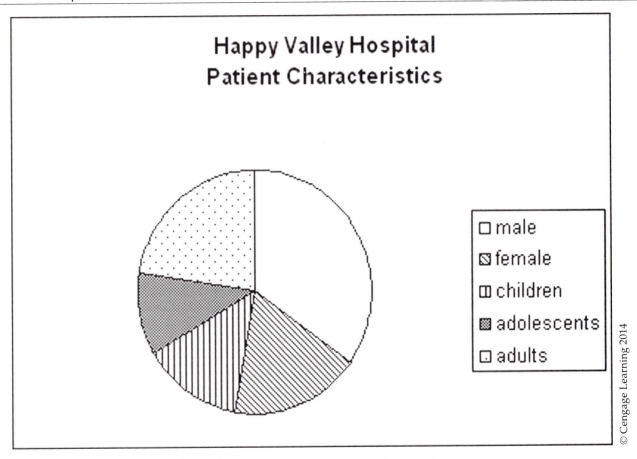

Happy Valley Hospital Patient Characteristics

Legend:
- □ male
- ⊠ female
- ⊞ children
- ▨ adolescents
- ⊡ adults

65. What is the biggest problem with the pie graph displayed above?
    A. There is not enough variation in the patterns to clearly distinguish between females and children.
    B. The total males and females do not equal the total children, adolescents, and adults.
    C. There are no definitions for children, adolescents, and adults.
    D. There is more than one variable displayed on the chart.

REFERENCE: McWay, pp 201–203
                     Horton, pp 210–211
                     Koch, pp 273–274
                     LaTour and Eichenwald-Maki, pp 446, 448

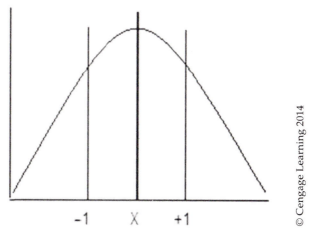

66. The chart above shows a normal distribution. What percentage of the cases fall within the two lines showing the standard distribution between −1 and +1 on either side of the mean?
   A. 68%
   B. 75%
   C. 95%
   D. 99%

REFERENCE: Horton, pp 184–186
              Koch, pp 238–243
              LaTour and Eichenwald-Maki, pp 457–458
              Shaw, pp 54–56

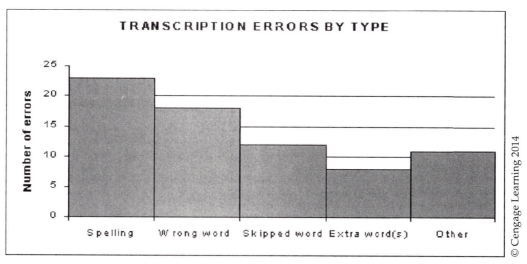

67. A transcription supervisor collected the data displayed above. What kind of data display is it? And how many errors are attributed to skipped words?
   A. This is a Pareto diagram; twelve (12) errors were due to skipped words.
   B. This is a bar chart; eighteen (18) errors were due to skipped words.
   C. This is a Pareto diagram; eighteen (18) errors were due to skipped words.
   D. This is a bar chart; twelve (12) errors were due to skipped words.

REFERENCE: McWay, pp 148–149, 274
              LaTour and Eichenwald-Maki, p 705
              Abdelhak, pp 382–385
              Shaw, pp 48–51, 57–63

68. A fetal death occurring during the 21st week of pregnancy, weighing 1,000 g is considered to be a(n)
    A. early fetal death.
    B. preterm neonate.
    C. intermediate fetal death.
    D. late fetal death.

REFERENCE: Johns, p 558
                      LaTour and Eichenwald-Maki, pp 431–432
                      Horton, p 88
                      Koch, pp 142–144

Section IV—Research, Financial Statistics, Etc.

You will use your statistics skills for a number of HIM functions. As usual, you must be prepared for that nebulous category we call "other." For these questions, use your basic problem-solving skills along with the terminology you learned in your statistics class. Many of these questions deal primarily with research and budgeting matters, so they are typically considered more appropriate for the RHIA than the RHIT. The RHIA questions are listed last and are so labeled.

69. Harry H. Potter was admitted to your hospital to receive a second round of chemotherapy for an invasive tumor. Four days after admission, Harry complained of a sore throat and developed a fever. Harry's throat culture was positive for strep. His strep throat will be
    A. added to the denominator of the hospital's nosocomial infection rate.
    B. added to the numerator of the hospital's community-acquired infection rate.
    C. considered separately because Harry H. Potter is immune suppressed from chemotherapy.
    D. added to the numerator of the hospital's nosocomial infection rate.

REFERENCE: McWay, p 199
               Abdelhak, pp 376–378
               Koch, p 179
               Johns, pp 564–565
               LaTour and Eichenwald-Maki, pp 434–435
               Horton, pp 116–117

70. Twelve new cases of a certain disease occurred during the month of August. If 4,000 persons were at risk during August, then the
    A. prevalence was 3 per 1,000 persons.
    B. prevalence was 6 per 1,000 persons.
    C. incidence was 3 per 1,000 persons.
    D. incidence was 6 per 1,000 persons.

REFERENCE: McWay, pp 198–199
               Abdelhak, pp 376–378
               Johns, pp 576, 1161
               Layman and Watzlaf, pp 131–132, 138
               Koch, p 205
               LaTour and Eichenwald-Maki, pp 442–443

71. The primary difference between an experimental (randomized) clinical trial and other observational study designs in epidemiology is that in an experimental trial, the
    A. study is prospective.
    B. investigator determines who is and who is not exposed.
    C. study is case controlled.
    D. study and control maps are selected on the basis of exposure to the suspected causal factor.

REFERENCE: Abdelhak, pp 424–427
               McWay, pp 243–244
               Shi, pp 166–167, 182–186
               Horton, pp 232–234
               Layman and Watzlaf, pp 44–46, 48–49

72. The ability to obtain the same results from different studies using different methodologies and different populations is
    A. reliability.
    B. validity.
    C. confidence.
    D. specificity.

REFERENCE: McWay, p 231
               Shi, pp 291, 297–300
               Horton, pp 232–233
               Abdelhak, pp 410–412
               LaTour and Eichenwald-Maki, pp 486–487
               Layman and Watzlaf, pp 221–222

73. You have been conducting productivity studies on your coders and find that 20% of their time is devoted to querying physicians about missing or unclear diagnoses. Assuming your coders work a 7-hour day, how many minutes do they spend per day querying physicians?
    A. 21
    B. 56
    C. 84
    D. 140

REFERENCE: Koch, pp 56–57
               Horton, pp 147–148

Use these data to calculate answers to questions 74 and 75.

Venice Bay Health Center collected the data displayed below concerning its four highest volume MS-DRGs.

MS-DRG A		MS-DRG B		MS-DRG C		MS-DRG D	
CMS WEIGHT	NUMBER PATIENTS WITH THIS MS-DRG	CMS WEIGHT	NUMBER PATIENTS WITH THIS MS-DRG	CMS WEIGHT	NUMBER PATIENTS WITH THIS MS-DRG	CMS WEIGHT	NUMBER PATIENTS WITH THIS MS-DRG
2.023	323	0.987	489	1.925	402	1.243	386

74. The MS-DRG that generated the most revenue for Venice Bay Health Center is
A. MS-DRG A.
B. MS-DRG B.
C. MS-DRG C.
D. MS-DRG D.

REFERENCE: McWay, pp 130–132, 135–136, 209, 357
Johns, p 324
Horton, pp 158–159

75. CMS has increased the weight for MS-DRG A by 14%, increased the weight for MS-DRG B by 20%, and decreased the weight for MS-DRG D by 10%. Given these new weights, which MS-DRG generated the most revenue for Venice Bay Health Center?
A. MS-DRG A
B. MS-DRG B
C. MS-DRG C
D. MS-DRG D

REFERENCE: Johns, p 324
Horton, pp 158–159

Use these data to answer questions 76 and 77.

Sea Side Clinic (SSC) provides episode of care service for four insurance companies. Data on services provided and reimbursement received are provided below.

COMPANY	UNITS OF SERVICE A	REIMBURSEMENT FOR SERVICE A	UNITS OF SERVICE B	REIMBURSEMENT FOR SERVICE B	TOTAL REIMBURSEMENT
Lifecare	259	31,196.55	812	163,577.40	194,773.95
Get Well	786	100,859.52	465	96,929.25	197,788.77
SureHealth	462	54,631.50	509	107,093.60	161,725.10
Be Healthy	219	26,991.75	417	89,425.65	116,417.40

76. It would be most profitable for Sea Side Clinic to increase episode of care service with
    A. Lifecare.
    B. Get Well.
    C. SureHealth.
    D. BeHealthy.

REFERENCE: Koch, pp 234–237
               Johns, pp 526–532
               Horton, pp 175–180
               LaTour and Eichenwald-Maki, pp 454–456

77. The most profitable insurance company for the units of services Sea Side Clinic performs is
    A. service A with Lifecare.
    B. service B with GetWell.
    C. service A with SureHealth.
    D. service B with BeHealthy.

REFERENCE: Koch, pp 234–237
               Johns, pp 529–532
               Horton, pp 175–180
               LaTour and Eichenwald-Maki, pp 454–456

Use these statistics to calculate answers to questions 78 and 79.

The physicians at Sunset Shore Clinic reported the following statistics last Tuesday.

PHYSICIAN	SERVICE A	SERVICE B	SERVICE C
Truba	10	18	14
Wooley	14	22	9
Howe	18	5	6
Masters	12	20	7

78. The physician who performed the highest number of services overall last Tuesday was Doctor
    A. Truba.
    B. Wooley.
    C. Howe.
    D. Masters.

REFERENCE: Koch, pp 56–57
               Horton, pp 147–148

79. It takes twice as long to perform Service C, so the doctors decided Service C should count as two services for the purpose of calculating workload. If Service C counts twice as much as Service A or Service B, then the physician who provided the most services was Doctor
    A. Truba.
    B. Wooley.
    C. Howe.
    D. Masters.

REFERENCE: Koch, pp 56–57
               Horton, pp 147–148

The following questions begin advanced competencies.

80. Your facility conducted a study of patient satisfaction, but you question the reliability of the questionnaire you used. The high degree of patient satisfaction expressed on the questionnaire just does not match the large number of complaints you have been receiving. You decide to try switching to an investigative strategy that will give you an immediate opportunity to review patient responses and correct errors. You have decided to use

A. samples.
B. interviews.
C. observations.
D. questionnaires.

REFERENCE: LaTour and Eichenwald-Maki, pp 477–479
Horton, pp 232–233
Shaw, pp 91–103

The next five questions are based on this study and the data collected for it.

The American Health Information Management Association conducted a study on job stress and job satisfaction in HIM professionals with more than 5 years of experience. The data they collected are displayed below.

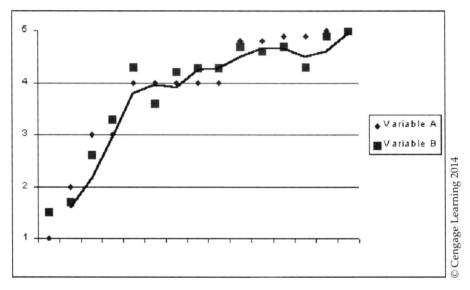

81. The researchers at AHIMA started by assuming there was no relationship between job stress and job satisfaction. This statement is generally called the

A. study statement.
B. false assumption.
C. null hypothesis.
D. correlation statement.

REFERENCE: McWay, p 195
Abdelhak, pp 389–391
Horton, pp 231–232
Layman and Watzlaf, pp 28–34
LaTour and Eichenwald-Maki, pp 484–486

82. Based on the data displayed in the graph AHIMA created,
    A. you can assume there is a positive relationship between variable A and variable B.
    B. you can assume there is a negative relationship between variable A and variable B.
    C. you can assume there is a causal relationship between variable A and variable B.
    D. you cannot make any assumptions without additional data.

REFERENCE: LaTour and Eichenwald-Maki, pp 449, 451–452
               Horton, pp 216–219
               Johns, p 632
               McWay, pp 203–204
               Layman and Watzlaf, pp 28–31
               Koch, pp 238–240

Very Dissatisfied	Somewhat Dissatisfied	Neutral	Somewhat Satisfied	Very Satisfied
1	2	3	4	5

83. The researchers at AHIMA who had professionals with 5 or more years' HIM experience rate their stress on a scale of 1–5, as shown in the chart above. Both job satisfaction and job stress are continuous variables. If the AHIMA researchers want to assess both the direction and the degree of the relationship between these two continuous variables, they may choose to compute the
    A. variable correlation coefficient.
    B. Pearson correlation coefficient.
    C. continuous correlation coefficient.
    D. Danbury correlation coefficient.

REFERENCE: McWay, pp 208–209
               Shi, pp 366–367
               Layman and Watzlaf, pp 28–31
               Abdelhak, p 393

84. There were some HIM professionals who refused to participate in a job stress/job satisfaction study. This is of great concern to the AHIMA researchers, who worry about the introduction of
    A. recall bias.   C. interviewer bias.
    B. selection bias.   D. nonresponse bias.

REFERENCE: Abdelhak, pp 412–414
               LaTour and Eichenwald-Maki, pp 492–493
               Shi, p 382
               Layman and Watzlaf, pp 228, 230

85. A researcher has repeated the same study 10 times. Each time the study is repeated, the p value decreases. As the p value approaches zero, the
    A. size of the sample increases.
    B. value of the study decreases.
    C. chance that the results are due to a sampling error decreases.
    D. chance that the results are due to a sampling error increases.

REFERENCE: Abdelhak, pp 389–391
               Horton, pp 250–253
               LaTour and Eichenwald-Maki, pp 485–486

86. You and your colleague are designing a study to try to determine the ideal mean cost for a discretionary service. You will market your service to a very large population. Your colleague thinks you will get the best data if you take lots of small samples. You think the data will be more reliable if you take one or two very large samples.
    A. Your colleague is right—the mean of multiple samples will yield more reliable results.
    B. You are right—the means of a few large samples will yield more reliable results.
    C. You are equally correct—there is little difference in the reliability of these sampling methods.
    D. You are equally wrong—unless you use stratified sampling, you cannot expect reliable results.

REFERENCE: Abdelhak, pp 396–398
                LaTour and Eichenwald-Maki, p 491
                Horton, pp 241–242
                Shi, pp 279–280, 282–284
                Layman and Watzlaf, pp 68–69, 237–238

87. You are conducting a patient satisfaction survey in your outpatient clinic using interviewers who administer a questionnaire. Because you typically see about 300 people per day in the clinic, you decide to have the interviewers administer the questionnaire on every tenth patient. You are using
    A. systematic sampling.   C. variable sampling.
    B. stratified sampling.   D. convenience sampling.

REFERENCE: Abdelhak, pp 396–398
                Horton, pp 242–246
                LaTour and Eichenwald-Maki, pp 490–491
                Shi, pp 272–274
                Layman and Watzlaf, pp 68, 235–238

88. The people of Treasure Island Beach have been struck with a rash that seems to be infecting almost everyone in town. The staff of the hospital is working to design a study of this mysterious disease. They decide to do a cross-sectional study because cross-sectional or prevalence studies are known for
    A. quickly identifying cause and effect relationships that can serve as a basis for treatment.
    B. concurrently describing characteristics and health outcomes at one specific point in time.
    C. providing the information necessary to test for the most effective treatment of an illness or condition.
    D. supplying entire populations with therapeutic interventions on an epidemiologically sound basis.

REFERENCE: Abdelhak, pp 413–414
                LaTour and Eichenwald-Maki, p 476
                Layman and Watzlaf, pp 129–133
                Koch, p 205
                McWay, pp 198–199
                Shi, p 61

89. You are planning a prospective study to try to prove a cause and effect relationship between dipping snuff and throat cancer. First, you identify subjects who regularly dip snuff and who are free of any signs of throat cancer. Next, you need to identify subjects who
    A. dip snuff regularly and who currently have throat cancer.
    B. dip snuff regularly and who currently have significant signs of throat cancer.
    C. do not dip snuff and who currently have significant signs of throat cancer.
    D. do not dip snuff and who are free of any signs of throat cancer.

REFERENCE: Abdelhak, pp 420–423
               LaTour and Eichenwald-Maki, p 476
               McWay, p 227
               Shi, pp 15–16, 371–374
               Layman and Watzlaf, pp 130–131, 134, 138–139

90. Your administrator is concerned about the snuff study (see question 88). The administrator would like to consider using a case–control study model rather than the prospective one you are planning. One of the biggest reasons the administrator is promoting the case–control model is because case–control is
    A. more likely to be free of design errors than a prospective study.
    B. the best way to analytically test the hypothesis of cause and effect.
    C. more likely to decrease recall bias errors than prospective studies.
    D. less expensive than prospective studies because it uses existing records.

REFERENCE: Abdelhak, pp 420–422
               LaTour and Eichenwald-Maki, p 476
               McWay, p 228

91. You point out to your administrator that the study model generally accepted to be the best method to determine the magnitude of risk in the population with the characteristic or suspected risk factor is the
    A. descriptive study design.   C. prospective study design.
    B. analytic study design.   D. case–control study design.

REFERENCE: Abdelhak, pp 420–426
               LaTour and Eichenwald-Maki, p 476
               McWay, p 227
               Layman and Watzlaf, pp 130–131, 134, 138–139

92. Investigator A claims that his results are statistically significant at the 10% level. Investigator B argues that significance should be announced only if the results are statistically significant at the 5% level. From this we can conclude that
    A. if investigator A has significant results at the 10% level, they will never be significant at the 5% level.
    B. it will be more difficult for investigator A to reject statistical null hypotheses if he always works at the 10% level compared with investigator B who works at the 5% level.
    C. if investigator A has significant results at the 10% level, they will also be significant at the 5% level.
    D. it will be less difficult for investigator A to reject statistical null hypotheses if he always works at the 10% level compared with investigator B who works at the 5% level.

REFERENCE: Abdelhak, pp 389–391
               McWay, p 95
               Shi, p 371
               LaTour and Eichenwald-Maki, pp 484–486
               Layman and Watzlaf, p 210

93. John Parker surveyed members of AHIMA's student COP regarding the relationship between clinical experiences and job opportunities. All respondents were seniors in HIA programs and each one expected to graduate and take the national exam within the next 6 months. Fifteen of the eighteen respondents indicated that at least one clinical rotation had resulted in a job offer. Based on this information, Parker expects to be offered a job during senior clinical rotations. John is basing this expectation on
    A. scientific inquiry.   C. inductive reasoning.
    B. empiricism.   D. deductive reasoning.

REFERENCE: LaTour and Eichenwald-Maki, pp 464–465
               Shi, pp 6, 35
               McWay, p 190

Use the formula below as a resource to answer questions 94 and 95.

FORMULA FOR CALCULATING SAMPLE SIZE

$$n = \frac{Np\,(1-p)}{(N-1)\,\frac{(B^2)}{4} + (p)\,(1-p)}$$

94. If population size (N) = 1,200 and the proportion of subjects needed (p) = 0.5 and the acceptable amount of error (B) = 0.05, then sample size (n) =
    A. 200.   C. 400.
    B. 300.   D. 600.

REFERENCE: LaTour and Eichenwald-Maki, pp 491–492
               Abdelhak, pp 396–398
               Shi, pp 279–280, 282–283
               Layman and Watzlaf, p 210

95. After the researchers see the number of subjects they will have to interview, they reexamine their criteria. The researchers could decrease the number of subjects while having the least impact on the reliability of the study by
    A. increasing p and decreasing B.
    B. increasing p or decreasing B.
    C. decreasing p and increasing B.
    D. decreasing p or increasing B.

REFERENCE:　　LaTour and Eichenwald-Maki, pp 484–486
　　　　　　　　Abdelhak, pp 396–398
　　　　　　　　Shi, pp 279–280, 282–283
　　　　　　　　Layman and Watzlaf, p 210

96. Which statistical analysis would be the best technique to use on the following problem?

> A study compared the effects of retesting on the scores of students who failed a writing test. Students who did not pass on their first attempt were allowed to retest. Results showed that students had higher mean scores at retest whether they attended additional training before retesting or not.

    A. descriptive stats
    B. ANOVA
    C. regression
    D. T test

REFERENCE:　　Abdelhak, pp 389–394
　　　　　　　　Horton, pp 250–257
　　　　　　　　McWay, pp 195–196

97. The name given to the error committed when the null hypothesis is rejected and it is actually true is
    A. type II error.
    B. selection bias.
    C. type I error.
    D. alternative hypothesis.

REFERENCE:　　Abdelhak, pp 389–391
　　　　　　　　McWay, p 212
　　　　　　　　LaTour and Eichenwald-Maki, p 485

98. The major purpose of random assignment in a clinical trial is to
   A. reduce selection bias in allocation of treatment.
   B. help ensure that study subjects are representative of the general population.
   C. facilitate double-blinding.
   D. ensure that the study groups are comparable on baseline characteristics.

REFERENCE: Abdelhak, pp 422–426
               LaTour and Eichenwald-Maki, pp 484, 577
               McWay, p 227
               Shi, pp 155–157

99. In statistics, the notation "ΣXY" means
   A. summed all the values of the X variable and then multiplied this result times the values of the Y variable.
   B. summed all the values of the X variable, all the values of the Y variable, then multiplied all of these results.
   C. multiplied each pair of the X and Y scores, then summed their values.
   D. variation of the X and Y variable is multiplied then squared.

REFERENCE: Horton, p 183
               Koch, p 234
               Johns, p 530
               LaTour and Eichenwald-Maki, p 455

100. A major disadvantage of cross-sectional studies is that
   A. the time sequence of exposure and disease is usually not known.
   B. they are usually more expensive and can take a long time to complete.
   C. prevalence rates cannot be calculated.
   D. they cannot provide information on both exposure and disease status in the same individual.

REFERENCE: Abdelhak, pp 313–315
               LaTour and Eichenwald-Maki, p 476
               Shi, pp 75, 131, 191
               Layman and Watzlaf, p 132

101. A study found that liver cancer rates per 100,000 males among cigarette smokers and nonsmokers in a major U.S. city were 48.0 and 25.4, respectively. The relative risk of developing liver cancer for male smokers compared to nonsmokers is

A. 1.89.   C. 22.6.
B. 15.6.   D. 48.0.

REFERENCE: Abdelhak, pp 420–422
                  LaTour and Eichenwald-Maki, p 578
                  McWay, p 241
                  Shi, pp 371–373
                  Layman and Watzlaf, p 138

102. The standard deviation of a particular set of measures was found to be 20.00. The sample variance would then be:

A. 20
B. 5
C. 400
D. 10

REFERENCE: LaTour and Eichenwald-Maki, p 457
                  Koch, pp 246–247
                  Shi, p 361
                  Horton, pp 182–185

103. If a constant is added to all measurements within a sample

A. the mean remains the same.
B. the standard deviation remains the same.
C. both A and B are true.
D. both A and B are false.

REFERENCE: Horton, pp 182–185
                  Koch, pp 246–247
                  LaTour and Eichenwald-Maki, p 457

104. Measurements within sample A are assumed to be more variable than measurements within sample B when

A. sample A and sample B have the same mean.
B. individuals within sample A are more alike than individuals within sample B.
C. individuals within sample A differ more from one another than individuals within sample B.
D. sample A and sample B have the same standard deviation.

REFERENCE: Horton, pp 182–185
                  Koch, pp 246–247
                  LaTour and Eichenwald-Maki, p 457

105. _____ refers to the flatness or peakedness of one distribution in relation to another distribution.
    A. Skewness
    B. Correlation
    C. Central tendency
    D. Kurtosis

REFERENCE: Horton, pp 187–189
                Koch, pp 238–243
                LaTour and Eichenwald-Maki, pp 457–458

106. Given a positively skewed frequency distribution
    A. the frequencies are identical between the mean, median, and mode.
    B. larger frequencies are concentrated at the low end of the variable.
    C. larger frequencies are concentrated at the high end of the variable.
    D. largest frequencies occur at both low and high ends of the variable.

REFERENCE: Horton, pp 187–189
                Koch, pp 238–243
                LaTour and Eichenwald-Maki, pp 457–458

Answer Key for Health Statistics and Research

ANSWER   EXPLANATION

1.   C $(27 \times 100) / 1,652 = 1.6\%$

2.   D   Calculate the answer as follows:

PHYSICIAN NAME	NUMBER OF HOURS WORKED	NUMBER OF PATIENTS SEEN	NUMBER OF PATIENTS SEEN PER HOUR WORKED
Robinson	32	185	185/32 = 5.78
Beasley	30	161	161/30 = 5.37
Hiltz	35	200	200/35 = 5.71
Wolf	26	157	157/26 = 6.04

3.   A   3,545 requested records $\times$ 100 / 150,000 total records = 354,500/150,000 = 2.36 = 2.4%.

4.   D

5.   A   Calculations: 95% of the observations fall within two standard deviations of the mean, so the cost of a lunch at Bon Appetite will be between $6.50
$[8 - (2 \times 0.75)]$ and $9.50 $[8 + (2 \times 0.75)]$.
         Lunch at Mario's will be between $5.50 $[7.5 - (2 \times 1)]$ and $9.50 $[7.5 + (2 \times 1)]$.
         Lunch at Au Courant will cost too much $[\$9 + (2 \times 1.25) = \$11.50]$.
         As will the Windy City Grill $[\$7.50 (2 \times 1.5) = \$10.50]$.

6.   B

7.   A

8.   C   Calculations:

	Records under Review	Same Code on Self-Coding Review	Intrarater Reliability Percentage	Same Code on Peer-Coding Review	Interrater Reliability Percentage	Mean Reliability Percentage
Coder A	28	22	78.57	20	71.43	75.00
Coder B	18	16	88.89	16	88.89	88.89
Coder C	45	42	93.33	43	95.56	94.44
Coder D	17	15	88.24	16	94.12	91.18

9   D

10.   C

11.   D

12.   B

13.   B   Calculation: $5 + 9 + 8 + 12 + 6 + 7 + 5 + 10 + 7 + 9 + 11 = 89/11 = 8.09$

14.   B   Calculate the mean time each physician spent with patients as follows:

PHYSICIAN	TIMES WITH PATIENTS	AVERAGE (MEAN) TIME WITH PATIENTS
Beasley	8, 6, 7	7
Robinson	5, 9, 9	7.7
Baumstark	10, 7	8.5
Wolf	12, 5, 11	9.3

15.   A

16.   A

Answer Key for Health Statistics and Research

ANSWER   EXPLANATION

17. C

18. A

19. B

20 C

21. D

22. D

23. B

24. B $40 + 10 + 5 + 2 = 57$

25. D $67 + 2 = 69$ admissions/discharges same day

(Transfers to other facilities and deaths are forms of discharge.)

26. A $(75,860 + 7,100) / 365 = 227$

(Note: Average daily census includes adult and pediatrics, but NOT newborns.)

27. B

28. B   The day of admission is counted as an inpatient service day, but the day of discharge is not.

29. A $1/24 – 31 = 8$ days $+ 2/1$ through $2/8 = 8$ days so $8 + 8 = 16$
(Count the day of admission but not discharge.)

30. B $(12,345 \times 100) / (500 \times 28) = 88.2\%$

31. B $9,457$ discharge days$/1,351$ discharges $= 7$ days

(Count the day of admission but not discharge.)

32. D   Only two answers, A and D, are correctly calculated. Should you choose to include the unusually long LOS, you should make a note to avoid confusing readers, which makes the answer "A" a poor choice. Should you choose to eliminate the potentially confusing LOS, you must subtract both the patient from the total discharges and the discharge days from the total discharge days.

33. B $$\frac{(28,690 + 27,400 + 19,250) \times 100}{(151 \times 200) + (137 \times 250) + (77 \times 275)} = 88.0 = 88\%$$

34. C   Use the direct method, bed turnover.
$16,570$ adult and peds discharges$/200$ adult and peds beds $= 82.85 = 82.9\%$

35. A 200 beds $\times 365$ days in a nonleap year $= 73,000$ (Note: Bassinets are excluded.)

36. C $$\frac{(5 \times 100)}{(225 + 5)} = 2.2\%$$

37. C $50 + (3$ sets of twins $\times 2$ births per set$) = 56$ births

38. B   Multiple births are one delivery; fetal deaths are counted as deliveries
$50 + 3 + 1 + 1 = 55$

39. D

40. D

41. C   Calculations: 361 total inpatient deaths $\times 100/6614$ total discharges $= 5.45 = 5.5\%$
Fetal deaths and outpatient deaths are not included in this calculation.

Answer Key for Health Statistics and Research

ANSWER   EXPLANATION

42. B   Calculations:

$$\frac{(108\ \text{total inpatient deaths} > 48\ \text{hours}) \times 100}{(6{,}614\ \text{total discharges} - 253\ \text{deaths} <48\ \text{hours})} = \frac{10800}{6{,}361} = 1.697 = 1.7\%$$

43. B   48 – 38 deaths over 48 hours = 10 deaths less than 48 hours. $\dfrac{(48 - 10)\ (100)}{(1{,}382 - 10)}$

44. B

45. B

46. C   LOS would increase through the year and drop when patient is discharged.

47. A $\dfrac{(72\ \text{intermediate and late fetal deaths} \times 100)}{(980\ \text{births} + 72\ \text{intermediate and late fetal deaths})} = \dfrac{7{,}200}{1{,}052} = 6.8\%$

48. C $(3{,}699 \times 100) / 20{,}932 = 17.7\%$

49. A

50. C

51. D

52. C

53. B

54. C

55. A

56. A

57. D

58. B

59. B

60. A

61. A

62. A

63. D

64. C

65. D

66. A

67. A

68. D

69. D

70. C

71. B

72. A

73. C   7 hours per day × 60 minutes per hour = 420 minutes per day. 20% of 420 = 84

Answer Key for Health Statistics and Research

ANSWER   EXPLANATION

74. C   Calculations:
- MS-DRG A = 2.023 × 323 = 653.43
- MS-DRG B = 0.987 × 489 = 482.64
- MS-DRG C = 1.925 × 402 = 773.85
- MS-DRG D = 1.243 × 386 = 479.80

75. C   Calculations:
- MS-DRG A = 2.023 × 0.14 = 0.283;   0.283 + 2.023 = 2.306 × 323 = 744.84
- MS-DRG B = 0.987 × 0.20 = 0.197;   0.987 + 0.197 = 1.184 × 489 = 578.98
- MS-DRG C = 1.925 × 402 = 773.85
- MS-DRG D = 1.243 × 0.10 = 0.124;   1.243 − 0.124 = 1.119 × 386 = 431.93

76. D   Arrive at the answer by calculating the reimbursement per unit for each service and averaging those answers, as shown below.

INSURANCE COMPANY	UNITS OF SERVICE A	REIMBURSE-MENT FOR SERVICE A	REIMBURSE-MENT PER UNIT FOR SERVICE A	UNITS OF SERVICE B	REIMBURSE-MENT FOR SERVICE B	REIMBURSE-MENT PER UNIT FOR SERVICE B	TOTAL REIMBURSE MENT	AVERAGE REIMBURSE-MENT PER UNIT OF SERVICE
Lifecare	259	31,196.55	120.45	812	163,577.40	201.45	194,773.95	160.95
Get-Well	786	100,859.52	128.32	465	96,929.25	208.45	197,788.77	168.39
SureHealth	462	54,631.50	118.25	509	107,093.60	210.40	161,725.10	164.33
Be-Healthy	219	26,991.75	123.25	417	89,425.65	214.45	116,417.40	168.85

77. D   Reference the table above.

78. B   Calculate by adding total services.

PHYSICIAN	SERVICE A	SERVICE B	SERVICE C	TOTAL SERVICES
Truba	10	22	10	42
Wooley	14	22	9	45
Howe	18	5	6	29
Masters	12	20	7	39

79. A   Double Service C in the table above.

80. B

81. C

82. A

83. C

84. D

85. C

86. B

87. A

88. B

89. D

90. D

91. C

Answer Key for Health Statistics and Research

ANSWER   EXPLANATION

92. B

93. C

94. B

$$n = \frac{(1200)\,(0.5)\,(1-0.5)}{(1200-1)\,\dfrac{(0.05^2)}{4} + (0.5)\,(1-0.5)}.$$

$$n = \frac{300}{(1199)\,(0.000625) + 0.25}.$$

$$n = \frac{300}{0.749 + 0.25} = \frac{300}{1} = 300$$

95. D

96. D

97. C

98. A

99. C

100. A

101. A   RR = risk exposed divided by risk not exposed = 48 divided by 25.4 = 1.89

102. C

103. B

104. C

105. D

106. B

REFERENCES

Abdelhak, M., Grostick, S., Hanken, M. A., & Jacobs, E. (Eds.). (2011). *Health information: Management of a strategic resource* (4th ed.). St. Louis, MO: Saunders Elsevier.

Horton, L. (2012). *Calculating and reporting health care statistics* (4th ed.). Chicago: American Health Information Management Association (AHIMA).

Johns, M. L. (2010). *Health information management technology: An applied approach* (3rd ed.). Chicago: American Health Information Management Association (AHIMA).

Koch, G. (2008). *Basic allied health statistics and analysis* (3rd ed.). Clifton Park, NY: Delmar Cengage Learning.

LaTour, K., & Eichenwald-Maki, S. (2010). *Health information management: Concepts, principles, and practice* (3rd ed.). Chicago: American Health Information Management Association (AHIMA).

Layman, E. J., & Watzlaf, V. J. (2009). *Health informatics research methods, principles and practice.* Chicago: American Health Information Management Association (AHIMA).

McWay, D. C. (2008). *Today's health information management: An integrated approach.* Clifton Park, NY: Delmar Cengage Learning.

Shaw, P., Elliot, C., Isaacson, P., & Murphy, E. (2012). *Quality and performance improvement in health care* (5th ed.). Chicago: American Health Information Management Association (AHIMA).

Shi, L. (2008). *Health services research methods* (2nd ed.). Clifton Park, NY: Delmar Cengage Learning.

Health Statistics and Research Competency Domains

COMPETENCIES FOR HEALTH STATISTICS AND RESEARCH							
Question		RHIA Domain Competencies					
	1	2	3	4	5	6	
1–106		X					

COMPETENCIES FOR HEALTH STATISTICS AND RESEARCH								
Question	RHIT Domain Competencies							
	1	2	3	4	5	6	7	
1	X							
2	X							
3					X			
4					X			
5					X			
6	X							
7	X							
8	X							
9	X							
10					X			
11					X			
12	X							
13	X							
14	X							
15	X							
16	X							
17	X							
18	X							
19	X							
20	X							
21	X							
22	X							
23	X							
24	X							
25	X							
26	X							
27	X							
28	X							
29	X							
30	X							
31	X							
32	X							
33	X							
34	X							
35	X							
36	X							
37	X							
38	X							
39	X							
40	X							
41	X							
42	X							
43	X							
44					X			
45					X			

Question		RHIT Domain Competencies							
	1	2	3	4	5	6	7		
46					X				
47	X								
48	X								
49					X				
50	X								
51					X				
52					X				
53					X				
54					X				
55					X				
56					X				
57					X				
58					X				
59					X				
60					X				
61					X				
62					X				
63					X				
64					X				
65					X				
66					X				
67					X				
68	X								
69					X				
70					X				
71					X				
72					X				
73		X							
74		X							
75		X							
76		X							
77		X							
78		X							
79		X							

XIV. Quality and Performance Improvement

Charlotte McCuen, MS, RHIA

1. What process assists a health care facility in continuously looking at the ways that problems develop and seeking ways to prevent problems from happening in the future?
   A. risk management
   B. quality control
   C. utilization management
   D. performance improvement

REFERENCE: McWay, pp 143, 157
               Abdelhak, pp 438, 447, 460, 462
               Shaw, p 4
               Johns, pp 607, 610
               LaTour and Eichenwald-Maki, pp 518, 537

2. The current hospital policy time frame for authenticating verbal orders adheres to the CMS COP that requires the ordering physician, or another health care practitioner responsible for the care of the patient, to write orders according to hospital policy and authenticate
   A. based on federal and state law.
   B. within 48 hours if a state law time frame doesn't exist.
   C. within 24 hours if a state law time frame doesn't exist.
   D. both A and B

REFERENCE: Federal Register, pp 17–18
               AHIMA (1)

3. The Blood Usage Review Committee has a quality monitor established to review all blood transfusion reaction cases. The HIM Director will be working with the committee to identify and abstract patient outcome information for committee evaluation. What data should be collected?
   A. effects of transfusion reaction (e.g., rash, death, etc.)
   B. type and cross-match accuracy
   C. justification for the transfusion
   D. all of the above

REFERENCE: Shaw, pp 136–137
               LaTour and Eichenwald-Maki, p 545

4. As supervisor of the record completion function of the HIM department, you are asked for record completion statistics for specific physicians who are being evaluated for reappointment to the medical staff. Which of the following information elements would you report for each physician?
   A. physician education and training
   B. number of delinquent records
   C. state licensure expiration date
   D. prior physician malpractice claims history

REFERENCE: McWay, pp 21–22
               Abdelhak, pp 468–469
               Shaw, p 296
               LaTour and Eichenwald-Maki, pp 213, 544

5. The HIM department is asked to pull records for review by the Quality Improvement Organization (QIO). The QIO reviewers analyze records to ensure that health care services are
   A. rendered according to appropriate professional standards.
   B. medically necessary.
   C. performed in the most efficient, effective, and economical manner.
   D. all of the above.

REFERENCE: McWay, p 160
                      Abdelhak, pp 70–71, 438
                      Johns, pp 31–33
                      LaTour and Eichenwald-Maki, pp 17, 33–34, 526–527
                      Shaw, p 333

6. The coding supervisor is responsible for reviewing a random sample of each coder's work and reporting on the error rate for each coder. A check sheet is used to collect the number of charts reviewed, the number of errors for each coder, and the type of errors. What types of graphs or charts could be used to report the information gathered?
   A. bar graphs
   B. Pareto charts
   C. histograms
   D. all of the above

REFERENCE: McWay, pp 149–151
                      Abdelhak, pp 386, 452–453
                      Shaw, pp 47, 57–58
                      Johns, pp 450, 619–620
                      LaTour and Eichenwald-Maki, pp 704–706

7. Clinical privileges are granted to the physician for an interval specified in the medical staff by laws, but not longer than
   A. 6 months.
   B. 1 year.
   C. 2 years.
   D. 3 years.

REFERENCE: Shaw, p 296
                      LaTour and Eichenwald-Maki, p 544

8. The hospital implemented an electronic query system to allow more effective communication with physicians and other health practitioners to improve clinical documentation in the patient record. This program is known as
   A. core measure reporting.
   B. CDI.
   C. TR.
   D. evidence-based medicine.

REFERENCE: AHIMA (2)

9. Requirements for monitoring the quality and appropriateness of inpatient services to Medicare beneficiaries and federally funded patients are outlined in the
   A. Peer Review Improvement Act.
   B. QIO Scope of Work.
   C. Manual of National Healthcare Policy.
   D. National Practitioner Data Bank.

REFERENCE: McWay, p 160
                    Abdelhak, pp 70–71, 438
                    LaTour and Eichenwald-Maki, pp 523, 526
                    Shaw, p 333

10. What quality indicator would prove useful in tracking customer satisfaction in the correspondence/release of information function?
    A. the number of medical record personnel required to perform the function
    B. the amount of overtime necessary to stay current
    C. the number of charts pulled for correspondence requests
    D. the turnaround time from the date a request is received to the date the information is provided to the requester

REFERENCE: Shaw, pp 118–119
                    LaTour and Eichenwald-Maki, pp 689–690, 699

11. Most acute care facilities use this type of screening criteria for utilization review purposes to determine the need for inpatient services and justification for continued stay.
    A. severity of illness/intensity of service criteria (SI/IS)
    B. critical pathways
    C. Joint Commission defined and developed criteria
    D. Health Plan Employer Data & Information (HEDIS) measures

REFERENCE: Abdelhak, pp 463–465
                    Shaw, p 119
                    Johns, p 650
                    LaTour and Eichenwald-Maki, p 523

12. The process of comparing the outcomes of HIM abstracting functions at your facility with those of comparable departments of superior performance in other health care facilities to help improve accuracy and quality is referred to as
    A. focused review.   C. peer review.
    B. benchmarking.   D. occurrence screening.

REFERENCE: McWay, p 148
                    Abdelhak, pp 446–447, 613
                    Shaw, p 16
                    Johns, pp 579–580
                    LaTour and Eichenwald-Maki, pp 518, 691

13. With the passage of Medicare (Title XVIII of the Social Security Act) in 1965, which of the following functions became mandatory?
   A. quality improvement
   B. risk management
   C. quality assessment
   D. utilization review

REFERENCE: McWay, p 160
               Abdelhak, p 462
               Shaw, p xxv
               Johns, pp 650–651, 690
               LaTour and Eichenwald-Maki, pp 518, 547

14. An ophthalmologist has requested permission to perform specialized laser procedures within the hospital. His request is evaluated by the Credentials Committee through a process to determine the specific procedures and services this physician can perform. This is known as
   A. discharge planning.
   B. medical staff evaluation.
   C. delineation of privileges.
   D. reappointment.

REFERENCE: McWay, p 21
               Abdelhak, pp 23, 467
               Shaw, p 294
               LaTour and Eichenwald-Maki, pp 498–499, 861–862
               Johns, p 681

15. Major responsibilities of the Risk Manager generally include
   A. loss prevention and reduction.
   B. liability claims management.
   C. participating in safety and security programs.
   D. all of the above.

REFERENCE: McWay, p 158
               Abdelhak, pp 460–461
               Shaw, pp 189, 196–200
               LaTour and Eichenwald-Maki, pp 549–550
               Johns, p 654

16. Needlesticks, patient or employee falls, medication errors, or any event not consistent with routine patient care activities would require risk reporting documentation in the form of an
   A. operative report.
   B. emergency room report.
   C. incident report.
   D. insurance claim.

REFERENCE: McWay, pp 110, 158
               Abdelhak, p 653
               Shaw, p 189
               LaTour and Eichenwald-Maki, pp 301–302, 550
               Johns, p 653

17. The responsibility for performing quality monitoring and evaluation activities in a departmentalized hospital is delegated to the
    A. director of utilization management.
    B. chairman of the board of trustees.
    C. clinical chairpersons of medical staff committees or ancillary department directors.
    D. chief executive officer.

REFERENCE: Shaw, pp 318, 320
               LaTour and Eichenwald-Maki, pp 542, 552

18. What criterion is critical in selecting performance indicators for a health information management department?
    A. The indicators must include the most important aspects of performance.
    B. Indicators must correlate with Deming's 14 points.
    C. Identify at least 25 indicators that are reflective of all department functions.
    D. Select only indicators that reflect positively on the department.

REFERENCE: Shaw, pp 6–7
               LaTour and Eichenwald-Maki, pp 532–536
               Johns, pp 607–610

19. In the Act phase of the PDSA method, what step can assist in implementing change in a department?
    A. incorporating changes into a policy statement or new standard
    B. distributing new policies and procedures to people affected by the changes and explaining the rationale for the changes
    C. informing all affected parties about the changes
    D. all of the above

REFERENCE: McWay, pp 143, 153
               Abdelhak, p 447
               LaTour and Eichenwald-Maki, pp 701–702

20. What feature distinguishes the Nominal Group Technique (NGT) from brainstorming?
    A. NGT can be accomplished by mail.
    B. NGT uses a visual device like a flip chart to keep track of responses.
    C. NGT draws responses from a large group of people.
    D. NGT determines the importance of responses through a rating system.

REFERENCE: McWay, p 148
               Abdelhak, p 450
               Shaw, pp 20–21
               LaTour and Eichenwald-Maki, p 704
               Johns, pp 633–635

21. When the policy and procedures manual no longer reflect current practices, it creates a situation that becomes a risk management issue because
    A. supervisory time and effort will be wasted to correct the manual.
    B. training of new personnel will not be standardized.
    C. broad and permissive policy statements cannot commit the organization to a course of action.
    D. policy and procedures should represent the normal course of business.

REFERENCE: LaTour and Eichenwald-Maki, pp 549, 554–555
              Shaw, p 189

22. The medical malpractice crisis of the 1970s prompted the development of _____ in health care facilities.
    A. utilization management   C. quality improvement programs
    B. financial analysis programs   D. risk management

REFERENCE: McWay, p 158
              Abdelhak, p 461
              LaTour and Eichenwald-Maki, p 549
              Shaw, p 426

23. The best protection against injuries and ensuing financial liability is
    A. risk reporting.   C. occurrence screening.
    B. risk settlement.   D. risk prevention.

REFERENCE: McWay, p 158
              Abdelhak, p 461
              LaTour and Eichenwald-Maki, p 550
              Shaw, pp 186–188
              Johns, pp 652–653

24. The hospital Quality Department adopted the Lean Management quality model using JIT, which ensures required process items and resources are
    A. available at the right place and the right time.
    B. for the correct patient, using the correct procedure, at the correct site.
    C. always kept stocked in Central Processing.
    D. automatically restocked to maintain a surplus.

REFERENCE: Johns, p 1059
              LaTour and Eichenwald-Maki, pp 708–710

25. The Utilization Review Coordinator reviews inpatient records at regular intervals to justify necessity and appropriateness of care to warrant further hospitalization. Which of the following utilization review activities is being performed?
    A. admission review   C. retrospective review
    B. preadmission   D. continued stay review

REFERENCE: McWay, p 161
              Abdelhak, p 463
              LaTour and Eichenwald-Maki, p 547
              Johns, p 651
              Shaw, p 113

26. The Joint Commission recently surveyed an acute care hospital. The hospital just received the survey report and the accreditation decision. Which of the following categories should the hospital leaders address first?
    A. Requirements for Improvement
    B. Grid Elements
    C. Written Progress Reports
    D. Triennial Exception Rules

REFERENCE: Shaw, p 341

27. What feature is a trademark of an effective PI program?
    A. a one-time cure—all for a facility's problems
    B. an unmanageable project that is too expensive
    C. a cost-containment effort
    D. a continuous cycle of improvement projects over time

REFERENCE: McWay, p 157
              Shaw, pp 4–5
              LaTour and Eichenwald-Maki, pp 700–701
              Johns, p 610

28. What QI tool uses criteria to weigh different alternatives? This display would assist in viewing all relevant information at the same time.
    A. the PDSA method
    B. a decision matrix
    C. a flowchart
    D. a customer satisfaction survey

REFERENCE: Abdelhak, p 451
              LaTour and Eichenwald-Maki, p 636

29. The quality improvement (QI) plan for your hospital requires each coder maintain a minimum of 94.5% accuracy in coding. You manage the coding department, and the past year's average accuracy rating was 95.3%. The QI plan allows a standard deviation (SD) of ±2 against best practices of 97% accuracy. Did your coding staff's overall average meet within standard deviation range?
    A. Yes, within ±2 below SD
    B. Yes, within ±2 above SD
    C. No, because it is >±2 below SD
    D. No, because it is >±2 above SD

REFERENCE: Shaw, p 442
              Abdelhak, pp 448–449
              McWay, p 144

30. Surgical case review includes all the following EXCEPT
    A. determination of surgical justification based on clinical indication(s) in cases where no tissue has been removed.
    B. cases with elements missing in the preoperative anesthesia consultation.
    C. cases where there is a significant discrepancy between preoperative, postoperative, and pathological diagnoses.
    D. cases with serious surgical complications or surgical mortalities.

REFERENCE: LaTour and Eichenwald-Maki, p 545

31. Joint Commission requires that medical record review be performed to evaluate adequacy, accuracy, completeness, and quality of documentation
    A. annually.
    B. every 2 years.
    C. on an ongoing basis.
    D. quarterly.

REFERENCE: Shaw, pp 6–7
                LaTour and Eichenwald-Maki, p 544
                Johns, pp 458–460

32. Which of the following established legal liability for hospitals in 1965?
    A. P.L. 92–603
    B. Health Care Financing Administration (HCFA)
    C. Joint Commission on Accreditation of Health care Organizations (Joint Commission)
    D. *Darling v. Charleston Community Memorial Hospital*

REFERENCE: Abdelhak, p 506
                LaTour and Eichenwald-Maki, p 522

33. The Credentials Committee of the medical staff reviews information about applicants for staff membership and makes recommendations for staff appointment and reappointment to the
    A. QI/UR Committee.
    B. Medical Record Committee.
    C. facility's governing body.
    D. Director of Health Information Management Services.

REFERENCE: McWay, p 22
                Abdelhak, p 466
                Shaw, p 296
                LaTour and Eichenwald-Maki, pp 542–543
                Johns, p 681

34. Reporting the number of incomplete charts over a 6-month period using a run or line chart will prove valuable in which of the following two ways?
    A. The run or line chart data can show how much and how far service goes.
    B. Over time, the data can reveal trends and point out areas for improvement.
    C. The data in the run or line chart can indicate the level of customer satisfaction related to transcription errors.
    D. Over time, the data can reveal an increase in office morale and productivity.

REFERENCE: McWay, pp 149, 151, 201–202
                Abdelhak, pp 452–453, 453f
                LaTour and Eichenwald-Maki, p 706
                Johns, p 623

35. As an HIM coding supervisor, you are asked to compare the current coding process with a proposed concurrent coding process. What visual tool would be the best to identify all the logical steps and sequence of each procedure?
   A. decision matrix
   B. cause and effect diagram
   C. flowchart
   D. checksheet

REFERENCE: McWay, p 273
               Abdelhak, pp 450–451, 618
               Shaw, pp 166–172
               LaTour and Eichenwald-Maki, pp 688, 704
               Johns, pp 626–627

36. Physicians who are members of the Surgery Committee meet to review surgical cases referred for quality issues and deviations from standard care norms. This type of review in which a physician's record is reviewed by his or her professional colleagues is known as
   A. concurrent review.
   B. clinical pertinence review.
   C. incident screening.
   D. peer review.

REFERENCE: Abdelhak, p 407
               Shaw, pp 324–325
               LaTour and Eichenwald-Maki, pp 34, 544–546
               Johns, p 717

37. Patient mortality, infection and complication rates, adherence to living will requirements, adequate pain control, and other documentation that describe end results of care or a measurable change in the patient's health are examples of
   A. outcome measures.
   B. threshold level.
   C. sentinel events.
   D. incident reports.

REFERENCE: McWay, p 153
               Abdelhak, p 442
               Shaw, pp 14, 16
               LaTour and Eichenwald-Maki, pp 537, 985
               Johns, pp 610, 644

38. In quality review activities, departments are directed to focus on clinical processes that are
   A. high volume.
   B. high risk.
   C. problem prone.
   D. all of the above

REFERENCE: Shaw, pp 6, 17
               LaTour and Eichenwald-Maki, p 551

39. The HIM department frequently experiences a backlog in loose report filing. A quality improvement team is assembled to identify the outcome variables and the major or root causes. What visual QI tool is helpful to report the findings?
   A. PDCA method
   B. run chart
   C. fishbone (cause and effect) diagram
   D. scatter diagram

REFERENCE: McWay, p 148
               Abdelhak, p 451
               Shaw, pp 201–202
               LaTour and Eichenwald-Maki, pp 551, 704–705
               Johns, pp 628–629

40. What action(s) would assist the manager of a medical record department in improving customer perception of the quality of services provided by the department?
    A. Establish a 2-week turnaround time for all dictated reports.
    B. Refuse to fax patient information to protect confidentiality.
    C. Have physicians and hospital staff retrieve their own medical records.
    D. Identify specific customer needs in order to design value-added services.

REFERENCE: Shaw, pp 6, 89–90
                LaTour and Eichenwald-Maki, p 699

41. As based in case law decisions and the Joint Commission standards, who is ultimately responsible to ensure quality and appropriateness of patient care in a health care facility?
    A. chief executive officer   C. governing body or board of trustees
    B. medical staff   D. hospital attorney

REFERENCE: McWay, pp 17–18
                Abdelhak, pp 21–22
                Shaw, pp 318–320
                LaTour and Eichenwald-Maki, p 520
                Johns, p 638

42. You sit on the quality improvement team for the Nursing department that meets to generate ideas to address verbal order documentation problems about the "Read Back Verbal Order" policy. What QI tool would prove useful in sharing input and various recommendations for solving this problem?
    A. flowchart   C. check sheet
    B. scatter diagram   D. brainstorming

REFERENCE: McWay, p 148
                Abdelhak, p 450
                Shaw, p 20
                LaTour and Eichenwald-Maki, pp 703–704
                Johns, pp 633–634

43. A histogram is a valuable tool for representing
    A. the solution to a problem.
    B. priorities in problem solving.
    C. a frequency distribution with continuous-interval data.
    D. the root causes of a problem.

REFERENCE: McWay, p 149
                Abdelhak, pp 386, 452
                Shaw, pp 57–58
                LaTour and Eichenwald-Maki, p 706
                Johns, pp 630–631

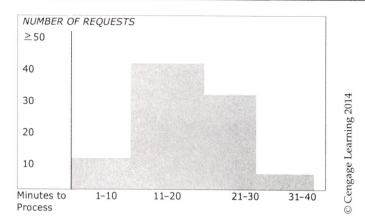

44. Eighty (80) requests for records to be pulled for the emergency room were processed in January. From the histogram provided above, what was the most frequent amount of time taken to process a request?
   A. 1–10 minutes
   B. 11–20 minutes
   C. 21–30 minutes
   D. 31–40 minutes

REFERENCE: McWay, p 149
               Abdelhak, p 386
               Shaw, pp 57–58
               LaTour and Eichenwald-Maki, p 706
               Johns, pp 630–631

45. Which quality management theorist focused on zero defects as the goal of performance improvement efforts?
   A. Kaizen
   B. Crosby
   C. Peters
   D. Deming

REFERENCE: Johns, p 607

46. As Director of the HIM department, you are asked to chair a committee that will recommend a pharmacy information system. The information has been collected, and you bring your committee together to prioritize their suggestions. This method of working with information is known as
   A. force field analysis.
   B. Delphi process.
   C. nominal group process.
   D. correlation analysis.

REFERENCE: McWay, pp 148, 273
               Shaw, pp 20–21
               LaTour and Eichenwald-Maki, p 704

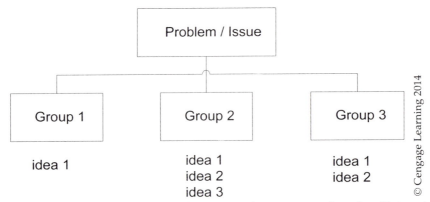

47. The performance tool shown above is used to provide structure by classifying information into smaller groups. What is the name of this chart/diagram?
    A. flowchart
    B. matrix
    C. affinity diagram
    D. arrow diagram

REFERENCE: McWay, p 148
               Abdelhak, p 450
               Shaw, p 20
               LaTour and Eichenwald-Maki, p 704
               Johns, p 634

48. Which quality management theorist believed that merit raises, formal evaluations, and quotas established through benchmarking hinder worker productivity and growth?
    A. Brian Joiner
    B. Philip Crosby
    C. Joseph Juran
    D. W. Edwards Deming

REFERENCE: Johns, p 606
               Shaw, p xxvii
               LaTour and Eichenwald-Maki, pp 628–629

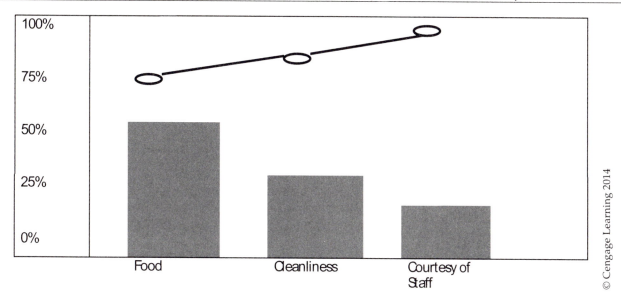

49. As head of the Performance Improvement Department, you are asked to evaluate patient satisfaction and offer recommendations for action. The performance tool shown above is used to graphically display the results. What is the name of this chart?
    A. Pareto chart
    B. line chart
    C. bar chart
    D. run chart

REFERENCE: McWay, p 148
               Abdelhak, p 453
               Shaw, pp 58–59
               LaTour and Eichenwald-Maki, p 705
               Johns, pp 632–633

50. Based on the previous graphic chart, which two areas should you recommend be acted upon first in order to address 80% of the patients' complaints?
    A. food and cleanliness
    B. food and courtesy of staff
    C. cleanliness and courtesy of staff
    D. not enough information to determine

REFERENCE: McWay, p 148
               Shaw, pp 58–59
               LaTour and Eichenwald-Maki, p 705
               Johns, pp 632–633

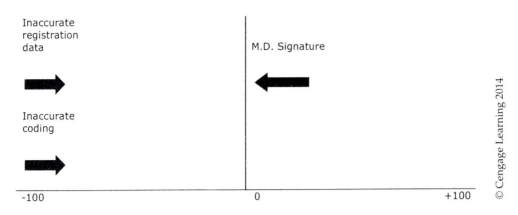

Inaccurate
registration
data

M.D. Signature

Inaccurate
coding

-100   0   +100

© Cengage Learning 2014

51. As Director of the HIM department, it is your responsibility to reduce the turnaround time for your organization's accounts receivable balance. The performance improvement tool shown above was used to add weights in order to prioritize ideas. What is it called?
    A. fishbone diagram
    B. precision matrix
    C. flowchart
    D. force field analysis

REFERENCE: McWay, p 273
                Abdelhak, p 452
                LaTour and Eichenwald-Maki, p 705
                Johns, p 629

52. Which of the following processes is mandatory for health care facilities?
    A. accreditation
    B. certification
    C. AHA registration
    D. licensure

REFERENCE: McWay, p 17
                Abdelhak, p 12
                Shaw, p 330
                LaTour and Eichenwald-Maki, p 35
                Johns, pp 61, 648, 721

53. A surgeon left a clamp in a patient, resulting in a return to the operating room. In an integrated organizational quality management model, all of the following entities would receive data about the investigation EXCEPT the
    A. Tissue Committee.
    B. Credentials Committee.
    C. Risk Management Program.
    D. Pharmacy and Therapeutics Committee.

REFERENCE: Shaw, p 198
                LaTour and Eichenwald-Maki, p 545

54. The Joint Commission requires health care facilities manage the environment of care by implementing seven (7) various safety plans, which must be evaluated at least
    A. monthly.
    C. biannually.
    B. quarterly.
    D. annually.

REFERENCE: Shaw, p 271

55. The type of indicator about the placement and number of fire extinguishers would be a(n)
    A. process.
    C. structure.
    B. outcome.
    D. regulation.

REFERENCE: Abdelhak, p 442
               Shaw, pp xxviii, 14
               LaTour and Eichenwald-Maki, pp 536–537

56. The Joint Commission on Accreditation of Health Care Facilities has a standard stating that a hospital must plan and design information management processes to meet _____ information needs.
    A. internal
    C. both internal and external
    B. external
    D. patient record

REFERENCE: Shaw, p 366
               Johns, pp 644–645
               LaTour and Eichenwald-Maki, pp 112–116
               Abdelhak, pp 128–129
               http://www.jointcommission.org

57. HEDIS gathers data in which of the following areas?
    A. measures of access (e.g., at least one visit to a provider within 3 years)
    B. measures of quality (e.g., cholesterol screenings)
    C. measures of member satisfaction (e.g., cost per member)
    D. all of the above

REFERENCE: McWay, pp 179–180
               Abdelhak, pp 692–693
               Shaw, pp 332–333
               Johns, pp 210–211, 309–310
               LaTour and Eichenwald-Maki, pp 533–534

58. If administrators of a home health agency wanted to measure the outcomes of adult patients receiving their agency's services, which tool would they use?
    A. OASIS
    B. HEDIS
    C. ORYX
    D. QAI

REFERENCE: McWay, pp 100, 209–210, 333
               Abdelhak, pp 137–138
               LaTour and Eichenwald-Maki, pp 169, 394
               Johns, pp 100, 209–210, 333
               Shaw, p 151

59. Your hospital is required by the Joint Commission and CMS to participate in national benchmarking on specific disease entities for quality of care measurement. This required collection and reporting of disease-specific data is considered
    A. an environment of care.
    B. a group of sentinel events.
    C. a series of core measures.
    D. risk assessment.

REFERENCE: Shaw, pp 132, 359
               Johns, pp 211–212
               LaTour and Eichenwald-Maki, pp 538–539

60. Continuous quality improvement is best described by the following statements EXCEPT
    A. corrective action targets clinicians more so than processes.
    B. standards are defined, measured, and systematically applied.
    C. monitoring is ongoing with periodic feedback.
    D. all personnel support quality improvement efforts, including top management and the governing body.

REFERENCE: McWay, p 142
               Abdelhak pp 441–442
               Shaw, pp 4–9
               LaTour and Eichenwald-Maki, pp 700–702
               Johns, pp 610–611, 613–614, 718

61. Which of the following is a disadvantage of retrospective data collection?
    A. Data are all available.
    B. Fewer data collectors are required.
    C. Deficiencies in documentation can effect reimbursement.
    D. Reviewer bias is reduced.

REFERENCE: McWay, pp 104–106, 152
               LaTour and Eichenwald-Maki, p 548

62. According to current theory in the quality management field, should concurrent data collection or retrospective data collection be utilized?
    A. Concurrent and retrospective data collection methods are both necessary in order to effect meaningful interventions and contain costs.
    B. Concurrent data collection methods alone are meaningful because they emulate health practitioner training.
    C. Concurrent data collection methods alone are meaningful because interventions must always be immediate.
    D. Retrospective data collection methods alone are appropriate in the reimbursement realities of this decade.

REFERENCE: McWay, pp 104–106, 152
               LaTour and Eichenwald-Maki, p 298

63. You are determining the sample size for a quality study. Which of the following factors should you consider first?
    A. cost   C. size of the target population
    B. personnel   D. confidentiality of the record

REFERENCE: Abdelhak, pp 399–400
               LaTour and Eichenwald-Maki, p 491
               Shaw, p 46

64. The Anesthesia Department is adding a new indicator to its plan. The Chief Anesthesiologist has come to you, the Director of Quality Management, to help her design a data collection methodology. The two of you are now considering who will be doing the data collection. All of the following are factors in your deliberations EXCEPT
    A. quality management organizational model of the institution.
    B. Joint Commission standards and required characteristics.
    C. the location of data.
    D. the expertise of the staff.

REFERENCE: McWay, p 143
               Shaw, pp 46–47

65. The manager of the utilization review department wants to monitor and evaluate the prevention of inappropriate admissions. When would the manager need to collect data?
    A. prospective review   C. retrospective review
    B. concurrent review   D. long-term care review

REFERENCE: McWay, p 227
               Abdelhak, p 463
               LaTour and Eichenwald-Maki, pp 547–548
               Johns, pp 649–652

66. The manager of the Quality Department is listing various sources of data. Which of the following data sources would be an example of an external source?
    A. emergency room logs
    B. incident reports
    C. patient registration and admission, discharge, transfer (ADT) information
    D. quality improvement organization (QIO) information

REFERENCE: McWay, pp 142, 160
                       Abdelhak, p 438
                       Shaw, p 46
                       Johns, pp 640–648

67. The primary advantage of concurrent quality data collection is that
    A. multiple chart reviews eliminate collector bias.
    B. patient care problems can be remedied immediately.
    C. practitioners receive immediate feedback about patient processes and outcomes.
    D. staffing is decreased.

REFERENCE: McWay, pp 104, 161

SUMMARY OF SELECTED BLOOD PRODUCT REVIEW

Monitoring Element	Packed Red Blood Cells		Fresh Frozen Plasma		Platelets	
(N = 295)	(N = 256)		(N = 29)		(N = 10)	
	Met N (%)	Unmet N (%)	Met N (%)	Unmet N (%)	Met N (%)	Unmet N (%)
Indications	232 (91%)	24 (9%)	7 (24%)	22 (76%)	10 (100%)	0 (0%)

68. Refer to the Summary of Selected Blood Product Review table shown above. Which blood component or derivative had the most units reviewed?
    A. packed red blood cells
    B. fresh frozen plasma
    C. platelets
    D. unable to determine from the table

REFERENCE: McWay, pp 192–193, 218
               Abdelhak, pp 384, 386
               Shaw, pp 53–54
               LaTour and Eichenwald-Maki, pp 424–425, 445, 454–455

69. Refer to the Summary of Selected Blood Product Review table shown above. Which quality improvement function would prompt the production of the table?
    A. pharmacy and therapeutics function
    B. drug usage evaluation
    C. medical record review
    D. blood usage review

REFERENCE: LaTour and Eichenwald-Maki, p 545

70. Refer to the Summary of Selected Blood Product Review table shown above. What percent of the fresh frozen plasma units met indications?
    A. 7%
    B. 24%
    C. 22%
    D. 76%

REFERENCE: McWay, pp 192–193, 218
               Abdelhak, pp 384, 386
               Shaw, pp 53–54, 119
               LaTour and Eichenwald-Maki, pp 424–425, 445, 454–455

71. Refer to the Summary of Selected Blood Product Review table shown above. Based on the results reported in the table, which blood component or derivative should first be the topic of an in-depth study?
    A. packed red blood cells
    B. fresh frozen plasma
    C. platelets
    D. unable to determine from the table

REFERENCE: Abdelhak, pp 384, 386, 452
               LaTour and Eichenwald-Maki, pp 545, 424–425, 445, 454–455
               Shaw, pp 47–48, 57

CASE STUDY #1

Upon employment at your facility, all new employees read, demonstrate understanding, and sign Confidentiality Statements. Disclosure of confidential information is grounds for immediate dismissal. Each year, during the annual performance evaluation, every employee again reads, demonstrates understanding, and signs the Confidentiality Statement.

You are the Director of the Quality Department. Your department has found that the femoral-popliteal bypass failure rate of one of your vascular surgeons, Dr. Z, is twice that of the national average. Members of the surgery department have reviewed that vascular surgeon's performance both by reading the medical records and by watching videos of her surgery. The Surgery Department and the Executive Committee have decided to deny reappointment for this surgeon.

Lucille X, the mother of one of your quality coordinators, has severe peripheral vascular disease. She was admitted to your facility and had an angiogram. The angiogram shows that she should have a femoral-popliteal bypass. She had told you that she would be in your facility and asked you to visit her. You are now fulfilling that promise and are also bringing her flowers. While pausing to knock on her door, you hear your employee, Mary G, vehemently state to her mother, "Mom, Dr. Z is a quack; half of her bypass surgeries fail. You must have Dr. DoGood!"

72. Referring to Case Study #1, what do you do as Director of the Quality Department?
    A. Seek the advice of the facility's legal counsel.
    B. Immediately dismiss Mary G upon her arrival back in the department.
    C. Walk into Lucille's room and state that Dr. Z is a fine surgeon and also advise Mary G to lower her voice.
    D. Upon Mary G's arrival back in the department, give her a written warning.

REFERENCE: McWay, pp 79, 81–84, 94
               Abdelhak, pp 521, 534–536
               LaTour and Eichenwald-Maki, pp 309–310, 552

73. Referring to Case Study #1, are the meeting minutes about the decisions regarding Dr. Z of the Department of Surgery and of the Executive Committee admissible in court?
    A. Yes, federal amendments to the Medicare Act require release of peer review.
    B. Yes, state laws allow discovery of medical review committee records.
    C. No, the federal Freedom of Information Act and state "sunshine laws" protect peer review.
    D. No, under state laws, records of medical review committees are not subject to introduction into evidence.

REFERENCE: Abdelhak, pp 534–536
               Shaw, p 429
               LaTour and Eichenwald-Maki, pp 298–299

CASE STUDY #2

You are helping the nursing department to write indicators to determine appropriate formulas for ratios and to determine data collection time frames. One important aspect of care is the documentation of education of patients. More specifically, the nursing department would like to assess its documentation of education on colostomy care for patients with new colostomies.

74. Referring to Case Study #2, what would be the most cost-effective and appropriate data collection time frame?
   A. prospective
   B. concurrent
   C. retrospective
   D. long-term care review

REFERENCE: McWay, p 152
               LaTour and Eichenwald-Maki, p 298

75. Referring to Case Study #2, which of the following ratios would you recommend?
   A. <u>Number of records with documentation of colostomy-care teaching</u>
      Total number of patients on surgery unit
   B. <u>Number of records with documentation of teaching</u>
      Total number of discharges
   C. <u>Number of records with documentation of colostomy-care teaching</u>
      Total number of patients with new colostomy
   D. <u>Number of records reviewed with documentation of colostomy-care teaching</u>
      Total number of records reviewed

REFERENCE: McWay, pp 198–200
               Abdelhak, p 373
               Johns, p 526
               LaTour and Eichenwald-Maki, p 424
               Shaw, p 119

76. A culture and sensitivity report was returned to the inpatient unit of Brian Hospital. The sensitivity showed bacterial resistance to the current antibiotic the patient was receiving. The patient continued on the same antibiotic without improvement. A generic quality screen identified this case for review. At a minimum, which committee should review this case?
   A. Surgical Case Review
   B. Safety Committee
   C. Information Management Committee
   D. Pharmacy and Therapeutics Committee

REFERENCE: Shaw, p 219
               LaTour and Eichenwald-Maki, p 545

77. The outpatient coding staff has been working to improve coding accuracy. The standard for the number of cases that must be coded has been raised four times in the past year. The staff said, "the more cases that must be coded, the greater the error rate will be for the corresponding time period." The department keeps statistics on both the numbers of cases coded and the corresponding error rate. What is the best QI tool for testing the coding staff's theory?
   A. control chart
   B. Pareto chart
   C. run chart
   D. scatter diagram

REFERENCE: McWay, pp 149–151
               LaTour and Eichenwald-Maki, pp 706–707
               Johns, p 632

78. The health information reception desk is experiencing a huge influx of phone calls on Monday, Tuesday, and Wednesday mornings. This is creating a problem in getting requested patient information out within an acceptable time frame. The reception staff work group has agreed to start recording the reason for the phone calls for the next 4 weeks. They want to focus on solving the response-time problem by reducing the turnaround time for the largest category of phone calls. Which QI tool best supports this goal?

A. control chart
B. Pareto chart
C. run chart
D. scatter diagram

REFERENCE: McWay, pp 148–151
Abdelhak, p 453
Shaw, pp 58–59
LaTour and Eichenwald-Maki, p 705
Johns, pp 632–633

79. The board of directors of a 400-bed women's hospital receives a report of key quality indicator results on a periodic basis. The report always includes the quarterly cesarean section rate. This reporting period, they see a rise in the rate and want to know if it is a significant increase. What is the best QI tool for this purpose?

A. control chart
B. Pareto chart
C. run chart
D. scatter diagram

REFERENCE: McWay, pp 148–151
Abdelhak, p 453
Johns, pp 623–624
LaTour and Eichenwald-Maki, pp 705–707
Shaw, pp 62–63

80. What is the best tool for differentiating between common cause variation and special cause variation?

A. control chart
B. Pareto chart
C. run chart
D. scatter diagram

REFERENCE: McWay, pp 211–212
Abdelhak, pp 453–454
Johns, p 623
LaTour and Eichenwald-Maki, p 707
Shaw, pp 62–63

81. Which department will most likely be responsible for taking corrective action regarding the following quality indicator?

> QUALITY INDICATOR:
> Ninety-five percent (95%) of physician appointments/reappointments will be completed within 90 days of receipt of all required materials.

A. Admissions
B. Business Office
C. Health Information Department
D. Medical Staff Office

REFERENCE: Abdelhak, pp 443, 467–468
Shaw, p 294
LaTour and Eichenwald-Maki, pp 542–544

82. Which department will most likely be responsible for taking corrective action regarding the following quality indicator?

> QUALITY INDICATOR:
> The number of DRG validation changes made by the QIO will not exceed 2%.

A. Admissions
B. Business Office
C. Health Information Department
D. Medical Staff Office

REFERENCE: Abdelhak, pp 442, 659

83. All of the following are among the Joint Commission's initial core measure sets for hospitals EXCEPT
A. acute myocardial infarction.
B. diabetes.
C. pneumonia.
D. surgical infection prevention.

REFERENCE: Shaw, pp 131–132
LaTour and Eichenwald-Maki, p 538

84. Which department will most likely be responsible for taking corrective action regarding the following quality indicator?

> QUALITY INDICATOR:
> Number of insurance claims requiring resubmission due to errors (not related to coding) will not exceed 3%.

A. Admissions
B. Business Office
C. Health Information Department
D. Medical Staff Office

REFERENCE: Abdelhak, p 657

85. What quality indicator would identify improvement needs in hospital electronic transmission of health care claims and remittances to allow interoperability with ICD-10 codes?
A. an increase in requests for operative reports
B. denied requests for medical record copies for continued care
C. an increase in hospital-acquired infections
D. an increase in 5010 rejections

REFERENCE: AHIMA (3)

86. Historic accomplishments impacting quality in medical care include all EXCEPT
A. ensuring competent practitioners.
B. *Darling v. Charleston Community Hospital.*
C. implementation of OTRA.
D. medical education reform (Flexner report findings).

REFERENCE: McWay, p 142
Abdelhak, pp 7–8, 438–439
LaTour and Eichenwald-Maki, pp 9–10, 297, 522
Johns, pp 674–680

87. An accreditation agency counterpart to the Joint Commission for managed care organizations is the

A. AHRQ.

B. AHCPR.

C. IOM.

D. NCQA.

REFERENCE: McWay, p 48
                Abdelhak, pp 14, 439
                Shaw, p 145
                LaTour and Eichenwald-Maki, pp 533–534
                Johns, pp 111, 310

88. Quality requirements of providers participating in the Medicare program are found in all EXCEPT the

A. Conditions of Participation.

B. Federal Register.

C. ORYX.

D. QIO regulations governing work scope

REFERENCE: Abdelhak, p 438
                Shaw, p 333
                LaTour and Eichenwald-Maki, pp 522–523
                Johns, pp 141, 211

89. Which data bank is a result of HIPAA legislation?

A. Fraud and Abuse Data Bank

B. Health Care Integrity and Protection Data Bank

C. National Practitioner Data Bank

D. Privacy Information Breach Data Bank

REFERENCE: McWay, pp 58–59
                Abdelhak, p 468
                Johns, p 499
                LaTour and Eichenwald-Maki, p 338
                Shaw, p 295

90. The following "sentinel events" must be available for Joint Commission review EXCEPT

A. infant abduction.

B. petechiae due to adverse drug reaction.

C. rape.

D. surgery on wrong patient or wrong body part.

REFERENCE: McWay, p 159
                Abdelhak, pp 456, 459
                Shaw, pp 187–188
                Johns, p 658

Year 2012 Month	Percent Patients with Unacceptable Waiting Time (%)
January	5
February	4
March	3
April	5
May	3
June	10
July	5
August	2
September	1
October	2
November	1
December	3

91. Use the information shown in the table above. Calculate the average percentage of patients for the entire year who waited longer than an acceptable amount of waiting time. (The sample size for each month's data is 100.)
   A. 3.1%
   B. 3.6%
   C. 3.7%
   D. 4.0%

REFERENCE: McWay, p 194
                Abdelhak, pp 389–390
                LaTour and Eichenwald-Maki, pp 454–455
                Johns, pp 528–529

92. Which of the following is incorrect about the use of control charts?
   A. Control charts can be used to measure key processes over time.
   B. The upper and lower control limits are always ± 2 standard deviations.
   C. The lower control limits are always ± 2 standard deviations.
   D. The upper control limits are always ± 1.8 standard deviations.

REFERENCE: McWay, pp 149, 151, 211–212
                Shaw, pp 62–63
                Johns, pp 623–624

93. The average percent of patients exceeding acceptable waiting time was 3.7% (see table for question 91). The calculated UCL (upper control limit) is 9.4. When you plot the upper and lower limits, what would you suggest as the reason for the June variation?
   A. common cause variation
   B. root cause variation
   C. special cause variation
   D. unable to determine with the data given

REFERENCE: McWay, pp 211–212
                Abdelhak, pp 453–454
                Shaw, p 62

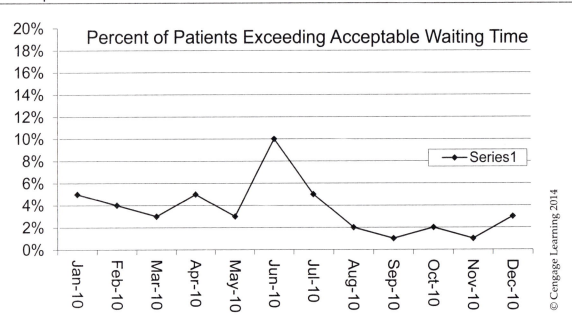

94. Adding the UCL (upper control limit) and LCL (lower control limit) to the chart above (from question 93) creates a
    A. control chart.   C. run chart.
    B. frequency distribution. D. variation graph.

REFERENCE: McWay, pp 149, 211–212
                Abdelhak, pp 452–454
                Shaw, pp 62–63
                Johns, p 623
                LaTour and Eichenwald-Maki, p 707

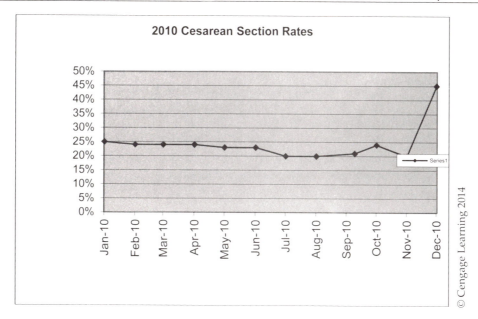

© Cengage Learning 2014

95. You are the Quality Coordinator for the medical staff. Analyze the chart above and determine the steps to be taken next.
    A. Plot the control limits, check the indicator threshold, and take the December charts to the OB/GYN Committee if the threshold is exceeded.
    B. Plot the control limits and take the December charts to the OB/GYN Committee if the December data point exceeds UCL.
    C. Plot the control limits, pull the charts for December, and do a focused review screening.
    D. Plot the control limits and refer to the Medical Executive Committee for variation review.

REFERENCE: McWay, pp 211–212
               Abdelhak, pp 386, 453–454
               Johns, pp 623–624
               LaTour and Eichenwald-Maki, p 707
               Shaw, pp 62–63

96. The U.S. federal government's CMS substitutes compliance of its Conditions of Participation requirements to hospitals that already have accreditation awarded by various other agencies that include the Joint Commission, CARF, AOA, or AAAHC. This is known as
    A. deemed status.   C. contingent statutory.
    B. due process.   D. waiver status.

REFERENCE: Shaw, p 334
               LaTour and Eichenwald-Maki, p 36
               Johns, pp 109, 458
               Abdelhak, p 12
               McWay, p 47

97. Dr. Jeremy is establishing a clinical trial research study for his patients with lung cancer wishing to participate in a chemotherapy clinical trial. As Assistant Director, you are responsible for clinical abstract of data and advise him to first seek approval of research involving human subjects through the

A. medical staff.
B. governing board.
C. institutional review board (IRB).
D. Office of National Coordinator (ONC).

REFERENCE: Shaw, p 92
Johns, pp 587–589, 847
LaTour and Eichenwald-Maki, pp 563–564
Abdelhak, pp 521–522
McWay, p 231

98. The Joint Commission on-site survey process incorporates tracer methodology, which emphasizes surveyor review by means of

A. patient tracers.
B. system tracers.
C. both system tracers and patient tracers.
D. policy and procedure manual reviews.

REFERENCE: Shaw, pp 336–337
Johns, pp 644–645
McWay, p 9

99. Storyboards are a method used in health care that

A. graphically display a performance improvement project conducted.
B. serve as a documentation format in patient records.
C. serve as a teaching tool for customers and staff.
D. both A and C

REFERENCE: Shaw, p 74–75
Johns, p 611

100. The Six Sigma methodology differs from other quality improvement models by defining improvement opportunities using

A. scientific management.
B. critical quality tree.
C. nonvalue activities/processes.
D. brainstorming.

REFERENCE: Shaw, p 443
LaTour and Eichenwald-Maki, pp 710–711
Abdelhak, pp 448–449
McWay, pp 144–145

101. The FOCUS PDCA model used in performance improvement is best known for its change strategy technique of

A. Business Process Engineering.
B. Plan, Do, Study, Act.
C. Input, Through-Put, Output.
D. Cause and Effect Diagramming.

REFERENCE: LaTour and Eichenwald-Maki, pp 701–702
Abdelhak, p 447
McWay, p 143

102. The quality review process of invasive and noninvasive procedures to ensure performance of appropriate procedure, preparation of patient, monitoring and postoperative care, and education of patient describes

A. universal protocol.
B. infection review.
C. surgical review.
D. blood and blood component usage.

REFERENCE: LaTour and Eichenwald-Maki, p 545
               Abdelhak, p 465
               McWay, pp 157–158

103. The Institute of Medicine (IOM) published report titled *To Err Is Human: Building a Safer Health System*, heightened concern by the U.S. government and accrediting agencies. This led the Joint Commission to place emphasis on improving patient safety and sentinel event occurrences through its safety program, known as

A. ORYX Initiative Set.
B. National Patient Safety Goals (NPSG).
C. Health Care Quality Improvement Program (HCQIP).
D. Health Plan Employer Data & Information (HEDIS).

REFERENCE: Shaw, pp 185–188
               Johns, p 644
               LaTour and Eichenwald-Maki, pp 532, 539–540
               Abdelhak, pp 454–455
               McWay, p 159

104. When a decision is made to restrict or deny clinical privileges during the recredentialing or reappointment process to a medical staff member, a _____ must be offered.

A. privilege suspension
B. revocation of license
C. due process
D. crisis intervention

REFERENCE: Shaw, p 296
               LaTour and Eichenwald-Maki, p 544
               Abdelhak, pp 467–468
               McWay, p 22

105. A patient satisfaction survey conducted after discharge is a method of quality measurement through

A. prospective indicator.
B. structure indicator.
C. process indicator.
D. outcomes indicator.

REFERENCE: Shaw, pp 14, 95–96
               Johns, pp 610–611
               LaTour and Eichenwald-Maki, p 580
               Abdelhak, pp 489–490
               McWay, p 153

106. The Joint Commission's emphasis on improving quality of patient care for a participating facility is exemplary through the required self-assessment known as
A. continuous quality improvement (CQI).
B. accreditation denial.
C. periodic performance review (PPR).
D. total quality management (TQM).

REFERENCE: Johns, pp 607–608, 610–611
Joint Commission,
http://www.jointcommission.org/AboutUs/Fact_Sheets/PPR_QA.htm

107. During the Utilization Review Committee meeting, a case presented for discussion involved a surgical case resulting in unexpected loss of lower extremity below the knee due to complications requiring extended length of stay. Being a sentinel event, the committee requested that an investigation and reporting was required to identify the cause and prevention of future occurrences. This investigation and required reporting to the Joint Commission is known as
A. root cause analysis.   C. medication review.
B. potential compensable event. D. report card.

REFERENCE: Shaw, pp 146, 157, 187–189
Johns, pp 628–629
LaTour and Eichenwald-Maki, p 551
Abdelhak, pp 458–459, 704–705
McWay, p 159

Answer Key for Quality and Performance Improvement

1.	D		47.	C	
2.	D		48.	D	
3.	D		49.	A	
4.	B		50.	A	
5.	D		51.	D	
6.	D		52.	D	
7.	C		53.	D	
8.	B		54.	D	
9.	B		55.	C	
10.	D		56.	C	
11.	A	Definition: HEDIS is Health Plan Employer Data and Information Set	57.	D	
12.	B		58.	A	
13.	D		59.	C	
14.	C		60.	A	
15.	D		61.	C	
16.	C		62.	A	
17.	C		63.	C	
18.	A		64.	B	
19.	D		65.	A	
20.	D		66.	D	
21.	D		67.	B	
22.	D		68.	A	
23.	D		69.	D	
24.	A		70.	B	
25.	D		71.	B	
26.	A		72.	B	
27.	D		73.	D	
28.	B		74.	C	
29.	C		75.	C	Number of times an event occurred divided by number of times the event could have occurred
30.	B				
31.	C				
32.	D		76.	D	
33.	C		77.	D	
34.	B		78.	B	
35.	C		79.	A	
36.	D		80.	A	
37.	A		81.	D	
38.	D		82.	C	
39.	C		83.	B	
40.	D		84.	B	
41.	C		85.	D	
42.	D		86.	C	
43.	C		87.	D	
44.	B		88.	C	
45.	B		89.	B	
46.	C		90.	B	

Answer Key for Quality and Performance Improvement

91. C (5 + 4 + 3 + 5 + 3 + 10 + 5 + 2 + 1 + 2
+ 1 + 3) ÷ 12 = 3.66 = 3.7
92. D
93. C Data points that lie outside the upper or lower control limits may signal special cause variation.
94. A
95. A
96. A
97. C
98. C
99. D
100. B
101. B
102. C
103. B
104 C
105. D
106. C
107. A

REFERENCES

Abdelhak, M., Grostick, S., Hanken, M. A., & Jacobs, E. (2012). *Health information: Management of a strategic resource* (4th ed.). Philadelphia: W. B. Saunders.

AHIMA (1). Practice Brief http://AHIMA.org, Book of Knowledge - Practice Brief, Verbal/Telephone Order Authentication and Time Frames (Updated), 8/15/12.

AHIMA (2) Practice Brief http://AHIMA.org Book of Knowledge - Practice Brief, Electronic Documentation Templates Support ICD-10-CM/PCS, 10/2/12.

AHIMA (3) Journal of AHIMA 80, no. 9 http://AHIMA.org, Three Short Years Organizations Lagging in 5010 and ICD-10 Progress, September 2010.

CMS Federal Register, pp 17–18 http://www.gpo.gov/fdsys/pkg/CFR-2011-title42-vol5/pdf/CFR-2011-title42-vol5.pdf.

Johns, M. L. (2011). *Health information management technology: An applied approach* (3rd ed.). Chicago: American Health Information Management Association (AHIMA).

Joint Commission. http://www.jointcommission.org/AboutUs/Fact_Sheets/PPR_QA.htm

LaTour, K., & Eichenwald-Maki, S. (2010). *Health information management: Concepts, principles, and practice* (3rd ed.). Chicago: American Health Information Management Association (AHIMA).

McWay, D. (2008). *Today's health information management: An integrated approach.* Clifton Park, NY: Delmar Cengage Learning.

Shaw, P. (2010). *Quality and performance improvement in health care: A tool for programmed learning* (4th ed.). Chicago: American Health Information Management Association (AHIMA).

Quality and Performance Improvement Competencies

Question	RHIA Domain	RHIT Domain
1–107	2	5

XV. Organization and Management

Anita Hazelwood, MLS, RHIA, FAHIMA

Carol A. Venable, MPH, RHIA, FAHIMA

1. The manager of a Health Information Department has many training and development methods available for the departmental and nondepartmental staff. Consider the following situation. The department's working hours are 8:00 AM to 6:00 PM. After 6:00 PM, if a record is needed in the emergency room for a possible readmission, the ER clerk has access to the HID in order to retrieve the record. On the occasions when the ER clerk has retrieved a record, she has left the department open, the records have been pulled and not replaced, and it appears as if the clerk was viewing records unnecessarily. What would be the best training or development method for the ER clerk in order to rectify this situation?
   A. receive training by an ER coworker
   B. receive training by an expert in record documentation
   C. attend an outside workshop or seminar
   D. receive training by the supervisor of files

REFERENCE: McWay, p 290
               LaTour and Eichenwald-Maki, pp 742, 745–746
               Abdelhak, pp 607–608

2. Strong lateral relationships within a facility are most likely when
   A. vertical relationships are less than adequate.
   B. individual departments cooperate together to achieve organizational goals.
   C. individual departments are only interested in their internal goals.
   D. individual departments avoid one another.

REFERENCE: LaTour and Eichenwald-Maki, pp 630–631

3. The Director of the Health Information Services Department has asked that the supervisor of coding institute a method to monitor the accuracy of coding. What method would be the most effective approach?
   A. Perform a 100% review of one of the employees' work each day.
   B. Review a sample of each employee's work annually.
   C. Review a random sample of each employee's work monthly.
   D. Have each employee check each other's work and report any problems to the supervisor.

REFERENCE: McWay, pp 264–265
               LaTour and Eichenwald-Maki, pp 691–693
               Abdelhak, pp 619–621
               Davis and LaCour, pp 156, 291

4. You are the Coding Supervisor and wish to know the amount of time spent on coding by eight employees this month. You have the following productivity log. What percentage of time was spent on coding?

Productivity Log January			
Number of Employees	Charts Coded	Standard	Hours Worked
8	725	12 minutes per chart	1,280

   A. 14.7%   C. 8.8%
   B. 6.8%   D. 11.3%

REFERENCE: McWay, pp 264–265
               Davis and LaCour, p 390
               Abdelhak, pp 619–621

5. The Director of Health Information Services has asked the supervisor over files to determine productivity standards for the file clerks. In initiating this process, the supervisor has determined that the best way to institute work standards is to
   A. determine which employee can work the fastest.
   B. perform time and motion studies.
   C. improve employee morale.
   D. develop standards based on professional standards and industry benchmarks.

REFERENCE: McWay, pp 264–265
               Davis and LaCour, pp 293, 390
               Abdelhak, pp 619–621

6. A new health information management clerk has been on staff for 2 days. She has thus far analyzed charts incorrectly, sent out confidential information improperly, and used the copy machine inappropriately. Evaluate this situation and determine the best resolution.
   A. Review the job description and job procedure with the clerk and follow up with an in-service.
   B. Review the job procedure with the clerk and have the analysis supervisor monitor her progress.
   C. Review the job description and job procedure with the clerk and follow up with a merit evaluation.
   D. Review job procedures with the clerk and follow up with an in-service.

REFERENCE: McWay, pp 264–265
               LaTour and Eichenwald-Maki, p 743
               Davis and LaCour, p 432
               Abdelhak, p 608

7. "Qualified employees should be given priority when vacancies within the organization occur" is an example of
   A. a policy of the organization.
   B. an objective for the organization.
   C. a rule for the organization.
   D. a procedure for the organization.

REFERENCE: McWay, pp 252, 260–261
               LaTour and Eichenwald-Maki, pp 728, 743
               Davis and LaCour, pp 398–399
               Abdelhak, p 646

8. A rule is helpful to both managers and the employees in the decision-making process. A rule
   A. allows judgments to be made.
   B. requires interpretation.
   C. predecides issues.
   D. provides the necessary details.

REFERENCE: McWay, pp 21, 45
               Davis and LaCour, pp 398–399
               LaTour and Eichenwald-Maki, p 637

9. Which of the following statements describes a method?
    A. Medical records requested by the emergency room will be retrieved and delivered within 30 minutes.
    B. Multiple-page discharge summaries are stapled together in the left-hand corner.
    C. Transcription turnaround time is established as 24 hours following completion of dictation by the physician.
    D. Only HIM personnel have access to the medical record filing area.

REFERENCE: McWay, pp 21, 45, 230
               LaTour and Eichenwald-Maki, pp 728–729
               Davis and LaCour, pp 398–399
               Abdelhak, pp 623–624

10. The supervisor of retention and retrieval was receiving frequent complaints from the file clerks regarding the discharge clerk's job performance. The file clerks stated that it was becoming difficult to maintain their productivity levels because the discharge clerk was not processing the requisition slips in a timely manner. In order to get a clearer understanding of the situation, the supervisor asked the file clerks and the discharge clerk to complete a task list for a 2-week period. The supervisor is constructing a
    A. flow process chart.
    B. movement diagram.
    C. work distribution chart.
    D. procedure flowchart.

REFERENCE: McWay, p 260
               LaTour and Eichenwald-Maki, pp 684, 702
               Abdelhak, pp 614–619

11. In a filing system containing a total of 1,255 records, 48 records are identified as misfiles. What is the percentage of filing accuracy for this area?
    A. 26.14%   C. 3.82%
    B. 74%   D. 96%

REFERENCE: McWay, pp 264–265
               LaTour and Eichenwald-Maki, pp 681, 691–692
               Davis and LaCour, pp 258–259

12. The standard for record retrieval is 200 work units per month. Based on the table below, what is the variance from standard for the month of May?

May Productivity Report—Chart Retrieval			
Week 1	Week 2	Week 3	Week 4
30	40	25	35

    A. 75%   C. 53%
    B. 65%   D. 15%

REFERENCE: McWay, pp 264–265

13. Ms. Wolf, supervisor of coding and abstracting, would like to determine the coders' accuracy. Which type of management tool would provide her with the information she needs?
    A.   a stopwatch study
    B.   a coding audit
    C.   an employee-reported log
    D.   a time log

REFERENCE: McWay, pp 264–265
               Davis and LaCour, pp 293, 390
               LaTour and Eichenwald-Maki, pp 691–692, 696–698

14. After a work sampling study was completed, it was found that 20% of a coder's time was devoted to pulling records for physicians with missing diagnoses. How many minutes of a 7-hour day are taken up with this activity?
    A.   140   C.   21
    B.   84   D.   56

REFERENCE: McWay, pp 264–265
               Abdelhak, pp 619–621
               LaTour and Eichenwald-Maki, pp 692–695

15. Written documents that assist an organization in achieving its objectives and carrying out its mission statement are known as
    A.   strategic plans.   C.   tactical plans.
    B.   game plans.   D.   operational plans.

REFERENCE: McWay, p 249
               Shortell and Kaluzny, pp 460–461
               Davis and LaCour, p 394
               Abdelhak, pp 636–637
               LaTour and Eichenwald-Maki, pp 823–827

16. Anna Kathryn is attending budget training for new supervisors. The representative from Finance explains that _____ costs will vary in direct proportion to changes in the volume of care provided.
    A.   fixed   C.   variable
    B.   periodic   D.   semivariable

REFERENCE: McLean, p 129
               Abdelhak, p 675
               LaTour and Eichenwald-Maki, p 790

17. The organizing process determines how the work in a particular department will be divided and accomplished. In order to be in the best position to organize the work effectively, the manager must first engage in which management function?
    A.   staffing   B.   directing
    C.   planning   D.   controlling

REFERENCE: McWay, pp 254, 277, 349
               Davis and LaCour, pp 393–397
               LaTour and Eichenwald-Maki, p 630

18. The director of a Health Information Department has discovered that the department's policy regarding the usage of the copy machine has been consistently abused by the majority of the staff. To put an end to this inappropriate use of the copy machine, the director should institute a department

A. method.   C. objective.

B. rule.   D. procedure.

REFERENCE: McWay, pp 21, 45
              LaTour and Eichenwald-Maki, p 637

19. The average number of transcribed lines per month at Bent Tree Hospital is 142,500. The daily production standard is 950 lines per day. With 20 workdays in the month, calculate the minimum number of FTEs needed for this volume.

A. 13   C. 6

B. 8   D. 7.5

REFERENCE: Davis and LaCour, pp 391–392, 401–402
              LaTour and Eichenwald-Maki, pp 684–685, 697–698

20. The supervisor of release of information in a Health Information Department is preparing a work distribution chart in the hopes of identifying some problem areas. Although the work distribution chart can provide the supervisor with a great deal of information concerning the work performed by her staff, it will not indicate

A. if a task is divided among employees disproportionately.

B. the solution to a specific problem area.

C. if the skills of each employee are utilized appropriately.

D. the appropriate method of work division.

REFERENCE: McWay, p 260
              LaTour and Eichenwald-Maki, p 684
              Abdelhak, pp 614–619

21. Emma Grace is a transcriptionist. Her productivity level, as determined by line count per day, has dropped significantly over the past 2 weeks. As a result, there is a backlog in transcription of history and physical reports and surgical reports. Several doctors and the operating room supervisor have complained. An appropriate initial course of action for the Supervisor of Transcription is to

A. counsel the transcriptionist privately.

B. fire the transcriptionist immediately.

C. refer the matter to the Human Resources Department.

D. suspend the transcriptionist without pay for 3 days.

REFERENCE: McWay, pp 301–302
              LaTour and Eichenwald-Maki, p 735
              Davis and LaCour, pp 406–409

22. The Director of the Health Information Services Department has determined that an in-service for department supervisors on improving productivity levels in their respective areas is needed. As an outcome of this in-service, the director would like the supervisors to understand that when setting productivity levels, a supervisor must
    A. tailor any training needs to each individual employee to achieve the productivity levels.
    B. direct training needs to the most efficient employee within the department in order to achieve the productivity levels.
    C. determine the productivity standards for each area and job function.
    D. consider only quantity and not quality.

REFERENCE: McWay, p 300
              Davis and LaCour, pp 391–392, 401–402, 436
              LaTour and Eichenwald-Maki, pp 696–697, 728–729

23. The coding supervisor reviewed the productivity logs of four newly hired coders after their first month. The report below illustrates each coder's output. Based on analysis of this report, which employee will require additional assistance in order to meet the coding standards?

PRODUCTIVITY REPORT Coding Standard: 20 charts per day				
Coder	Week 1	Week 2	Week 3	Week 4
1	90	100	95	100
2	100	105	105	95
3	70	75	90	85
4	85	85	90	100

    A. Coder 1
    B. Coder 2
    C. Coder 3
    D. Coder 4

REFERENCE: McWay, p 300
              Davis and LaCour, pp 390–391

24. Which of the following statements best describes the scalar or chain of command principle?
    A. Effective organization is made up of people who perform the work assigned.
    B. There is a clear flow of authority from superior to subordinate throughout the organization.
    C. The objectives of a business or a group of functions within the business must be clearly defined and understood.
    D. The number of subordinates under the immediate supervision of the supervisor should be limited.

REFERENCE: McWay, pp 255–258
              LaTour and Eichenwald-Maki, pp 626, 719

The following questions represent advanced competencies.

IMPLEMENTATION PROCESS OF A HID COMPUTER SYSTEM

Planned

Actual

ACTIVITY *Weeks*	OCTOBER 1 2 3 4	NOVEMBER 1 2 3 4	DECEMBER 1 2 3 4
1. organize staff [Nancy]			
2. select & order equipment [Mary]			
3. develop training plan [Bob]			
4. conduct training [Joe]			

© Cengage Learning 2014

25. Based on the Gantt chart shown above, which planned activities can be done simultaneously?
    A. activities 1 and 2
    B. activities 3 and 4
    C. activities 1, 3, and 4
    D. activities 2 and 3

REFERENCE: McWay, p 254
                LaTour and Eichenwald-Maki, p 625

26. In order to improve efficiency and productivity, which of the following sequence of steps is the most effective?
    A. Break down the work into component activities, assign personnel, and delegate authority.
    B. Delegate authority, assign personnel, and define individual job duties.
    C. Know the objective; assign personnel and group activities into proper organizational units.
    D. Know the objective; break down the work into component activities, and the group activities into proper organizational units.

REFERENCE: McWay, p 255

27. Amelia Claire is a CNA and an RHIA who is a clinical documentation trainer for a large health system. The results of a quality improvement study indicated that an informed consent was not obtained for 25% of the surgical procedures performed. Amelia has discussed the problem with the director of the Health Information Department and they have decided to begin corrective action by providing an in-service. The most important participants who should attend this in-service are
    A. nurses and unit clerks.
    B. medical record and quality improvement personnel.
    C. physicians and residents.
    D. administrators.

REFERENCE: McWay, p 265
                LaTour and Eichenwald-Maki, pp 748–750
                Davis and LaCour, p 436

28. The Director of Health Information Services has recently received approval to purchase the necessary equipment to place all inactive records on optical disc. The director plans to redo the department layout to accommodate the equipment and to ensure that the equipment is placed in the most appropriate area of the department. Which of the following tools will best assist the director with this new layout?
    A. proximity chart
    B. frequency chart
    C. Gantt chart
    D. replacement chart

REFERENCE: Abdelhak, p 647

29. One of your first tasks as the new Manager of Health Information Services is to review the department policy and procedure manual. You have determined that several policy statements are incongruent with appropriate current employee practices. Proper management conventions require
    A. leaving the policy as written in the manual.
    B. contacting the hospital attorney to decide what action to take.
    C. enforcing the existing policy.
    D. revising the policy appropriately and documenting the date of the change.

REFERENCE: McWay, p 252
              LaTour and Eichenwald-Maki, pp 727–729
              Davis and LaCour, pp 398–400

30. Elizabeth Home is the Chief Executive Officer (CEO) at St. Augustine Medical Center. At the beginning of each fiscal year, she begins a formal planning cycle. Her annual planning process should begin with which of the following?
    A. revising the institutional mission
    B. developing strategic plans
    C. establishing the annual organizational objectives
    D. developing strategic goals

REFERENCE: McWay, pp 251–252
              LaTour and Eichenwald-Maki, p 630
              Davis and LaCour, pp 394–395

31. Which of the following statements is false in regard to departmental reengineering?
    A. It is mainly done to reduce departmental costs.
    B. It is intended to make small or minor changes in order to improve a function or process.
    C. It is intended to improve departmental productivity.
    D. It is intended to ensure satisfied customers.

REFERENCE: McWay, pp 676–677
              LaTour and Eichenwald-Maki, pp 707–709

32. In preparing a capital budget request, the first priority will be to document
    A. the specific type of equipment requested.
    B. where the new equipment will be located.
    C. the need for the new equipment.
    D. the cost of the new equipment.

REFERENCE: McWay, p 341
              McLean, p 152
              Davis and LaCour, pp 395–396

33. Based on the information displayed in the decision matrix below, which vendor would you recommend for the purchase of a copy machine?

Criteria	Weight	Vendor A Rating	Vendor B Rating	Vendor C Rating	Vendor D Rating
Quality	5	4	3	3	3
Speed	4	3	1	3	2
Service	2	3	3	5	2

A. Vendor A   C. Vendor C
B. Vendor B   D. Vendor D

REFERENCE: McWay, pp 261–262, 318
                  LaTour and Eichenwald-Maki, pp 635–636
                  Davis and LaCour, pp 306–307

34. As the Director of the Health Information Department, you are preparing a request for approval for the purchase of an encoding system. Because this is considered a capital request, you are required to submit the cost–benefit ratio. The software and license cost $6,000, hardware maintenance is $1,500, and the training of two employees will cost $500. It is expected that the encoding system will increase reimbursement by $10,000. The cost–benefit ratio is
A. 0.8.   C. 1.25.
B. 1.7.   D. 1.33.

REFERENCE: McWay, p 337
                  Abdelhak, p 332

35. What two types of budgets are often prepared by managers of health information departments?
A. capital budget and the finance budget
B. capital budget and the operational or revenue and expense budget
C. profit and loss budget and the finance budget
D. finance budget and the revenue and expense budget

REFERENCE: McLean, pp 151–152
                  Davis and LaCour, pp 395–396

36. Both Mary and Sue are employed as medical transcriptionists at All Children's Hospital. They are able to set their own work hours provided the department is covered by one of them during regular office hours. This kind of work arrangement is referred to as
A. compressed work week.   C. flex time.
B. job sharing.   D. telecommuting.

REFERENCE: LaTour and Eichenwald-Maki, pp 685–686, 759–760

37. The most important consideration in planning the office layout for a Health Information Services department is the
A. number of employees.   C. types of furniture to be purchased.
B. cost.   D. workflow.

REFERENCE: LaTour and Eichenwald-Maki, pp 680, 711–712
                  Davis and LaCour, p 389

38. Allison has conducted a timely performance evaluation for one of her employees and awarded the employee a 4% merit increase. She is currently completing the paperwork to submit to Human Resources. If the employee's hourly salary is presently $7.10, what will the hourly salary be with this increase?
    A. $7.33
    B. $7.38
    C. $7.80
    D. $7.54

REFERENCE: Abdelhak, pp 594–595

39. The span of control in an organization refers to the
    A. number of supervisors for each functional area.
    B. amount of space assigned to one supervisor.
    C. amount of work expected of an employee.
    D. number of people who report to one supervisor.

REFERENCE: Davis and LaCour, pp 385–386
               LaTour and Eichenwald-Maki, pp 630–631, 719

40. A work environment that is not ergonomically sound could lead to
    A. injuries.
    B. conflict among departments.
    C. employee arguments.
    D. increases in department equipment budgets.

REFERENCE: McWay, p 260
               LaTour and Eichenwald-Maki, pp 682–683
               Davis and LaCour, pp 420–421

41. Jessica is the leader of a project team working on the definition of the women's health service line. Several departments are so enthusiastic about the progress that they ask for additions to the project. This is not uncommon, and is known as
    A. add-ons.
    B. scope creep.
    C. effort expansion.
    D. deliverable increase.

REFERENCE: McWay, p 318
               LaTour and Eichenwald-Maki, p 809

42. The transcription production for February was 225,333 lines. The total work hours for all transcriptionists for the same period was 2,000. The average hourly cost was $13.50. Determine the cost per line for operating this service for this month.
    A. $1.20
    B. $0.24
    C. $2.40
    D. $0.12

REFERENCE: Davis and LaCour, pp 401–405, 408
               Abdelhak, pp 619–621

HEALTH INFORMATION DEPARTMENT MONTHLY BUDGET JANUARY		
Items	Budget	Actual
Supplies	495	675
Travel	300	150
Rental Equipment	1,250	1,250
Service Contracts	900	1,130

43. Based on the budget illustrated above, what is the monthly budget variance percent for supplies?
   A. 13.6%
   B. 36%
   C. 26.6%
   D. 11.9%

REFERENCE: McWay, p 342
                        McLean, pp 156–157

44. The most realistic approach that could encourage increased productivity in the tedious record file/retrieval area is to
   A. shorten the workday by 1 hour.
   B. vary and rotate the work assigned to each file clerk.
   C. have all the file clerks work on a part-time basis.
   D. arrange for all the file clerks to have flex time.

REFERENCE: McWay, pp 265–266

45. The HIM Department of a local hospital will experience a 20% increase in the number of discharges processed per day as the result of a merger with a smaller facility. This 20% increase is projected as 120 additional records per day. The standard time for coding a record is 15 minutes. Compute the number of FTEs required to process this increased volume in coding based on an 8-hour day.
   A. 3.75
   B. 2.8
   C. 6.5
   D. 5.25

REFERENCE: LaTour and Eichenwald-Maki, pp 689–691

46. Cheryl is the Director of the Health Information Services Department and Suzanne is the Assistant Director. Cheryl notices one of Suzanne's subordinates leaving the department for an unscheduled break. When the employee returns, Cheryl immediately asks the employee to step into her office and begins discussing the unauthorized break. Which organizational principle is this director violating?
   A. organizational function
   B. grievance procedure
   C. span of control
   D. unity of command

REFERENCE: Davis and LaCour, pp 385–386
                        LaTour and Eichenwald-Maki, pp 626, 719

47. As the Director of Health Information Services, you manage the department with the assistance of four supervisors. One day you observe a coder coding charts from the face sheet without reviewing the record for additional documentation. The most appropriate course of action would be to
    A. discuss your concerns with the Supervisor of Coding and direct her to address this issue immediately.
    B. discuss the problem with the CFO.
    C. discuss the matter directly with the coder and instruct him to review the entire record for correct assignment of codes.
    D. do nothing because the coding area is extremely productive.

REFERENCE: Davis and LaCour, p 386
LaTour and Eichenwald-Maki, p 719

48. During the month of May, there were 800 discharge abstracts processed at a cost of $0.90 per abstract for a total of $720.00. In June, 732 discharge abstracts were processed for a total cost of $658.80. This type of cost is known as
    A. semivariable.   B. adjustable rate.
    C. fixed.   D. variable.

REFERENCE: McLean, p 129
McWay, p 342

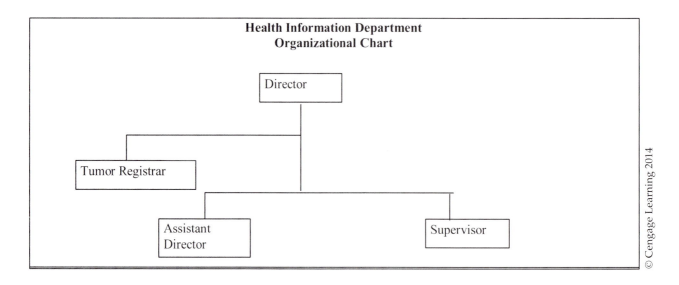

49. Which statement is an inaccurate description of the organization chart shown above?
    A. The director has authority over others in the department.
    B. The director has subordinates.
    C. The assistant director and the supervisor have a lateral relationship.
    D. The tumor registrar has authority over the assistant director.

REFERENCE: McWay, pp 256–258
LaTour and Eichenwald-Maki, p 719
Davis and LaCour, pp 384–389

50. The Director of a Health Information Department has received the quarterly variance budget report. The report indicates the "overtime" category is unfavorable. The director is required to justify this overtime expense. Which of the following would be considered an acceptable explanation for this expenditure? Overtime is unfavorable this quarter due to
    A. the annual purging of inactive files.
    B. a chronic backlog in transcription.
    C. a decrease in admissions this quarter.
    D. a lack of supervision in the file area.

REFERENCE: McWay, pp 265, 342
              LaTour and Eichenwald-Maki, pp 799–800

51. The director of a Health Information Department has asked the department supervisors to review and revise all job descriptions. Missy Harris, the supervisor over coding and analysis, has determined that the job description for the senior coders must be revised. Ms. Harris' decision to revise the job description is probably due to a change in the
    A. number of coders.
    B. recruitment practices for coders.
    C. scope of coding responsibilities.
    D. method in which the coders' performance is evaluated.

REFERENCE: McWay, pp 263–265, 300–301
              LaTour and Eichenwald-Maki, pp 727–728
              Davis and LaCour, pp 401–403

52. Which of the following is false in regard to budget variances?
    A. Variances are often calculated on the monthly budget report.
    B. Permanent budget variances do not resolve during the current fiscal year.
    C. A variance analysis identifies whether the variance is favorable or unfavorable.
    D. Temporary budget variances are expected to continue in subsequent months.

REFERENCE: McWay, pp 265, 342
              LaTour and Eichenwald-Maki, pp 799–800

53. The expense budget is also known as the
    A. production budget.   C. contract budget.
    B. operating budget.   D. profit and loss budget.

REFERENCE: Davis and LaCour, pp 395–396
              LaTour and Eichenwald-Maki, p 797

54. The Supervisor of a Health Information Department has aspirations of becoming the HID director. She works very long hours so that she can address all department issues herself rather than relying on her staff to assist her. Which type of management skills is she in need of improving in order to attain her goal of department director?
    A. delegating skills   C. motivating skills
    B. leadership skills   D. political skills

REFERENCE: McWay, pp 262–263
              LaTour and Eichenwald-Maki, pp 733, 763–764
              Davis and LaCour, p 386

55. The supervisor over release of information has requested a meeting with her superior, the Director of Health Information Services. She begins the meeting by describing how overwhelmed she is feeling. She is extremely behind in her work and she does not know what she can do to change the situation. In advising the supervisor, the director suggests that perhaps she should begin addressing her problem by attending a management workshop. Which of the following workshop topics is more likely to help the supervisor with her problem?
    A. "Leadership Styles for Women Managers and Supervisors"
    B. "The Nature of Delegation"
    C. "Understanding Your Employee"
    D. "Writing Skills for the Release of Information Supervisor"

REFERENCE: McWay, pp 262–263
             LaTour and Eichenwald-Maki, pp 733, 763–764
             Davis and LaCour, p 386

56. The Director of the Health Information Services Department is developing a plan to convert their existing filing system to a terminal digit filing system. The tool that is most useful to the director in displaying the steps and completion schedule for each phase of the conversion is a
    A. work distribution chart.   C. procedure flowchart.
    B. Gantt chart.   D. flow process chart.

REFERENCE: McWay, pp 148, 254, 271
             LaTour and Eichenwald-Maki, p 625

57. Mr. Beasley determined that the rate of absenteeism with three of his employees was 15%. He felt that this was unacceptable and decided that there were two different ways he could handle this situation. He evaluated these alternatives and thought the best thing to do would be to suspend all three for 2 days. Once he implemented this idea, he analyzed the consequences. How would you label this process?
    A. decision making   B. planning
    C. crisis management   D. communicating

REFERENCE: McWay, pp 85–87, 261–262
             LaTour and Eichenwald-Maki, pp 635–636

58. The Project Manager is responsible for all of the following functions, EXCEPT
    A. approval of the budget for the project.   B. creation of project plan.
    C. recruitment of project team.   D. recommending plan revisions.

REFERENCE: McWay, p 271
             LaTour and Eichenwald-Maki, pp 812–814

59. A basic concept of office layout and workflow is that the
    A. paper and employee move to a predetermined location.
    B. employee moves to the paper.
    C. office layout and workflow should be revised frequently.
    D. paper moves to the employee.

REFERENCE: Davis and LaCour, pp 389–393
             LaTour and Eichenwald-Maki, pp 687–689

60. Which of the following tasks is the most appropriate for the Health Information Services Director to delegate to the Supervisor of Record Processing and Statistics?
    A. formulating a record retention policy for the entire facility
    B. reviewing monthly statistical reports to verify accuracy
    C. interviewing applicants for the position of Tumor Registrar
    D. completing a performance rating on the Assistant Director of the department

REFERENCE: McWay, pp 35–36
              LaTour and Eichenwald-Maki, pp 763–764

61. When interviewing a prospective employee, which question would be inappropriate to ask?
    A. "Can you type?"
    B. "Where may we contact you?"
    C. "What language other than English can you speak or write?"
    D. "Do you own a home?"

REFERENCE: LaTour and Eichenwald-Maki, pp 729–732

62. If the budgeted payroll expense was $24,300 and the actual payroll expense was $25,800, what is the percentage of cost variance?
    A. 6.0%   C. 6.17%
    B. 0.58%   D. 6.7%

REFERENCE: McLean, pp 156–157

63. Which of the following actions illustrates the use of a participative management style?
    A. discussing suggested approaches of improving productivity and performance with employees
    B. basing decisions on information found in the manual of operations
    C. providing supervision only when requested by employees
    D. micromanaging all aspects and functions performed in the department

REFERENCE: McWay, p 269
              LaTour and Eichenwald-Maki, p 628
              Davis and LaCour, p 386

64. In deciding to purchase or lease a new dictation system, the Director of Health Information Services calculated the payback period and rate of return on the investment. The hospital's required payback period is 3 years with a required rate of return of 20%. If the equipment costs $32,000 and generates $8,000 per year in savings, what would the payback period for this equipment be?
    A. 2 years   C. 3 years
    B. 5 years   D. 4 years

REFERENCE: McWay, p 334
              LaTour and Eichenwald-Maki, pp 802–803

65. The Director of a Health Information Department prepared a document in which the following information could be obtained: job title, reporting line, span of control, and routes of promotion. The document she was preparing was a(n)
    A. job description.   C. work distribution chart.
    B. organizational chart.   D. job procedure.

REFERENCE: McWay, pp 256–258
              LaTour and Eichenwald-Maki, pp 720–721
              Davis and LaCour, pp 384–389

66. The Director of the Health Information Department had to resign immediately due to a family crisis requiring her to leave the country. Her superior, the Administrator of Support Services, must appoint an Acting Director as soon as possible but is questioning who might be the best individual for this temporary role. What tool would assist the administrator with this decision?
    A. staffing table
    B. replacement chart
    C. proximity chart
    D. frequency chart

REFERENCE: Abdelhak, pp 584–585

67. The file section supervisor is preparing the staffing budget for the coming fiscal year. Presently, the staff is filing approximately 500 charts per day. By the time the fiscal year begins, this is expected to increase to 650 charts per day. Currently, it takes nine FTEs to file 500 charts. The supervisor should project an FTE increase for the coming year's budget of
    A. 13%.
    B. 76%.
    C. 23%.
    D. 55%.

REFERENCE: Calculation

68. Lizzie O'Leary, Director of the Health Information Services Department, is writing a memo about a recent problem the department has had with a contracted copy service when she is notified of an emergency, hospital-wide department-head meeting. Because it is necessary that the memo be completed by the end of the day, it is most appropriate for the director to delegate its completion to the supervisor of
    A. storage and retrieval.
    B. transcription.
    C. coding and abstracting.
    D. release of information.

REFERENCE: McWay, pp 259, 262–263, 336
LaTour and Eichenwald-Maki, pp 733–734

69. Of the following, which is NOT considered justification to approve overtime? Overtime is not justified
    A. for unpredictable fluctuations in volume.
    B. when there is unusually high absenteeism.
    C. when there is a temporary change of work methods.
    D. for employees who want to supplement their wages.

REFERENCE: LaTour and Eichenwald-Maki, pp 799–800

70. A job analysis includes the
    A. summation of the qualifications needed in a worker for a specific job.
    B. collection of data to determine the content of a job.
    C. title of the job and summary of the basic tasks making up a job.
    D. goals to be achieved by a worker over a specified period.

REFERENCE: McWay, p 258
Abdelhak, pp 586–587
Davis and LaCour, pp 400–401, 402, 404

71. The Director of the Health Information Services Department is preparing the department's budget for the coming year. She has included the costs for the coding staff to attend at least two workshops in the budget. What portion of the department's budget will the cost of the workshops be allocated to?
    A. staffing budget
    B. revenue budget
    C. personnel budget
    D. expense budget

REFERENCE: McLean, p 152

72. The manager of a transcription agency is preparing December's staffing schedule. Because this month has several holidays, there are more requests for vacation and personal days than usual. Additionally, it is apparent to the supervisor that she will not be able to approve all requests for time off. It will be best for the supervisor to construct the schedule by
    A. processing requests based on seniority.
    B. granting requests on a first-come basis.
    C. adhering to the hospital and department policy regarding requests for time off.
    D. not approving any time off, thus eliminating any conflicts.

REFERENCE: McWay, p 252
               LaTour and Eichenwald-Maki, p 684–685, 727

73. The supervisor over the file section has discovered an enormous backlog of loose lab reports. The first step that the supervisor should take in attempting to resolve this matter is to
    A. analyze possible courses of action.
    B. gather relevant data regarding the problem.
    C. identify and clarify the problem.
    D. choose the best course of action.

REFERENCE: McWay, p 262
               LaTour and Eichenwald-Maki, pp 635–636

74. New equipment has just been purchased for a Health Information Services Department. Prior to its arrival and placement in the department, it is important for the manager to adhere to the rules and regulations governed by
    A. FDA.
    B. OSHA.
    C. CMS.
    D. SSA.

REFERENCE: McWay, pp 260, 297
               LaTour and Eichenwald-Maki, p 726
               Davis and LaCour, pp 216–217

75. The best source for obtaining data for a job analysis is the
    A. department director.
    B. supervisor of the job.
    C. the person who performs the job.
    D. procedures manual.

REFERENCE: McWay, p 258
               Abdelhak, pp 586–587

76. Mike is an information specialist in the Department of Information Technology. He has been asked to assist with the Joint Commission survey process, which accounts for approximately 75% of his time. He also receives project assignments from the HIM director, his immediate supervisor, as well as the overall project manager. This refers to what type of authority relationship?
    A. functional
    B. parallel
    C. matrix
    D. divisional

REFERENCE: Shortell and Kaluzny, p 77

77. The department director is responsible for budget costs that are controllable. Which of the following costs would be out of the director's control?
    A. equipment purchases
    B. fringe benefit cost per employee
    C. supply requisitions
    D. overtime authorizations

REFERENCE: McWay, pp 339–342
Davis and LaCour, pp 395–396

78. Kim Khoury is planning a luncheon for the team members and stakeholders on the CPOE implementation to celebrate reaching a major milestone. Which of the following is true?
    A. Acknowledging accomplishments and milestones motivates teams.
    B. Budgets rarely permit these extra expenses.
    C. Celebrations are only appropriate at the close of a project.
    D. Professionals are self-motivated, making celebrations unnecessary.

REFERENCE: McWay, p 266
LaTour and Eichenwald-Maki, p 821

79. Beth Huber, Director of Health Information, has been selected to participate in a strategic planning retreat for her health system. In preparation, she refreshes her understanding of strategic planning. Which of the following will likely be included in the retreat?

    A. improvement of existing programs and services
    B. opportunities to review internal structures and systems
    C. enhancing customer and patient satisfaction
    D. focus on the organization's fit with the external environment

REFERENCE: McWay, pp 249–251
LaTour and Eichenwald-Maki, pp 825–827

80. The project definition justifies the need for the new project. What would you expect to see in the project justification?
    A. project scope, resources needed, and amount of time required
    B. project scope, resources needed, and developing the solution
    C. resources needed, amount of time required, and preparing supporting documentation for the system chosen
    D. amount of time required, alternative analysis, and implementation review

REFERENCE: McWay, pp 270–271, 318–319
LaTour and Eichenwald-Maki, pp 812–814

81. Roberta Little Eagle is the new HIM supervisor at a large South Dakota reservation clinic. In order to become familiar with the specific steps currently used in record processing, she uses which graphic tool?
    A. force field analysis   C. fishbone analysis
    B. histogram   D. flowchart

REFERENCE: McWay, p 263
LaTour and Eichenwald-Maki, pp 687–689
Davis and LaCour, pp 307–308

82. Megan is the new Director of Health Information at Blue Ridge Rehabilitation Associates, a large multispecialty clinic. Her initial assessment of the department's functioning is that there is considerable duplication of effort. To collect information on the systems used in the current functions and to analyze and improve the process, she chose to use a
    A. work process flowchart.
    B. systems diagram.
    C. decision tree.
    D. Pareto chart.

REFERENCE: McWay, pp 260–261, 263

83. Which of the following would NOT be a scientific method of establishing standards?
    A. stopwatch studies
    B. work sampling
    C. personal experience
    D. time-log studies

REFERENCE: McWay, pp 264–265
              LaTour and Eichenwald-Maki, pp 689–695

84. Lucy Ann manages a claims review unit for an insurance company. Her staff keys a high volume of data daily. She has scheduled a staff physical therapist to do the annual ergonomics presentation to help prevent repetitive strain injuries. All of the following would be included EXCEPT
    A. using a footrest.
    B. wrists should be elevated.
    C. monitor placed directly in front and elevated.
    D. lumbar support provided.

REFERENCE: Marreel and McLellan, pp 171–177
              Davis and LaCour, pp 420–421, 429
              LaTour and Eichenwald-Maki, pp 682–683

85. South Beach Medical Center is preparing to open as a new 250-bed acute care hospital. This facility is located in a growing area of the city and is projected to have 85% occupancy within 3 years. To determine the number of employees needed in the HIM department, the director must first
    A. determine employee salary ranges.
    B. develop a departmental organizational chart.
    C. collect data from hospitals that are of comparable size.
    D. identify the departmental functions to be performed.

REFERENCE: McWay, p 252
              Davis and LaCour, pp 386–390
              LaTour and Eichenwald-Maki, p 725

86. A national HIM publication routinely requests that practitioners submit statistics from their facility regarding department functions. These are then summarized and published in graphic form, providing a tool for which of the following activities?
    A. benchmarking
    B. work standards
    C. job evaluation
    D. job redesign

REFERENCE: McWay, pp 148, 153, 157
              Davis and LaCour, p 293
              LaTour and Eichenwald-Maki, pp 691–692

87. In project management, the series of specific tasks that determine the overall project duration is referred to as
    A. project network.
    B. critical path.
    C. risk analysis.
    D. project definition.

REFERENCE: LaTour and Eichenwald-Maki, p 816

88. The formalized road map that describes how your institution executes the chosen strategy defines
    A. operations improvement.
    B. strategic thinking.
    C. operational mission.
    D. strategic planning.

REFERENCE: LaTour and Eichenwald-Maki, p 824

89. Which of the following is a tool for strategic thinking?
    A. storytelling
    B. driving force
    C. innovations
    D. critical issues

REFERENCE: LaTour and Eichenwald-Maki, p 831

90. Which of the following helps the organization prioritize investment opportunities?
    A. return on investment
    B. profitability index
    C. net present value
    D. internal rate of return

REFERENCE: LaTour and Eichenwald-Maki, p 804

91. Which of the following emphasizes the work climate in which harmony and cohesion promote good work?
    A. effectiveness
    B. chain of command
    C. scalar chain
    D. esprit de corps

REFERENCE: LaTour and Eichenwald-Maki, p 626

92. Which of the following is often characterized as a manager's version of a pilot's cockpit as it contains all the critical information for leading the organization?
    A. balanced scorecard
    B. revenge effect
    C. executive dashboard
    D. groupthink

REFERENCE: LaTour and Eichenwald-Maki, p 632

93. The statement "Managers must understand the informal organization of workers (groups, group sentiments, team work), the need of workers to be listened to and to participate in the design of their work" is characteristic of which of the following schools of management?
    A. Classical School of Administration
    B. Human Relations School
    C. Scientific Management School
    D. Decision-making School

REFERENCE: Shortell & Kaluzny, pp 16–17

94. Units that provide support services to the organization, such as human resources, finances, and information systems, are referred to as
    A. line managers.
    B. integrated delivery systems.
    C. matrix organization.
    D. staff departments.

REFERENCE: Shortell & Kaluzny, p 79

95. In Maslow's "hierarchy or needs," the term that describes the need for a positive self-image or self-respect, and the need for recognition and respect from others best describes
    A. belonging needs.
    B. security needs.
    C. esteem needs.
    D. self-actualization needs.

REFERENCE: Shortell & Kaluzny, pp 97–98

96. The Occupational Safety and Health Act of 1970, the Americans with Disability Act, and the Vocational Rehabilitation Act are all federal legislation designed to
    A. prevent sexual harassment.
    B. ensure equal pay for equal work.
    C. keep the workplace safe and accessible to all employees and customers.
    D. protect child labor.

REFERENCE: Abdelhak, p 577

97. Which of the following methods of performance appraisal requires the supervisor to document exceptional behavior by the employee?
    A. Behaviorally Anchored Rating
    B. Graphic Rating Scales
    C. Goal Setting
    D. Critical Incident Method

REFERENCE: Abdelhak, pp 594–595

98. The HIM employee is consistently late for work. Her supervisor has given her an oral warning. According to the definition of progressive discipline, what would the next step be?
    A. written warning and reprimand
    B. meeting with the supervisor of her supervisor
    C. suspension
    D. termination

REFERENCE: Abdelhak, p 601

99. There are several methods used to evaluate jobs. Which of the following is the simplest but the least precise?
    A. factor comparison   C. job grading
    B. job ranking   D. point system

REFERENCE: Abdelhak, p 605-606

100. An example of a communication network that is suitable to use when you have to communicate with several people who have no need to communicate directly with each other describes
    A. wheel.   C. circle.
    B. chain.   D. a "Y" pattern.

REFERENCE: Shortell & Kaluzny, p 181

101. A type of job evaluation that requires the identification of essential factors or elements common to all jobs and the comparison of jobs on the basis of rating those elements (not the job as a whole), refers to
    A. job ranking.   C. factor comparison.
    B. job grading.   D. point system.

REFERENCE: Abdelhak, p 607

102. The mechanism that provides a communication and problem-solving tool for employees to express a complaint that management has violated one of its own policies, and caused adverse consequences to the employee, refers to
    A. employee discipline   C. involuntary retirement
    B. the grievance process   D. employee counseling

REFERENCE: Abdelhak, p 601

103. The National Labor Relations Act (NLRA), which serves as the foundation for U.S. labor laws and collective bargaining, is also known as
    A. the Equal Pay Act.
    B. the Fair Labor Standards Act.
    C. the Family and Medical Leave Act.
    D. the Wagner Act.

REFERENCE: Abdelhak, p 578

104. Which of the following examples would NOT be considered "reasonable accommodation" under the Americans with Disabilities Act?
    A. completely renovating an entire department to accommodate a disabled employee
    B. providing qualified readers or interpreters
    C. reassigning a current employee to a vacant position
    D. acquiring or modifying equipment

REFERENCE: Abdelhak, p 576

105. An amendment to the Civil Rights Act of 1964 that extends the 180-day statute of limitations previously applied to the filing of an equal-pay lawsuit refers to the
    A. Americans with Disabilities Act.
    B. Lilly Ledbetter Fair Pay Act.
    C. Age Discrimination in Employment Act.
    D. Family and Medical Leave Act.

REFERERNCE: Abdelhak, p 573

106. Which of the following is NOT a main objective of reengineering?
    A. to improve quality
    B. to increase revenue
    C. to increase cost
    D. to reduce risk

REFERENCE: Abdelhak, p 645

Answer Key for Organization and Management

ANSWER   EXPLANATION

NOTE: Explanations are provided for those questions that require mathematical calculations and questions that are not clearly explained in the references that are cited.

1. D

2. B   The reference pages indicated do not answer the question directly. The references relate to discussions of the organizational structure and design. Based on that information, assumptions regarding organizational relationships (vertical, lateral, matrix, etc.) can be made.

3. C

4. D   Remember to convert the hours to minutes.
725×12 minutes = 8,700 minutes
1,280 hours $\times$ 60 minutes = 76,800 minutes
8,700 minutes on coding/76,800 minutes worked = 11.3% spent on coding

5. D

6. B   This is clearly a problem of not understanding the procedures of the tasks; therefore, reviewing the job description probably will not be of much help. This rules out answers A and C. This also does not seem to be a problem that would require an in-service, thereby ruling out answer D. Therefore, the best solution is to review the procedures with her and have the analysis clerk monitor her progress to ensure that she fully understands the procedures.

7. A

8. C

9. B   Answers A and C describe a standard. Answer D describes a rule.

10. C

11. D $1,255 - 48 = 1,207$; $1,207 / 1,255 = 0.96 \times 100 = 96\%$

12. B   Formula: Total actual work units $\times$ 100/ Standard work units = variance percent
$(30 + 40 + 25 + 35) \times 100 = 13,000$ $13,000/200 = 65\%$

13. B

14. B   The hours must first be converted to minutes.
7 hours $\times$ 60 = 420 minutes
420 minutes $\times$ 0.20 = 84 minutes

15. A

16. C

17. C

18. B

19. D $950 \times 20 = 19,000$; $142,500/19,000 = 7.5$ FTEs

20. B

21. A

22. C

23. C   20 charts $\times$ 5 days = 100 per week $\times$ 4 weeks = 400
A standard of 400 charts coded over 4 weeks per coder.
Coder 3 has coded only 320 charts over the 4 weeks.

24. B

25. D

26. D

27. C   It is the physician's responsibility to ensure that a patient has consented to a surgical procedure.

Answer Key for Organization and Management

ANSWER   EXPLANATION

28. A
29. D
30. C   Although a CEO is involved in all of the options given, only the organizational objectives are completed annually. The mission statement is reviewed to ensure that the organizational objectives are consistent with it, but it is not revised annually. Strategic goals and objectives are completed on a long-term basis, not annually.
31. B
32. C
33. A   In order to determine which vendor to choose, each vendor's scores are added. The vendor that scores the highest for all three criteria is chosen. Calculations: Multiply the weight for each criterion by the rating. After this is done, each column is totaled. Vendor A scores 38; Vendor B, 25; Vendor C, 37; Vendor D, 27.
34. C   Costs = $6,000 + $1,500 + $500 = $8,000.
         Benefits = $10,000. (That is the increase in reimbursement.)
         10,000/8,000 = 1.25. Benefits/Costs Ratio = 1.25. (This also known as the cost–benefit figure.) In other words, for every dollar invested in the encoding system, it will have a return of $1.25 after one year.
35. B
36. C
37. D
38. B $7.10 \times 0.04 = 0.284 + $7.10 = $7.384
39. D
40. A
41. B
42. D $2,000 \times $13.50 = $27,000; $27,000/225,333 = 0.1198$, rounded to 0.12
43. B   The formula for budget variance percent is actual minus budget divided by budget.
         675 − 495 = 180
         (180 × 100)/495 = 36%
44. B
45. A   To determine the number of employees needed for a specific job, first determine how much time the work requires. In this case, we know we will have an additional 120 records per day and each record will average about 15 minutes. To figure the amount of total time, multiply 120 × 15 = 1,800 minutes. Compute this to hours by dividing by 60 (60 minutes in an hour): 1,800/60 = 30 hours. Based on the 8-hour day, divide 30 hours by 8 = 3.75 FTEs.
46. D
47. A
48. D
49. D
50. A
51. C
52. D
53. B
54. A
55. B
56. B   A Gantt chart is a scheduling tool.
57. A

Answer Key for Organization and Management
ANSWER EXPLANATION

58. A
59. D
60. B
61. D One must be familiar with the various labor laws to ensure that an interviewee is not asked questions that could be considered discriminating or illegal.
62. C $25,800 - 24,300 = 1,500; 1,500/24,300 = 0.0617 \times 100 = 6.17\%$
63. A
64. D Formula: initial investment/annual cash flow = payback period $32,000/$8,000 = 4 years
65. B
66. B
67. C Currently, each FTE files 55.5 charts (500/9 = 55.5).
- Since there will be 150 more charts per day needing filing (150/55.5 = 2.70), you will need 2.70 FTEs for filing the extra charts.
- Add current 9 FTE to the 2.70 FTE increase needed = 11.7 FTE.
- Divide by the increase of 2.7 FTE by the 11.7 total FTE needed to get the percentage increase in FTE. (2.7/11.7 = 23% increase).

For an anticipated increase from 500 to 650 you need to increase your filing FTE staff by 23%.
68. D
69. D
70. B
71. D
72. C
73. C
74. B
75. C
76. C
77. B
78. A
79. D
80. A
81. D
82. A
83. C Personal experience is subjective. A, B, and D rely on objective measurement of job performance.
84. B Wrists should be in a neutral position.
85. D
86. A
87. B
88. D
89. A
90. B
91. D
92. C
93. B
94. D
95. C
96. C

Answer Key for Organization and Management
ANSWER EXPLANATION

97. D
98. A
99. B
100. A
101. C
102. B
103. D
104. A
105. B
106. C

REFERENCES

Abdelhak, M., Grostick, S., Hanken, M. A., & Jacobs, E. (2012). *Health information: Management of a strategic resource* (4th ed.). Philadelphia: W. B. Saunders.

Davis, N., & LaCour, M. (2007). *Health information technology* (2nd ed.). Philadelphia: W. B. Saunders.

LaTour, K., & Eichenwald-Maki, S. (2010). *Health information management: Concepts, principles, and practice* (3rd ed.). Chicago: American Health Information Management Association (AHIMA).

McLean, R. (2003). *Financial management in health care organizations.* Clifton Park, NY: Delmar Cengage Learning.

McWay, D. (2008). *Today's health information management: An integrated approach.* Clifton Park, NY: Delmar Cengage Learning.

Shortell, S., & Kaluzny, A. (2012). *Health care management: Organization design and behavior.* Clifton Park, NY: Delmar Cengage Learning.

Competency Domains for Organization and Management

Question	RHIA Domain	RHIT Domain
1–106	4	
1–24		1

XVI. Human Resources

Mary Spivey Teslow, MLIS, RHIA

Use the following information to answer questions 1–3.

The training staff in the Human Resources Department is proposing a computer-based training program for 200 employees and needs to prepare a budget for the time and cost of the training.
- The training program will be 30 minutes in length.
- The employees can take the training online at any time.
- There are 200 employees to be trained.
- The rate of pay for 50 of the employees is $15.50 per hour.
- The rate of pay for 50 employees is $12.00 per hour.
- The rate of pay for the other 100 employees is $18.00.

1. How many employee clock hours will be needed to complete the training?
   A. 200 hours
   B. 150 hours
   C. 100 hours
   D. 50 hours

REFERENCE: Horton, pp 136–139
                Davis and LaCour, pp 382–383
                Koch, pp 55–56
                Liebler and McConnell, pp 243, 385–387

2. When submitting the cost of training, how much should the training staff request in the budget for doing the computer-based training program?
   A. $3,175.00
   B. $1,975.00
   C. $1,887.50
   D. $1,587.50

REFERENCE: Horton, pp 136–139, 150–151
                Davis and LaCour, pp 382–383
                Koch, pp 55–56
                Liebler and McConnell, pp 243, 385–387

3. What would be the average cost for training an employee?
   A. $7.94
   B. $9.00
   C. $15.50
   D. $15.87

REFERENCE: Horton, pp 136–139
                Davis and LaCour, pp 382–383
                Koch, pp 55–56

4. At Great Plains Regional Hospital, record processing takes approximately 18 minutes. If there are 15,620 discharges for the month, how many personnel hours are needed for this volume of work?
   A. 2,891
   B. 4,686
   C. 5,496
   D. 3,394

REFERENCE: Abdelhak, p 584
                Koch, pp 55–56
                Horton, pp 146–147
                Davis and LaCour, pp 382–383
                LaTour and Eichenwald-Maki, p 690
                Liebler and McConnell, pp 243, 385–387
                McConnell, pp 350–351

5. The advantages of teams or committees over individuals in complex situations include all of the following EXCEPT:
   A. Decision making is accomplished more quickly.
   B. Complex problems can be better assessed.
   C. Authority can be counterbalanced.
   D. Coordination and cooperation can be increased.

REFERENCE: McWay, pp 304–305
                       Johns, pp 1036–1037

6. Mallory, the coding supervisor, must determine the number of full-time employees (FTEs) needed to code 600 discharges per week. It takes an average of 20 minutes to code each record and each coder will work 40 hours per week. How many coders are needed?
   A. 6.0
   B. 5.0
   C. 12.0
   D. 4.5

REFERENCE: Abdelhak, p 584
                       Koch, pp 55–56
                       Horton, pp 146–147
                       LaTour and Eichenwald-Maki, p 690
                       Davis and LaCour, pp 382–383
                       McConnell, pp 350–351
                       Liebler and McConnell, p 243

7. Under the Americans with Disabilities Act (ADA), prior to employment, it is illegal to require a
   A. math aptitude test.
   B. typing skill test.
   C. coding proficiency test.
   D. physical exam.

REFERENCE: McWay, pp 295–297
                       Abdelhak, pp 575–576
                       Johns, p 863

8. Jason, an HIM educator, plans to lecture on department design and the legislative act or agency that was created to ensure that workers have a safe and healthy work environment. Which of the following legal issue will he describe?
   A. OSHA Act
   B. Wagner Act
   C. Taft-Hartley Law
   D. Labor Management Relations Act

REFERENCE: McWay, pp 293, 297–298
                       Abdelhak, p 577
                       Davis and LaCour, pp 216–217
                       Johns, p 863
                       LaTour and Eichenwald-Maki, p 726

9. Dana has prepared a performance appraisal for one of her employees. As the HIM director reviews the evaluation, he notes that the employee received an overall rating of "needs improvement." After reading the comments, the director asks Dana to document specific performance improvement recommendations. Dana is unable to do so because she is basing her assessment on her memory of incidents that have occurred over the past year. The director suggests that Dana reassess the employee's evaluation because, ideally, performance appraisals should occur
   A. at the end of the 90-day probationary period.
   B. when the employee needs counseling.
   C. on a continuous basis.
   D. once a year.

REFERENCE: McWay, pp 300–304
               Abdelhak, pp 590–594
               Davis and LaCour, pp 406–409
               LaTour and Eichenwald-Maki, p 735
               McConnell, p 205

10. Trevor is a new scanning technician. To fulfill your responsibility as a supervisor and to help him learn and complete his work correctly, the best training resource to use would be a
    A. job description.
    B. method.
    C. policy.
    D. procedure.

REFERENCE: Abdelhak, p 646
               Johns, pp 1031–1032
               LaTour & Maki, p 687

11. Gregg is a recent graduate who has applied for a Trauma Registry position at a Chicago hospital while he prepares to apply to graduate school. In making the decision, he considers the offer of $15 per hour for a 40-hour week, benefits of 27.5% of his salary, and tuition waivers of six credits per year at $145. He calculated that his total compensation would be
    A. $40,650.00.
    B. $39,563.25.
    C. $38,599.00.
    D. $31,030.00.

REFERENCE: Koch, pp 55–56

12. Yanique is a new supervisor at a mental health facility. She discovers that one of her employees has shared her password with a coworker. This action violates policies and procedures and is the first occasion of difficulty with this employee. Disciplinary action should be taken by
    A. waiting for another occurrence to act.
    B. referring the action to Human Resources.
    C. asking for guidance from Human Resources and then acting.
    D. immediately dismissing the employee.

REFERENCE: McWay, pp 302–303
               Abdelhak, pp 601–603
               Liebler and McConnell, pp 425–426

13. Conflict is inevitable. What is the LEAST effective way to manage conflict?
    A. Acknowledge that creative solutions often come from conflict and do not intervene.
    B. Encourage the parties to compromise by each willing to lose part of their position.
    B. Limit or control interaction when emotions are intense.
    C. Use an objective third party to seek a constructive outcome for both parties.

REFERENCE: Johns, pp 1046–1048
               LaTour and Eichenwald-Maki, p 736
               Liebler and McConnell, p 333

14. The HIPAA Privacy and Security Rule requires that training be documented. What methods of documenting training efforts need to be used?
    A. retention of training aids and handouts
    B. meeting handouts and minutes
    C. training content, training dates, and attendee names
    D. signed confidentiality statements

REFERENCE: AHIMA Practice Brief

15. Holly is the day supervisor who works from 7:00 AM to 4:00 PM. Kim is the evening supervisor who works from 2:00 PM to 11:00 PM. Sarah is a transcriptionist who works from 10:00 AM to 7:00 PM, which overlaps the day and evening shifts. Sarah asked Holly, the day supervisor, if she could leave early for personal reasons. Holly said Sarah could leave early if Kim, the evening supervisor, agrees. Which theory of management does this situation violate?
    A. span of control   C. specialization of labor
    B. formal theory of authority   D. unity of command

REFERENCE: Davis and LaCour, p 386
               LaTour and Eichenwald-Maki, p 719
               McConnell, pp 56–57
               Liebler and McConnell, p 130

16. You are preparing a training program for specific functional areas of the department (e.g. coding, transcription, etc.). Which of the following is the primary factor to consider in developing an effective training program?
    A. credentials of the employees
    B. objectives of each functional area
    C. cost of training the employees
    D. number of employees to be trained

REFERENCE: McWay, pp 286–290
               Abdelhak, p 607
               Davis and LaCour, pp 432–436
               LaTour and Eichenwald-Maki, p 745

17. Grace Holt, RHIA, is the HIM Department Manager. She is reviewing interviewing techniques with Maria Hernandez, RHIT, as she prepares to interview for a new analyst. Grace recommends that Maria should
    A. ask questions that encourage a "yes" or "no" response.
    B. politely interrupt occasionally to seek clarification.
    C. talk down to the applicant to show authority.
    D. phrase questions so the expected answer is encouraged.

REFERENCE: McWay, pp 284–286
               Abdelhak, pp 591–592
               Davis and LaCour, pp 411–416
               Johns, pp 1039–1040
               McConnell, pp 139–141

18. Your job description states that as Assistant Director of the HIM Department, you will supervise day-to-day operations for the record processing, transcription, and release of information areas. What principle of management is described?
    A. specialization   C. span of control
    B. centralized authority   D. delegation

REFERENCE: Davis and LaCour, pp 485–486
               LaTour and Eichenwald-Maki, pp 630–631
               Liebler and McConnell, pp 131–132
               McConnell, p 57

19. Rachel's work performance has diminished over the last 2 weeks. In addition, she has uncharacteristic mood swings and has exhibited difficulty concentrating. She is also having difficulties with tardiness and attendance. As her supervisor, you meet with Rachel to discuss your concerns. She reveals that she is struggling financially. What action should you take?
    A. Tell her that as long as she can perform her job acceptably, her personal life is none of your concern.
    B. Put her on probation.
    C. Refer her to the Employee Assistance Program.
    D. Terminate her.

REFERENCE: McWay, pp 301–302
               Abdelhak, p 601
               McConnell, pp 244–245

20. Nancy arrives for work Monday through Friday any time between 7:00 and 9:00 AM, is on the job until at least 3:00 PM, and then may leave any time between 3:00 and 6:00 PM. Nancy's schedule is an example of
    A. the 8/80 work week.
    B. the staggered work hours program.
    C. variable work schedule.
    D. flextime.

REFERENCE: Abdelhak, pp 568–599
               Johns, p 1062
               LaTour and Eichenwald-Maki, pp 759–760

21. Use the following statistics from Utah Home Health to calculate the absenteeism rate.

Month: January	
Number of employees	20
Number of workdays	22
Total work days lost	25

    A. 0.44%   C. 5.8%

    B. 5.68%   D. 0.568%

REFERENCE: McWay, p 198
                        Horton, pp 16–19

22. As an HIM supervisor, one of your employees reports that a coworker has returned from lunch on numerous occasions with the smell of alcohol on his breath. What is the best approach in handling this problem?
    A. Confront the employee and place him on suspension for 1 week.
    B. Terminate the employee immediately.
    C. Ignore the report because it is hearsay.
    D. Handle the situation as you would any other disease that affects an employee's work.

REFERENCE: McWay, pp 301–303
                        Abdelhak, p 601
                        McConnell, pp 243–245

23. Gary's primary concern is job continuity and adequate health insurance for his large family. What level of Maslow's hierarchy of needs does Gary operate from?
    A. physiological   C. esteem
    B. self-actualization   D. safety

REFERENCE: McWay, pp 265–266
                        LaTour and Eichenwald-Maki, p 627
                        McConnell, pp 180–182

24. Employers may be able to demonstrate that age is a reasonable requirement for a position. Such an exception to the Age Discrimination in Employment Act (ADEA) is called a
    A. job description essential.
    B. bona fide occupational qualification.
    C. essential element for employment.
    D. there is no such exception to ADEA.

REFERENCE: McWay, p 295
                        Abdelhak, pp 576–577
                        McConnell, pp 456–457

25. Julian supervises the department's coding section. He notices that the coding technician is working 30 additional minutes each day before clocking in at her scheduled starting time. After discussing her timecard with her, he discovers that she is starting work early in order to check the unbilled account report. Under which act are you required to pay her for all hours worked?
   A. ERISA
   B. Fair Labor Standards Act
   C. National Labor Relations Act
   D. Equal Pay Act

REFERENCE: McWay, pp 446–451
               Abdelhak, p 578
               LaTour and Eichenwald-Maki, p 734
               McConnell, pp 551–553

26. Puget Sound Health System has set hiring goals and taken steps to guarantee equal employment opportunities for members of protected groups (e.g., American Indians, veterans, etc.). It is complying with
   A. Affirmative Action.
   B. Equal Pay Act.
   C. Minority Hiring Act.
   D. Civil Rights Act.

REFERENCE: McWay, p 307
               Abdelhak, pp 574–575
               McConnell, pp 453–454

27. Southwest Health System has numerous semiretired staff. The Human Resources Department has provided training regarding the Age Discrimination in Employment Act (ADEA). They emphasized that it protects employees and applicants between what ages?
   A. 50 and 75
   B. 45 and 99
   C. 62 and 85
   D. 40 and over

REFERENCE: McWay, p 295
               Abdelhak, pp 576–577
               Johns, p 863
               McConnell, pp 456–457

28. Which of the following HIPAA components would the general New Employee Orientation training most likely cover?
   A. marketing issues
   B. business associate agreements
   C. physical/workstation security
   D. job-specific training (e.g., patient's right to amend record)

REFERENCE: AHIMA Practice Brief

29. Krista combined her HIM and legal education and is now a Risk Manager. An employee has a complaint that may be considered a grievance. She should listen to the employee and then
   A. put the complaint aside to see if other employees complain about the same issue.
   B. deal with the issue as if it were a bona fide grievance.
   C. deal with the complaint only if the employee seldom complains.
   D. ignore the complaint until it is in writing.

REFERENCE: McWay, pp 302–303
               Abdelhak, pp 603–604
               Johns, p 1048
               LaTour and Eichenwald-Maki, p 736

30. Human Resources provide training for new supervisors. It includes discussion of the Equal Pay Act, which was passed to eliminate discrimination based on which of the following?
    A. merit of the employee
    B. seniority of the employee
    C. employee gender
    D. personal productivity, such as in a incentive compensation system

REFERENCE: McWay, pp 302–303
                Abdelhak, p 578
                Davis and LaCour, pp 416–417
                John, p 863
                McConnell, p 456

31. The transcription area has an opening for a transcriptionist with demonstrated skill in medical and surgical reports. Which of the following types of tests should be administered?
    A. performance   C. intelligence
    B. aptitude   D. stress

REFERENCE: McWay, p 285
                Abdelhak, p 591
                Davis and LaCour, pp 416–417
                LaTour and Eichenwald-Maki, p 731
                McConnell, p 135

32. As manager of release of information, you supervise an employee who has been a correspondence clerk for many years. Her performance has gradually diminished and has become substandard. What method would most likely prove to be INEFFECTIVE in assisting this employee in improving her performance?
    A. threatening to fire the employee
    B. asking the employee to cross-train with other employees
    C. delegation of special assignments
    D. creating an action plan with the employee

REFERENCE: McWay, pp 303–304
                Abdelhak, pp 601–602
                LaTour and Eichenwald-Maki, p 735
                McConnell, pp 224–225

33. The HIM clerical supervisor, Debbie, is concerned that some employees are not utilizing their talents and skills effectively. Which of the following should Debbie consider first?
    A. revising job descriptions
    B. performing a job analysis
    C. observing the workers more closely
    D. giving the employees additional responsibilities

REFERENCE: McWay, pp 303–304
                Abdelhak, pp 586–587
                Liebler and McConnell, pp 155–156
                McConnell, pp 190–191

34. After receiving completed requisitions to fill positions within the HIM Department, Human Resources can be most effective in recruiting qualified applicants with the assistance of a
    A. departmental organizational chart.
    B. current job description.
    C. salary schedule.
    D. employee benefits handbook.

REFERENCE: McWay, pp 259, 300
               Abdelhak, pp 587–588
               Davis and LaCour, pp 401–402
               Johns, p 1063
               LaTour and Eichenwald-Maki, pp 727–728
               Liebler and McConnell, pp 159–161
               McConnell, p 259

35. You are interviewing a candidate for a position for handling subpoenas in the release of information section. Which of the following is the LEAST appropriate information to ask an interviewee to provide?
    A. Do you have transportation for attendance at depositions and court?
    B. Please share an experience where you had to determine applicable state law.
    C. Please provide a copy of your most recent CE certificate and AHIMA membership.
    D. Do you have family responsibilities that would keep you from remaining at a trial?

REFERENCE: McWay, pp 284–286
               Johns, pp 1039–1040
               McConnell, pp 136–137

36. Carlos has noted increased complaints by employees of headaches and fatigue. Which of the following factors should he consider?
    A. room temperature   C. lighting
    B. humidity   D. air quality

REFERENCE: McWay, p 13
               Abdelhak, pp 653–656
               LaTour and Eichenwald-Maki, p 682

37. Which of the following describes the act that requires employers to make reasonable accommodations in the workplace for individuals to perform essential job functions?
    A. Age Discrimination Act
    B. Americans with Disabilities Act
    C. Rehabilitation Act
    D. Equal Opportunity Employment Act

REFERENCE: McWay, pp 295–297
               Abdelhak, pp 575–576
               Johns, p 863
               LaTour and Eichenwald-Maki, p 754
               Liebler and McConnell, pp 455–456
               McConnell, pp 457–458
               Davis and LaCour, p 417

38. Eva Pulaski supervises the electronic document management (EDM) section. She is preparing a report that includes a graphic that displays data over time and provides an excellent visualization of quality and quantity trends. This style of a report is called a(n)
    A. Pareto chart.
    B. correlation analysis.
    C. run or line chart.
    D. scatter diagram.

REFERENCE: McWay, pp 149, 151, 201
              Abdelhak, pp 382–385
              Johns, p 623
              Koch, pp 247–278
              LaTour and Eichenwald-Maki, pp 136–138, 450
              Liebler and McConnell, p 216

39. Kari works 40 hours per week at Rio Grande Radiology, which pays time-and-a-half for overtime and double-time for holidays. During the past week, Kari took six hours of unpaid personal leave and worked an eight-hour holiday. How many hours will Kari be paid?
    A. 34
    B. 42
    C. 48
    D. 50

REFERENCE: McConnell, pp 448–451
              Koch, pp 55–56

40. Natalie was an orientation counselor in college and knows that a well-designed program can help those new to a setting feel comfortable. As a new manager, she continues her commitment and contributes to new employee orientation. Which of the following statements about orientation programs is NOT true?
    A. A good orientation program can substitute for a job-specific departmental training.
    B. The most meaningful training program includes a "show and tell" format by peers.
    C. The orientation assists the employee in learning about the workplace culture.
    D. Proper training can enhance employee satisfaction.

REFERENCE: McWay, pp 286–290
              Abdelhak, pp 593–594
              Johns, pp 1040–1042
              LaTour and Eichenwald-Maki, pp 743–744
              Davis and LaCour, pp 427–432

41. Gina is the HIPAA Privacy and Security Officer and primary trainer for a regional health system. In determining how a person in a position in a department uses health information, she must certainly review the
    A. past performance evaluations of persons in the position.
    B. position or job description.
    C. facility policy on protecting health information.
    D. facility policy and procedure on documenting training.

REFERENCE: McWay, pp 259, 300
              AHIMA Practice Brief
              LaTour and Eichenwald-Maki, p 766

42. Mary Ellen Smith has been an excellent biller for the past 5 years. Lately, you have noticed that she has the highest error rate and the lowest productivity rate of the entire billing section. She also seems to be distracted and unhappy. You have a conversation with her and she confides that she is having many "personal problems" that are causing her enormous stress. As her supervisor, you
    A. accept this explanation and determine that it is probably a temporary situation.
    B. issue a verbal warning to Mary Ellen to shape up.
    C. issue a written warning with a date to review her progress.
    D. refer her to the Employee Assistance Program.

REFERENCE: McWay, pp 301–302
               Abdelhak, p 601
               McConnell, pp 244–245

43. At Orientation a new employee receives the Employee Handbook. All of the following information about the Employee Handbook is true, EXCEPT that
    A. it provides a contractual obligation to continued employment.
    B. it provides policies and procedures developed by management.
    C. a receipt must be documented in writing.
    D. it must be reviewed periodically by legal counsel to avoid legal risk.

REFERENCE: Abdelhak, pp 588–589
               LaTour and Eichenwald, pp 726, 732–733, 743–745
               Davis and LaCour, pp 427–432

44. Fareeda's methods improvement objectives are to use an organized approach to determine how to accomplish a task with less effort in less time or at a lower cost while maintaining or improving the quality of the outcome. Frequently, methods improvement is referred to as
    A. benchmarking.   C. work simplification.
    B. work distribution.   D. data quality improvement.

REFERENCE: McWay, p 263
               Abdelhak, pp 623–624

45. You work in a unionized organization and have filed a grievance. Which of the following will most likely take place?
    A. You can be terminated for registering a grievance.
    B. The grievance procedure regulations stipulated in the union contract will be followed.
    C. Follow facility policies and procedures for prompt and fair action on any grievance.
    D. The time from complaint to resolution should be no longer than 90 days.

REFERENCE: McWay, pp 298–299, 302–303
               Abdelhak, pp 603–604
               LaTour and Eichenwald-Maki, p 736
               Johns, p 1048

46. Bay Area Home Care utilizes a discipline system that provides for stronger penalties for each successive repeat offense. They are most likely using
    A. corrective discipline.
    B. preventive discipline.
    C. progressive discipline.
    D. terminating discipline.

REFERENCE: McWay, p 302
              Abdelhak, pp 601–603
              Johns, p 1045
              LaTour and Eichenwald-Maki, p 735
              Liebler and McConnell, pp 413–416
              McConnell, p 219

47. When analyzing discipline problems, which of the following should be considered?
    A. the prior performance of the employee in question
    B. the frequency of the problem
    C. the seriousness of the problem
    D. all of the above

REFERENCE: Abdelhak, pp 601–603
              McWay, pp 302–303
              LaTour and Eichenwald-Maki, p 735
              Liebler and McConnell, pp 413–416
              McConnell, pp 225–227

48 Chris and Amy, two coders on your team, have come to you complaining that Jane, the discharge clerk, is deliberately holding back charts, causing a coding backlog. You are not sure Jane is really the cause of this problem because Chris and Amy have a history of blaming others for their work-related delays. To determine if Jane is truly a "problem employee" it would be best to first
    A. determine the source of the conflict.
    B. discretely ask other employees if they are having similar problems with Jane.
    C. request assistance from the Human Resources Department.
    D. observe Jane's interaction with others.

REFERENCE: McWay, pp 267–268
              Abdelhak, pp 600–603
              Johns, pp 1046–1048
              LaTour and Eichenwald-Maki, p 736

49. There is an opening for a coder in a 150-bed acute care hospital. The position requires someone who can code from a wide variety of medical records using both ICD and CPT. Of the following candidates interviewing for this position, which would be the most appropriate to hire?
    A. a high-school graduate who has applied for entry into the 2-year college RHIT program
    B. a recent graduate of a 4-year HIM program, RHIA eligible, who hopes to become a department manager within 1 year
    C. a graduate of a 2-year community college HIT program, RHIT eligible, with 1 year of outpatient coding experience
    D. an RHIA with 5 years of supervisory experience in medical records who recently moved to this city and can find no other available position as a supervisor at this time

REFERENCE: McWay, p 285
              Abdelhak, pp 591–593
              Johns, pp 1039–1040
              LaTour and Eichenwald-Maki, p 731

50. Your department's productivity and morale have been steadily deteriorating, while absenteeism and turnover are increasing. As you go through the department, you notice that there are some questionable jokes pinned on the department corkboard. The source of the problems you are experiencing in the department could likely be
    A. cutbacks in staffing.
    B. a need for job enrichment.
    C. boredom.
    D. sexual harassment in the workplace.

REFERENCE: McWay, p 294
               LaTour and Eichenwald, p 726
               Abdelhak, p 575
               Leibler and McConnell, pp 456–457

51. One of your new employees has just completed orientation, receiving basic HIPAA training. You are now providing more specific training related to her job. She asks whether the information she provided during the hiring process, as well as benefits claims, are also protected under HIPAA. Which of the following can you assure her that the Human Resources Department protects?
    A. all personal health information (PHI)
    B. benefits enrollment
    C. Employee Assistance Program contacts
    D. OSHA information

REFERENCE: McWay, p 299
               Abdelhak, p 577
               LaTour and Eichenwald-Maki, p 736
               McConnell, pp 272, 477

The following questions represent advanced competencies.

52. The management assumption that work and the opportunity to utilize skills, knowledge, and talents are basic human needs was presented in McGregor's
    A. Theory X.   C. Delphi Process.
    B. Theory Y.   D. Managerial Grid Model.

REFERENCE: McWay, p 269
               LaTour and Eichenwald-Maki, p 627
               Liebler and McConnell, pp 513–514

53. Emma Miller, RHIA, interviewed one applicant for the new position of data analyst and subsequently hired the applicant. During the 20-minute interview, she told the applicant about the department and hospital and what the job entailed. Much to Emma's disappointment, this newly hired employee did not work out. What went wrong?
    A. Emma asked too many questions during the interview.
    B. Emma should not have told the applicant anything about the hospital because that is the responsibility of Human Resources.
    C. Emma failed to interview enough applicants.
    D. Emma did not allow enough time for the interview.

REFERENCE: Abdelhak, pp 590–593
              Johns, pp 1038–1039
              LaTour and Eichenwald-Maki, p 731
              McConnell, pp 129–130

54. Carrie Ann provides a dynamic and effective orientation to the HIM Department. It includes all of the following EXCEPT
    A. the role and function of the department.
    B. facility emergency procedures.
    C. department policies, procedures, and rules.
    D. the organization of the department.

REFERENCE: McWay, pp 286–290
              Abdelhak, pp 593–594
              LaTour and Eichenwald-Maki, pp 744–745
              Davis and LaCour, pp 427–432

55. One of the most common rater biases that affect an employee's evaluation is the halo effect. The halo effect suggests that the supervisor
    A. rates everyone as average.
    B. is too lenient or too strict in rating employee performance.
    C. rates the employee on the basis of a strong like or dislike of the person.
    D. bases the employee evaluation on behavior in the most recent period rather than the entire evaluation period.

REFERENCE: Abdelhak, pp 598–599
              McConnell, p 199

56. Elizabeth is the manager of the state cancer registry. In developing a training "to-do list," she is reviewing the staff and what general training and specialized training topics would be necessary. What tool would be most helpful in organizing this information?
    A. Gantt chart to show who gets trained when
    B. spreadsheet with grids identifying who needs what type of training
    C. a "train-the-trainers" training manual to help in consistency in training
    D. documentation of previous orientation training to see what has already been covered

REFERENCE: AHIMA Practice Brief
              LaTour and Eichenwald-Maki, p 748

57. To ensure consistency of coverage among trainers, you may want to develop
    A. training manuals.
    B. meeting handouts and minutes.
    C. signed confidentiality statements acknowledging receipt and understanding of any training attended.
    D. ongoing training to keep the issues in front of the workforce.

REFERENCE: AHIMA Practice Brief

58. Mark Beck is a new graduate preparing for an interview. In school, he had the opportunity to role-play a technique that requires applicants to give specific examples of how they have performed a specific task or handled a specific problem in the past. This technique is becoming more popular and is known as a(n)
    A. audition interview.
    B. behavioral interview.
    C. structured interview.
    D. targeted interview.

REFERENCE: Abdelhak, pp 591–593
               LaTour and Eichenwald-Maki, p 731

59. Which of the following is NOT an advantage of committee meetings?
    A. Group judgment improves decision making.
    B. Group process stimulates creativity.
    C. Committees enhance acceptance.
    D. Committees are economical.

REFERENCE: Liebler and McConnell, pp 290–295
               McConnell, p 326

60. All of the following principles are illustrated in an organizational chart EXCEPT
    A. chain of authority.
    B. unity of command.
    C. unity of direction.
    D. span of control.

REFERENCE: LaTour and Eichenwald-Maki, pp 720–721
               Davis and LaCour, pp 427–432
               Liebler and McConnell, pp 150–151

61. As the manager of the billing department, Jessica has heard from her employees that rumors have been circulating throughout the hospital concerning centralization and layoffs. At a meeting with the CFO, all departments were asked to cut back 15%. What should Jessica tell her employees?
    A. nothing, because it would only depress them
    B. that no one in the HIM department will be laid off
    C. share with employees the facts because she knows them from the meeting
    D. tell one employee who likes to spread rumors so employees will learn from each other

REFERENCE: McWay, p 268
               Abdelhak, p 593
               LaTour and Eichenwald-Maki, pp 639–640
               Davis and LaCour, pp 439–443
               McConnell, pp 304–346

62. Which appraisal method places the employees into a set of ordered groups (e.g., top 10%, above average 20%, middle 40%) on the basis of a global measure?
    A. critical incident method
    B. behaviorally anchored ranking scales
    C. Management by Objectives
    D. forced ranking

REFERENCE: Abdelhak, pp 595–596
               McConnell, pp 189–191

63. Members of the clinical documentation improvement team have developed an extensive communication grapevine throughout the hospital. Which of the following is the least effective approach for a manager to take over this type of informal communication?
    A. be acutely aware of the grapevine
    B. control and limit interaction as best you can.
    C. check out any disturbing content or comments
    D. feed in some real, positive facts when possible

REFERENCE: Liebler and McConnell, p 493
               McConnell, pp 495–496

64. A union is engaged in an organizing campaign in a hospital facility. Which activity should management personnel AVOID during this time?
    A. telling employees that they are free to join or not to join any organization without threat to their status with the facility
    B. telling employees of the disadvantages that may result from belonging to a union
    C. promising employees a pay increase or promotion if they vote against the union
    D. telling employees the benefits they presently enjoy

REFERENCE: Abdelhak, pp 578–580
               McConnell, pp 505–507

65. Kimberly Wolf wants a Mercedes and the position of Vice President of Information Services. She feels that achieving these goals will provide her with a sense of achievement, prestige, and reputation in the eyes of others. At what level of Maslow's hierarchy of needs is she operating?
    A. esteem   C. self-actualization
    B. safety   D. basic physiological

REFERENCE: McWay, pp 265–266
               LaTour and Eichenwald-Maki, p 627
               McConnell, pp 180–181

66. Research has shown that productivity increases with all of the following interventions EXCEPT when
    A. employees are rewarded for extra output.
    B. it becomes the primary goal of management.
    C. it is measured.
    D. the office environment is reengineered.

REFERENCE: McWay, p 269
               Abdelhak, p 621

67. Human Resource managers increasingly advise which of the following as the best approach for obtaining a legally sound and reliable reference?
    A. a telephone reference from a personal friend of the applicant
    B. a written reference from a former supervisor of the applicant
    C. a telephone reference from a former supervisor of the applicant
    D. a written reference from the HR Department of the applicant's former employer

REFERENCE: McWay, pp 284–285
              Abdelhak, p 591
              LaTour and Eichenwald-Maki, p 731
              McConnell, p 139

68. In your new position as Director of Health Information Services, you have noticed that department supervisors arbitrarily allow employees to make up missed time due to absences. You decide that you need a policy to reinforce the attendance policy and cut down on tardiness and absences. Which policy statement would support your overall departmental goals?
    A. Advance approval is required for changes in work schedules and depend upon departmental operations.
    B. Sick days can be used in lieu of time missed due to tardiness or absences.
    C. No make-up time for absences and tardiness is allowed.
    D. Changes in work schedules must be approved in advance and depend upon departmental operations.

REFERENCE: McWay, p 252
              Abdelhak, pp 645–646
              LaTour and Eichenwald-Maki, pp 728–729
              McConnell, pp 240–243

69. As HIM Director, you receive a call from the CEO informing you that she has received a complaint from a patient. The patient reported that one of the coders in your department revealed his diagnosis to his neighbor. What action is recommended?
    A. Gather all the facts prior to meeting with the employee.
    B. Give the employee a written warning.
    C. Terminate the employee immediately for violation of the confidentiality policy.
    D. Immediately call a departmental meeting to discuss the importance of maintaining confidentiality.

REFERENCE: McWay, pp 301–303
              Abdelhak, pp 601–602
              McConnell, p 226

70. Miranda has decided to accept a position as a manager in a large health system. A key factor was the opportunity to work for a transformational leader. She recognizes all but one of the following characteristics observed that the Health Information Director is a transformational leader. Which of the following characteristics would be least likely to support her decision?
    A. risk taking   C. charisma
    B. mentoring   D. dependency

REFERENCE: LaTour and Eichenwald-Maki, p 659

71. Human Resources has recently provided training for and implemented a new performance appraisal system that includes input from managers, peers, and staff. This approach is typically known as
    A. 360-degree evaluation.   C. holistic appraisal.
    B. group appraisal.   D. multifactor evaluation.

REFERENCE: McWay, p 301
                 LaTour and Eichenwald-Maki, p 735

72. Employee turnover is expensive and stressful on staff. The best defense against employee dissatisfaction is
    A. the employee handbook.
    B. open and honest communication.
    C. written policies and procedures.
    D. weekly departmental meetings.

REFERENCE: McWay, p 268
                 LaTour and Eichenwald-Maki, p 639
                 Liebler and McConnell, pp 491–496
                 McConnell, pp 149–150
                 Davis and LaCour, pp 439–443

73. Human Resources use a systematic procedure to determine the relative worth of a position to the organization. When this approach is used, compensation for the position is most likely based on
    A. job evaluation.   C. job survey.
    B. job planning.   D. job ranking.

REFERENCE: McWay, p 259
                 LaTour and Eichenwald-Maki, pp 734–735
                 Liebler and McConnell, p 195

74. Summer is the document imaging manager. She has had a meeting with the scanning clerks. They are complaining that the pay rate for their position is too low in their facility. What would be the best way to deal with this complaint?
    A. Submit a request for merit raises for all scanning clerks.
    B. Work with Human Resources on a job evaluation and current wage and salary survey.
    C. Explain to the scanning clerks that health care cost containment means little money for raises.
    D. Ignore the complaint.

REFERENCE: McWay, p 259
                 Abdelhak, pp 606–607
                 LaTour and Eichenwald-Maki, p 734
                 McConnell, p 256

75. The teaching method selected by an instructor influences the student's ability to understand the material. Instructor-led classrooms work best when
    A. in-depth training and interaction are desired.
    B. there are three shifts of employees to train.
    C. you want to minimize the cost for training.
    D. employees from all departments must be trained.

REFERENCE: AHIMA Practice Brief
                    LaTour and Eichenwald-Maki, pp 755–756

76. Which of the following scenarios best describes job enrichment as a motivational technique?
    A. Anna is an effective data analyst. In addition to her regular job duties, her supervisor has assigned her to special projects and committee assignments.
    B. Becky prefers to work where she can be active and have personal contacts. The supervisor rotates her through all clerical jobs in the department so that she can have variety in her work.
    C. Cheryl's job keeps her fully occupied all day. In fact, she frequently has to rush to get the work completed daily. Cheryl's supervisor decides to remove some responsibility from her job so she has less stress.
    D. Derek has worked in the department for several years. His supervisor decided to combine several jobs and add other tasks to enable Derek to use his knowledge and skills gained in school. With these increased responsibilities he is increasing his chances of being promoted.

REFERENCE: McWay, pp 266–267
                    McConnell, pp 187–188

77. Amanda, an EHR implementation manager, wants to increase her staff's problem-solving skills. Which of the following approaches is likely to have the best and most long-lasting results?
    A. hiring a consultant to assess the EHR implementation strategies
    B. developing an EHR implementation work team
    C. taking a field trip to a neighboring facility known for project management
    D. request that Human Resources conduct a training session on program solving

REFERENCE: McWay, pp 304–305
                    LaTour and Eichenwald-Maki, p 733
                    Liebler and McConnell, pp 358–360

78. According to Frederick Herzberg, challenging work, recognition of workers and their accomplishments, and employee self-improvement are examples of
    A. maintenance factors.
    B. needs.
    C. motivators.
    D. hygienic factors.

REFERENCE: McWay, p 266
                    Liebler and McConnell, p 370
                    McConnell, pp 177–179

79. Tina, the Coding Supervisor at Highlands Hospital, has heard rumors that her facility is starting a coding training program. Rumor also has it that the HIM Director is trying to recruit the coding supervisor from a neighboring hospital to head up the training position. Tina makes the following statement to the assistant director: "I'm obviously not good enough for the training position. Perhaps I should resign." How should the assistant director respond?
    A. ignore Tina's statement
    B. refer Tina to the Employee Assistance Program
    C. assist Tina in developing her career goals
    D. guarantee Tina that she will be considered for the position

REFERENCE: McWay, pp 290–291, 303–304
               Abdelhak, pp 607–609
               LaTour and Eichenwald-Maki, p 732
               Liebler and McConnell, p 240

80. HIM professionals should be prepared with a clear statement of their department's functions and value that can be delivered during a brief encounter. This is typically called a/an
    A. e-alert   C. public relations pitch
    B. elevator speech   D. value proposition

REFERENCE: McConnell, p 375

81. Your organization's employees consist of a mixture of women and men. The women are of all ages, some are single mothers, others are married women with no children, and still others are women who care for older parents at home. The men also have varying personal lifestyles. Human Resources have designed a new benefit program that allows employees to choose from an array of benefits based on their own needs or lifestyle. The new benefit program is called a(n)
    A. prepaid benefit plan.
    B. cafeteria benefit plan.
    C. flexible benefit plan.
    D. employee-driven benefit plan.

REFERENCE: Abdelhak, pp 568–569

82. Samantha is the evening discharge analysis clerk. As the evening supervisor, you personally trained her regarding the correct job procedures and policies. Within the last 2 months, Samantha has received an oral and written warning for failure to follow job procedures. Your facility utilizes a progressive discipline system. What is the next appropriate step?
    A. demotion
    B. suspension
    C. oral reprimand from the evening supervisor
    D. written warning from the director of the department

REFERENCE: McWay, pp 302–303
               Abdelhak, pp 602–603
               LaTour and Eichenwald-Maki, p 735
               McConnell, pp 215–219
               Liebler and McConnell, pp 415–416

83. In your department employee performance is rated using a continuous scale range of unsatisfactory through average to outstanding. Some other departments use a discrete system in which the supervisor assigns "fails to meet standards," "meets standards," and "exceeds standards." Both systems being used are
    A. rating scales.
    B. checklists.
    C. critical incident methods.
    D. ranking methods.

REFERENCE: McWay, pp 300–301
              Abdelhak, pp 595–598
              McConnell, pp 194–195

84. Virginia is the Record Processing Coordinator, which is a lead position. She has an excellent work record and is able to assist in most work areas of the department. She knows that she could easily get another job within the hospital for the asking. Recently she has been arriving late and has been uncooperative in dealing with others. As her immediate supervisor, what is the BEST first step in dealing with this situation?
    A. Institute progressive discipline.
    B. Ignore the situation and hope she will improve because she is a good employee.
    C. Counsel her by encouraging self-analysis and problem-solving processes.
    D. Suggest that she transfer to another department.

REFERENCE: McWay, pp 301–304
              Abdelhak, pp 601–603
              LaTour and Eichenwald-Maki, p 735
              McConnell, p 220
              Johns, p 1045

85. Health care is known for rapid change. Melissa, an RHIA who has just been hired as a systems analyst in Information Technology, understands the importance of change management and being a positive change agent. Which of the following approaches would be LEAST likely to support her approach?
    A. being available to listen to staff
    B. holding on to the vision
    C. measuring and celebrating success
    D. easing up on delegating

REFERENCE: McWay, p 270
              Johns, p 1073
              LaTour and Eichenwald-Maki, p 671
              Liebler and McConnell, pp 48–49

86. HIM professionals increasingly participate on project teams. Tuckman has developed a model describing predictable stages. Which of the following reflects the stage where teams may experience disequilibrium?
    A. forming
    B. storming
    C. norming
    D. performing

REFERENCE: Johns, p 1035
              Liebler and McConnell, pp 352–354
              Umiker, pp 119–120

87. Rita Mizner, MBA, RHIA, is Director of Information Services for Mt. Sinai Medical Center. She is well respected for a management style that empowers her staff. All of the following are characteristics of effective delegation, EXCEPT
    A. explaining exactly what needs to be done.
    B. agreeing on performance standards.
    C. providing necessary resources.
    D. retaining authority to make key decisions.

REFERENCE: McWay, pp 262–263
                      LaTour and Eichenwald-Maki, p 763
                      McConnell, p 180

88. Tara is an RHIA who works at a large academic medical center. Her salary of $37,540 is paid 60% from research grants as clinical trial coordinator and 40% by HIM as a database manager. The hospital's fringe benefit rate is 23%. How much must the HIM director include in the budget (rounded to the nearest dollar) to cover Sarah's database management role?
    A. $15,016   C. $22,524
    B. $18,470   D. $27,705

REFERENCE: Koch, pp 55–56
                      Horton, pp 136–137

89. Christina is a pharmacy tech who recently earned her RHIA. She is interviewing to become a representative of an international pharmaceutical firm. She would work from home, login to the corporate Web site several times a day, and make calls on various pharmacies in her territory. She would visit headquarters about once a quarter. This proposed work arrangement can best be described as
    A. flextime.   C.   consulting.
    B. outsourcing.   D.   telecommuting.

REFERENCE: LaTour and Eichenwald-Maki, pp 760–762
                      Liebler and McConnell, pp 147–150

90. Which of the following employees is exempt under the Fair Labor Standards Act?
    A. an RHIA who performs record analysis and coding 90% of the time and who supervises three employees
    B. an RHIT who manages the Health Information Services department and is involved with planning and decision-making activities 90% of the time
    C. the department secretary who spends 100% of her time performing clerical duties for the Director of Health Information Services
    D. a file clerk who spends 100% of the time on filing activities

REFERENCE: McWay, p 298
                      Abdelhak, p 578
                      Davis and LaCour, pp 416–417
                      McConnell, pp 446–448

91. Charles Jones is employed as a regional coding consultant by a corporate hospital chain. In the organization chart, this position would be
    A. shown as a line position.
    B. shown as a staff position.
    C. not shown, because it is a consulting position.
    D. not shown, because this function is outsourced.

REFERENCE: Liebler and McConnell, pp 134–136
                 McConnell, pp 51–52

92. Keith is director at a medical center that includes a daycare center and has several employees who have young children. He knows that it is important to be familiar with the provisions of the Family Medical Leave Act (FMLA), which includes all the following provisions EXCEPT
    A. ensuring any job the employee is qualified for upon return.
    B. that both men and women qualify under the FMLA.
    C. that it covers leave to care for a spouse, child, or parent.
    D. that it provides up to 12 weeks of unpaid leave annually.

REFERENCE: McWay, pp 92, 298
                 Abdelhak, pp 578
                 Liebler and McConnell, p 156

93. Ty Ngynn is Assistant Director in Information Services. He has made an appointment with the Director of Human Resources to discuss his recent trip to the state HIM meeting with his Director, Wendy Richards. During the trip, Wendy repeatedly asked Ty to her room, suggesting they work on new plans for the department. When Ty declined, Wendy suggested it might not be worthwhile for him to attend future state meetings. The HR Director should
    A. explain that off-site events are outside the scope of the HR Department.
    B. provide Ty with additional training on resisting unwanted advances.
    C. take the complaint seriously and begin a sexual harassment investigation.
    D. explain that it is the Director's right to select who attends professional meetings.

REFERENCE: McWay, p 294
                 Abdelhak, p 575
                 Liebler and McConnell, pp 456–457

94. Which of the following types of members is best for a committee?
    A. individuals of equal rank and authority
    B. a diverse group with widely varied rank and authority
    C. a blend of managers and entry level staff
    D. There is no clear benefit to one form or another.

REFERENCE: Liebler and McConnell, pp 297–298

95. As a new RHIA and coding manager, how likely is it that you will participate on committees?
    A. Infrequently until you are promoted to a higher position.
    B. You should expect committee participation to be a regular part of your job.
    C. Occasionally, mostly with your staff.
    D. It depends on whether your organization chooses to use the committee structure.

REFERENCE: Liebler and McConnell, pp 327–328
                 Umiker, p 446

96. Niagra Falls Health Center needs occasional help in coding to remain current. Rena, the coding manager, is seeking an individual who is available evenings and weekends and will be responsible for his or her own actions. At a regional HIM meeting, Rena announces that she is looking for a(n)
    A. consultant.
    C. part-time employee.
    B. statutory employee.
    D. independent contractor.

REFERENCE: Umiker, p 446
               Leibler and McConnell, p 181

97. Under the Immigration Reform and Control Act, all of the following apply EXCEPT
    A. undocumented workers may not be hired.
    B. U.S. citizens must be given preference.
    C. noncitizens may not be discriminated against.
    D. applicant must have I-9 documentation.

REFERENCE: Abdelhak, p 577
               Umiker, p 446
               McConnell, p 462

98. Using Donabedian's framework for quality assessment (structure, process, and outcome), which of the following is an appropriate human resource outcome?
    A. absenteeism rate
    B. organizational climate
    C. salary and benefit compared with competitors
    D. None, Donabedian is a clinical framework.

REFERENCE: Abdelhak, pp 444–445
               LaTour and Eichenwald-Maki, pp 536–537

99. Nina is participating in Human Resources training for new supervisors and has a question for the presenter. "I have an employee who is at the top of the pay scale for her position. Do I still need to do a performance evaluation?" The presenter most likely answers
    A. "Yes, at this stage, she should be asked to participate in evaluating other staff."
    B. "Yes, every employee deserves to know how he or she is performing and to set goals."
    C. "No, once no salary increase can be provided, an evaluation is not necessary."
    D. "Maybe, it is typically an optional process at this stage of employment."

REFERENCE: Abdelhak, pp 594–595
               LaTour and Eichenwald-Maki, p 735

100. Postage charges for Health Information Services have increased over the last quarter. As the Director, you have seen mail envelopes that have been meter-stamped that did not appear to be official hospital business. The best course of action is to
    A. remove the postage meter from the department.
    B. keep a watchful eye to see who is using the postage meter improperly.
    C. call a department meeting and issue employee warnings.
    D. put one person in charge of the meter.

REFERENCE: McWay, pp 363–365
               LaTour and Eichenwald-Maki, pp 696–697
               McConnell, pp 58–59

Answer Key for Human Resources

ANSWER   EXPLANATION

NOTE: Explanations are provided for those questions that require mathematical calculations and questions that are not clearly explained in the references that are cited.

1.   C $200 \times 30/60 = 100$ hours total

2.   D   50 employees × \$15.50 per hour × ½ hour   =   387.50
             50 employees × \$12.00 per hour × ½ hour   =   300.00
             100 employees × \$18.00 per hour × ½ hour   =   900.00
             \$387.50 + \$300.00 + \$900.00   = \$1,587.50

3.   A   Calculate by time: \$1,587.50 total cost for training/100 hours needed to train = \$15.88 per hour/2 to get cost for ½ hour of training = 7.938 =\$7.94
                              OR
             Calculate by employee: \$1,587.50/200 employees = 7.938 =\$7.94

4.   B   To determine the number of hours needed to perform a volume of work or "service units," in this case discharges (15,620) are multiplied by the "time standard" (18 minutes) and then divided by the number of minutes per hour (60).
             (15,620 × 18) = 281,160 divided by 60 = 4,686.

5.   D

6.   B   To determine the number of employees needed for a specific position, you must first determine how much time is being spent on work currently being done. The "service units," in this case discharges (600), are multiplied by the "time factor," 20 minutes. (600 × 20 = 12,000 minutes) Because this problem's time factor is in minutes, you must also compute the number of available minutes per week. The "actual hours" in this case, 40 hours, is multiplied by 60 (60 minutes per hour) (40 × 60 = 2,400). The earned time, 12,000 minutes, is then divided by the actual minutes, 2,400, to determine the number of employees needed to perform a specific job duty. So, 12,000 divided by 2,400 = 5.

7.   D

8.   A

9.   C   Dana should be assessing employee performance on an ongoing basis. Without proper documentation, an evaluation of "needs improvement" will be difficult to justify.

10.   D

11.   A   Calculation: \$15.00 × 2,080 hours per year = \$31,200 × 27.5% = \$8,580
             Tuition waiver = 6 credits at \$145 = \$870
             Therefore, \$31,200, + \$8,580 + \$870 = \$40,650

12.   C

13.   A

14.   C   You are required to document the training content, dates, and attendees.

15.   D

16.   B

17.   B

18.   C

19.   C

20.   D

Answer Key for Human Resources

ANSWER	EXPLANATION

21.   B   To calculate the absenteeism rate, use the following formula as suggested by the U.S. Department of Labor:

$$\frac{\text{Worker-days lost during period} \times 100}{(\text{Avg. number of workers})\,(\text{Number of days in period})} \qquad \frac{25 \times 100}{20 \times 22} = 5.68\%$$

22.   D

23.   D

24.   B

25.   B

26.   A

27.   D

28.   C   Physical/workstation security training would be appropriate for all employees in general orientation training. Answers A and B are higher level functions that would not be performed by all new employees. Answer D. Job-specific training would be better suited to training in the department in which the employee will work.

29.   B

30.   C

31.   A

32.   A

33.   B

34.   B   Job descriptions should be reviewed and updated before beginning the hiring process.

35.   D

36.   D   Although all of these environmental conditions can contribute to the employees' well-being, air pollution, such as stale or dusty air, is a known contributor to headaches and fatigue.

37.   B

38.   C

39.   B   Kari took 6 hours unpaid leave (40 − 6 = 34), but worked a holiday at double-time (8 × 2 = 16). Because 8 hours of the holiday are already figured in the work week, add an additional 8 hours for holiday pay. So, 34 + 8 = 42.

40.   A

41.   B   A well-written job description includes what and how health information is used in a position. The job description would be the document Gina would review for choosing appropriate training levels for staff members in different positions.

42.   D

43.   A

44.   C

45.   B   It is illegal for an organization to fire an employee for filing a grievance. The union contract stipulates the policy and procedures for resolving grievances. You would need to refer to the union contract for any specific time boundaries.

46.   C

47.   D

48.   A

49.   C

50.   D   Cutbacks in staffing, the need for job enrichment, and boredom could account for some of the problems in the department, but having potentially offensive jokes would certainly lead to an investigation of possible sexual harassment in the department.

Answer Key for Human Resources

	ANSWER	EXPLANATION

51. A

52. B Theory "Y" can be recalled as answering "yes" to the question: Do employees fundamentally want to do a good job and contribute to the organization?

53. C

54. B In the department orientation, the new employee should also be oriented to the location of various facilities (restrooms, cafeteria) and to the general position tasks to be performed. In addition to the department orientation, there is usually a facility-wide orientation meeting for all new hires. The facility emergency procedures are usually covered at this facility-wide orientation meeting.

55. C

56. B A spreadsheet with grids identifying who needs what type of training would help in defining the department privacy and security training plan.

57. A Training manuals would help ensure consistency of coverage of the materials among trainers. B and C serve to help in documenting the training that was given. D. In addition to initial training, the security rule requires ongoing training/reminders.

58. B

59. D Employee salary expense is significant.

60. C All three are among Fayol's 14 principles, though unity of direction refers to all workers being aligned toward one single outcome.

61. C Managers should not attempt to "water down" information, even if it is bad news. Fueling the grapevine can also lead to additional misinformation. Managers should make every effort to communicate factual information to their employees in a calm and timely manner.

62. D

63. A Directing or telling is associated with the low maturity level and/or low experience level of a group.

64. C

65. A

66. D

67. C Increasing legal challenges have made this an area best left to HR professionals.

68. D

69. A Even though a serious incident such as this could result in termination of an employee, it is important to gather all the facts prior to meeting with the employee to substantiate any claims.

70. D

71. A

72. B Weekly department meetings, having an employee handbook, and written policies and procedures are all part of the necessary open and honest communication.

73. A

74. B A common and easy solution to this problem is to ignore the complaint, although this will not solve the problem; it will only prolong it. If the clerks complain that their job rate is too low, a job evaluation seeks to determine the position's relative worth to maintain pay equity within the organization and a wage and salary survey helps in determining the market value of the position.

Answer Key for Human Resources

ANSWER   EXPLANATION

75.   B   In-depth training and interaction are best obtained in an instructor-led classroom style of training. Answers B, C, and D are disadvantages of instructor-led training. Instructor-led training becomes expensive and time intensive when scheduling and training many shifts of employees from all departments.

76.   A   Job enrichment involves assigning more challenging tasks and responsibilities without combining jobs, which is called job enlargement. Switching job tasks among employees is called job rotation. All of these are attempts to diversify work and motivate employees. Redesigning a job by removing responsibility, however, would probably not be a motivational factor.

77.   B

78.   C

79.   C

80.   B

81.   B

82.   B

83.   A

84.   C

85.   D

86.   C

87.   D   To be effective, authority needs to be delegated along with responsibility.

88.   B   Calculations: $37,540 × 123% = $46,174.20
          HIM pays 40% or $46,174.20 × .40 = $18,469.68, rounded to $18,470

89.   D

90.   B

91.   B

92.   A

93.   C

94.   A

95.   C

96.   D

97.   B

98.   A

99.   B

100. D   Although putting one person in charge of the meter may not stop the abuse of the postage meter, it is the best first course of action to take. Answers A and C are too drastic, and answer B is not efficient use of a manager's time.

REFERENCES

Abdelhak, M., Grostick, S., Hanken, M. A., & Jacobs, E. (Eds.). (2011). *Health information: Management of a strategic resource* (4th ed.). Philadelphia: W. B. Saunders.

AHIMA Practice Brief HIPAA Privacy and Security Training. (November 2010). Chicago: American Health Information Management Association. (Updated). Retrieved from http://www.ahima.org, November 5, 2012.

Davis, N., & LaCour, M. (2007). *Introduction to health information technology* (2nd ed.). Philadelphia: W. B. Saunders.

Horton, L. (2010). *Calculating and reporting health care statistics* (3rd ed.). Chicago: American Health Information Management Association (AHIMA).

Johns, M. L. (2011). *Health information technology: An applied approach* (3rd ed.). Chicago: American Health Information Management Association (AHIMA).

Koch, P. G. (2008). *Basic allied health statistics and analysis* (3rd ed.). Clifton Park, NY: Delmar Cengage Learning.

LaTour, K., & Eichenwald-Maki, S. (2010). *Health information management: Concepts, principles and practice* (3rd ed.). Chicago: American Health Information Management Association (AHIMA).

Liebler, J. G., & McConnell, C. R. (2012). *Management principles for health professionals* (6th ed.). Sudbury, MA: Jones & Bartlett.

McConnell, C. *The effective health care supervisor* (6th ed.). Sudbury, MA: Jones & Bartlett.

McWay, D. C. (2008). *Today's health information management, an integrated approach*. Clifton Park, NY: Delmar Cengage Learning.

Human Resources Competencies

Question	RHIA Domain Competencies					
	1	2	3	4	5	6
1–100				X		

Question	RHIT Domain Competencies							
	1	2	3	4	5	6	7	
1	X							
2	X							
3	X							
4	X							
5	X							
6	X							
7						X		
8						X		
9	X							
10	X							
11	X							
12						X		
13	X							
14						X		
15	X							
16	X							
17	X							
18	X							
19	X							
20	X							
21	X							
22						X		
23	X							
24						X		
25		X						
26						X		
27						X		
28						X		
29						X		
30						X		
31	X							
32	X							
33	X							
34	X							
35						X		
36	X							
37						X		
38					X			
39					X			
40	X							
41						X		
42						X		
43	X							
44					X			
45						X		
46						X		
47	X							
48	X							
49		X						
50	X							
51						X		

XVII. Mock Examination

Debra W. Cook, MAEd, RHIA

Sheila Carlon, PhD, RHIA, FAHIMA

NOTE:
If you are taking the mock for the RHIT examination, you may choose to complete the first 150 questions. The mock for the RHIA examination has 180 questions to complete. In timing your speed at answering questions, allow about 1.35 minutes per question. For example, if you are taking the entire mock exam in one sitting, you should allow about 4 hours and 3 minutes (180 questions × 1.35 minutes for a total of 243 minutes = 4 hours and 3 minutes).

GULFSIDE HEALTHCARE CENTER AVERAGE CLINIC WAITING TIME BY TIME BLOCK DECEMBER 2012				
TIME BLOCK	PEDIATRICS	OBSTETRICS	CARDIOLOGY	ORTHOPEDICS
8:00–11:00	12	18	10	9
11:01–2:00	8	10	8	14
2:01–5:00	10	7	7	12

1. Each month, the staff of the clinic with the lowest overall waiting time is awarded a free dessert in the Gulfside Healthcare Center cafeteria. Take a look at the information listed above. The winner will be selected based on
    A   demonstrative clinical data.   C.   objective individual data.
    B. comparative aggregate data.   D.   duplicate thematic data.

REFERENCE: McWay, p 226
                  Abdelhak, pp 380–382
                  LaTour and Eichenwald-Maki, p 164

2. A union campaign is being conducted at your facility. As a department manager, it is appropriate for you to tell employees that
    A. a strike is inevitable if the union wins.
    B. wages will increase if the union is defeated.
    C. you need the names of those involved in union activities.
    D. you are opposed to the union.

REFERENCE: Abdelhak, pp 579–580

3. As the Coding Supervisor, your job description includes working with agents who have been charged with detecting and correcting overpayments made to your hospital in the Medicare Fee for Service program. You will need to develop a professional relationship with
    A. the OIG.
    B. MEDPAR representatives.
    C. QIO physicians.
    D. recovery audit contractors.

REFERENCE: Green and Bowie, pp 325–326
                  Johns, pp 364–365

4. Employing the SOAP style of progress notes, choose the "assessment" statement from the following:
   A. Patient states low back pain with sciatica is as severe as it was on admission.
   B. Patient moving about very cautiously appears to be in pain.
   C. Adjust pain medication; begin physical therapy tomorrow.
   D. Sciatica unimproved with hot pack therapy.

REFERENCE: Abdelhak, p 119
               Green and Bowie, pp 90–92
               LaTour and Eichenwald-Maki, p 204
               McWay, p 103

5. In preparation for an EHR, you are conducting a total facility inventory of all forms currently used. You must name each form for bar coding and indexing. The unnamed document in front of you includes a checklist for assessing an obstetric patient's lochia, fundus, and perineum. The document type you give to this form is
   A. prenatal record.   C. delivery room record.
   B. labor record.   D. postpartum record.

REFERENCE: Abdelhak, p 113
               Green and Bowie, p 182

SAMPLE MS-DRG REPORT		
MS-DRG IDENTIFIER	RELATIVE WEIGHT	NUMBER OF PATIENTS WITH THIS MS-DRG
A	1.234	12
B	3.122	10
C	2.165	19
D	5.118	16

6. Based on the MS-DRG report above, what is the case-mix index for this facility?
   A. 0.204193   C. 11.639
   B. 2.965807   D. 57

REFERENCE: Johns, p 324
               LaTour and Eichenwald-Maki, pp 436–437
               Green and Bowie, pp 316–317
               McWay, pp 135–136, 209, 357

7. The special form or view that plays the central role in planning and providing care at nursing, psychiatric, and rehabilitation facilities is the
   A. interdisciplinary patient care plan.
   B. medical history and review of systems.
   C. interval summary.
   D. problem list.

REFERENCE: Abdelhak, p 142
               LaTour and Eichenwald-Maki, p 203
               Johns, pp 98–103

8. Four patients were discharged from Crestview Hospital yesterday. A final progress note is an appropriate discharge summary for
   A. Howard, who died within 24 hours after his admission for a second heart attack in 2 weeks.
   B. Jackson, who had no comorbidities or complications during this admission for replacement of a pacemaker battery.
   C. Fieldstone, who was admitted just 15 days following a heart attack for the acute onset of chest pain.
   D. Babson, who delivered a healthy 8-pound boy without complications for either mother or child, and was discharged within 36 hours of admission.

REFERENCE: Abdelhak, p 113
                Green and Bowie, pp 142–144
                LaTour and Eichenwald-Maki, pp 201–202

Use the information in the tables below to answer the next two questions.

Make Me Better Clinic (MMBC) provides well child visits and childhood immunizations for four insurance companies. Data on the services they provided and the reimbursement they received from the four companies are listed in the two tables below.

Table 1 Well Child Visits

INSURANCE COMPANY	NUMBER OF WELL CHILD VISITS	REIMBURSEMENT FROM PAYER
Lifecare	259	$ 31,196.55
Getwell	786	$100,859.52
SureHealth	462	$ 54,631.50
BeHealthy	219	$ 26,991.75

Table 2 Immunizations

INSURANCE COMPANY	NUMBER OF IMMUNIZATIONS	TOTAL REIMBURSEMENT FROM PAYER
Lifecare	412	2,175.36
Getwell	1,465	9,053.70
SureHealth	609	3,580.92
BeHealthy	417	2,118.36

9. MMBC receives the best reimbursement for well child visits from
   A. Lifecare.   C. SureHealth.
   B. Getwell.   D. BeHealthy.

REFERENCE: Math Calculation

10. Most of the children who are seen at MMBC will have a well child visit and two immunizations. If you add the reimbursement for two immunizations to the reimbursement for each well child visit, which insurance company benefits MMBC most?
    A. Lifecare   C. SureHealth
    B. Getwell   D. BeHealthy

REFERENCE: Math Calculation

11. You are calculating the fee schedule payment amount for physician services covered under Medicare Part B. You already have the relative value unit figure. The only other information you need is
    A. the facility's case-mix index.
    C. the facility's base rate.
    B. a national conversion factor.
    D. MS-DRG relative weights.

REFERENCE: Johns, pp 326–328
              Green, pp 795–796
              LaTour and Eichenwald-Maki, pp 393–394

KEY WEST HOSPITAL FOUR HIGHEST MS-DRGs							
MS-DRG A		MS-DRG B		MS-DRG C		MS-DRG D	
CMS WEIGHT	NUMBER OF PATIENTS WITH MS-DRG A	CMS WEIGHT	NUMBER OF PATIENTS WITH MS-DRG B	CMS WEIGHT	NUMBER OF PATIENTS WITH MS-DRG C	CMS WEIGHT	NUMBER OF PATIENTS WITH MS-DRG D
2.023	323	0.987	489	1.925	402	1.243	386

12. Key West Hospital collected the data displayed above concerning its four highest volume MS-DRGs. Which MS-DRG generated the most revenue for the hospital?
    A. MS-DRG A
    C. MS-DRG C
    B. MS-DRG B
    D. MS-DRG D

REFERENCE: Abdelhak, p 661
              Johns, pp 322–325
              LaTour and Eichenwald-Maki, pp 436–437

13. In reviewing a health record for coding purposes, the coder notes that the patient was put on Keflex post-surgery. There is no mention of a postoperative complication in the attending physician's discharge summary. Before querying the doctor, the coder will seek to confirm the infection by reviewing the
    A. lab report.
    C. operative report.
    B. nurses' notes.
    D. pathology report.

REFERENCE: Johns, pp 44, 71
              Green, pp 14–16
              LaTour and Eichenwald-Maki, p 410

14. Stan works in an acute care general hospital, Fran works for a skilled nursing facility, Ann is employed at an assisted living facility, and Dan works for a home care provider. Which people are employed in facilities that may seek Joint Commission accreditation?
    A. only Stan and Fran
    C. only Fran and Dan
    B. only Stan and Dan
    D. Dan, Stan, and Fran

REFERENCE: Abdelhak, p 14
              Johns, pp 109–110, 699–701
              LaTour and Eichenwald-Maki, p 36
              McWay, pp 7, 102, 180, 354

15. Sunset Beach Clinic allows patients to communicate by e-mail to ask questions regarding their treatment and request appointment changes. E-mails and text messages are
   A. considered health care business records and are subject to the same regulations as records created in face-to-face patient encounters.
   B. considered proof of patient contact and should be summarized in a progress note in the patient record.
   C. generally maintained in a facility's electronic mail system until the next face-to-face patient encounter.
   D. not typically maintained or documented as patient encounters.

REFERENCE: Brodnik, pp 124–128

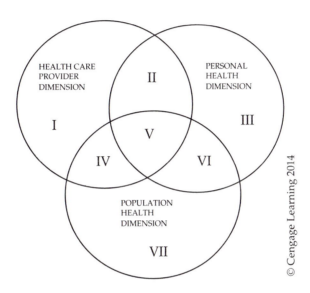

16. The proposed National Healthcare Information Network (NHIN) dimensions are graphically depicted in the diagram above. Roman numerals are added to allow for the identification of specific areas. Where would information concerning a patient's health insurance be located on this chart?
   A. I   C. III
   B. II   D. V

REFERENCE: LaTour and Eichenwald-Maki, pp 169–176
                Johns, pp 152, 213

17. The facility's policy for physician's verbal orders in accordance with state law and regulations needs updating. The first area of investigation is the qualifications of those individuals who have been authorized to record verbal orders. For this information you will consult the
    A. policy and procedure manual.
    B. hospital's Quality Management Plan.
    C. data dictionary.
    D. hospital bylaws, rules, and regulations.

REFERENCE: Green and Bowie, pp 14–16
LaTour and Eichenwald-Maki, pp 25, 197, 214, 522, 542, 544
Johns, pp 68, 107, 710–711
McWay, pp 20–23

18. Parker has type 1 diabetes with hypertension that is currently controlled with medication. Parker was admitted through the ED for an emergency appendectomy. Following surgery, the patient developed an infection at the wound site that was treated with antibiotics. When making decisions about sequencing the codes for this case, the coder should rely on definitions found in the
    A. UHDDS.
    B. Coding Clinic.
    C. CMS Coding Guidelines.
    D. Federal Register.

REFERENCE: Green and Bowie, pp 124–128
Green, p 230

19. Parker has type 1 diabetes with hypertension that is currently controlled with medication. Parker was admitted through the ED for an emergency appendectomy. Following surgery, the patient developed an infection at the wound site that was treated with antibiotics. Parker's principal diagnosis is the
    A. complications of hypertension.
    B. comorbidity of the wound infection.
    C. comorbidity of type 1 diabetes.
    D. acute appendicitis.

REFERENCE: Green, p 230
Green and Bowie, pp 124–128

20. Dr. Reed tried to explain wound care to Mr. Baker prior to discharge, but Baker (who is 104 and moderately senile) just could not seem to understand or remember what the doctor said. Mr. Baker's daughter was with him, so Dr. Reed explained Mr. Baker's aftercare to his daughter. Dr. Reed should document discharge instructions
    A. in the discharge summary.
    B. on a patient instructions form signed by Dr. Reed and Mr. Baker and filed in Mr. Baker's medical record.
    C. in the discharge summary and on a patient instructions form signed by Dr. Reed and Mr. Baker and filed in Baker's medical record.
    D. in the discharge summary and on a patient instructions form signed by Dr. Reed and Mr. Baker's daughter and filed in Mr. Baker's medical record.

REFERENCE: Abdelhak, p 113
Johns, p 78
LaTour and Eichenwald-Maki, pp 200–201
Green and Bowie, pp 143–145

21. The physician has documented the final diagnoses as acute myocardial infarction, COPD, CHF, hypertension, atrial fibrillation, and status-post cholecystectomy. The following conditions should be reported:

401.1	Essential Hypertension, benign
401.9	Essential Hypertension, unspecified
402.91	Hypertension, heart disease, unspecified as to malignant or benign, with heart failure
410.91	Acute myocardial infarction, unspecified site, initial episode of care
427.31	Atrial fibrillation
428.0	Congestive heart failure, unspecified
496	Chronic obstructive pulmonary disease
V45.79	Acquired absence of gallbladder

A. 410.9, 496, 402.91, 427.31, V45.79
B. 410.91, 496, 428.0, 401.9, 427.31
C. 410.91, 496, 428.0, 401.9, 427.31, V45.79
D. 410.91, 496, 428.0, 401.1, 427.31

REFERENCE: Bowie and Schaffer (2012), pp 191–195, 197–199, 214–215
    Green, pp 157–163
    Johnson and Linker, pp 39–45, 51–53
    Brown, pp 186–187, 333–334, 339–340, 347–348
    Hazelwood and Venable, pp 163–170, 174, 187–188

22. Mary is 6 weeks postmastectomy for carcinoma of the breast. She is admitted for chemotherapy. What is the correct sequencing of the codes?

174.9	Malignant neoplasm of the breast
V10.3	Personal history of malignant neoplasm of breast
V58.11	Encounter for antineoplastic chemotherapy
V67.00	Follow-up exam after surgery

A. V58.11, 174.9   C. V67.00, V58.11
B. V58.11, V10.3   D. V10.3

REFERENCE: Bowie and Schaffer (2012), p 120
    Green, pp 212–213
    Brown, pp 229, 393–394
    Johnson and Linker, pp 52, 63–64

23. Which of the following is coded as an adverse effect in ICD-9-CM?
    A. tinnitus due to allergic reaction after administration of eardrops
    B. mental retardation due to intracranial abscess
    C. rejection of transplanted kidney
    D. nonfunctioning pacemaker due to defective soldering

REFERENCE: Green, pp 190–192, 196
              Johnson and Linker, pp 73–75
              Brown, pp 441–445
              Bowie and Schaffer (2012), pp 35–37

24. Which of the following scenarios identifies a pathologic fracture?
    A. greenstick fracture secondary to fall from a bed
    B. compression fracture of the skull after being hit with a baseball bat
    C. vertebral fracture with cord compression following a car accident
    D. compression fracture of the vertebrae as a result of bone metastasis

REFERENCE: Bowie and Shaffer (2012), p 289
              Brown, pp 255, 415
              Green, pp 188–189, 522
              Johnson and Linker, pp 70, 250, 255–256

25. If the same condition is described as both acute and chronic and separate subentries exist in the ICD-9-CM alphabetic index at the same indentation level,
    A. they should both be coded, acute sequenced first.
    B. they should both be coded, chronic sequenced first.
    C. only the acute condition should be coded.
    D. only the chronic condition should be coded.

REFERENCE: Bowie and Schaffer (2012), p 61
              Brown, pp 57–58
              Green, p 120
              Johnson and Linker, p 79

26. Which of the following statements is true?
    A. A surgical procedure may include one or more surgical operations.
    B. The terms *surgical operation* and *surgical procedure* are synonymous.
    C. A surgical operation may include one or more surgical procedures.
    D. The term *surgical procedure* is an incorrect term and should not be used.

REFERENCE: Koch, p 180

27. Which of the following would be coded as a poisoning?
    A. Coumadin intoxication due to a cumulative effect
    B. idiosyncratic reaction to Artane
    C. interaction between Aldomet and a vasodilating agent
    D. reaction between Coumadin and an over-the-counter medication

REFERENCE: Brown, pp 445–446, 450
               Green, pp 189–193

28. Which of the following diagnoses or procedures would prevent the normal delivery code, 650, from being assigned?
    A. occiput presentation   C. episiotomy
    B. single liveborn   D. low forceps

REFERENCE: Bowie and Schaffer (2012), p 260
               Brown, pp 272–273
               Green, pp 172, 174
               Johnson and Linker, pp 54–55

29. Which of the following are considered late effects regardless of time?
    A. congenital defect   C. nonhealing fracture
    B. nonunion   D. poisoning

REFERENCE: Bowie and Shaffer (2012), pp 63–64
               Brown, p 425
               Johnson and Linker, pp 78–79

30. Four people were seen in your emergency department yesterday. Which one will be coded as a poisoning?

- Josh was diagnosed with digitalis intoxication.
- Ben had an allergic reaction to a dye administered for a pyelogram.
- Bryan developed syncope after taking Contac pills with a double scotch.
- Matthew had an idiosyncratic reaction between two properly administered prescription drugs.

    A. Josh   C. Bryan
    B. Ben   D. Matthew

REFERENCE: Brown, pp 445–446, 450
               Green, pp 165–167, 170–171
               Johnson and Linker, pp 73–75

31. Patient is admitted for elective cholecystectomy for treatment of chronic cholecystitis with cholelithiasis. Prior to administration of general anesthesia, patient suffers cerebral thrombosis. Surgery is subsequently canceled. Code and sequence the coding from the following codes.

434.00	Cerebral thrombosis without cerebral infarction
574.10	Chronic cholecystitis with cholelithiasis
V64.1	Surgery canceled, contraindication
997.02	Iatrogenic cerebrovascular infarction or hemorrhage
51.22	Cholecystectomy, total

A. 997.02, 574.10, 51.22   C. 997.02, 434.00, V64.1
B. 574.10, 434.00, V64.1   D. 434.00, V64.1

REFERENCE: Bowie and Shaffer (2012), p 375
               Brown, pp 72–73
               Green, pp 202, 211–212

32. The discharge diagnosis for this inpatient encounter is "rule out myocardial infarction." The coder would assign
    A. a code for a myocardial infarction.
    B. a code for the patient's symptoms.
    C. a code for an impending myocardial infarction.
    D. no code for this condition.

REFERENCE: Bowie and Schaffer (2012), p 67
               Johnson and Linker, p 35
               Brown, pp 56–57
               Green, pp 124, 233

33. Staging
    A. refers to the monitoring of incidence and trends associated with a disease.
    B. is continued medical surveillance of a case.
    C. is a system for documenting the extent or spread of cancer.
    D. designates the degree of differentiation of cells.

REFERENCE: Abdelhak, p 488
               LaTour and Eichenwald-Maki, p 332
               Johns, p 487

34. Which of these conditions are always considered "present on admission" (POA)?
    A. congenital conditions
    B. E codes
    C. acute conditions
    D. possible, probable, or suspected conditions

REFERENCE: Brown, pp 526–528
               LaTour and Eichenwald-Maki, p 391

35. In your state, it is legal for minors to seek medical treatment for a sexually transmitted disease without parental consent. When this occurs, who would be expected to authorize the release of the medical information documented in this episode of care to the patient's insurers?
    A. the patient
    B. a court-appointed guardian on behalf of the patient
    C. the custodial parent of the patient
    D. the patient's doctor on behalf of the patient

REFERENCE: Brodnik, pp 137–139

36. A patient is admitted through the emergency department. Three days after admission, the physician documents uncontrolled diabetes mellitus. What is the "present on admission" (POA) indicator for uncontrolled diabetes mellitus?
    A. "Y"   C. "W"
    B. "U"   D. "N"

REFERENCE: Brown, pp 541–544
                Bowie and Schaffer (2012), pp 73–74

37. The patient had a thrombectomy, without catheter, of the peroneal artery, by leg incision.

34203	Embolectomy or thrombectomy, with or without catheter; popliteal-tibioperoneal artery, by leg incision
35226	Repair blood vessel, direct; lower extremity
35302	Thromboendarterectomy, including patch graft if performed; superficial femoral artery
37799	Unlisted procedure, vascular surgery

    A. 34203   C. 35302
    B. 37799   D. 35226

REFERENCE: Bowie and Schaffer (2011), pp 190–191
                Green, pp 576, 578

38. Patient was seen for excision of two interdigital neuromas from the left foot.

28080	Excision, interdigital (Morton) neuroma, single, each
64774	Excision of neuroma; cutaneous nerve, surgically identifiable
64776	Excision of neuroma; digital nerve, one or both, same digit

    A. 64774   C. 28080
    B. 64776   D. 28080, 28080

REFERENCE: AMA CPT (2012)

39. Patient was seen in the Emergency Department with lacerations on the left arm. Two lacerations, one 7 cm and one 9 cm, were closed with layered sutures.

12002	Simple repair of superficial wounds of scalp, neck, axillae, external genitalia, trunk and/or extremities (including hands and feet); 2.6–7.5 cm
12004	Simple repair of superficial wounds of scalp, neck, axillae, external genitalia, trunk and/or extremities (including hands and feet); 7.6–12.5 cm
12035	Layer closure of wounds of scalp, axillae, trunk and/or extremities (excluding hands and feet); 12.6–20.0 cm
12045	Layer closure of wounds of neck, hands, feet and/or external genitalia; 12.6–20.0 cm

   A. 12045   C. 12002, 12004

   B. 12035   D. 12004

REFERENCE: Bowie and Schaffer (2011), pp 106–108
                Green, p 500
                Johnson and Linker, pp 224–226
                AMA, pp 131–132

40. Office visit for 43-year-old male, new patient, with no complaints. Patient is applying for life insurance and requests a physical examination. A detailed health and family history was obtained and a basic physical was done. Physician completed life insurance physical form at patient's request. Blood and urine were collected.

99381	Initial comprehensive preventive medicine evaluation and management of an individual including an age and gender appropriate history, examination, counseling/anticipatory guidance/risk factor reduction interventions, and the ordering of appropriate immunization(s), laboratory/diagnostic procedures, new patient; infant (age under 1 year)
99386	Initial comprehensive preventive medicine evaluation and management of an individual including a comprehensive history, a comprehensive examination, counseling/anticipatory guidance/risk factor reduction interventions, and the ordering of appropriate immunization(s), laboratory/diagnostic procedures, new patient; 40–64 years
99396	Periodic comprehensive preventive medicine reevaluation and management of an individual including an age and gender appropriate history, examination, counseling/anticipatory guidance/risk factor reduction interventions, and the ordering of appropriate immunization(s), laboratory/diagnostic procedures, established patient; 40–64 years
99450	Basic life and/or disability examination that includes completion of a medical history following a life insurance pro forma

   A. 99450   C. 99396

   B. 99386   D. 99381

REFERENCE: Bowie and Schaffer (2013), p 79
                Green, p 424
                Johnson and Linker, pp 164–165
                AMA CPT (2012), p 37

41. Patient was seen today for regular hemodialysis. No problems reported, tolerated procedure well.

90935	Hemodialysis procedure with single physician evaluation
90937	Hemodialysis procedure requiring repeated evaluations(s) with or without substantial revision of dialysis prescription
90945	Dialysis procedure other than hemodialysis (e.g., peritoneal dialysis, hemofiltration, or other continuous renal replacement therapies), with single physician evaluation
+99354	Prolonged physician service in the office or other outpatient setting requiring direct (face-to-face) contact beyond the usual service; first hour (list separately in addition to code for office or other outpatient Evaluation and Management service)

A. 90937   C. 90945
B. 99354   D. 90935

REFERENCE: Bowie and Schaffer (2011), pp 383–385
Green, pp 777–778
Johnson and Linker, pp 432–433
AMA, p 405

42. An established patient was seen by the physician in the office for DTaP vaccine and Hib.

90471	Immunization administration (includes percutaneous, intradermal, subcutaneous, intramuscular injections); one vaccine (single or combination vaccine/toxoid)
90700	Diphtheria, tetanus toxoids, and acellular pertussis vaccine (DTaP), when administered to individuals younger than 7 years, for intramuscular use
90720	Diphtheria, tetanus toxoids, and whole cell pertussis vaccine and Hemophilus influenza B vaccine (DTP-Hib), for intramuscular use
90721	Diphtheria, tetanus toxoids, and acellular pertussis vaccine and Hemophilus influenza B vaccine (DTaP-Hib), for intramuscular use
90748	Hepatitis B and Hemophilus influenza b vaccine (HepB-Hib), for intramuscular use
99211	Office or other outpatient visit for the evaluation and management of an established patient, which may not require the presence of a physician. Usually, the presenting problem(s) are minimal. Typically, 5 minutes are spent performing or supervising these services.

A. 90721   C. 90700, 90748, 99211
B. 90720, 90471   D. 90471, 90721

REFERENCE: Bowie and Schaffer (2013), pp 425–426
AMA CPT (2012), pp 449–453
AMA, pp 394–395, 398
Green, pp 772–773
Johnson and Linker, p 429

43. A patient with lung cancer and bone metastasis is seen for complex treatment planning by a radiation oncologist.

77263	Therapeutic radiology treatment planning; complex
77290	Therapeutic radiology simulation-aided field setting; complex
77315	Teletherapy, isodose plan (whether hand or computer calculated); complex (mantle or inverted Y, tangential ports, the use of wedges, compensators, complex blocking, rotational beam, or special beam considerations)
77334	Treatment devices, design and construction; complex (irregular blocks, special shields, compensators, wedges, molds, or casts)

A. 77315   C. 77290
B. 77263   D. 77334

REFERENCE: Bowie and Schaffer (2013), pp 406–407
Green, pp 723–725
AMA CPT (2012), pp 388–389
AMA, pp 269, 282, 344–345

44. A 4-year-old had a repair of an incarcerated inguinal hernia. This is the first time this child had been treated for this condition.

49496	Repair initial inguinal hernia full-term infant, under age 6 months, or preterm infant over 50 weeks' post conception age and under 6 months at the time of surgery, with or without hydrocelectomy; incarcerated or strangulated
49501	Repair initial inguinal hernia, age 6 months to under 5 years, with or without hydrocelectomy; incarcerated or strangulated
49521	Repair recurrent inguinal hernia, any age; incarcerated or strangulated
49553	Repair initial femoral hernia, any age; incarcerated or strangulated

A. 49553   C. 49521
B. 49496   D. 49501

REFERENCE: Bowie and Schaffer (2011), p 242
Green, pp 625–626
Johnson and Linker, pp 192–193
AMA, pp 229–230

45. A quantitative drug assay was performed for a patient to determine digoxin level.

80050	General health panel
80101	Drug screen, qualitative; single drug class method (e.g., immunoassay, enzyme assay), each drug class
80162	Digoxin (therapeutic drug assay, quantitative examination)
80166	Doxepin (therapeutic drug assay, quantitative examination)

A. 80101
B. 80050
C. 80166
D. 80162

REFERENCE: Bowie and Schaffer (2011), p 373
Green, pp 748–749
AMA, pp 362–365
Johnson and Linker, p 415

46. Provide the CPT code for anesthesia services for the transvenous insertion of a pacemaker.

00530	Anesthesia for permanent transvenous pacemaker insertion
00560	Anesthesia for procedures on heart, pericardial sac, and great vessels of chest; without pump oxygenator
33202	Insertion of epicardial electrode(s); open incision
33206	Insertion or replacement of permanent pacemaker with transvenous electrode(s); atrial

A. 00560
B. 33202, 00530
C. 00530
D. 33206, 00560

REFERENCE: Bowie and Schaffer (2013), pp 89–91
Green, p 459
AMA, pp 99–103

47. The transcriptionists have collected data on the number and types of problems with the dictation equipment. The best tool to display the data they collected is a
A. flowchart.
B. Pareto chart.
C. Gantt chart.
D. PERT chart.

REFERENCE: McWay, pp 148–149
LaTour and Eichenwald-Maki, p 705

48. Based on the information below, what was the net death rate at Seaside Hospital in January?

SEASIDE HOSPITAL SELECTED STATISTICS JANUARY				
Admissions	Discharged to Home	Discharge Transfers	Deaths <48 hours	Deaths >48 hours
280	212	28	8	6

   A. 2.4%   C. 3.8%
   B. 2.8%   D. 5.8%

REFERENCE: Koch, pp 120–121
               Horton, pp 75–76
               LaTour and Eichenwald-Maki, p 431
               Johns, pp 556–557

49. The formula used to calculate the percentage of ambulatory care visits made with same day appointments is
   A. $\dfrac{\text{number of patients seen with same day appointments for a period} \times 100}{\text{number of patients seen with advance appointments for the same period}}$
   B. $\dfrac{\text{number of patients seen with advance appointments for a period} \times 100}{\text{number of patients seen with same day appointments for the same period}}$
   C. $\dfrac{\text{number of patients seen with same day appointments for a period} \times 100}{\text{number of patients seen in the same period}}$
   D. $\dfrac{\text{number of patients seen with advance appointments for a period} \times 100}{\text{number of patients seen in the same period}}$

REFERENCE: McWay, p 192
               Koch, p 178
               LaTour and Eichenwald-Maki, pp 424–425
               Horton, pp 14–18
               Johns, pp 526–527

50. An HIM Department Budget Report for May shows a payroll budget of $25,000 and an actual payroll expense of $22,345. The percentage of budget variance for the month is
   A. $2,655.   C. $265.
   B. 11%.   D. 0.9%.

REFERENCE: LaTour and Eichenwald-Maki, pp 799–800

51. Your large office practice has decided to try an e-health initiative. They have established a practice Web site and encourage patients to submit questions electronically instead of calling the advice nurse. After an initial surge in interest, very few patients use the service. The Web site is attractive and easy to navigate. Questions submitted via the site are answered by the nursing staff within 2 working days. You suspect few patients use the service because
   A. most of your patients are too old to be Internet savvy.
   B. the turnaround time is too long to replace the advice nurse.
   C. the nurses may be using language that is too technical for patients.
   D. most patients just prefer the personal touch they get on the phone.

REFERENCE: LaTour and Eichenwald-Maki, pp 71–72

52. Your facility is engaged in a research project concerning patients newly diagnosed with type 2 diabetes. The researchers notice older patients have a longer length of stay than younger patients. They have seen a
    A. positive correlation between age and length of stay.
    B. negative correlation between age and length of stay.
    C. causal relationship between age and length of stay.
    D. homologous relationship between age and length of stay.

REFERENCE: McWay, pp 203–206
                Johns, p 632
                Koch, pp 274–248

53. Johnston City was set upon by a swarm of killer bees. All 5,000 residents are at risk of a bee attack. If 25 residents were attacked by the bees, the incidence of bee attacks
    A. is 5 in 1,000.   C. is 25 in 1,000.
    B. is 5 in 5,000.   D. cannot be determined at this time.

REFERENCE: Koch, p 205
                McWay, pp 227–228
                Abdelhak, p 378
                LaTour and Eichenwald-Maki, pp 442–443

54. A 335-bed hospital opened a new wing on June 1 of a nonleap year, increasing its bed count to 350 beds. The total bed count days for the year at the hospital was
    A. 122,275.
    B. 125,485.
    C. 127,750.
    D. The answer cannot be calculated with the information provided.

REFERENCE: Koch, p 86
                Johns, pp 550–551
                LaTour and Eichenwald-Maki, p 428

55. A patient who was admitted to the hospital on January 14 and discharged on March 2 in a nonleap year has a length of stay of
    A. 45 days.   C. 47 days.
    B. 46 days.   D. 48 days.

REFERENCE: Koch, p 102
                LaTour and Eichenwald-Maki, pp 429–431
                Johns, pp 553–554

56. Release of information has increased its use of part-time prn clerical support in order to respond to increased requests for release of information. The budget variance report will reflect
    A. the increase in the cost of part-time clerical support for ROI but not the increase in revenue from this area.
    B. the increase in revenue from increased volume in ROI but not the increased costs of part-time clerical support.
    C. both the increases in revenue and increased costs for clerical support in ROI.
    D. neither the increased costs nor increased revenue, as temporary changes are rarely reflected on variance reports.

REFERENCE: Abdelhak, pp 676–677
               LaTour and Eichenwald-Maki, pp 799–800

57. You are heading a research study that includes a patient questionnaire. Five of the questions will be answered using the following scale:

1	Strongly disagree
2	Disagree
3	No opinion
4	Agree
5	Strongly agree

You would like to display the study in your report. If you'd like to include responses to all five questions on one display, you should use a
    A. stacked bar graph.   C. frequency table.
    B. pie chart.   D. frequency polygon.

REFERENCE: Abdelhak, p 382
               LaTour and Eichenwald-Maki, pp 451, 453

58. Your HMO manager has requested a report on the number of patient visits per year for preschool children. Which of the age groupings below will you use for your report?

A. 0–1 year	B. < 12 months	C. >12 months	D. 0–2 years
1–2 years	12–24 months	12–24 months	3–4 years
2–3 years	25–37 months	25–37 months	5 years
3–4 years	38–50 months	38–50 months	
4–5 years	51–63 months	< 51 months	

REFERENCE: Koch, p 260
               LaTour and Eichenwald-Maki, pp 445–446
               Johns, pp 534–535

59. Collins Family Hospital had a bed count of 150 for the first 6 months of the year. On June 1, it added 15 beds when it opened a new wing. If you are given the average length of stay for the year, can you calculate the annual bed turnover rate? How?
   A. Yes, using the direct method.
   B. Yes, using the indirect method.
   C. Yes, using the Joint Commission method.
   D. No, there is insufficient data to complete the calculation.

REFERENCE: Koch, pp 185–186
                Abdelhak, p 378
                LaTour and Eichenwald-Maki, p 429
                Horton, pp 52–53

60. In a research study that includes a patient questionnaire, five of the questions will be answered using the following scale:

1	Strongly disagree
2	Disagree
3	No opinion
4	Agree
5	Strongly agree

The data collected using this scale are called
   A. cardinal data.
   B. ordinal data.
   C. nominal data.
   D. continuous data.

REFERENCE: McWay, p 201
                Koch, p 13
                Abdelhak, p 380
                LaTour and Eichenwald-Maki, p 423
                Horton, p 197
                Sui, p 293

61. Gail Smith has presented to the ER in a coma with injuries sustained in a motor vehicle accident. According to her sister, Gail has had a recent medical history taken at the public health department. The physician on call is grateful that she can access this patient information using the area's
   A. EDMS system.
   B. CPOE.
   C. expert system.
   D. RHIO.

REFERENCE: Green and Bowie, p 112
                Johns, pp 150–151

62. The patient's family asked the attending physician to keep the patient in the hospital for a few days more until they could make arrangements for the patient's home care. Because the patient no longer meets criteria for continued stay, if the physician complies with the family's request, this would be considered
    A. the best utilization of the hospital's resources.
    B. an inappropriate use of hospital resources.
    C. a compassionate use of the hospital's resources.
    D. appropriate provided it is limited to a few days.

REFERENCE: Abdelhak, p 467
                    LaTour and Eichenwald-Maki, pp 547–548
                    Johns, pp 649–652

63. The state is considering the closure of the Arcadia Hospital. In reviewing the hospital statistics, which indicator will best help state officials determine whether closure is warranted?
    A. daily census   C. inpatient service days
    B. percentage of occupancy   D. average length of stay

REFERENCE: LaTour and Eichenwald-Maki, pp 426, 428
                    Johns, pp 549–551
                    Koch, p 84

64. The census taken at midnight on August 1 showed 99 patients remaining in the hospital. On August 2, four patients were admitted, there was one fetal death, one DOA, and seven patients were discharged. One of these patients was admitted in the morning and remained only 8 hours. How many inpatient service days were rendered on August 2?
    A. 94   C. 96
    B. 95   D. 97

REFERENCE: Abdelhak, p 379
                    Koch, pp 64–67
                    LaTour and Eichenwald-Maki, p 427
                    Johns, pp 553–554

65. You are implementing a quality improvement plan that utilizes the PDSA cycle. If you correctly implement PDSA, which phase of the project will take the most of your time?
    A. P   C. S
    B. D   D. A

REFERENCE: Johns, pp 569–570
                    LaTour and Eichenwald-Maki, p 702
                    McWay, p 143

66. A run or line chart would be most useful for collecting data on
    A. waiting time in the Pediatrics Clinic.
    B. patient satisfaction with the food.
    C. delays in scheduling elective surgical procedures.
    D. medication errors and their causes.

REFERENCE: Koch, pp 274–275
                    McWay, pp 149, 151, 201
                    LaTour and Eichenwald-Maki, p 707
                    Johns, pp 550–541, 623–624

Number of Visits and Wait Times in the ER

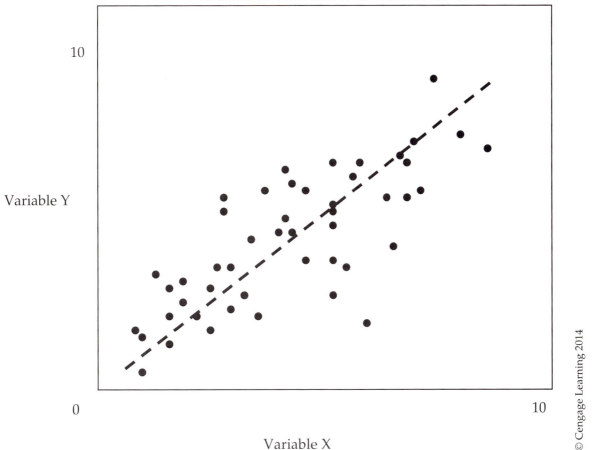

67. The ER staff has collected the data on the number of visits and corresponding wait times in the ER. The data are displayed on the chart shown above. Based on this information, what kind of correlation do you see between the number of visits (Variable X) and the wait times (Variable Y)?
    A. a positive correlation between Variable X and Variable Y
    B. a negative correlation between Variable X and Variable Y
    C. a conjunctive correlation between Variable X and Variable Y
    D. a causative correlation between Variable X and Variable Y

REFERENCE: McWay, pp 203–204
                LaTour and Eichenwald-Maki, pp 449–451
                Johns, p 632
                Koch, pp 247–248

68. Fred is recovering nicely, so he asks Dr. Jones if he can go home for the weekend. Dr. Jones approves a two-night leave of absence (LOA). Chances are Fred is a patient in
    A. an acute care facility; his LOA will decrease the month's average daily inpatient census.
    B. a long-term care facility; his LOA will increase the month's percentage of occupancy.
    C. an acute care facility; his LOA will increase the month's total discharge days.
    D. a long-term care facility; his LOA will decrease the month's total inpatient service days.

REFERENCE: Horton, p 27
               Koch, pp 111–112

69. Community Hospital reported an average LOS in December of 3.7 days with a standard deviation of 23. This information indicates that
    A. there was a small variation in the LOS at Community Hospital.
    B. there was a large variation in the LOS at Community Hospital.
    C. most of the patients at Community Hospital stay 3 to 4 days.
    D. patients stay longer at Community than at most hospitals.

REFERENCE: McWay, p 198
               LaTour and Eichenwald-Maki, p 457
               Koch, pp 246–247

70. Four HIT students are working on a LOS project at their clinical site. To describe the variability of the data, Smithson suggests using range because it is the most exact. Donaldson wants to use the mean because it is easy to calculate. Franklin recommends variance because it is the most popular measure of variability. Howell proposes the use of standard deviation because it is the most preferred and has better interpretive uses. Who made the best suggestion?
    A. Smithson   C. Franklin
    B. Donaldson   D. Howell

REFERENCE: McWay, pp 194–195
               Koch, p 246
               LaTour and Eichenwald-Maki, pp 454–457
               Johns, pp 532–533

71. Sun City reported 12 cases of chronic heart disease in a population of 8,000 in 2008. In 2011, Sun City reported there were still 12 cases of chronic heart disease, but its population had decreased to 6,000. This represents an increase in the
    A. prevalence of chronic heart disease in Sun City.
    B. incidence of chronic heart disease in Sun City.
    C. reliability of reporting chronic heart disease in Sun City.
    D. occurrence of chronic heart disease in Sun City.

REFERENCE: McWay, pp 198–199
               Koch, pp 145–146, 205
               LaTour and Eichenwald-Maki, pp 442–443

72. Community Hospital Administration decided to change the number of adult and children beds from 300 to 375 effective July 1. The total number of inpatient service days for adults and children for the year was 111,963. What was the percentage of occupancy rate for adults and children for the entire year?
    A. 0.9%
    B. 45.4%
    C. 90.8%
    D. 91.0%

REFERENCE: LaTour and Eichenwald-Maki, pp 428–429
                Horton, pp 49–50
                Koch, pp 91–92

73. When checking the census data at South Beach Women's Center, you see that just yesterday, there were four sets of triplets, five sets of twins, and eight single births. Yesterday, South Beach Women's Center had
    A. 17 deliveries.
    B. 25 deliveries.
    C. 30 deliveries.
    D. 39 deliveries.

REFERENCE: Koch, p 140
                Horton, p 124

74. In preparing the retention schedule for health records, the most concrete guidance in determining when records may be destroyed will be
    A. the average readmission rate for the facility.
    B. the available options for inactive records.
    C. the statute of limitations in your state.
    D. Joint Commission and AOA standards regarding minimum retention periods.

REFERENCE: Brodnik, pp 186–187
                LaTour and Eichenwald-Maki, pp 221–223
                Johns, pp 403, 423, 802–803

The Credentialing Committee reviewed Dr. Hernandez's application for renewal of his medical staff privileges. They noted that Dr. Hernandez had a high incidence of nosocomial infections after hip replacement surgery. The committee recommended renewal of Dr. Hernandez's general medical staff privileges but suspended his permission to perform hip replacement surgery until he completed an AMA-approved course on infection control and successfully demonstrated improved technique to the department chair.

75. The Credentialing Committee discovered the problems with Dr. Hernandez's hip replacements by
    A. sampling and reviewing Dr. Hernandez's patient records.
    B. reviewing Dr. Hernandez's physician profile.
    C. querying the National Physician Data Bank.
    D. interviewing the Chief of Surgery.

REFERENCE: Abdelhak, pp 464–465
                LaTour and Eichenwald-Maki, pp 542–545

76. You are starting your new job as the sole HIM professional at a small psychiatric practice. The practice uses DSM for billing purposes. You find this "theoretically" reasonable because DSM
    A. is a widely used and accepted classification system.
    B. codes are also valid ICD-9-CM codes.
    C. codes are also valid CPT codes.
    D. is the industry standard for psychiatric billing systems.

REFERENCE: Green and Bowie, p 307
               LaTour and Eichenwald-Maki, p 354

77. As the Information Security Officer at your facility, you have been asked to provide examples of the physical safeguards used to manage data security measures throughout the organization. Which of the following would you provide?
    A. audit controls   C. chain-of-trust partner agreements
    B. entity authentication   D. workstation use and location

REFERENCE: Green and Bowie, pp 270–271
               LaTour and Eichenwald-Maki, p 254
               Brodnik, p 280

78. The MS-DRG weight in a particular case is 2.0671 and the hospital's payment rate is $3,027. How much would the hospital receive as reimbursement in this case?
    A. $3,027.00   C. $6,257.11
    B. $5,094.10   D. $960.00

REFERENCE: Johns, pp 322–234
               Abdelhak, p 661

79. A patient's husband slipped and fell in your HIM reception area and now he is suing the facility. You have to prepare detailed written answers to a long list of questions and send them to your hospital attorney. You will spend the afternoon working on
    A. affidavits.   C. interrogatories.
    B. allocutions.   D. depositions.

REFERENCE: Brodnik, pp 35–36
               LaTour and Eichenwald-Maki, p 274
               Abdelhak, pp 541–542

Use the information on errors in indexing of scanned material that you have collected and presented in the table below to answer the next two questions.

TYPE OF MATERIAL	NUMBER SCANNED	NUMBER INDEXING ERRORS
CONSULTATION REPORTS	2,879	431
LAB SLIPS	15,242	458
CORRESPONDENCE	1,426	114
OTHER	6,271	313

80. If you want to begin with the type of material that has the highest error rate, you will start by working on problems with
    A. consultation reports.
    B. lab slips.
    C. correspondence.
    D. other.

REFERENCE: Koch, p 48
               Abdelhak, p 368

81. Referring again to the data collected on scanning errors, if you want to work on the type of material with the highest volume, you will work on problems with
    A. consultation reports.
    B. lab slips.
    C. correspondence.
    D. other.

REFERENCE: Koch, p 48
               Abdelhak, p 378

82. You are providing an educational session to new hires at your hospital. You tell the new employees that hospital records may be used as evidence in court even though hearsay laws bar the use of most evidence that does not represent personal knowledge of the witness. That is because the hospital record
    A. is written rather than spoken.
    B. was kept in the regular course of business.
    C. has not been tampered with in any way.
    D. is accurate and complete.

REFERENCE: Brodnik, p 54
               Abdelhak, p 525
               LaTour and Eichenwald-Maki, pp 292–293
               Pozgar, pp 119–120

83. Which of the following responsibilities would you expect to find on the job description of a facility's Information Security Officer but NOT on the job description of Chief Privacy Officer?
    A. Cooperate with the Office of Civil Rights in compliance investigations.
    B. Conduct audit trails to monitor inappropriate access to system information.
    C. Oversee the patient's right to inspect, amend, and restrict access to protected health information.
    D. Monitor the facility's business associate agreements.

REFERENCE: McWay, pp 36, 57–61, 324
               Green and Bowie, pp 42, 280
               LaTour and Eichenwald-Maki, pp 254–256
               Johns, pp 510, 963–964

84. Sally is a HIM professional with many years of experience. Unlike some of her colleagues, Sally loves the challenge of adapting to change. She is happy that HIPAA empowers the Secretary of DHHS to adopt standards for electronically maintained health information. Sally hopes that the standardization under HIPAA will make it easier to design safeguards for electronic data, to protect against unauthorized access, to
    A. make and use copies of the data, and to guard against unauthorized data integration.
    B. protect electronic records from corruption, and to prosecute hackers under federal law.
    C. prevent the corruption of electronically stored data, and to protect the integrity of the information itself.
    D. submit revisions of claims as they are denied, and to track third-party payers.

REFERENCE: McWay, pp 57, 322–324
               Abdelhak, p 209
               LaTour and Eichenwald-Maki, pp 254–255
               Johns, pp 510, 819–820

85. An 11-year-old female is brought to the emergency room with a compound, comminuted fracture of the right tibia and fibula. Her mother was very seriously injured in the same accident and is unconscious. What should be done?
    A. Nothing, until consent can be obtained from the nearest relative.
    B. The mother can be treated under implied consent but not the child.
    C. The hospital should quickly seek a court-appointed guardian for the child.
    D. Both patients can be treated under implied consent.

REFERENCE: Brodnik, pp 136–138
               Pozgar, p 314
               Johns, p 62

86. A pharmacist at your facility was caught running a drug ring. The pharmacist filled orders of valuable medications with cheap outdated ones purchased on the Internet and then sold the good drugs for profit. Patients have been injured and the lawsuits are starting. Unfortunately, your facility is going to be held responsible for the pharmacist's negligent acts under the doctrine of
    A. adjudicus res.   C. respondeat superior.
    B. res ipsa loquitur.   D. stare decisis.

REFERENCE: Brodnik, p 96
               Pozgar, p 149

87. A patient was treated for meningitis at age 3 (15 years ago). The patient is now 18. The patient's attorney is requesting information on the admission. You tell the clerk the information is
    A. no longer available because your facility retains information for 10 years after the last patient visit.
    B. available, but the attorney will have to obtain a court order before you will release it.
    C. available, but the patient's parents will have to sign a consent for you to release it.
    D. available, and the patient may sign consent to release the information in the record.

REFERENCE: Brodnik, p 178
               Abdelhak, pp 196–197
               LaTour and Eichenwald-Maki, p 287

88. A patient has written to request a copy of his own record. When the clerk checked the record, it was noted that the patient was last admitted to the psychiatric unit of the facility. You advise the clerk to
    A. comply with the request immediately.
    B. contact the patient's attending physician before complying.
    C. ignore the request and advise you if it is repeated.
    D. ask the patient to send the required fee prior to the release.

REFERENCE: Green and Bowie, pp 294–295
               Abdelhak, pp 538–539
               LaTour and Eichenwald-Maki, pp 283–285
               Johns, pp 87–89, 826–828
               Brodnik, p 338

89. Your HIS Department receives an authorization for Sara May's medical history to be sent to her attorney, but the expiration date noted on the authorization has passed. What action is appropriate according to HIPAA privacy rules?
    A. Do not honor because the authorization is invalid.
    B. Contact the patient to get permission to respond.
    C. Contact the attending physician for permission to respond.
    D. Honor the authorization since the patient obviously approves of the release.

REFERENCE: Brodnik, p 159
               Johns, p 840

90. The hospital's strategic plan calls for having the entire health record content recorded in discrete form within the next 10 years. Which system will the HIM Director most likely recommend in the early stages of the project as a transition strategy?
    A. electronic document management system
    B. clinical data repository system
    C. CPOE system
    D. speech recognition system

REFERENCE: Sayles and Trawick, p 153
               Abdelhak, p 196
               Amatayakul, pp 440–443
               McWay, pp 128, 132

91. As the Information Security Officer at your facility, you have been asked to provide examples of technical security safeguards adopted as a result of HIPAA legislation. Which of the following would you provide?
    A. audit controls
    B. evidence of security awareness training
    C. surge protectors
    D. workstation use and location

REFERENCE: McWay, p 323
              Brodnik, pp 281–282
              Green and Bowie, p 283
              Johns, pp 1005–1006
              LaTour and Eichenwald-Maki, pp 254–256
              Eichenwald and Petterson, p 38
              Miaoulis, pp 18–20

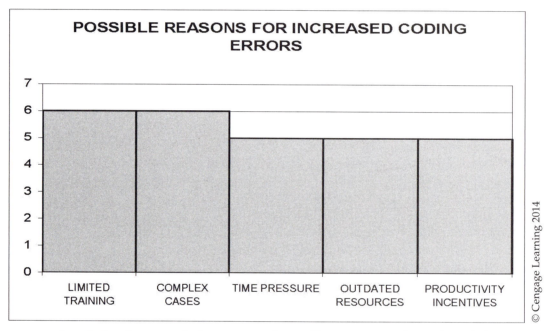

92. After your coders helped you rank the reasons for coding errors in the order of their importance, you then plotted the results on the chart above. The results of your work surprise you because
    A. you expected the coders to put more emphasis on time pressure.
    B. you thought limited training was the primary reason for the errors.
    C. the rankings show surprising disagreement on the issue.
    D. the results appear to violate the Pareto principle.

REFERENCE: McWay, pp 148–149, 274
              LaTour and Eichenwald-Maki, p 705

93. Joanie Howell presents to Dr. Franklin requesting rhinoplasty. Because Howell is covered by Medicare, Dr. Franklin must provide Howell with
    A. a Notice of Exclusion, because rhinoplasty is not a Medicare covered service.
    B. an Advance Beneficiary Notice, because rhinoplasty is not a Medicare covered service.
    C. a Notice of Exclusion, because Howell's rhinoplasty may not be medically necessary.
    D. an Advance Beneficiary Notice, because Howell's rhinoplasty may not be medically necessary.

REFERENCE: Green and Rowell, pp 463–465
               LaTour and Eichenwald-Maki, pp 405–406
               Johns, pp 350–351

94. A 19-year-old former patient faxes a request to your facility requesting the release of his medical records of all episodes of care to the Army. The release of information clerk should
    A. send the records as requested.
    B. inform the young man that specific reports must be identified in his request.
    C. send a letter informing him that faxed requests are not accepted.
    D. deny the request.

REFERENCE: Brodnik, pp 357–359
               Abdelhak, p 539
               LaTour and Eichenwald-Maki, p 290

95. A 16-year-old male was treated at your facility for a closed head injury. The patient's 18-year-old wife accompanied him to the hospital and signed the consent for admission and treatment because of the patient's incapacity at the time. The patient has requested that copies of his medical records be sent to his attorney. Who should sign the authorization to release the records?
    A. the patient
    B. either of the patient's parents
    C. the patient's parent or legal guardian
    D. the patient's wife

REFERENCE: Brodnik, pp 154–155
               Abdelhak, p 538
               LaTour and Eichenwald-Maki, pp 283–291

96. When a patient is admitted because of a primary neoplasm with metastasis and treatment is directed toward the secondary neoplasm only,
    A. code only the primary neoplasm as the principal diagnosis.
    B. the primary neoplasm is coded as the principal diagnosis, and the secondary neoplasm is coded as an additional diagnosis.
    C. the secondary diagnosis is coded as the principal diagnosis, and the primary neoplasm is coded as an additional diagnosis.
    D. code only the secondary neoplasm as the principal diagnosis.

REFERENCE: Bowie and Schaffer (2012), pp 116–117
               Brown, pp 391–392

97. During her hospitalization for her third delivery, Calee had a sterilization procedure performed. When the record is coded, the V code for sterilization, V25.2, is
    A. not used.
    B. used and sequenced as the principal diagnosis.
    C. used and sequenced as a secondary diagnosis.
    D. the only code used.

REFERENCE: Brown, pp 283–284

98. A transcription unit has been asked to tally the number of times they have to leave sections of a report blank for various reasons (poor dictation technique, background noise, etc.). The quality improvement tool most likely to help collect these data would be
    A. force field analysis.   C. flowchart.
    B. decision matrix.   D. check sheet.

REFERENCE: LaTour and Eichenwald-Maki, pp 705–706
              Johns, pp 619–620

99. As the Director of a Health Information Technology Program, your community college has been selected to participate in the workforce development of electronic health record specialists as outlined by ARRA and HITECH. In order to keep abreast of changes in this program, you will need to regularly access the Web site of which governmental agency?
    A. ONC
    B. CMS
    C. OSHA
    D. CDC

REFERENCE: Johns, p 221

100. The Chief of Staff, Chief of Medicine, President of the Governing Body, and most departmental managers have already completed CQI training. Unfortunately, the hospital administrator has not been to training, refuses to get involved with CQI, and refuses to let the administrative departmental staff get training.
    A. This level of involvement is enough to meet Joint Commission standards.
    B. The Joint Commission only expects involvement from clinical staff.
    C. This will not do because it violates Joint Commission standards and CQI philosophy.
    D. If you can talk him into training his staff, you can let him skip the training.

REFERENCE: McWay, pp 142–144
              LaTour and Eichenwald-Maki, p 544
              Johns, pp 616, 638–640

RECORD COMPLETION INFORMATION FOR DECEMBER				
INCOMPLETE RECORDS	DELINQUENT RECORDS	AVERAGE MONTHLY DISCHARGES	AVERAGE MONTHLY OPERATIVE PROCEDURES	DELINQUENT OPERATIVE REPORTS
604	304	845	526	14

101. Use the information provided in the table above to calculate the delinquent rate. The delinquent rate
   A. cannot be determined.
   B. is 36%.
   C. is 50%.
   D. is 71%.

REFERENCE: Abdelhak, p 128
               Green and Bowie, p 84
               LaTour and Eichenwald-Maki, pp 215–216, 424–425

102. The percentage of records delinquent due to the absence of an operative report
   A. is 1.7%.
   B. is 2.7%.
   C. is 4.6%.
   D. cannot be determined from the information given.

Answer sheet is wrong on this one

REFERENCE: Abdelhak, p 128
               Green and Bowie, p 84
               LaTour and Eichenwald-Maki, pp 215–216, 424–425

103. The purpose of the Correct Coding Initiative is to
   A. increase fines and penalties for bundling services into comprehensive CPT codes.
   B. restrict Medicare reimbursement to hospitals for ancillary services.
   C. teach coders how to unbundle codes.
   D. detect and prevent payment for improperly coded services.

REFERENCE: Green, pp 11, 372–376, 849
               Hazelwood and Venable, p 328

104. Access to radiologic images has been improved through the use of which of the following?
   A. LOINC
   B. PACS
   C. EDMS
   D. CPOE

REFERENCE: Sayles and Trawick, pp 229–230
               Abdelhak, p 229
               Johns, p 948

105. The difference between an Institutional Review Board (IRB) and a hospital's Ethics Committee is that
    A. the IRB focuses on patient care only, and the Ethics Committee addresses both patient care and business practices.
    B. the Ethics Committee reviews ethics complaints, and the IRB focuses on developing policies and procedures.
    C. the IRB deals with the ethical treatment of human research subjects, and the Ethics Committee covers a wide range of issues.
    D. the IRB is made up entirely of patient care providers, and the Ethics Committee is multidisciplinary.

REFERENCE: McWay, pp 84, 231–232
              LaTour and Eichenwald-Maki, p 564
              Johns, pp 587–588

106. A common goal of the Office of the National Coordinator for Health Information Technology, RHIOs, and a national infrastructure for information is
    A. translating images into a digital format.
    B. sharing information among providers.
    C. transferring health information within a hospital system.
    D. promoting telemedicine.

REFERENCE: Sayles and Trawick, pp 336–367
              LaTour and Eichenwald-Maki, p 145

107. You are considering the classification of two patients discharged from your hospital yesterday. Both patients had a length of stay that was increased due to comorbidities and/or complications described below,

- Fred's hospitalization for gallbladder surgery was extended because Fred has brittle diabetes. True to form, Fred's blood glucose dropped to alarming levels and his hospital stay was extended until it was back under control.
- Ted also has diabetes, but his sugar is typically well controlled. After Ted's surgery, the physician prescribed a broad-spectrum antibiotic prophylactically. Ted had a severe reaction to the medication and had to spend an additional night in the hospital.

The best way to describe these two cases would be to say that
    A. both Fred and Ted have concomitant chronic comorbidities; Fred also had a nosocomial complication.
    B. both Fred and Ted have concomitant chronic comorbidities; Ted also had an iatrogenic complication.
    C. Fred had a concomitant chronic comorbidity; Ted had a concomitant complication.
    D. Fred had a concomitant chronic complication; Ted had a concomitant comorbidity.

REFERENCE: Green and Bowie, pp 128–129
              Green, p 238

108. Your facility would like to improve physician documentation in order to allow improved coding. As coding supervisor, you have found it very effective to provide the physicians with
    A. a copy of the facility coding guidelines, along with written information on improved documentation.
    B. the UHDDS and information on where each data element is collected and/or verified in your facility.
    C. regular in-service presentations on documentation, including its importance and tips for improvement.
    D. feedback on specific instances when improved documentation would improve coding.

REFERENCE: Green, pp 14–16
             Abdelhak, p 132

109. A piece of objective data collected upon initial assessment of the patient is the
    A. review of systems.   C. chief complaint.
    B. history of present illness.   D. vital signs.

REFERENCE: Green and Bowie, pp 145–148
             Abdelhak, pp 108–109
             LaTour and Eichenwald-Maki, p 204

110. The use of computer key signatures requires the same administrative controls as
    A. rubber stamp signatures.   C. signatures made by interns and residents.
    B. computer passwords.   D. use of faxed signatures.

REFERENCE: Green and Bowie, pp 79–80
             Abdelhak, p 528
             LaTour and Eichenwald-Maki, pp 213–214

111. A number of key elements for your facility's computerized patient record are still input by clerical staff from handwritten data entry sheets. You are concerned about the transfer of data. If the vital signs stored in the database are not what were originally recorded, the impact on patient care could be severe. You are concerned about the
    A. stability of the data.   C. legitimacy of the data.
    B. validity of the data.   D. reliability of the data.

REFERENCE: Green and Bowie, p 257
             McWay, p 143
             Koch, p 249
             Abdelhak, pp 410–411
             LaTour and Eichenwald-Maki, pp 342–343
             Johns, p 509

112. ORYX is a program that was developed by
    A. CMS to track Medicare costs.
    B. Joint Commission to link patient outcomes to accreditation.
    C. NIH to track communicable diseases.
    D. AMA to allow for rapid CPT updates.

REFERENCE: McWay, pp 157–158, 180
             Green and Bowie, p 30
             LaTour and Eichenwald-Maki, p 170
             Johns, pp 211–212

113. In preparation for conversion to a computerized patient record, a committee at your facility is defining each of the data elements in a patient record to determine which elements should be required and to set parameters for each element. The committee is working on the data
    A. edits.
    C. dictionary.
    B. reasonableness.
    D. feasibility.

REFERENCE: McWay, p 170
            Green and Bowie, pp 250–253
            Eichenwald-Maki and Peterson, pp 37–38
            Abdelhak, pp 502–503
            Johns, pp 169, 199–200, 904–907
            LaTour and Eichenwald-Maki, pp 131–133

114. An effective means of protecting the security of computerized health information would be to
    A. require all facility employees to change their passwords at least once a month.
    B. write detailed procedures for the entry of data into the computerized information system.
    C. install a system that would require fingerprint scanning and recognition for data access.
    D. develop clear policies on data security that are supported by the top management of the facility.

REFERENCE: McWay, pp 322–323
            Brodnik, pp 278–280
            Johns, p 919
            LaTour and Eichenwald-Maki, pp 134–135

115. In reviewing the policies on release of information in respect to the privacy rules, you note that it is still acceptable to allow release of protected health information without patient permission to
    A. the patient's spouse.
    B. a health care provider interested in the case.
    C. the quality assurance committee for review purposes.
    D. a third-party payer with a direct interest in the case.

REFERENCE: Brodnik, p 359
            LaTour and Eichenwald-Maki, pp 253–254

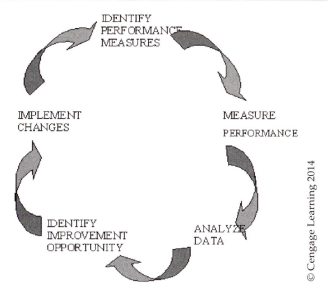

116. Your facility has a team that has been working to develop a strong performance improvement model, and they have come up with the model shown above. The team asks if you see anything missing from the model. You tell them they
   A. are missing a step requiring regular employee input into the process.
   B. are missing a step requiring reporting to the board of directors.
   C. are missing a step requiring ongoing monitoring and reassessment.
   D. aren't missing any steps; the model is a good one.

REFERENCE: Johns, p 608
             McWay, p 152

117. Part of your job description is to educate physicians regarding proper documentation policies and standards. You are the
   A. Information Security Manager.   C. Health Information Manager.
   B. Clinical Data Specialist.   D. Risk Manager.

REFERENCE: Green and Bowie, pp 98–99
             Johns, pp 659, 755, 775–778

118. Your hospital has purchased a number of outpatient facilities. You have been assigned to chair an interdisciplinary committee that will write record retention policies for the new corporation. You begin by telling the committee their primary consideration when making retention decisions must be
   A. space considerations.   C. provider preferences.
   B. statutory requirements.   D. professional standards.

REFERENCE: Brodnik, pp 189–190
             McWay, pp 112–113
             Abdelhak, pp 196–197
             Johns, pp 403–405, 815–818
             LaTour and Eichenwald-Maki, pp 221–202

119. A major drug company wants to promote a fundraiser targeting patients with congestive heart failure. The drug company representative has requested a list of patients treated at your facility. As privacy and security officer, you tell them that
A. they just need to send a written request for the list.
B. a prior authorization is required before any PHI can be released.
C. you will need to confer with the medical director.
D. if the fundraising was conducted by a business associate without authorization, and the funds were to benefit your facility (the covered entity), that you could disclose the information.

REFERENCE: Brodnik, p 359
LaTour and Eichenwald-Maki, p 287

120. Your facility is storing scanned records for long-term storage on optical disk. The Risk Management Committee's Disaster Task Force has recommended that copies of the disks be stored at a facility across town. The administrator is concerned that records may be altered on the disks stored off-site. You tell the administrator
A. this is a legitimate concern; it should be addressed in the contract written with the storage facility.
B. this is not a concern because WORM technology makes it impossible to alter the documents.
C. this is a legitimate concern; perhaps the committee should consider storing duplicates in two locations in this facility.
D. this is not a concern; there is really no need to make and store duplicate disks as they are difficult to damage.

REFERENCE: LaTour and Eichenwald-Maki, p 224
Abdelhak, pp 190–191

121. The Pharmacy and Therapeutics Committee has asked you to find out more about a computerized order entry system that calculates drug dosages based on patient parameters (weight, age, etc.) and even suggests the best drug given the patient's diagnosis and current treatment. The committee is asking for information on a(n)
A. application system.
B. clinical decision support system.
C. ordering system.
D. practice parameters system.

REFERENCE: Eichenwald-Maki and Petterson, pp 126–133
Abdelhak, pp 179–180
LaTour and Eichenwald-Maki, pp 600–601
Johns, pp 881, 949–951, 1132

122. A portion of a deficiency slip is reproduced below. This patient was discharged yesterday. Your greatest concern regarding deficiencies on this record would be the missing

Physician: Hunter, J. T.				
Missing Signatures			Missing Reports	
X	History			Diagnoses/Procedure
	Physical			History
	Consultative Report			Physical
X	Operative Report			Consultation Report
	Discharge Summary		X	Operative Report
	X-ray Report			Discharge Summary
	Other			X-ray Report
				Others

   A. signature on the physical exam.
   B. signature on the discharge summary.
   C. diagnoses and procedures.
   D. operative report.

REFERENCE: Green and Bowie, pp 99, 165
                Abdelhak, p 129

123. In the past, Joint Commission standards have focused on promoting the use of a facility approved abbreviation list to be used by hospital care providers. With the advent of the Commission's national patient safety goals, the focus has shifted to the
   A. prohibited use of any abbreviations.
   B. flagrant use of specialty-specific abbreviations.
   C. use of prohibited or "dangerous" abbreviations.
   D. use of abbreviations used in the final diagnoses.

REFERENCE: Abdelhak, p 117

124. Annual costs for the only Release of Information Clerk at Jacksonville Beach Healthcare Center (salary and benefits) are $36,429. The monthly cost for the copier used solely for ROI is $89 (supplies and repairs). It costs the department $0.95 on average for ROI mailings (envelopes and postage). There were 687 requests filled for ROI last month. The cost per request for release of information last month was
   A. $4.42.   C. $4.63.
   B. $4.55.   D. $5.50.

REFERENCE: Horton, p 140

125. The decision makers in the HIM department have decided to use the decision analysis matrix method to select coding software. Use of this method will help ensure
   A. all alternatives/vendors are evaluated subjectively.
   B. the personalities of individual vendors will not influence the decision.
   C. consistent criteria are used to evaluate the alternatives/vendors.
   D. the level of software support will be considered in the decision.

REFERENCE: Abdelhak, p 626
                McWay, pp 157–158, 318

126. Many of the departments in your facility create and modify forms often. A major key to forms control in this setting is
    A. consistent formatting of each page of each form.
    B. capturing every data item required by UHDDS.
    C. giving each form or view an identifiable name, number, and revision date.
    D. providing instructions when necessary for appropriate data fields.

REFERENCE: Green and Bowie, pp 201–202
             McWay, pp 109–110
             Abdelhak, pp 119–120
             LaTour and Eichenwald-Maki, pp 216–217
             Johns, pp 414–417

Record #	Patient Last Name	Date of Birth	Date of Service
32-15-65	Smith	02/3/76	3/20/2011
02-45-77	Cook	09/12/86	10/21/2011
10-88-48	Baker	01/23/24	11/14/2011

127. Which means of data modeling is illustrated in the table shown above?
    A. entity-relationship model   C. data management model
    B. object-oriented model   D. relational data model

REFERENCE: Abdelhak, pp 268–270

128. Which of the following is the unique identifier in the database illustrated in the table for question 127?
    A. record number   C. date of birth
    B. patient's last name   D. date of service

REFERENCE: Abdelhak, p 190

129. Stage I of meaningful use focuses on data capture and sharing. Which of the following is included in the menu set of objectives for eligible hospitals in this stage?
    A. Use CPOE for medication orders
    B. Smoking cessation counseling for MI patients
    C. Appropriate use of HL-7 standards
    D. Establish critical pathways for complex, high-dollar cases

REFERENCE: HealthIT.hhs.gov

130. As supervisor of the cancer registry, you report the registry's annual caseload to administration. The most efficient way to retrieve this information would be to use
    A. patient abstracts.
    C. accession register.
    B. patient index.
    D. follow-up files.

REFERENCE: Johns, p 487
          LaTour and Eichenwald-Maki, p 332

131. A supervisor reviews a job to determine the required content, skills, knowledge, abilities, and responsibilities for the position. The tasks are grouped and lines of responsibility and authority are defined. The supervisor is writing a job
    A. description.
    C. process.
    B. analysis.
    D. detail.

REFERENCE: McWay, p 300
          Abdelhak, pp 586–587
          LaTour and Eichenwald-Maki, p 743

132. The emergency department staff has complained that the clerical staff in your department is delaying stat reports. You decide to meet with your staff and develop a cause and effect diagram to determine possible reasons for the delay. You have explained the issue to your staff and have set up a blank cause and effect diagram. The next step is to
    A. discuss the importance of prompt delivery of stat reports.
    B. determine whether there are internal conflicts in the area.
    C. brainstorm possible reasons for delays in delivering the reports.
    D. design a new system that will support prompt report delivery.

REFERENCE: McWay, p 274
          Abdelhak, p 455
          LaTour and Eichenwald-Maki, pp 703–705
          Johns, pp 628–629

133. As your meeting with the clerical staff on the stat report continues, one clerk suggests a possible reason for the delays is a lack of training concerning the nature of stat reports. On the cause and effect diagram, this would most appropriately be listed under
    A. personnel.
    C. materials.
    B. equipment.
    D. methods.

REFERENCE: McWay, p 274
          Abdelhak, p 455
          LaTour and Eichenwald-Maki, pp 703–705
          Johns, pp 628–629

	Rule 1	Rule 2	Rule 3	Rule 4
Condition 1				
Condition 1				
Condition 1				
Condition 1				
Action1				
Action 2				
Action 3				
Action 4				

134. You stop by the office to meet a friend for lunch. Looking on her desk, you see the grid above. Your friend is trying to
    A. plan a conversion.
    B. design a system.
    C. analyze a workflow.
    D. make a decision.

REFERENCE: Abdelhak, pp 626–627
             LaTour and Eichenwald-Maki, pp 635–637
             McWay, pp 86–87, 262

SAINT JOSEPH HOSPITAL CODING PRODUCTIVITY WEEK ENDING JANUARY 4, 2012			
EMPLOYEE NUMBER	INPATIENT	OUTPATIENT PROCEDURE	EMERGENCY OR OBSERVATION
425	120	35	16
426	48	89	95
427	80	92	4
428	65	109	16

135. The performance standard for coders is 28–33 workload units per day. Workload units are calculated as follows:
    Inpatient record = 1 workload unit
    Outpatient surgical procedure records = 0.75 workload units
    Outpatient observation/emergency records = 0.50 workload units
One week's productivity information is shown in the table above. What percentage of the coders is meeting the productivity standards?
    A. 100%
    B. 75%
    C. 50%
    D. 25%

REFERENCE: Abdelhak, p 619
             McWay, pp 209–214

136. The coding supervisor tends to deal with issues as they come up, prioritizing only when problems are pressing or appear to be important to upper management. This crisis manager is particularly weak in which management function?
   A. planning
   B. organizing
   C. controlling
   D. budgeting

REFERENCE: McWay, p 249
             Abdelhak, p 616
             LaTour and Eichenwald-Maki, p 630

137. As a new HIM manager, you recognize that employee development is a necessary investment for the long-term survival and growth of the organization. Your goal is to design and implement a staff development program for your employees, so one of your first steps is to
   A.   implement training programs that emphasize teamwork.
   B.   establish a budget for all hospital employee training.
   C.   survey the HIM employees to assess their need for new skills or knowledge.
   D.   establish HIPAA training programs hospital-wide.

REFERENCE: McWay, pp 290, 303–304
             Abdelhak, p 585
             LaTour and Eichenwald-Maki, pp 732–733

138. Now that the EHR has been fully implemented, you are ready to move old records to basement storage. You are ordering shelving for those old paper files. You have 18,000 records. The files average is three files per filing inch. The shelf units you have selected have six shelves that will hold 34 inches per shelf. You will have to plan for a 20% expansion rate to accommodate miscellaneous paper records over the next 10 years. How many shelving units should you order?
   A. 30
   B. 31
   C. 35
   D. 36

REFERENCE: Green and Bowie, pp 218–219
             LaTour and Eichenwald-Maki, pp 220–221
             Johns, pp 397–399

139. Postage charges in the Health Information Department have increased during the last quarter. The department director has seen metered envelopes in the mail bin that do not appear to be those used for departmental business. The best course of action for the director would be to
   A. remove the postage meter from the department.
   B. keep a watchful eye on the meter and who uses it.
   C. issue employee warnings at the next departmental meeting.
   D. assign responsibility for the postage meter to one employee.

REFERENCE: LaTour and Eichenwald-Maki, p 632
             McWay, pp 299–300

140. A clerk's work performance has diminished dramatically during the past 2 weeks. The supervisor initiates a discussion with the clerk, during which the clerk reveals that he recently accepted that he has an alcohol addiction. The clerk states an intention to quit drinking completely. The supervisor should
    A. terminate the clerk if it can be proved that alcohol was used on the job.
    B. suspend the clerk if alcohol has diminished the clerk's job performance.
    C. give the clerk a leave of absence until these problems can be resolved.
    D. refer the clerk to the facility's Employee Assistance Program.

REFERENCE: McWay, p 302
              Abdelhak, p 602
              LaTour and Eichenwald-Maki, p 735

141. Everyone in the Health Information Department has been working overtime to complete a major record conversion. The supervisor will have to plan for overtime pay for all personnel who are not
    A. hourly employees.   C. salaried nonexempt employees.
    B. salaried exempt employees.   D. temporary employees.

REFERENCE: McWay, p 298
              Abdelhak, p 578
              LaTour and Eichenwald-Maki, p 734

142. The coder works 7.5 hours per day. If a time standard is determined from sample observations to be 2.50 minutes per record for coding emergency room records, what is the daily standard for the number of records coded when a 15% fatigue factor is allowed?
    A. 153 records per day   C. 192 records per day
    B. 180 records per day   D. 200 records per day

REFERENCE: McWay, p 264
              Horton, pp 135–140

143. The correspondence section of your department receives an average of 50 requests per day for release of information. It takes an average of 30 minutes to fulfill each request. Using 6.5 productive hours per day as your standard, calculate the staffing needs for the correspondence section.
    A. 3.8 FTE   C. 3 FTE
    B. 2.5 FTE   D. 4 FTE

REFERENCE: Koch, p 55
              Horton, pp 14, 18

144. Your hospital takes advantage of the 8/80 exemption for health care facilities. Assuming that no employee worked more than 8 hours in a day, which of the employees listed in the table below will be paid overtime this pay period?

EMPLOYEE NUMBER	SCHEDULED HOURS PER WEEK	ACTUAL HOURS THIS WEEK	ACTUAL HOURS LAST WEEK
101	40	42	40
102	40	38	42
103	30	40	40
104	20	22	24
105	40	40	48

   A. Employees 101 and 105
   B. Employees 101, 102, and 105
   C. Employees 101, 104, and 105
   D. Employees 101, 103, 104, and 105

REFERENCE: Abdelhak, p 578
                  LaTour and Eichenwald-Maki, p 734

145. During the work sampling of a file clerk's activity, it is noted that the employee is speaking on the telephone during 76 of 300 observations. How much of the employee's time is spent on the phone if the employee works 7 hours a day?
   A. 1.77 hours
   B. 3.28%
   C. 3.94 hours
   D. 9.2%

REFERENCE: Koch, pp 52–54
                  Horton, p 14

146. You are conducting an educational session on benchmarking. You tell your audience that the key to benchmarking is to use the comparison to
   A. implement your QI process.
   B. make recommendations for improvement.
   C. improve your department's processes.
   D. compare your department with another.

REFERENCE: McWay, pp 148, 153, 157
                  LaTour and Eichenwald-Maki, p 691
                  Abdelhak, p 452

147. In conducting an educational session for your staff about implementing a benchmarking program, you tell your staff that when an organization uses benchmarking, it is important to compare your facility's outcomes to
   A. nationally known facilities.
   B. larger facilities.
   C. facilities within your corporation.
   D. facilities with superior performance.

REFERENCE: McWay, pp 148, 153, 157
                  Abdelhak, p 452
                  LaTour and Eichenwald-Maki, p 691

148. You supervise five clerical employees who will be moving when a new wing of your facility is completed. When you meet with the architect to plan their space, you will ask for
   A. 200 square feet of space for your clerical staff.
   B. 250 square feet of space for your clerical staff.
   C. 300 square feet of space for your clerical staff.
   D. 350 square feet of space for your clerical staff.

REFERENCE: Abdelhak, pp 647–649

149. How long will it take to complete the project described below?

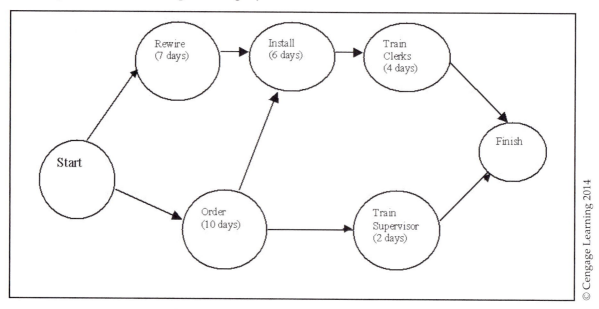

   A. 12 days   C. 20 days
   B. 17 days   D. 29 days

REFERENCE: McWay, p 254
          Abdelhak, pp 638–640

150. The file clerks in your department's main file area report that they are able to locate 400 out of 450 requested records during the past month. There are a total of 4,500 records in the main file. What is the area's accuracy rate?
   A. 1.1%   C. 10.0%
   B. 8.9%   D. 88.9%

REFERENCE: Calculation

END OF THE RHIT MOCK EXAMINATION

FOR THE RHIA MOCK EXAMINATION CONTINUE TESTING AND COMPLETE THE REMAINING 30 QUESTIONS.

151. Encoding software was installed at your hospital 2 years ago. The coders are well trained on it and like using it. It functions well and only requires ICD code updates yearly. In terms of the Information Systems Life Cycle phases, the coding system is likely in the
   A. design phase.
   B. implementation phase.
   C. operation and maintenance phase.
   D. obsolescence or decline phase.

REFERENCE: McWay, pp 317–318
             Abdelhak, pp 303–307
             LaTour and Eichenwald-Maki, pp 148–152

152. A clerical-level employee reports an incident in which the clerk felt the first-line supervisor discriminated on the basis of the clerk's gender. The best action for you to take at this time is to
   A. thoroughly investigate the matter and document your findings.
   B. talk with the first-line supervisor to determine what happened.
   C. ask the other clerical level staff if they have had similar experiences.
   D. ask the clerk to provide objective evidence of the discrimination.

REFERENCE: Abdelhak, pp 601–603
             LaTour and Eichenwald-Maki, pp 732–733

153. A section of a job description states that the incumbent will handle day-to-day operations in the transcription and release of information areas. This section defines the
   A. skills required to perform the job.
   B. time required for each function.
   C. authority associated with the job.
   D. scope of responsibility in the job.

REFERENCE: McWay, pp 259, 300–301
             Abdelhak, pp 587–588
             LaTour and Eichenwald-Maki, pp 727–728

154. There are 15 employees in your department. There were 21 working days last month. There were a total of 12 lost workdays last month due to absenteeism of all types. The absenteeism rate for your department last month was
   A. 21%.
   B. 57%.
   C. 4%.
   D. 5%.

REFERENCE: Calculation

155. You have been the supervisor in quality management at Naples Hospital for almost a year now and your appraisal is right around the corner. Your director has asked the members of your staff and the physicians on the committees you service to complete forms that will provide input into the appraisal process. In addition, you have been asked to formally assess your own progress in this new position. It is time–consuming and more than a little intimidating, but you suppose it will provide you with some good insights into the quality of your work. Because you are, after all, the supervisor in QM, it is only fair that you participate fully in your facility's commitment to
    A. participative evaluation.
    B. 360-degree evaluation.
    C. conductive evaluation.
    D. managed evaluation.

REFERENCE: McWay, pp 300–301
                      Abdelhak pp 594–599
                      LaTour and Eichenwald-Maki, p 735

156. You are a new supervisor in the HIM department and find it difficult to deal with performance issues. Laney, an employee in the Release of Information section, has been late several times this month. She has already been given a verbal warning. She was late again today. According to the progressive discipline process, your next step will be to
    A. reinforce the institution's policies.
    B. reissue the verbal warning.
    C. suspend the employee.
    D. issue a written warning.

REFERENCE: McWay, p 302
                      Abdelhak, pp 601–603
                      LaTour and Eichenwald-Maki, p 735

157. The CFO of your facility asks you to prepare a budget for the fiscal year based on the past volume and expected capacity for the coming year. This process is an example of using the "_____" budgeting method.
    A. rolling budget
    B. fixed budget
    C. flexible or statistics budget
    D. zero-based budget

REFERENCE: McWay, p 341
                      LaTour and Eichenwald-Maki, p 797

158. The committee that is preparing your acute care hospital for an electronic health record is planning for an imaging system for record archiving in the immediate future. They are looking for a solution for data interfacing or integration of the imaging system into other computer systems. You recommend
    A. data dictionary guidelines.
    B. Health Level 7 standards.
    C. Regional Health Information Organization guidelines.
    D. Joint Commission standards.

REFERENCE: McWay, p 174
                      LaTour and Eichenwald-Maki, pp 178–179
                      Abdelhak, pp 168–170
                      Eichenwald-Maki and Petterson, p 2

159. Your facility has decided to purchase an integrated patient information system. Your part in the initial work plan is to develop system specifications that will ultimately be sent out to vendors who will potentially submit a bid on your system. You are working on the systems specs that will become part of the

A. CPR.   C. RFP.
B. IRB.   D. CRS.

REFERENCE: McWay, pp 344–345
             Abdelhak, pp 337–346
             LaTour and Eichenwald-Maki, pp 149–150, 264, 991

160. Reference checks are conducted on potential employees to help assess the applicant's fit with the position and also to

A. confirm the accuracy of information provided on the application.
B. uncover skills the applicant may have neglected to report.
C. get another opinion on the applicant's emotional stability.
D. alert the past employer that the applicant is job hunting.

REFERENCE: McWay, pp 284–285
             Abdelhak, pp 590–593
             LaTour and Eichenwald-Maki, p 731

161. In order to perform their jobs, facility employees should have full and timely access only to the information they need to complete the task at hand. This is similar to HIPAA's provision for

A. a Notice of Privacy Practices (NOPP).
B. amending a record.
C. accessing need to know information only.
D. an informed consent.

REFERENCE: Abdelhak, p 529
             LaTour and Eichenwald-Maki, p 281

162. Authentication is one of the components necessary to produce a legal document in an EHR. This means

A. tracking changes in the EHR system.
B. establishing access controls for individual employees.
C. creating audit trails.
D. identifying who created a document and when.

REFERENCE: Abdelhak, p 191
             LaTour and Eichenwald-Maki, p 213

Patients with diabetes participated in a study to determine the effectiveness of a new drug, Glucodown.

The drug was taken at bedtime. The drug company expected patients taking Glucodown to have a normal early morning fasting blood sugar level. The null hypothesis for the study follows.

There will be no difference in fasting early morning blood sugar levels between patients taking Glucodown and patients taking a placebo.

Half the patients were given Glucodown. Half were given a placebo.

Early morning fasting blood sugar levels are reported below.

Patient	STUDY GROUP (patients receiving Glucodown)					CONTROL GROUP (patients receiving placebo)				
	1	2	3	4	5	6	7	8	9	10
Day 1	102	89	114	95	114	143	160	128	128	106
Day 2	100	83	112	98	99	147	165	111	125	110
Day 3	106	84	103	99	95	139	156	106	115	111
Day 4	100	86	114	102	98	150	168	110	128	114
Day 5	98	88	109	98	91	142	159	102	122	110

163. Based on this information, you would expect the researchers to
   A. accept the null hypothesis.
   B. reject the null hypothesis.
   C. restate the null hypothesis.
   D. draw no conclusions.

REFERENCE: McWay, p 195
                    LaTour and Eichenwald-Maki, p 485

164. The researchers in the previous question wonder if there is any relationship between patient age and average fasting blood sugar. The best data display tool the researchers could use to look for a possible relationship would be a
   A. Pareto diagram.
   B. line graph.
   C. scatter diagram.
   D. cause and effect diagram.

REFERENCE: McWay, pp 149–150, 152
                    LaTour and Eichenwald-Maki, p 449
                    Johns, pp 630–633

165. You have been asked to reduce your department's operating budget by 20%. In order to do so, you will have to effect reductions in your largest budget line. You will have to make cuts in
   A. equipment.
   B. personnel.
   C. supplies.
   D. contracts.

REFERENCE: Abdelhak, pp 676–677
                    LaTour and Eichenwald-Maki, pp 799–800

166. Take a look at the comparison of the two life cycles below.

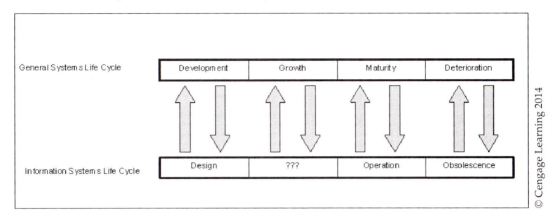

Look at the cell in the Information Systems Life Cycle that is filled with question marks. Which of the following should replace those question marks to make a complete, correct comparison?

A. Growth
B. Installation
C. Implementation
D. Reevaluation

REFERENCE: McWay, pp 317–319
LaTour and Eichenwald-Maki, pp 148–152

167. All of the following are "covered entities" under HIPAA EXCEPT a

A. hospital.
B. health plan.
C. clinic.
D. transcription service.

REFERENCE: LaTour and Eichenwald-Maki, pp 98–99

168. In your job as Chief Security Officer, you are evaluating software programs that will support your policy on sound terminal controls within your facility. One of the features you include in your request for information to vendors is

A. auto log off.
B. encryption.
C. voice recognition feature.
D. unique identifier for log-on.

REFERENCE: Brodnik, pp 278–280
LaTour and Eichenwald-Maki, pp 252–256

169. The most sophisticated level of interoperability of an EHR and other such systems is the
_____ level.
    A. basic
    B. functional
    C. semantic
    D. exchange

REFERENCE: Abdelhak, pp 218–219
             LaTour & Eichenwald-Maki, p 244

170. As the Project Manager for the upcoming EHR implementation, you ask your assistant to develop
a work breakdown structure (WBS). Critical to implementations and project success, the WBS
    A. lists steps needed to complete the project.
    B. determines dependencies among project tasks.
    C. describes project responsibilities.
    D. defines the project's critical path.

REFERENCE: Abdelhak, p 639
             LaTour and Eichenwald-Maki, p 814

171. As the HIM manager in charge of your department's budget, you are mandated to report on
variances of more than 6% either positive or negative to your Chief Financial Officer and include
the reasons for the variance and any action plans necessary. Based on the table below for the
December variance report, what category would you be required to report on to the CFO?

Variance Report for December			
Description	December Budget	December Actual	Variance
Office Supplies	5,120	5,550	(430)
Contract Services	8,500	8,340	160
Travel	3,500	3,700	(200)
Education	2,500	2,400	100

    A. office supplies   C.   travel
    B. contract services   D.   education

REFERENCE: McWay, p 342
             Abdelhak, p 676
             LaTour and Eichenwald-Maki, pp 799–800

172. Evidence-based management and decision making is an emerging model now used to make more
informed decisions. The premise of this model is
    A. using intuition based on previous experience.
    B. using a decision tree with branches that show the alternatives.
    C. using the best clinical and research practices available.
    D. using an alternative that meets minimum requirements.

REFERENCE: McWay, p 145
             LaTour and Eichenwald-Maki, pp 634–635
             Abdelhak, p 444

Document Imaging Implementation						
Beginning Date:	December 2012		**Planning Date:**	October	2012	
Activity	**Assigned:**	**October 2012**	**November 2012**	**December 2012**	**January 9, 2013**	**February 9, 2013**
Kickoff	Team	•				
RFP	PM	•				
System Anal	PM	•				
Design	ITS		•			
RFP eval	Team			•		
Select Vendor	Team			•		
Purchase	CFO/ITS				•	
Build System	ITS				•	
Implement	Team					•

173. As a member of the project team for document imaging implementation, you were asked to provide the information in the grid above. This is an example of a
A. PERT diagram.
B. Gantt chart.
C. PMBOK chart.
D. work flow diagram.

REFERENCE: McWay, p 254
Abdelhak, p 640
LaTour and Eichenwald-Maki, p 625

174. A tool that is used to illustrate the various applications, support structures, and sequencing of implementation phases for a system is a
A. work flow diagram.
B. migration path.
C. milestone chart.
D. PERTT diagram.

REFERENCE: Amatayakul, p 174
LaTour and Eichenwald-Maki, pp 234–235

175 A _____uses a private tunnel through the Internet as a transport medium between locations for secure access and transmission.
A. TCPIP protocol
B. firewall
C. hub
D. VPN

REFERENCE: Amatayakul pp 298–299
Abdelhak, pp 283–284
LaTour and Eichenwald-Maki, p 256

176. A technique that uncovers new information from existing information by probing data sets is known as
A. data mining.
B. systems query language (SQL).
C. neural network analysis.
D. data warehousing.

REFERENCE: Amatayakul, p 30
                Abdelhak, p 292
                LaTour and Eichenwald-Maki, p 66

177. Your HIM department is moving to a new location and in order to arrange your employees and functions for optimal work flow efficiency and to decide which employees need to be placed close to each other, the tool you decide to use is a
A. data flow diagram.
B. PERT chart.
C. proximity chart or movement diagram.
D. flow process chart.

REFERENCE: LaTour and Eichenwald-Maki, pp 680–681, 703, 712

178. A p value of less than 0.05 is what researchers commonly use to reject the null hypothesis. A smaller p value may place interpretation of the results of the study at risk for a
A. sampling error.
B. stratification error.
C. type 1 (a) error.
D. type 2 (b) error.

REFERENCE: Abdelhak, p 389
                LaTour and Eichenwald-Maki, pp 484–485

179. Which of the following employees would be considered exempt under the Fair Labor Standards Act?
A. the head of the Department of Health Information Services who is involved in decision making and planning 90% of the time
B. the coding supervisor who has responsibility for three employees and performs analysis and coding 80% of the time
C. the departmental secretary who is responsible for performing a variety of clerical and administrative tasks
D. the sole employee in the physician's workroom who has responsibility for maintaining and tracking medical record deficiencies

REFERENCE: McWay, p 298
                Abdelhak, p 578
                Brodnik, p 478
                LaTour and Eichenwald-Maki, p 734

180. In order to prevent the accidental introduction of a virus into your facility's local area network, your facility has a policy that strictly prohibits
A. doing personal work on the computer system, even during personal time.
B. sharing disks from one workstation to another within the facility.
C. downloading executable files from electronic bulletin boards.
D. sending or receiving e-mail from addresses that have not been authorized.

REFERENCES: Miaoulia, pp 145–147
                Brodnik, pp 278–280

END OF RHIA MOCK EXAMINATION

Answer Key for the Mock Examination

ANSWER   EXPLANATION

1. B
2. D
3. D
4. D   Progress note elements written in the acronym "SOAP" style are:
   S-subjective; records what the patient states is the problem
   O-objective; records what the practitioner identifies through history, physical examination, and diagnostic tests
   A-assessment; combines the subjective and objective into a conclusion
   P-plan; what approach is going to be taken to resolve the problem
5. D
6. B   Calculation: $\dfrac{169.051 \text{ total relative weight}}{57 \text{ total patients seen}} = 2.965807$

7. A   The interdisciplinary care plan is the foundation around which patient care is organized. It contains input from the unique perspective of each discipline involved. It includes an assessment, statement of goals, identification of specific activities, or strategies to achieve those goals and periodic assessment of goal attainment.
8. D
9. B   Calculations: Reimbursement from payor for one well child visit equals total reimbursement divided by number of visits to the clinic.

INSURANCE COMPANY	NUMBER OF WELL CHILD VISITS	REIMBURSEMENT FROM PAYER FOR WELL CHILD VISITS	REIMBURSEMENT FROM PAYER FOR ONE WELL CHILD VISIT (TOTAL REIMBURSEMENT/ NUMBER OF VISITS)
Lifecare	259	$31,196.55	$120.45
Getwell	786	$100,859.52	$128.32
SureHealth	462	$54,631.50	$118.25
BeHealthy	219	$26,991.75	$123.25

Answer Key for the Mock Examination

ANSWER   EXPLANATION

10. B   CALCULATIONS:

Reimbursement for one well child visit = total reimbursement divided by number of visits.

Reimbursements for two immunizations = total reimbursement divided by number of immunizations x 2.

Total reimbursement for one average visit = reimbursement for one well child visit + reimbursement for two immunizations.

INSURANCE COMPANY	REIMBURSEMENT FOR ONE WELL CHILD VISIT	REIMBURSEMENT FOR TWO IMMUNIZATIONS [(TOTAL REIMBURSEMENT/NUMBER OF IMMUNIZATIONS) x 2]	TOTAL REIMBURSEMENT FOR ONE AVERAGE VISIT (REIMBURSEMENT FOR ONE WELL CHILD VISIT + REIMBURSEMENT FOR TWO IMMUNIZATIONS)
Lifecare	$120.45	$10.56	$131.01
Getwell	$128.32	$12.36	$140.68
SureHealth	$118.25	$11.76	$130.01
BeHealthy	$123.25	$10.16	$133.41

11. B

12. C   Calculations:

MS-DRG A $2.023 \times 323 = 653.43$
MS-DRG B $0.987 \times 489 = 485.65$
MS-DRG C $1.925 \times 402 = 773.85$
MS-DRG D $1.243 \times 386 = 479.80$

13. A

14. D

15. A

16. B

17. D

18. A

19. D

20. D

21. B   The category V45.7X, acquired absence of organ, is intended to be used for patient care where the absence of an organ affects treatment.

22. A   The cancer is coded as a current condition as long as the patient is receiving adjunct therapy.

23. A

24. D

25. A

26. C   A surgical operation is one or more surgical procedures performed at one time for one patient using a common approach or for a common purpose.

27. D

28. D

29. B

Answer Key for the Mock Examination

ANSWER EXPLANATION

30. C The condition should be coded as a poisoning when there is an interaction of an over-the-counter drug and alcohol. Answers A, B, and D are adverse effects of a correctly administered prescription drug.

31. B

32. A When a diagnosis is preceded by the phrase "rule out" in the inpatient setting, the condition is coded as though it is confirmed.

33. C *Staging* is a term used to refer to the progression of cancer. In accessing most types of cancer, a method (staging) is used to determine how far the cancer has progressed. The cancer is described in terms of how large the main tumor is, the degree to which it has invaded surrounding tissue, and the extent to which it has spread to lymph glands or other areas of the body. Staging not only helps to assess outlook but also the most appropriate treatment.

34. A

35. A

36. D Not all of the components of the combination code were POA.
"Y" = yes, present on admission.
"U"= no information in the record.
"W"= clinically undetermined.
"N" = no, not present on admission.

37. A

38. D Look up in CPT codebook index under foot, neuroma.

39. B The sizes of the layered wound repairs of the same body area are added together in order to select the correct CPT code.

40. A The codes in this subsection are used to report evaluations for life or disability insurance baseline information.

41. D *Dialysis* is the main term to be referenced in the CPT manual index.

42. D If the immunization is the only service that the patient receives, then two codes are used to report the service. The immunization administration code is first and then the code for the vaccine/toxoid.

43. B

44. D

45. D

46. C

47. B

48. A Calculation: $\dfrac{(6 \times 100)}{(212 + 28 + 6)} = 2.4\%$

49. C

50. B Calculation: $\$2{,}655 \times 100$ divided by $\$25{,}000 = 10.6 = 11\%$

51. B

52. A

53. A

54. B Calculation: $(335 \times 151) + (350 \times 214) = 125{,}485$

55. C Calculation: $31 - 14 + 28 + 2 = 47$ days

56. A

57. C

Answer Key for the Mock Examination

ANSWER   EXPLANATION

58. B
59. D
60. B
61. D
62. B
63. B
64. D   Calculation:

Remaining at midnight 8/1	99
Admissions	+4
Discharges	−7
In and Out Same Day	+1
Inpatient Service Days 8/2	97

Fetal Deaths and DOA have no impact on inpatient service days.
65. A
66. A
67. A
68. D
69. B
70. D
71. A
72. C   Calculation:

$$\frac{(111{,}963 \times 100)}{(300 \times 181) + (375 \times 184)} = 90.8\%$$

73. A   Multiple births are still considered one delivery for statistical purposes.
74. C
75. B
76. B
77. D
78. C   Calculation: $\$3{,}027 \times 2.0671 = \$6{,}257.11$
79. C
80. A   Calculation: $(431 \times 100)/2{,}879 = 14.97\%$
    $(458 \times 100)/15{,}242 = 3\%$
    $(114 \times 100)/1{,}426 = 8\%$
    $(313 \times 100)/6{,}271 = 5\%$

The highest percentage of error is in consultation reports.
81. B   The highest volume (number) of errors is in lab slips.
82. B
83. B
84. C
85. D
86. C
87. D
88. B
89. A
90. A   Many hospitals use the EDMS as a transition strategy to support their EHR effort.
91. A
92. D
93. D

Answer Key for the Mock Examination

ANSWER	EXPLANATION
94. A	
95. A	
96. C	
97. C	
98. D	
99. A	
100. C	It is the responsibility of organizational leaders to participate in the QI process.
101. B	Calculation: $(304 \times 100)/845 = 36\%$
102. C	Calculation: $(14 \times 100)/526 = 2.66\%$ or 2.7%
103. D	
104. B	Picture archiving and communication systems provide a means to store and rapidly access digitized file images.
105. C	
106. B	Health information exchange is a term used to refer to a "plan in which health information is shared among providers."
107. B	
108. D	
109. D	
110. A	
111. B	
112. B	
113. C	
114. D	
115. C	
116. C	
117. C	
118. B	
119. B	
120. B	
121. B	
122. D	
123. C	The Joint Commission requires hospitals to prohibit abbreviations that have caused confusion or problems in their handwritten form (e.g., "U" for unit, which can be mistaken for "0" (zero) or "4"). Spelling out "unit" is preferred.
124. D	Calculations: • $36,429 annual labor costs/12 = $3,035.75 cost per month • $3,035.75 + $89 copier cost = $3,124.75 monthly costs/687 • ROI last month = 4.548 or $4.55 unit cost (not counting mailing) • $4.55 + 0.95 average mailing cost = $5.50 per ROI
125. C	
126. C	
127. D	
128. A	
129. C	
130. C	
131. A	

Answer Key for the Mock Examination

ANSWER   EXPLANATION

132. C

133. A

134. D

135. A   employee # 425: 120 + (35 × 0.75) + (16 × 0.5) = 154.25
         154.25/5 = 30.85 average work units per day
       employee # 426: 48 + (89 × 0.75) + (95 × 0.5) = 162.25
         162.25/5 = 32.45 average work units per day
       employee # 427: 80 + (92 × 0.75) + (4 × 0.5) = 151
         151/5 = 30.2 average work units per day
       employee # 428: 65 + (109 × 0.75) + (16 × 0.5) = 154.75
         154.75 = 30.95 average work units per day

136. A

137. C

138. D   Calculation: (You can only purchase whole shelf units.)
       34 × 3 = 102 records per shelf
       102 × 6 = 612 records per filing unit
       18,000 × 0.20 = 3,600 records for projected expansion
       18,000 + 3,600 = 21,600 total records
       21,600/612 = 35.29 = 36 total filing units needed

139. D

140. D

141. B

142. A   Calculation: 7.5 hours × 60 minutes per hour = 450 minutes per day
       450 × 15% = 67.5   450 − 67.5 = 382.5   382.5/2.5 = 153

143. A   Calculation: 50 × 30 = 1,500   1,500/60 = 25   25/6.5 = 3.8

144. A   Although employees 103 and 104 worked more hours than scheduled, they still did not work overtime using the 8/80 rules.

145. A   Calculation: 76/300 = 0.253   0.253 × 7 hours = 1.77 hours

146. C   Benchmarking involves comparing your department to other departments or organizations known to be excellent in one or more areas. The success of benchmarking involves finding out how the other department functions and then incorporating their ideas into your department.

147. D

148. C   Generally, allow 60 sq ft per employee. However, as time progresses, less area is being allotted for personal space.

149. C

150. D   Calculation: (400 × 100)/450 = 88.9%

151. C

152. A

153. D

154. C   Calculation: (12 × 100) / (15 × 21) = 3.80 = 4%

155. B

156. D

157. B

158. B

Answer Key for the Mock Examination

ANSWER   EXPLANATION

159. C
160. A
161. C
162. D
163. B
164. C
165. B
166. C
167. D
168. A
169. C
170. A
171. C
172. C
173. B
174. B
175. D
176. A
177. D
178. A
179. A
180. C

REFERENCES

Abdelhak, M., Grostick, S., Hanken, M. A., & Jacobs, E. (Eds.). (2012). *Health information: Management of a strategic resource* (4th ed.). Philadelphia: Elsevier.

Amatayakul, M. (2009). *Electronic Health Records. A practical guide for professionals and organizations,* (5th ed.). Chicago: American Health Information Management Association (AHIMA).

American Medical Association (AMA). (2012). *Physicians' current procedural terminology: CPT 2013, professional edition.* Chicago: Author.

American Medical Association (AMA). (2010). *Principles of CPT coding* (6th ed.). Chicago: Author.

Bowie, M. J., & Schaffer, R. M. (2013). *Understanding procedural coding: A worktext* (3rd ed.). Clifton Park, NY: Delmar Cengage Learning.

Brodnik, M. S., McCain, M. C., Rinehart-Thompson, L. A., & Reynolds, R. B. (2009).*Fundamentals of law for health informatics and information management.* Chicago: American Health Information Management Association (AHIMA).

Brown, F. (2012). *ICD-9-CM coding handbook 2012 with answers.* Chicago: American Hospital Association (AHA). Centers for Medicare & Medicaid Services: https://www.cms.gov/Regulations- and-Guidance/Legislation/EHRIncentivePrograms/index.html?redirect=/ehrincentiveprograms

Eichenwald-Maki, S., & Petterson, B. (2008). *Using the electronic health record in the health care provider practice.* Clifton Park, NY: Delmar Cengage Learning.

Green, M. A. (2012). *3-2-1 code it!* (3rd ed.). Clifton Park, NY: Delmar Cengage Learning.

Green, M. A., & Bowie, M. J. (2011). *Essentials of health information management: Principles and practice* (2nd. ed.). Clifton Park, NY: Delmar Cengage Learning.

Green, M. A., & Rowell J. C. (2011). *Understanding health insurance: A guide to billing and reimbursement* (10th ed.).Clifton Park, NY: Delmar Cengage Learning.

Horton, L. (2011). *Calculating and reporting health care statistics* (4th ed.). Chicago: American Health Information Management Association (AHIMA).

ICD-9-CM code book, professional edition 2012. Salt Lake City, UT: INGENIX.

Koch, G. (2008). *Basic allied health statistics and analysis* (3rd ed.). Clifton Park, NY: Delmar Cengage Learning.

Johns, M. L. (2010). *Health information technology: An applied approach* (3rd ed.). Chicago: American Health Information Management Association (AHIMA).
[NOTE: All references to this book have been listed as "Johns."]

Johnson, S. L., & Linker, R. (2013). *Understanding medical coding: A comprehensive guide* (3rd ed.). Clifton Park, NY: Delmar Cengage Learning.

LaTour, K., & Eichenwald-Maki, S. (2010). *Health information management: Concepts, principles and practice* (3rd ed.). Chicago: American Health Information Management Association (AHIMA).

McLendon, W. K., & Lowe, M. R. (2011). The legal health record: Regulations, policies, and guidance (2nd ed.). Chicago: AHIMA.

McWay, D. C. (2008). *Today's health information management: An integrated approach.* Clifton Park, NY: Delmar Cengage Learning.

Pozgar, G. G. (2012). *Legal aspects of health care administration* (11th ed.). Sudbury, MA: Jones & Bartlett Learning, LLC.

Sayles N. B., & Trawick, K. (2010). *Introduction to computer systems for health information technology.* Chicago: American Health Information Management Association (AHIMA).

RHIA AND RHIT COMPETENCIES BY QUESTION FOR MOCK EXAMINATION

Question	RHIA Domain Competencies							RHIT Domain Competencies						
	1	2	3	4	5	6		1	2	3	4	5	6	7
1		X						X						
2						X							X	
3			X											X
4	X							X						
5			X						X					
6	X							X						
7	X							X						
8	X							X						
9	X													X
10	X													X
11	X													X
12	X													X
13	X								X					
14	X									X				
15						X						X		
16		X									X			
17						X					X			
18	X								X					
19	X								X					
20	X							X						
21	X								X					
22	X								X					
23	X								X					
24	X								X					
25	X								X					
26	X							X						
27	X								X					
28	X								X					
29	X								X					
30	X								X					
31	X								X					
32	X								X					
33	X							X						
34	X								X					
35						X							X	
36	X								X					
37	X								X					
38	X								X					
39	X								X					
40	X								X					